Coding

ALL-IN-ONE

Coding

ALL-IN-ONE

2nd Edition

**by Chris Minnick, Nikhil Abraham,
Barry Burd, Eva Holland, Luca Massaron,
and John Paul Mueller**

A Wiley Brand

Coding All-in-One For Dummies®, 2nd Edition

Published by: **John Wiley & Sons, Inc.**, 111 River Street, Hoboken, NJ 07030-5774, www.wiley.com

Copyright © 2022 by John Wiley & Sons, Inc., Hoboken, New Jersey

Media and software compilation copyright © 2022 by John Wiley & Sons, Inc. All rights reserved.

Published simultaneously in Canada

For general information on our other products and services, please contact our Customer Care Department within the U.S. at 877-762-2974, outside the U.S. at 317-572-3993, or fax 317-572-4002. For technical support, please visit https://hub.wiley.com/community/support/dummies.

Wiley publishes in a variety of print and electronic formats and by print-on-demand. Some material included with standard print versions of this book may not be included in e-books or in print-on-demand. If this book refers to media such as a CD or DVD that is not included in the version you purchased, you may download this material at http://booksupport.wiley.com. For more information about Wiley products, visit www.wiley.com.

Library of Congress Control Number: 2022939031

ISBN 978-1-119-88956-4 (pbk); 978-1-119-88957-1 (epub); 978-1-119-89535-0 (epdf)

SKY10044181_030823

Contents at a Glance

Table of Contents

Introduction

The ability to read, write, and understand code has never been more important, useful, or lucrative than it is today. Computer code has forever changed our lives. Many people can't even make it through the day without interacting with something built with code. Even so, for many people, the world of coding seems complex and inaccessible. Maybe you participated in a tech-related business meeting and did not fully understand the conversation. Perhaps you tried to build a web page for your family and friends, but ran into problems displaying pictures or aligning text. Maybe you're even intimidated by the unrecognizable words on the covers of books about coding, words such as HTML, CSS, JavaScript, Python, or Ruby.

If you've previously been in these situations, then *Coding All-in-One For Dummies,* 2nd Edition is for you. This book explains basic concepts so you can participate in technical conversations and ask the right questions, and it goes even further than *Coding For Dummies* by covering additional topics in mobile app development, data science, and coding careers. Don't worry — this book assumes you're starting with little to no previous coding knowledge, and I haven't tried to cram every possible coding concept into these pages. Additionally, I encourage you here to learn by doing and by actually creating your own programs. Instead of a website or mobile app, imagine that you want to build a house. You could spend eight years studying to be an architect, or you could start today by learning a little bit about foundations and framing. This book kick-starts your coding journey today.

The importance of coding is ever-increasing. As author and technologist Douglas Rushkoff famously said, "program or be programmed." When humans invented languages and then the alphabet, people learned to listen and speak, and then read and write. In our increasingly digital world, it's important to learn not just how to use programs but also how to make them. For example, observe this transition in music. For over a century, music labels decided what songs the public could listen to and purchase. In 2005, three coders created YouTube, which allowed anyone to release songs. Today more songs have been uploaded to YouTube than have been released by all the record labels combined in the past century.

About This Book

This book is designed for readers with little to no coding experience and gives an overview of programming to non-programmers. In plain English, you learn how code is used to create websites and mobile apps, who makes those programs, and the processes they use. The topics covered include

>> Explaining what coding is and answering the common questions related to code

>> Building basic websites using the three most common languages: HTML, CSS, and JavaScript

>> Surveying other programming languages such as Python and Dart

>> Creating mobile apps for iOS and Android devices using Flutter

>> Working with data using Python

>> Exploring coding careers paths and different ways to learn how to code

As you read this book, keep the following in mind:

>> The book can be read from beginning to end, but feel free to skip around if you like. If a topic interests you, start there. You can always return to the previous chapters, if necessary.

>> At some point, you will get stuck, and the code you write will not work as intended. Do not fear! There are many resources to help you, including support forums, others on the Internet, and me! Using Twitter, you can send me a public message at @chrisminnick with the hashtag #codingFD. Additionally, you can sign up for book updates and explanations for changes to programming language commands by visiting https://tinyletter.com/codingallinone.

>> Code in the book appears in a monospaced font like this: `<h1>Hi there!</h1>`.

Foolish Assumptions

I do not make many assumptions about you, the reader, but I do make a few.

I assume you don't have previous programming experience. To follow along, then, you only need to be able to read, type, and follow directions. I try to explain as many concepts as possible using examples and analogies you already know.

I assume you have a computer running the latest version of Google Chrome. The examples in the book have been tested and optimized for the Chrome browser, which is available for free from Google. Even so, the examples also work in the latest version of Firefox, Safari, or Microsoft Edge.

I assume you have access to an Internet connection. Some of the examples in the book can be done without an Internet connection, but most require one.

For the books on Python and data analysis, I assume you are able to download and install the Python programming language and its associated programming libraries, both of which are available for free.

Icons Used in This Book

Here are the icons used in the book to flag text that should be given extra attention or that can be skipped.

TIP

This icon flags useful information or explains a shortcut to help you understand a concept.

TECHNICAL STUFF

This icon explains technical details about the concept being explained. The details might be informative or interesting, but are not essential to your understanding of the concept at this stage.

REMEMBER

Try not to forget the material marked with this icon. It signals an important concept or process that you should keep in mind.

WARNING

Watch out! This icon flags common mistakes and problems that can be avoided if you heed the warning.

Beyond the Book

A lot of extra content that you won't find in this book is available at www.dummies.com. Go online to find the following:

>> **The source code for the examples in this book:** You can find it at www.dummies.com/go/codingallinonefd2e.

The source code is organized by book and chapter. The best way to work with a chapter is to download all the source code for it at one time.

>> **The book's cheat sheet.** Simply navigate to www.dummies.com and search for "Coding All-in-One For Dummies Cheat Sheet." From there, you'll be able to access several helpful articles about coding, including general web development terms and advice for preparing for a job interview, among other useful tidbits.

>> **Updates:** Code and specifications are constantly changing, so the commands and syntax that work today may not work tomorrow. You can find any updates or corrections by visiting http://www.dummies.com/go/codingallinonefd2e or https://tinyletter.com/codingallinone.

Where to Go from Here

All right, now that all the administrative stuff is out of the way, it's time to get started. You can totally do this. Congratulations on taking your first step into the world of coding!

1

Getting Started with Coding

Contents at a Glance

» Touring your first program using code

» Understanding programming languages used to write code

Chapter **1**

What Is Coding?

"A million dollars isn't cool, you know what's cool? A billion dollars."

— SEAN PARKER, THE SOCIAL NETWORK

Every week the newspapers report on another technology company that has raised capital or sold for millions of dollars. Sometimes, in the case of companies like Zoom, Coinbase, and Squarespace, the amount in the headline is for billions of dollars. These articles may pique your curiosity, and you may want to see how code is used to build the applications that experience these financial outcomes. Alternatively, your interests may lie closer to work. Perhaps you work in an industry in decline or in a function that technology is rapidly changing. Whether you are thinking about switching to a new career or improving your current career, understanding computer programming or "coding" can help with your professional development. Finally, your interest may be more personal — perhaps you have an idea, a burning desire to create something, a website or an app, to solve a problem you have experienced, and you know reading and writing code is the first step to building your solution. Whatever your motivation, this book will shed light on coding and programmers, and help you think of both not as mysterious and complex but approachable and something you can do yourself.

In this chapter, you will understand what code is, what industries are affected by computer software, the different types of programming languages used to write code, and take a tour of a web app built with code.

Defining What Code Is

Computer code is not a cryptic activity reserved for geniuses and oracles. In fact, in a few minutes you will be writing some computer code yourself! Most computer code performs a range of tasks in our lives from the mundane to the extraordinary. Code runs our traffic lights and pedestrian signals, the elevators in our buildings, the cell phone towers that transmit our phone signals, and the space ships headed for outer space. We also interact with code on a more personal level, on our phones and computers, and usually to check email or the weather.

Following instructions

Computer code is a set of statements, like sentences in English, and each statement directs the computer to perform a single step or instruction. Each of these steps is very precise, and followed to the letter. For example, if you are in a restaurant and ask a waiter to direct you to the restroom, they might say, "head to the back, and try the middle door." To a computer, these directions are so vague as to be unusable. Instead, if the waiter gave instructions to you as if you were a computer program they might say, "From this table, walk northeast for 40 paces. Then turn right 90 degrees, walk 5 paces, turn left 90 degrees, and walk 5 paces. Open the door directly in front of you, and enter the restroom." Figure 1-1 shows lines of code from the popular game, Pong. Do not worry about trying to understand what every single line does, or feel intimated. You will soon be reading and writing your own code.

```
1   launchPong(function () {
2       function colour_random() {
3           var num = Math.floor(Math.random() * Math.pow(2, 24));
4           return '#' + ('00000' + num.toString(16)).substr(-6);
5       }
6
7
8       pongSettings.ball.size = 15;
9       pongSettings.ball.color = colour_random();
10      pongSettings.ball.velocity[0] = 15;
11      pongSettings.ball.velocity[1] = 15;
12
13  });
14
15
```

FIGURE 1-1: Computer code from the game Pong.

One rough way to measure a program's complexity is to count its statements or lines of code. Basic applications like the Pong game have 5,000 lines of code, while more complex applications like Facebook currently have over 10 million lines of code. Whether few or many lines of code, the computer follows each instruction exactly and effortlessly, never tiring like the waiter might when asked for the 100th time for the location of the restroom.

TIP Be careful of only using lines of code as a measure for a program's complexity. Just like when writing in English, 100 well written lines of code can perform the same functionality as 1,000 poorly written lines of code.

Writing code with some Angry Birds

If you have never written code before, now is your chance to try! Go to https://hourofcode.com/us/learn and under the "Beginners" heading, scroll down (or use the search box) to find the "Write Your First Computer Program" link with the Angry Birds icon, as shown in Figure 1-2. This tutorial is meant for those with no previous computer programming experience, and it introduces the basic building blocks used by all computer programs. The most important take-away from the tutorial is to understand that computer programs use code to literally and exactly tell the computer to execute a set of instructions.

FIGURE 1-2: Write your first computer program with a game-like tutorial using Angry Birds.

© John Wiley & Sons

TIP The Hour of Code is an annual program dedicated to elevating the profile of computer science during one week in December. In the past, President Obama, Bill Gates, basketball player Stephen Curry, singer Shakira, and even your humble author of this book have supported and encouraged people from the United States and around the world to participate.

Understanding What Coding Can Do for You

Coding can be used to perform tasks and solve problems that you experience every day. The "everyday" situations in which programs or apps can provide assistance continues to grow at an exponential pace, but this was not always the case. The rise of web applications, Internet connectivity, and mobile phones have inserted software programs into daily life and lowered the barrier for you to become a creator, solving personal and professional problems with code.

Eating the world with software

In 2011, Marc Andreessen, creator of one of the first web browsers, Netscape Navigator, and now a venture capitalist, noted that "software is eating the world." He predicted that software companies would disrupt existing companies at a rapid pace. Traditionally, code powered software used on desktops and laptops. The software had to first be installed, and then you had to supply data to the program. Three trends have dramatically increased the use of code in everyday life:

>> **Web-based software:** This software operates in the browser without requiring installation. For example, if you wanted to check your email, you previously had to install an email client either by downloading the software or from a CD-ROM. Sometimes, issues arose when the software was not available for your operating system, or conflicted with your operating system version. Hotmail, a web-based email client, rose to popularity, in part, because it allowed users visiting www.hotmail.com to instantly check their email without worrying about installation or software compatibility. Web applications increased consumer appetite to try more applications, and developers in turn were incentivized to write more applications.

>> **Internet broadband connectivity:** Broadband connectivity has increased, providing a fast Internet connection to more people in the last few years than in the previous decade. Today, more than two billion people can access web-based software, up from approximately 50 million only a decade ago.

>> **Mobile phones:** Today's smartphones bring programs with you wherever you go and help supply data to programs. Many software programs became more useful when accessed on-the-go than when limited to a desktop computer. For instance, use of maps applications greatly increased thanks to mobile phones because users need directions the most when lost, not just when planning a trip at home on the computer. In addition, mobile phones are equipped with sensors that measure and supply data to programs like orientation, acceleration, and current location through GPS. Now instead of

having to input all the data to programs yourself, mobile devices can help. For instance, a fitness application like Runkeeper does not require you to input start and end times to keep track of your runs. You can press start at the beginning of your run, and the phone will automatically track your distance, speed, and time.

The combination of these trends have created software companies that have upended incumbents in almost every industry, especially ones typically immune to technology. Some notable examples include:

- » **Airbnb:** Airbnb is a peer-to-peer lodging company that owns no rooms, yet books more nights than the Hilton and Intercontinental, the largest hotel chains in the world. (See Figure 1-3.)

- » **Uber:** Uber is a car transportation company that owns no vehicles, books more trips, and has more drivers in the largest 200 cities than any other car or taxi service.

- » **Groupon:** Groupon, the daily deals company, generated almost $1 billion after just two years in business, growing faster than any other company in history, let alone any other traditional direct marketing company.

FIGURE 1-3: Airbnb booked 5 million nights after 3.5 years, and its next 5 million nights 6 months later.

© John Wiley & Sons

Coding on the job

Coding can be useful in the workplace as well. Outside the technology sector, coding in the workplace is common for some professions like financial traders, economists, and scientists. However, for most professionals outside the technology sector, coding is just beginning to penetrate the workplace, and gradually starting to increase in relevance. Here are areas where coding is playing a larger role on the job:

>> **Advertising:** Spend is shifting from print and TV to digital campaigns, and search engine advertising and optimization relies on keywords to bring visitors to websites. Advertisers who understand code see successful keywords used by competitors, and use that data to create more effective campaigns.

>> **Marketing:** When promoting products, personalizing communication is one strategy that often increases results. Marketers who code can query customer databases and create personalized communications that include customer names and products tailored to specific interests.

>> **Sales:** The sales process always starts with leads. Salespeople who code retrieve their own leads from web pages and directories, and then sort and qualify those leads.

TIP

Retrieving information by copying text on web pages and in directories is referred to as *scraping*.

>> **Design:** After creating a web page or a digital design, designers must persuade other designers and eventually developers to actually program their drawings into the product. Designers who code can more easily bring their designs to life, and can more effectively advocate for specific designs by creating working prototypes that others can interact with.

>> **Public relations:** Companies constantly measure how customers and the public react to announcements and news. For instance, if a celebrity spokesperson for a company does or says something offensive, should the company dump the celebrity? Public relations people who code query social media networks like Twitter or Facebook, and analyze hundreds of thousands of individual messages to understand market sentiment.

>> **Operations:** Additional profit can be generated, in part, by analyzing a company's costs. Operations people who code write programs to try millions of combinations to optimize packaging methods, loading routines, and delivery routes.

Book 7 has lots more information about careers in coding.

Scratching your own itch (and becoming rich and famous)

Using code built by others and coding in the workplace may cause you to think of problems you personally face that you could solve with code of your own. You may have an idea for a social network website, a better fitness app, or something new altogether. The path from idea to functioning prototype used by others involves a good amount of time and work, but might be more achievable than you think. For example, take Coffitivity, a productivity website that streams ambient coffee shop sounds to create white noise. The website was created by two people who had just learned how to program a few months prior. Shortly after Coffitivity launched, *TIME* magazine named the website one of 50 Best Websites of 2013, and the *Wall Street Journal* also reviewed the website. While not every startup or app will initially receive this much media coverage, it can be helpful to know what is possible when a solution really solves a problem.

Having a goal, like a website or app you want to build, is one of the best ways to learn how to code. When facing a difficult bug or a hard concept, the idea of bringing your website to life will provide the motivation you need to keep going. Just as important, do not learn how to code to become rich and famous, as the probability of your website or app becoming successful is largely due to factors out of your control.

TIP

The characteristics that make a website or app addictive are described using the Hook Model at https://www.nirandfar.com/how-to-manufacture-desire/. Products are usually made by companies, and the characteristics of an enduring company are described at https://articles.sequoiacap.com/elements-of-enduring-companies, based on a review of companies funded by Sequoia, one of the most successful venture capital firms in the world and early investors in Apple, Google, and PayPal.

Surveying the Types of Programming Languages

Code comes in different flavors called *programming languages*. It's estimated that there are about 9,000 different programming languages, so clearly we can't talk about them all. Some of the most popular ones are JavaScript, Python, Java, Rust, Ruby, Go, Kotlin, R, PHP, C, C++, Dart, and Swift.

You can think of programming languages just like spoken languages, as they both share many of the same characteristics, such as:

>> **Functionality across languages:** Programming languages can all create the same functionality similar to how spoken languages can all express the same objects, phrases, and emotions.

>> **Syntax and structure:** Commands in programming languages can overlap just like words in spoken languages overlap. To output text to screen in Python or Ruby you use the `print` command, just like imprimer and imprimir are the verbs for "print" in French and Spanish.

>> **Natural lifespan:** Programming languages are born when a programmer thinks of a new or easier way to express a computational concept. If other programmers agree, they adopt the language for their own programs and the programming language spreads. However, just like Latin or Aramaic, if the programming language is not adopted by other programmers or a better language comes along, then the programming language slowly dies from lack of use.

Despite these similarities, programming languages also differ from spoken languages in a few key ways:

>> **One creator:** Unlike spoken languages, programming languages can be created by one person in a short period of time, sometimes in just a few days. Popular languages with a single creator include JavaScript (Brendan Eich), Python (Guido van Rossum), and Ruby (Yukihiro Matsumoto).

>> **Written in English:** Unlike spoken languages (except, of course, English), almost all programming languages are written in English. Whether they're programming in HTML, JavaScript, Python, or Ruby, Brazilian, French, or Chinese programmers all use the same English keywords and syntax in their code. Some non-English programming languages exist, such as languages in Hindi or Arabic, but none of these languages are widespread or mainstream.

Comparing low-level and high-level programming languages

One way to classify programming languages is either as low-level languages or high-level languages. Low-level languages interact directly with the computer processor or CPU, are capable of performing very basic commands, and are generally hard to read. Machine code, one example of a low-level language, uses code that consists of just two numbers — 0 and 1. Figure 1-4 shows an example of machine code. Assembly language, another low-level language, uses keywords to perform basic commands like read data, move data, and store data.

```
0110101001101010001011011001001010110010101010100101010
0111100010101111000110111011100010101001010100110101010
0101010001001001011010100010100101110001001010100100110
0011010101011110101101111010010010001011010101010000101
0011010100110101000101101100100101011001010101010101010
1011110001010111000110111011100010101001010100110101010
0010101000100100101101010001010010111000110010101010011
0001101010101111010110111101001001000101101010101000010
0011010100110101000101101100100101011001010101010101010
1011110001010111000110111011100010101001010100110101010
0010101000100100101101010001010010111000110010101010011
0001101010101111010110111101001001000101101010101000010
0011010100110101000101101100100101011001010101010101010
1011110001010111000110111011100010101001010100110101010
0010101000100100101101010001010010111000110010101010011
0001101010101111010110111101001001000101101010101000010
0011010100110101000101101100100101011001010101010101010
1011110001010111000110111011100010101001010100110101010
0010101000100100101101010001010010111000110010101010011
0001101010101111010110111101001001000101101010101000010
0011010100110101000101101100100101011001010101010101010
1011110001010111000110111011100010101001010100110101010
```

FIGURE 1-4:
Machine code
consists of 0s
and 1s.

By contrast, high-level languages use natural language so it is easier for people to read and write. Once code is written in a high-level language, like C++, Python, or Ruby, an interpreter or compiler translates this high-level language into low-level code a computer can understand.

Contrasting compiled code and interpreted code

High-level programming languages must be converted to low-level programming languages using an interpreter or compiler, depending on the language. Interpreted languages are considered more portable than compiled languages, while compiled languages execute faster than interpreted languages. However, the speed advantage compiled languages have is starting to fade in importance as improving processor speeds make performance differences between interpreted and compiled languages negligible.

High-level programming languages like JavaScript, Python, and Ruby are interpreted. For these languages the interpreter executes the program directly, translating each statement *one line at a time* into machine code. High-level programming languages like C++, COBOL, and Visual Basic are compiled. For these languages, after the code is written a compiler translates *all* the code into machine code, and an executable file is created. This executable file is then distributed via a website or app store and run. Software you install on your computer, smartphone, or tablet, like Microsoft Office or Adobe Photoshop, are coded using compiled languages.

Programming for the web

Software accessible on websites is gradually starting to take over installed software. Think of the last time you downloaded and installed software for your computer — you may not even remember! Installed software like Windows Media Player and Winamp that play music and movies have been replaced with websites like YouTube and Netflix. Traditional installed word processor and spreadsheet software like Microsoft Word and Excel are competing with web software like Google Docs and Sheets. The Google Chromebook doesn't contain installed software (other than Google's Chrome browser) and instead relies exclusively on web software to provide functionality.

Much of this book will focus on developing and creating web software, not just because web software is growing rapidly, but also because programs for the web are easier to learn and launch than traditional installed software.

Taking a Tour of a Web App Built with Code

With all this talk of programming, let us actually take a look at a web application built with code. Yelp.com is a website that allows you to search and find crowd-sourced reviews for local businesses like restaurants, nightlife, and shopping. As shown in Figure 1-5, Yelp did not always look as polished as it does today, but its purpose has stayed relatively constant over the years.

FIGURE 1-5: Yelp's website in 2004 and in 2022

Defining the app's purpose and scope

Once you understand an app's purpose, you can identify a few actionable tasks a user should be able to perform to achieve that purpose. Regardless of design, the Yelp's website has always allowed users to

>> Search local listings based on venue type and location.

>> Browse listing results for address, hours, reviews, photos, and location on a map.

Successful web applications generally allow for completing only a few key tasks when using the app. Adding too many features to an app dilutes the strength of the existing features, and so is avoided by most developers. For example, it took Yelp, which has 30,000 restaurant reviews, exactly one decade after its founding to allow users to make reservations at those restaurants directly on its website. Whether you are using or building an app, have a clear sense of the app's purpose.

Standing on the shoulders of giants

Developers make strategic choices and decide which parts of the app to code themselves, and which parts of the app to use code built by others. Developers often turn to third-party providers for functionality that is either not core to the business or not an area of strength. In this way, apps stand on the shoulders of others, and benefit from others who have come before and solved challenging problems.

Yelp, for instance, displays local listing reviews and places every listing on a map. While Yelp solicits the reviews and writes the code to display basic listing data, it is Google, as shown in Figure 1-6, which develops the maps used on Yelp's website. By using Google's map application instead of building its own, Yelp created the first version of the app with fewer engineers than otherwise would have been required.

FIGURE 1-6:
Google maps used for the Yelp web application.

© John Wiley & Sons

IN THIS CHAPTER

» Seeing the code powering websites
you use every day

» Understanding the languages used to
make websites

» Learning how applications are
created for mobile devices

Chapter **2**

Programming for the Web

There was a time when people felt the Internet was another world, but now people realize it's a tool that we use in this world.

—TIM BERNERS-LEE

Programming for the web allows you to reach massive audiences around the world faster than ever before. Four years after its 2004 launch, Facebook had 100 million users, and by 2012 it had over a billion. By contrast, it took desktop software years to reach even 1 million people. These days, mobile phones are increasing the reach of web applications. Although roughly 250 million desktop and laptop computers are sold every year, more than 1.5 billion mobile phones are sold in that time.

In this chapter you learn how websites are displayed on your computer or mobile device. I introduce the languages used to program websites and show you how mobile-device applications are made.

Displaying Web Pages on Your Desktop and Mobile Device

On desktop computers and mobile devices, web pages are displayed by applications called *browsers*. The most popular web browsers include Google Chrome, Mozilla Firefox, Microsoft Edge, and Apple Safari. Until now, you have likely interacted with websites you visit as an obedient user, and followed the rules the website has created by pointing and clicking when allowed. The first step to becoming a producer and programmer of websites is to peel back the web page and see and play with the code underneath it all.

Hacking your favorite news website

What's your favorite news website? By following a few steps, you can see and even modify the code used to create that website. (No need to worry, you won't be breaking any rules by following these instructions.)

TIP

Although you can use almost any modern browser to inspect a website's code, these instructions assume you're using the Google Chrome browser. Install the latest version by going to www.google.com/chrome/.

To "hack" your favorite news website, follow these steps:

1. **Open your favorite news website using the Chrome browser. (In this example, I use www.huffpost.com.)**

2. **Place your mouse cursor over any static fixed headline and right-click once, which opens a contextual menu. Then, left-click once on the Inspect menu choice. (See Figure 2-1.)**

TIP

If you're using a Macintosh computer, you can right-click by holding down the Control key and clicking once.

The Developer Tools panel opens at the bottom of your browser (or on the right side). This panel shows you the code used to create this web page! You can resize this window by dragging its top edge. The specific code used to create the headline where you originally put your mouse cursor is highlighted. (See Figure 2-2.)

TIP

Look at the left edge of the highlighted code. If you see a right arrow, left-click once on the arrow to expand the code.

FIGURE 2-1:
Right-click on
a headline and
select Inspect
from the menu.

© John Wiley & Sons

FIGURE 2-2:
The highlighted
code is used to
create the web
page headline.

© John Wiley & Sons

3. **Scan the highlighted code carefully for the text of your headline. When you find it, double-click on the headline text. This allows you to edit the headline. (See Figure 2-3.)**

Be careful not to click on anything that begins with http, which is the headline link. Clicking on a headline link will open a new window or tab and load the link.

FIGURE 2-3:
Double-click the
headline text to
edit it with your
own headline.

4. **Insert your name in the headline and press Enter.**

   Your name now appears on the actual web page. (See Figure 2-4.) Enjoy your newfound fame!

TIP

If you were unable to edit the headline after following these steps, visit `https://x-ray-goggles.mouse.org/` for instructions on installing the Mozilla X-Ray Goggles tool. It's a teaching aid that shows that any code on the Internet can be modified. On that page, follow the instructions to install the X-Ray Goggles bookmark, then visit any other website and click on the bookmark. Try using X-Ray Goggles to hack your favorite news website.

FIGURE 2-4:
You successfully
changed the
headline of a
major news
website.

© John Wiley & Sons

If you successfully completed the steps above and changed the original headline, it's time for your 15 minutes of fame to come to an end. Reload the web page and the original headline reappears. What just happened? Did your changes appear to everyone visiting the web page? And why did your edited headline disappear?

To answer these questions, you first need to understand how the Internet delivers web pages to your computer.

Understanding how the World Wide Web works

After you type a URL, such as huffpost.com, into your browser, the following steps happen behind the scenes in the seconds before your page loads (see Figure 2-5):

1. Your computer sends your request for the web page to a router. The router distributes Internet access throughout your home or workplace.

2. The router passes your request onto your Internet service provider (ISP). In the United States, your ISP is a company like Comcast, Time Warner, AT&T, or Verizon.

3. Your ISP then converts the words and characters in your URL — "huffpost. com" in my example — into a numerical address called the *Internet protocol address* (or, more commonly, *IP address*). An IP address is a set of four numbers separated by periods (such as, for example, 192.168.1.1). Just like your physical address, this number is unique, and every computer has one. Your ISP has a digital phonebook, similar to a physical phonebook, called a *domain name server* that's used to convert text URLs into IP addresses.

4. With the IP address located, your ISP knows which server on the Internet to forward your request to, and your personal IP address is included in this request.

5. The website server receives your request and sends a copy of the web page code to your computer for your browser to display.

6. Your web browser renders the code onto the screen.

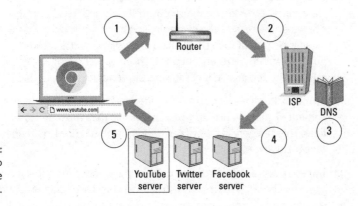

FIGURE 2-5:
Steps followed to deliver a website to your browser.

When you edited the website code using the Developer Tools, you modified only the copy of the website code that exists on your computer, so only you could see the change. When you reloaded the page, you started Steps 1 through 6 again and retrieved a fresh copy of the code from the server, overwriting any changes you made on your computer.

TIP

You may have heard of a software tool called an *ad blocker.* Ad blockers work by editing the local copy of website code, just as you did above, to remove website advertisements. Ad blockers are controversial because websites use advertising revenue to pay for operating costs. If ad blockers continue rising in popularity, ad revenue could dry up, and websites would have to demand that readers pay to see their content.

Watching out for your frontend and backend

Now that you know how your browser accesses websites, let's dive deeper into the way the actual website is constructed. As shown in Figure 2-6, the code for websites, and for programs in general, can be divided into four categories, according to the code's function:

>> **Appearance:** Appearance is the visible part of the website, including content layout and any applied styling, such font size, font typeface, and image size. This category is called the *frontend* and is created using languages like HTML, CSS, and JavaScript.

>> **Logic:** Logic determines what content to show and when. For example, a New Yorker accessing a news website should see New York weather, whereas Chicagoans accessing the same site should see Chicago weather. This category is part of the group called the *backend* and is created using languages like Ruby, Python, and PHP. These backend languages can modify the HTML, CSS, and JavaScript that is displayed to the user.

>> **Storage:** Storage saves any data generated by the site and its users. User-generated content, preferences, and profile data must be stored for retrieval later. This category is part of the backend and is stored in databases like MongoDB and MySQL.

>> **Infrastructure:** Infrastructure delivers the website from the server to you, the client machine. When the infrastructure is properly configured, no one notices it, but it can *become* noticeable when a website becomes unavailable due to high traffic from events like presidential elections, the Super Bowl, and natural disasters.

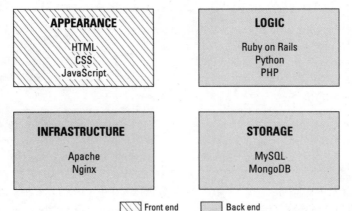

FIGURE 2-6:
Every website is made up of four different parts.

Usually, website developers specialize in one or at most two of these categories. For example, an engineer might really understand the frontend and logic languages, or specialize in only databases. Website developers have strengths and specializations, and outside of these areas their expertise is limited, much in the same way that Jerry Seinfeld, a terrific comedy writer, would likely make a terrible romance novelist.

TECHNICAL STUFF

The rare website developer proficient in all four of these categories is referred to as a *full stack developer*. Usually, smaller companies hire full stack developers, whereas larger companies require the expertise that comes with specialization.

Defining web and mobile applications

Web applications are websites you visit using a web browser on any device. Websites optimized for use on a mobile device, like a phone or tablet, are called *mobile web applications*. By contrast, *native mobile applications* cannot be viewed using a web browser. Instead, native mobile applications are downloaded from an app store like the Apple App Store or Google Play, and designed to run on a specific device such as an iPhone or an Android tablet. Historically, desktop computers outnumbered and outsold mobile devices, but two major trends in mobile usage have occurred:

» Starting in 2014, people with mobile devices outnumbered people with desktop computers. This gap is projected to continue increasing, as shown in Figure 2-7.

» Mobile-device users spend 80 percent of their time using native mobile applications and 20 percent of their time browsing mobile websites.

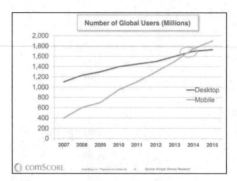
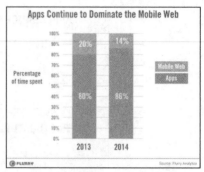

The increase in mobile devices has happened so quickly over the last 15 years that many companies are becoming "mobile first," designing and developing the mobile version of their applications before the desktop version. WhatsApp and Instagram, two popular mobile applications, first built mobile applications, which continue to have more functionality then their regular websites.

Coding Web Applications

Web applications are easier to build than mobile applications, require little to no additional software to develop and test, and run on all devices, including desktop, laptops, and mobile. Although mobile applications can perform many common web-application tasks, such as email, some tasks are still easier to perform using web applications. For example, booking travel is easier using web applications, especially since the steps necessary — reviewing flights, hotels, and rental cars, and then purchasing all three — are best achieved with multiple windows, access to a calendar, and the entry of substantial personal and payment information.

The programming languages used to code basic web applications, further defined in the following sections, include HTML (Hypertext Markup Language), CSS (Cascading Style Sheets), and JavaScript. Additional features can be added to these websites using languages like Python, Ruby, or PHP.

Starting with HTML, CSS, and JavaScript

Simple websites, such as the one shown in Figure 2-8, are coded using HTML, CSS, and JavaScript. HTML is used to place text on the page, CSS is used to style that text, and JavaScript is used to add interactive effects like the Twitter or Facebook Share button that allows you to share content on social networks and updates the number of other people who have also shared the same content. Websites conveying mainly static, unchanging information are often coded only in these three languages. You will learn about each of these languages in later chapters.

FIGURE 2-8:
The lindaliukas.
com website from
2014, built using
HTML, CSS, and
JavaScript.

Adding logic with Python, Ruby, or PHP

Websites with more advanced functionality, such as user accounts, file uploads, and e-commerce, typically require a programming language to implement these features. Although Python, Ruby, and PHP are not the only programming languages these sites can use, they are among the most popular. This popularity means there are large online communities of developers who program in these languages, freely post code that you can copy to build common features, and host public online discussions that you can read for solutions to common issues.

Each of these languages also has popular and well documented frameworks. A *framework* is a collection of generic components, such as user accounts and authentication schemes that are reused frequently, allowing developers to build, test, and launch websites more quickly. You can think of a framework as similar to the collection of templates that comes with a word processor. You can design your resume, greeting card, or calendar from scratch, but using the built-in template for each of these document types helps you create your document faster and with greater consistency. Popular frameworks for these languages include

>> Django and Flask for Python

>> Rails and Sinatra for Ruby

>> Zend and Laravel for PHP

Coding Mobile Applications

Mobile applications are hot topics today, in part because mobile apps such as WhatsApp and Instagram were acquired for billions of dollars, and mobile app companies like Rovio, makers of Angry Birds, and King Digital, makers of Candy Crush, generate annual revenues of hundreds of millions to billions of dollars.

When coding mobile applications, developers can either build

>> Mobile web applications, using HTML, CSS, and JavaScript.

>> Native mobile applications using a specific language. For example, Apple devices are programmed using Objective-C or Swift, and Android devices are programmed using Java, Kotlin, or Dart.

The choice between these two options may seem simple, but there are a few factors at play. Consider the following:

>> Companies developing mobile web applications must make sure the mobile version works across different browsers, different screen sizes, and even different manufacturers, such as Apple, Samsung, RIM, and Microsoft. This results in thousands of possible phone combinations, which can greatly increase the complexity of testing needed before launch. Native mobile apps run only on one phone platform, so there is less variation to account for.

>> Despite running on only one platform, native mobile apps are more expensive and take longer to build than mobile web apps.

>> Some developers have reported that mobile web applications have more performance issues and load more slowly than native mobile applications.

>> As mentioned, users are spending more time using native mobile applications and less time using browser-based mobile web apps.

>> Native mobile apps are distributed through an app store, which may require approval from the app store owner, whereas mobile web apps are accessible from any web browser. For example, Apple has a strict approval policy and takes up to six days to approve an app for inclusion in the Apple App Store, while Google has a more relaxed approval policy and takes two hours to approve an app.

TECHNICAL STUFF

In one famous example of an app rejected from an app store, Apple blocked Google from launching the Google Voice app in the Apple App Store because it overlapped with Apple's own phone functionality. Google responded by creating a mobile web app accessible from any browser, and Apple could do nothing to block it.

If you're making this choice, consider the complexity of your application. Simple applications, like schedules or menus, can likely be cheaply developed with a mobile web app, whereas more complex applications, like messaging and social networking, may benefit from having a native mobile app. Even well-established technology companies struggle with this choice. Initially, Facebook and LinkedIn created mobile web applications, but both have since shifted to primarily promoting and supporting native mobile apps. The companies cited better speed, memory management, and Developer Tools as some of the reasons for making the switch.

Building mobile web apps

Although any website can be viewed with a mobile browser, those websites not optimized for mobile devices look a little weird, as if the regular website font size and image dimensions were decreased to fit on a mobile screen. (See Figure 2-9.) By contrast, websites optimized for mobile devices have fonts that are readable, images that scale to the mobile device screen, and a vertical layout suitable for a mobile phone.

FIGURE 2-9: Left: starbucks.com not optimized for mobile. Right: starbucks.com optimized for mobile.

© John Wiley & Sons

Building mobile web apps is done using HTML, CSS, and JavaScript. CSS controls the website appearance across devices based on the screen width. Screens with a small width, such as those on phones, are assigned one vertically-based layout, whereas screens with a larger width, like those on tablets, are assigned another, horizontally-based layout. Because mobile web apps are accessed from the browser and are not installed on the user's device, these web apps can't send push notifications (alerts) to your phone, run in the background while the browser is minimized, or communicate with other apps.

Although you can write the HTML, CSS, and JavaScript for your mobile web app from scratch, mobile web frameworks allow you to develop from a base of pre-written code, much like the frameworks for programming languages I mentioned earlier. These mobile web frameworks include a collection of generic components that are reused frequently, and allow developers to build, test, and launch websites more quickly. Bootstrap is one such mobile web framework, which I introduce in Book 2.

Building native mobile apps

Native mobile apps can be faster, more reliable, and look more polished than mobile web apps, as shown in Figure 2-10. Built using Java for use on Android devices, and Objective-C or Swift for use on Apple devices (iOS), native mobile apps must be uploaded to an app store, which may require approvals. The main benefit of an app store is its centralized distribution, and the app may be featured in parts of the app store that can drive downloads. Also, since native mobile applications are programs that are installed on the mobile device, they can be used in more situations without an Internet connection. Finally, and most importantly, users appear to prefer native mobile apps to mobile web apps by a wide margin, one that continues to increase.

FIGURE 2-10: Left: facebook. com native mobile app. Right: facebook. com mobile web app.

© John Wiley & Sons

Native mobile apps can take advantage of features that run in the background while the app is minimized, such as push notifications, and communicate with other apps, and these features are not available when creating a mobile web app. Additionally, native mobile apps perform better when handling graphics-intensive applications, such as games. To be clear, native mobile apps offer better performance and a greater number of features, but they require longer development times and are more expensive to build than mobile web apps.

There is an alternative way to build a native mobile app — a hybrid approach that involves building an app using one framework and then compiling that code for multiple mobile operating systems. Two popular cross-platform frameworks are Fluttter and React Native. Both allow you to write cross-platform code, either using JavaScript (in the case of React Native) or Dart (in the case of Flutter). After you've built one version of the app, you can use that version to create apps for multiple platforms, including Android, iOS, and the web. The major advantage to using this hybrid approach is building your app once, and then releasing it to multiple platforms simultaneously.

TIP

Imagine you knew how to play the piano, but you wanted to also learn how to play the violin. One way you could do this is to buy a violin and start learning how to play. Another option is to buy a synthesizer keyboard, set the tone to violin, and play the keyboard to sound like a violin. This is similar to the hybrid approach, except, in this example, the piano is the language used by the cross-platform framework, the violin is a native iOS app, and the synthesizer keyboard is React Native or Flutter. Just like the synthesizer keyboard can be set to violin, cello, or guitar, so too can React Native and Flutter create apps for Apple, Android, and other platforms.

Deploying Web Applications in the Cloud

In the early days of the web and mobile apps, making your web applications and mobile applications available to the world meant that you needed to buy, configure, and maintain enough physical hardware (in the form of expensive web servers) to be able to handle your busiest days. This generally meant that anyone who built a web app or mobile app had an enormous amount of computing power that was going unused most of the time.

Servers are expensive to purchase, but they also require dedicated staff to install upgrades and repair. If a web app or mobile app suddenly became so popular that the servers hosting it slowed down during peak times, the only solution was to purchase yet more hardware.

In recent years, this dependency of backend services on physical hardware owned by the creator of the software has been reduced or eliminated through the use of *cloud computing*. Cloud computing is revolutionizing how software runs over the web by making computing power available as a service. What that means is that instead of the creator of an app needing to anticipate and monitor demand for their app and increase (or decrease) the power of the computers running the app, cloud computing makes computing power more like a utility.

For example, when you turn on multiple appliances in your home, your electric bill goes up. But when you turn off appliances and lights, your bill goes down rather than you always having to pay for the maximum amount of electricity you might use.

Cloud computing, in its most basic form, is simply the use of computers you don't own to run computer programs.

WHAT ABOUT ALL THOSE OTHER PROGRAMMING LANGUAGES? (C, JAVA, AND SO ON)

You may wonder why so many languages exist, and what they all do. Programming languages are created when a developer sees a need not addressed by the current languages. For example, Apple created the Swift programming language to make developing iPhone and iPad apps easier than Objective-C, the previous programming language used. After they're created, programming languages are very similar to spoken languages, like English or Latin. If developers code using the new language, then it thrives and grows in popularity, like English has over the last six centuries; otherwise, the programming language suffers the same fate as Latin, and becomes a dead language.

You may remember languages like C++, Java, and FORTRAN. These languages still exist today, and they're used in more places than you might think. C++ is preferred when speed and performance is extremely important, and is used to program web browsers, such as Chrome, Firefox, and Safari, along with games like Minecraft and Counter Strike. Java is preferred by many large-scale businesses, and is also one language used to program apps for the Android phone. Finally, FORTRAN is not as widespread or popular as it once was, but it is still popular within the scientific community, and it powers some functionality in the financial sector, especially at some of the largest banks in the world, many of which continue to have old code.

As long as programmers think of faster and better ways to program, new programming languages will continue to be created, while older languages fall out of favor.

Chapter **3**

Becoming a Programmer

"The way to get started is to quit talking and begin doing."

— WALT DISNEY

rogramming is a skill that can be learned by anyone. You might be a student in college wondering how to start learning or a professional hoping to find a new job or improve your performance at your current job. In just about every case, the best way to grasp how to code is pretty straightforward:

» Have a goal of what you would like to build.

» Actually start coding.

In this chapter, you discover the processes every programmer follows when programming, and the different roles programmers play to create a program — whether it's a desktop application, a web application, or a mobile app. You also find out about the tools to use when coding either offline or online.

Writing Code Using a Process

Writing code is much like painting, furniture making, or cooking — it isn't always obvious how the end product was created. However, all programs, even mysterious ones, are created using a process. Here are two of the most popular processes used today:

>> **Waterfall:** A set of *sequential* steps followed to create a program.

>> **Agile:** A set of *iterative* steps followed to create a program. (See Figure 3-1.)

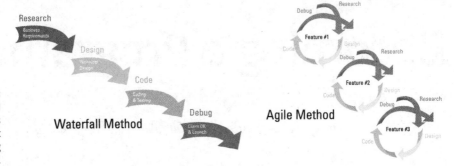

FIGURE 3-1:
The waterfall and agile processes are two different ways of creating software.

Let me describe a specific scenario to explain how these two processes work. Imagine that you want to build a restaurant app that does the following two things:

>> It displays restaurant information, such as the hours of operation and the menu.

>> It allows users to make or cancel reservations.

Using the waterfall method, you define everything the app needs to do: You design both the information-display and the reservation parts of the app, code the entire app, and then release the app to users. In contrast, using the agile method, you define, design, and code only the information-display portion of the app, release it to users, and collect feedback. Based on the feedback collected, you then redesign and make changes to the information-display to address major concerns. When you're satisfied with the information-display piece, you then define, design, and build the reservation part of the app. Again, you collect feedback and refine the reservation feature to address major concerns.

The agile methodology stresses shorter development times and has increased in popularity as the pace of technological change has increased. The waterfall approach, on the other hand, demands that the developer code and release the entire app at once, but since completing a large project takes an enormous amount of time, changes in technology may occur before the finished product arrives. If you use the waterfall method to create the restaurant-app example, the technology needed to take reservations may change by the time you get around to coding that portion of the app. Still, the waterfall approach remains popular in certain contexts, such as with financial and government software, where requirements and approval are obtained at the beginning of a project, and whose documentation of a project must be complete.

TECHNICAL STUFF

The `healthcare.gov` website, released in October 2013, was developed using a waterfall style process. Testing of all the code occurred in September 2013, when the entire system was assembled. Unfortunately, the tests occurred too late and weren't comprehensive, resulting in not enough time to fix errors before launching the site publicly.

Regardless of whether you pick the agile or waterfall methodology, coding an app involves four steps:

1. Researching what you want to build

2. Designing your app

3. Coding your app

4. Debugging your code

REMEMBER

On average, you'll spend much more time researching, designing, and debugging your app than doing the actual coding, which is the opposite of what you might expect.

These steps are described in the sections that follow.

Researching what you want to build

You have an idea for a web or mobile application and usually it starts with, "Wouldn't it be great if. . . ." Before writing any code, it helps to do some investigating. Consider the possibilities in your project as you answer the following questions:

>> What similar website/app already exists? What technology was used to build it?

>> Which features should I include — and more importantly exclude — in my app?

>> Which providers can help create these features? For example, companies like Google, Yahoo, Microsoft, or others may have software that you could incorporate into your app.

To illustrate, consider the restaurant app I discussed earlier. When conducting market research and answering the three preceding questions, using Google to search is usually the best choice. Searching for *restaurant reservation app* shows existing restaurant apps that include OpenTable, Yelp, and Reserve with Google. OpenTable, for example, allows users to reserve a table from restaurants displayed on a map using Google Maps.

In the restaurant app example, you want to research exactly what kinds of restaurant information you need to provide and how extensive the reservation system portion of the app should be. In addition, for each of these questions, you must decide whether to build the feature from scratch or to use an existing provider. For example, when providing restaurant information, do you want to show only name, cuisine, address, telephone number, and hours of operation, or do you also want to show restaurant menus? When showing restaurant data, do you prefer extensive coverage of a single geographical area, or do you want national coverage even if that means you cover fewer restaurants in any specific area?

Designing your app

Your app's visual design incorporates all of your research and describes exactly how your users will interact with every page and feature. Because your users will be accessing your site from desktop, laptop, and mobile devices, you want to make sure you create a responsive (multi-device) design and carefully consider how your site will look on all these devices. At this stage of the process, a general web designer, illustrator, or user interface specialist will help create visual designs for the app.

TIP

Many responsive app designs and templates can be found on the Internet and used freely. For specific examples, see Book 2, Chapter 6, or search Google using the query *responsive website design examples*.

There are two types of visual designs (see Figure 3-2):

>> **Wireframes:** These are low-fidelity website drawings that show structurally the ways your content and your site's interface interact.

>> **Mockups:** These are high-fidelity website previews that include colors, images, and logos.

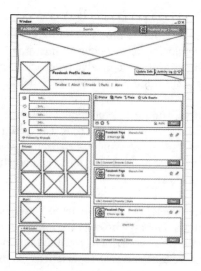

FIGURE 3-2:
Wireframes (left) are simple site renderings, whereas mockups (right) show full site previews.

TIP

Balsamiq is a popular tool used to create wireframes, and Photoshop is a popular tool to create mockups. However, you can avoid paying for additional software by using PowerPoint (PC), Keynote (Mac), or the free and open-source OpenOffice to create your app designs.

TECHNICAL STUFF

Professional designers create mockups with Adobe Photoshop and use *layers*, which isolate individual site elements. A properly created layered Photoshop file helps developers more easily write the code for those website elements.

In addition to visual design, complex apps also have technical designs and decisions to finalize. For example, if your app stores and retrieves user data, you need a database to perform these tasks. Initial decisions here include the type of database to add, the specific database provider to use, and the best way to integrate the database into the application. Additionally, developers must design the database by choosing the fields to store. The process is similar to the process of creating a spreadsheet to model a company's income — you first decide the number of columns to use, whether you'll include fields as a percentage of revenue or a numerical value, and so on. Similarly, other features like user logins or credit card payments all require you to make choices for how to implement these features.

Coding your app

With research and design done, you're now ready to code your application. In everyday web development, you begin by choosing which pages and features to start coding.

Knowing how much to code and when to stop can be tough. Developers call the first iteration of an app the *minimum viable product* — meaning you've coded just enough to test your app with real users and receive feedback. If no one likes your app or thinks it's useful, it's best to find out as soon as possible.

An app is the sum of its features, and for any individual feature, it's a good idea to write the minimum code necessary and then add to it. For example, your restaurant app may have a toolbar at the top of the page with drop-down menus. Instead of trying to create the whole menu at once, it's better to just create the main menu and then later create the drop-down menu.

Projects can involve frontend developers, who write code to design the appearance of the app, and backend developers, who code the logic and create databases. A "full stack developer" is one who can do both frontend and backend development. On large projects, it's more common to see specialized frontend and backend developers, along with project managers who ensure everyone is communicating with each other and adhering to the schedule so that the project finishes on time.

Debugging your code

Debugging is going to be a natural part of creating an application. The computer always follows your instructions exactly, yet no program ever works as you expect it to. Debugging can be frustrating. Three of the more common mistakes to watch out for are

>> **Syntax errors:** These are errors caused by misspelling words/commands, by omitting characters, or by including extra characters. Some languages, such as HTML and CSS, are forgiving of these errors, and your code will still work even with some syntax errors; whereas other languages, such as JavaScript, are more particular, and your code won't run when even one such error is present.

>> **Logic errors:** These are harder to fix. With logic errors, your syntax is correct, but the program behaves differently than you expected, such as when the prices of the items in the shopping cart of an e-commerce site don't add up to the correct total.

>> **Display errors:** These are common mainly in web applications. With display errors, your program might run and work properly, but it won't appear properly. Web apps today run on many devices, browsers, and screen sizes, so extensive testing is the only way to catch these types of errors.

The word *debugging* was popularized in the 1940s by Grace Hopper, who fixed a computer error by literally removing a moth from a computer.

TECHNICAL STUFF

Picking Tools for the Job

Now you're ready to actually start coding. You can develop websites either offline, by working with an editor, or online, with a web service such as CodeSandbox. io. CodeSandbox.io is an example of a code playground. Other code playgrounds include JSFiddle, Codepen, JSBin, PlayCode, and Plunker. Each code playground has its own strengths, and it's a good idea to experiment with several of them.

As of this writing, each of these code sandboxes is free to use (at least for the basic features). Because it's the web, however, that's subject to change at any time. Fortunately, almost any code sandbox will work fine for getting started with coding. CodeSandbox is one of the newer options, and it features support for version control as well as for collaboration and many modern web programming tools.

TIP

Especially if you haven't done any coding before, I strongly recommend that you code with access to an Internet connection using CodeSandbox.io or another code playground. That way, you don't have to download and install any software to start coding, you don't have to find a web host to serve your web pages, and you don't need to upload your web page to a web host.

Working offline

To code offline, you need the following:

>> **Editor:** This refers to the text editor you use to write all the code this book covers, including HTML, CSS, JavaScript, Ruby, Python, and PHP.

The editor you use will depend on the type of computer you have:

- *PC:* To get started, use the preinstalled Notepad or install Notepad++, a free editor available for download at notepad-plus-plus.org. A popular (and free) professional code editor is Microsoft's Visual Studio Code (also known as VSCode), which can be downloaded from https://code. visualstudio.com.

- *Mac:* Use the preinstalled TextEdit or install TextMate 2.0, an open-source editor available for download at macromates.com. Visual Studio Code also works on macOS.

>> **Browser:** Many browsers exist, including Chrome, Firefox, Safari, Microsoft Edge, and Opera.

TIP

The latest version of any of the web browsers listed here will work fine for this book. In most cases, the screenshots in this book were taken using Google Chrome.

>> **Web host:** In order for your website code to be accessible to everyone on the Internet, you need to host your website online. Freemium web hosts include Weebly (www.weebly.com) and Wix (www.wix.com); these sites offer basic hosting but charge for additional features such as additional storage or removal of ads. Google provides free web hosting through Google Sites (http://sites.google.com) and Google Drive (http://drive.google.com).

Working online with CodeSandbox.io

CodeSandbox.io is one of the easiest ways to start coding online and to share your creations with the world. The site doesn't require you to install a code editor or sign up for a web host before you start coding, and it's free to individual users like you. Once you've visited CodeSandbox for the first time, it's also possible to use it offline.

Follow these steps to get started using CodeSandbox:

1. Open https://codesandbox.io in your web browser. If you've never visited the site before, you'll see a screen similar to Figure 3-3.

FIGURE 3-3:
CodeSandbox.io's
homepage

2. **Click the button labeled Start Coding for Free. The Welcome screen, shown in Figure 3-4, will open.**

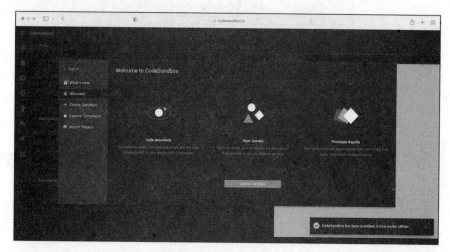

FIGURE 3-4: CodeSandbox.io's welcome page

3. **Click Create Sandbox to get to the list of templates you can choose from to make a project, as shown in Figure 3-5.**

FIGURE 3-5 The template selection screen in CodeSandbox

4. **For your first project, find the template called *static* and click it to open a basic project, as shown in Figure 3-6.**

You're now ready to start coding!

FIGURE 3-6
A new static
project in
CodeSandbox

2

Basic Web Coding

Contents at a Glance

Chapter **1**

Exploring Basic HTML

"A chain is no stronger than its weakest link, and life is after all a chain."

— WILLIAM JAMES

HTML, or *HyperText Markup Language*, is used in every single web page you browse on the Internet. Because the language is so foundational, a good first step for you is to start learning HTML.

In this chapter, you discover the HTML basics, including basic HTML structure and how to make text appear in the browser. Next, you find out how to format text and display images in a web browser. Finally, you create your own, and possibly first, HTML website. You may find that HTML without any additional styling appears to be very plain, and doesn't look like the websites you normally visit on the Internet. After you code a basic website using HTML, you will use additional languages in later chapters to add even more style and functionality to your websites.

What Does HTML Do?

HTML is the language used to give structure to a website. HTML was originally designed for creating structured documents, such as a letter, a book, or a scientific paper you might create using a word processor. Whether you use Microsoft Word or WordPad, Apple Pages, or another application, your word processor has a main window in which you type text content, and a menu or toolbar with multiple options to structure and style that text (see Figure 1-1). Using your word processor, you can create headings and sub-headings, write paragraphs, insert pictures, create footers, and so forth. Similarly, you can use HTML to structure text that appears on websites.

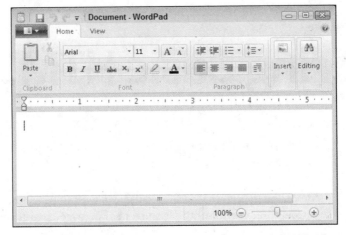

FIGURE 1-1:
The layout of a
word processor.

© John Wiley & Sons

Markup language documents, like HTML documents, are just plain text files. Unlike documents created with a word processor, you can view an HTML file using any web browser on any type of computer.

REMEMBER

HTML files are plain text files that appear styled only when viewed with a browser. By contrast, the rich text file format used by word processors adds unseen formatting commands to the file. As a result, HTML written in a rich text file won't render correctly in the browser.

Understanding HTML Structure

HTML follows a few rules to ensure that a website always displays in the same way no matter which browser or computer is used. Once you understand these rules, you'll be better able to predict how the browser will display your HTML pages, and to diagnose your mistakes when the browser displays your web page differently than you expected.

TIP

You can use any browser to display your HTML files, though I strongly recommend you download, install, and use Chrome or Firefox. Both of these browsers are updated often, are generally fast, and support and consistently render the widest variety of HTML tags.

Identifying elements

The basic building blocks of HTML are called *elements*. Elements give meaning and structure to web pages. The browser recognizes an element if the following three conditions exist:

>> The element has a name that's a letter, word, or phrase with special meaning. For example, h1 is an element recognized by the browser to mark text as a header. By default, a header will display in a browser with bold text and an enlarged font size.

>> The element's name is enclosed with a left-angle bracket (<) and right-angle bracket (>). An element enclosed in this way is called a *tag* (such as <h1>).

>> An opening tag (<element>) is followed by a closing tag (</element>). Note that the closing tag differs from the opening tag by the addition of a forward slash after the first left bracket and before the element (such as </h1>).

REMEMBER

Some HTML elements are self-closing, and don't need separate closing tags, only a forward slash in the opening tag. For more about this topic, see the section, "Getting Familiar with Common HTML Tasks and Elements," later in this chapter.

When all three conditions are met, web browsers will display the text between the opening and closing tags using some predefined style, or the browser will take some other action based on the content of the element. If one of these conditions is not met, the browser will try to figure out what you meant to do, but the result may not be what you expect.

For a better understanding of these three conditions, see the following example code:

```
<h1>This is a big heading with all three conditions</h1>
h1 This is text without the < and > sign surrounding the tag /h1
<rockstar>This is text with a tag that has no meaning to the browser</rockstar>
This is regular text
```

You can see how a browser displays this code in Figure 1-2.

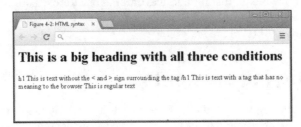

FIGURE 1-2:
The example
code displayed in
a browser.

© John Wiley & Sons

The browser applies a header effect to "This is a big heading with all three conditions" because h1 is a header element and all three conditions for a valid HTML element exist:

>> The browser recognizes the h1 element.

>> The h1 element name is surrounded with a left- (<) and right-angle bracket (>).

>> The opening tag (<h1>) is followed by text and then a closing tag (</h1>).

TIP

Notice how the h1 tags do not display in the heading. The browser will never display the actual text of a tag in a properly formatted HTML element.

The remaining lines of code display as plain text because they each are missing one of the conditions. On the second line of code, the <h1> tag is missing the left and right brackets, which violates the second condition. The third line of code violates the first condition because rockstar is not a recognized HTML element. (Once you finish this chapter, however, you may feel like a rockstar!) Finally, the fourth line of code displays as plain text because it has no opening tag preceding the text, and no closing tag following the text, which violates the third condition.

REMEMBER

Every left-angle bracket must be followed after the element name with a right-angle bracket. In addition, every opening HTML tag must be followed with a closing HTML tag.

Over 100 HTML elements exist, and you'll learn about the most important elements in the following sections. For now, don't worry about memorizing individual element names.

HTML is a forgiving language, and browsers may properly render it even if you're missing pieces of code, like a closing tag. However, if you leave in too many errors, your page won't display correctly.

Featuring your best attribute

Attributes provide additional ways to modify the behavior of an element or specify additional information. Usually, but not always, you set an attribute equal to a value enclosed in quotes. Here's an example using the `title` attribute and the `hidden` attribute:

```
<h1 title="United States of America">USA</h1>
<h1 hidden>New York City</h1>
```

The `title` attribute provides advisory information about the element that appears when the mouse cursor hovers over the affected text (in other words, a *tooltip*). In this example, the word USA is styled as a header using the `<h1>` tag with a `title` attribute set equal to `"United States of America"`. In a browser, when you place your mouse cursor over the word USA, the text `United States of America` displays as a tooltip. (See Figure 1-3.)

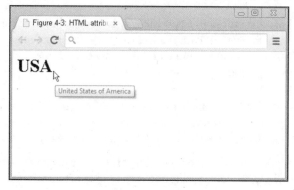

FIGURE 1-3:
A heading with title attribute has a tooltip.

© John Wiley & Sons

The `hidden` attribute indicates that the element is not relevant, so the browser won't render any elements with this attribute. In this example, the words New York City never appear in the browser window because the `hidden` attribute is in

Exploring Basic HTML

the opening `<h1>` tag. More practically, `hidden` attributes are often used to hide form fields from users so they can't edit them. For example, an RSVP website may want to include but hide from users' view a date and time field.

You don't have to use one attribute at a time. You can include multiple attributes in the opening HTML tag, like this:

```
<h1 title="United States of America" lang="en">USA</h1>
```

This example uses the `title` attribute and the `lang` attribute. The `lang` attribute is set to "en" to specify that the content of the element is in the English language.

When including multiple attributes, separate each attribute with one space.

Keep the following rules in mind when using attributes:

>> If using an attribute, always include the attribute in the opening HTML tag.

>> Multiple attributes can modify a single element.

>> If the attribute has a value, then use the equals sign (=) and enclose the value in quotes.

Standing head, title, and body above the rest

HTML files are structured in a specific way so browsers can correctly interpret the file's information. Every HTML file has the same five elements: four whose opening and closing tags appear once and only once, and one that appears once and doesn't need a closing tag. These are as follows:

>> `!DOCTYPE html` must appear first in your HTML file, and it appears only once. This tag lets browsers know which version of HTML you're using. In this case, it's the latest version, HTML5. No closing tag is necessary for this element.

>> `html` represents the *root* or beginning of an HTML document. The `<html>` tag is followed by first an opening and closing `<head>` tag, and then an opening and closing `<body>` tag.

>> `head` contains other elements that specify general information about the page, including the title.

>> `title` defines the title in the browser's title bar or page tab.

Search engines like Google use `title` to rank websites in search results.

>> body contains the main content of an HTML document. Text, images, and other content listed between the opening and closing body tag are displayed by the browser.

Here is an example of a properly structured HTML file with these five elements (see Figure 1-4):

```
<!DOCTYPE html>
<html>
<head>
   <title>Favorite Movie Quotes</title>
</head>
<body>
   <h1>"I'm going to make him an offer he can't refuse"</h1>
   <h1>"Houston, we have a problem"</h1>
   <h1>"May the Force be with you"</h1>
   <h1>"You talking to me?"</h1>
</body>
</html>
```

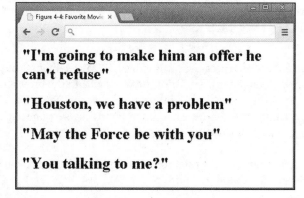

FIGURE 1-4:
A web page created with basic HTML elements.

© John Wiley & Sons

TIP

Using spaces to indent and separate your tags is highly recommended. It helps you and others read and understand your code. These spaces are only for you and any other human that reads the code, however. Your browser won't care. As far as your browser is concerned, you could run all your HTML together on one line. (Don't do this, though. The next person who reads your code will be most unhappy.)

REMEMBER

The example had many h1 elements but only one opening and closing html, head, title, and body tag.

HISTORY OF HTML

A computer engineer, Tim Berners-Lee, wanted academics to easily access academic papers and collaborate with each other. To accomplish this goal, in 1989 Mr. Berners-Lee created the first version of HTML, which had the same hyperlink elements you find in this chapter, and hosted the first website in 1991. Unlike with most other computer software, Mr. Berners-Lee made HTML available royalty-free, allowing widespread adoption and use around the world. Shortly after creating the first iteration of HTML, Mr. Berners-Lee formed the W3C (World Wide Web Consortium), which is a group of people from academic institutions and corporations who define and maintain the HTML language. The W3C continues to develop the HTML language and has defined more than 100 HTML elements, far more than the 18 that Mr. Berners-Lee originally created. The latest version of HTML is HTML5, and it has considerable functionality. In addition to supporting elements from previous HTML versions, HTML5 allows developers to write code for browsers to play audio and video files, easily locate a user's physical location, and build charts and graphs.

Getting Familiar with Common HTML Tasks and Elements

Your browser can interpret over a hundred HTML elements, but most websites use just a few elements to do most of the work within the browser. To understand this, let's try a little exercise: Think of your favorite news website. Have one in mind? Now connect to the Internet, open your browser, and type the address of that website. Bring this book with you, and take your time — I can wait!

In the event you can't access the Internet right now, take a look at the article from *The New York Times*, found in Figure 1-5.

Look closely at the news website on your screen (or look at the one in Figure 1-5). Four HTML elements are used to create the majority of the page:

>> **Headlines:** Headlines are displayed in bold and have a larger font size than the surrounding text.

>> **Paragraphs:** Each story is organized into paragraphs with whitespace dividing each paragraph.

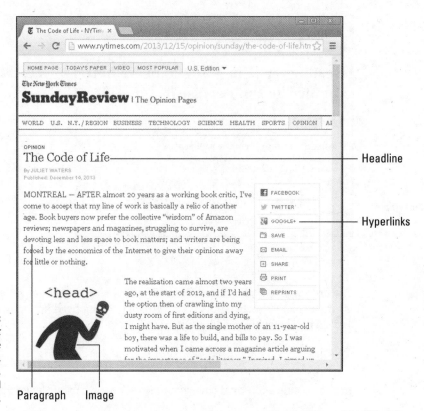

FIGURE 1-5:
The New York Times article with headline, paragraphs, hyperlinks, and images.

© John Wiley & Sons

>> **Hyperlinks:** The site's homepage and article pages have links to other stories, and links to share the story on social networks like Facebook and Twitter.

>> **Images:** Writers place images throughout the story, but also look for site images like icons and logos.

The following sections explain how to write code to create these common HTML features.

Writing headlines

Use headlines to describe a section of your page. HTML has six levels of headings (see Figure 1-6):

>> h1, which is used for the most important headings

>> h2, which is used for subheadings

>> h3 to h6, which are used for less important headings

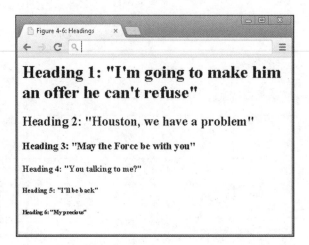

FIGURE 1-6:
Headings created
using elements
h1 through h6.

The browser renders h1 headings with a font size larger than h2's, which in turn is larger than h3's. Headings start with an opening heading tag, the heading text, and then the closing heading tag, as follows:

```
<h1>Heading text here</h1>
```

Here are some additional code examples showing various headings:

```
<h1>Heading 1: "I'm going to make him an offer he can't refuse"</h1>
<h2>Heading 2: "Houston, we have a problem"</h2>
<h3>Heading 3: "May the Force be with you"</h3>
<h4>Heading 4: "You talking to me?"</h4>
<h5>Heading 5: "I'll be back"</h5>
<h6>Heading 6: "My precious"</h6>
```

REMEMBER

Always close what you open. With headings, remember to include a closing heading tag, such as </h1>.

Organizing text in paragraphs

To display text in paragraphs, you can use the p element: Place an opening <p> tag before the paragraph, and a closing tag after it. The p element takes text and inserts a line break after the closing tag.

TIP

To insert a single line break after any element, use the <br> tag. The <br> tag is self-closing so no closing tag is needed, and </br> isn't used.

Paragraphs start with an opening paragraph tag, the paragraph text, and then the closing paragraph tag:

```
<p>Paragraph text here</p>
```

Here are some additional examples of coding a paragraph (see Figure 1-7):

```
<p>Armstrong: Okay. I'm going to step off the LM now.</p>
<p>Armstrong: That's one small step for man; one giant leap for mankind.</p>
<p>Armstrong: Yes, the surface is fine and powdery. I can kick it up loosely
            with my toe. It does adhere in fine layers, like powdered
            charcoal, to the sole and sides of my boots.</p>
```

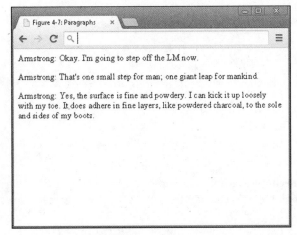

FIGURE 1-7:
Text displayed in paragraphs using the p element.

Linking to your (heart's) content

Hyperlinks are one of HTML's most valuable features. Web pages that include hyperlinked references to other sources allow the reader to access those sources with just a click, a big advantage over printed pages.

Hyperlinks have two parts:

>> **Link destination:** The web page the browser visits once the link is clicked.

   To define the link destination in HTML, start with an opening anchor tag (<a>) that has an href attribute. Then add the value of the href attribute, which is the website the browser will go to once the link is clicked.

>> **Link description:** The words used to describe the link.

To create a hyperlink, add text to describe the link after the opening anchor tag, and then add the closing anchor tag.

The resulting HTML should look something like this:

```
<a href="website url">Link description</a>
```

Here are three more examples of coding a hyperlink (see Figure 1-8):

```
<a href="http://www.amazon.com">Purchase anything</a>
<a href="http://www.airbnb.com">Rent a place to stay from a local host</a>
<a href="http://www.techcrunch.com">Tech industry blog</a>
```

FIGURE 1-8:
Three hyperlinks created using the a element.

When rendering hyperlinks, the browser, by default, will underline the link and color the link blue. To change these default properties, see Book 2, Chapter 3.

The `<a>` tag does not include a line break after the link.

REMEMBER

Google's search engine ranks web pages partly based on the words used to describe a web page between the opening and closing `<a>` tags. This improved on search results from previous methods, which relied primarily on analyzing page content.

TECHNICAL
STUFF

Adding images

Images spruce up otherwise plain HTML text pages. To include an image on your web page — your own or someone else's — you must obtain the image's web address. Websites like Google Images (images.google.com) and Flickr (www.flickr.com) allow you to search for online images based on keywords. When you find an image you like, right-click on the image and select Copy Image URL.

WARNING

Make sure you have permission to use an online image. Flickr has tools that allow you to search for images with few to no license restrictions. Additionally, websites pay to host images and incur charges when a website directly links to an image. For this reason, some websites do not allow *hotlinking*, or linking directly from third-party websites to an image.

TIP

If you want to use an image that has not already been uploaded to the Internet, you can use a site like www.imgur.com to upload the image. After uploading, you will be able to copy the image URL and use it in your HTML.

To include an image, start with an opening image tag `<img>`, define the source of the image using the `src` attribute, and include a forward slash at the end of the opening tag to close the tag (see Figure 1-9):

```
<img src="http://upload.wikimedia.org/wikipedia/commons/5/55/Grace_Hopper.jpg"/>
<img src="http://upload.wikimedia.org/wikipedia/commons/b/bd/Bill_Gates.jpg"/>
```

FIGURE 1-9:
Images of
Grace Hopper,
a U.S. Navy
rear admiral,
and Bill Gates,
the cofounder
of Microsoft,
rendered using
`<img>`.

Bill Gates photo credit https://commons.wikimedia.org/wiki/
File:Dts_news_bill_gates_wikipedia.JPG

TIP

The image tag is self-closing, which means a separate `</img>` closing image tag is not used. The image tag is one of the exceptions to the always-close-what-you-open rule!

Exploring Basic HTML

Styling Me Pretty

Now that you know how to display basic text and images in a browser, you should understand how to further customize and style them. HTML has basic capabilities to style content, and later chapters show you how to use CSS to style and position your content down to the last pixel. Here, however, I explain how to do some basic text formatting in HTML, and then you'll build your first web page.

Highlighting with bold, italics, underline, and strikethrough

HTML allows for basic text styling using the following elements:

» strong marks important text, which the browser displays as bold

» em marks emphasized text, which the browser displays as italicized

» u marks text as underlined

» del marks deleted text, which the browser displays as strikethrough

REMEMBER

The underline element is not typically used for text because it can lead to confusion. Hyperlinks, after all, are underlined by default.

To use these elements, start with the element's opening tag, followed by the affected text, and then a closing tag, as follows:

```
<element name>Affected text</element name>
```

Here are some examples (see Figure 1-10):

```
Grace Hopper, <strong> a US Navy rear admiral </strong>, popularized the term
"debugging."
Bill Gates co-founded a company called <em>Microsoft</em>.
Stuart Russell and Peter Norvig wrote a book called <u>Artificial Intelligence:
A Modern Approach</u>.
Mark Zuckerberg created a website called <del>Nosebook</del> Facebook.
Steve Jobs co-founded a company called <del><em>Peach</em></del> <em>Apple</em>
```

TIP

You can apply multiple effects to text by using multiple HTML tags. Always close the most recently opened tag first and then the next most recently used tag. For an example, look at the last line of code in Figure 1-10 and the tags applied to the word *Peach*.

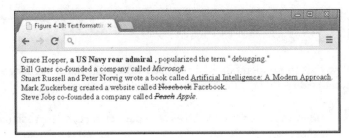

FIGURE 1-10:
Sentences
formatted using
bold, italics,
underline, and
strikethrough.

© John Wiley & Sons

Raising and lowering text with superscript and subscript

Reference works like *Wikipedia* and technical papers often use superscript for footnotes and subscript for chemical names. To apply these styles, use the elements

» sup for text marked as superscript

» sub for text marked as subscript

To use these elements, start with the element's opening tag, followed by the affected text, and then a closing tag as follows:

```
<element name>Affected text</element name>
```

Here are two examples (see Figure 1-11):

```
<p>The University of Pennsylvania announced to the public the first
electronic general-purpose computer, named ENIAC, on February 14,
1946.<sup>1</sup></p>
<p>The Centers for Disease Control and Prevention recommends drinking
several glasses of H<sub>2</sub>0 per day.</p>
```

TIP

When using the superscript element to mark footnotes, use an ‹a› anchor tag to link directly to the footnote so the reader can view the footnote easily.

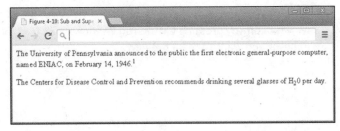

FIGURE 1-11:
Text formatted to
show superscript
and subscript
effects.

© John Wiley & Sons

Building Your First Website Using HTML

Now that you understand the basics, you can put that knowledge to use. You can practice directly on your computer by following these steps:

1. **Open any text editor, such as Notepad (on a PC) or TextEdit (on a Mac).**

   On a PC running Microsoft Windows, you can access Notepad by clicking the Start button and selecting Run; in the search box, type **Notepad**.

   On a Macintosh, select the Spotlight Search (hourglass icon on the top-right corner of the toolbar), and type **TextEdit**.

2. **Enter into the text editor any of the code samples you have seen in this chapter or create your own combination of the code.**

3. **Once you have finished, save the file and make sure to include** `.html` **at the end of the filename.**

4. **Double-click the file to open it in your default browser.**

TIP

Visual Studio Code is a specialized text editor created specifically for writing code. You can download it (for macOS, Windows, or Linux) at code.visualstudio.com.

If you want to practice your HTML online, you can use the CodeSandbox.io website. It's a code playground that you can use to code websites and web apps without installing or downloading any software. (See Figure 1-12.) Practice all the tags (and a few more) that you find in this chapter by following these steps:

1. **Open your browser and go to** codesandbox.io.

2. **If you have a codesandbox account, sign in.**

   Signing up is discussed in Book 1, Chapter 3.

   Creating an account allows you to save your progress as you work, but it's optional.

TECHNICAL STUFF

3. **Create a new sandbox using the static template.**

4. **Edit the** index.html **file using the elements you've learned about in this chapter.**

5. **Save your code by pressing CMD+S (on Windows) or CTL+S (on macOS) whenever you want to see a preview.**

FIGURE 1-12:
The Code
Sandbox.io
interface

© John Wiley & Sons

Exploring Basic HTML

Chapter **2**

Getting More Out of HTML

"I'm controlling, and I want everything orderly, and I need lists."

— SANDRA BULLOCK

E ven your best content needs structure to increase readability for your users. This book is no exception. Consider the "In This Chapter" bulleted list of items at the top of this chapter, or the table of contents at the beginning of the book. Lists and tables make things easier for you to understand at a glance. By mirroring the structure you find in a book or magazine, web elements let you precisely define how content, such as text and images, appear on the web.

In this chapter, you find out how to use HTML elements such as lists, tables, and forms, and how to know when these elements are appropriate for your content.

Organizing Content on the Page

Readability is the most important principle for organizing and displaying content on your web page. Your web page should allow visitors to easily read, understand, and act on your content. The desired action you have in mind for your visitors may be to click on and read additional content, share the content with others, or perhaps make a purchase. Poorly organized content will lead users to leave your website before engaging with your content long enough to complete the desired action.

Figures 2-1 and 2-2 show two examples of website readability. Figure 2-1 shows a search at Craigslist.org for an apartment in Portland, Oregon. The search results are structured like a list, and you can limit the content displayed using the filters and search forms. Each listing has multiple attributes, such as a description, the number of bedrooms, the neighborhood, and, most importantly, the price. Comparing similar attributes from different listings takes some effort — notice the jagged line your eye must follow.

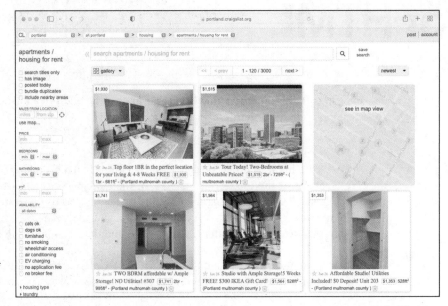

FIGURE 2-1:
A Craigslist.org listing of apartments in Portland.

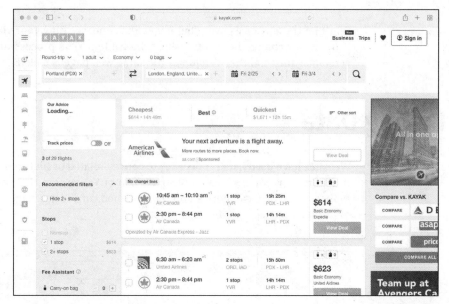

FIGURE 2-2:
A Kayak.com
listing of flights
from Portland to
London.

Figure 2-2 shows the results of a search at Kayak.com for flights from Portland to London. As with the Craigslist search results, you can limit the content displayed using the filters and search forms. Additionally, each flight listing has multiple attributes, including price, carrier, departure time, landing time, and duration, which are similar to the attributes of the apartment listings. Comparing similar attributes from different flights is much easier with the Kayak layout, however. Notice how the content, in contrast to Craigslist's, has a layout that allows your eye to follow a straight line down the page, so you can easily rank and compare different options.

TIP

Don't underestimate the power of simplicity when displaying content. Although Craigslist's content layout may look almost too simple, the site is one of the top 50 most visited websites in the world. Reddit.com is another example of a top 50 website with a simple layout.

Before displaying your content, ask yourself a few questions first:

>> **Does your content have one attribute with related data, or does it follow sequential steps?** If so, consider using lists.

>> **Does your content have multiple attributes suitable for comparison?** If so, consider using tables.

>> **Do you need to collect input from the visitor?** If so, consider using forms.

Don't let these choices overwhelm you. Pick one, see how your visitors react, and if necessary change how you display the content. The process of evaluating one version against another version of the same web page is called *A/B testing*.

Listing Data

Websites have used lists for decades to convey related or hierarchical information. In Figure 2-3, you can see an older version of Yahoo.com that uses bulleted lists to display various categories and today's Food.com recipe page, which uses lists to display various ingredients.

Lists begin with a symbol, an indentation, and then the list item. The symbol used can be a number, letter, bullet, or no symbol at all.

Creating ordered and unordered lists

Here are the two most popular types of lists:

>> **Ordered:** Ordered lists are numerical or alphabetical lists in which the sequence of list items is important.

>> **Unordered:** These lists are usually bulleted lists in which the sequence of list items has no importance.

You create lists by specifying the type of list as ordered or unordered and then adding each list item using the `li` tag, as shown in the following steps:

1. **Specify the type of list.**

   Add opening and closing list tags that specify either an ordered (ol) or unordered (ul) list, as follows:

   - ol to specify the beginning and end of an ordered list

   - ul to specify the beginning and end of an unordered list

2. **Add an opening and closing tag (that is, <li> and </li>) for each item in the list.**

   For example, here's an ordered list:

```
<ol>
    <li> List item #1 </li>
    <li> List item #2 </li>
    <li> List item #3 </li>
</ol>
```

Nesting lists

Additionally, you can nest lists within lists. A list of any type can be nested inside another list; to nest a list, replace the list item tag <li> with a list type tag, either <ol> or <ul>.

The example code in Figure 2-4 shows various list types including a nested list. (See Figures 2-4 and 2-5.)

```
1  <!--Ordinary list-->
2  <h1>Tasks for today</h1>
3  <ol>
4      <li>Schedule a product meeting</li>
5      <li>Have lunch with Arun</li>
6      <li>Draft client presentation</li>
7  </ol>
8
9  <!--Nested list-->
10 <h1>Tasks for tomorrow</h1>
11 <ul>
12     <li>Send sketches to London office</li>
13     <li>File expense reports</li>
14     <ol>
15         <li>Trip to San Francisco</li>
16         <li>Trip to Los Angeles</li>
17     </ol>
18 </ul>
```

FIGURE 2-4: Coding an ordered list and a nested list.

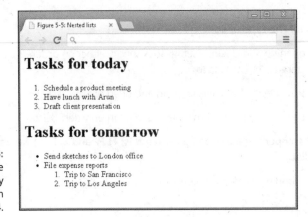

FIGURE 2-5:
The page produced by the code in Figure 2-4.

© John Wiley & Sons

TIP

The <h1> tag shown in this code sample is not necessary to create a list. I use it here only to name each list.

Every opening list or list item tag must be followed with a closing list or list item tag.

Putting Data in Tables

Tables help further organize text and tabular data on the page. (See Figure 2-6.) The table format is especially appropriate when displaying pricing information, comparing features across products, or in any situation where the columns or rows share a common attribute. Tables act as containers and can hold and display any type of content, including text, such as heading and lists and images. For example, the table in Figure 2-6 includes additional content and styling like icons at the top of each column, gray background shading, and rounded buttons. This content and styling can make tables you see online differ from tables you ordinarily see in books.

TIP

Avoid using tables to create page layouts. In the past, developers created multi-column layouts using tables, but today developers use CSS (see Book 2, Chapters 3 and 4) for layout-related tasks.

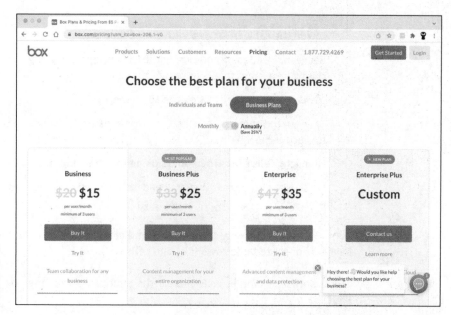

FIGURE 2-6:
Box.com
uses tables to
display pricing
information.

Basic table structuring

Tables comprise several parts, like the one shown in Figure 2-7.

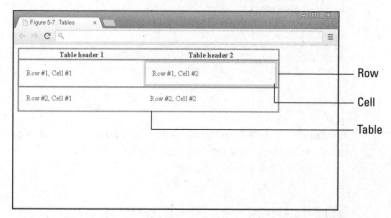

FIGURE 2-7:
The different
parts of a table.

You create a table by following these steps:

1. **Define a table with the `table` element.**

To do this, add the opening and closing `<table>` tags.

2. **Divide the table into rows with the tr element.**

Between the opening and closing table tags, create opening `<tr>` tags and closing `</tr>` tags for each row of your table.

3. **Divide rows into cells using the td element.**

Between the opening and closing tr tags, create opening and closing td tags for each cell in the row.

4. **Highlight cells that are headers using the th element.**

Finally, specify any cells that are headers by replacing the td element with a th element.

Your table will have only one opening and closing `<table>` tag; however, you can have one or more table rows (tr) and cells (td).

The following example code shows the syntax for creating the table shown in Figure 2-7.

```
<table>
   <tr>
     <th>Table header 1</th>
     <th>Table header 2</th>
   </tr>
   <tr>
     <td>Row #1, Cell #1</td>
     <td>Row #1, Cell #2</td>
   </tr>
   <tr>
     <td>Row #2, Cell #1</td>
     <td>Row #2, Cell #2</td>
   </tr>
</table>>
```

After you've decided how many rows and columns your table will have, make sure to use an opening and closing `<tr>` tag for each row and an opening and closing `<td>` tag for each cell in the row.

Stretching table columns and rows

Take a look at the table describing Facebook's income statement in Figure 2-8. Each year appears in individual columns of equal-sized width. Now look at Total Revenue, which appears in a cell that stretches or spans across several columns.

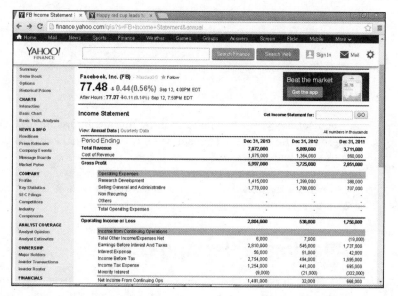

FIGURE 2-8:
An income
statement in a
table with
columns of
different sizes.

© John Wiley & Sons

TECHNICAL
STUFF

Stretching a cell across columns or rows is called *spanning*.

The colspan attribute spans a column over subsequent vertical columns. The value of the colspan attribute is set equal to the number of columns you want to span. You always span a column from left to right. Similarly, the rowspan attribute spans a row over subsequent horizontal rows. Set rowspan equal to the number of rows you want to span.

The following code generates a part of the table shown in Figure 2-8. You can see the colspan attribute spans the Total Revenue cell across two columns. As described in Book 2, Chapter 1, the <strong> tag is used to mark important text and is shown as bold by the browser.

```
<tr>
    <td colspan="2">
        <strong>Total Revenue</strong>
    </td>
    <td>
        <strong>112,330,000</strong>
    </td>
    <td>
        <strong>85,965,000</strong>
    </td>
    <td>
        <strong>70,697,000</strong>
    </td>
```

```
<td>
    <strong>55,838,000</strong>
</td>

</tr>
```

REMEMBER

If you set a column or row to span by more columns or rows than are actually present in the table, the browser will insert additional columns or rows, changing your table layout.

TIP

CSS helps size individual columns and rows, as well as entire tables. See Book 2, Chapters 3 and 4.

Aligning tables and cells

WARNING

The latest version of HTML does not support the tags and attributes in this section. Although your browser may correctly render this code, there is no guarantee your browser will correctly render it in the future. I include these attributes because, as of this writing, HTML code on the Internet still uses these deprecated (older) attributes in tables. This code is similar to expletives — recognize them but try not to use them. Refer to Book 2, Chapter 3 to see modern techniques using Cascading Style Sheets (CSS) for achieving the identical effects.

The `table` element has three deprecated attributes you need to know — `align`, `width`, and `border`. These attributes are described in Table 2-1.

TABLE 2-1

Table Attributes Replaced by CSS

Attribute Name	Possible Values	Description
`align`	`left` `center` `right`	Position of table relative to the containing document according to the value of the attribute. For example, `align="right"` positions the table on the right side of the web page.
`width`	`pixels (#)` `%`	Width of table measured either in pixels on-screen or as a percentage of the browser window or container tag.
`border`	`pixels (#)`	Width of table border in pixels.

The following example code shows the syntax for creating the table in Figure 2-9 with `align`, `width`, and `border` attributes.

FIGURE 2-9:
A table with
deprecated
align, width,
and border
attributes.

The Social Network | Generation Like
Tron | War Games

© John Wiley & Sons

```
<table align="right" width=50% border=1>
    <tr>
        <td>The Social Network</td>
        <td>Generation Like</td>
    </tr>
    <tr>
        <td>Tron</td>
    <td>War Games</td>
    </tr>
</table>>
```

REMEMBER

Always insert attributes inside the opening <html> tag and enclose words in quotes.

The tr element has two deprecated attributes you need to know — align and valign. These are described in Table 2-2.

TABLE 2-2

Table Row Attributes Replaced by CSS

Attribute Name	Possible Values	Description
align	left right center justify	Horizontal alignment of a row's cell contents according to the value of the attribute. For example, align="right" positions a row's cell contents on the right side of each cell.
valign	top middle bottom	Vertical alignment of a row's cell contents according to the value of the attribute. For example, align="bottom" positions a row's cell contents on the bottom of each cell.

The td element has four deprecated attributes you need to know — align, valign, width, and height. These are described in Table 2-3.

TABLE 2-3 **Table Cell Attributes Replaced by CSS**

Attribute Name	Possible Values	Description
align	left right center justify	Horizontal alignment of a cell's contents according to the value of the attribute. For example, align="center" positions the cell's contents in the center of the cell.
valign	top middle bottom	Vertical alignment of a cell's contents according to the value of the attribute. For example, align="middle" positions a cell's contents in the middle of the cell.
width	pixels (#) %	Width of a cell measured either in pixels on-screen or as a percentage of the table width.
height	pixels (#) %	Height of a cell measured either in pixels on-screen or as a percentage of the table width.

The following example code shows the syntax for creating the table in Figure 2-10 with the align, valign, width, and height attributes.

```
<table align="right" width=50% border=1>
    <tr align="right" valign="bottom">
      <td height=100>The Social Network</td>
      <td>Generation Like</td>
    </tr>
    <tr>
      <td height=200 align="center" valign="middle">Tron</td>
      <td align="center" valign="top" width=20%>War Games</td>
    </tr>
</table>>
```

WARNING

Remember, these attributes are no longer supported and should not be used in your code.

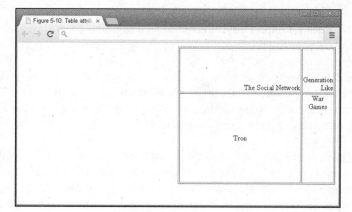

FIGURE 2-10:
A table with deprecated `align`, `valign`, `width`, and `height` attributes.

Filling Out Forms

Forms allow you to capture input from your website visitors. Until now we have displayed content as-is, but capturing input from visitors allows you to do the following:

>> **Modify existing content on the page.** For example, price and date filters on airline websites allow for finding a desired flight more quickly.

>> **Store the input for later use.** For example, a website may use a registration form to collect your email, username, and password information to allow you to access it at a later date.

Understanding how forms work

Forms pass information entered by a user to a server by using the following process:

1. The browser displays a form on the client machine.

2. The user completes the form and presses the Submit button.

3. The browser submits the data collected from the form to a server.

4. The server processes and stores the data and sends a response to the client machine.

5. The browser displays the response, usually indicating whether the submission was successful.

See Book 1, Chapter 2 for an additional discussion about the relationship between the client and server.

TIP

REMEMBER

A full description of how the server receives and stores data (Steps 3 to 5) is beyond the scope of this book. For now, all you need to know is that server-side programming languages such as Python, PHP, and Ruby are used to write scripts that receive and store form submissions.

Forms are very flexible and can record a variety of user inputs. Input fields used in forms can include free text fields, radio buttons, checkboxes, drop-down menus, range sliders, dates, phone numbers, and more. (See Table 2-4.) Additionally, input fields can be set to initial default values without any user input.

TABLE 2-4

Selected Form Attributes

Attribute Name	Possible Values	Description
type	checkbox email submit text password radio (a complete list of values has been omitted here for brevity)	Defines the type of input field to display in the form. For example, text is used for free text fields, and submit is used to create a Submit button.
value	text	The initial value of the input control.

View the entire list of form input types and example code at www.w3schools.com/tags/att_input_type.asp.

TIP

Creating basic forms

You create a basic form by following these steps

1. **Define a form with the form element.**

   Start by adding an opening ‹form› tag and closing ‹/form› tag.

2. **Using the** `action` **attribute, specify in the** `form` **element where to send form data.**

Add an `action` attribute to your opening `<form>` tag and set it equal to the URL of a script that will process and store the user input.

3. **Using the** `method` **attribute, specify in the** `form` **element how to send form data.**

Add a `method` attribute to your opening `<form>` tag and set it equal to `POST`.

The `method` attribute is set equal to `GET` or `POST`. The technicalities of each are beyond the scope of this book, but, in general, `POST` is used for storing sensitive information (such as credit card numbers), whereas `GET` is used to allow users to bookmark or share with others the results of a submitted form (for example, airline flight listings).

4. **Provide a way for users to input and submit responses with the** `input` **element.**

Between the opening `<form>` and closing `</form>` tags, create one `<input>` tag.

Your form will have only one opening and closing `<form>` tag; however, you will have at least two `<input>` tags to collect and submit user data.

5. **Specify input types using the** `type` **attribute in the** `input` **element.**

For this example, set the `type` attribute equal to `"text"`.

The `<input>` tag doesn't have a closing tag, which is an exception to the "close every tag you open" rule. These tags are called self-closing tags, and you can see more examples in Book 2, Chapter 1.

6. **Finally, create another** `<input>` **tag and set the** `type` **attribute equal to** `submit`.

The following example code shows the syntax for creating the form shown in Figure 2-11.

```
<form action="mailto:chris@minnick.com" method="POST">
    <input type="text" value="Type a short message here">
    <input type="submit">
</form>
```

The `action` attribute in this form is set equal to `mailto`, which signals to the browser to send an email using your default mail client (such as Outlook or Gmail). If your browser isn't configured to handle email links, this form won't work. Ordinarily, forms are submitted to a server to process and store the form's contents, but in this example form, the contents are submitted to the user's email application.

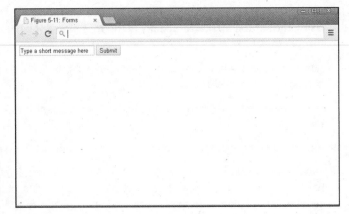

FIGURE 2-11:
A form with one
user input and a
Submit button.

Practicing More with HTML

Practice your HTML online using the CodeSandbox.io website (or one of the other code playgrounds listed in Book 1). Practice all the tags that you find in this chapter by following these steps:

1. **Open your browser and go to** `codesandbox.io`.

2. **If you have a codesandbox account, sign in.**

   Signing up is discussed in Book 1, Chapter 3.

   Creating an account allows you to save your progress as you work, but it's optional.

**TECHNICAL
STUFF**

3. **Create a new sandbox using the static template, or open the sandbox that you created in Book 2, Chapter 1.**

4. **Edit the** `index.html` **file using the elements you learned about in this chapter. For example, create a list of your favorite songs or try creating a table containing seven columns (one for each day of the week). Inside each column, create a list of things you need to do on that day of the week.**

5. **Save your code by pressing CMD+S (on Windows) or CTL+S (on macOS) whenever you want to see a preview.**

» **Formatting text size, color, and style**

» **Styling images**

» **Using CSS in three different contexts**

Chapter **3**

Getting Stylish with CSS

"Create your own style . . . let it be unique for yourself and yet identifiable for others."

— ANNA WINTOUR

The website code examples in the preceding chapters resemble websites you may have seen from a previous era. Websites you browse today are different, and they have a more polished look and feel. Numerous factors enabled this change. Twenty years ago you might have browsed the Internet with a dial-up modem, but today you likely use a very fast Internet connection and a more powerful computer. Programmers have used this extra bandwidth and speed to write code to further customize and style websites.

In this chapter you discover modern techniques to style websites using Cascading Style Sheets (CSS). First, you'll learn basic CSS structure and then the CSS rules to style your content. Finally, you'll see how to apply these rules to your websites.

What Does CSS Do?

CSS styles HTML elements with greater control than HTML does. Take a look at Figure 3-1. On the left, Facebook appears as it currently exists; on the right, however, the same Facebook page is shown without all the CSS styling. Without the CSS, all the images and text appear left-justified, borders and shading disappear, and text has minimal formatting.

FIGURE 3-1:
Left Facebook
with CSS.
Right: Facebook
without CSS.

CSS can style almost any HTML tag that creates a visible element on the page, including all the HTML tags used to create headings, paragraphs, links, images, lists, and tables that you learned about in previous chapters. Specifically, CSS allows you to style

>> Text size, color, style, typeface, and alignment

>> Link color and style

>> Image size and alignment

>> List bullet styles and indentation

>> Table size, shading, borders, and alignment

REMEMBER

CSS styles and positions the HTML elements that appear on a web page. However, some HTML elements (for example, `<head>`) aren't visible on the page and aren't styled using CSS.

You may wonder why creating a separate language like CSS to handle styling was considered a better approach than expanding the capabilities of HTML. There are three reasons:

>> **History:** CSS was created four years after HTML as an experiment to see whether developers and consumers wanted extra styling effects. At the time, it was unclear whether CSS would be useful and only some major browsers supported it. As a result, CSS was created separately from HTML to allow developers to build sites using just HTML.

>> **Code management:** Initially, some CSS functionality overlapped with existing HTML functionality. However, specifying styling effects in HTML results in cluttered and messy code. For example, specifying a particular font typeface in HTML requires that you include the font typeface attribute in every paragraph (`<p>`) tag. Styling a single paragraph this way is easy, but applying the font to a series of paragraphs (or an entire page or website) quickly becomes tedious. By contrast, CSS requires the typeface to be specified only once, and it automatically applies to all paragraphs. This feature makes it easier for developers to write and maintain code. In addition, separating the styling of the content from the actual content itself has allowed search engines and other automated website agents to more easily process the content on web pages.

>> **Accessibility:** Web browsers aren't the only place where web pages are used. In addition to traditional web browsers, web pages may also be used by screen readers for the blind, text-to-speech applications, smart speakers, and much more. Different kinds of devices require different types of styling. By separating style (CSS) from structure (HTML) web pages become much more flexible and the content of the web page can be used more easily by more people.

CSS Structure

CSS follows a set of rules to ensure that websites will be displayed in the same way no matter the browser or computer used. Sometimes, because of varying support of the CSS standard, browsers can and do display web pages differently. Nevertheless, generally speaking, CSS ensures that users have a consistent experience across all browsers.

TIP

Every web browser will interpret CSS rules to style your HTML, though you should be sure to download, install, and use the latest version of Chrome, Safari, Firefox, Edge, or Opera for the best experience.

Choosing the element to style

CSS continues to evolve and support increased functionality, but the basic syntax for defining CSS rules remains the same. CSS modifies HTML elements with rules that apply to each element. These rules are written as follows:

```
selector {
  property: value;
}
```

A CSS rule is comprised of three parts:

>> **Selector:** The HTML element you want to style.

>> **Property:** The feature of the HTML element you want to style. For example, font typeface, image height, or color.

>> **Value:** The options for the property that the CSS rule sets. For example, if color were the property, the value would be red.

The selector identifies which HTML element you want to style. In HTML, an element is surrounded by angle brackets, but in CSS, the selector stands alone. The selector is followed by a space, an opening left curly bracket ({), property with a value, and then a closing right curly bracket (}). The line break after the opening curly bracket, and before the closing curly bracket is not required by CSS — in fact, you could put all your code on one line with no line breaks or spaces. Using line breaks is the convention followed by developers to make CSS easier to modify and read.

You can find curly brackets on most keyboards to the right of the P key.

The following code shows you an example of CSS modifying a specific HTML element. The CSS code appears first, followed by the HTML code that it modifies:

The CSS:

```
h1 {
    font-family: cursive;
}
```

And now the HTML:

```
<h1>
    Largest IPOs in US History
</h1>
<ul>
    <li>2014: Alibaba - $20B</li>
    <li>2008: Visa - $18B</li>
</ul>
```

The CSS selector targets and styles the HTML element with the same name (in this case, ‹h1› tags). For example, in Figure 3-2, the heading "Largest IPOs in US History," created using the opening and closing ‹h1› tag is styled using the h1 selector, and the font-family property with cursive value.

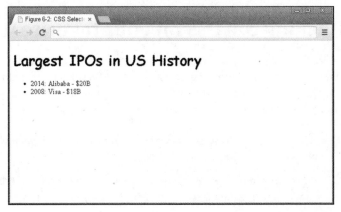

FIGURE 3-2:
CSS targeting
the heading h1
element.

© John Wiley & Sons

CSS uses a colon instead of the equals sign (=) to set values of CSS properties.

REMEMBER

The font in Figure 3-2 likely doesn't appear to be cursive, as defined in the preceding code, because cursive is the name of a generic font family, not a specific font. Generic font families are described later in this chapter.

TIP

My property has value

CSS syntax requires that a CSS property and its value appear within opening and closing curly brackets. After each property is a colon, and after each value is a semicolon. This combination of property and value together is called a *declaration*, and a group of properties and values is called a *declaration block*.

Let's look at a specific example with multiple properties and values:

```
h1 {
    font-size: 15px;
    color: blue;
}
```

In this example, CSS styles the h1 element, changing the font-size property to 15px, and the color property to blue.

TIP

You can improve the readability of your code by putting each declaration (each property/value combination) on its own line. Additionally, adding spaces or tabs to indent the declarations also improves the readability. Adding these line breaks and indentions doesn't affect browser performance in any way, but it will make it easier for you and others to read your code.

Hacking the CSS on your favorite website

In Book 1, Chapter 2, you modified a news website's HTML code. In this chapter, you modify its CSS. Let's take a look at some CSS rules in the wild. In this example, you change the CSS on huffpost.com (or your news website of choice) using the Chrome browser. Just follow these steps:

1. **Using a Chrome browser, navigate to your favorite news website, ideally one with many headlines. (See Figure 3-3.)**

2. **Place your mouse pointer over a headline and right-click. From the menu that appears, select Inspect. (See Figure 3-4.)**

   A window opens at the bottom of your browser.

3. **Click the Styles tab on the right side of this window to see the CSS rules being applied to HTML elements.**

4. **Change the color of the headline using CSS.**

   To do this, first find the color property in the element.style section; note the square color box within that property that displays a sample of the current color. Click this box and change the value by selecting a new color from the pop-up menu, and then press Enter.

   Your headline now appears in the color you picked. (See Figure 3-5.)

TIP

If the element.style section is blank and no color property appears, you can still add it manually. To do so, click once in the element.style section, and when the blinking cursor appears, type **color: purple**. The headline changes to purple.

TIP

As with HTML, you can modify any website's CSS using Chrome's Inspect feature. Most modern browsers, including Firefox, Edge, Safari, and Opera, have a similar feature.

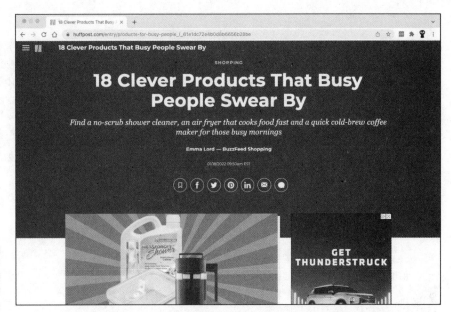

FIGURE 3-3:
The Huffington
Post website
before
modification.

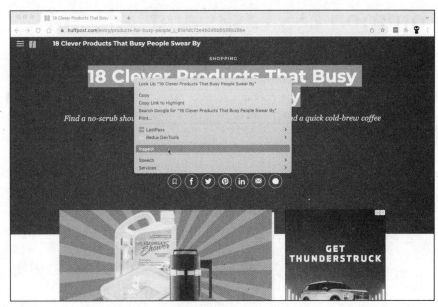

FIGURE 3-4:
Inspecting
the website's
headline.

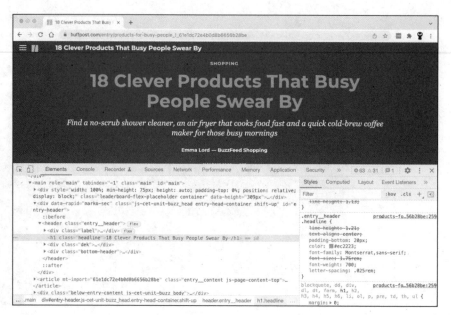

FIGURE 3-5:
Changing the CSS changes the color of the headline.

Common CSS Tasks and Selectors

Although CSS includes over 150 properties and many values for each property, on modern websites, a handful of CSS properties and values do the majority of the work. In the previous section, when you "hacked" the CSS on a live website, you changed the heading color — a common task in CSS. Other common tasks performed with CSS include

>> Changing font size, style, font family, and decoration

>> Customizing links including color, background color, and link state

>> Adding background images and formatting foreground images

Font gymnastics: Size, color, style, family, and decoration

CSS lets you control text in many HTML elements. The most common text-related CSS properties and values are shown in Table 3-1. I describe these properties and values more fully in the sections that follow.

TABLE 3-1 ## Common CSS Properties and Values for Styling Text

Property Name	Possible Values	Description
font-size	pixels (#px) % em (#em)	Specifies the size of text measured either in pixels as a percentage of the containing element's font size or with an em value, which is calculated by desired pixel value divided by containing element font size in pixels. Example: font-size: 16px;
color	name hex code rgb value	Changes the color of the text specified using names (color: blue;), hexadecimal code (color: #0000FF;), or RGB (red, green, and blue) value (color: rgb(0,0,255);).
font-style	normal italic	Sets font to appear in italics (or not).
font-weight	normal bold	Sets font to appear as bold (or not).
font-family	font name	Sets the font typeface. Example: font-family: serif;
text-decoration	none underline line-through	Sets font to have an underline or strikethrough (or not).

Setting the font-size

As in a word processor, you can set the size of the font you're using with CSS's font-size property. You have a few options for setting the font size, and the most common one is to use pixels, as in the following:

```
p {
   font-size: 16px;
}
```

In this example, I used the p selector to size the paragraph text to 16 pixels. One disadvantage of using pixels to size your font occurs when users who prefer a large font size for readability have changed their browser settings to a default font size value that's larger than the one you specify on your site. In these situations, the font size specified in the browser takes precedence, and the fonts on your site will not scale to adjust to these preferences.

Percentage-sizing and em values, the other options to size your fonts, are considered more accessibility-friendly. The default browser font size of normal text is 16 pixels. With percentage-sizing and em values, fonts can be sized relative to the user-specified default. For example, the CSS for percentage-sizing looks like this:

```
p {
   font-size: 150%;
}
```

In this example, I used the p selector to size the paragraph text to 150 percent of the default size. If the browser's default font size was set at 16 pixels, this paragraph's font would appear sized at 24 pixels (150 percent of 16).

TECHNICAL STUFF

A font-size equal to 1px is equivalent to one pixel on your monitor, so the actual size of the text displayed varies according to the size of the monitor. Accordingly, for a fixed font size in pixels, the text appears smaller as you increase the screen resolution.

Setting the color

The color property sets the color in one of three ways:

» **Name:** One hundred forty-seven colors can be referenced by name. You can reference common colors, such as black, blue, and red, along with uncommon colors, such as burlywood, lemon chiffon, thistle, and rebeccapurple.

TECHNICAL STUFF

Rebecca Meyer, the daughter of prominent CSS standards author Eric Meyer, passed away in 2014 from brain cancer at the age of six. In response, the CSS standardization committee approved adding a shade of purple called rebeccapurple to the CSS specification in Rebecca's honor. All major Internet browsers have implemented support for the color.

» **Hex code:** Colors can be defined by component parts of red, green, and blue, and when hexadecimal code is used, over 16 million colors can be referenced. In the code example, I set the h1 color equal to #FF0000. After the hashtag, the first two digits (FF) refer to the red in the color, the next two digits (00) refer to the green in the color, and the final two digits (00) refer to the blue in the color.

» **RGB value:** Just like hex codes, RGB values specify the red, green, and blue component parts for over 16 million colors. RGB values are the decimal equivalent to hexadecimal values.

TIP

Don't worry about trying to remember hex codes or RGB values. You can easily identify colors using an online color picker such as the one at www.w3schools.com/colors/colors_picker.asp.

The following example shows all three types of color changes:

```
p {
  color: red
}
h1 {
  color: #FF0000
}
li {
  color: rgb(255,0,0)
}
```

li is the element name for a list item in ordered and unordered lists.

All three colors in the preceding code example reference the same shade of red. For the full list of colors that can be referenced by name go to www.w3.org/TR/css3-color/#svg-color.

Setting the font-style and font-weight

The font-style property can set text to italics, and the font-weight property can set text to bold. For each of these properties, the default is normal, which doesn't need to be specified. In the following example, the paragraph is styled so that the font appears italicized and bold. Here's an example of each:

```
p {
  font-style: italics;
  font-weight: bold;
}
```

Setting the font-family

The font-family property sets the typeface used for text. The property is set equal to one font, or to a list of fonts separated by commas. Your website visitors will have a variety of different fonts installed on their computers, but the font-family property displays your specified font only if that font is already installed on their system.

The font-family property can be set equal to two types of values:

>> **Font name:** Specific font names such as Times New Roman, Arial, and Courier.

>> **Generic font family:** Modern browsers usually define one installed font for each generic font family. These five generic font families include

- **Serif** (Times New Roman, Palantino)
- **Sans-serif** (Helvetica, Verdana)
- **Monospace** (Courier, Andale Mono)
- **Cursive** (Comic Sans, Florence)
- **Fantasy** (Impact, Oldtown)

When using `font-family`, it's best to define two or three specific fonts followed by a generic font family as a fallback in case the fonts you specify aren't installed, as in the following example:

```
p {
    font-family: "Times New Roman", Times, serif;
}
```

In this example, the paragraph's font family is defined as Times New Roman. If Times New Roman isn't installed on the user's computer, the browser then uses Times. If Times isn't installed, the browser will use any available font in the generic serif font family.

TIP

When using a font name with multiple words (such as Times New Roman), enclose the font name in quotes.

Setting the text-decoration

The `text-decoration` property sets any font underlining or strikethrough. By default, the property is equal to none, which doesn't have to be specified. In the following example, any text with an h1 heading is underlined, whereas any text inside a paragraph tag is made strikethrough:

```
h1 {
    text-decoration: underline;
}
p {
    text-decoration: line-through;
}
```

Customizing links

In general, browsers display links as blue underlined text. Originally, this default behavior minimized the confusion between content on the page and an interactive link. Today, almost every website styles links in its own way. Some websites don't underline links; others retain the underlining but style links in colors other than blue; and so on.

REMEMBER

The HTML anchor element (a) is used to create links. The text between the opening and closing anchor tag is the link description, and the URL set in the `href` attribute is the address the browser visits when the link is clicked.

The anchor tag has four states:

» `link`: A link that a user hasn't clicked or visited

» `visited`: A link that a user has clicked or visited

» `hover`: A link that the user hovers the mouse cursor over without clicking

» `active`: A link the user has begun to click but hasn't yet released the mouse button

CSS can style each of these four states, most often by using the properties and values shown in Table 3-2.

TABLE 3-2   **Common CSS Properties and Values for Styling Links**

Property Name	Possible Values	Description
color	name hex code rgb value	Link color specified using names (`color: blue;`), hexadecimal code (`color: #0000FF;`), or RGB value (`color: rgb(0,0,255);`).
text-decoration	none underline	Sets link to have an underline (or not).

The following example styles links in a way that's similar to the way they're styled in articles at Wikipedia, where links appear blue by default, underlined on mouse hover, and orange when active. As shown in Figure 3-6, the first link to Chief Technology Officer of the United States appears underlined as it would if my mouse was hovering over it. Also, the link to Google appears orange as it would if it were active and my mouse were clicking it.

```
a:link{
    color: rgb(6,69,173);
    text-decoration: none;
}
```

```
a:visited {
    color: rgb(11,0,128)
}
a:hover {
    text-decoration: underline
}
a:active {
    color: rgb(250,167,0)
}
```

FIGURE 3-6:
Wikipedia.org
page showing
link, visited,
hover, and active
states.

© John Wiley & Sons

REMEMBER

Remember to include the colon between the a selector and the link state.

Although explaining why is beyond the scope of this book, CSS specifications insist that you define the various link states in the order shown here — link, visited, hover, and then active. However, it is acceptable to not define a link state, as long as this order is preserved.

TECHNICAL STUFF

The various link states are known as *pseudo-class selectors*. Pseudo-class selectors add a keyword to CSS selectors and allow you to style a special state of the selected element.

Adding background images and styling foreground images

You can use CSS to add background images behind HTML elements. Most commonly, the background-image property is used to add background images to individual HTML elements such as div, table, and p, or (when applied to the body element) to entire web pages.

TIP

Background images with smaller file sizes load more quickly than larger images. This is especially important if your visitors commonly browse your website using a mobile phone, which typically has a slower data connection.

The properties and values in Table 3-3 show the options for adding background images.

Setting the background-image

As shown in the following example, the background-image property can set the background image for the entire web page or a specific element.

```
body {
    background-image:
    url("http://upload.wikimedia.org/wikipedia/commons/e/e5/
    Chrysler_Building_Midtown_Manhattan_New_York_City_1932.jpg
    ");
}
```

TIP

You can find background images at sites such as images.google.com, www.flickr.com, or publicdomainarchive.com.

WARNING

Check image copyright information to see if you have permission to use the image, and comply with image's licensing terms, which can include attributing or identifying the author. Additionally, directly linking to images on other servers is called *hotlinking.* It is preferable to download the image and host and link to the image on your own server.

TIP

If you prefer a single-color background instead of an image, use the background-color property. This property is defined in much the same way as the background-image property. Just set it equal to a color name, RGB value, or hex code, as I describe earlier in this chapter in the section "Setting the color."

TABLE 3-3   ## CSS Properties and Values for Background Images

Property Name	Possible Values	Description
background-image	url("URL")	Adds a background image from the image link specified at *URL*.
background-size	auto contain cover width height (#px, %)	Sets background size according to the value: auto (default value) displays the image as originally sized. contain scales the image's width and height so that it fits inside element. cover scales the image so element background isn't visible. Background size can also be set by specifying width and height in pixels or as a percentage.
background-position	keywords position (#px, %)	Positions the background in element using keywords or exact position. *Keywords* comprise horizontal keywords (left, right, center) and vertical keywords (top, center, and bottom). The placement of the background can also be exactly defined using pixels or a percentage to describe the horizontal and vertical position relative to the element.
background-repeat	repeat repeat-x repeat-y no-repeat	Sets the background image to *tile*, or repeat, as follows: horizontally (repeat-x) vertically (repeat-y) horizontally and vertically (repeat) don't repeat at all (no-repeat).
background-attachment	scroll fixed	Sets the background to scroll with other content (scroll), or to remain fixed (fixed).

Setting the background-size

By specifying exact dimensions using pixels or percentages, the background-size property can scale background images to be smaller or larger, as needed. In addition, this property has three dimensions commonly used on web pages, as follows (see Figure 3-7):

>> auto: This value maintains the original dimensions of an image.

>> cover: This value scales an image so all dimensions are greater than or equal to the size of the container or HTML element.

>> `contain`: This value scales an image so all dimensions are less than or equal to the size of the container or HTML element.

FIGURE 3-7:
Setting the
background size
to three different
values.

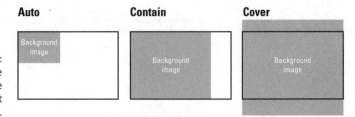

Auto   **Contain**   **Cover**

Setting the background-position

The `background-position` property sets the initial position of the background image. The default initial position is in the top-left corner of the web page or specific element. You change the default position by specifying a pair of keywords or position values, as follows:

>> **Keywords:** The first keyword (`left`, `center`, or `right`) represents the horizontal position, and the second keyword (`top`, `center`, or `bottom`) represents the vertical position.

>> **Position:** The first position value represents the horizontal position, and the second value represents the vertical. Each value is defined using pixels or percentages, representing the distance from the top-left of the browser or the specified element. For example, `background-position: center center` is equal to `background-position: 50% 50%`. (See Figure 3-8.)

Setting the background-repeat

The `background-repeat` property sets the direction the background will tile as follows:

>> `repeat`: This value (the default) repeats the background image both horizontally and vertically.

>> `repeat-x`: This value repeats the background image only horizontally.

>> `repeat-y`: This repeats the background image only vertically.

>> `no-repeat`: This value prevents the background from repeating at all.

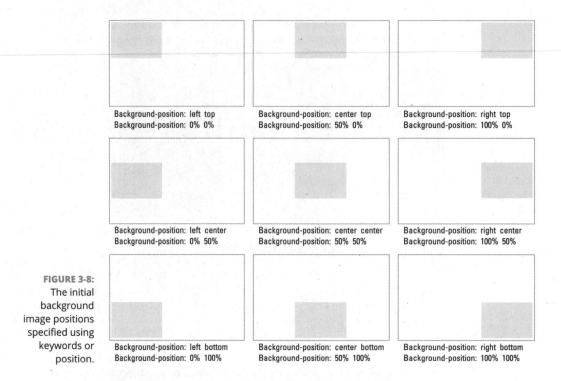

Background-position: left top
Background-position: 0% 0%

Background-position: center top
Background-position: 50% 0%

Background-position: right top
Background-position: 100% 0%

Background-position: left center
Background-position: 0% 50%

Background-position: center center
Background-position: 50% 50%

Background-position: right center
Background-position: 100% 50%

Background-position: left bottom
Background-position: 0% 100%

Background-position: center bottom
Background-position: 50% 100%

Background-position: right bottom
Background-position: 100% 100%

FIGURE 3-8:
The initial background image positions specified using keywords or position.

Setting the background-attachment

The `background-attachment` property sets the background image to move (or not) when the user scrolls through content on the page. The property can be set to

>> `scroll`: The background image moves when the user scrolls.

>> `fixed`: The background image doesn't move when the user scrolls.

The following code segment uses several of the properties discussed earlier to add a background image that stretches across the entire web page, is aligned in the center, does not repeat, and does not move when the user scrolls. (See Figure 3-9.)

```
body {
    background-image:
    "http://upload.wikimedia.org/wikipedia/commons/thumb/a/a0/
    USMC-090807-M-8097K-022.jpg/640px-USMC-090807-M-8097K-022.jpg");
    background-size: cover;
    background-position: center center;
    background-repeat: no-repeat;
    background-attachment: fixed;
}
```

FIGURE 3-9:
An image set as
the background
for entire page.

Getting Stylish

The CSS rules discussed in this chapter give you a taste of a few common styling properties and values. Although you aren't likely to remember every property and value, with practice, the property and value names will come to you naturally. After you understand the basic syntax, the next step is to actually incorporate CSS into your web page and try your hand at styling HTML elements.

Adding CSS to your HTML

There are three ways to apply CSS to a website to style HTML elements:

» **Inline CSS:** CSS can be specified within an HTML file on the same line as the HTML element it styles. This method requires placing the `style` attribute inside the opening HTML tag. Generally, inline CSS is the least preferred way of styling a website because the styling rules are frequently repeated. Here's an example of inline CSS:

```
<!DOCTYPE html>
<html>
<head>
    <title>Record IPOs</title>
</head>
<body>
```

```
    <h1 style="color: red;">Alibaba IPO expected to be biggest IPO of all
      time</h1>
  </body>
</html>
```

>> **Embedded CSS:** With this approach, CSS appears within the HTML file, but separated from the HTML tags it modifies. The CSS code appears within the HTML file between an opening and closing `<style>` tag, which itself is located between an opening and closing `<head>` tag. Embedded CSS is usually used when styling a single HTML page differently than the rest of your website.

In this example, the embedded CSS styles the header red, just like the preceding inline CSS does.

```
<!DOCTYPE html>
<html>
<head>
 <title>Record IPOs</title>
 <style type="text/css">
 h1 {
      color: red;
 }
 </style>
</head>
<body>
  <h1>Alibaba IPO expected to be biggest IPO of all time</h1>
</body>
</html>
```

>> **Separate style sheets:** CSS can be specified in a separate *style sheet* — that is, in a separate file. Using a separate style sheet is the preferred approach to storing your CSS because it makes maintaining the HTML file easier and allows you to quickly make changes. In the HTML file, the `<link>` tag is used to refer to the separate style sheet and has three attributes:

- `href`: Specifies the CSS filename.

- `rel`: Should be set equal to `"stylesheet"`.

- `type`: Should be set equal to `"text/css"`.

With three different ways of styling HTML elements with CSS, all three ways could be used with contradictory styles. For example, say your inline CSS styles h1 elements as red, whereas embedded CSS styles them as blue, and a separate style sheet styles them as green. To resolve these conflicts, inline CSS has the highest priority and overrides all other CSS rules. If no inline CSS is specified, then embedded CSS has the next highest priority, and finally in the absence of inline or embedded CSS, the styles in a separate style sheet are used. In the example, with the presence of all three styles, the h1 element text would appear red because inline CSS has the highest priority and overrides the embedded CSS blue styling and the separate CSS green styling.

The following example uses a separate CSS style sheet to style the header red, as in the previous two examples:

CSS: style.css

```
h1 {
    color: red;
}
```

HTML: index.html

```
<DOCTYPE html>
<html>
<head>
 <title>Record IPOs</title>
 <link href="style.css" type="text/css" rel="stylesheet">
</head>
<body>
   <h1>Alibaba IPO expected to be biggest IPO of all time</h1>
</body>
</html>
```

Practicing with CSS

Practice your CSS online using the CodeSandbox.io website (or one of the other code playgrounds listed in Book 1). Practice using all the CSS properties that you find in this chapter by following these steps:

1. **Open your browser and go to codesandbox.io.**

2. **If you have a codesandbox account, sign in.**

   Signing up is discussed in Book 1, Chapter 3.

   Creating an account allows you to save your progress as you work, but it's optional.

   TECHNICAL
   STUFF

3. **Create a new sandbox using the static template or open the sandbox that you created in a previous chapter.**

4. Add an opening `<style>` tag and a closing `</style>` tag inside the head element of your HTML file.

5. Define styles for some of the elements in your HTML document. For example, to make all the text in your web page red, you can use the following CSS rule:

```
body {
  color: red;
}
```

6. Make as many CSS rules as you like, using what you've learned in this chapter, and save your file to see them in the preview window.

7. Create a new file in your project and give it a name ending with `.css` (such as `styles.css`).

8. Replace your embedded CSS in `index.html` with a link to your new `.css` file. For example, if your CSS file is named `styles.css` (and if it's in the same folder as your HTML file), your link tag would look like this:

```
<link href="styles.css" type="text/css" rel="stylesheet">
```

Chapter **4**

Next Steps with CSS

"Design is not just what it looks like and feels like. Design is how it works."

—STEVE JOBS

n this chapter, you continue building on the CSS you worked with in Book 2, Chapter 3. So far, the CSS rules you've seen in the previous chapter applied to the entire web page, but now they get more specific. You find out how to style several more HTML elements, including lists, tables, and forms, and how to select and style specific parts of a web page, such as the first paragraph in a story or the last row of a table. Finally, you read about how professional web developers use CSS and the box model to control, down to the pixel, the positioning of elements on the page.

Before diving in, remember the big picture: HTML puts content on the web page, and CSS further styles and positions that content. Instead of trying to memorize every rule, use this chapter to understand CSS basics. CSS selectors have properties and values that modify HTML elements.

TIP

There is no better way to learn than by doing, so feel free to try out new style properties you learn about in CodeSandbox (or another code playground) as you go through this chapter. If you've built a web page already, you can use this chapter as a reference when you have questions about specific elements you're trying to style.

Styling (More) Elements on Your Page

In this section, you discover common ways to style lists and tables. In the previous chapter, the CSS properties and rules you saw, like color and font-family, can apply to any HTML element containing text. By contrast, some of the CSS shown here is used only to style lists, tables, and forms.

Styling lists

In Book 2, Chapter 2 you created ordered lists, which start with markers like letters or numbers, and unordered lists, which start with markers like bullet points. By default, list items in an ordered list use numbers (for example, 1, 2, 3), whereas list items in unordered lists use a solid black circle (●).

These defaults may not be appropriate for all circumstances. In fact, the two most common tasks when styling a list include the following:

>> **Changing the marker used to create a list:** For unordered lists, like this one, you can use a solid disc, empty circle, or square bullet point. For ordered lists, you can use numbers, Roman numerals (upper- or lowercase), or case letters (upper or lower).

>> **Specifying an image to use as the bullet point:** You can create your own marker for ordered and unordered lists instead of using the default option. For example, if you create an unordered bulleted list for a burger restaurant, instead of using a solid circle as a bullet point, you could use a color hamburger icon image.

You can accomplish either of these tasks by using the properties in Table 4-1 with an ol or ul selector to modify the list type.

REMEMBER

CSS selectors using properties and rules modify HTML elements by the same name. For example, Figure 4-1 has HTML <ul> tags that are referred to in CSS with the ul selector and styled using the properties and rules in Table 4-1.

CSS properties and values apply to a CSS selector and modify an HTML element. In the following example, embedded CSS (between the opening and closing <style> tags) and inline CSS (defined with the style attribute in the HTML) are used to

>> Change the marker in an unordered list to a square using list-style-type.

>> Change the marker in an ordered list to uppercase Roman numerals again using list-style-type.

>> Set a custom marker to an icon using list-style-image.

TABLE 4-1

Common CSS Properties and Values for Styling Lists

Property Name	Possible Values	Description
list–style–type (unordered list)	disc circle square none	Sets the markers used to create list items in an unordered list to disc (●), circle (o), square (■), or none.
list–style–type (ordered list)	decimal upper–roman lower–roman upper–alpha lower–alpha	Sets the markers used to create list items in an ordered list to decimal (1, 2, 3), uppercase Roman numerals (I, II, III), lowercase Roman numerals (i, ii, iii), uppercase letters (A, B, C), or lowercase letters (a, b, c).
list–style–image	url("URL")	When URL is replaced with the image link, the property sets an image as the marker used to create a list item.

```html
1  <html>
2  <head>
3  <title>Figure 7-1: Lists</title>
4  <style>
5  ul {
6      list-style-type: square;
7  }
8  ol {
9      list-style-type: upper-roman;
10 }
11
12 li {
13     font-size: 27px;
14 }
15 </style>
16 </head>
17 <body>
18 <h1>Ridesharing startups</h1>
19 <ul>
20     <li>Hailo: book a taxi on your phone</li>
21     <li>Lyft: request a peer to peer ride</li>
22     <li style="list-style-image: url('car.png');">Uber: request a drivers for hire</li>
23 </ul>
24 <h1>Food startups</h1>
25 <ol>
26     <li>Grubhub: order takeout food online</li>
27     <li style="list-style-image: url('burger.png');">Blue Apron: subscribe to weekly meal
        delivery</li>
28     <li>Instacart: request groceries delivered the same day</li>
29 </ol>
30 </body>
31 </html>
```

FIGURE 4-1: Embedded and inline CSS.

The code for embedded and inline CSS is shown next and in Figure 4-1. Figure 4-2 shows this code rendered in the browser.

```html
<html>
<head>
```

```
<title>Figure 4-1: Lists</title>
<style>
ul {
    list-style-type: square;
}


ol {
    list-style-type: upper-roman;
}


li {
font-size: 27px;
}
</style>
</head>
<body>

<h1>Ridesharing startups</h1>
<ul>
    <li>Hailo: book a taxi on your phone</li>
    <li>Lyft: request a peer-to-peer ride</li>
    <li style="list-style-image: url('car.png');">Uber: hire a driver</li>
</ul>

<h1>Food startups</h1>
<ol>
    <li>Grubhub: order takeout food online</li>
    <li style="list-style-image: url(&apos;burger.png&apos;);">Blue Apron:
    subscribe to weekly meal delivery</li>
    <li>Instacart: request groceries delivered the same day</li>
</ol>
</body>
</html>
```

Ridesharing startups

- Hailo: book a taxi on your phone
- Lyft: request a peer-to-peer ride
- Uber: request a driver for hire

Food startups

I. Grubhub: order takeout food online

Blue Apron: subscribe to weekly meal delivery

III. Instacart: request groceries delivered the same day

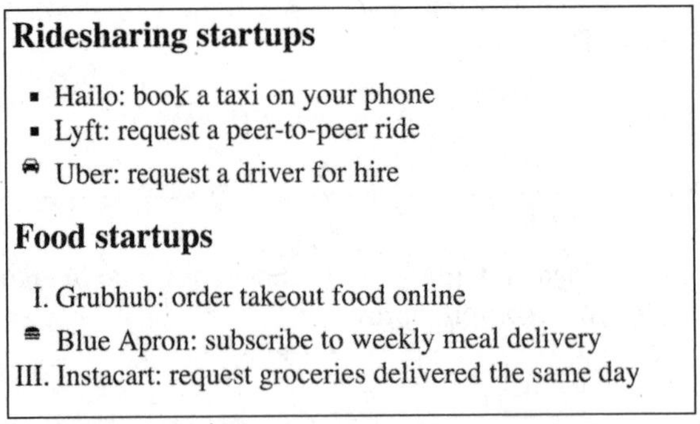

FIGURE 4-2:
Ordered and
unordered
lists modified
to change the
marker type.

TIP

If the custom image for your marker is larger than the text, your text may not align vertically with the marker. To fix this problem, you can either increase the font size of each list item using `font-size` (as shown in the example) and increase the margin between each list item using `margin`, or you can set `list-style-type` to none and set a background image on the `ul` element using `background-image`.

REMEMBER

There are three ways to apply CSS — with inline CSS using the `style` attribute, with embedded CSS using an opening and closing `<style>` tag, and in a separate CSS style sheet.

Designing tables

In Book 2, Chapter 2, you found out how to create basic tables. By default, the width of these tables expands to fit content inside the table, content in individual cells is left-aligned, and no borders are displayed.

These defaults may not be appropriate for all circumstances. Deprecated (unsupported) HTML attributes can modify these defaults, but if at any time browsers stop recognizing these attributes, tables created with these attributes will display incorrectly. As a safer alternative, CSS can style tables with greater control. Three common tasks CSS can perform for tables include the following:

>> Setting the width of a table, table row, or individual table cell with the `width` property

>> Aligning text within the table with the `text-align` property

>> Displaying borders within the table with the `border` property (See Table 4-2.)

TABLE 4-2   **Common CSS Properties and Values for Styling Tables**

Property Name	Possible Values	Description
`width`	*pixels* (`#px`) `%`	Width of the table measured either in pixels on-screen or as a percentage of the browser window or container tag.

`text-align`	`left`
	`right`
	`center`
	`justify`
		Position of text relative to the table according to the value of the attribute. For example, `text-align="center"` positions the text in the center of the table cell.

`border`	`width`
	`style`
	`color`
		Defines three properties in one — `border-width`, `border-style`, and `border-color`. The values must be specified in this order: Width (pixel), style (none, dotted, dashed, solid), and color (name, hexadecimal code, RBG value). For example, `border: 1px solid red`.

In the following example, the table is wider than the text in any cell, the text in each cell is centered, and the table border is applied to header cells:

```html
<html>
<head>
<title>Figure 4-3: Tables</title>
<style>
   table {
     width: 700px;
   }

   table, td {
     text-align: center;
     border: 1px solid black;
     border-collapse: collapse;
   }

</style>
</head>
<body>
  <table>
    <caption>Desktop browser market share (December 2021)</caption>
    <tr>
      <th>Source</th>
      <th>Chrome</th>
      <th>Safari</th>
      <th>IE and Edge</th>
      <th>Firefox</th>
      <th>Opera</th>
    </tr>
    <tr>
      <td>StatCounter</td>
      <td>66.6%</td>
      <td>9.56%</td>
      <td>9.22%</td>
      <td>8.49%</td>
      <td>2.95%</td>
    </tr>
    <tr>
      <td>W3Counter</td>
      <td>66%</td>
      <td>16.8%</td>
      <td>5.2%</td>
      <td>3.2%</td>
      <td>1.5%</td>
    </tr>
  </table>>
</body>
</html>
```

TIP

The HTML tag `<caption>` and the CSS property `border-collapse` further style the preceding table. The `<caption>` tag adds a title to the table. Although you can create a similar effect using the `<h1>` tag, `<caption>` associates the title with the table. The CSS `border-collapse` property can have a value of `separate` or `collapse`. The `separate` value renders each border separately (refer to Book 2, Chapter 2, Figure 2-9), whereas `collapse` draws a single border when possible (see Figure 4-3).

FIGURE 4-3:
Table with width, text alignment, and border modified using CSS.

	127.0.0.1				

Desktop browser market share (December 2021)

Source	Chrome	Safari	IE and Edge	Firefox	Opera
StatCounter	66.6%	9.56%	9.22%	8.49%	2.95%
W3Counter	66%	16.8%	5.2%	3.2%	1.5%

Selecting Elements to Style

Currently, the CSS you have seen styles every HTML element that matches the CSS selector. For example, in Figure 4-3 the `table` and `td` selectors have a `text-align` property that centers text in every table cell. Depending on the content, you may want to center only the text in the header row, but left-align text in subsequent rows. Here are two ways to do so:

>> Styling specific HTML elements based on position to other elements

>> Naming HTML elements and styling elements only by name

Styling specific elements

When styling specific elements, it is helpful to visualize the HTML code as a family tree with parents, children, and siblings. In the following code example (also shown in Figure 4-4), the tree starts with the `html` element, which has two children `head` and `body`. The `head` has a child element called `title`. The `body` has `h1`, `ul`, and `p` elements as children. Finally, the `ul` element has `li` elements as children, and the `p` element has `a` elements as children. Figure 4-4 shows how the following code appears in the browser, and Figure 4-5 shows a depiction of the following code using the tree metaphor. Note that Figure 4-6 shows each relationship once. For example, in the following code, an a element is inside each of three li elements, and Figure 4-6 shows this ul li a relationship once.

```html
<html>
<head>
    <title>Figure 4-4: DOM</title>
</head>
<body>

<h1>Parody Tech Twitter Accounts</h1>
<ul>
    <li>
    <a href="http://twitter.com/BoredElonMusk">Bored Elon Musk</a>
    </li>
    <li>
    <a href="http://twitter.com/VinodColeslaw">Vinod Coleslaw</a>
    </li>
    <li>
    <a href=" https://twitter.com/sarcasticrover">Sarcastic Rover</a>
    </li>
    </ul>

<h1>Parody Non-Tech Twitter Accounts</h1>
<p><a href="https://twitter.com/JurassicPark2go">Jurassic Park Updates </a></p>
<p><a href="http://twitter.com/Lord_Voldemort7">Lord_Voldemort7</a></p>

</body>
</html>
```

TIP

Bored Elon Musk is a parody of Elon Musk, the founder of PayPal, Tesla, and SpaceX. Vinod Coleslaw is a parody of Vinod Khosla, the Sun Microsystems cofounder and venture capitalist. Sarcastic Rover imagines the unfiltered thoughts of the Mars Curiosity Rover.

TECHNICAL STUFF

The HTML tree is called the *DOM* or *document object model*.

Child selector

The Parody Non-Tech Twitter account anchor tags are immediate children of the paragraph tags. If you want to style just the Parody Non-Tech Twitter accounts, you can use the *child selector,* which selects the immediate children of a specified element. A child selector is created by first listing the parent selector, then a greater-than sign (>), and finally the child selector.

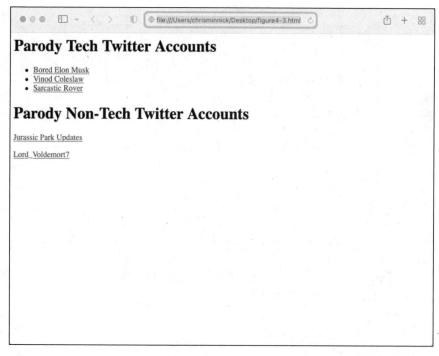

```
<> figure0404.html U ×
BOOK_2_BASIC_WEB_CODING > Chapter04 > <> figure0404.html > ⊗ html > ⊗ head > ⊗ title
  1   <html>
  2     <head>
  3       <title>Figure 4-4: DOM</title>
  4     </head>
  5     <body>
  6       <h1>Parody Tech Twitter Accounts</h1>
  7       <ul>
  8         <li>
  9           <a href="http://twitter.com/BoredElonMusk">Bored Elon Musk</a>
 10         </li>
 11         <li>
 12           <a href="http://twitter.com/VinodColeslaw">Vinod Coleslaw</a>
 13         </li>
 14         <li>
 15           <a href=" https://twitter.com/sarcasticrover">Sarcastic Rover</a>
 16         </li>
 17       </ul>
 18
 19       <h1>Parody Non-Tech Twitter Accounts</h1>
 20       <p>
 21         <a href="https://twitter.com/JurassicPark2go">Jurassic Park Updates </a>
 22       </p>
 23       <p><a href="http://twitter.com/Lord_Voldemort7">Lord_Voldemort7</a></p>
 24     </body>
 25   </html>
 26
```

FIGURE 4-4:
Styling a family
tree of elements.

file:///Users/chrisminnick/Desktop/figure4-3.html

Parody Tech Twitter Accounts

- Bored Elon Musk
- Vinod Coleslaw
- Sarcastic Rover

Parody Non-Tech Twitter Accounts

Jurassic Park Updates

Lord_Voldemort7

FIGURE 4-5:
Parody Tech
and Non-Tech
Twitter accounts
(browser view).

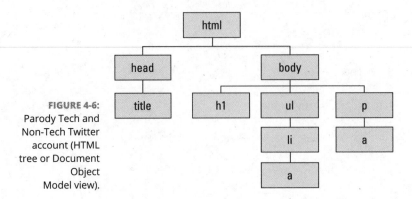

FIGURE 4-6:
Parody Tech and
Non-Tech Twitter
account (HTML
tree or Document
Object
Model view).

In the following example, the anchor tags that are immediate children of the paragraph tags are selected, and those hyperlinks are styled with a red font color and without any underline. The Parody Tech Twitter accounts are not styled because they are direct children of the list item tag. (See Figure 4-7.)

```
p > a {
    color: red;
    text-decoration: none;
}
```

FIGURE 4-7:
Child selector
used to style the
Parody Non-Tech
Twitter accounts.

© John Wiley & Sons

If you use just the a selector here, all the links on the page would be styled instead of just a selection.

REMEMBER

Descendant selector

The Parody Tech Twitter account anchor tags are descendants, or located within, the unordered list. If you want to style just the Parody Tech Twitter accounts, you can use the *descendant selector*, which selects not just immediate children of a specified element but all elements nested within the specified element. A descendant selector is created by first listing the parent selector, a space, and finally the descendant selector you want to target.

In the following example, as shown in Figure 4-8, the anchor tags that are descendants of the unordered list are selected, and those hyperlinks are styled with a blue font color and are crossed out. The Parody Non-Tech Twitter accounts aren't styled because they aren't descendants of an unordered list.

```
ul a {
    color: blue;
    text-decoration: line-through;
}
```

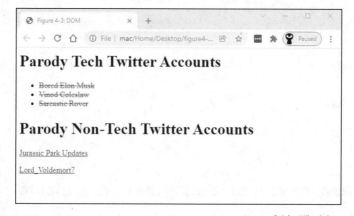

FIGURE 4-8: Child selector used to style the Parody Tech Twitter accounts.

© John Wiley & Sons

TIP

Interested in styling just the first anchor tag within a list, like the Jurassic Park Updates Twitter account, or the second list item, like the Vinod Coleslaw Twitter account? Go to w3schools.com and read more about the first-child (www.w3schools.com/cssref/sel_firstchild.asp) and nth-child selectors (www.w3schools.com/cssref/sel_nth-child.asp).

Naming HTML elements

The other way of styling specific elements in CSS is to name your HTML elements. You name your code by using either the id or class attribute and then style your code by referring to the id or class selector.

Naming your code using the id attribute

Use the id attribute to style one specific element on your web page. The id attribute can name any HTML element, and it is always placed in the opening HTML tag. Additionally, each element can have only one id attribute value, and the attribute value must appear only once within the HTML file. After you define the attribute in the HTML file, you refer to the HTML element in your CSS by writing a hashtag (#) followed by the attribute value.

Using the id attribute, the following code styles the Jurassic Park Updates Twitter link the color red with a yellow background:

HTML:

```
<p><a href="https://twitter.com/JurassicPark2go" id="jurassic">Jurassic Park
    Updates </a></p>
```

CSS:

```
#jurassic {
    color: red;
    background-color: yellow;
}
```

Naming your code using the class attribute

Use the class attribute to style multiple elements on your web page. The class attribute can name any HTML element and is always placed in the opening HTML tag. The attribute value need not be unique within the HTML file. After you define the attribute in the HTML file, you refer to the HTML element by writing a period (.) followed by the attribute value.

With the class attribute, the following code styles all the Parody Tech Twitter account links the color red with no underline:

HTML:

```
<ul>
<li>
```

```
<a href="http://twitter.com/BoredElonMusk" class="tech">Bored Elon Musk</a>
</li>
<li>
<a href="http://twitter.com/VinodColeslaw" class="tech">Vinod Coleslaw</a>
</li>
<li>
<a href=" https://twitter.com/sarcasticrover class="tech">Sarcastic Rover</a>
</li>
</ul>
```

CSS:

```
.tech {
   color: red;
   text-decoration: none;
}
```

TIP

Proactively use a search engine, such as Google, to search for additional CSS effects. For example, if you want to increase the spacing between each list item, open your browser and search for *list item line spacing css.* Links appearing in the top ten results should include:

>> www.w3schools.com: A beginner tutorial site

>> www.stackoverflow.com: A discussion board for experienced developers

>> developer.mozilla.org: A reference guide initially created by the foundation that maintains the Firefox browser and now maintained by a community of developers

Each of these sites is a good place to start; be sure to look for answers that include example code.

Aligning and Laying Out Your Elements

CSS not only allows control over the formatting of HTML elements, it also allows control over the placement of these elements on the page, known as *page layout.* Historically, developers used HTML tables to create page layouts. HTML table page layouts were tedious to create and required that developers write a great deal of code to ensure consistency across browsers. CSS eliminated the need to use tables to create layouts, helped reduce code bloat, and increased control of page layouts.

Organizing data on the page

Before diving into code, let's look at Figure 4-9 and review some of the basic ways we can structure the page and the content on it. Layouts have evolved over time, with some layouts working well on desktop computers but not displaying optimally on tablet or mobile devices.

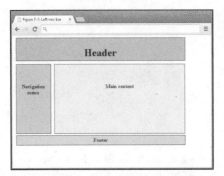

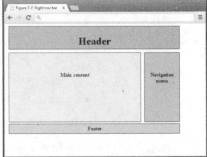

FIGURE 4-9:
Vertical and horizontal navigation layouts.

© John Wiley & Sons

TIP

Always ask yourself how your intended layout will appear on desktop, tablet, and mobile devices.

Hundreds of different layouts exist, and a few selected page layouts appear here along with example websites.

TIP

Left and right navigation toolbars aren't usually seen on mobile devices. Top navigation toolbars are used on both desktop and mobile devices, and bottom navigation toolbars are most common on mobile devices.

The following examples show real websites with these layouts:

>> Vertical navigation, as shown in Figure 4-10, aids reader understanding when a hierarchy or relationship exists between navigational topics.

In the w3schools.com example, HTML, JavaScript, Server Side, and XML relate to one another, and underneath each topic heading are related subtopics.

>> Horizontal or menu navigation, as shown in Figure 4-11, helps reader navigation with weak or disparate relationships between navigational topics.

In the eBay example, the Motors, Fashion, and Electronics menu items have different products and appeal to different audiences.

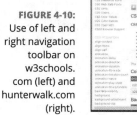

TIP

Don't spend too much time worrying about what layout to pick. You can always pick one, observe whether your visitors can navigate your website quickly and easily and change the layout if necessary.

Shaping the div

The preceding page layouts are collections of elements grouped together. These elements are grouped together using rectangular containers created with an opening and closing <div> tag, and all of the layouts can be created with these <div> tags. By itself, the <div> tag doesn't render anything on the screen, but instead serves as a container for content of any type, such as HTML headings, lists, tables, or images. To see the <div> tag in action, take a look at the Codecademy.com homepage in Figure 4-12.

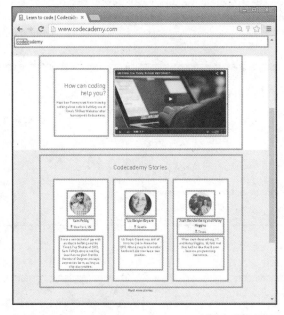

FIGURE 4-12: Codecademy.com homepage with visible borders for the <div> tags.

© John Wiley & Sons

Notice how the page can be divided into three parts — the navigation header, the middle video testimonial, and then additional text user testimonials. <div> tags are used to outline these major content areas, and additional nested <div> tags within each part are used to group content such as images and text.

In the following example, as shown in Figure 4-13, HTML code is used to create two containers using <div> tags, the id attribute names each div, and CSS sizes and colors the div.

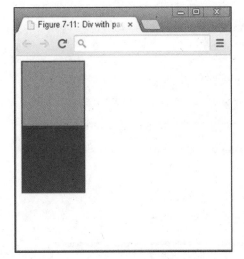

FIGURE 4-13:
Two boxes
created with
HTML <div> tag
and styled
using CSS.

HTML:

```
<div id="first"/></div>
<div id="second"/></div>
```

CSS:

```
div {
    height: 100px;
    width: 100px;
    border: 2px solid purple;
}

#first {
    background-color: red;
}

#second {
    background-color: blue;
}
```

Understanding the box model

Just as we created boxes with the preceding tags, CSS creates a box around each and every single element on the page, even text. Figure 4-14 shows the box model for an image that says, "This is an element." These boxes may not always be visible, but comprise four parts:

» `content`: HTML tag that is rendered in the browser

» `padding`: Optional spacing between content and the border

» `border`: Marks the edge of the padding and varies in width and visibility

» `margin`: Transparent optional spacing surrounding the border

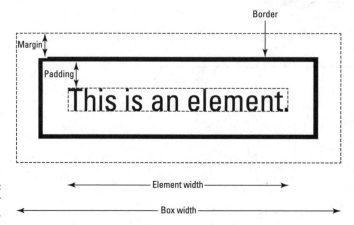

FIGURE 4-14:
Box model for
`img` element.

TIP

Using the Chrome browser, navigate to your favorite news website, then right-click an image and choose Inspect from the context menu. On the right side of the screen, you see three tabs; click the Computed tab. The box model is displayed for the image you right-clicked, showing the content dimensions, and then dimensions for the padding, border, and margin.

The padding, border, and margin are CSS properties, and the value is usually expressed in pixels. In the following code, shown in Figure 4-15, padding and margins are added to separate each `div`.

```
div {
    height: 100px;
    width: 100px;
    border: 1px solid black;
    padding: 10px;
    margin: 10px;
}
```

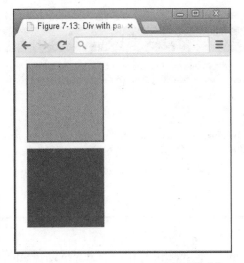

FIGURE 4-15:
Padding and
margin added to
separate
each `div`.

Positioning the boxes

Now that you understand how to group elements using HTML and how CSS views elements, the final piece is to position these elements on the page. Various techniques can be used for page layouts, and a comprehensive overview of each technique is beyond the scope of this book. However, one technique to create the layouts shown in Figure 4-16 is to use the `float` and `clear` properties (as described in Table 4-3).

FIGURE 4-16:
Left navigation
web page layout
created using
`<div>` tags.

TABLE 4-3 **Select CSS Properties and Values for Page Layouts**

Property Name	Possible Values	Description
float	left right none	Sends an element to the left or right of the container it is in. The none value specifies that the element should not float.
clear	left right both none	Specifies on which side of an element not to have other floating elements.

If the width of an element is specified, the float property allows elements that would normally appear on separate lines to appear next to each other, such as navigation toolbars and a main content window. The clear property is used to prevent any other elements from floating on one or both sides of current element, and the property is commonly set to both to place web page footers below other elements.

The following example code uses ‹div› tags, float, and clear to create a simple left navigation layout. (See Figure 4-16.) Typically, after grouping your content using ‹div› tags, you name each ‹div› tag using class or id attributes, and then style the div in CSS. A lot of code follows, so let's break it down into segments:

>> The CSS is embedded between the opening and closing ‹style› tags, and the HTML is between the opening and closing ‹body› tags.

>> Between the opening and closing ‹body› tags, using ‹div› tags, the page is divided into four parts with header, navigation bar, content, and footer.

>> The navigation menu is created with an unordered list, which is left-aligned, with no marker.

>> CSS styles size and color and align each ‹div› tag.

>> CSS properties, float and clear, are used to place the left navigation layout to the left, and the footer below the other elements.

```
<!DOCTYPE html>
<html>
<head>
  <title>Figure 4-14: Layout</title>
  <style>
```

```
    #header{
      background-color: #FF8C8C;
      border: 1px solid black;
      padding: 5px;
      margin: 5px;
      text-align: center;
    }

    #navbar {
      background-color: #00E0FF;
      height: 200px;
      width: 100px;
      float: left;
      border: 1px solid black;
      padding: 5px;
      margin: 5px;
      text-align: left;
    }

    #content {
      background-color: #EEEEEE;
      height: 200px;
      width: 412px;
      float: left;
      border: 1px solid black;
      padding: 5px;
      margin: 5px;
      text-align: center;
    }

    #footer{
      background-color: #FFBD47;
      clear: both;
      text-align: center;
      border: 1px solid black;
      padding: 5px;
      margin: 5px;
    }

    ul {
      list-style-type: none;
      line-height: 25px;
      padding: 0px;
    }
  </style>
</head>
<body>
<div id="header"><h1>Nik's Tapas Restaurant</h1></div>
```

```
<div id="navbar">
 <ul>
   <li>About us</li>
   <li>Reservations</li>
   <li>Menus</li>
   <li>Gallery</li>
   <li>Events</li>
   <li>Catering</li>
   <li>Press</li>
 </ul>
</div>

<div id="content"><img src="food.jpg" alt="Nik's Tapas"></div>

<div id="footer">Copyright &amp;copy; Nik's Tapas</div>
</body>
</html>
```

Writing More Advanced CSS

Practice your CSS online using the CodeSandbox.io website (or one of the other code playgrounds listed in Book 1). Practice using all the CSS properties that you find in this chapter by following these steps:

1. **Open your browser and go to codesandbox.io.**

2. **If you have a codesandbox account, sign in.**

    Signing up is discussed in Book 1, Chapter 3.

    Creating an account allows you to save your progress as you work, but it's optional.

TECHNICAL STUFF

3. **Create a new sandbox using the static template or open the sandbox that you created in the previous chapter.**

4. **Use an HTML document from this chapter or make your own. Examples of HTML documents you might try writing include your favorite recipe, your resume (or even a fictitious one), or a web page that explains the steps for fixing a leaky sink or planting a garden.**

5. **Make a `style.css` file and link it to your HTML file.**

6. **Try using some of the new style properties you learned in this chapter, as well as ID and class selectors, to style elements in your HTML document.**

Chapter **5**

Responsive Layouts with Flexbox

"The measure of intelligence is the ability to change."

—ALBERT EINSTEIN

n this chapter, you continue building on the knowledge of CSS you gained in Book 2, Chapters 3 and 4. You previously learned how to apply styles to elements and how to do basic web page layout using CSS. Now it's time to learn one of the newest and most useful features of the latest version of CSS to easily make web pages that look good in any browser: including on desktop, tablet, or mobile devices.

TIP

Flexbox can be confusing at first, until you do some hands-on work with it. Use a code playground such as CodeSandbox as you go through this chapter to experiment with the examples provided. If you've built a web page already, you can use this chapter as a reference when you have questions about specific Flexbox properties.

Introducing Responsive Design

Responsive design is the practice of making web pages and web apps that adjust to fit the width of the browser window in which they appear. In this section, you'll learn the terminology behind responsive design as well as the reasons for designing responsive web pages.

The web is mobile

In the years since the first edition of this book came out, the web passed a major milestone. In 2016, the number of web pages viewed on mobile devices surpassed the number of web pages viewed on desktop (including laptop) devices globally. Since then, this trend has continued. Today, around two-thirds of all web page views come from mobile devices. This fact is significant, because many web pages still don't work well on mobile devices.

Why are so many sites mobile-unfriendly?

Since most web development is done using desktop computers (it's so much easier to code with a large monitor, or even better, with multiple monitors!), there is an inherent bias in web development toward desktop browsers. Many web developers still treat testing their websites on mobile as an afterthought.

WARNING

A website built without taking mobile browsers into consideration from the very beginning is likely to not work as well on mobile devices as it does on desktop, or to not be usable at all on mobile. When so many more web pages are being browsed on mobile devices, leaving them behind can result in significantly less traffic to your website and in unhappy customers.

Introducing mobile-first design

In recent years, the trend in web development has begun to reflect reality, and we've entered the age of "mobile-first" design. In mobile-first design, instead of making a web page that's optimized for desktop devices and then scaling it down for mobile devices, we design web pages first for mobile and then scale them up for desktop devices.

Making responsive web pages with the viewport meta tag

The simplest way to design a responsive web page is to write a simple web page that uses the browser's default styling, with no additional positioning CSS or element widths specified, and then add a `viewport` meta tag to the head element.

A `viewport` meta tag is an instruction for the web browser that tells it how to scale the virtual window in which web pages display, which is called the *viewport*.

For example, the following HTML document will look just fine (if a bit boring) on desktop devices.

```
<!DOCTYPE html>
<html>
  <head>
    <title>What's the cat up to?</title>
  </head>
  <body>
    <h1>Here are some of the things my cat is doing this morning:</h1>
    <ul>
      <li>Playing with catnip mouse</li>
      <li>Hiding from the dog</li>
      <li>Jumping on the table</li>
      <li>Getting into the salad</li>
      <li>Rolling on the floor</li>
      <li>Sleeping on the dresser</li>
    </ul>
  </body>
</html>
```

Figure 5-1 shows how this web page looks in Chrome on a desktop computer.

When you open this same web page on a mobile device, however, it appears very small, as shown in Figure 5-2.

The reason the web page looks so small on a mobile device is that mobile devices display more pixels per inch than desktop devices. To get more details about the reasons behind this and how using a `viewport` meta tag adjusts for this, view the excellent video about the browser viewports at `https://www.youtube.com/watch?v=XrMTuTzX4co`.

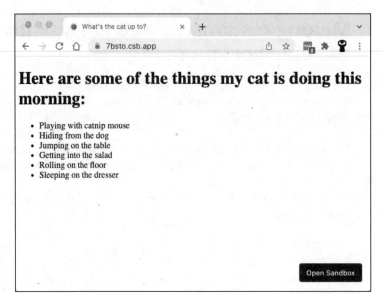

FIGURE 5-1:
A simple web
page in a desktop
browser.

FIGURE 5-2:
A non-optimized
web page in a
mobile browser.

The `viewport` meta tag you can use to make a simple web page display correctly on mobile devices is as follows:

```
<meta name="viewport" content="width=device-width,
    initial-scale=1.0">
```

If this tag looks familiar, that's because it's always added to the default `index.html` file that gets created in codesandbox.io when you make a new project. The `viewport` meta tag is almost always the same as the one shown above, and it's so useful that you should add it to every web page you make in the future.

What this `viewport` meta tag does is to adjust the size of the content to fit the size of the viewport.

TECHNICAL STUFF

A full explanation of how the `viewport` tag works is much easier to understand from a video. Check out the link from a few paragraphs ago to learn more.

With the `viewport` meta tag added, here's how the preceding simple web page's code now looks:

```
<!DOCTYPE html>
<html>
  <head>
    <title>What's the cat up to?</title>
    <meta name="viewport" content="width=device-width, initial-scale=1.0">
  </head>
  <body>
    <h1>Here are some of the things my cat is doing this morning:</h1>
    <ul>
      <li>Playing with catnip mouse</li>
      <li>Hiding from the dog</li>
      <li>Jumping on the table</li>
      <li>Getting into the salad</li>
      <li>Rolling on the floor</li>
      <li>Sleeping on the dresser</li>
    </ul>
  </body>
</html>
```

This page will look the same in a desktop browser as it did in Figure 5-1. Figure 5-3 shows how it looks in a mobile browser now.

REMEMBER

If you want to try this out for yourself, go to codesandbox.io and enter this code into an HTML page. Then open the preview URL in your mobile phone's web browser.

FIGURE 5-3:
A simple mobile
web page.

Using Flexbox

By default, web browsers display the elements in an HTML document from left to right and from top to bottom. This is what's called the *normal flow.* By using the CSS `float` and `position` properties, you can modify this normal flow of HTML or even remove elements from the normal flow of a document and position them wherever you want in the viewport. However, these positioning tools can be complex, and achieving the results you want and getting them to work correctly on different devices can be tricky — especially when you're trying to align elements or create responsive layouts.

Another problem with normal flow is that not all languages are written from left to right. So-called normal flow is backward to the Arabic-speaking world, for example.

Flexbox was created to fix the many issues with web page layout using older CSS properties like `float` and `position`. The first things you need to know about Flexbox are:

» All Flexbox layout happens in Flexbox containers (also known as *boxes*).

» Flexbox is one-dimensional. When you work with Flexbox, you only deal with the x axis (rows) or the y axis (columns) at any one time.

» Flexbox doesn't assume that the text direction (also known as the *writing mode*) is left-to-right.

» Flexbox containers and the items inside them are flexible (it's right there in the name!).

In the following sections, you'll learn more about each of these points and you'll see plenty of example code you can try out on your own to help you get comfortable with using Flexbox.

Creating boxes

To get started with Flexbox, you first need to define what part or parts of your web page will use it. The way to do this is to set the display property of an element to flex. By default, a container will flow elements inside it horizontally (in a row). For example, in the following code, the div element with the id of gallery is a Flexbox that will flow horizontally.

```
<!DOCTYPE html>
<html>
  <head>
    <title>Creating a container</title>
    <style>
      #gallery {
        display: flex;
      }
    </style>
  </head>
  <body>
    <div id="gallery"></div>
  </body>
</html>
```

The preceding code won't display anything in the browser just yet, because there's no content in the Flexbox container. To see what Flexbox can do, you can put something in the Flexbox. An element that's inside a Flexbox container is called an *item*.

Just as a cardboard box doesn't make a lot of sense for holding just one thing (unless you're a certain online retailer, in which case the bigger the box and the smaller the item inside it the better!), a Flexbox with only one item isn't impressive. To see what simply creating a container and putting things in it can do, we'll need several items in the box. The following example code creates three `div` elements in the flex container and styles them with a solid black border and margins of 10 pixels.

```
<!DOCTYPE html>
<html>
  <head>
    <title>A flexible row of boxes</title>
    <style>
      #gallery {
        display: flex;
      }
      .box {
        border: 4px solid black;
        margin: 10px;
        width: 100px;
        height: 100px;
        font-size: 36px;
      }
    </style>
  </head>
  <body>
    <div id="gallery">
      <div class="box">1</div>
      <div class="box">2</div>
      <div class="box">3</div>
    </div>
  </body>
</html>
```

When displayed in a web browser, the preceding code will show three boxes arranged in a neat row, as shown in Figure 5-4.

Thinking in one dimension

When we say that Flexbox layout is one-dimensional, what we mean is that Flexbox only deals with either layout in rows or layout in columns. This is different from a grid layout, in which you can position objects in rows or columns at the same time.

The property to change the dimension that a container flows its items in is `flex-direction`. The `flex-direction` property has four possible values: `row` (the default), `row-reverse`, `column`, and `column-reverse`.

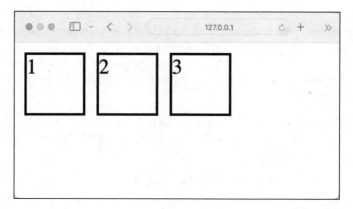

FIGURE 5-4:
Little boxes all
the same.

The following code changes the layout direction of the items to `column`, which makes them display as vertically stacked boxes.

```html
<!DOCTYPE html>
<html>
  <head>
    <title>Demonstrating flex-direction</title>
    <style>
      #gallery {
        display: flex;
        flex-direction: column;
      }
      .box {
        border: 4px solid black;
        margin: 10px;
        width: 100px;
        height: 100px;
        font-size: 36px;
      }
    </style>
  </head>
<body>
  <div id="gallery">
    <div class="box">1</div>
    <div class="box">2</div>
    <div class="box">3</div>
  </div>
</body>
</html>
```

To reverse the order of the items in the box, use one of the –reverse values, as shown in the following code and in Figure 5-5:

```
<!DOCTYPE html>
<html>
  <head>
    <title>Demonstrating flex-direction</title>
    <style>
      #gallery {
        display: flex;
        flex-direction: row-reverse;
      }
      .box {
        border: 4px solid black;
        margin: 10px;
        width: 100px;
        height: 100px;
        font-size: 36px;
      }
    </style>
  </head>
  <body>
    <div id="gallery">
      <div class="box">1</div>
      <div class="box">2</div>
      <div class="box">3</div>
    </div>
  </body>
</html>
```

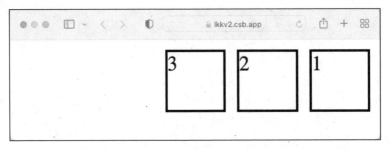

FIGURE 5-5:
Reversing a flex container

© John Wiley & Sons

Using multi-line containers

By default, the items in a flex container will all be on one line. If you want to create a multi-line container in which items will wrap to new lines in the container when a line of items in a container fills up, you can use the `flex-wrap` property.

In the following code, the `flex-wrap` property is set to `wrap`, which will cause an additional line to be created when the previous line fills up with items.

```html
<!DOCTYPE html>
<html>
  <head>
    <title>Demonstrating flex-wrap</title>
    <style>
      #gallery {
        display: flex;
        flex-wrap: wrap;
      }
      .box {
        border: 4px solid black;
        margin: 10px;
        font-size: 36px;
        width: 100px;
        height: 100px;
        font-size: 36px;
      }
    </style>
  </head>
  <body>
    <div id="gallery">
      <div class="box">1</div>
      <div class="box">2</div>
      <div class="box">3</div>
      <div class="box">4</div>
      <div class="box">5</div>
      <div class="box">6</div>
    </div>
  </body>
</html>
```

Figure 5-6 shows what the preceding code looks like rendered in a browser whose viewport is less than the total width of the six items in the container.

TIP

Wrapping items in a container is one of the best ways to create a responsive layout with Flexbox. With wrapping, when a multiple-column layout doesn't fit the width of the viewport, the items that don't fit will just drop down to a new line, rather than going off the page or shrinking down to fit.

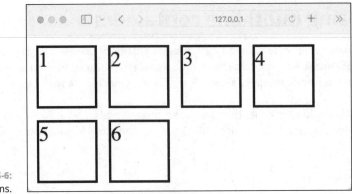

FIGURE 5-6:
Wrapping items.

Make no assumptions

If you're working in a language with a left-to-right writing mode, your Flexbox containers will flow their items from left to right by default. If you're working in a language with a right-to-left writing mode, your Flexbox containers will flow their items from right to left by default.

The terminology used by Flexbox is careful not to play favorites. When we talk about the position where a row or column of items begin, we use the term "start." Likewise, when we talk about the position where a row or column of items stops, we use the term "end." The start and end positions could be at the top, bottom, left, or right of the screen. All that's important is that the items in a flex container flow from the start to the end by default. If you use a -reverse value for the flex-direction property, the items will flow from the end to the start.

By default, items are aligned to the start position on their axis. You can see that in Figure 5-4, where the row of boxes starts at the left and moves to the right.

Aligning on the cross-axis

One of the greatest features of Flexbox is that you can modify the alignment of items on their axis or on their cross-axis. The cross-axis refers to the other axis. To set the cross-axis alignment of items, use the align-items property. The align-items property can have one of four possible values:

» stretch

» flex-start

» flex-end

» center

The default value is stretch, which makes all the items the same size (along the cross-axis) as the largest one. For example, Figure 5-7 shows three boxes of different sizes. Using the stretch value of align-items, all the boxes will be the same height as the tallest one.

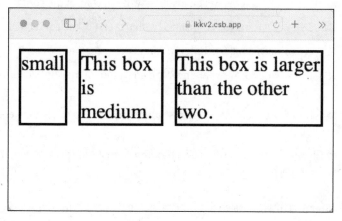

FIGURE 5-7: Stretching items.

If you set align-items to flex-start, the items will be different heights and their start points will be aligned. If you set align-items to flex-end, their end points will align. Setting align-items to center will center the items vertically if the flex-direction is set to row or row-reverse, as shown in Figure 5-8.

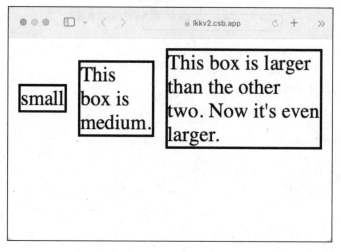

FIGURE 5-8: Centering on the cross-axis.

Responsive Layouts with Flexbox

Aligning on the main axis

To align items on their main axis, use the `justify-content` property. The possible values of `justify-content` are:

» `flex-start`: Items will be justified with the start of the container.

» `flex-end`: Items will be justified with the end of the container.

» `center`: Items will be centered within the container.

» `space-around`: Items are evenly distributed on the line with equal space around each item.

» `space-between`: Items are distributed so that the space between them is equal.

» `space-evenly`: Items are distributed so that the space between the items and the space to the edges is even.

Figure 5-9 illustrates each of the possible values of the `justify-content` property.

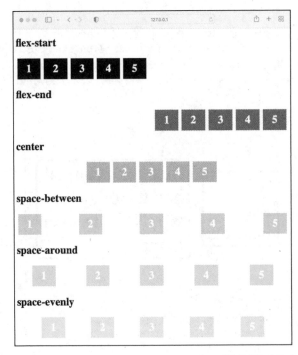

FIGURE 5-9: The different ways to justify content within a container.

Modifying flexible boxes

All the Flexbox properties you've seen so far are applied to the container. Each item within the container can also have Flexbox properties applied to it. For example, you may want to modify the sizes or the relative sizes of items within a Flexbox. The three properties that can be applied flex items to affect their size are:

>> `flex-basis`

>> `flex-grow`

>> `flex-shrink`

These three properties tell items how to adjust when there's extra space (also known as *available space*) within the container. For example, if you have three items that are each 100 pixels wide, and the container around them is 500 pixels wide, there will be 200 pixels of available space (assuming that the items don't have margins between them, of course).

flex-basis

The `flex-basis` property specifies the initial size of an item before the available space in the container is taken into consideration. By default, `flex-basis` is set to `auto`, which tells the item to look at its `width` or `height` property. You can also set the `flex-basis` property to any other size by specifying a `length` (for example, 100px or 80%).

flex-grow

The `flex-grow` property is a number that indicates what share of the available space an item will get when it's distributed. For example, if each item in the container has `flex-grow` set to 1 (which is the default value), the available space will be distributed evenly between them. But, if there are three items and two of them have `flex-grow` set to 1 and the other has `flex-grow` set to 2, the one with `flex-grow` set to 2 will get twice as much of the available space as the others, as shown in the following code and in Figure 5-10.

```
<div style="display: flex;">
  <div class="box" style="flex-grow: 1;"></div>
  <div class="box" style="flex-grow: 2;"></div>
  <div class="box" style="flex-grow: 1;"></div>
</div>
```

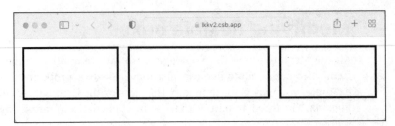

© John Wiley & Sons

FIGURE 5-10:
Distributing
available space
with flex-grow.

flex-shrink

The flex-shrink property behaves the same way as flex-grow, but it determines how much an item will shrink if there isn't enough space available for the items. In the following code and example, the middle item will shrink twice as much as the other two, as shown in Figure 5-11.

```
<div style="display: flex;">
  <div class="box" style="flex-shrink: 1;"></div>
  <div class="box" style="flex-shrink: 2;"></div>
  <div class="box" style="flex-shrink: 1;"></div>
</div>
```

© John Wiley & Sons

FIGURE 5-11:
Using
flex-shrink.

The flex property

Although you can specify the flex-basis, flex-grow, and flex-shrink properties individually for each item, it's more common for developers to use a shorthand property that sets all three at the same time. The shorthand property for setting these three is the flex property.

The flex property takes up to three values. The first one is the only value required, and it's the number for the flex-grow property. The second one is the number for the flex-shrink property. The third value is the value for flex-basis. There's no difference between using the shorthand property or using the individual properties, except in the amount of typing you need to do.

Here's how you can set flex-grow to 2, flex-shrink to 1, and flex-basis to 100px, all in one line of CSS:

```
flex: 2 1 100px;
```

If you only want to set the flex-grow property, you can just use one number:

```
flex: 1;
```

If you only want to set flex-grow and flex-basis, you can use two values:

```
flex: 1 100px;
```

TECHNICAL STUFF

Notice that there's no way to use two values to set only flex-shrink and flex-basis. If that's what you want to do, you need to use three values and set flex-grow as well.

Changing the order of items

The order in which items appear in a container will be in the same order in which they appear in the code, by default. If you want to modify the order of the items, you can do so using the order property.

The order property takes a number value, which is the order in which the item should appear. Items that have the same number for the order property will be laid out in the order that they appear in the source code. By default, all items have an order value of 0.

The following code and Figure 5-12 demonstrate the use of order to make an element that comes last in the source code appear first in the browser window.

```
<!DOCTYPE html>
<html>
  <head>
    <title>The order property</title>
    <style>
      #gallery {
        display: flex;
```

```
      }
   .box {
      border: 4px solid black;
      margin: 10px;
      font-size: 36px;
      width: 100px;
      height: 100px;
   }
   </style>
</head>
<body>
   <div id="gallery">
      <div class="box" style="order: 2;">
         1
      </div>
      <div class="box" style="order: 3;">
         2
      </div>
      <div class="box" style="order: 1;">
         3
      </div>
   </div>
</body>
</html>
```

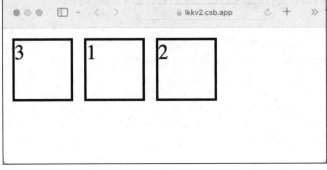

FIGURE 5-12:
Changing the
order of items in
a container.

Experimenting with Flexbox

Practice using Flexbox online using the CodeSandbox.io website (or one of the
other code playgrounds listed in Book 1) by following these steps:

1. **Open your browser and go to codesandbox.io.**

2. **If you have a codesandbox account, sign in.**

   Signing up is discussed in Book 1, Chapter 3.

   TECHNICAL STUFF

   Creating an account allows you to save your progress as you work, but it's optional.

3. **Create a new sandbox using the static template or open the sandbox that you created in the previous chapter.**

4. **Use an HTML document from this chapter or make your own.**

5. **Make a `style.css` file and link it to your HTML file.**

6. **Make a Flexbox container and then try using some of the properties you learned in this chapter. Test your web page on both a desktop browser and a mobile browser and get it to look good on both.**

Responsive Layouts
with Flexbox

Chapter **6**

Styling with Bootstrap

"None of us got where we are solely by pulling ourselves up by our bootstraps. We got here because somebody — a parent, a teacher, an Ivy League crony, or a few nuns — bent down and helped us pick up our boots."

— THURGOOD MARSHALL

Bootstrap is a free toolkit that allows users to create web pages quickly and with great consistency. In 2011 two Twitter developers, Mark Otto and Jacob Thornton, created the toolkit for internal use at Twitter and soon afterward released it to the general public. Before Bootstrap, developers would create common web page features over and over again and each time slightly differently, leading to increased time spent on maintenance. Bootstrap has become one of the most popular tools used in creating websites and is used by NASA and *Newsweek* for their websites. With a basic understanding of HTML and CSS, you can use and customize Bootstrap layouts and elements for your own projects.

In this chapter, you discover what Bootstrap does and how to use it. You also discover the various layouts and elements that you can quickly and easily create when using Bootstrap.

Figuring Out What Bootstrap Does

Imagine you're the online layout developer for *The Washington Post*, responsible for coding the front page of the print newspaper (see Figure 6-1) into a digital website version. The newspaper consistently uses the same font size and typeface for the main headline, captions, and bylines. Similarly, there are a set number of layouts to choose from, usually with the main headline at the top of the page accompanied by a photo.

FIGURE 6-1:
The front page of *The Washington Post* (January 25, 2022).

© John Wiley & Sons

Every day you could write your CSS code from scratch, defining font typeface, sizes, paragraph layouts, and the like. However, given that the newspaper follows a largely defined format, it would be easier to define this styling ahead of time in your CSS file with class names and when necessary refer to the styling you want by name. At its core, this is how Bootstrap functions.

Bootstrap is a collection of standardized prewritten HTML, CSS, and JavaScript code that you can reference using class names (for a refresher, see Book 2, Chapter 4) and then further customize. Bootstrap allows you to create and gives you the following:

>> **Layouts:** Define your web page content and elements in a grid pattern.

>> **Components:** Use existing buttons, menus, and icons that have been tested on hundreds of millions of users.

>> **Responsiveness:** A fancy word for whether your site will work on mobile phones and tablets in addition to desktop computers. Ordinarily, you would write additional code so your website appears properly on these different screen sizes, but Bootstrap code is already optimized to do this for you, as shown in Figure 6-2. Behind the scenes, Bootstrap uses Flexbox, which you learned about in Book 2, Chapter 5, to make responsive layouts.

>> **Cross-browser compatibility:** Chrome, Firefox, Safari, Edge, and other browsers all vary in the way they render certain HTML elements and CSS properties. Bootstrap code is optimized so your web page appears consistently no matter the browser used.

FIGURE 6-2:
The Super Mario Odyssey page optimized for mobile, tablet, and desktop using Bootstrap.

© John Wiley & Sons

Installing Bootstrap

Install and add Bootstrap to your HTML file by following these steps:

1. **Open your web browser and go to** `https://getbootstrap.com`.

2. **Click the Download button. You'll see the Download Bootstrap page.**

3. **Scroll down the page (or use the navigation link on the right side of the page) to find the section called CDN via jsDelivr, as shown in Figure 6-3.**

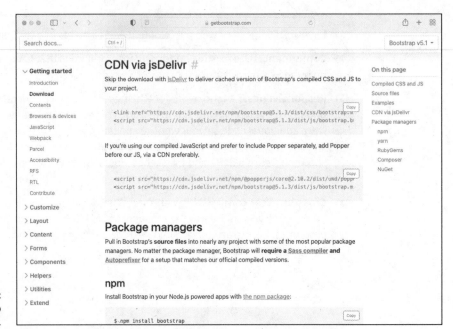

FIGURE 6-3:
The Bootstrap
CDN links.

4. **Click the first Copy button in the CDN via jsDelivr section to copy the code for including Bootstrap in your web page.**

5. **Paste the code you just copied between your opening and closing `<head>` tag.**

TIP

The `<link>` and `<script>` tags download Bootstrap from a content delivery network (CDN), which is a network that's optimized for serving code and media files to users quickly no matter where they're located.

TIP

If you want to try Bootstrap using CodeSandbox.io, you can create a new project with the static template (or use one that you've already created) and paste the CDN links into the `<head>` element, as shown in Figure 6-4. When you save the file, your page will have Bootstrap styles applied to it. Try changing the default text on the page and see how simply adding Bootstrap to a page makes it look better.

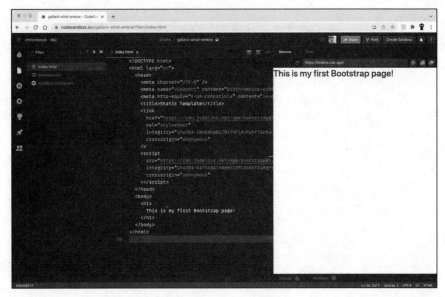

FIGURE 6-4:
Using
Bootstrap in
CodeSandbox.io

Understanding the Layout Options

Bootstrap allows you to lay out content quickly and easily using a grid system. You have three options when using this grid system:

>> **Code yourself.** After you learn how the grid is organized, you can write code to create any layout you wish.

>> **Code with a Bootstrap editor.** Instead of writing code in a text editor, drag and drop components and elements to generate Bootstrap code. You can then download and use this code.

>> **Code with a prebuilt theme.** Download free Bootstrap themes or buy a theme where the website has already been created, and you fill in your own content.

Lining up on the grid system

Bootstrap divides the screen into a grid system of 12 equally sized columns. These columns follow a few rules:

>> **Columns must sum to a width of 12 columns.** You can use one column that is 12 columns wide, 12 columns that are each one column wide, or anything in between.

>> **Columns can contain content or spaces.** For example, you could have a 4-column-wide column, a space of 4 columns, and another 4-column-wide column.

Unless you specify otherwise, these columns will automatically stack into a single column on smaller browser sizes or screens like mobile devices, and expand horizontally on larger browser sizes or screens like laptop and desktop screens. (See Figure 6-5.)

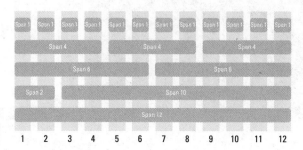

FIGURE 6-5:
Sample Bootstrap
layouts.

Now that you have a sense for how these layouts appear on the screen, take a look at example code used to generate these layouts. To create any layout, follow these steps:

1. **Create a ‹div› tag with the attribute** `class="container"`.

2. **Inside the first ‹div› tag, create another nested ‹div› tag with the attribute** `class="row"`.

3. **For each row you want to create, create another ‹div› tag with the attribute** `class="col-md-X"`. **Set X equal to the number of columns you want the row to span.**

   For example, to have a row span four columns, write ‹div class= "col-md-4"›. The md targets the column width for desktops, and I show you how to target other devices later in this section.

WARNING

You must include ‹div class="container"› at the beginning of your page and have a closing ‹/div› tag, or your page will not render properly.

The following code, as shown in Figure 6-6, creates a simple three-column centered layout:

```
<div class="container">
  <!-- Example row of columns -->
```

```
<div class="row">
 <div class="col-md-4">
   <h2>Heading</h2>
   <p>Lorem ipsum dolor sit amet, consectetur adipisicing elit, sed do
   eiusmod tempor incididunt ut labore et dolore magna aliqua. Ut enim
   ad minim veniam, quis nostrud exercitation ullamco laboris nisi ut
   aliquip ex ea commodo consequat.
</p>
 </div>
 <div class="col-md-4">
   <h2>Heading</h2>
   <p>Lorem ipsum dolor sit amet, consectetur adipisicing elit, sed do eiusmod
   Tempor incididunt ut labore et dolore magna aliqua. Ut enim ad minim veniam,
   quis nostrud exercitation ullamco laboris nisi ut aliquip ex ea commodo
   consequat.
</p>
 </div>
 <div class="col-md-4">
   <h2>Heading</h2>
   <p>Lorem ipsum dolor sit amet, consectetur adipisicing elit, sed do eiusmod
   tempor incididunt ut labore et dolore magna aliqua. Ut enim ad minim veniam,
   quis nostrud exercitation ullamco laboris nisi ut aliquip ex ea commodo
   consequat.
</p>
  </div>
  </div>
</div>
```

FIGURE 6-6: Bootstrap three-column layout with desktop (left) and mobile (right) versions.

© John Wiley & Sons

To see another example, go to the Zoom.us site and resize the browser window. You will notice that as you make the browser window smaller, the columns automatically stack on top of one another in order to be readable. Also, the columns are automatically centered. Without Bootstrap, you would need more code to achieve these same effects.

TECHNICAL STUFF

The Lorem Ipsum text you see in the preceding code is commonly used to create filler text. Although the words don't mean anything, the quotation originates from a first-century BC Latin text by Cicero. You can generate filler text when creating your own websites by using the dummy text you find at www.lipsum.org.

Dragging and dropping to a website

After looking at the preceding code, you may want an even easier way to generate the code without having to type it yourself. Bootstrap editors allow you to drag and drop components to create a layout, after which the editor will generate Bootstrap code for your use.

Bootstrap editors that you can use include the following:

>> **Layoutit.com:** Free online Bootstrap editor (as shown in Figure 6-7) that allows you to drag and drop components and then download the source code

>> **Pingendo.com:** Free downloadable drag-and-drop Bootstrap editor

>> **Codeply.com:** Free online code editor with built-in support for Bootstrap

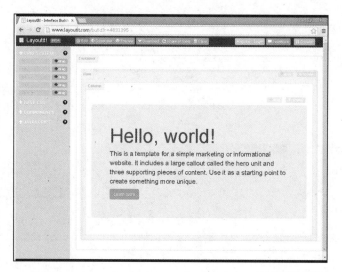

FIGURE 6-7:
Layoutit.com
interface with
drag-and-drop
Bootstrap
components.

© John Wiley & Sons

TIP

These sites are free and may stop working without notice. You can find additional options by using any search engine to search for *Bootstrap editors*.

Using predefined templates

Sites exist with ready-to-use Bootstrap themes; all you need to do is add your own content. Of course, you can also modify the theme if you wish. Here are some of these Bootstrap theme websites:

- » www.bootstrapzero.com: Collection of free, open-source Bootstrap templates

- » www.bootswatch.com and www.bootsnipp.com: Include prebuilt Bootstrap components that you can assemble for your own site

- » www.wrapbootstrap.com: Bootstrap templates available for purchase

TIP

Bootstrap themes may be available for free, but follow the licensing terms. The author may require attribution, email registration, or a tweet.

Adapting layout for mobile, tablet, and desktop

The Bootstrap grid is mobile first. What this means is that the default behavior for items within a Bootstrap container is for each one to take up the full 12 columns. If you want to have multiple columns on larger devices, you can use the col-xx-xx classes. In responsive design, we call the screen sizes at which the layout shifts *breakpoints*. There are six breakpoints you can target — extra small, small, medium, large, extra large, and extra extra large. As shown in Table 6-1, Bootstrap uses a different class prefix to target each breakpoint except the extra small one, which is the default.

TABLE 6-1   **Bootstrap Code for Various Screen Sizes**

	Extra Small (<576px)	Small (≥576px)	Medium (≥768px)	Large (≥992 px)	Extra Large (≥1200px)	Extra Extra Large (≥1400px)
Class prefix	col-xs-	col-sm-	col-md-	col-lg-	col-xl-	col-xxl-
Example device	Phones	Tablets	Laptops	Desktops	Large screens	Extra large screens, TVs

REMEMBER

Because Bootstrap is mobile first, you only need to use the col-xs- breakpoint if you want to divide a mobile screen into multiple columns. If you want to display your layout in a single column on small screens (which is generally a good idea), you don't need to specify the col-xs-12 breakpoint, as it's implied.

Based on Table 6-1, if you want your website to have two equally sized columns on tablets, desktops, large desktops, and TVs, you use the col-sm- class name as follows:

```
<div class="container">
  <div class="row">
    <div class="col-sm-6">Column 1</div>
    <div class="col-sm-6">Column 2</div>
  </div>
</div>
```

After viewing your code on all three devices, you decide that on desktops and larger devices you prefer unequal instead of equal columns so that the left column is half the size of the right column. You target desktop devices using the col-md- class name and add it to the class name immediately after col-sm-:

```
<div class="container">
  <div class="row">
    <div class="col-sm-6 col-md-4">Column 1</div>
    <div class="col-sm-6 col-md-8">Column 2</div>
  </div>
</div>
```

TIP

HTML elements can have multiple classes. This allows you to add multiple effects, such as changing the way a column is displayed, to the element. To define multiple classes, use the class attribute and set it equal to each class; separate each class with a space. For an example, refer to the preceding code: The third and fourth <div> elements have two classes, col-sm-6 and col-md-4.

Finally, you decide that on large desktop screens and TVs, you want the left column to be two columns wide. You target large desktop screens using the col-lg- class name, as shown in Figure 6-8, and add to your existing class attribute values:

```
<div class="container">
  <div class="row">
    <div class="col-sm-6 col-md-4 col-lg-2">Column 1</div>
    <div class="col-sm-6 col-md-8 col-lg-10">Column 2</div>
  </div>
</div>
```

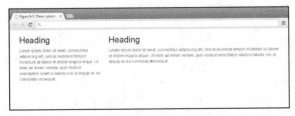

FIGURE 6-8:
A two-column
site displayed on
tablet, desktop,
and large
desktop.

© John Wiley & Sons

Coding Basic Web Page Elements

In addition to responsive layouts, Bootstrap can also create web page components found on almost every website. The idea here is the same as when working with layouts — instead of re-creating the wheel every time by designing your own button or toolbar, it would be better to use prebuilt code, which has already been tested across multiple browsers and devices.

The following examples show how to quickly create common web components.

Designing buttons

Buttons are a basic element on many web pages, but usually can be difficult to set up and style. As shown in Table 6-2, buttons can have various types and sizes.

TABLE 6-2　Bootstrap Code for Creating Buttons

Attribute	Class Prefix	Description
Button type	`btn-primary`	Blue button with hover effect
	`btn-secondary`	Gray button with hover effect
	`btn-success`	Green button with hover effect
	`btn-danger btn-warning`	Red button with hover effect
	btn-info	Yellow button with hover effect
	btn-light	Light blue button with hover effect
	btn-dark	Light gray button with hover effect
		Black button with hover effect
Button size	`btn-lg btn-sm`	Large button size
		Default button size
		Small button size

To create a button, write the following HTML:

1. **Begin with the** `button` **HTML element.**

2. **In the opening** `<button>` **tag, include** `type="button"`.

3. **Include the** `class` **attribute with the** `btn` **class attribute value and add class prefixes based on the effect you want.**

4. **To add styles, continue adding the class prefix name into the HTML** `class` **attribute.**

As shown in Figure 6-9, the following code combines the button type and button size:

```
<p>
  <button type="button" class="btn btn-primary btn-lg">Large primary button
  </button>
  <button type="button" class="btn btn-danger btn-lg">Large danger button
  </button>
</p>
<p>
  <button type="button" class="btn btn-success">Default success button</button>
  <button type="button" class="btn btn-info">Default info button</button>
</p>
<p>
  <button type="button" class="btn btn-warning btn-sm">Small warning button
```

```
    </button>
    <button type="button" class="btn btn-dark btn-sm">Small dark button
    </button>
</p>
```

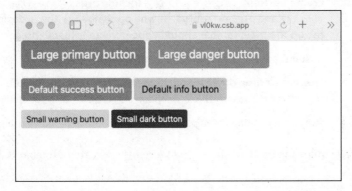

FIGURE 6-9:
Bootstrap button
types and sizes.

TIP

For additional button type, button size, and other button options, see `https://getbootstrap.com/docs/5.1/components/buttons/`.

Navigating with toolbars

Web pages with multiple pages or views usually have one or more toolbars to help users with navigation. Some toolbar options are shown in Table 6-3.

TABLE 6-3   **Bootstrap Code for Creating Navigation Toolbars**

Attribute	Class Prefix	Description
Toolbar type	nav-tabs	Tabbed navigation toolbar
	nav-pills	Pill, or solid button navigation toolbar
Toolbar button type	dropdown	Button or tab as drop-down menu
	caret dropdown-menu	Down-arrow drop-down menu icon
		Drop-down menu items

To create a pill or solid button navigation toolbar, write the following HTML:

1. **Begin an unordered list using the** `ul` **element.**

2. **In the opening** `<ul>` **tag, include** `class="nav nav-pills"`.

3. **Create buttons using the** `<li>` **tag. Include** `class="nav-item"` **in each** `<li>` **tag and** `class="active"` **in one opening** `<li>` **tag to designate which tab on the main toolbar should appear visually highlighted.**

4. **Include** `class="nav-link"` **in each** `<a>` **tag.**

5. **To create a drop-down menu, nest an unordered list. See the code next to "More" with class prefixes** `"dropdown"`, `"caret"`, **and** `"dropdown-menu"`.

   You can link to other web pages in your drop-down menu by using the `<a>` tag.

The following code, as shown in Figure 6-10, creates a toolbar using Bootstrap:

```html
<ul class="nav nav-pills">
    <li class="nav-item">
      <a class="nav-link active" href="timeline.html">Timeline</a>
    </li>
    <li class="nav-item">
      <a class="nav-link" href="about.html">About</a>
    </li>
    <li class="nav-item">
      <a class="nav-link" href="photos.html">Photos</a>
    </li>
    <li class="nav-item">
      <a class="nav-link" href="friends.html">Friends</a>
    </li>
    <li class="nav-item dropdown">
      <a class="nav-link dropdown-toggle" data-bs-toggle="dropdown" href="#"
        >More
        <span class="caret"></span>
      </a>
      <ul class="dropdown-menu">
        <li class="nav-item">
          <a class="nav-link" href="places.html">Places</a>
        </li>
        <li class="nav-item">
          <a class="nav-link" href="sports.html">Sports</a>
        </li>
        <li class="nav-item">
          <a class="nav-link" href="music.html">Music</a>
        </li>
      </ul>
    </li>
  </ul>
```

FIGURE 6-10:
Bootstrap toolbar
with drop-down
menus.

© John Wiley & Sons

TIP

The `dropdown-toggle` class and the `data-bs-toggle="dropdown"` attribute and value work together to add drop-down menus to elements such as links. For additional toolbar options, see `https://getbootstrap.com/docs/5.1/components/navs-tabs/`.

Adding icons

Icons are frequently used with buttons to help convey some type of action. For example, your email program likely uses a button with a trash can icon to delete emails. Icons quickly communicate a suggested action to users without much explanation.

Bootstrap Icons is a free and open-source library of over 1,500 icons. To use Bootstrap Icons, you first need to link to the icon library. One way to do this is by putting the following link to the Bootstrap Icons CDN URL in the ‹head› of your HTML page.

```
<link rel="stylesheet" href="https://cdn.jsdelivr.net/npm/bootstrap-icons@1.7.2/
    font/bootstrap-icons.css">
```

Once you've included the Bootstrap Icons in your page, you can browse the icons at `https://icons.getbootstrap.com/` to find the icon you want. To use the icon, give an element the `bi` class along with the `bi-[icon-name]` class. As shown in Figure 6-11, the following example code creates three buttons with a star, paperclip, and trash can icon.

TECHNICAL
STUFF

Although you can include the entire library in your web page, if you're only going to use one of two, you can improve the loading time of your website by only importing the icons you use. You can get the code for importing individual icons at `icons.getbootstrap.com/#install`.

```
<button type="button" class="btn btn-light">Star
<i class="bi bi-star"></i>
```

```
  </button>
  <button type="button" class="btn btn-light">Attach
  <i class="bi bi-paperclip"></i>
  </button>
  <button type="button" class="btn btn-light">Trash
  <i class="bi bi-trash"></i>
  </button>
```

FIGURE 6-11:
Bootstrap buttons with icons.

Practicing with Bootstrap

You can practice using Bootstrap online with the CodeSandbox.io website (or one of the other code playgrounds listed in Book 1) by following these steps:

1. **Open your browser and go to codesandbox.io.**

2. **If you have a codesandbox account, sign in.**

    Signing up is discussed in Book 1, Chapter 3.

    Creating an account allows you to save your progress as you work, but it's optional.

TECHNICAL STUFF

3. **Create a new sandbox using the static template or open the sandbox that you created in the previous chapter.**

4. **Use an HTML document from this chapter or make your own.**

5. **Follow the instructions in this chapter to include Bootstrap in your page.**

6. **Make a Bootstrap container and then try using some of the Bootstrap classes you learned in this chapter. Test your web page on a desktop browser and a mobile browser and get it to look good on both.**

3

Advanced Web Coding

Contents at a Glance

Chapter **1**

What Is JavaScript?

"People understand me so poorly that they don't even understand my complaint about them not understanding me."

— SØREN KIERKEGAARD

JavaScript hasn't always been as highly regarded as it is today. Some people have called it the best and worst programming language in the world. Over the last few years, there have been a great number of improvements made to the way programmers write JavaScript and to JavaScript interpreters. These improvements have made JavaScript a much better language today than it's been in the past.

In this chapter, you discover what JavaScript is and a little bit of the history of the language. You also find out what JavaScript does and why you need to know it.

What Is JavaScript?

Back in the very early days of the web, browsers were simple readers for web pages (see Figure 1-1). They had virtually no capabilities themselves, except for the ability to display text in various sized fonts. As soon as Microsoft released its

Internet Explorer browser, the browser wars were on, and the features started flying! One browser introduced the ability to display images, then another introduced the capability to have different fonts, and then blinking text, moving text, and all sorts of other wacky capabilities were introduced!

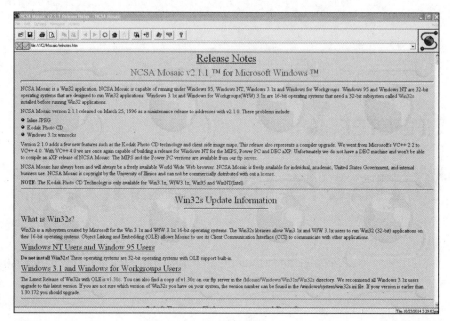

FIGURE 1-1:
The first web browsers weren't much to look at.

It wasn't long before someone got the idea that browsers could actually do useful things themselves, rather than just acting as fancy document display programs.

The Eich-man cometh

JavaScript got its start back in 1995 at Netscape. The creator of JavaScript, Brandon Eich, wrote JavaScript in record time (some say in as few as ten days!) by borrowing many of the best features from various other programming languages. The rush to market also created some interesting quirks (or, less politely described, mistakes) in the design of the language. The result is a sort of Esperanto-like language that looks deceptively familiar to people who are experienced with other programming languages.

Mocha-licious

The original name of JavaScript was Mocha. It was renamed LiveScript with the first beta deployment of Netscape Navigator and was then changed to JavaScript when it was built into the Netscape 2 browser in 1995. Microsoft very quickly reverse-engineered JavaScript and introduced an exact clone of it in Internet Explorer, calling it Jscript to get around trademark issues.

Netscape submitted JavaScript to the standards organization known as Ecma International, and it was adopted and standardized as ECMAScript in 1997.

TECHNICAL STUFF

Brandon Eich, the creator of JavaScript, famously commented about the name of the standardized language, stating that ECMAScript was an "unwanted trade name that sounds like a skin disease."

WARNING

Not only is ECMAScript an unappealing name for a programming language, the name given to the language by Netscape and which most people refer to it as, is rather unfortunate as well. If you already know how to program in Java or if you learn how to at some point, it's a very good idea to keep in mind that the two languages may have some similarities, but they are, in fact, quite different animals.

We need more effects!

When JavaScript debuted, it quickly became very popular as a way to make web pages more dynamic. So-called Dynamic HTML (DHTML) was an early result of JavaScript being built into web browsers, and it enabled all sorts of fun effects, like the falling snowflake effect (see Figure 1-2), popup windows, and curling web page corners, but also more useful things like drop-down menus and form validation.

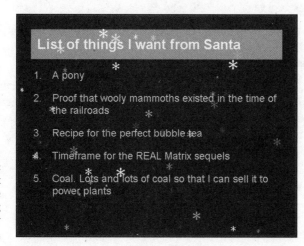

FIGURE 1-2:
JavaScript made it possible to have snowflakes falling on your web page.

JavaScript Grows Up

In the years since those early days, JavaScript has become the world's most widely used programming language and virtually every personal computer in the world has at least one browser on it that can run JavaScript code.

JavaScript is flexible enough that it can be used and learned by nonprogrammers, but powerful enough that it can (and is) used by professional programmers to enable functionality on nearly every website on the Internet today, ranging from single-page sites to gigantic sites like Google, Amazon, Facebook, and many, many others!

COMMON MISCONCEPTIONS ABOUT JAVASCRIPT

Over the years, JavaScript has had some pretty nasty things said about it. While sometimes rumors are interesting, they aren't always true. The following list explains some common misconceptions about JavaScript:

- **Myth:** JavaScript is not a real programming language. **Reality:** JavaScript is often used for trivial tasks in web browsers, but that doesn't make it any less of a programming language. In fact, JavaScript has many advanced features that have raised the bar for programming languages and are now being imitated in languages such as PHP, C++, and even Java.

- **Myth:** JavaScript is related to Java. **Reality:** Nope. The name JavaScript was invented purely as a marketing strategy because Java was incredibly popular at the time JavaScript came out.

- **Myth:** JavaScript is new. **Reality:** JavaScript has been around for over a quarter of a century! Many awesome JavaScript programmers today weren't even born when JavaScript was created.

- **Myth:** JavaScript is buggy and runs differently in different browsers. **Reality:** While this used to be true in some cases, browser makers decided to support the standardized version of JavaScript long ago. Every browser will run JavaScript the same today.

Dynamic scripting language

JavaScript is often described as a *dynamic scripting language.* To understand what this means, you'll first need to learn a couple of terms and get some context.

Computer programs are sets of instructions that cause computers to do things. Every computer programming language has a set of instructions and a certain way that humans must write those instructions. The computer can't understand these instructions directly. For a computer to understand a programming language, it needs to go through a conversion process that translates human-readable (and writable) instructions into machine language. Depending on when this translation takes place, programming languages can be roughly divided into two types: compiled and interpreted (see Figure 1-3).

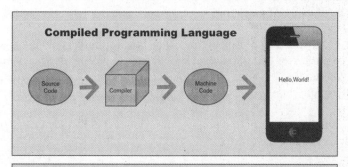

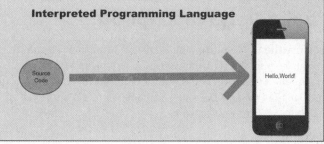

FIGURE 1-3: Programming languages are classified according to when the compilation takes place.

Compiled programming languages

Compiled programming languages are languages in which a programmer must write the code and then run it through a special program called a *compiler* that interprets the given code and then converts it into machine language. The computer can then execute the compiled program.

Examples of compiled languages include C, C++, Fortran, Java, Objective-C, and COBOL.

Interpreted programming languages

Interpreted languages are technically still compiled by the computer into machine language, but the compiling takes place by the user's web browser right as the program is being run. Programmers who write interpreted languages don't need to go through the step of compiling their code prior to handing it off to the computer to run.

The benefit of programming in an interpreted language is that it's easy to make changes to the program at any time. The downside, however, is that compiling code as it's being run creates another step in the process and can slow down the performance of programs.

Partially because of this performance factor, interpreted languages have gotten a reputation for being less than serious programming languages. However, because of better just-in-time compilers and faster computer processors, this perception is rapidly changing. JavaScript is having a big impact in this regard.

Examples of interpreted programming languages include PHP, Perl, Haskell, Ruby and of course, JavaScript.

What does JavaScript do?

If you use the web, you're making use of JavaScript all the time. The list of things that can be enabled with JavaScript is extensive and ranges from simple notices you get when you forget to fill out a required field on a form to complex applications, such as Google Docs or Facebook. Here's a short list of the most common uses for JavaScript on the web:

>> Nifty effects

>> Input validation

>> Rollover effects

>> Drop-down/fly-out menus

>> Drag and drop features

>> Infinitely scrolling web pages

>> Autocomplete

>> Progress bars

>> Tabs within web pages

>> Sortable lists

>> Magic Zoom (see Figure 1-4)

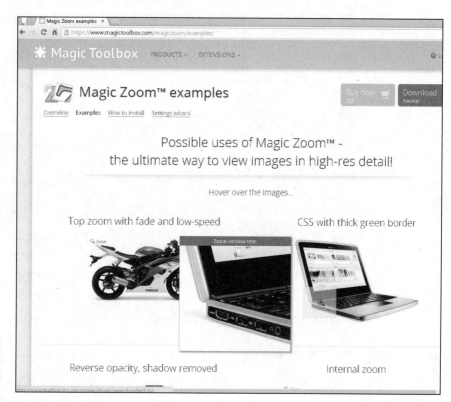

FIGURE 1-4:
So-called Magic Zoom effects are enabled using JavaScript.

Why JavaScript?

JavaScript has become the standard for creating dynamic user interfaces for the web. Pretty much any time you visit a web page with animation, live data, a button that changes when you hover over it, or a drop-down menu, JavaScript is at work. Because of its power and ability to run in any web browser, JavaScript coding is the most popular and necessary skill for a modern web developer to have.

JavaScript is easy to learn!

Keep in mind that programming languages were created to give people a simple way to talk to computers and tell them what to do. Compared with machine language, the language that the computer's CPU speaks, every programming language is easy and understandable. To give you a sample of what sort of instructions your computer is actually obeying, here is a machine language program to write out "Hello World".

```
b8    21 0a 00 00
a3    0c 10 00 06
b8    6f 72 6c 64
a3    08 10 00 06
b8    6f 2c 20 57
a3    04 10 00 06
b8    48 65 6c
a3    00 10 00 06
b9    00 10 00 06
ba    10 00 00 00
bb    01 00 00 00
b8    04 00 00 00
cd    80
b8    01 00 00 00
cd    80
```

Now look at one way you can accomplish this simple task with JavaScript:

```
alert("Hello World");
```

Much easier, yes?

Once you learn the basic rules of the road (called the *syntax*), such as when to use parentheses and when to use curly brackets ({}), JavaScript resembles plain old English.

The first step in learning any language, including programming languages, is to get over your fear of getting started. JavaScript makes this easy. There are thousands of sample bits of JavaScript code on the web that anyone can just pick up and start messing around with. You already have all the tools you need (see Book 3, Chapter 2), and it's easy to start small with JavaScript and gradually build up to making great and wonderful things.

JavaScript is everywhere!

Although JavaScript was originally designed to be used in web browsers, it has found a home in many other places. Today, JavaScript runs on smartphones and tablets, on web servers, in desktop applications, and in all sorts of portable devices.

The most common place to find JavaScript, and what it was originally designed to do, is running in web browsers. When JavaScript runs in this way, it's called *client-side JavaScript.*

Client-side JavaScript adds interactivity to web pages. It accomplishes this in several ways:

>> By controlling the browser itself or making use of functionality of the browser

>> By manipulating the structure and content of web pages

>> By manipulating the styles (such as fonts and layout) of web pages

>> By accessing data from other sources

To understand how JavaScript can manipulate the structure and style of web pages, you need to know a little bit about HTML5 and CSS3.

HTML5

Hypertext Markup Language (HTML) is the language used to structure web pages. It works by marking up content (text and images) to give web browsers information about the content, such as what is a heading, what is a paragraph, where an image goes, and so on. Listing 1-1 shows a simple HTML document. Figure 1-5 shows how a web browser displays this document.

| LISTING 1-1: | A Simple HTML Document |

```
<!DOCTYPE html>
<html>
  <head>
    <title>Hello, HTML!</title>
  </head>
  <body>
    <h1>This is HTML</h1>
    <p id="introduction">
```

(continued)

LISTING 1-1: *(continued)*

```
        This simple document was written with Hypertext Markup
   Language.
</p>
   </body>
</html>
```

FIGURE 1-5:
Web browsers use HTML to render web pages.

Here's a quick review of everything you need to know about HTML right now to move forward with learning JavaScript:

» In HTML, the characters surrounded by angle brackets are called *tags.*

» The *ending tag* (which comes after the content being marked up) has a slash after the first angle bracket. For example ⟨/p⟩ is an ending tag.

» A group of two tags (beginning and ending), plus the content in between them, is called an *element.*

» Elements are generally organized in a hierarchal way (with elements nested within elements).

» Elements may contain name/value pairs, called *attributes.* If an element has attributes, they go in the beginning tag. *Name/value pairs* assign values, in quotes, to names (which aren't in quotes) by putting an equals sign between them. For example, in the following tag, width and height are both attributes of the div element:

```
<div width="100" height="100"></div>
```

>> Some elements don't have content and therefore don't need an ending tag. For example, the `img` tag, which simply inserts an image into a web page, looks like this:

```
<img src="myimage.jpg" width="320" height="200" alt="Here
    is a picture of my dog.">
```

All the data necessary to show the image is included in the beginning tag using attributes, so the `img` tag doesn't require an ending tag.

When you write a web page with HTML, you can include JavaScript code directly in that document, or you can reference JavaScript code files (which end in `.js`) from the HTML document. Either way, your viewer's web browser will download the JavaScript code and run it when a user accesses a web page containing that JavaScript.

REMEMBER

Client-side JavaScript runs inside of your users' web browsers.

CSS3

Cascading Style Sheets (CSS) is the language used to add formatting and different layouts to web pages. The word *style,* when used in CSS, refers to many aspects of how the HTML document is presented to the user, including

>> Typefaces (or font faces)

>> Type size

>> Colors

>> Arrangement of elements in the browser window

>> Sizes of elements

>> Borders

>> Backgrounds

>> Creation of rounded corners on element borders

Like JavaScript, CSS can be either placed directly into an HTML document, or it can be linked to from the HTML document. Once it's downloaded, it immediately does its thing and formats the document according to your specifications.

Style sheets in CSS are made up of CSS rules, which contain properties and values that should be applied to an element or a group of elements. Here's an example of a CSS rule:

```
p{font-size: 14px; font-color: black; font-family: Arial,
    sans-serif}
```

This rule, reading from left to right, specifies that all p elements (which indicate paragraphs in HTML) should be displayed in text that is 14px large, black, and using the Arial font. If Arial isn't available on the user's computer, it should be displayed in some sans-serif typeface.

The part of the CSS rule that's outside of the curly brackets is called the *selector*. It selects the elements that the properties within the curly brackets apply to.

TECHNICAL STUFF

Throughout Book 3, you find out how to use JavaScript with HTML and CSS. We provide just enough information here to be able to show you how HTML and CSS work. If you need to learn more, you can review Book 2.

JavaScript is powerful!

JavaScript running in a web browser used to be slow, and JavaScript got a bad reputation early on among programmers. According to Google, JavaScript code runs up to 80 percent as fast as compiled code. And, it keeps getting faster all the time. What this means is that today's JavaScript is much more powerful than the JavaScript of just a few years ago. And, it's many times more powerful than the JavaScript that was introduced in 1995.

JavaScript is in demand!

JavaScript is not only the most widely known programming language, it's also the most in-demand skill in the information technology (IT) job market. It's projected that the job market for JavaScript programmers will increase by 13 percent between 2020 and 2030. Exciting things are happening with JavaScript, and there has never been a better time than right now to learn it.

Chapter **2**

Writing Your First JavaScript Program

"The secret of getting ahead is getting started."

— MARK TWAIN

Simple JavaScript programming isn't difficult to understand. In this chapter, you go through the process of setting up your computer for writing JavaScript. You also write your first JavaScript program and get to know the basic syntax behind everything you'll do with JavaScript in your future as a programmer.

Setting Up Your Development Environment

It's important to have all your tools set up and in place before beginning to write your first JavaScript program. The first step, if you haven't already done it, is to go through the process of downloading and installing JavaScript development tools.

If you have preferred tools other than the ones recommended in this chapter, please feel free to use those. However, you should still read this section of the book to learn about some of the most popular JavaScript tools and to make your own decisions about whether to use them.

REMEMBER

If you don't want to install any additional tools, you can continue to work in CodeSandbox.io. The template you'll want to use for JavaScript programs is called Vanilla.

After you install each of the tools, you'll learn some tips and tricks for how to get the most out of each of them.

Downloading and installing Chrome

All browsers will run JavaScript very fast and correctly. However, some of the instructions in this book will be specific to Google Chrome, so you should at least go through the process of installing it on your computer in this chapter. This book uses Google Chrome because it offers excellent tools for making JavaScript programmers' jobs easier and because it's currently the most widely used web browser on the Internet.

If you don't have Chrome installed, follow these steps to install it:

1. **Go to www.google.com/chrome.**

   Figure 2-1 shows you what the download page for Google Chrome looks like.

2. **Click Download Chrome and the appropriate version for your computer will be downloaded.**

3. **Open the downloaded file and follow the instructions to install Chrome.**

Downloading and installing a code editor

A *source code editor*, commonly referred to as code editor, is a text editor with added functionality that helps you write and edit programming code. The one you'll learn about in this book is Visual Studio Code.

FIGURE 2-1:
Installing Chrome
is easy on Mac or
Windows.

TIP

There are many code editors to choose from, so if you already have a favorite that you like to use and that you're comfortable with, please use it! A programmer's code editor is a very personal choice, and many people will find that they just feel more comfortable with a specific one. If you find that Visual Studio Code (also known as VS Code) just doesn't fit your style, Table 2-1 lists some other options.

VS Code is popular among JavaScript programmers, and it provides a simple user interface along with many plugins for handling more advanced programming tasks as you gain more programming experience.

NOW YOU HAVE A SUPERCHARGED JAVASCRIPT ENGINE!

Google Chrome uses Google's V8 JavaScript engine to parse, compile, and run JavaScript code. Depending on whose benchmarking test you believe, Chrome is either the fastest way to run JavaScript in a browser, or it's one of the fastest. The major browser makers are constantly competing to outdo each other. It doesn't matter too much who is the fastest at any one time; the competition has increased the speed of every browser's JavaScript engine by leaps and bounds in recent years.

TABLE 2-1

Examples of Other Code Editors

Name	Location	Compatible with . . .
Brackets	brackets.io	Mac, Windows, Linux
Atom	www.atom.io	Mac, Windows, Linux
Sublime Text	sublimetext.com	Mac, Windows, Linux
Nova	nova.app	Mac only
Notepad++	http://notepad-plus-plus.org	Windows only
TextMate	http://macromates.com	Mac only
BBEdit	www.barebones.com/products/bbedit	Mac only
EMacs	www.gnu.org/software/emacs	Mac, Windows, Linux
TextPad	www.textpad.com	Windows only
vim	www.vim.org	Mac, Windows, Linux
Netbeans	https://netbeans.org	Mac, Windows, Linux

To install VS Code, follow these steps:

1. Go to http://code.visualstudio.com and choose the appropriate version for your operating system.

2. Open the downloaded file and follow the instructions for installing VS Code.

Getting started with VS code

When you first open VS Code, you'll have an option to choose a color theme, as shown in Figure 2-2. If you want to skip this for now, you can click the Get Started link in the upper left to go to the main Get Started screen (see Figure 2-3).

If you've used VS Code before, you'll have the option to open a recent project from the Get Started page. Otherwise, you can choose one of the options under the Start heading on the Get Started screen: New File, Open (which opens an existing folder), or Clone Git Repository.

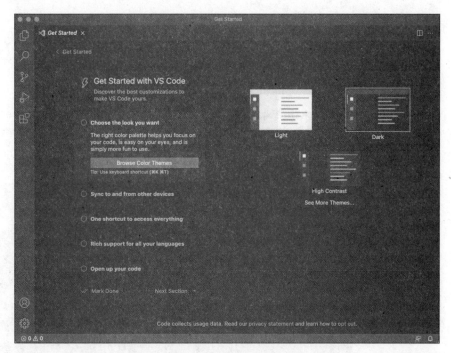

FIGURE 2-2:
The Color Theme
preferences
window.

© John Wiley & Sons

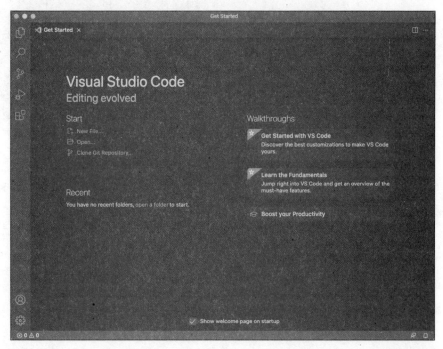

FIGURE 2-3:
The Get Started
page.

© John Wiley & Sons

To get started with your first VS Code project, follow these steps:

1. **Click New File from the Get Started Screen.**

   A blank and untitled page will appear.

2. **Click the Explorer icon (it looks like a magnifying glass) in the left toolbar. The Explorer pane will open on the left and it will tell you that you haven't opened a folder yet, as shown in Figure 2-4.**

FIGURE 2-4:
The Explorer pane.

3. **Click Open Folder and find a folder (or create a new one) on your computer that you want to keep your JavaScript files in.**

4. **Save your untitled file in your new folder and name it** myFirstProgram. html.

Choosing a syntax color scheme

VS Code syntax colors are based on the type of code that you're writing and the file extension. Input the following HTML and JavaScript code shown in Listing 2-1 into the file you've just created to see the default color scheme.

WARNING

As you're about to find out, JavaScript is finicky. Make sure that you capitalize and spell everything exactly as it is in the listing, or your script may not work correctly or at all.

LISTING 2-1: **A Sample HTML File Containing JavaScript**

```html
<!DOCTYPE html>
<html>
<head>
  <title>Hello, HTML!</title>
  <script>
    function countToTen(){
      let count = 0;
      while (count < 10) {
        count++;
        document.getElementById("theCount").innerHTML += count +
  "<br>";
      }
    }
</script>
</head>
<body onload="countToTen();">
  <h1>Let's Count to 10 with JavaScript!</h1>
  <p id="theCount"></p>
</body>
</html>
```

Figure 2-5 shows what the file looks like in VS Code.

TIP

If you don't like the color scheme that's currently selected, you can change it by choosing Preferences ⇨ Color Theme and then selecting another color scheme.

Try out a few of the other color schemes and find one you like.

FIGURE 2-5: VS Code applies colors to all of the different parts of your code.

```
index.html — javascript
EXPLORER                    index.html  ×
JAVASCRIPT                  index.html >  html
  index.html          1   <!DOCTYPE html>
                      2   <html>
                      3   <head>
                      4     <title>Hello, HTML!</title>
                      5     <script>
                      6       function countToTen(){
                      7         var count = 0;
                      8         while (count < 10) {
                      9           count++;
                     10           document.getElementById("theCount").innerHTML += count +
                                  "<br>";
                     11         }
                     12       }
                     13     </script>
                     14   </head>
                     15   <body onload="countToTen();">
                     16     <h1>Let's Count to 10 with JavaScript!</h1>
                     17     <p id="theCount"></p>
                     18   </body>
                     19   </html>
                     20
  OUTLINE
  0  0    Cloud Code   minikube          Ln 19, Col 8   Spaces: 2   UTF-8   LF   HTML   Port : 5500   Prettier
```

If you'd like to try out the program you've just typed, follow these steps:

1. **Save the file by choosing File ⇨ Save.**

2. **Open your Chrome browser and press Ctrl+O.**

   An Open File window appears.

3. **Navigate to the file on your computer and select it.**

4. **Click the Open button.**

   The file will open in your browser.

Your browser should look just like Figure 2-6. If it doesn't, very carefully check your code — you probably have a small typo somewhere. Don't forget to save your file after making any changes!

TECHNICAL STUFF

You can also save your file by pressing Command+S (on the Mac) or Control+S (On Windows). Once you become proficient with them, keyboard shortcuts will save you a lot of time.

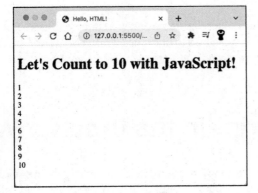

FIGURE 2-6:
Running a simple counting program in Chrome.

© John Wiley & Sons

Reading JavaScript Code

Before you get started with writing JavaScript programs, you need to be aware of a few rules of JavaScript:

» **JavaScript is case-sensitive.** Mistakes in capitalization are probably the most common errors that those who are new to JavaScript make. They're also one of the more difficult bugs to track down. Remember, to JavaScript, the words pants and Pants are completely different.

» **JavaScript doesn't care much about whitespace.** Whitespace includes spaces, tabs, and line breaks — any character that doesn't have a visual representation. When you're writing JavaScript code, it doesn't matter if you use one space, two spaces, a tab, or even a line break (in most cases) within the code. JavaScript will ignore whitespace. The one exception is when you're writing out text that you want JavaScript to print to the screen. In this case, the whitespace you use will show up in the end result. The best practice, with regards to whitespace in your code, is to use enough space that your code is easy to read and to also be consistent with how you use this space.

» **Watch out for reserved words.** JavaScript has a list of words that have special meaning to the language. We list these words in Book 3, Chapter 3. For now, just be aware that some words, such as function, while, break, and with, have special meanings.

» **JavaScript likes semicolons.** JavaScript code is made up of statements. You can think of statements as sentences. They are fundamental building blocks for JavaScript programs in the same way that sentences are the building blocks of paragraphs. In JavaScript, statements end with a semicolon.

WARNING

If you don't use a semicolon at the end of a statement, JavaScript will put it there for you. This can lead to unexpected results, however, so it's considered a best practice to always end statements with a semicolon.

Running JavaScript in the Browser Window

Although it's seen in many different environments, the most common place to see JavaScript in the wild is running in web browsers. Controlling inputs and outputs, manipulating web pages, handling common browser events such as clicks and scrolls, and controlling the different features of web browsers is what JavaScript was born to do!

To run JavaScript in a web browser, you have three options, all of which will be shown in the following pages:

>> Put it directly in an HTML event attribute

>> Put it between an opening and closing script tag

>> Put it in a separate document and include it in your HTML document

Many times, you'll use a combination of all three techniques within any one web page. However, knowing when to use each is important and is a skill that you'll learn with more practice.

Using JavaScript in an HTML event attribute

HTML has several special attributes that are designed for triggering JavaScript when something happens in the web browser or when the user does something. Here's an example of an HTML button with an event attribute that responds to mouse click events:

```
<button id="bigButton" onclick="alert('Hello World!');">Click
    Here</button>
```

In this case, when a user clicks on the button created by this HTML element, a popup will appear with the words "Hello World!".

HTML has over 70 different event attributes. Table 2-2 shows the most commonly used ones.

TABLE 2-2

Commonly Used HTML Event Attributes

Attribute	Description
onload	Runs the script after the page finishes loading
onfocus	Runs the script when the element gets focus (such as when a text box is active)
onblur	Runs the script when the element loses focus (such as when the user clicks a new text box in a form)
onchange	Runs the script when the value of an element is changed
onselect	Runs the script when text has been submitted
onsubmit	Runs the script when a form has been submitted
onkeydown	Runs the script when a user is pressing a key
onkeypress	Runs the script when a user presses a key
onkeyup	Runs the script when a user releases a key
onclick	Runs the script when a user mouse clicks an element
ondrag	Runs the script when an element is dragged
ondrop	Runs the script when a dragged element is being dropped
onmouseover	Runs the script when a user moves a mouse pointer over an element

WARNING

Although they're easy to use, using event attributes is considered a less-than-ideal practice by many JavaScript programmers. You learn them in this book because they are so widely used and easy to learn. However, for now, just be aware that there is a better way to write JavaScript code that responds to events than to use event attributes. You'll learn about this better method in Book 3, Chapter 11.

Using JavaScript in a script element

The HTML script element allows you to embed JavaScript into an HTML document. Often script elements are placed within the head element, and, in fact, this placement was often stated as a requirement. Today, however, script elements are used within the head element as well as in the body of web pages.

The format of the script element is very simple:

```
<script>
  (insert your JavaScript here)
</script>
```

You saw an example of this type of script embedding in Listing 2-1. Listing 2-2 shows another example of an HTML document with a script tag containing JavaScript. In this case, however, the script element is at the bottom of the body element.

LISTING 2-2: **Embedding JavaScript within a Script Element**

```html
<!DOCTYPE html>
<html>
<head>
 <title>Hello, HTML!</title>
</head>
<body>
 <h1>Let's Count to 10 with JavaScript!</h1>
 <p id="theCount"></p>
 <script>
   let count = 0;
   while (count < 10) {
    count++;
    document.getElementById("theCount").innerHTML += count +
   "<br>";
   }
 </script>
</body>
</html>
```

If you create a new file in VS Code, input Listing 2-2 into it, and then open it in a web browser, you'll notice that it does exactly the same thing as Listing 2-1.

Script placement and JavaScript execution

Web browsers normally load and execute scripts as they are loaded. A web page always gets read by the browser from the top down, just as you would read a page of text. Sometimes you'll want to wait until the browser is done loading the contents of the web page before the script runs. In Listing 2-1, we accomplished this by using the onload event attribute in the body element. Another common way to delay execution is to simply place the code to be executed at the end of the code, as in Listing 2-2.

Limitations of JavaScript in <script> elements

While much more commonly used and more widely accepted than inline scripting (putting JavaScript into event attributes), embedding JavaScript into a script element has some serious limitations.

The biggest limitation is that scripts embedded in this way can be used only within the web page where they live. In other words, if you put your JavaScript into a `script` element, you need to copy and paste that `script` element exactly into every page where it exists. With some websites containing many hundreds of web pages, you can see how this can become a maintenance nightmare.

When to use JavaScript in <script> elements

This method of embedding JavaScript does have its uses. For bits of JavaScript that simply call other bits of JavaScript and that rarely (or preferably, never) change, it is acceptable and can even speed up the loading and display of your web pages by causing the web server to have to make fewer requests to the server.

Single page apps, which (as the name implies) contain only a single HTML page, are also great candidates for the use of this type of embedding because there will only ever be one place to update the script.

As a rule, however, you should seek to minimize the amount of JavaScript that you embed directly into an HTML document. The results will be easier maintenance and better organization of your code.

Including external JavaScript files

The third and most popular way to include JavaScript in HTML documents is by using the `src` attribute of the `script` element.

A `script` element with a `src` attribute works exactly like a `script` element with JavaScript between the tags, except that if you use the `src` attribute, the JavaScript is loaded into the HTML document from a separate file. Here's an example of a `script` element with a `src` attribute:

```
<script src="myScript.js"></script>
```

In this case, you would have a separate file, named `myScript.js`, that would reside in the same folder as your HTML document. The benefits of using external JavaScript files are that using them:

» Keeps your HTML files neater and less cluttered

» Makes your life easier because you need to modify JavaScript in only one place when something changes or when you make a bug fix

Creating a .js file

Creating an external JavaScript file is like creating an HTML file or another type of file. To replace the embedded JavaScript in Listing 2-1 with an external JavaScript file, follow these steps:

1. **In VS Code, choose File ⇨ New File.**

2. **Copy everything between `<script>` and `</script>` from the file you created for Listing 2-1 and paste it into your new .js file.**

   Notice that external JavaScript files don't contain `<script>` elements, just the JavaScript.

3. **Save your new file as `countToTen.js` in the same folder as your `.html` files.**

4. **In your `.html` file, modify your `script` element to add a `src` attribute, like this:**

   ```
   <script src="countToTen.js"></script>
   ```

Your copy of `MyFirstProgram.html` should now look like this:

```
<!DOCTYPE html>
<html>
  <head>
    <title>Hello, HTML!</title>
    <script src="countToTen.js"></script>
  </head>
  <body onload="countToTen();">
    <h1>Let's Count to 10 with JavaScript!</h1>
    <p id="theCount"></p>
  </body>
</html>
```

Your new file, `countToTen.js`, should look like this:

```
function countToTen(){
 let count = 0;
 while (count < 10) {
   count++;
   document.getElementById("theCount").innerHTML += count +
   "<br>";
 }
}
```

After you've saved both files, you should see them inside your project in the VS Code explorer pane, as shown in Figure 2-7.

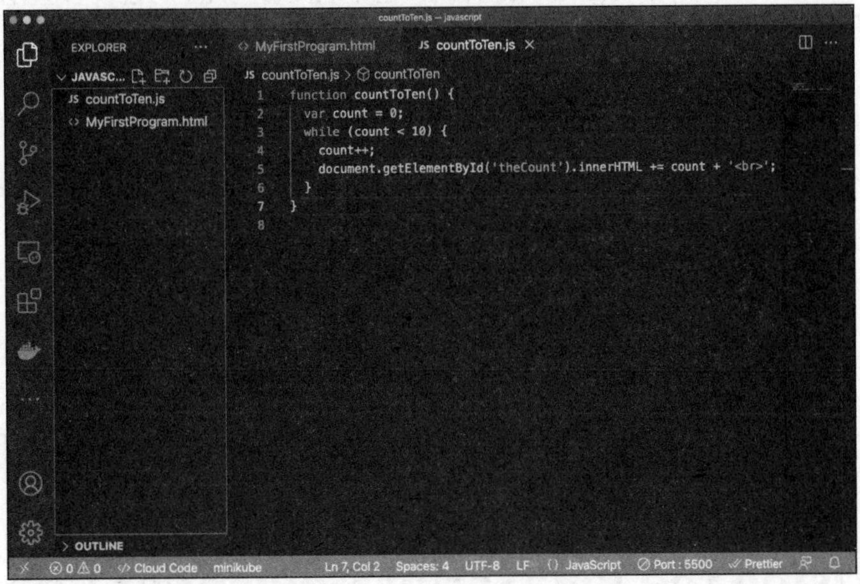

FIGURE 2-7:
Viewing multiple files in your project folder in VS Code.

Keeping your .js files organized

External JavaScript files can sometimes get to be very large. In many cases, it's a good idea to break them up into smaller files, organized by the type of functions they contain. For example, one JavaScript file may contain scripts related to the user login capabilities of your program, while another may contain scripts related to the blogging capabilities.

For small programs, however, it's usually sufficient to have just one file, and many people will name their single JavaScript file something generic, such as `app.js`, `main.js`, or `scripts.js`.

JavaScript files don't need to be in the same folder as the HTML file that includes them. In fact, we recommend that you create a new folder specifically for storing your external JavaScript files. Most people call this something like `js`.

Follow these steps to create a `js` folder inside of your VS Code project and move your `js` file into it:

1. **Click the New Folder icon at the top of the VS Code Explorer pane.**

2. **A blank text area will appear in the explorer.**

3. **Enter `js` into the folder name text field and press Enter.**

4. **A new folder called `js` appears in the sidebar.**

5. **Click and drag `countToTen.js` in the Explorer to put it in the `js` folder.**

6. **Open `MyFirstProgram.js` and change your `script` element to reflect the new location of your `js` file, like this:**

```
<script src="js/countToTen.js"></script>
```

When you open `MyFirstProgram.html` in your browser (or simply click refresh), it should look exactly like it did before you moved the JavaScript file into its own folder.

Using the JavaScript Developer Console

Sometimes, it's helpful to be able to run JavaScript commands without creating an HTML page and including separate scripts or creating `<script>` blocks. For these times, you can use the Chrome browser's JavaScript Console (see Figure 2-8).

To access the JavaScript Console, find the Chrome menu in the upper-right corner of your browser. It looks like three dots stacked on top of each other.

TECHNICAL STUFF

A menu icon made of three stacked dots like the Chrome menu is sometimes called a "Kebab" menu, because it looks a little like three things on a skewer.

Click the Chrome menu and then find More Tools in the drop-down menu. Under More Tools, choose Developer Tools from the drop-down menu. When the Developer Tools opens (at the bottom of the screen or on the right), click the Console tab at the top of it.

And, yes, there is a faster way to open the JavaScript Console. Simply press Alt+Command+J (on Mac) or Control+Shift+J (on Windows).

FIGURE 2-8:
JavaScript
Console in the
Chrome browser.

**TECHNICAL
STUFF**

The JavaScript Console is perhaps the best friend of the JavaScript developer. Besides allowing you to test and run JavaScript code quickly and easily, it also is where errors in your code are reported, and it has features that will help you track down and solve problems with your code.

Once you've opened the JavaScript Console, you can start inputting commands into it, which will run as soon as you press Enter. To try it out, open the JavaScript Console and then type the following commands, pressing Enter after each one:

```
1080/33
40 + 2
40 * 34
100%3
34++
34--
```

Commenting Your Code

As you learn more JavaScript commands and start to write larger programs, it's often helpful to be able to leave yourself little reminders of what you were thinking or what certain things do. Programmers call these tiny notes to themselves (or to anyone else who may work with your code) *comments*. The process of writing these notes is called *commenting*.

REMEMBER

The JavaScript engine completely ignores comments. They are there just for people. This is your time to explain things, clarify things, describe your thinking, or even leave reminders to yourself about things you want to do in the future.

It is always a good idea to comment your code. Even if you think that your code is self-explanatory at the time that you write it, chances are good that you won't think that eight months down the road when you need to modify it.

JavaScript gives you two ways to denote something as a comment:

» The single-line comment

» The multi-line comment

Single-line comments

Single-line comments start with //. Everything after these two slashes and up until the end of the line will be ignored by the JavaScript parser.

Single-line comments don't need to start at the beginning of a line. It's quite common to see a single-line comment used on the same line as a piece of code that is not commented. For example:

```
pizzas = pizza + 1; // add one more pizza
```

Multi-line comments

Multi-line comments start with /* and tell the JavaScript parser to ignore everything up to */. Multi-line comments are useful for more extensive documentation of code. For example:

```
/* The countToTen function does the following things:
  * Initializes a variable called count
  * Starts a loop by checking the value of count to make sure
  it's less than 10
  * Adds 1 to the value of count
  * Appends the current value of count, followed by a line
  break, to the paragraph with id='theCount'
  * Starts the loop over
*/
```

Using comments to prevent code execution

Besides being useful for documenting code, comments are often useful for isolating pieces of code to find problems. For example, if you wanted to see what the countToTen function would do if you removed the line from the loop that increments the value of count, you could comment out that line using a single-line comment, like this:

```javascript
function countToTen(){
  let count = 0;
  while (count < 10) {
    // count++;
    document.getElementById("theCount").innerHTML += count +
    "<br>";
  }
}
```

When you run this program, the line count++; will no longer run, and the program will print out 0s forever (or until you close the browser window).

WARNING

What you just created is called an *infinite loop.* If you do run a modified version of this program, it won't do any harm to your computer, but it will likely take your CPU for a wild ride of spinning in circles as fast as it can until you shut down the browser tab.

Chapter **3**

Working with Variables

"Beauty is variable, ugliness is constant."

— DOUGLAS HORTON (1891 – 1968)

n this chapter, you discover how to create variables, fill them with values, use functions to find out what type of data is in your variables, convert between different data types, and manipulate the data in your variables.

Understanding Variables

Variables are representative names in a program. Just as *x* may stand for some as-yet-unknown value in algebra, or *x* may mark the spot where the treasure is buried on a pirate's map, variables are used in programming to represent something else.

You can think about variables as containers that contain data. You can give these containers names, and later you can recall and change the data in a variable by using its name.

Without variables, every computer program would have only one purpose. For example, the following one-line program doesn't use variables:

```
alert(3 + 7);
```

Its purpose is to add together the numbers 3 and 7 and to print out the result in a browser popup window.

The program isn't of much use, however (unless you happen to need to recall the sum of 3 and 7 on a regular basis). With variables, you can make a general purpose program that can add together any two numbers and print out the result, like the following example:

```
let firstNumber = 3;
let secondNumber = 7;
let total = Number(firstNumber) +
            Number(secondNumber);
alert (total);
```

Taken a step further, you can expand this program to ask the user for two numbers and then add them together, like the following example:

```
let firstNumber = prompt("Enter the first number");
let secondNumber = prompt("Enter the second number");
let total = Number(firstNumber) + Number(secondNumber);
alert (total);
```

Try out this program for yourself! (Book 3, Chapter 2 shows how to use your code editor.) Follow these steps:

1. **Open your code editor and create a basic HTML template.**

2. **Between <body> and </body>, insert an opening <script> tag and a closing </script> tag.**

3. **Between the opening and closing script tags, enter the preceding example code.**

Your document should now look like this:

```
<html>
  <head></head>
  <body>
    <script>
```

```
      let firstNumber = prompt('Enter the first number');
      let secondNumber = prompt('Enter the second number');
      let total = Number(firstNumber) + Number(secondNumber);
      alert(total);
    </script>
  </body>
</html>
```

1. **Save your new HTML document as** `addtwo.html`.

2. **Open your HTML document in your web browser.**

   You should be prompted for a first number, as shown in Figure 3-1.

3. **Enter the first number.**

   After you enter that number, you'll be prompted for a second number.

4. **Enter the second number.**

   After you give the program the second number, the result of adding the two numbers together will be displayed on the screen.

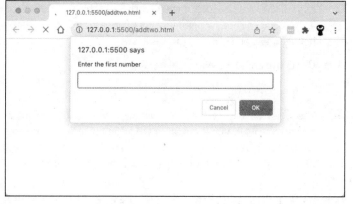

FIGURE 3-1: A general-purpose program for adding two user-submitted numbers.

© John Wiley & Sons

Initializing Variables

Initializing a variable is the technical term that's used to describe the process of first creating a variable in a program and giving it an initial value.

Variables in JavaScript can be initialized in one of three ways:

>> **Using a** `var` **keyword:**

```
var myName;
```

A variable created using a `var` keyword will have an initial value of undefined unless you give it a value when you create it, such as

```
var myName = "Chris";
```

It's also possible to use the `var` keyword without using the `var` keyword (sounds strange, right?), like this:

```
myName = "Chris";
```

When you create a variable without a `var` keyword, it becomes a global variable. (To understand what a global variable means, see the next section.)

WARNING

Creating global variables is a bad practice that should be avoided.

>> **Using a** `let` **keyword:**

```
let myName = "Chris";
```

As with the `var` keyword, if you create a variable without specifically assigning it a value, it will have a default value of undefined. You'll learn the difference between `let` and `var` in a moment.

>> **Using the** `const` **keyword:**

```
const myName = "Chris";
```

The `const` keyword creates a constant. Once created, a constant can't be assigned a new value. Constants are great for making sure your program won't accidentally change something that shouldn't be changed — the value of pi or the recipe for mom's vegetable soup, for example.

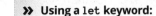

TECHNICAL STUFF

Notice the quotes around the value on the right in the preceding examples. These quotes indicate that the value should be treated as text, rather than as a number, a JavaScript keyword, or another variable. See the section on data types later in this chapter for more information about how and when to use quotes.

WHEN IS EQUAL NOT EQUAL?

In English, it's common and correct to read statements containing "=" as "var myName equals Chris". However, this interpretation is not correct in programming.

Take, for example,

```
var myName = 'Chris';
```

The character that looks like an equals sign between the variable name (myName) and the value (Chris) in the preceding example may look exactly like an equals sign, and it's even produced using the key that is commonly called equals sign on the keyboard. However, in JavaScript, the equals sign is actually called the *assignment operator*.

The difference between an assignment operator and an "equals to" is vital to understand:

- The assignment operator sets the thing to the left of it equal to the thing to the right of it, like this:

```
var myName = 'Chris';
```

- "Equals" compares the value on the left to the value on the right and determines whether or not they are the same. Equals in JavaScript is written as ===.

Understanding Global and Local Scope

How and where you declare a variable determines how and where your program can make use of that variable. This concept is called *variable scope*. JavaScript has three types of scope:

>> *Global scoped variables* can be used anywhere inside of a program.

>> *Function scoped* variables are variables that you create using the var keyword inside of a protected program within a program, called a function.

>> *Block scoped* variables are variables created using the let or const keyword. Block scoped variables can be used within the "block" where they're initialized. A block in JavaScript is a unit of code created using a left curly bracket ({) and a right curly bracket (}).

WARNING

THE TRAGIC TALE OF THE MISSING VAR

There is really never a reason to create a variable without using the var, let, or const keyword, and doing so will cause you problems. If you leave out the var, let, or const keyword, it just looks like you forgot it, so don't do it!

The following example shows the kind of problem and confusion that can happen from creating a global variable. It also demonstrates the use of a more advanced programming tool, called a function, which we cover in much more detail in Book 3, Chapter 7. In short, functions let you put smaller programs within your programs.

In this first example, the programmer wants to have a variable called movie that is global, and a separate variable with the same name that is only valid within the function called showBadMovie. This is a perfectly normal thing to do, and under normal circumstances, the movie variable inside the function wouldn't affect the global variable. However, if you forget to use the var or let keyword when declaring the movie variable inside the function, bad things happen.

```
var movie = "The Godfather";
function showGoodMovie () {
 alert (movie + " is a good movie!");
}
function showBadMovie () {
 movie = "Speed 2: Cruise Control";
 alert (movie + " is a bad movie!");
}
```

Notice that the var keyword is missing from before the movie variable in showBad-Movie(). JavaScript assumes that you want to override the global movie variable, rather than create a local function variable. The results are positively disastrous!

```
showGoodMovie(); // pops up "The Godfather is a good movie!"
showBadMovie(); // pops up "Speed 2: Cruise Control is a bad
    movie!"
/* Oh no! The global variable is now Speed 2: Cruise Control,
    not the good movie name anymore! */
showGoodMovie(); // pops up "Speed 2: Cruise Control is a good
    movie!"
```

© John Wiley & Sons

TIP

Using block scoped variables is preferable to using function scoped variables because limiting the scope of variables reduces the chance that you'll accidentally overwrite the value of a variable with another variable of the same name.

The use of function scoped variables and globals can create problems in your program that can be difficult to track down and fix. Most JavaScript programmers agree that you should avoid creating globals whenever possible, and that it's a far better practice to use block scoped variables (created using let or const) than to use var.

Naming Variables

Variable names can start with the following characters:

>> Upper- or lowercase letter

>> An underscore (_)

>> A dollar sign ($)

Although you can use an underscore or dollar sign to start a variable, it's best to begin with a letter. Unexpected characters can often cause your code to look confusing and difficult to read, especially if you are new to JavaScript coding.

GUIDELINES FOR CREATING GOOD VARIABLE NAMES

Although JavaScript gives you a lot of freedom in how you name your variables, it's best to decide on some basic rules for yourself before you start programming. For example, do you start your variable names with a lowercase or uppercase letter? Do you use underscores between multiple words within a variable name, or do you use camelCase? As your code becomes more complex, the importance of correct naming becomes apparent.

Fortunately, you're not on your own when you're deciding on your style. There are some best practices that many professional JavaScript programmers agree upon and use when naming variables:

- Do not use names that are too short! Simple one letter names or nonsensical names are not a good option when naming variables.
- Use multiword names to be as precise as possible.
- In multiword names, always put adjectives to the left, as in `let greenPython;`.

Pick a style for multiple word names and be consistent. There are two ways to join words to create a name: camelCase and under_score. JavaScript is a flexible language, and you can use either method, although camelCase is generally the more commonly employed.

Some words cannot be used as variable names. The following is a list of reserved words that cannot be used as JavaScript variables, functions, methods, loop labels, or object names.

abstract	else	instanceof	switch
boolean	enum	int	synchronized
break	export	interface	this
byte	extends	long	throw
case	false	native	throws
catch	final	new	transient
char	finally	null	true
class	float	package	try

const	for	private	typeof
continue	function	protected	var
debugger	goto	public	void
default	if	return	volatile
delete	implements	short	while
do	import	static	with
double	in	super	

After the first character, you can use any letter or number in your variable name, and it can be any length. JavaScript variables cannot contain spaces, mathematical operators, or punctuation (other than the underscore).

WARNING

Always remember that JavaScript is case-sensitive. A variable named `myname` is not the same variable as `Myname` or `myName`.

Variable names are identifiers; the best thing you can do is name a variable something precise and relevant. This naming convention may sometimes result in very long names, but as a rule, a longer name that accurately represents the variable is more useful than a shorter name that is vague.

TIP

Of course, there are limits to how long variable names can be without making your life more difficult. If you need to use 20 characters to accurately describe your variable, go for it. But, if you're creating variable names like `nameOfPerson-WhoJustFilledOutTheFormOnMyWebsite`, you may want to see whether you can simplify your life (as well as that of anyone else who may need to work with your code) by shortening to something more like `personName`.

Creating Constants Using the const Keyword

Occasionally, your program may have a need for variables that can't be changed. In these cases, you can declare your variable using the `const` keyword. For example:

```
const heightOfTheEmpireStateBuilding = 1454;
const speedOfLight = 299792458;
```

```
const numberOfProblems = 99;
const meanNumberofBooksReadIn2022 = 12;
```

Constants abide by the same rules as other variables, but once you create a constant, its value cannot be changed during its lifetime (which lasts as long as the script is running).

Working with Data Types

A variable's data type is the kind of data the variable can hold and what operations can be done with the value of the variable. The number 10, used in a sentence, is different than the number 10 used in an equation, for example. Data types are the way JavaScript distinguishes between values that are meant to be words and values that are meant to be treated as mathematical expressions.

If you think about all the types of data that you work with on a daily basis — pie charts, recipes, short stories, newspaper articles, and so on — you'll see just how much potential there is for things to get very complicated when it comes to data. The generous creators of JavaScript decided to make things very simple for you. It has seven basic data types.

Furthermore, JavaScript is what's called a loosely typed language. What *loosely typed* means is that you don't even need to tell JavaScript, or even know, whether a variable you're creating will hold a word, a paragraph, a number, or a different type of data.

Loosely typed doesn't mean that JavaScript doesn't distinguish between words and numbers. JavaScript is friendly about it and handles the work of figuring out what type of data you store in your variables largely behind the scenes.

JavaScript recognizes seven basic, or primitive, types of data.

Number data type

Numbers in JavaScript are stored as 64-bit, floating point values. What this means, in English, is that numbers can range from 5e-324 (that's -5 followed by 324 zeros) to 1.7976931348623157e+308 (move the decimal 308 spots to the right to see this giant number). Any number may have decimal points or not. Unlike most programming languages, JavaScript doesn't have separate data types for integers (positive or negative numbers without a fractional part) and floating points (decimals).

TECHNICAL STUFF

Just how big is the biggest number JavaScript can use? Here it is, written out without scientific notation:

17976931348623157000

TECHNICAL STUFF

In practice, however, the biggest number that's "safe" to use in JavaScript is 9007199254740991. If you compare two numbers that are larger than this number using JavaScript, you'll get incorrect results. If you need to use a larger number, consider using the bigInt data type instead of number. You learn about bigInt in the next section.

When you declare a number variable, you compile it from all of the following elements:

>> The var, let, or const keyword

>> The name you want to give your variable

>> The assignment operator

>> A number (or an equation that resolves to a number)

>> A semicolon

Here are some examples of valid number variables declarations:

```
let numberOfDucks = 4;
```

```
var populationOfSpain = 47200000;
```

```
const howManyTacos = 8;
```

Number functions

JavaScript includes a built-in Number function for converting values to numbers. To use the Number function, simply put the value (or a variable holding the value) that you want to convert to a number between the parentheses after the Number function.

The Number function produces four kinds of output:

>> Numbers that are formatted as text strings are converted to numbers that can be used for calculations, like this:

```
Number("42") // returns the number 42
```

>> Text strings that can't be converted to numbers return the value NaN, like this:

```
Number("eggs") // returns NaN
```

>> The Boolean value `true` returns the number 1, like this:

```
Number(true) // returns 1
```

>> The Boolean value `false` returns the number 0, like this:

```
Number(false) // returns 0
```

parseInt function

To JavaScript, all numbers are actually floating point numbers. However, you can use the `parseInt` function to tell JavaScript to consider only the nonfractional part of the number (the integer), discarding everything after the decimal point.

```
parseInt(100.33); // returns 100
```

parseFloat function

You can use `parseFloat` to specifically tell JavaScript to treat a number as a float. Or, you can even use it to convert a string to a number. For example:

```
parseFloat("10"); // returns 10
parseFloat(100.00); //returns 100.00
parseFloat("10"); //returns 10
```

Examples

Now you can play around with some numbers and number functions. Try entering the following expressions into the JavaScript Console in your Chrome browser to see what results they produce.

TIP

You can open the JavaScript Console in Chrome by pressing Command+Option+J (Mac) or Ctrl+Shift+J (Windows).

```
1 + 1
3 * 3
parseFloat("839");
parseInt("33.333333");
12 + "12"
"12" + 12
"12" * 2
```

Number variables must be declared without quotation marks. "10" is not the same as 10. The former is a string (which is covered in the next section), and if you accidentally declare a number variable inside of quotes, you'll get unexpected results.

If you're following along, you may have noticed some odd behaviors with the previous examples. For example, when you add "12" (a string) to 12 (a number), the result is "1212" (a string). But, when you multiply "12" (a string) by 2 (a number) the result is 24 (a number). This is a case where JavaScript is really using its head!

In the first example, when you add, JavaScript guesses that, because one of the values in the addition equation is a string, you meant for both of them to be. So, it converts the number to a string and treats the plus symbol as a *concatenation operator*.

In the second example, when you multiply, one of the values in the operation is a number, and there's no way to multiply strings together. JavaScript converts the string to a number and then proceeds with the multiplication. But, what happens when you try to multiple two strings together?

```
"sassafras" * "orange"
```

The result is NaN (not a number). There's just no way to convert sassafras or orange into a number, so JavaScript throws up its hands.

bigInt data type

The bigInt data type doesn't have an upper limit. If you need to use numbers larger than the maximum safe integer (9007199254740991), bigInt is the way to go.

To create a bigInt, just add an *n* to the end of a number. For example, here's a number that's larger than the maximum safe number, safely stored in a bigInt:

```
let reallyBigNumber = 9007199254740992n;
```

String data type

Strings can be made up of any characters:

>> Letter

>> Number

>> Punctuation (such as commas and periods)

>> Special characters that can be written using a backslash followed by character

Some characters, such as quotes, have special meaning in JavaScript or require a special combination of characters, such as a tab or new line, to represent inside of a string. We call these *special characters*. Table 3-1 lists the special characters that you can use inside JavaScript strings.

TABLE 3-1

JavaScript Special Characters

Code	Outputs
\'	Single quote
\"	Double quote
\\	Backslash
\n	New line
\r	Carriage return
\t	Tab
\b	backspace
\f	Form feed

You create a string variable by enclosing it in single or double quotes, like this:

```
let myString = "Hi, I'm a string.";
```

It doesn't matter whether you use single or double quotes, as long as the beginning and ending quotes surrounding the string match up.

If you surround your string with single quotes, you can use double quotes within that string without a problem. The same goes for if you surround your strings with double quotes; you can use single quotes within the string without a problem.

WARNING

If you create a string and surround it with one type of quote, you can't use that type of quote inside the string, or the JavaScript parser will think you mean to end the string and will generate an error.

Escaping quotes

The solution to the problem of not being able to include quotes inside of a string surrounded with that type of quotes is to preface the quotes with a \. Adding a backslash before a quote is called *escaping* the quotes.

String functions

JavaScript includes many helpful functions for working with and converting strings.

Here's a list of the most frequently used built-in string functions:

>> charAt produces the character at a specified position. Note that the counting of characters starts with 0:

```
let watzThisString = 'JavaScript is Fun!';
console.log (watzThisString.charAt(3));
// returns a
```

>> concat combines one or more strings and returns the incorporated string:

```
let watzThisString = 'JavaScript is Fun!';
console.log (watzThisString.concat(' We love
    JavaScript!'));
// returns JavaScript is Fun! We love JavaScript!
```

>> indexOf searches and returns the position of the first occurrence of the searched character or substring within the string:

```
let watzThisString = 'JavaScript is Fun!';
console.log (watzThisString.indexOf('Fun');
// returns 14
```

>> split splits strings into an array of substrings:

```
let watzThisString = 'JavaScript is Fun!';
console.log (watzThisString.split('F'));
// returns ["JavaScript is ", "un!"]
```

>> substr extracts a portion of a string beginning at "start" through a specified length:

```
let watzThisString = 'JavaScript is Fun!';
console.log (watzThisString.substr(2,5));
// returns vaScr
```

» substring extracts the characters within a string between two specified positions:

```
let watzThisString = 'JavaScript is Fun!';
console.log (watzThisString.substring(2,5));
// returns Vas
```

» toLowerCase produces the string with all of its characters converted to lowercase:

```
let watzThisString = 'JavaScript is Fun!';
console.log (watzThisString.toLowerCase());
// returns javascript is fun!
```

» toUpperCase produces the string with all of its characters converted to uppercase:

```
let watzThisString = 'JavaScript is Fun!';
console.log (watzThisString.toUpperCase());
// returns JAVASCRIPT IS FUN!
```

Boolean data type

Boolean variables store one of two possible values: either true or false.

TECHNICAL STUFF

The term *Boolean* is named after George Boole (1815–1864), who created an algebraic system of logic. Because it's named after a person, you generally write it with an initial capital letter.

Boolean variables are often used for storing the results of comparisons. You can find out the Boolean value of a comparison or convert any value in JavaScript into a Boolean value by using the Boolean function. For example:

```
let isItGreater = Boolean (3 > 20);
alert (isItGreater); // returns false
let areTheySame = Boolean ("tiger" === "Tiger");
alert (areTheySame); // returns false
```

The result of converting a value in JavaScript into a Boolean value using the Boolean function depends on the value:

» In JavaScript, the following values always evaluate to a Boolean false value:

- NaN
- undefined

- 0 (numeric value zero)

- −0

- "" (empty string)

- false

» Anything that is not one of the preceding values evaluates to a Boolean true. For example:

- 74

- "Eva"

- "10"

- "NaN"

The number character "0" is not the same as the numeric value 0 (zero). While 0 will always result in a Boolean value of false, the string "0" will always result in a Boolean true.

Boolean values are primarily used with conditional expressions. The following program creates a Boolean variable and then tests its value using an if/then statement (which you can find out about in Book 3, Chapter 5).

```
let b = true;
if (b == true) {
  alert ("It is true!");
  } else {
  alert ("It is false.");
}
```

Boolean values are written without quotes around them, like this:

```
let myVar = true
```

On the other hand, let myVar = "true" creates a string variable.

NaN data type

NaN stands for Not a Number. It's the result that you get when you try to do math with a string, or when a calculation fails or can't be done. For example, it's impossible to calculate the square root of a negative number. Trying to do so will result in NaN.

Working with Variables

A more common occurrence that will produce NaN is an attempt to perform mathematical operations using strings that can't be converted to numbers.

Undefined data type

Even if you create a variable in JavaScript and don't specifically give it a value, it still has a default value. This value is undefined.

Symbol data type

The Symbol data type is used to create unique identifiers in JavaScript. Unlike the other data types, even if two symbols appear to be identical and have the same name, JavaScript guarantees that they'll be unique. To test this, enter the following code into your Chrome Developer Console:

```
let id1 = Symbol("id");
let id2 = Symbol("id");
alert(id1 === id2);
```

The result will be an alert window with the Boolean false value displayed in it.

Chapter **4**

Understanding Arrays

"I am large. I contain multitudes."

— WALT WHITMAN

Arrays are a fundamental part of any programming language. In this chapter, you discover what they are, how to use them, and what makes JavaScript arrays distinct from arrays in other programming languages. You work with arrays to create lists, order lists, and add and remove items from lists.

Making a List

The earlier chapters in this book involve working with variables that are stand-alone pieces of data, such as: const myName = "Chris", let firstNumber = "3", and var how ManyTacos = 8. There are often times in programming (and in life) where you want to store related data under a single name. For example, consider the following types of lists:

>> A list of your favorite artists

>> A program that selects and displays a different quote from a list of quotes each time it's run

- » A holiday card mailing list
- » A list of your top music albums of the year
- » A list of all your family and friends' birthdays
- » A shopping list
- » A to-do list
- » A list of New Year's resolutions

Using single-value variables (see Book 3, Chapter 3), you would need to create and keep track of multiple variables in order to accomplish any of these tasks. Here is an example of a list created using single-value variables:

```
let artist1 = "Alphonse Mucha";
let artist2 = "Chiara Bautista";
let artist3 = "Claude Monet";
let artist4 = "Sandro Botticelli";
let artist5 = "Andy Warhol";
let artist6 = "Jill McVarish";
let artist7 = "Vincent Van Gough";
let artist8 = "Paul Klee";
let artist9 = "William Blake";
let artist10 = "Egon Schiele";
let artist11 = "Salvador Dali";
let artist12 = "Paul Cezanne";
let artist13 = "Diego Rivera";
let artist14 = "Pablo Picasso";
```

This approach could work in the short term, but you'd quickly run into difficulties. For example, what if you wanted to sort the list alphabetically and move artists into the correct variable names based on their position in the alphabetical sort? You'd need to first move Mucha out of the artist1 variable (maybe into a temporary holding variable) and then move Bautista into the artist1 variable. The artist2 spot would then be free for Blake, but don't forget that Mucha is still in that temporary slot! Blake's removal from artist9 frees that up for you to move someone else into the temporary variable, and so on. Creating a list in this way quickly becomes complicated and confusing.

Fortunately, JavaScript supports the creation of variables containing multiple values, called *arrays*.

Arrays are a way to store groups of related data inside of a single variable. With arrays, you can create lists containing any mix of string values, numbers, Boolean values, objects, functions, any other type of data, and even other arrays!

Array Fundamentals

An array consists of array elements. Array elements are made up of the array name and then an index number that is contained in square brackets. The individual value within an array is called an *array element*. Arrays use numbers (called the *index numbers*) to access those elements. The following example illustrates how arrays use index numbers to access elements:

```
myArray[0] = "yellow balloon";
myArray[1] = "red balloon";
myArray[2] = "blue balloon";
myArray[3] = "pink balloon";
```

In this example, the element with the index number of 0 has a value of "yellow balloon". The element with an index number 3 has a value of "pink balloon". Just as with any variable, you can give an array any name that complies with the rules of naming JavaScript variables. By assigning index numbers in arrays, JavaScript gives you the ability to make a single variable name hold a nearly unlimited list of values.

TECHNICAL STUFF

Just so you don't get too carried away, there actually is a limit to the number of elements that you can have in an array, although you're very unlikely to ever reach it. The limit is 4,294,967,295 elements.

In addition to naming requirements (which are the same for any type of variable, as described in Book 3, Chapter 3), arrays have a couple of other rules and special properties that you need to be familiar with:

>> Arrays are zero-indexed

>> Arrays can store any type of data

Arrays are zero-indexed

JavaScript doesn't have fingers or toes. As such, it doesn't need to abide by our crazy human rules about starting counting at 1. The first element in a JavaScript array always has an index number of 0 (see Figure 4-1).

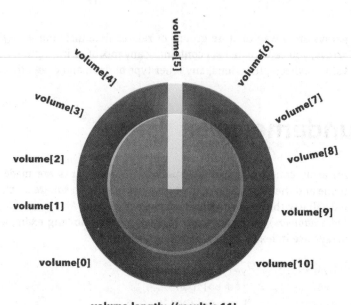

volume.length; //result is 11!

FIGURE 4-1:
JavaScript is
similar to a
volume knob. It
starts counting at
zero!

What this means for you is that `myArray[3]` is actually the fourth element in the array.

Zero-based numbering is a frequent cause of bugs and confusion for those new to programming, but once you get used to it, it will become quite natural. You may even discover that there are benefits to it, such as the ability to turn your guitar amp up to the 11th level.

Arrays can store any type of data

Each element in an array can store any of the data types (see Book 3, Chapter 3), as well as other arrays. Array elements can also contain functions and JavaScript objects (see Book 3, Chapters 7 and 8).

While you can store any type of data in an array, you can also store elements that contain different types of data, together, within one array, as shown in Listing 4-1.

LISTING 4-1: **Storing Different Types of Data in an Array**

```
item[0] = "apple";
item[1] = 4+8;
item[2] = 3;
item[3] = item[2] * item[1];
```

Creating Arrays

JavaScript provides two ways for you to create new arrays:

> » new keyword
>
> » Array literal notation

Using the new keyword method

The new keyword method uses new Array to create an array and add values to it.

```
let catNames = new Array("Larry", "Fuzzball", "Mr. Furly");
```

You may see this method used in your career as a programmer, and it's a perfectly acceptable way to create an array.

WARNING

Many JavaScript experts recommend against using this method, however. The biggest problem with using the new keyword is what happens when you forget to include it. Forgetting to use the new keyword can dramatically change the way your program operates.

Array literal

A much simpler and safer way to create arrays is to use what is called the array literal method of notation. This is what it looks like:

```
let dogNames =["Shaggy", "Tennessee", "Dr. Spock"];
```

That's all there is to it. The use of square brackets and no special keywords means that you're less likely to accidentally leave something out. The array literal method also uses less characters than the new keyword method — and when you're trying to keep your JavaScript as tidy as possible, every little bit helps!

Populating Arrays

You can add values to an array when it is first created, or you can simply create an array and then add elements to it at a later time. Adding elements to an array works exactly the same as creating or modifying a variable, except that you specify the index number of the element that you want to create or modify. Listing 4-2 shows an example of creating an empty array and adding elements to it.

LISTING 4-2: **Populating an Empty Array**

```
let peopleList =[];
peopleList[0] = "Chris Minnick";
peopleList[1] = "Eva Holland";
peopleList[2] = "Abraham Lincoln";
```

You don't always need to add elements sequentially. It is perfectly legal in JavaScript to create a new element out of sequence. For example, in the array in Listing 4-2, you could add the following:

```
peopleList[99] = "Tina Turner";
```

Creating an array out of sequence like this effectively creates blank elements for all of the indexes in between peopleList[2] and peopleList[99].

So, if you check the length property of the peopleList array after adding an element with an index of 99, something interesting happens:

```
peopleList.length // returns 100
```

Even though you've only created four elements, JavaScript will say that the length of an array is 100 because the length is based on the highest numbered index, rather than on how many elements you've actually created.

Understanding Multidimensional Arrays

Not only can you store arrays inside of arrays, you can even put arrays inside of arrays inside of arrays. This can go on and on.

An array that contains an array is called a *multidimensional array*. To write a multidimensional array, you simply add more sets of square brackets to a variable name. For example:

```
let listOfLists[0][0];
```

Multidimensional arrays can be difficult to visualize when you first start working with them. Figure 4-2 shows a pictorial representation of a multidimensional array.

You can also visualize multidimensional arrays as hierarchal lists or outlines. For example:

Top Albums by Genre

1. Country

> **1.1** Johnny Cash:Live at Folsom Prison
>
> **1.2** Patsy Cline:Sentimentally Yours
>
> **1.3** Hank Williams:I'm Blue Inside

2. Rock

> **2.1** T-Rex:Slider
>
> **2.2** Nirvana:Nevermind
>
> **2.3** Lou Reed:Transformer

3. Punk

> **3.1** Flipper:Generic
>
> **3.2** The Dead Milkmen:Big Lizard in my Backyard
>
> **3.3** Patti Smith:Easter

Here is a code that would create an array based on Figure 4-2:

```
let bestAlbumsByGenre = []
bestAlbumsByGenre[0] = "Country";
bestAlbumsByGenre[0][0] = "Johnny Cash:Live at Folsom Prison"
bestAlbumsByGenre[0][1] = "Patsy Cline:Sentimentally Yours";
bestAlbumsByGenre[0][2] = "Hank Williams:I'm Blue Inside";
bestAlbumsByGenre[1] = "Rock";
bestAlbumsByGenre[1][0] = "T-Rex:Slider";
bestAlbumsByGenre[1][1] = "Nirvana:Nevermind";
bestAlbumsByGenre[1][2] = "Lou Reed:Tranformer";
bestAlbumsByGenre[2] = "Punk";
bestAlbumsByGenre[2][0] = "Flipper:Generic";
bestAlbumsByGenre[2][1] = "The Dead Milkmen:Big Lizard in my
    Backyard";
bestAlbumsByGenre[2][2] = "Patti Smith:Easter";
```

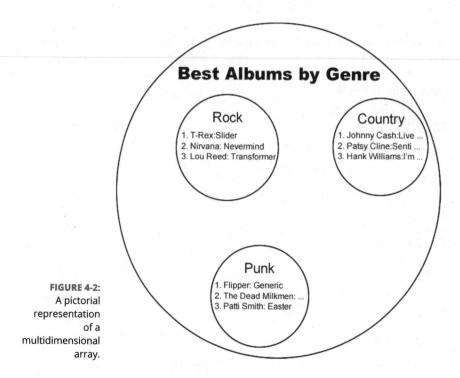

FIGURE 4-2:
A pictorial
representation
of a
multidimensional
array.

Accessing Array Elements

You can access the elements of arrays in the same way that you set them, using square brackets and the index number. For example, to access the third element in any array called myArray, you would use the following:

```
myArray[2];
```

To access elements in a multidimensional array, just add more square brackets to get to the element you want:

```
bestAlbumsByGenre[0][1]; // returns "Patsy_Cline:Sentimentally
    Yours";
```

To test out setting and accessing the elements of an array, follow these steps:

TIP

1. **Open your Chrome browser and then open the JavaScript Console.**

   You can open your JavaScript Console using the Chrome menu or by pressing Command+Option+J on Mac or Ctrl+Shift+J in Windows.

2. **In the console, type the following statement, followed by the Return or Enter key, to create an array called** `lengthsOfString`:

```
let lengthsOfString = [2,4,1.5,80];
```

3. **Type the array name followed by the index number in square brackets to retrieve the value of each array element.**

For example:

```
lengthsOfString[0];
lengthsOfString[3];
lengthsOfString[2];
```

4. **Enter an index number that doesn't exist in the array.**

For example:

```
lengthsOfString[4];
```

Notice that the value of this array element is undefined.

5. **Type the following command to create a new variable to hold the total length of string that you have:**

```
let totalLength = lengthsOfString[0] + lengthsOfString[1] +
    lengthsOfString[2] + lengthsOfString[3];
```

6. **Finally, get the value of** `totalLength` **with this command:**

```
totalLength;
```

Looping through arrays

As you can imagine, working with multiple values of arrays by typing the array name and the index number can get tiring for your fingers after a while. Fortunately, there are easier ways to work with all of the elements in an array. The most common method is to use a programming construct called a *loop*. (We cover loops in much more detail in Book 3, Chapter 6.)

It's also possible to work with multiple elements in an array by using JavaScript's built-in array functions.

Array properties

You can access certain data about an array by accessing array properties. The way to access array properties in JavaScript is by using *dot notation*. To use dot notation, you type the name of the array, followed by a period, followed by the property you want to access. (You can find out much more about properties in Book 3, Chapter 8.) Table 4-1 lists all of the properties of JavaScript arrays.

TABLE 4-1 **JavaScript's Array Properties**

Property	Return Value
prototype	Allows the addition of properties and methods to an Array object
constructor	A reference to the function that created the Array object's prototype
length	Either returns or sets the number of elements in an array

The most commonly used array property is `length`. You have already seen the `length` property in action. Its purpose is to provide the number of elements in an array, whether defined or undefined. For example:

```
let myArray = [];
myArray[2000] = "surprise!";
myArray.length; // returns 2001
```

You can also use the `length` property to truncate an array:

```
myArray.length; // returns 2001
myArray.length = 10;
myArray.length; // returns 10
```

Array methods

JavaScript array methods (also known as array functions) provide handy ways to manipulate and work with arrays. Table 4-2 shows a list of the most commonly used array methods, along with descriptions of what they do or the values they produce.

TABLE 4-2   JavaScript Array Methods

Method	Return Value
concat	A new array made up of the current array, joined with other array(s) and/or value(s)
every	true if every element in the given array satisfies the provided testing function
filter	A new array with all of the elements of a current array that test true by the given function
forEach	Completes the function once for each element in the array
indexOf	The first occurrence of the specified value within the array. Returns –1 if the value is not found
join	Joins all the elements of an array into a string
lastIndexOf	The last occurrence of the specified value within the array. Returns –1 if value is not found
map	A new array with the result of a provided function on every element in the array
pop	Removes the last element in an array
push	Adds new items to the end of an array
reduce	Reduces two values of an array to a single value by applying a function to them (from left to right)
reduceRight	Reduces two values of an array to a single value by applying a function to them simultaneously (from right to left)
reverse	Reverses the order of elements in an array
shift	Removes the first element from an array and returns that element, resulting in a change in length of an array
slice	Selects a portion of an array and returns it as a new array
some	Returns true if one or more elements satisfy the provided testing function
sort	Returns an array after the elements in an array are sorted (default sort order is alphabetical and ascending)
splice	Returns a new array comprised of elements that were added or removed from a given array
toString	Converts an array to a string
unshift	Returns a new array with a new length by the addition of one or more elements

Using array methods

The syntax for using array methods differs depending on the particular method you are trying to use. You do, however, access the functionality of every array method the same way that you access array properties: by using dot notation.

For a complete reference to JavaScript array methods, with examples, visit https://developer.mozilla.org/en-US/docs/Web/JavaScript/Reference/ Global_Objects/Array.

Listing 4-3 shows some examples of how to use JavaScript array methods.

LISTING 4-3: Commonly Used JavaScript Array Methods in Action

```html
<html>
  <head>
    <title>common array methods</title>
  </head>
  <body>
  <script>
    let animals = ['tiger', 'bear'];
    let fruit = ['cantaloupe', 'orange'];
    let dishes = ['plate', 'bowl', 'cup'];
    let fruitsAndAnimals = fruit.concat(animals);
    document.write(fruitsAndAnimals + '<br>');
    let whereIsTheTiger = animals.indexOf('tiger');
    document.write(
      'The tiger has an index number of: ' + whereIsTheTiger +
        '<br>'
    );
  </script>
  </body>
</html>
```

Figure 4-3 shows the result of Listing 4-3 when run in a browser.

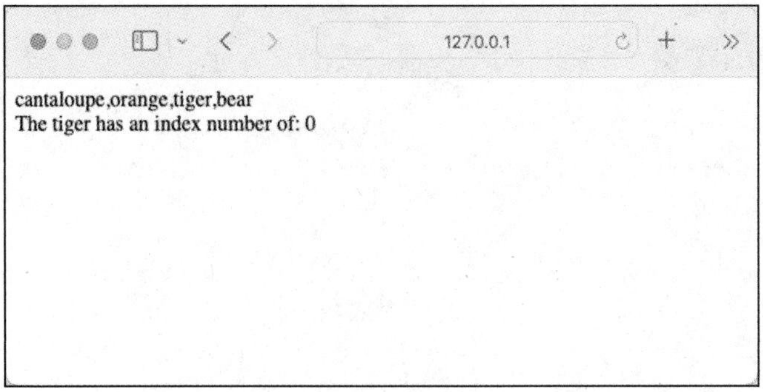

FIGURE 4-3:
Commonly used
JavaScript array
methods in
action.

© John Wiley & Sons

Chapter 5

Working with Operators, Expressions, and Statements

"Hello Operator. Can you give me number 9?"

— THE WHITE STRIPES

JavaScript operators, expressions, and statements are the basic building blocks of programs. They help you manipulate and change values, perform math, compare two or more values, and much, much more.

In this chapter, you discover how operators, expressions, and statements do their work and how you can best use them to your advantage.

Express Yourself

An *expression* is a piece of code that resolves to a value. Expressions can either assign a value to a variable, or they can simply have a value. For example, both of the following are examples of valid expressions:

```
1 + 1
```

```
a = 1;
```

Expressions can be short and simple, as illustrated in these examples, or they can be quite complicated.

The pieces of data (1 or a in these examples) in an expression are called *operands*.

Hello, Operator

The engines that make expressions do their work are called *operators*. They operate on data to produce different results. The = and + in the preceding expressions are examples of operators.

Operator precedence

A single expression often will contain several operators. Consider the following example:

```
a = 1 + 2 * 3 / 4;
```

Depending on the order in which you perform the different calculations, the final value of a could be any one of the following:

```
a = 1.75
```

```
a = 2.5
```

```
a = 2.25
```

In fact, the actual result of this expression will be 2.5. But how do you know this? Depending on the person doing the math, the division could be done first (3 / 4), the addition could be done first (1 + 2), or the multiplication could be done first (2 * 3).

Clearly, there must be a better way to figure out the answer, and there is! This is where *operator precedence* comes in. Operator precedence is the order in which operators in an expression are evaluated.

Operators are divided into groups of different levels of precedence, numbered from 0 to 19, as shown in Table 5-1.

TECHNICAL STUFF

The operator with the lowest number is said to have the highest precedence. This may seem confusing at first, but if you think of it in terms of the first person in a line (whoever is in spot 0, in this case) being the first person to get a delicious sandwich or cup of coffee, you'll have no problem keeping it straight.

When an expression contains two or more operators that have the same precedence, they are evaluated according to their *associativity*. Associativity determines whether the operators are evaluated from left to right or right to left.

Using parentheses

The operator with the highest precedence in an expression is parentheses. In most cases, you can ignore the rules of operator precedence simply by grouping operations into subexpressions using parentheses. For example, the previous multi-operator expression can be fully clarified in the following ways:

```
a = (1 + 2) * (3 / 4); // result: 2.25
a = (1 + (2 * 3)) / 4; // result: 1.75
a = ((1 + 2) *3) / 4; // result: 2.25
a = 1 + ((2 * 3) / 4); // result: 2.5
```

Parentheses in expressions force the JavaScript interpreter to evaluate the contents of the parentheses first, from the innermost parentheses to the outermost, before performing the operations outside of the parentheses.

Upon consulting Table 5-1, you'll see that the actual order of the precedence for the preceding expression is

```
a = 1 + ((2 * 3) / 4);
```

This statement makes the actual operator precedence explicit. Multiplication is done first, followed by division, followed by the addition.

TABLE 5-1   ## Operator Precedence

Operator	Use	Operator Associativity	Precedence	Sample Use
(..)	Grouping	n/a	0 — highest precedence	(1 + 3)
. . . . .	Operator property access	Left to right	1	myCar.color
[..]	Array access	Left to right	1	thingsToDo[4]
new ...()	Creates an object (with arguments list)	n/a	1	new Car ("red")
function ...()	Function call	Left to right	2	function sum (1,2)
new ...	Creates an object (without a list)	Right to left	2	new Car
...++	Postfix increment	n/a	3	number++
...--	Postfix decrement	n/a	3	number--
! ...	Logical not	Right to left	4	!myVal
~ ...	Bitwise not	Right to left	4	~myVal
- ...	Negation	Right to left	4	-aNumber
++ ...	Prefix increment	Right to left	4	++aNumber
-- ...	Prefix decrement	Right to left	4	--aNumber
typeof ...	typeof	Right to left	4	typeof myVar
void ...	void	Right to left	4	void(0)
delete ...	delete	Right to left	4	delete object.property
... * ...	Multiplication	Left to right	5	result = 3 * 7
... / ...	Division	Left to right	5	result = 3 / 7
... % ...	Remainder	Left to right	5	result = 7 % 3
... + ...	Addition	Left to right	6	result = 3 + 7
... - ...	Subtraction	Left to right	6	result = 3 - 7
... << ...	Bitwise left shift	Left to right	7	result = 3 << 7
... >> ...	Bitwise right shift	Left to right	7	result = 3 >> 7

Operator	Use	Operator Associativity	Precedence	Sample Use
... >>> ...	Bitwise unsigned right shift	Left to right	7	`result = 3 >>> 7`
... < ...	Less than	Left to right	8	`a < b`
... <= ...	Less than or equal to	Left to right	8	`a <= b`
... > ...	Greater than	Left to right	8	`a > b`
... >= ...	Greater than or equal to	Left to right	8	`a >= b`
... in ...	in	Left to right	8	`value in values`
... instanceof ...	instanceof	Left to right	8	`myCar instanceof car`
... == ...	Equality	Left to right	9	`3 == "3"`
... != ...	Inequality	Left to right	9	`3 != "3"`
... === ...	Strict equality	Left to right	9	`3 === "3"`
... !== ...	Strict inequality	Left to right	9	`3 !== "3"`
... & ...	Bitwise and	Left to right	10	`result = a & b`
... ^ ...	Bitwise xor	Left to right	11	`result = a ^ b`
... | ...	Bitwise or	Left to right	12	`result = a | b`
... && ...	Logical and	Left to right	13	`a && b`
... || ...	Logical or	Left to right	14	`a || b`
... ? ... : ...	Conditional	Right to left	15	`a ? 3 : 7`
... = ...	Assignment	Right to left	16	`a = 3`
... += ...	Assignment	Right to left	16	`a += 3`
... -= ...	Assignment	Right to left	16	`a -= 3`
... *= ...	Assignment	Right to left	16	`a *= 3`
... /= ...	Assignment	Right to left	16	`a /= 3`
... %= ...	Assignment	Right to left	16	`a %= 3`
... <<= ...	Assignment	Right to left	16	`a <<= 3`

(continued)

CHAPTER 5 **Working with Operators, Expressions, and Statements** 229

TABLE 5-1 *(continued)*

Operator	Use	Operator Associativity	Precedence	Sample Use
... >>= ...	Assignment	Right to left	16	a >>= 3
... >>>= ...	Assignment	Right to left	16	a >>>= 3
... &= ...	Assignment	Right to left	16	a &= 3
... ^= ...	Assignment	Right to left	16	a ^= 3
... |= ...	Assignment	Right to left	16	a |= 3
yield ...	Yield	Right to left	17	yield [expression]
... , ...	Comma / sequence	Left to right	18	a + b, c + d

Types of Operators

JavaScript has several types of operators. This section discusses the most used types of operators.

Assignment operators

The *assignment operator* assigns the value of the operand on the right to the operand on the left:

```
a = 5;
```

After this expression runs, the variable a will have a value of 5. You can also chain assignment operators together to assign the same value to multiple variables, as in the following example:

```
a = b = c = 5;
```

Because the operator's associativity is right to left (see Table 5-1), 5 will first be assigned to c, then the value of c will be assigned to b, and then the value of b will be assigned to a. The result of this expression is that a, b, and c all have a value of 5.

What do you think the end value of a will be after these expressions are evaluated?

```
let b = 1;
```

```
let a = b += c = 5;
```

To find out, open the JavaScript Console in Chrome and type each line, followed by Return or Enter. The result of this statement is that a will be equal to 6.

TIP

You can find a complete list of the different assignment operators in in the "Combining operators" section, later in this chapter.

Comparison operators

Comparison operators test for equality or difference between operands and return a true or false value.

Table 5-2 shows a complete list of the JavaScript comparison operators.

TABLE 5-2

JavaScript Comparison Operators

Operator	Description	Example
==	Equality	3 == "3" // true
!=	Inequality	3 != 3 // false
===	Strict equality	3 === "3" // false
!==	Strict inequality	3 !== "3" // true
>	Greater than	7 > 1 // true
>=	Greater than or equal to	7 >= 7 // true
<	Less than	7 < 10 // true
<=	Less than or equal to	2 <= 2 // true

Arithmetic operators

Arithmetic operators perform mathematical operations on operands and return the result. Table 5-3 shows a complete list of arithmetic operators.

TABLE 5-3

Arithmetic Operators

Operator	Description	Example
+	Addition	a = 1 + 1
–	Subtraction	a = 10 – 1
*	Multiplication	a = 2 * 2
/	Division	a = 8 / 2
%	Modulus	a = 5 % 2
++	Increment	a = ++b a = b++ a++
––	Decrement	a = ––b a = b–– a––

Listing 5-1 shows arithmetic operators at work.

LISTING 5-1: ## Using Arithmetic Operators

```
<html>
<head>
  <title>arithmetic operators</title>
</head>
<body>
  <h1>Wild Birthday Game</h1>
  <p>
  <ul>
    <li>Enter the number 7</li>
    <li>Multiply by the month of your birth</li>
    <li>Subtract 1</li>
    <li>Multiply by 13</li>
    <li>Add the day of your birth</li>
    <li>Add 3</li>
    <li>Multiply by 11</li>
    <li>Subtract the month of your birth</li>
    <li>Subtract the day of your birth</li>
    <li>Divide by 10</li>
    <li>Add 11</li>
    <li>Divide by 100</li>
  </ul>
  </p>
```

```
<script>
    let numberSeven = Number(prompt('Enter the number 7'));
    let birthMonth = Number(prompt('Enter your birth month'));
    let calculation = numberSeven * birthMonth;
    calculation = calculation - 1;
    calculation = calculation * 13;
    let birthDay = Number(prompt('Enter the day of your birth'));
    calculation = calculation + birthDay;
    calculation = calculation + 3;
    calculation = calculation * 11
    calculation = calculation - birthMonth;
    calculation = calculation - birthDay;
    calculation = calculation / 10;
    calculation = calculation + 11;
    calculation = calculation / 100;
    document.write("Your birthday is " + calculation);
</script>
</body>
</html>
```

The result of running Listing 5-1 in a browser is shown in Figure 5-1.

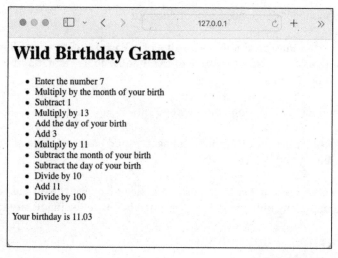

FIGURE 5-1: The wild arithmetic game.

© John Wiley & Sons

String operator

The *string operator* performs operations using two strings. When used with strings, the + operator becomes the concatenation operator. Its purpose is to join strings. Note that when you're joining strings with the concatenation operator, no spaces are added. Thus, it's very common to see statements like the following, where strings containing nothing but a blank space are concatenated between other strings or spaces are added to the end or beginning of strings (before the quotation mark) to form a coherent sentence:

```
let greeting = "Hello, " + firstName + ". I'm" + " " + mood + "
   to see you.";
```

Bitwise operators

Bitwise operators treat operands as signed 32-bit binary representations of numbers in twos complement format. Here's what that means, starting with the term *binary*.

Binary numbers are strings of 1s or 0s, with the position of the digit determining the value of a 1 in that position. For example, here's how to write the number 1 as a 32-bit binary number:

00000000000000000000000000000001

The rightmost position has a value of 1. Each position to the left of this position has a value of twice the value of the number to its right. So, the following binary number is equal to 5:

00000000000000000000000000000101

Signed integers means that both negative and positive whole numbers can be represented in this form.

To change a number from positive to negative, just flip all the bits and add 1. For example, the number -5 is represented by the following binary number:

11111111111111111111111111111011

TECHNICAL STUFF

Bitwise operators convert numbers to these 32-bit binary numbers and then convert them back to what we would consider normal numbers after the operation has been done.

Bitwise operators are difficult to understand at first. They're not very commonly used in JavaScript, but they're included here for the sake of completeness. Table 5-4 lists the JavaScript bitwise operators.

TABLE 5-4   JavaScript Bitwise Operators

Operator	Usage	Description
Bitwise AND	a & b	Returns a 1 in each bit position for which the corresponding bits of both operands are 1s.
Bitwise OR	a | b	Returns a 1 in each bit position for which the corresponding bits of either or both operands are 1s.
Bitwise XOR	a ^ b	Returns a 1 in each bit position for which the corresponding bits of either but not both operands are 1s.
Bitwise NOT	~a	Inverts the bits of its operand.
Left shift	a << b	Shifts a in binary representation b (<32) bits to the left, shifting in zeros from the right.
Sign-propagating right shift	a >> b	Shifts a in binary representation b (<32) bits to the right, discarding bits shifted off.
Zero-fill right shift	a >>> b	Shifts a in binary representation b (<32) bits to the right, discarding bits shifted off and shifting in zeros from the left.

Figure 5-2 shows a demonstration of each of the bitwise operators in the Chrome JavaScript Console.

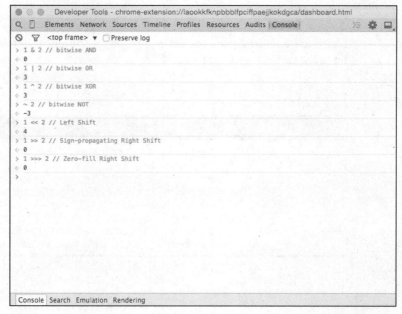

FIGURE 5-2:
The JavaScript bitwise operators.

© John Wiley & Sons

Logical operators

The terms *truthy* and *falsy* in JavaScript refer to the value that's returned when you evaluate something as a Boolean. The following values evaluate to Boolean `false` values and are thus considered falsy values:

» `false`

» `0`

» `-0`

» `''` (empty string)

» `null`

» `undefined`

» NaN

Everything else evaluates to a Boolean `true` value, and is thus considered truthy. You can find out whether a value or expression is truthy or falsy by surrounding it with the `Boolean()` function, as in these examples:

```
Boolean(0) // returns false
Boolean("0") // returns true
Boolean(1+1) //returns true
```

Logical operators evaluate a logical expression for truthiness or falsiness. There are three logical operators, shown in Table 5-5.

TABLE 5-5

Logical Operators

Operator	Meaning	Description
&&	And	Returns the first falsy operand. Otherwise, it returns the second operand.
||	Or	Returns the first operand if it is `true`. Otherwise, it returns the second operand.
!	Not	Takes only one operand. Returns `false` if its operand can be converted to `true`. Otherwise, it returns `false`.

**TECHNICAL
STUFF**

You can also use the OR operator to set a default value for variables. For example, in the following expression, the value of myVar will be set to the value of x unless x evaluates to a false value (for example, if x is undefined). Otherwise, it will be set to the default value of 0.

```
let myVar = x||0;
```

Special operators

JavaScript's special operators are a hodge-podge of miscellaneous other symbols and words that perform other important functions.

Conditional operator

The *conditional operator* (also known as the *ternary operator*) uses three operands. It evaluates a logical expression and then returns a value based on whether that expression is true or false. The conditional operator is the only operator that requires three operands. For example:

```
let isItBiggerThanTen = (value > 10) ? "greater than 10" : "not
   greater than 10";
```

Comma operator

The *comma operator* evaluates two operands and returns the value of the second one. It's most often used to perform multiple assignments or other operations within loops. It can also serve as a shorthand for initializing variables. For example:

```
let a = 10 , b = 0;
```

Because the comma has the lowest precedence of the operators, its operands are always evaluated separately.

delete operator

The delete operator removes a property from an object or an element from an array.

WARNING

When you use the delete operator to remove an element from an array, the length of the array stays the same. The removed element will have a value of undefined.

```
let animals = ["dog","cat","bird","octopus"];
console.log (animals[3]); // returns "octopus"
```

```
delete animals[3];
console.log (animals[3]); // returns "undefined"
```

in operator

The in operator returns true if the specified value exists in an array or object.

```
let animals = ["dog","cat","bird","octopus"];
if (3 in animals) {
 console.log ("it's in there");
 }
```

In this example, if the animals array has an element with the index of 3, the string "it's in there" will print out to the JavaScript Console.

instanceof operator

The instanceof operator returns true if the object you specify is the type of object that has been specified.

```
let myString = new String();
if (myString instanceof String) {
 console.log("yup, it's a string!");
 }
```

new operator

The new operator creates an instance of an object. As you can see in Book 3, Chapter 8, JavaScript has several built-in object types, and you can also define your own. In the following example, Date is a built-in JavaScript object, while Pet and Flower are examples of objects that a programmer could create to serve custom purposes within a program.

```
let today = new Date();
let bird = new Pet();
let daisy = new Flower();
```

this operator

The `this` operator refers to the current object. It's frequently used for retrieving properties within an object.

Book 3, Chapter 8 covers the `this` operator in more detail.

typeof operator

The `typeof` operator returns a string containing the type of the operand:

```
let businessName = "Harry's Watch Repair";
console.log(typeof businessName); // returns "string"
```

void operator

The `void` operator evaluates an expression and then returns `undefined`. The place where you most often see `void` used is in HTML documents when a link is needed, but the creator of the link wants to override the default behavior of the link using JavaScript:

```
<a href="javascript:void(0);">
This is a link, but it won't do anything
</a>
```

Combining operators

You can combine assignment operators with the other operators as a shorthand method of assigning the result of an expression to a variable. For example, the following two examples have the same result:

```
a = a + 10;
```

```
a += 10;
```

Table 5-6 lists all the possible combinations of the assignment operators with other operators.

TABLE 5-6 ## Combining the Assignment Operators and Other Operators

Name	Shorthand	Standard Operator
Assignment	x = y	x = y
Addition assignment	x += y	x = x + y
Subtraction assignment	x -= y	x = x - y
Multiplication assignment	x *= y	x = x * y
Division assignment	x /= y	x = x / y
Remainder assignment	x %= y	x = x % y
Left shift assignment	x <<= y	x = x << y
Right shift assignment	x >>= y	x = x >> y
Unassigned right shift assignment	x >>>= y	x = x <<< y
Bitwise AND assignment	x &= y	x = x & y
Bitwise XOR assignment	x ^= y	x = x ^ y
Bitwise OR assignment	x |= y	x = x	y

Chapter **6**

Getting into the Flow with Loops and Branches

"It's not hard to make decisions when you know what your values are."

— ROY DISNEY

In earlier chapters of this book, you learned about linear JavaScript code. However, more often than not, there comes a time (many times, actually) in a program where you need a choice to be made or where you need to alter the straight-ahead logic of a program to repeat statements multiple times with different values. In this chapter, you learn about looping and branching statements.

Branching Out

Looping and *branching statements* are called control statements because they control the order in which JavaScript statements are run. You can use *branching statements* to create different paths for the execution of JavaScript code, depending on conditional logic. *Loops* are the simplest way to group JavaScript statements together in a program.

The logic of a JavaScript program often comes to a point where a choice must be made that will make all the difference. Figure 6-1 demonstrates, using JavaScript, a real-world decision that can be solved using branching.

FIGURE 6-1:
Branching
chooses the path.

if . . . else statements

The if and else statements work together to evaluate a logical expression and run different statements based on the result. if statements can be, and often are, used by themselves. else statements must always be used in conjunction with an if statement.

The basic syntax for an if statement is

```
if (condition) {
...
}
```

The condition here is any expression that evaluates to a Boolean (true or false) value. If the result of the expression is true, the statements between the brackets will be executed. If it's false, they will just be skipped over.

The else statement comes in when you want to do something if the condition evaluates to false. For example:

```
let age = 19;
if (age < 21){
  document.write ("You are under the legal drinking age in the
  U.S.");
} else {
  document.write ("What'll it be?");
}
```

Many other programming languages have a combination keyword called the elseif, which can be used multiple times in an if . . . else statement until a true value occurs. JavaScript doesn't have an elseif keyword.

However, you can get the same functionality as an elseif keyword by using if and else together with a space between them. For example:

```
if (time < 12){
 document.write ("Good Morning!");
} else if (time < 17){
 document.write ("Good Afternoon!");
} else if (time < 20){
 document.write ("Good Evening!");
} else {
 document.write ("Good Night!");
}
```

Notice the use of line breaks and spaces in the preceding examples. Many people have different styles for how to write if . . . else statements. You may also see them written with fewer line breaks or without space between the keywords and brackets. These will work, too. However, whenever possible, it is preferable to choose ease of reading over brevity.

Switch statements

The switch statement chooses between multiple statements to execute based on possible values of a single expression. Each of these values in a switch statement is called a case. In English, you may say, for example:

> "In the case that we are expecting six guests, order three pizzas. In the case that we are expecting 12 guests, order six pizzas. In the case that we're expecting more than 20 guests, freak out."

UNDERSTANDING IF . . . ELSE SHORTHAND

You should be aware of a couple of shortcuts for using if . . . else statements. The first is to use a ternary operator in place of the if . . . else. This is somewhat more difficult to read than a standard if . . . else:

```
let whatToSay = (time < 12 ? "Good Morning" : "Hello");
```

In this case, the value of whatToSay is set to "Good Morning" if time is less than 12 and it's set to "Hello" if time is not less than 12.

Another shorthand method for writing if . . . else statements uses the logical AND (&&) operator. Remember that the logical AND will only evaluate the second operand if the first evaluates to true. Programmers call this *short-circuiting* because it's not necessary for the second operand to be evaluated in a logical AND operation if the first operand results in a false value.

```
time < 12 && console.log ("Good Morning!");
```

In the preceding example, the && statement first looks at whether time is less than 12. If it is, the string "Good Morning" will be written to the console. If it isn't, nothing will be done because of the short-circuiting side effect of the && operator.

The syntax for the switch statement is

```
switch (expression) {
  case value1:
  // Statements
  break;
  case value2:
  // Statements
  break;
  case value3:
  // Statements
  break;
  default:
  // Statements
  break;
}
```

Notice the break statement after the statements associated with each case. The break statement tells the switch statement to stop and exit the switch statement.

Without the `break`, the `switch` statement would continue and run the statements in the next clause, regardless of whether the expression meets the conditions of that case.

WARNING

Forgetting a `break` statement within a switch can cause big problems, so be sure to always use it. Because a `switch` statement will run any statements within any case clause after a clause that evaluates to `true`, unpredictable results can occur when you forget a `break` statement. Problems caused by missing `break` statements are not easy to identify because they generally won't produce errors, but will frequently produce incorrect results.

If no match is found in any of the `case` clauses, the `switch` statement will look for a `default` clause and execute the statement it contains.

TECHNICAL STUFF

The exception to the rule that you should always use a `break` statement between case clauses is the `default` clause. As long as the `default` clause is the last statement in your switch (which it should be), you can safely omit the `break` after it because the program will break out of the switch after the last statement anyway.

Listing 6-1 shows an example of how you might use a `switch` statement.

LISTING 6-1: **Using a switch Statement to Personalize a Greeting**

```
let languagePreference = "Spanish";
switch (languagePreference){
 case "English":
   console.log("Hello!");
   break;
 case "Spanish":
   console.log("Hola!");
   break;
 case "German":
   console.log("Guten Tag!");
   break;
 case "French":
   console.log("Bon Jour!");
   break;
 default:
   console.log("I'm Sorry, I don't speak" + languagePreferance +
   "!");
}
```

Here We Go: Loop De Loop

Loops execute the same statement multiple times. JavaScript has several different types of loops:

» `for`

» `for . . . in`

» `do . . . while`

» `while`

for loops

The `for` statement creates a loop using three expressions:

» **Initialization:** The initial value of a variable, typically a counter.

» **Condition:** A Boolean expression to be evaluated with each iteration of the loop.

» **Final expression:** An expression to be evaluated after each loop iteration.

Although it's not required to use all three expressions in a `for` loop, all three of them are nearly always included. The `for` loop is usually used to run code a pre-determined number of times.

The following is an example of a simple `for` loop:

```
for (let x = 1; x < 10; x++){
console.log(x);
}
```

Broken down, this is how the preceding `for` loop example works:

1. **A new variable, in this case x, is initiated with the value of 1.**

2. **A test is performed to determine whether x is less than 10.**

   If it is, the statements inside the loop are executed (in this case, a console.log statement).

   If not, the value of x is incremented using the increment operator (++).

3. The test is done again to determine whether x is less than 10.

If so, the statements inside the loop are executed.

4. The test repeats, until the condition expression no longer evaluates to true.

Figure 6-2 shows the result of running this for statement in the Chrome developer tools.

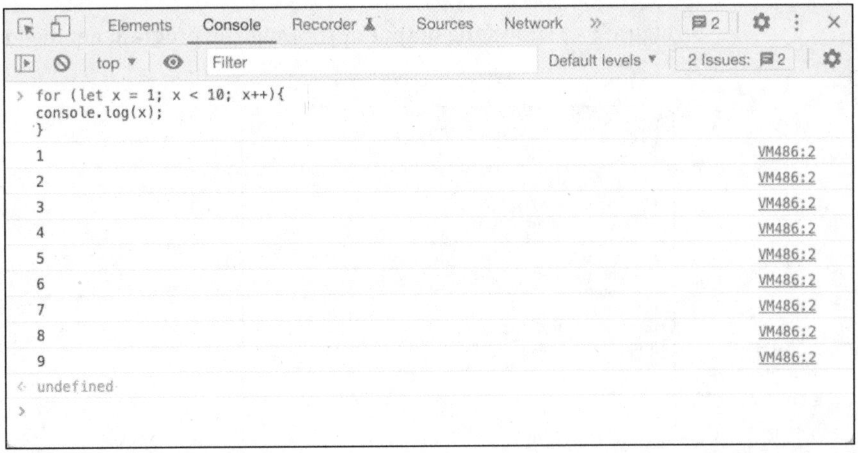

© John Wiley & Sons

FIGURE 6-2:
A loop that counts from 1 to 9.

Looping through an array

You can use for loops to list the contents of an array by testing the value of the counter against the value of the length property of the array. Be sure to remember that JavaScript arrays are zero-indexed, so the value of any array.length will be one more than the highest index numbered element in the array. That is why we subtract 1 in Listing 6-2.

LISTING 6-2: **Listing the Contents of an Array with for Loop**

```html
<html>
<head>
 <title>Different Area Codes</title>
</head>
<body>
 <script>
   let areaCodes = ["770", "404", "718", "202", "901", "305",
   "312", "313", "215", "803"];
```

(continued)

LISTING 6-2: *(continued)*

```
for (x=0; x < areaCodes.length - 1; x++){
  document.write("Different Area Code:" + areaCodes[x] +
"<br>");
      }
</script>
</body>
</html>
```

Figure 6-3 shows the output of running the program detailed in Listing 6-2.

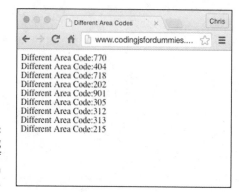

FIGURE 6-3: Output of listing the contents of an array with a for loop.

© John Wiley & Sons

for . . . in loops

The for . . . in statements loop through the properties in an object. You can also use a for . . . in statement to loop through the values of an array.

WARNING

The for . . . in loop has an interesting quirk. It doesn't care about the order of properties or elements that it's looping through. For this reason, and because using for . . . in loop is slower, you're better off using a standard for loop to loop through array elements.

Objects are data containers that have properties (what they are) and methods (what they do). Web browsers have a set of built-in objects that programmers can use to control the function of the browser. The most basic of these is the Document object. The write method of the Document object, for example, tells your browser to insert a specified value into the HTML document.

The Document object also has properties that it uses to track and give programmers information about the current document. The Document.images collection, for example, contains all of the img tags in the current HTML document.

In Listing 6-3, the for...in loop is used to list all the properties of the Document object.

LISTING 6-3: **Looping through the Document object with for...in**

```html
<html>
  <head>
    <title>document properties</title>
    <style>
      .columns {
        column-count: 6;
      }
    </style>
  </head>
  <body>
    <div class="columns">
      <script>
        for (var prop in document) {
          document.write(prop + '<br>');
        }
      </script>
    </div>
  </body>
</html>
```

The results of running Listing 6-3 are shown in Figure 6-4.

You can also use a for...in loop to output the values that are in the properties of the object, rather than just the property name. Listing 6-4 is a program that outputs the current values of each of the Document object's properties.

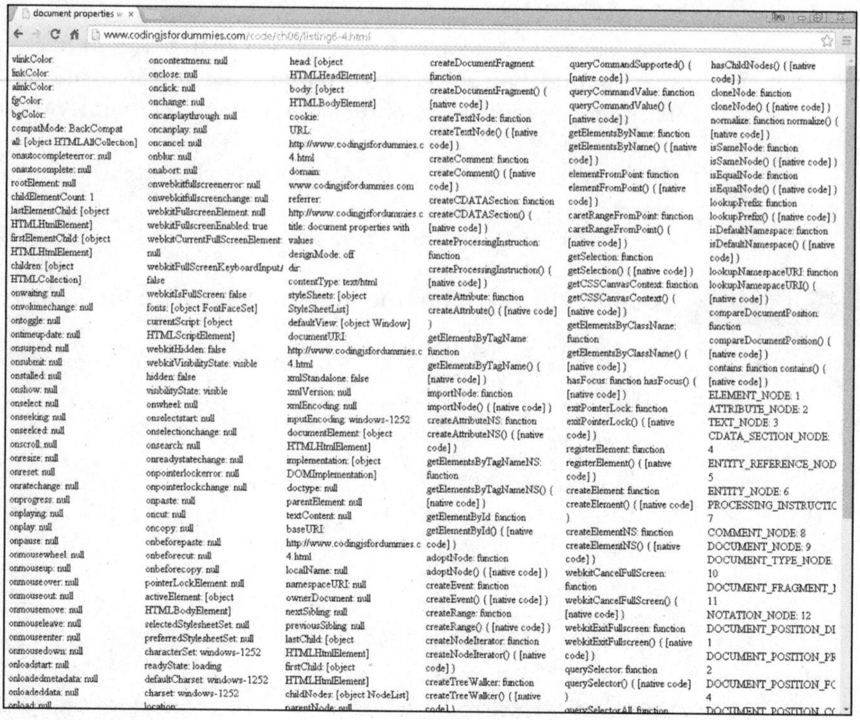

FIGURE 6-4:
A list of all the properties of a Document object using the for . . . in loop.

© John Wiley & Sons

LISTING 6-4: **Outputting the Property Names and Values of the Document Object with for . . . in**

```html
<html>
  <head>
    <title>document properties with values</title>
    <style>
      .columns {
        column-count: 6;
      }
    </style>
  </head>
  <body>
    <div class="columns">
      <script>
        for (var prop in document) {
          document.write(prop + ': ' + document[prop] + '<br>');
        }
```

```
      </script>
    </div>
  </body>
</html>
```

Figure 6-5 shows the output of Listing 6-4.

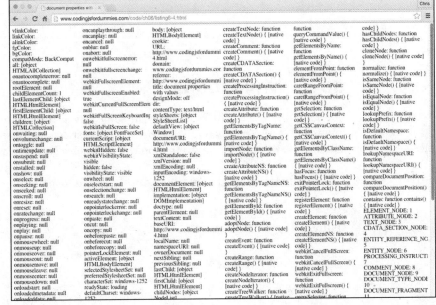

FIGURE 6-5:
Results of outputting the property names and values of the Document object with for . . . in.

© John Wiley & Sons

while loops

The `while` statement creates a loop that runs as long as a condition evaluates to true. Listing 6-5 shows a web page containing an example of the `while` loop.

LISTING 6-5: **Using a while Loop**

```
<html>
  <head>
    <title>Guess the Word</title>
  </head>
  <body>
    <script>
```

(continued)

LISTING 6-5: *(continued)*

```
      let guessedWord = prompt('What word am I thinking of?');
      while (guessedWord != 'sandwich') {
        // as long as the guessed word is not sandwich
        guessedWord = prompt("No. That's not it. Try again.");
      }
      alert("Congratulations! That's exactly right!"); // do this
    after exiting the loop
      </script>
    </body>
</html>
```

do . . . while loops

The do . . . while loop works in much the same way as the while loop, except that it puts the statements before the expression to test against. The effect is that the statements within a do . . . while loop will always execute as least once.

Listing 6-6 demonstrates the use of a do . . . while loop.

LISTING 6-6: **Using a do . . . while Loop**

```
<html>
  <head>
    <title>Let's Count</title>
  </head>
  <body>
    <script>
      let i = 0;
      do {
        i++;
        document.write(i + '<br>');
      } while (i < 10);
    </script>
  </body>
</html>
```

break and continue statements

You can use break and continue to interrupt the execution of a loop. The break statement was shown previously in this chapter in the context of a switch statement, where it serves to break out of the switch after a successful match.

In a loop, break does much the same thing. It causes the program to immediately exit the loop, no matter whether the conditions for the completion of the loop have been met.

For example, in Listing 6-7, the word-guessing game will progress just as it does in Listing 6-5, but the loop will immediately terminate if no value is entered.

LISTING 6-7: **Using a break in a while Loop**

```
<html>
  <head>
    <title>Guess the Word</title>
  </head>
  <body>
    <script>
      let guessedWord = prompt('What word am I thinking of?');
      while (guessedWord != 'sandwich') {
        if (guessedWord == '') {
          break;
        } // exit the loop right away if user doesn't enter a
value
        guessedWord = prompt("No. That's not it. Try again.");
      }
      alert("Congratulations! That's exactly right!");
    </script>
  </body>
</html>
```

The continue statement causes the current iteration of the loop to stop and tells the program to start up again with the next iteration of the loop, skipping the statements that come after the continue statement.

Listing 6-8 shows a program that counts from 1 to 20, but only prints out even numbers. Notice that the program determines whether a number is even by using the modulus operator to test whether the current value of the counter is divisible by two.

LISTING 6-8: **Counting and Using continue to Display Even Numbers**

```html
<html>
<head>
 <title>Count and show me even numbers</title>
</head>
<body>
 <script>
   for (let i = 0; i <= 20; i++){
     if (i%2 != 0){
       continue;
     }
     document.write (i + " is an even number.<br>");
   }
 </script>
</body>
</html>
```

When used in this way, continue can replace the functionality of an else statement. Figure 6-6 shows the result of running Listing 6-8 in a browser.

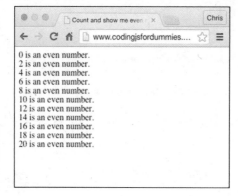

FIGURE 6-6:
Counting and
using continue
to display even
numbers.

© John Wiley & Sons

WARNING

The break and continue statements can be useful, but they can also be dangerous. Their small size and great power make them easy to overlook when reading through code. For this reason, some programmers consider using them inside of a loop to be a bad practice. For more information on why and the complexities of the issue, read this discussion: http://programmers.stackexchange.com/questions/58237/are-break-and-continue-bad-programming-practices.

Chapter **7**

Getting Functional

"I write as a function. Without it I would fall ill and die. It's much a part of one as the liver or intestine, and just about as glamorous."

— CHARLES BUKOWSKI

Functions help you reduce code repetition by turning frequently used bits of code into reusable parts. In this chapter, you write some functions and use them to make otherwise tedious tasks easy and fun!

Understanding the Function of Functions

Functions are mini programs within your programs. Functions serve to handle tasks within the main program that may be required multiple times by different parts of the program.

If you've read any of the preceding chapters, you've seen a few functions in action. The following example is a simple function that, when run, simply adds a z to the end of a string.

```
function addZ(aString) {
  aString += "z";
  return aString;
}
```

To try this function, follow these steps:

1. **Open the JavaScript Console in Chrome.**

2. **Type in the function.**

   You can type it all on one line, or you can press Shift+Enter or Shift+Return after each line to create a line break without executing the code.

3. Press Return or Enter after the final curly brace.

   The console should write out undefined.

4. Type the following command, followed by Return or Enter, to run the function:

   ```
   addZ("I have JavaScript skill");
   ```

   The result of running this function is shown in Figure 7-1.

FIGURE 7-1:
Running your first function in the JavaScript Console.

Functions are a fundamental part of JavaScript programming, and they have a lot of rules and special powers that you need to be aware of as a JavaScript coder. Don't worry if you aren't able to memorize each detail about functions. It will take some practice to understand some of the more abstract concepts, and you may even need to read this chapter again. Eventually, everything will become clear to you, so just stick with it!

Using Function Terminology

Programmers have a number of words that are important to understand when they talk about functions. We use these words extensively in this chapter and throughout this book. The following list is a quick summary of some of the lingo you'll run into when you're working with functions.

Defining a function

When a function appears in JavaScript code, it doesn't run. It's simply created and made available for use later. The creation of the function so that it can be used later on is called *defining* a function.

REMEMBER

You only need to define a function once in a program or on a web page. If you accidentally define the same function more than once, however, JavaScript won't complain. It will simply use the most recently defined version of the function.

For example:

```
function myFunction(){
};
```

Function head

The *function head* is the part of the function definition that includes the function keyword, the function name, and the parentheses.

For example:

```
function myFunction()
```

Function body

The *function body* is made up of the statements between the curly braces of the function.

For example:

```
{
  // function body
}
```

Calling a function

When you use a function, it's called *calling* the function. Calling a function causes the statements in the function body to be executed.

For example:

```
myFunction();
```

Defining parameters and passing arguments

Parameters are names that you give to pieces of data that are provided to a function when it's called. *Arguments* are the values you provide to functions. When a function is called with arguments (according to the specified parameters of the function), programmers refer to that as *passing* the arguments into the function.

The syntax for defining a parameter is as follows:

```
function myFunction(parameter) {
```

The syntax for calling a function with an argument is as follows:

```
myFunction(myArgument);
```

Returning a value

In addition to being able to accept input from the outside world, functions can also send back values after they're finished running. When a function sends back something, it's called *returning a value.*

To return a value, use the `return` keyword inside the function. For example:

```
return myValue;
```

The Benefits of Using Functions

Listing 7-1 shows a program that adds numbers together. It works great and does exactly what it's supposed to do, using a `for ... in` loop (see Book 3, Chapter 6).

LISTING 7-1: **A Program for Adding Numbers Using the for . . . in Loop**

```html
<html>
<head>
  <title>Get the total</title>
</head>
<body>
  <script>
    let myNumbers = [2,4,2,7];
    let total = 0;
    for (oneNumber in myNumbers){
      total = total + myNumbers[oneNumber];
    }
    document.write(total);
  </script>
</body>
</html>
```

If you had multiple sets of numbers to add together, however, you'd need to write a new loop statement specifically for each new array of numbers.

Listing 7-2 turns the program from Listing 7-1 into a function and then uses that function to find the sums of the elements in several different arrays.

LISTING 7-2: **A Function for Adding Numbers from an Array**

```html
<html>
<head>
  <title>Get the sum</title>
</head>
<body>
  <script>
    /**
    *Adds elements in an array
    *@param {Array.<number>} numbersToAdd
    *@return {Number} sum
    */
    function addNumbers(numbersToAdd) {
      let sum = 0;
      for (oneNumber in numbersToAdd) {
        sum = sum + numbersToAdd[oneNumber];
      }
```

(continued)

LISTING 7-2: *(continued)*

```
        return sum;
    }
    let myNumbers = [2,4,2,7];
    let myNumbers2 = [3333,222,111];
    let myNumbers3 = [777,555,777,555];
    let sum1 = addNumbers(myNumbers);
    let sum2 = addNumbers(myNumbers2);
    let sum3 = addNumbers(myNumbers3);
    document.write(sum1 + "<br>");
    document.write(sum2 + "<br>");
    document.write(sum3 + "<br>");
  </script>
</body>
</html>
```

DOCUMENTING JAVASCRIPT WITH JSDOC

It's a good practice to always document your JavaScript code using a standard system. The most widely used JavaScript documentation system, and thus the de-facto standard, is JSDoc.

The JSDoc language is a simple markup language that can be inserted inside of JavaScript files. JSDoc is based on the JavaDoc system that's used for documenting code written in the Java programming language.

After you've annotated your JavaScript files with JSDoc, you can use a documentation generator, such as `jsdoc-toolkit`, to create HTML files documenting the code.

JSDoc markup goes inside of special block comment tags. The only difference between JSDoc markup and regular JavaScript block comments is that JSDoc markup starts with `/**` and ends with `*/`, whereas normal block comments in JavaScript only require one asterisk after the beginning slash. The extra asterisk in JSDoc markup tags allows you to create normal comment blocks without having them be a part of the generated documentation.

The figure shows some code from the open-source AngularJS JavaScript framework that has been annotated using JSDoc.

© John Wiley & Sons

Different parts and aspects of a program can be documented with JSDoc using JSDoc tags. Here are the most popular tags:

JSDoc Tag	Explanation
@author	Programmer's name
@constructor	Indicates that a function is a constructor
@deprecated	Indicates the method is deprecated
@exception	Describes an exception thrown by a method; synonymous with @throws
@exports	Specifies a member that is exported by the module
@param	Describes a method parameter
@private	Indicates a member is private
@return	Describes a return value. Synonymous with @returns
@returns	Describes a return value. Synonymous with @return
@see	Records an association to another object

(continued)

Getting Functional

(continued)

JSDoc Tag	Explanation
@this	Specifies the types of the object to which the keyword this refers within a function
@throws	Describes an exception thrown by a method
@version	Indicates the version number of a library

TECHNICAL STUFF

The block comment that precedes the function in Listing 7-2 follows the format specified by the JavaScript documenting system, JSDoc. By commenting your functions using this format, you not only make your programs much easier to read, you also can use these comments to automatically generate documentation for your programs. You can read more about JSDoc in the sidebar "Documenting JavaScript with JSDoc" or at http://usejsdoc.org.

Functions are a great time, work, and space saver. Writing a useful function may initially take longer than writing JavaScript code outside of functions, but in the long term, your programs will be better organized, and you'll save yourself a lot of headaches if you get into the habit of writing functions.

Writing Functions

A function declaration consists of the following items, in this order:

>> Function keyword

>> Name of the function

>> Parentheses, which may contain one or more parameters

>> Pair of curly brackets containing statements

Sometimes, a function's whole purpose will be to write a message to the screen in a web page. An example of a time when it's useful to have a function like this is for displaying the current date. The following example function writes out the current date to the browser window:

```
function getTheDate(){
 let rightNow = new Date();
 document.write(rightNow.toDateString());
}
```

Follow these steps to try this function:

1. **Open the JavaScript Console in Chrome.**

2. **Type the function into the console.**

   Use Shift+Return (or Shift+Enter) after typing each line to create a line break in the console without executing the code.

3. **After you enter the final }, press Return (or Enter) to run the code.**

   Notice that nothing happens, except that the word undefined appears in the console, letting you know that the function has been accepted, but that it didn't return a value.

4. **Call the function by typing the name of the function (getTheDate) followed by parentheses, followed by a semicolon:**

   ```
   getTheDate();
   ```

   The function prints out the current date and time to the browser window, and then the console displays undefined because the function doesn't have a return value; its purpose is simply to print out the date to the browser window.

TECHNICAL STUFF

The default return value of functions is undefined, so technically, undefined is a return value.

Returning Values

In the example in the preceding section, we create a function that just prints a string to the browser window. After the single document.write statement executes, there are no more statements to run and so the program exits the function and continues with the next statement after the function call.

Most functions return a value (other than undefined) after their work is done. You can then use this value in the rest of the program. Listing 7-3 shows a function that returns a value. The return value of the function is then assigned to a variable and printed to the console.

LISTING 7-3: **Returning a Value from a Function**

```
function getHello(){
  return "Hello!";
}
let helloText = getHello();
console.log (helloText);
```

The return statement is generally the last statement in a function. When it executes, the function exits. You can use the return statement to send any type of literal value (such as "Hello!" or 3) outside of the function or to return the value of a variable, an expression, an array or object, or even another function! Listing 7-4 shows a function that returns the result of an expression.

LISTING 7-4: **Returning the Result of an Expression**

```
function getCircumference(){
  let radius = 12;
  return 2 * Math.PI * radius;
}
console.log (getCircumference());
```

Passing and Using Arguments

For functions to be able to do the same thing with different input, they need a way for programmers to give them input. In Listing 7-2, earlier in this chapter, the parentheses after the name of a function in its declaration are used to specify parameters for the function.

REMEMBER

The difference between parameters and arguments can be confusing at first. Here's how it works:

» Parameters are the names you specify in the function definition.

» Arguments are the values you pass to the function. They take on the names of the parameters when they are passed.

In the following function, you define two parameters for the myTacos function:

```
function myTacos(meat,produce){
...
}
```

When you call this function, you include data (arguments) in the places where the function definition has parameters. Note that the arguments passed to the function must be listed in the same order as the parameters in the function definition:

```
myTacos("beef","onions");
```

The values passed to the function will become the values of the local variables inside of the function and will be given the names of the function's parameters.

Listing 7-5 expands the myTacos function to print out the values of the two arguments to the console. Passing an argument is like initializing a variable inside of the function, except that the values come from outside of the function.

LISTING 7-5: **Referring to Arguments Inside a Function Using the Parameter Names**

```
function myTacos(meat,produce){
  console.log(meat); // writes "beef"
  console.log(produce); // writes "onions"
}
myTacos("beef","onions");
```

TECHNICAL STUFF

You can specify up to 255 parameters in a function definition. However, it's highly unusual to need to write a function that takes anywhere near that many parameters! Just for the sake of keeping your code clean and understandable, if you find you need a lot of parameters, you should think about whether there's a better way to do it.

Passing arguments by value

If you use a variable with one of the primitive data types to pass your argument, the argument passes *by value*. What this means is the new variable created inside the function is totally separate from the variable used to pass the argument, and no matter what happens after the value gets into the function, the variable outside of the function won't change.

REMEMBER

Primitive data types in JavaScript are `string`, `number`, `bigInt`, `Boolean`, `Symbol`, `undefined`, and `null`.

In Listing 7-6, you see that several variables are created, given values, and then passed into a function. In this case, the parameters of the function have the same names as the variables used to pass the arguments. Even though the values of the variables inside the function get changed, the values of the original variables remain the same.

LISTING 7-6: **Demonstration of Arguments Passed by Value**

```html
<html>
<head>
  <title>Arguments Passed By Value</title>
</head>
<body>
  <script>
    /**
     * Increments two numbers
     * @param {number} number1
     * @param {number} number2
     */
    function addToMyNumbers(number1,number2){
      number1++;
      number2++;
      console.log("number 1: " + number1);
      console.log("number 2: " + number2);
    }
    let number1 = 3;
    let number2 = 12;
    addToMyNumbers(number1,number2); // pass the arguments
    console.log("original number1: " + number1);
    console.log("original number2: " + number2);
  </script>
</body>
</html>
```

Figure 7-2 shows the output of this program in the JavaScript Console.

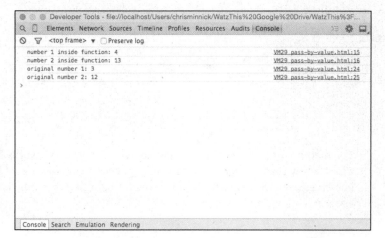

FIGURE 7-2:
Variables outside of a function aren't affected by what happens inside the function.

Passing arguments by reference

Whereas JavaScript primitive variables (strings, numbers, Boolean, undefined, and null) are passed to functions by value, JavaScript objects are passed by reference. What this means is that if you pass an object as an argument to a function, any changes to that object within the function will also change the value outside of the function. The implications and uses of passing by reference are beyond the scope of this chapter but are covered in Book 3, Chapter 8.

Calling a function without all the arguments

You don't need to always call a function with the same number of parameters as are listed in the function definition. If a function definition contains three parameters, but you call it with only two, the third parameter will create a variable with a value of undefined in the function.

Setting default parameter values

If you want arguments to default to something other than undefined, you can set default values. One way to do this is to test the arguments inside of the function value and set default values if the data type of the argument is undefined.

For example, in Listing 7-7, the function takes one parameter. Inside the function, a test is done to check whether the argument is undefined. If so, it will be set to a default value.

Getting Functional

LISTING 7-7: **Setting Default Argument Values**

```
function welcome(yourName){
 if (typeof yourName === 'undefined'){
   yourName = "friend";
 }
```

The method for setting default values shown in Listing 7-7 works fine, but there's a better way that's much more compact. Since the 2015 version of JavaScript (also known as ES6), you can set default values for parameters inside the function head, as shown in Listing 7-8.

LISTING 7-8: **Setting Default Arguments in the Function Head**

```
function welcome(yourName = "friend") {
 document.write("Hello," + yourName);
}
```

Calling a function with more arguments than parameters

If you call a function with more arguments than the number of parameters, local variables won't be created for the additional arguments because the function has no way of knowing what to call them.

There is a neat trick that you can use to retrieve the values of arguments that are passed to a function but don't have a matching parameter: the arguments object.

Getting into arguments with the arguments object

When you don't know how many arguments will be passed into a function, you can use the arguments object, which is built-in to functions by JavaScript, to retrieve all the arguments and make use of them.

The arguments object contains an array of all the arguments passed to a function. By looping through the array (using the for loop or the for ... in loop — see Book 3, Chapter 6), you can make use of every argument, even if the number of arguments may change each time the function is called.

Listing 7-9 demonstrates the use of the `arguments` object to present a welcome message to someone with two middle names as well as someone with one middle name.

LISTING 7-9: **Using the Arguments Object to Define a Function that Can Add an Arbitrary Number of Numbers**

```html
<html>
  <head>
    <title>Welcome Message</title>
  </head>
  <body>
    <script>
      /**
       *Flexible Welcome Message
       */
      function flexibleWelcome() {
        let welcome = 'Welcome,';
        for (i = 0; i < arguments.length; i++) {
          welcome = welcome + arguments[i] + '';
        }
        return welcome;
      }
      document.write(
        flexibleWelcome('John', 'Jacob', 'Jingleheimer', 'Schmidt') + '<br>'
      );
      document.write(
        flexibleWelcome('Christopher', 'James', 'Minnick') + '<br>'
      );
    </script>
  </body>
</html>
```

Understanding Function Scope

Variables created inside a function by passing arguments are only available within that function. Programmers call this feature of JavaScript *function scope.* Variables created inside of a function are destroyed when the function exits.

However, if you create a variable inside a function without using a `var`, `let`, or `const` keyword, that variable becomes a global variable and can be changed and accessed anywhere in your program.

WARNING

Accidentally creating a global variable is the source of many JavaScript bugs and errors, and it's recommended that you always properly scope variables and never create a global variable unless it's absolutely necessary. Most JavaScript programmers agree that *implicit* globals (globals created by not using var, let, or const when initializing a variable) are a bad practice. As such, most code-checking and testing tools specifically disallow their use.

Creating Anonymous Functions

The function name part of the function head isn't required, and you can create functions without names. This may seem like an odd thing to do because a function with no name is like a dog with no name; you have no way to call it! However, anonymous functions can be assigned to variables when they are created, which gives you the same capabilities as using a name within the function head:

```
let doTheThing = function(thingToDo) {
  document.write("I will do this thing: " + thingToDo);
}
```

Knowing the differences between anonymous and named functions

There are a couple important, and sometimes useful, differences between creating a named function and assigning an anonymous function to a variable. The first is that an anonymous function assigned to a variable only exists and can only be called after the program executes the assignment. Named functions can be accessed anywhere in a program.

The second difference between named functions and anonymous functions assigned to variables is that you can change the value of a variable and assign a different function to it at any point. That makes anonymous functions assigned to variables more flexible than named functions.

Arrow functions

Another way to write anonymous functions is as arrow functions. Arrow functions get their name from the combination of symbols used to write them. Instead of the function keyword, arrow functions use the characters => between the parameter list and the function body.

TECHNICAL STUFF

The combination of the = and the > operator is called a "fat arrow."

Arrow functions are always anonymous functions. They can be passed as arguments to other functions, or they can be assigned to variables. For example, here's an arrow function that squares a number:

```
let square = (num) => {
  return num * num;
}
```

One of the things that makes arrow functions useful is that they are more compact than using the `function` keyword. In fact, arrow functions have some special rules and shortcuts that can make them even more compact than the preceding example. These rules are:

» If the function only has one parameter, you don't need to use the parentheses around the parameter list.

» If the function doesn't do anything but return data, you don't need to include the `return` keyword.

» If you don't include the `return` keyword, you also don't include the curly brackets around the function body.

Using an arrow function, the preceding square function can be written as the following:

```
let square = num => num * num;
```

Doing it Again with Recursion

You can call functions from outside of the function or from within other functions. You can even call a function from within itself. When a function calls itself, it's using a programming technique called *recursion*.

You can use recursion in many of the same cases where you would use a loop, except that it repeats the statements within a function.

Listing 7-10 shows a simple recursive function. This recursive function has one big problem, however. Can you spot it?

LISTING 7-10:
A Fatally Flawed Recursive Function

```
function squareItUp(startingNumber) {
  var square = startingNumber * startingNumber;
  console.log(square);
  squareItUp(square);
}
```

Do you see the issue with this function? It never ends. It will just keep on multiplying numbers together until you stop it.

WARNING

Running this function will probably crash your browser, if not your computer. No permanent damage will be done, of course, but it's enough for you to just read the code and notice the problem here.

Listing 7-11 improves upon the squareItUp() function by providing what's called a *base case*. A base case is the condition under which a recursive function's job is done and it should halt. Every recursive function must have a base case.

LISTING 7-11:
A Recursive Function to Square Numbers Until the Number Is Greater than 1,000,000

```
function squareItUp(startingNumber) {
  square = startingNumber * startingNumber;

  if (square > 1000000) {
    console.log(square);
  } else {
    squareItUp(square);
  }
}
```

There. That's better! But, this function still has a big problem. What if someone passes a negative number, zero or 1 into it? The result of any of these cases would still be an infinite loop. To protect against such a situation, we need a termination condition. In Listing 7-12, a check to make sure that the argument isn't less than or equal to 1 and that it isn't something other than a number has been added. In both cases, the function will stop immediately.

LISTING 7-12: **A Recursive Function with Termination and Base Conditions**

```
function squareItUp(startingNumber) {
  // Termination conditions, invalid input
  if (typeof startingNumber != 'number' || startingNumber - Number <= 1) {
    return -1; // exit the function
  }
  square = startingNumber * startingNumber;
  // Base condition
  if (square > 1000000) {
    console.log(square); // Print the final value
  } else {
    // If the base condition isn't met, do it again.
    squareItUp(square);
  }
}
```

Functions within Functions

Functions can be declared within functions. Listing 7-13 demonstrates how this technique works and how it affects the scope of variables created within the functions.

LISTING 7-13: **Declaring Functions within Functions**

```
function turnIntoAMartian(myName) {
  function recallName(myName) {
    let martianName = myName + ' Martian';
  }
  recallName(myName);
  console.log(martianName);
}
turnIntoAMartian("Glenn"); // martianName is not defined
```

The preceding example demonstrates how nesting a function within a function creates another layer of scope. Variables created in the inner function aren't directly accessible to the containing function. In order to get their values, a return statement is needed, as shown in Listing 7-14.

Getting Functional

LISTING 7-14: **Returning Values from an Inner Function**

```
function turnIntoAMartian(myName) {
  function recallName(myName) {
    let martianName = myName + ' Martian';
    return martianName;
  }
  let martianName = recallName(myName);
  console.log(martianName);
}
turnIntoAMartian("Glenn"); // "Glenn Martian"
```

Chapter **8**

Making and Using Objects

"We cannot do anything with an object that has no name."

— MAURICE BLANCHOT, "LITERATURE AND THE RIGHT TO DEATH"

n this chapter, we show you why you should use objects, how to use them, and what special powers they have to make your programs and your programming better.

Object of My Desire

In addition to the seven primitive data types (see Book 3, Chapter 3,) JavaScript also has a data type called *object*. JavaScript *objects* encapsulate data and functionality in reusable components.

To understand what objects are and how they work, it's helpful to compare JavaScript objects with physical, real-life things. Take a guitar, for example.

A guitar has things that make up what it is and has things that it does. Here are a few facts about the guitar we're using for this example:

>> It has six strings.

>> It's black and white.

>> It's electric.

>> Its body is solid.

Some of the things this guitar can do (or that can be done to the guitar) are

>> Strum strings

>> Increase the volume

>> Decrease the volume

>> Tighten the strings

>> Adjust the tone

>> Loosen the strings

If this guitar were a JavaScript object instead of a real-life object, the things that it does would be called its *methods*, and the things that make up the guitar, such as its strings and body type, would be its *properties*.

Methods and properties in objects are both written the same way: as name–value pairs, with a colon separating the name and the value. When a property has a function as its value, it's known as a method.

TECHNICAL STUFF

In reality, everything within an object is a property. We just call a property with a function value by a different name: a method.

Listing 8-1 shows what our guitar's properties might look like as a JavaScript object.

LISTING 8-1: **A JavaScript Guitar Object**

```
let guitar = {
  bodyColor: "black",
  scratchPlateColor: "white",
  numberOfStrings: 6,
  brand: "Yamaha",
```

```
bodyType: "solid",
strum: function() {...},
tune: function() {...}
};
```

Creating Objects

JavaScript has four ways to create objects:

» By writing an object literal

» By using the object constructor method

» By using the Object.create method

» By using the class keyword

Which one you choose depends on the circumstances. In the next sections, you discover the pros and cons of each and when one is preferred over the other.

Defining objects with object literals

The object literal method of creating objects starts with a standard variable definition, using the var, let, or const keyword, followed by the assignment operator:

```
const person =
```

In the right side of the statement, however, you'll use curly braces with comma-separated name/value pairs:

```
const person = {eyes: 2, feet: 2, hands: 2, eyeColor: "blue"};
```

If you don't know the properties that your object will have when you create it or if your program requires that additional properties be added a later time, you can create the object with few, or even no properties, and then add properties to it later:

```
const person = {};
person.eyes = 2;
person.hair = "brown";
```

The methods in the examples earlier in this book have mostly been used to output text. `document.write` and `console.log` both use this method of separating properties with a period, so it may look familiar to you. The dot between the object name and the property indicates that the property belongs to that object. Dot notation is covered in more detail in the "Retrieving and Setting Object Properties" section, later of this chapter.

Another thing to notice about objects is that, like arrays, objects can contain multiple different data types as the values of properties.

TECHNICAL STUFF

The not-so-well-kept secret to really understanding JavaScript is in knowing that arrays and functions are types of objects and that the number, string, and Boolean primitive data types can also be used as objects. What this means is that they have all the properties of objects and can be assigned properties in the same way as objects.

TECHNICAL STUFF

Objects and arrays are often initialized using the `const` keyword, as in the preceding example. Using `const` to initialize arrays and objects still gives you the ability to change the elements or properties of the array or object, but it restricts the variable from being assigned a different or new object.

Defining objects with a constructor function

The second way to define an object is by using a constructor function. This method uses the `new` keyword to create an object from a function. An example of using an object constructor is shown in Listing 8-2.

LISTING 8-2: **Using a Constructor Function**

```
function Person(name,age){
  this.name = name;
  this.age = age;
}

const mom = new Person("Patricia",78);
```

A constructor function can be used to create multiple objects from the same template. Each object created using the `Person` function will have a property called `name` and a property called `age`.

Making objects with class

A *class* is a template for objects. If you think this sounds similar to the definition of a constructor function, you're right. Many other programming languages use classes to define object templates, but JavaScript never had the concept of a class when it was growing up.

That changed in 2015, when the `class` keyword and the syntax for writing classes officially became part of JavaScript. JavaScript classes are very similar to constructor functions in their purpose, but the language you use to write a class is somewhat different.

To write a JavaScript class, start with the `class` keyword, the name you want to give your class (it's traditional to give classes names that start with a capital letter), and then a left curly brace, like this:

```
class Person {
```

Once you've written the class header, you can write a constructor. This is a function, just like a normal constructor function, but you can write it using *method notation*, which omits the `function` keyword and the colon that would normally be required to write a function inside an object.

```
class Person {
  constructor(name,age) {
    this.name = name;
    this.age = age;
  }
}
```

Once you've defined your class, you create an object from a class the same way you create an object from a constructor function:

```
const neighbor = new Person('Murray',6);
```

One of the interesting things about using classes is that you can create new classes that are based on other classes. For example, if you wanted to create a new class called `Teacher` that had all the same properties as `Person`, plus some more, you could use the `extends` keyword to do it, like this:

```
const Teacher extends Person {
  constructor(name,age,subject) {
    super(name,age);
    this.subject = subject;
  }
}
```

To create a new object based on the Teacher class, just use the new keyword and pass the three arguments. Inside the constructor function, the class uses the super function to call the Person class and run its constructor function with the arguments provided to Teacher (the values of name and age, in this example).

```
const myTeacher = new Teacher('Jill',39,'art');
```

Using Object.create

The Object.create method of making objects takes an existing object as its parameter and returns a new object with the object it was created from as its prototype. For example, you might start with an object like the following to use as a prototype for other objects:

```
const cat = {
  sound: 'meow',
  sleep: function () {
    console.log('The cat is asleep');
  },
};
```

With Object.create, you can make a copy of this object that still has the sound and sleep properties and add properties to it, as shown in Listing 8-3.

LISTING 8-3: **Using object.create**

```
const cat = {
  sound: 'meow',
  sleep: function () {
    console.log('The cat is asleep');
  },
};
const sparky = object.create(cat);
sparky.name = 'Sparky';
sparky.age = 10;
```

Retrieving and Setting Object Properties

After you create an object and define its properties, you'll want to be able to retrieve and change those properties. The two ways to access object properties are by using dot notation or square brackets notation.

Using dot notation

In dot notation, the name of an object is followed by a period (or dot), followed by the name of the property that you want to get or set.

To create a new property called firstName in the person object or to modify the value of an existing firstName property, you would use a statement like the following:

```
person.firstName = "Glenn";
```

If the firstName property doesn't already exist, this statement will create it. If it does exist, it will update it with a new value.

To retrieve the value of a property using dot notation, you would use the exact same syntax, but you would move the object and property names (called the *property accessor*) into a different position in the statement. For example, if you want to concatenate the values of person.firstName and person.lastName and assign them to a new variable called fullName, you do the following:

```
let fullname = person.firstName + person.lastName;
```

Or, to write out the value of a person.firstName to your browser console, just use the property accessor as you would any variable; such as

```
console.log(person.firstName);
```

TIP

Dot notation is generally faster to type and easier to read. It's an easier way to set and retrieve object property values.

Using square bracket notation

Square bracket notation uses, you guessed it, square brackets after the object name in order to get and set property values. To set a property value with square bracket notation, put the name of the property in quotes inside square brackets, like this:

```
person["firstName"] = "Iggy";
```

Square bracket notation has a couple of capabilities that dot notation doesn't. The main one is that you can use variables inside of square bracket notation for cases where you don't know the name of the property that you want to retrieve when you're writing your program.

The following example does the exact same thing as the preceding example, but with a variable inside of the square brackets rather than a literal string. Using this technique, you can make a single statement that can function in many different circumstances, such as in a loop or a function:

```
let personProperty = "firstName";
person[personProperty] = "Iggy";
```

Listing 8-4 shows a simple program that creates an object called chair, then loops through each of the object's properties and asks the user to input values for each. Once the user has entered a value for each of the properties, the write-ChairReceipt function is called, which prints out each property along with the value the user entered.

LISTING 8-4: **Chair Configuration Script**

```
<html>
  <head>
    <title>The WatzThis? Chair Configurator</title>
  </head>
  <body>
    <script>
      let myChair = {
        cushionMaterial: '',
        numberOfLegs: '',
        legHeight: '',
      };

      function configureChair() {
        let userValue;
        for (const property in myChair) {
          if (myChair.hasOwnProperty(property)) {
            userValue = prompt('Enter a value for ' + property);
            myChair[property] = userValue;
          }
        }
      }
```

```
    function writeChairReceipt() {
       document.write(
         '<h2>Your chair will have the following
configuration:</h2>'
       );
       for (const property in myChair) {
          if (myChair.hasOwnProperty(property)) {
             document.write(property + ': ' + myChair[property] +
'<br>');
          }
       }
    }

    configureChair();
    writeChairReceipt();
  </script>
 </body>
</html>
```

Deleting Properties

You can delete properties from objects by using the delete operator. Listing 8-5 demonstrates how this operator works.

LISTING 8-5: **Using the delete Operator**

```
const myObject = {
 var1 : "the value",
 var2 : "another value",
 var3 : "yet another"
};

// delete var2 from myObject
delete myObject.var2;

// try to write the value of var2
document.write(myObject.var2); // result is an error
```

Working with Methods

Methods are properties with functions for their values. You define a method the same way that you define any function. The only difference is that a method is assigned to a property of an object. Listing 8-6 demonstrates the creation of an object with several properties, one of which is a method.

LISTING 8-6: **Creating a Method**

```
const sandwich = {
  meat: '',
  cheese: '',
  bread: '',
  condiment: '',
  makeSandwich: function (meat, cheese, bread, condiment) {
    sandwich.meat = meat;
    sandwich.cheese = cheese;
    sandwich.bread = bread;
    sandwich.condiment = condiment;
    let mySandwich =
      sandwich.bread +
      ', ' +
      sandwich.meat +
      ', ' +
      sandwich.cheese +
      ', ' +
      sandwich.condiment;
    return mySandwich;
  },
};
```

TECHNICAL STUFF

JavaScript has a newer way of creating strings that incorporate variables than the method shown in the preceding example. The newer method is called *template literals notation*. Template literals use the backtick character (which is in the upper-left corner of a desktop or laptop keyboard) around a string. Strings inside of backtick characters can include JavaScript expressions inside of curly braces preceded by a $. For example, the mySandwich variable in the makeSandwich method in Listing 8-6 can be rewritten like this:

```
let mySandwich = '${sandwich.bread}, ${sandwich.meat},
  ${sandwich.cheese}, ${sandwich.condiment}';
```

To call the makeSandwich method of the sandwich object, you can then use dot notation just as you would access a property, but with parentheses and parameters supplied after the method name, as shown in Listing 8-7.

LISTING 8-7: **Calling a Method**

```html
<html>
  <head>
    <title>Make me a sandwich</title>
  </head>
  <body>
    <script>
      const sandwich = {
        meat: '',
        cheese: '',
        bread: '',
        condiment: '',
        makeSandwich: function (meat, cheese, bread, condiment) {
          sandwich.meat = meat;
          sandwich.cheese = cheese;
          sandwich.bread = bread;
          sandwich.condiment = condiment;
          let mySandwich = `${sandwich.bread}, ${sandwich.meat},
${sandwich.cheese}, ${sandwich.condiment}`;
          return mySandwich;
        },
      };

      let sandwichOrder = sandwich.makeSandwich(
        'ham',
        'cheddar',
        'wheat',
        'spicy mustard'
      );
      document.write(sandwichOrder);
    </script>
  </body>
</html>
```

Using this

The `this` keyword is a shorthand for referencing the containing object of a method. For example, in Listing 8-8, every instance of the object name, sandwich, has been replaced with `this`. When the `makeSandwich` function is called as a method of the sandwich object, JavaScript understands that `this` refers to the sandwich object.

LISTING 8-8: **Using this Inside a Method**

```
<html>
<head>
 <title>Make a sandwich</title>
</head>
<body>
 <script>

   const sandwich = {
     meat:"",
     cheese:"",
     bread:"",
     condiment:"",
     makeSandwich: function(meat,cheese,bread,condiment){
       this.meat = meat;
       this.cheese = cheese;
       this.bread = bread;
       this.condiment = condiment;
       let mySandwich = `${sandwich.bread}, ${sandwich.meat},
   ${sandwich.cheese}, ${sandwich.condiment}`;
       return mySandwich;
       }
     }

     let sandwichOrder = sandwich.makeSandwich("ham","cheddar","wh
   eat","spicy mustard");
     document.write (sandwichOrder);

 </script>
</body>
</html>
```

The result of using the `this` keyword instead of the specific object name is exactly the same in this case.

Where `this` becomes very useful is when you have a function that may apply to multiple different objects. In that case, the `this` keyword will reference the object that it's called within, rather than being tied to a specific object.

In the next sections, you find out about constructor functions and inheritance, both of which are enabled by the humble `this` statement.

An Object-Oriented Way to Become Wealthy: Inheritance

When you create objects, you're not just limited to creating specific objects, such as your guitar, your car, your cat, or your sandwich. The real beauty of objects is that you can use them to create types of objects, from which other objects can be created.

Every JavaScript object is based on another JavaScript object, and that object may be based on another object. The objects that an object is based on is called its prototype. The prototype may also have a prototype. This goes on until you get to the base object in JavaScript that, eventually, all objects are based on. This is the `Object` object.

To better understand the idea of prototypes and inheritance, let's start at the top of the prototype chain and make some new objects. It's possible to use the `Object` constructor function to create a new object based on the base object:

```
const person = new Object();
```

Here, a new `person` object of the type `Object` is created. This new `person` object contains all the default properties and methods of the `Object` type, but with a new name. You can then add your own properties and methods to the `person` object to make it specifically describe what you mean by person.

```
const person = new Object();
person.eyes = 2;
person.ears = 2;
person.arms = 2;
person.hands = 2;
person.feet = 2;
person.legs = 2;
person.species = "Homo sapien";
```

Creating an object using inheritance

So, now you've set some specific properties of the person object. Imagine that you want to create a new object that's a specific person, like Willie Nelson. You could simply create a new object called willieNelson and give it all the same properties as the person object, plus the properties that make Willie Nelson unique.

```
const willieNelson = new Object();
willieNelson.eyes = 2;
willieNelson.ears = 2;
willieNelson.arms = 2;
willieNelson.hands = 2;
willieNelson.feet = 2;
willieNelson.legs = 2;
willieNelson.species = "Homo sapien";
willieNelson.occupation = "musician";
willieNelson.hometown = "Austin";
willieNelson.hair = "Long";
willieNelson.genre = "country";
```

This method of defining the willieNelson object is wasteful, however. It requires you to do a lot of work, and there's no indication here that Willie Nelson is a person. He just happens to have all the same properties as a person.

The solution is to create a new type of object, called Person and then make the willieNelson object be of the type Person.

TECHNICAL STUFF

Notice that when we talk about a type of object, we always capitalize the name of the object type. This isn't a requirement, but it is a nearly universal convention. For example, we say

```
const person = new Object();
```

or

```
const willieNelson = new Person();
```

This new willieNelson object will inherit all the properties of the person object. And, there's one more fascinating thing about the relationship between an object and its prototype: if you don't specifically set a value for a property of an object, when you try to access that property, JavaScript will look for a value for that property in the object's prototype, and the prototype's prototype, all the way up the chain.

In the `willieNelson` example, where `willieNelson` was created using the `Person` constructor, if you access `willieNelson.eyes`, it will return 2, because the `person` object has a property called `eyes` with a value of 2.

To test this, run the code in Listing 8-9 in a web browser.

LISTING 8-9: **Testing Inheritance**

```
<html>
<head>
 <title>Inheritance demo</title>
</head>
<body>
 <script>

   function Person(){
     this.eyes = 2;
     this.ears = 2;
     this.arms = 2;
     this.hands = 2;
     this.feet = 2;
     this.legs = 2;
     this.species = "Homo sapien";
   }
   const willieNelson = new Person();
   alert("Willie Nelson has " + willieNelson.feet + " feet!");
 </script>
</body>
</html>
```

The result of running Listing 8-9 in a browser is shown in Figure 8-1.

Modifying an object type

Suppose that you have your `Person` object type, which serves as the prototype for several objects. At some point you realize that the person, as well as all the objects that inherit from it, ought to have a few more properties.

© John Wiley & Sons

FIGURE 8-1:
Willie Nelson is a
Person.

To modify a prototype object, use the `prototype` property that every object inherits from `Object`. Listing 8-10 shows how this works.

LISTING 8-10: **Modifying a Prototype Object**

```
function Person(){
 this.eyes = 2;
 this.ears = 2;
 this.arms = 2;
 this.hands = 2;
 this.feet = 2;
 this.legs = 2;
 this.species = "Homo sapien";
}

const willieNelson = new Person();
const johnnyCash = new Person();
const patsyCline = new Person();

// Person needs more properties!
Person.prototype.knees = 2;
Person.prototype.toes = 10;
Person.prototype.elbows = 2;

// Check the values of existing objects for the new properties
document.write (patsyCline.toes); // outputs 10
```

Chapter **9**

Controlling the Browser with the Window Object

"In making theories, always keep a window open so that you can throw one out if necessary."

— BELA LUGOSI

The Browser Object Model (BOM) allows JavaScript to interact with the functionality of the web browser. Using the BOM, you can create and resize windows, display alert messages, and change the current page being displayed in the browser.

In this chapter, you discover what can be done with the browser window and how to use it to write better JavaScript programs.

Understanding the Browser Environment

Web browsers are complicated pieces of software. When they work well, they operate seamlessly and integrate all their functions into a smooth and seemingly simple web browsing experience. We all know that web browsers have an occasional hiccup and sometimes even crash. To understand why this happens, and to be able to make better use of browsers, it's important to know the many different parts of the web browser and how these parts interact with each other.

The user interface

The part of the web browser that you interact with when you type in an URL, click the home button, create or use a bookmark, or change your browser settings is called the user interface, or browser chrome (not to be confused with Google's Chrome browser).

The Chrome browser consists of the web browser's menus, window frames, toolbars, and buttons that are outside of the main content window where web pages load, as shown in Figure 9-1.

FIGURE 9-1:
The Chrome browser.

© John Wiley & Sons

Loader

The *loader* is the part of a web browser that communicates with web servers and downloads web pages, scripts, CSS, graphics, and all the other components of a web page. Most often, loading is the part of displaying a web page that creates the longest wait time for the user.

The *HTML page* is the first part of a web page that must be downloaded, as it contains links and embedded scripts and styles that need to be processed to display the page.

Figure 9-2 shows the Chrome Developer Tools' Network tab. It displays a graphical view of everything that happens during the loading of a web page, along with a timeline showing how long the loading of each part takes.

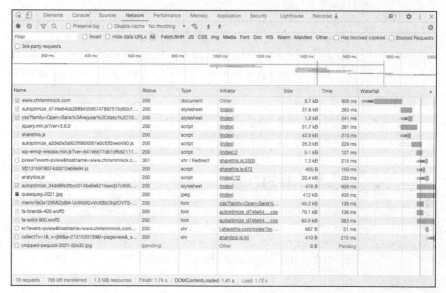

© John Wiley & Sons

FIGURE 9-2:
Web browser loading.

Once the HTML document is downloaded, browsers will open several connections to the server to download the other parts of the web page as quickly as possible. Generally, the parts of a web page that are linked from an HTML document (also known as the *resources*) are loaded in the order in which they appear in the HTML document. For example, a script that is linked in the head element of the page will be loaded before one that's linked at the bottom of the page.

The load order of resources is critical to the efficiency and speed at which the page can be displayed to the user. For a web page to be displayed correctly, the CSS styles that apply to that page need to be loaded and parsed. Because of this, CSS should always be loaded in the head element at the top of the web page.

JavaScript sometimes affects the display of a web page as well, but more often, it affects only the functionality. When a script will affect the display of a web page, it should be loaded in the head of the document (after the CSS). Scripts that aren't critical to how the web page appears should be linked from the very end of the body element (right before the </body>), to not create a blocking scenario in which the browser waits for scripts to load before displaying anything to the user.

HTML parsing

After a web page is downloaded, the HTML parsing component of the browser goes to work parsing the HTML to create a model (called the Document Object Model or DOM) of the web page. The DOM, which is covered in detail in Book 3, Chapter 10, is like a map of your web page. JavaScript programmers use this map to manipulate and access all the different parts of a web page.

Upon completion of the HTML parsing, the browser begins downloading the other components of the web page.

CSS parsing

Once the CSS for a web page is completely downloaded, the web browser will parse the styles and figure out which ones apply to the HTML document. CSS parsing is a complex process involving multiple passes over a document to apply each style correctly and to consider how the styles impact each other.

JavaScript parsing

The next step in displaying a web page is the JavaScript parsing. The JavaScript parser compiles and runs every script in your web page in the order in which it appears in the document. If your JavaScript code adds or removes elements, text, or styles within the HTML DOM, the browser will update the HTML and CSS renderings accordingly.

Layout and rendering

Finally, once all the web page's resources have been loaded and parsed, the browser determines how to display the page and then displays it. Unless you've specified that a script included earlier in the document should wait until the end to be executed, the layout and rendering of your scripts will occur in the order they're included in the document.

TIP

In general, it's better to display a web page to the user as quickly as possible, even if the page may not be fully functional when it first appears. Modern websites frequently employ this strategy specifically (called *deferred loading*) to improve the perceived performance of their pages. If you've ever opened a web page and had to wait for a moment before you can use a form or interactive element, you've seen deferred loading in action.

Investigating the BOM

JavaScript programmers can find out information about a user's web browser and control aspects of the user's experience through an API called the Browser Object Model (the BOM).

There is no official standard for the Browser Object Model. Different browsers implement it in different ways. However, there are some generally accepted standards for how JavaScript interacts with web browsers.

The Navigator object

The Navigator object provides JavaScript with access to information about the user's web browser. The Navigator object takes its name from the first web browser to implement it, Netscape Navigator. The Navigator object isn't built into JavaScript. Rather, it's a feature of web browsers that is accessible using JavaScript. Nearly every web browser (and every modern web browser) has adopted the same terminology to refer to this highest-level browser object.

The Navigator object accesses helpful information such as

>> The name of the web browser

>> The version of the web browser

>> The physical location of the computer the browser is running on (if the user allows the browser to access geolocation data)

>> The language of the browser

>> The type of computer the browser is running on

Table 9-1 shows all the properties of the Navigator object.

TABLE 9-1

The Properties of the Navigator Object

Property	Use
appCodeName	Gets the code name of the browser.
appName	Gets the name of the browser.
appVersion	Gets the browser version information.
cookieEnabled	Tells whether cookies are enabled in the browser.
geolocation	Locates the user's physical location.
language	Gets the language of the browser.
onLine	Identifies whether the browser is online.
platform	Gets the platform the browser was compiled for.
product	Gets the browser engine name of the browser.
userAgent	Gets the user-agent the browser sends to web servers.

To get the properties of the Navigator object, you use the same syntax used to get the properties of any object — namely, dot notation or brackets notation. Listing 9-1, when opened in a web browser, will display all the current properties and values of the Navigator object.

LISTING 9-1: **Properties of the Navigator Object and Their Values**

```
<html>
  <head>
    <style>
      .columns {
        column-count: 6;
      }
```

```
      </style>
    </head>
    <body>
      <div class="columns">
        <script>
          for (var prop in navigator) {
            document.write(prop + ': ' + navigator[prop] + '<br>');
          }
        </script>
      </div>
    </body>
</html>
```

Figure 9-3 shows the output of Listing 9-1 when opened in a web browser.

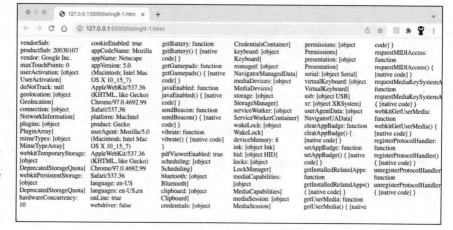

FIGURE 9-3:
Listing all the
properties of
the Navigator
object with
their values.

© John Wiley & Sons

If you run Listing 9-1 yourself, you'll notice something interesting about the output: The values for the appName and userAgent properties are seemingly just plain wrong. For example, the browser used to generate Figure 9-3 was Google Chrome, but appName lists it as Netscape.

This misleading value is a relic from the days when programmers used the properties of the Navigator object to detect whether a user was using a particular browser and supported certain features.

When new browsers, such as Chrome and Firefox, came along, those browsers adopted the Netscape browser appName value in order to make sure they were compatible with websites that detected features in this way.

WARNING

Today, browser detection isn't recommended, and you can use better ways to detect browser support for functionality than by looking at the appName property. The most common way to detect features today is by examining the DOM for objects associated with the feature you want to use. For example, if you want to find out if a browser supports the HTML5 audio element, you can use the following test:

```
let test_audio = document.createElement('audio');
if (test_audio.play) {
  console.log('Browser supports HTML5 audio');
} else {
  console.log("Browser doesn't support HTML5 audio");
}
```

The Window object

The main area of a web browser is called the *window.* This is the area into which HTML documents (and associated resources) load. Each tab in a web browser is represented in JavaScript by an instance of the Window object. The Window object's properties are listed in Table 9-2.

Some of the most common uses for the window properties include

>> Opening a new location in the browser window

>> Finding the size of a browser window

>> Returning to a previously open page (as in the Back button functionality)

Opening a web page with the window.location property

Getting the value of the window.location property will return the URL of the current page. Setting the value of the window.location property with a new URL causes the browser to load that web page in the window.

Listing 9-2 is a web page with a script that requests a web page address from the user and then loads that page in the current browser window.

TABLE 9-2

The Window Object's Properties

Property	Use
closed	A Boolean value indicating whether a window has been closed or not.
defaultStatus	Gets or sets the default text in the status bar of a window.
document	Refers to the document object for the window.
frameElement	Gets the element, such as <iframe> or <object>, that the window is embedded in.
frames	Lists all the subframes in the current window.
history	Gets the user's browser history for the current window.
innerHeight	Gets the inner height of the window.
innerWidth	Gets the inner width of the window.
length	Gets the number of frames in the window.
location	Gets the Location object for the window.
name	Gets or sets the name of the window.
navigator	Gets the Navigator object for the window.
opener	Gets the Window object that created the current window.
outerHeight	Gets the outer height of the window, including scrollbars and toolbars.
pageXOffset	Gets the number of pixels that have been scrolled horizontally in the window.
pageYOffset	Gets the number of pixels that have been scrolled vertically in the window.
parent	Refers to the parent of the current window.
screen	Refers to the Screen object of the window.
screenLeft	Gets the horizontal pixel distance from the left side of the main screen to the left side of the current window.
screenTop	Gets the vertical pixel distance from the top of the window relative to the top of the screen.
screenX	Gets the horizontal coordinate relative to the screen.
screenY	Gets the vertical coordinate relative to the screen.
self	Refers to the current window.
top	Refers to the topmost browser window.

LISTING 9-2: **A Script for Loading a Web Page in the Browser Window Using the window.location Property**

```html
<html>
  <head>
    <script>
      function loadNewPage(url) {
        window.location = url;
      }
    </script>
  </head>
  <body>
    <script>
      let newURL = prompt('
          Please enter a web page address!
        ');
      loadNewPage(newURL);
    </script>
  </body>
</html>
```

Figure 9-4 shows the output of Listing 9-2.

FIGURE 9-4:
The window.
location
property
in action.

© John Wiley & Sons

Determining the size of a browser window

When you're designing a website or a web application to work and function on different types of devices (a technique known as *responsive design*), knowing the size of the web browser, particularly the width, is critical.

The `window.innerWidth` and `window.innerHeight` properties give you this information, in pixels, for the current web browser window.

Using CSS to determine the size of a browser window is also possible and quite common. However, there are some differences in how CSS and JavaScript treat scrollbars that may influence which technique you decide to use.

Try a simple responsive design example using JavaScript. Run the program in Listing 9-3 in your web browser. If your web browser window width is below 500 pixels, one message will be displayed. If your window's width is greater than 500 pixels, a different message will be displayed.

LISTING 9-3: **Changing a Web Page Based on the Width of the Window**

```html
<html>
  <head>
    <title>Adapting to the window.innerWidth</title>
  </head>
  <body>
    <script>
      let currentWidth = window.innerWidth;
      if (currentWidth > 500) {
        document.write('<h1>Your window is big.</h1>');
      } else {
        document.write('<h1>Your window is small.</h1>');
      }
    </script>
  </body>
</html>
```

To test the responsive design example in Listing 9-3, follow these steps:

1. **In your web browser, open an HTML document containing the code in Listing 9-3.**

If your window is more than 500px wide when you open your page, you'll see a message that your window is big.

2. **Drag the lower-right corner of your browser to make the window as narrow as you can, as shown in Figure 9-5.**

3. **Click your browser's refresh button, or press Command+R (on Mac) or Ctrl+R (on Windows), to reload the page.**

   Notice that the message on the page now says your browser's window is small.

FIGURE 9-5:
Displaying a
different message
for narrow
browser width.

Creating a Back button using location and history

The `history` property of the `window` object is a read-only reference to the history object, which stores information about the pages the user has accessed in the current browser window. By far the most common use of the `history` object is to enable buttons that return the user to a previously viewed page, as shown in Listing 9-4.

LISTING 9-4: **Implementing a Back Button in a Web Application**

```html
<html>
  <head>
    <title>Creating a Back button</title>
    <script>
      function takeMeBack() {
        window.location(history.go(-1));
      }
      function getHistoryLength() {
        var l = window.history.length;
        return l;
      }
    </script>
  </head>
  <body>
    <script>
      var historyLength = getHistoryLength();
      document.write(
        "<p>Welcome! The number of pages you've visited in this
window is: " +
          historyLength +
          ".</p>"       );
    </script>
    <br/>
    <a href="javascript:void(0);" onclick="takeMeBack();">Go
Back</a>
  </body>
</html>
```

To use the Back button in Listing 9-4, follow these steps:

1. **Open a new browser window and visit any page you like, such as www.watzthis.com.**

2. **While in that same browser window, open an HTML document containing the code in Listing 9-4.**

3. **Click the Go Back link.**

Your browser will take you back to the last page you visited before the one containing the Back button.

TIP

Care to guess what happens if you open Listing 9-4 in a new browser tab before accessing any other web pages in that tab? If you guessed that nothing happens, you're correct! If only one page (the current one) has been displayed in a window, there's nothing to go back to.

Using the Window object's methods

In addition to its properties, the `Window` object also has some useful methods that JavaScript programmers should know and use. Table 9-3 shows the complete list of these methods.

TABLE 9-3

The Window Object's Methods

Method	Use
`alert()`	Displays an alert box with a message and an OK button.
`atob()`	Decodes a base-64 encoded string.
`blur()`	Causes the current window to lose focus.
`clearInterval()`	Cancels the timer set using `setInterval()`.
`clearTimeout()`	Cancels the timer set using `setTimeout()`.
`close()`	Closes the current window or notification.
`confirm()`	Displays a dialog box with an optional message and two buttons; OK and Cancel.
`createPopup()`	Creates a popup window.
`focus()`	Sets the current window into focus.
`moveBy()`	Moves the current window by a specified amount.
`moveTo()`	Relocates a window to a specified position.
`open()`	Opens a new window.
`print()`	Prints the contents of the current window.
`prompt()`	Displays a dialog box prompting the user for input.
`resizeBy()`	Resizes the window by a specified number of pixels.

Method	Use
resizeTo()	Resizes a window to a specified height and width.
scrollBy()	Scrolls the document by a specified amount.
scrollTo()	Scrolls the document to a specific set of coordinates.
setInterval()	Calls a function or executes an expression repeatedly at specified intervals (in milliseconds).
setTimeout()	Calls a function or executes an expression after a specified interval (in milliseconds).
stop()	Stops the current window from loading.

REMEMBER

A method is just another name for a function that's contained within an object.

Chapter **10**

Manipulating Documents with the DOM

"No object is mysterious. The mystery is your eye."

— ELISABETH BOWEN

U nderstanding the DOM is key to being able to manipulate the text or HTML in a web page. Using the DOM, you can create animations, update data without refreshing web pages, move objects around in a browser, and much more!

Understanding the DOM

The Document Object Model (DOM) is the interface for JavaScript to talk to and work with HTML documents inside of browser windows. The DOM can be visualized as an inverted tree, with each part of the HTML document branching off its containing part.

Listing 10-1 is the markup for a web page. The DOM representation is shown in Figure 10-1.

LISTING 10-1: **An HTML Document**

```html
<html>
<head>
  <title>Bob's Appliances</title>
</head>
<body>
  <header>
    <img src="logo.gif" width="100"
         height="100" alt="Site Logo">
  </header>
  <div>
    <h1>Welcome to Bob's</h1>
    <p>The home of quality appliances</p>
  </div>
  <footer>
    copyright &copy; Bob
  </footer>
</body>
</html>
```

A DOM tree is made up of individual components, called *nodes.* The main node, from which every other node springs, is called the *document node.* The node under the document node is the *root element node.* For HTML documents, the root node is the one created by the html element. After the root node, every element, attribute, and piece of content in the document is represented by a node in the tree that comes from another node in the tree.

The DOM has several different types of nodes:

» **Document node:** The entire HTML document is represented in this node

» **Element nodes:** The HTML elements

» **Attribute nodes:** The attributes associated with elements

» **Text nodes:** The text content of elements

» **Comment nodes:** The HTML comments in a document

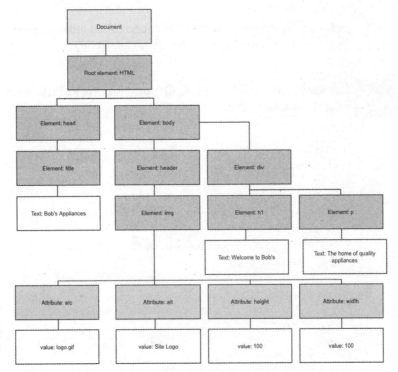

Understanding Node Relationships

HTML DOM trees resemble family trees in the hierarchical relationship between nodes. In fact, the technical terms used to describe relationships between nodes in a tree take their names from familial relationships.

>> Every node, except the root node, has one *parent*.

>> Each node may have any number of *children*.

>> Nodes with the same parent are *siblings*.

Because HTML documents often have multiple elements that are of the same type, the DOM allows you to access distinct elements in a node list using an index number. For example, you can refer to the first `<p>` element in a document as p[0], and the second `<p>` element node as p[1].

WARNING

Although a node list may look like an array, it's not. You can loop through the contents of a node list, but you can't use array methods on node lists.

In Listing 10-2, the three ⟨p⟩ elements are all children of the ⟨div⟩ element. Because they have the same parent, they are siblings.

LISTING 10-2: **Demonstration of Parent, Child, and Sibling Relationships in an HTML Document**

```
<html>
<head>
  <title>The HTML Family</title>
</head>
<body>
  <section> <!-- proud parent of 3 p elements, child of body -->
    <p>First</p>
  <!-- 1st child of section element, sibling of 2 p elements -->
    <p>Second</p>
  <!-- 2nd p child of section element, sibling of 2 p elements -->
    <p>Third</p>
  <!-- 3rd p child of section element, sibling of 2 p elements -->
  </section>
</body>
</html>
```

TECHNICAL STUFF

In Listing 10-2, the HTML comments are also children of the section element. The last comment before the closing section tag is called the *last child* of the section.

By understanding the relationships between document nodes, you can use the DOM tree to find any element within a document.

Listing 10-3 is an HTML document containing a script that outputs all the child nodes of the section element.

LISTING 10-3: **Displaying the Child Nodes of the section Element**

```
<html>
  <head>
    <title>The HTML Family</title>
  </head>
  <body>
    <section> <!-- proud parent of 3 p elements,
                 child of body -->
```

```
   <p>First</p> <!-- 1st child of section element,
                    sibling of 2 p elements -->
   <p>Second</p>
<!-- 2nd p child of section element,
                    sibling of 2 p elements -->
   <p>Third</p>
<!-- 3rd p child of section element,
                    sibling of 2 p elements -->
  </section>
  <h1>Nodes in the section element</h1>
  <script>
    let myNodelist = document.body.childNodes[1].childNodes;
    for (let i = 0; i < myNodelist.length; i++) {
      document.write(myNodelist[i] + '<br>');
    }
  </script>
 </body>
</html>
```

Figure 10-2 shows what the output of Listing 10-3 looks like in a browser. Notice that the first child node of the section element is a text node. If you look closely at the HTML markup in Listing 10-3, you'll see that there is a single space between the opening section tag and the comment. Even something as simple as a single space (or a tab or a line break) creates a node in the DOM tree. This fact needs to be taken into consideration when you're navigating the DOM using relationships between nodes.

The HTML DOM also provides a couple of keywords for navigating nodes using their positions relative to their siblings or parents. The relative properties are:

>> firstChild: References the first child of a node

>> lastChild: References the last child of the node

>> nextSibling: References the next node with the same parent node

>> previousSibling: References the previous node with the same parent node

Listing 10-4 shows how you can use these relative properties to traverse the DOM.

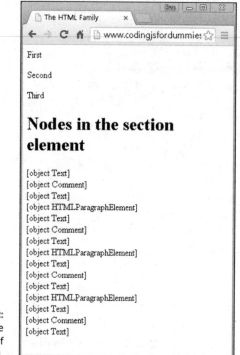

FIGURE 10-2:
Viewing the
output of
Listing 10-3.

© John Wiley & Sons

LISTING 10-4: **Using firstChild and lastChild to Highlight Navigation Links**

```html
<html>
  <head>
    <title>Iguanas Are No Fun</title>
    <script>
      function boldFirstAndLastNav() {
        document.body.childNodes[1].firstChild.style
          .fontWeight = 'bold';
        document.body.childNodes[1].lastChild.style
          .fontWeight = 'bold';
      }
    </script>
  </head>
  <body>
    <nav>
      <a href="home.html">Home</a> |
      <a href="why.html">Why Are Iguanas No Fun?</a> |
      <a href="what.html">What Can Be Done?</a> |
      <a href="contact.html">Contact Us</a>
```

```
    </nav>
    <p>Iguanas are no fun to be around. Use the links
       above to learn more.</p>
    <script>
      boldFirstAndLastNav();
    </script>
  </body>
</html>
```

Notice in Listing 10-4 that all the spacing must be removed between the elements within the `<nav>` element for the `firstChild` and `lastChild` properties to access the correct elements that we want to select and style.

Figure 10-3 shows what the document in Listing 10-4 looks like when previewed in a browser. Notice that just the first and last links in the navigation are bold.

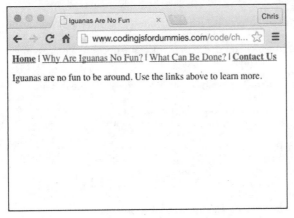

FIGURE 10-3:
Previewing
Listing 10-4 in a
browser.

© John Wiley & Sons

This is the first example in which we use the DOM to make a change to existing elements within the document. However, this method of selecting elements is almost never used. It's too prone to mistakes and too difficult to interpret and use.

In the next section, you see that the DOM provides you with much easier ways of traversing and manipulating nodes than counting children.

Using the Document Object's Properties and Methods

The Document object provides properties and methods for working with HTML documents. The complete list of Document object properties is shown in Table 10-1. The Document object's methods are shown in Table 10-2.

TABLE 10-1 The Document Object's Properties

Property	Use
anchors	Gets a list of all anchors (`<a>` elements with name attributes) in the document.
baseURI	Gets the base URI of the document.
body	Gets the `<body>` or `<frameset>` node of the document body.
cookie	Gets or sets the name/value pairs of cookies in the document.
doctype	Gets the Document Type Declaration associated with the document.
documentElement	Gets the element that is the root of the document (for example, the `<html>` element of an HTML document).
documentMode	Gets the mode used by the browser to render the document.
documentURI	Gets or sets the location of the document.
domain	Gets the domain name of the server that loaded the document.
embeds	Gets a list of all `<embed>` elements in the document.
forms	Gets a collection of all `<form>` elements in the document.
head	Gets the `<head>` element in the document.
images	Gets a list of all `<img>` elements in the document.
implementation	Gets the DOMImplementation object that handles the document.
lastModified	Gets the date and time the current document was last modified.
links	Gets a collection of all `<area>` and `<a>` elements in the document that contain the href attribute.
readyState	Gets the loading status of the document. Returns loading while the document is loading, interactive when it has finished parsing, and complete when it has completed loading.
referrer	Gets the URL of the page that the current document was linked from.

Property	Use
scripts	Gets a list of `<scripts>` elements in the document.
title	Gets or sets the title of the document.
URL	Gets the full URL of the document.

TABLE 10-2   **The Document Object's Methods**

Method	Use
addEventListener()	Assigns an event handler to the document.
adoptNode()	Adopts a node from an external document.
close()	Finishes the output writing stream of the document that was previously opened with document.open().
createAttribute()	Creates an attribute node.
createComment()	Creates a comment node.
createDocumentFragment()	Creates an empty document fragment.
createElement()	Creates an element node.
createTextNode()	Creates a text node.
getElementById()	Gets the element that has the specified ID attribute.
getElementsByClassName()	Gets all elements with the specified class name.
getElementsByName()	Gets all elements with the specified name.
getElementsByTagName()	Gets all elements with the specified tag name.
importNode()	Copies and imports a node from an external document.
normalize()	Clears the empty text nodes and joins adjacent nodes.
open()	Opens a document for writing.
querySelector()	Gets the first element that matches the specified group of selector(s) in the document.
querySelectorAll()	Gets a list of all the elements that match the specified selector(s) in the document.
removeEventListener()	Clears an event handler that had been added using the .addEventListener() method from the document.
renameNode()	Renames an existing node.
write()	Writes JavaScript code or HTML expressions to a document.
writeIn()	Writes JavaScript code or HTML expressions to a document and adds a new line character after each statement.

Using the Element Object's Properties and Methods

The Element object provides properties and methods for working with HTML elements within a document. Table 10-3 shows all the properties of the Element object. Table 10-4 lists all the methods of the Element object.

TABLE 10-3   The Element Object's properties

Method	Use
accessKey	Gets or sets the accesskey attribute of the element.
attributes	Gets a collection of all the element's attributes registered to the specified node (returns a NameNodeMap).
childElementCount	Gets the number of child elements in the specified node.
childNodes	Gets a list of the element's child nodes.
children	Gets a list of the element's child elements.
classList	Gets the class name(s) of the element.
className	Gets or sets the value of the class attribute of the element.
clientHeight	Gets the inner height of an element, including padding.
clientLeft	Gets the left border width of the element.
clientTop	Gets the top border width of the element.
clientWidth	Gets the width of the element, including padding.
contentEditable	Gets or sets whether the element is editable.
dir	Gets or sets the value of the dir attribute of the element.
firstChild	Gets the first child node of the element.
firstElementChild	Gets the first child element of the element.
id	Gets or sets the value of the id attribute of the element.
innerHTML	Gets or sets the content of the element.
isContentEditable	Returns true if the content of an element is editable; returns false if it is not editable.
lang	Gets or sets the base language of the elements attribute.
lastChild	Gets the last child node of the element.

Method	Use
lastElementChild	Gets the last child element of the element.
namespaceURI	Gets the namespace URI for the first node in the element.
nextSibling	Gets the next node at the same node level.
nextElement Sibling	Gets the next element at the same node level.
nodeName	Gets the current node's name.
nodeType	Gets the current node's type.
nodeValue	Gets or sets the value of the node.
offsetHeight	Gets the height of the element, including vertical padding, borders, and scrollbar.
offsetWidth	Gets the width of the element, including horizontal padding, borders, and scrollbar.
offsetLeft	Gets the horizontal offset position of the element.
offsetParent	Gets the offset container of the element.
offsetTop	Gets the vertical offset position of the element.
ownerDocument	Gets the root element (document node) for an element.
parentNode	Gets the parent node of the element.
parentElement	Gets the parent element node of the element.
previousSibling	Gets the previous node at the same node tree level.
previousElement Sibling	Gets the previous element node at the same node tree level.
scrollHeight	Gets the entire height of the element, including padding.
scrollLeft	Gets or sets the number of pixels the element's content is scrolled horizontally.
scrollTop	Gets or sets the number of pixels the element's content is scrolled vertically.
scrollWidth	Gets the entire width of the element, including padding.
style	Gets or sets the value of the style attribute of the element.
tabIndex	Gets or sets the value of the tabindex attribute of the element.
tagName	Gets the tag name of the element.
textContent	Gets or sets the textual content of the node and its descendants.
title	Gets or sets the value of the title attribute of the element.
length	Gets the number of nodes in the NodeList.

TABLE 10-4   **The Element Object's Methods**

Method	Use
addEventLIstener()	Registers an event handler to the element.
appendChild()	Inserts a new child node to the element (as a last child node).
blur()	Eliminates focus from the element.
click()	Replicates a mouse-click on the element.
cloneNode()	Clones the element.
compareDocumentPosition()	Compares the document position of two elements.
contains()	Yields true if the node is a descendant of a node; otherwise, yields false.
focus()	Gives focus to the element.
getAttribute()	Gets the specified attribute value of the element node.
getAttributeNode()	Gets the specified attribute node.
getElementsByClassName()	Gets a collection of all child elements with the stated class name.
getElementsByTagName()	Gets a collection of all the child elements with the stated tag name.
getFeature()	Gets an object that implements the APIs of the stated feature.
hasAttribute()	Yields true if the element has the stated attribute; otherwise, yields false.
hasAttributes()	Yields true if the element has any attributes; otherwise, yields false.
hasChildNodes()	Yields true if the element has any child nodes; otherwise, yields false.
insertBefore()	Enters a new child node before the stated existing node.
isDefaultNamespace()	Yields true if the stated namespaceURI is the default; otherwise, yields false.
isEqualNode()	Evaluates to see whether two elements are equal.
isSameNode()	Evaluates to see whether two elements are the same node.
isSupported()	Yields true if the stated feature is supported on the element.
normalize()	Joins the specified nodes with their adjacent nodes and removes any empty text nodes.
querySelector()	Gets the first child element that matches the stated CSS selector(s) of the element.

Method	Use
querySelectorAll()	Gets all the child elements that match the stated CSS selector(s) of the element.
removeAttribute()	Takes the stated attribute out of the element.
removeAttributeNode()	Takes the stated attribute node out of the element and retrieves the removed node.
removeChild()	Removes the stated child node.
replaceChild()	Replaces the specified child node with another.
removeEventListener()	Removes the specified event handler.
setAttribute()	Changes or sets the stated attribute to the specified value.
setAttributeNode()	Changes or sets the stated attribute node.
toString()	Changes an element to a string.
item()	Gets the node at the stated index in the NodeList.

Working with the Contents of Elements

You can display node types and node values by using the HTML DOM. You also can set property values of elements within the DOM using the Element object. When you use JavaScript to set the properties of DOM elements, the new values are reflected in real time within the HTML document.

Changing the properties of elements in a web document in order to reflect them instantly in the browser, without needing to refresh or reload the web page, is a cornerstone of what used to be called Web 2.0.

innerHTML

The most important property of an element that you can modify through the DOM is the innerHTML property.

The innerHTML property of an element contains everything between the beginning and ending tag of the element. For example, in the following code, the innerHTML property of the div element contains a p element and its text node child:

```
<body><div><p>This is some text.</p>
```

```
</div></body>
```

TECHNICAL STUFF

It's very common in web programming to create empty `div` elements in your HTML document and then use the `innerHTML` property to dynamically insert HTML into the elements.

To retrieve and display the value of the `innerHTML` property, you can use the following code:

```
let getTheInner = document.body.firstChild.innerHTML;
document.write (getTheInner);
```

In the preceding code, the value that will be output by the `document.write()` method is

```
<p>This is some text.</p>
```

Setting the `innerHTML` property is done in the same way that you set the property of any object:

```
document.body.firstChild.innerHTML = "Hi there!";
```

The result of running the preceding JavaScript will be that the `p` element and the sentence of text in the original markup will be replaced with the words `"Hi There!"` The original HTML document remains unchanged, but the DOM representation and the rendering of the web page will be updated to reflect the new value. Because the DOM representation of the HTML document is what the browser displays, the display of your web page will also be updated.

Setting attributes

To set the value of an HTML attribute, you can use the `setAttribute()` method:

```
document.body.firstChild.innerHTML.setAttribute("class",
   "myclass");
```

The result of running this statement is that the first child element of the body element will be given a new attribute named `"class"` with a value of `"myclass"`.

Getting Elements by ID, Tag Name, or Class

The `getElementBy` methods provide easy access to any element or groups of elements in a document without relying on parent/child relationships of nodes. The three most used ways to access elements are

» getElementById

» getElementsByTagName

» getElementsByClassName

getElementById

By far the most widely used method for selecting elements, getElementById is essential to modern web development. With this handy little tool, you can find and work with any element simply by referencing a unique id attribute. No matter what else happens in the HTML document, getElementById will always be there for you and will reliably select the exact element that you want.

Listing 10-5 demonstrates the awesome power of getElementById to enable you to keep all your JavaScript together in your document or to modularize your code. By using getElementById, you can work with any element, anywhere in your document just as long as you know its id.

LISTING 10-5: **Using getElementById to Select Elements**

```html
<html>
  <head>
    <title>Using getElementById</title>
    <script>
      function calculateMPG(miles, gallons) {
        document.getElementById('displayMiles').innerHTML = parseInt(miles);
        document.getElementById('displayGallons').innerHTML = parseInt(gallons);
        document.getElementById('displayMPG').innerHTML = miles / gallons;
      }
    </script>
  </head>
  <body>
    <p>You drove <span id="displayMiles">___</span> miles.</p>
    <p>You used <span id="displayGallons">___</span> gallons of gas.</p>
    <p>
      Your MPG is <span id="displayMPG">___</span>.
      <script>
        let milesDriven = prompt('Enter miles driven');
        let gallonsGas = prompt('Enter the gallons of gas used');
        calculateMPG(milesDriven, gallonsGas);
      </script>
    </p>
  </body>
</html>
```

---

getElementsByTagName

The getElementsByTagName method returns a node list of all the elements with the specified tag name. For example, in Listing 10-6, getElementsByTagName is used to select all h1 elements and change their innerHTML properties to sequential numbers.

LISTING 10-6: **Using getElementsByTagName to Select and Change Elements**

```html
<html>
  <head>
    <title>Using getElementsByTagName</title>
    <script>
      function numberElements(tagName) {
        let getTags = document.getElementsByTagName(tagName);
        for (let i = 0; i < getTags.length; i++) {
          getTags[i].innerHTML = i + 1;
        }
      }
    </script>
  </head>
  <body>
    <h1>this text will go away</h1>
    <h1>this will get overwritten</h1>
    <h1>JavaScript will erase this</h1>
    <script>
      numberElements('h1');
    </script>
  </body>
</html>
```

getElementsByClassName

The getElementsByClassName method works in much the same way as the getElementsByTagName, but it uses the values of the class attribute to select elements. The function in Listing 10-7 selects elements with a class of "error" and will change the value of their innerHTML property.

LISTING 10-7: **Using getElementsByClassName to Select and Change Elements**

```html
<html>
  <head>
    <title>Using getElementsByClassName</title>
    <script>
      function checkMath(result) {
        let userMath = document.getElementById('answer1').value;
        let errors = document.getElementsByClassName('error');
        if (parseInt(userMath) != parseInt(result)) {
          errors[0].innerHTML =
            'That\'s wrong. You entered ' +
            userMath +
            '. The answer is ' +
            result;
        } else {
          errors[0].innerHTML = 'Correct!';
        }
      }
    </script>
  </head>
  <body>
    <label for="number1">4+1 = </label
    ><input type="text" id="answer1" value=""/>
    <button id="submit" onclick="checkMath(4+1);">Check your math!</button>
    <h1 class="error"></h1>
  </body>
</html>
```

The result of running Listing 10-7 in a web browser and entering a wrong answer is shown in Figure 10-4.

TECHNICAL STUFF

Notice that Listing 10-7 uses an `onclick` attribute inside the `button` element. This is an example of a DOM event handler attribute. You can find out more about event handlers in Book 3, Chapter 11.

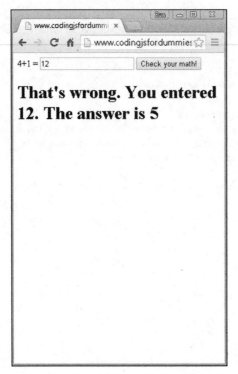

FIGURE 10-4:
Using the get
Elements
ByClassName to
select an element
for displaying an
error message.

Using the Attribute Object's Properties

The Attribute object provides properties for working with attributes within the HTML elements. Table 10-5 lists all the Attribute object's properties.

TABLE 10-5 ## The Attribute Object's Properties

Property	Use
isId	Yields true if the attribute is an id; otherwise, yields false.
name	Gets the name of the attribute.
value	Gets or sets the value of the attribute.
specified	Yields true if the attribute has been specified; otherwise, yields false.

Creating and Appending Elements

To create a new element in an HTML document, use the `document.create Element()` method. When you use `createElement()`, a new beginning and end tag of the type you specify will be created.

Listing 10-8 shows an example of how you can use this method to dynamically create a list in an HTML document from an array.

Using document.createElement() to Generate a Table from an Array

```html
<html>
  <head>
    <title>Generating a list</title>
  </head>
  <body>
    <h1>Here are some types of balls</h1>
    <ul id="ballList"></ul>
    <script>
      let typeOfBall = ['basket', 'base', 'soccer', 'foot', 'hand'];
      for (let i = 0; i < typeOfBall.length; i++) {
        let listElement = document.createElement('li');
        listElement.innerHTML = typeOfBall[i];
        document.getElementById('ballList').appendChild(listElement);
      }
    </script>
  </body>
</html>
```

Removing Elements

For all the great things that it lets you do with HTML documents, the HTML DOM is not highly regarded by professional JavaScript programmers. It has a number of oddities and tends to make some things more difficult than they should be.

One of the big faults with the DOM is that it doesn't provide a way to directly remove an element from a document. Instead, you have to tell the DOM to find the parent of the element you want to remove and then tell the parent to remove its child. It sounds a little confusing, but Listing 10-9 should clear it all up.

LISTING 10-9: **Removing an Element from a Document**

```html
<html>
  <head>
    <title>Remove an element</title>
    <script>
      function removeFirstParagraph() {
        let firstPara = document.getElementById('firstparagraph');
        firstPara.parentNode.removeChild(firstPara);
      }
    </script>
  </head>
  <body>
    <div id="gibberish">
      <p id="firstparagraph">
        Lorem ipsum dolor sit amet, consectetur adipiscing elit. Vestibulum
        molestie pulvinar ante, a volutpat est sodales et. Ut gravida justo ac
        leo euismod, et tempus magna posuere. Cum sociis natoque penatibus et
        magnis dis parturient montes, nascetur ridiculus mus. Integer non mi
        iaculis, facilisis risus et, vestibulum lorem. Sed quam ex, placerat nec
        tristique id, mattis fringilla ligula. Maecenas a pretium justo.
        Suspendisse sit amet nibh consectetur, tristique tellus quis, congue
        arcu. Etiam pellentesque dictum elit eget semper. Phasellus orci neque,
        semper ac tortor ac, laoreet ultricies enim.
      </p>
    </div>
    <button onclick="removeFirstParagraph();">That's Gibberish!</button>
  </body>
</html>
```

When you run Listing 10-9 in a browser and press the button, the `onclick` event calls the `removeFirstParagraph()` function.

The first thing `removeFirstParagraph()` does is select the element that you actually want to remove, the element with the `id = "firstparagraph"`. Then, the script selects the parent node of the first paragraph. It then uses the `removeChild()` method to remove the first paragraph.

Chapter **11**

Using Events in JavaScript

"And now, the sequence of events in no particular order:"

— DAN RATHER

Web pages are much more than just static displays of text and graphics. JavaScript gives web pages interactivity and the ability to perform useful work. An important part of JavaScript's ability to perform useful functions in the browser is its ability to respond to events.

Knowing Your Events

Events are the things that happen within the browser (such as a page loading) and things the user does (such as clicking, pressing keys on the keyboard, moving the mouse, and so on). Events happen all the time in the browser.

The HTML DOM gives JavaScript the ability to identify and respond to events in a web browser. Events can be divided into groups according to what HTML elements or browser objects they apply to. Table 11-1 lists events that are supported by every HTML element.

TABLE 11-1 **Events Supported by All HTML Elements**

Event	Occurs When . . .
abort	The loading of a file is aborted.
change	An elements value has changed since losing and regaining focus.
click	A mouse has been clicked on an element.
dblclick	A mouse has been clicked twice on an element.
input	The value of an <input> or <textarea> element is changed.
keydown	A key is pressed down.
keyup	A key is released after being pressed.
mousedown	A mouse button has been pressed down on an element.
mouseenter	A mouse pointer is moved onto the element that has the listener attached.
mouseleave	A mouse pointer is moved off of the element that has the listener attached.
mousemove	A mouse pointer is moved over an element.
mouseout	A mouse pointer is moved off the element or one of its children that has the listener attached.
mouseover	A mouse pointer is moved onto the element or one of its children that the listener is attached to.
mouseup	A mouse button is released over an element.
mousewheel	A wheel button of a mouse is rotated.
reset	A form is reset.
select	Text has been selected.
submit	A form is submitted.

Other types of events are supported by every element other than the body and frameset elements. These are listed in Table 11-2.

Table 11-3 shows the events that are supported by the window object.

In addition to these events, many other specifications define events that can happen. For example, the File API has a series of events related to file loading, and the HTML5 Media specification contains events related to audio and video playback. As you can see, a lot of things are going on (or can go on) in your browser!

TABLE 11-2   **Events Supported by Every Element Except <body> and <frameset>**

Event	Occurs When . . .
blur	An element has gone out of focus.
error	A file failed to load.
focus	An element has come into focus.
load	A file and its attached files have finished loading.
resize	The document has been resized.
scroll	The document or an element has been scrolled.

TABLE 11-3   **Events Supported by the Window Object**

Event	Occurs When . . .
afterprint	The document print preview has been closed or the document has started printing.
beforeprint	The document print preview is open or the document is about to be printed.
beforeunload	The window, the document, and its included files are about to be unloaded.
hashchange	The part of the URL after the number sign (#) changes.
pagehide	The browser leaves a page in the browser history.
pageshow	The browser goes to a page in the session history.
popstate	The active session history item changes.
unload	The document or included file is being unloaded.

For a complete list of events, you can visit https://developer.mozilla. org/en-US/docs/Web/Events.

Handling Events

When JavaScript does something in response to these events, it's called *event handling*.

Over the years, browser makers have implemented several ways for JavaScript programs to handle events. As a result, the landscape of JavaScript events has been one of incompatibilities between browsers.

Today, JavaScript is getting to the point where the old, inefficient techniques for handling events can soon be discarded. However, because these older techniques are still widely used, it's important that they are covered here.

Using inline event handlers

The first system for handling events was introduced along with the first versions of JavaScript. It relies on special event handler attributes in HTML, including the `onclick` event handler.

The inline event handler attributes are formed by adding the prefix on to an event. To use them, add the event attribute to an HTML element. When the specified event occurs, the JavaScript within the value of the attribute will be performed. For example, Listing 11-1 pops up an alert when the link is clicked.

LISTING 11-1: **Attaching an onclick Event Handler to a Link Using the Inline Method**

```
<a href="home.html" onclick="alert('Go Home!');">Click Here To Go
    Home</a>
```

If you put this markup into an HTML document and click the link, you see an alert window with the words Go Home! When you dismiss the alert window, the link proceeds with the default event handler associated with the a element — namely, following the link in the href attribute.

In many cases, you may not want the default action associated with an element to happen. For example, what if you just wanted the alert window in Listing 11-1 to pop up without doing anything else?

JavaScript programmers have come up with several different methods to prevent default actions. One technique is to make the default action be something that is inconsequential. For example, by changing the value of the href attribute to a #, the link will point to itself:

```
<a href="#" onclick="alert('Go Home!');">Click Here</a>
```

A better method, however, is to tell the event handler to return a Boolean false value, which tells the default action not to run:

```
<a href="homepage.html" onclick="alert('Go Home!');return
    false">Click Here</a>
```

Another method of preventing the default action is to use the void operator, which you learned about in Book 3, Chapter 5.

Event handling using element properties

One of the biggest problems with the older, inline technique of assigning events to elements is that it violates one of the most important rules of programming: keeping presentation (how something looks) separate from functionality (what it does). Mixing up your event handlers and HTML tags makes your web pages more difficult to maintain, debug, and understand.

With version 3 of their browser, Netscape introduced a new event model that allowed programmers to attach events to elements as properties. Listing 11-2 shows an example of how this model works.

LISTING 11-2: **Attaching Events to Elements Using Event Properties**

```html
<html>
  <head>
    <title>Counting App</title>
    <script>
      // wait until the window is loaded before registering the onclick event
      window.onload = initializer;
      // create a global counting variable
      var theCount = 0;
      /**
Registers onclick event
*/
      function initializer() {
        document.getElementById('incrementButton').onclick = increaseCount;
      }
      /**
Increments theCount and displays result.
*/
      function increaseCount() {
        theCount++;
        document.getElementById('currentCount').innerHTML = theCount;
      }
    </script>
  </head>
  <body>
    <h1>Click the button to count.</h1>
    <p>Current Number: <span id="currentCount">0</span></p>
    <button id="incrementButton">Increase Count</button>
  </body>
</html>
```

One thing to notice about Listing 11-2 is that function names that are assigned to the event handler don't have parentheses after them. What's going on here is that the whole function is assigned to the event handler and is telling it "run this when this event happens," rather than actually using a function call. If you add the parentheses after the function name, the function will be executed, and its result will be assigned to the onclick event, which is not what you want.

Event handling using addEventListener

Although the previous two methods of event handling are very commonly used and are supported by every browser, a more modern and flexible way to handle events (and the recommended way) is to use the addEventListener() method.

The addEventListener method listens for events on any DOM node and triggers actions based on those events. When the function specified as an action for the event runs, it automatically receives a single argument, the Event object. By convention, we name this argument e.

addEventListener() has several benefits over using the DOM event attributes:

>> You can apply more than one event listener to an element.

>> It works on any node in the DOM tree, not just on elements.

>> It gives you more control over when it's activated.

Listing 11-3 demonstrates the use of the addEventListener method. This example has the same counting function as Listing 11-2, but it adds a second event handler to the button that increases the size of the number each time it's clicked.

LISTING 11-3: **Assigning an Event with addEventListener()**

```
<html>
  <head>
    <title>Counting App</title>
    <script>
      // wait until the window is loaded before registering the onclick event
      window.addEventListener('load', registerEvents, false);
      // create a global counting variable
      var theCount = 0;
      /**
       Registers onclick events
       */
      function registerEvents(e) {
        document
```

```
            .getElementById('incrementButton')
            .addEventListener('click', increaseCount, false);
        document
            .getElementById('incrementButton')
            .addEventListener('click', changeSize, false);
    }


    /**
     Increments theCount and displays result.
     */
    function increaseCount(e) {
        theCount++;
        document.getElementById('currentCount').innerHTML = theCount;
    }
    /**
     Change the font size of the count text
     */
    function changeSize(e) {
        document.getElementById('currentCount').style.fontSize = theCount;
    }
    </script>
  </head>
  <body>
    <h1>Click the button to count.</h1>
    <p>Current Number: <span id="currentCount">0</span></p>
    <button id="incrementButton">Increase Count</button>
  </body>
</html>
```

Figure 11-1 shows what the page created by Listing 11-3 looks like after an exciting afternoon of clicking the button.

The addEventListener method is implemented by using three arguments.

The first argument is the event type. Unlike the other two event-handling methods, addEventListener just wants the name of the event, without the on prefix.

The second argument is the function to call when the event happens. As with the event properties method of event handling, it's important to not use the parentheses here in order for the function to be assigned to the event handler, rather than the result of running the function.

FIGURE 11-1:
Attaching two
events to the
same element
increases the
possibilities!

© John Wiley & Sons

The third argument is a Boolean value (`true` or `false`) that indicates the order in which event handlers execute when an element with an event has a parent element that also is associated with an event.

When elements are nested, it's important to know which one will happen first. Figure 11-2 illustrates a common problem: The outer square is clickable, but so is the inner circle. When you click on the inner circle, should the event attached to the square happen first, or should the event attached to the circle happen first?

FIGURE 11-2:
Events within
events.

Most people would say that it makes sense that the circle event should happen first. However, when Microsoft implemented its version of events in Internet Explorer, it decided that the outer event (the square) should happen first.

Microsoft eventually lost, and today the default way for events to be handled in a situation like the one in Figure 11-2 is called *bubbling up.* Events on the inside-most element happen first and then bubble up to the outermost elements.

The other way to handle this scenario is called the *capture* method. In capture mode, the outermost events happen first, and the innermost events happen last. To use the capture method, set the last argument of the addEventListener method to true. In most cases, however, omitting the last argument of addEventListener or specifically setting it to false is what you'll want to do.

Listing 11-4 shows an example demonstrating why knowing the order in which event handlers execute is important. The h1 elements have click events, but so do words within that header.

LISTING 11-4: **Demonstrating Event Capture and Event Bubbling**

```html
<html>
  <head>
    <title>Event capturing vs. Event bubbling</title>
    <style>
      #theText {
        font-size: 18px;
      }
      h1 {
        border: 1px solid #000;
        background-color: #dadada;
      }
      #capEvent,
      #bubEvent {
        background-color: #666;
      }
    </style>
    <script>
      // wait until the window is loaded before registering the events
      window.addEventListener('load', registerEvents, false);
      /**
       Registers onclick events
       */
      function registerEvents(e) {
        document
          .getElementById('capTitle')
          .addEventListener('click', makeTiny, true);
        document
          .getElementById('capEvent')
          .addEventListener('click', makeHuge, true);
        document
```

(continued)

LISTING 11-4: *(continued)*

```
      .getElementById('bubTitle')
      .addEventListener('click', makeTiny, false);
    document
      .getElementById('bubEvent')
      .addEventListener('click', makeHuge, false);
    }
    function makeHuge(e) {
      console.log('making the text huge');
      document.getElementById('theText').style.fontSize = '80px';
    }
    function makeTiny(e) {
      console.log('making the text tiny');
      document.getElementById('theText').style.fontSize = '10px';
    }
  </script>
 </head>
 <body>
   <h1 id="capTitle">Event <span id="capEvent">capturing </span></h1>
   <h1 id="bubTitle">Event <span id="bubEvent">bubbling </span></h1>
   <p id="theText">Hello, Events!</p>
 </body>
</html>
```

Figure 11-3 shows what Listing 11-4 looks like in a web browser.

In Figure 11-3, when the word *capturing* is clicked, the event registered to the larger container fires first, followed by the event registered to the event containing the word capturing.

When you click the word *bubbling*, the event registered to that span fires first, followed by the event on its parent element.

Stopping propagation

In addition to bubbling and capturing, you can handle nested events in a third way: just do the single event and then stop. You can turn off bubbling and capturing for an event (or even for all events) by using the stopPropagation method.

TIP

If you don't need event propagation in your script, it's a good idea to turn it off because all that bubbling and capturing does use system resources and can make your website slower.

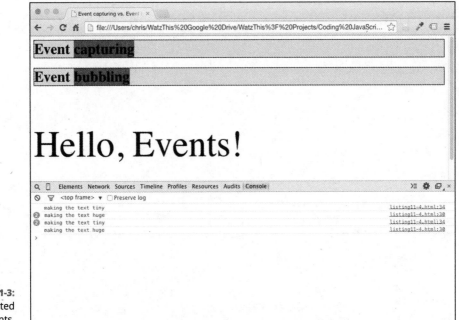

FIGURE 11-3:
Handling nested
events.

© John Wiley & Sons

Listing 11-5 demonstrates how to turn off event propagation.

LISTING 11-5: **Turning Off Event Propagation**

```
function load(e) {
  if (!e) var e = window.event; // set cancelBubble for IE 8 and earlier
  e.cancelBubble = true;
  if (e.stopPropagation) e.stopPropagation();
  document.getElementById('capTitle').addEventListener('click', makeTiny, true);
  document.getElementById('capEvent').addEventListener('click', makeHuge, true);
  document
    .getElementById('bubTitle')
    .addEventListener('click', makeTiny, false);
  document
    .getElementById('bubEvent')
    .addEventListener('click', makeHuge, false);
}
```

Chapter **12**

Integrating Input and Output

"Malfunction. Need Input."

— NUMBER 5, SHORT CIRCUIT (1986)

H andling user input and sending back results are basic and necessary functions for any computer program. In this chapter, you find out how JavaScript and HTML can work together to receive and output data.

Understanding HTML Forms

The primary way to get input from users of web applications is through HTML forms. HTML forms give web developers the ability to create text fields, drop-down selectors, radio buttons, checkboxes, and buttons. With CSS, you can adjust the look of a form to fit your particular website. JavaScript gives you the ability to enhance the functionality of your form.

The form element

All HTML forms are contained within a `form` element. The `form` element is the container that holds the input fields, buttons, checkboxes, and labels that make up a user input area. The `form` element acts much like any container element, such as a `div`, `article`, or `section`. But it also contains some attributes that tell the browser what to do with the user input from the form fields it contains.

Listing 12-1 shows an HTML form containing two input fields and a submit button.

LISTING 12-1: **Example of an HTML Page Containing a Form**

```
<html>
<head>
  <title>HTML form</title>
</head>
<body>
  <form action="subscribe.php" name="newsletterSubscribe"
  method="post">
    <label for="firstName">First Name: </label>
    <input type="text" name="firstName" id="firstName"><br>
    <label for="email">Email: <input type="text" name="email"
  id="email"></label><br>
    <input type="submit" value="Subscribe to our newsletter!">
  </form>
</body>
</html>
```

When you view this form in a web browser, it looks like Figure 12-1.

In the preceding example, the `form` element has three attributes:

» `action`: Tells the browser what to do with the user input. Often, the action is a server-side script.

» `name`: Specifies the name that the programmer assigned to this form. The name attribute of the form is useful for accessing the form using the DOM.

» `method`: Takes a value of either `get` or `post`, indicating whether the browser should send the data from the form in the URL or in the HTTP header.

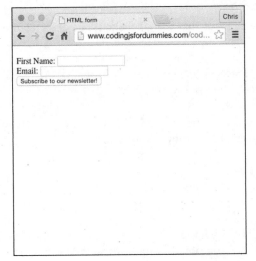

FIGURE 12-1:
An HTML form.

In addition to these three attributes, the `form` element can also contain several other attributes:

>> `accept–charset`: Indicates the character sets that the server accepts. Unless you're working with multilingual content, you can safely leave this attribute out.

>> `autocomplete`: Indicates whether the input elements of the form should use autocomplete in the browser.

>> `enctype`: Indicates the type of content that the form should submit to the server. For forms that are submitting only text data to the server, this should be set to `text/html`. If your form is submitting a file to the server (such as an uploaded graphic), the enctype should be `multipart/form–data`. The default value is `application/x–www–form–urlencoded`.

>> `novalidate`: A Boolean value indicating whether the input from the form should be validated by the browser on submit. If this attribute isn't specified, forms are validated by default.

>> `target`: Indicates where the response from the server should be displayed after the form is submitted. The default (`"_self"`) is to open the response in the same browser window where the form was. Another option is to open the response in a new window (`"_blank"`).

The label element

You can use the `label` element to associate an input field's description (label) with the input field. The `for` attribute of the `label` element takes the value of the id attribute of the element that the label should be associated with, as shown in this example:

```
<label for="firstName">First Name: </label>
<input type="text" name="firstName" id="firstName">
```

Another method for associating a label with a form field is to nest the form field within the label element, as shown in this example:

```
<label>First Name:
  <input type="text" name="firstName">
</label>
```

This method has the advantage of not requiring the input field to have an ID (which is often just a duplicate of its name attribute).

The input element

The HTML input element is the most fundamental form-related HTML element. Depending on the value of its type attribute, it causes the browser to display (or not display) several types of input fields.

Most commonly, the input element's type is set to "text", which creates a text input in the browser. The optional value attribute assigns a default value to the element, and the name attribute is the name that is paired with the value to form the name/value pair that can be accessed through the DOM and that is submitted along with the rest of the form values when the form is submitted.

A basic text input field looks like this:

```
<input type="text" name="streetAddress">
```

With HTML5, the input element gained a bunch of new possible type attribute values. These new values allow the web developer to more precisely specify the type of value that should be provided in the input. They also allow the web browser to provide controls that are better suited to the type of input that's required to do input validation and results in better web applications.

TECHNICAL STUFF

It may seem odd that this chapter focuses so much on the form capabilities of HTML, rather than jumping right into JavaScript. However, forms are an area where HTML can really reduce the workload of programmers, so it's vital that JavaScript programmers learn what can be accomplished with forms through HTML.

The input element's possible values for the type attribute are shown in Table 12-1.

TABLE 12-1

Possible Values for the input Element's type Attribute

Value	Description
button	A clickable button
checkbox	A checkbox
color	A color picker
date	A date control (year, month, and day)
datetime	A date and time control (year, month, day, hour, minute, second, and fraction of a second based on the UTC time zone)
datetime-local	A date and time control (year, month, day, hour, minute, second, and fraction of a second; no time zone)
email	A field for an email address
file	A file-select field and a Browse button
hidden	A hidden input field
image	A submit button using an image, rather that the default button
month	A month and year control
number	A number input field
password	A password filed
radio	A radio button
range	An input using a range of numbers, such as a slider control
reset	A reset button
search	A text field for entering a search string
submit	A submit button
tel	A field for entering a telephone number
text	Default; a single-line text field
time	A control for entering a time (no time zone)
url	A field for entering a URL
week	A week and year control (no time zone)

The select element

The HTML select element defines either a drop-down or a multiselect input. The select element contains option elements that are the choices that the user will have in the select control, as shown in Listing 12-2.

LISTING 12-2: **A Drop-Down Form Control, Created Using the select Element**

```
<select name="favoriteColor">
 <option value="red">red</option>
 <option value="blue">blue</option>
 <option value="green">green<option>
</select>
```

The form created by the markup in Listing 12-2 is shown in Figure 12-2.

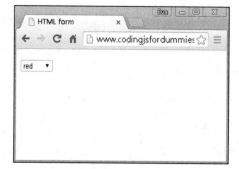

© John Wiley & Sons

FIGURE 12-2:
An HTML drop-down control.

The textarea element

The textarea element defines a multiline text input field:

```
<textarea name="description" rows="4" cols="30"></textarea>
```

The button element

The button element defines another way to create a clickable button:

```
<button name="myButton">Click The Button</button>
```

The button element can be used in place of input elements with the type attribute set to 'submit'. Or, you can use button elements anywhere you need a button, but where you don't want the submit action to happen.

WARNING

If you don't want the button to submit the form when clicked, you need to add a type attribute to it with the value of 'button'.

Working with the Form Object

The HTML DOM represents forms using the Form object. Through the Form object, you can get and set values of form fields, control the action that's taken when a user submits a form, and change the behavior of the form.

Using Form properties

The properties of the Form object match up with the attributes of the HTML form element (see the section earlier in this chapter called "The form element"). They're used for getting or setting the values of the HTML form element attributes with JavaScript. Table 12-2 lists all the properties of the Form object.

REMEMBER

DOM objects are representations of HTML pages. Their purpose is to give you access (also known as *programming interface*) to the different parts of the document through JavaScript. Anything within an HTML document can be accessed and changed with JavaScript by using the DOM.

You can find techniques for setting or getting the value of a form's properties in Book 3, Chapter 10. After referencing the form using one of these methods, you then access the property using dot notation or the square bracket method.

USING THE AUTOCOMPLETE ATTRIBUTE

The autocomplete attribute in an HTML form element sets the default autocomplete value for the input elements inside the form. If you want the browser to provide autocomplete functionality for every input in the form, set autocomplete to 'on'. If you want to be able to select which elements the browser can autocomplete or if your document provides its own autocomplete functionality (through JavaScript), set the form's autocomplete attribute to 'off', and then you can set the autocomplete attribute for each individual input element within the form.

TABLE 12-2   **Form Object Properties**

Property	Use
acceptCharset	Gets or sets a list of character sets that are supported by the server.
action	Gets or sets the value of the action attribute of the form element.
autocomplete	Gets or sets whether input elements can have their values automatically completed by the browser.
encoding	Tells the browser how to encode the form data (either as text or as a file). This property is synonymous with enctype.
enctype	Tells the browser how to encode the form data (either as text or as a file).
length	Gets the number of controls in the form.
method	Gets or sets the HTTP method the browser uses to submit the form.
name	Gets or sets the name of the form.
noValidate	Indicates that the form does not need to be validated upon submittal.
target	Indicates the place to display the results of a submitted form.

To get the value of the name property of the first form in a document, you could use the following statement:

```
document.getElementByTagName("form")[0].name
```

A more common way to access a form is by assigning it an id attribute and using getElementById to select it.

The DOM provides another, more convenient method for accessing forms: the forms collection. The forms collection lets you access the forms in a document in two different ways:

>> **By index number:** When a form element is created in the document, it is assigned an index number, starting with zero. To access the first form in the document, use document.forms[0].

>> **By name:** You can also access forms using the name attribute of the form element. For example, to get the value of the action property of a form with a name of subscribeForm, you would use document.forms.subscribeForm.action. Or you can use the square brackets method of accessing properties and write document.forms["subscribeForm"].action.

Using the Form object's methods

The Form object has two methods: reset and submit.

The reset method

The reset method clears any changes to the form's fields that were made after the page loaded and resets the default values. It does the same thing as the HTML reset button, which is created by using a type="reset" attribute with an input element, as shown in the following code:

```
<input type="reset" value="Clear the form">
```

The submit method

The submit method causes the form to submit its values according to the properties of the form (action, method, target, and so on). It does the same thing as the HTML submit button, which is created by using a type="submit" attribute with an input element, as shown in the following code:

```
<input type="submit" value="Submit the form">
```

Listing 12-3 demonstrates the use of the submit and reset methods, along with several of the Form object's properties.

LISTING 12-3: **Using the Form Object's Properties and Methods**

```
<html>
  <head>
    <title>Subscribe to our newsletter!</title>
    <script>
      function setFormDefaults() {
        document.forms.subscribeForm.method = 'post';
        document.forms.subscribeForm.target = '_blank';
        document.forms.subscribeForm.action =
          'http://watzthis.us9.list-manage.com/' +
          'subscribe/post?u=1e6d8741f7db587af747ec056&amp;id=663906e3ba';
        //register the button events
        document
          .getElementById('btnSubscribe')
          .addEventListener('click', submitForm);
        document
          .getElementById('btnReset')
          .addEventListener('click', resetForm);
      }
```

(continued)

LISTING 12-3: *(continued)*

```
     function submitForm() {
       document.forms.subscribeForm.submit();
     }
     function resetForm() {
       document.forms.subscribeForm.reset();
     }
  </script>
</head>
<body onload="setFormDefaults();">
  <form name="subscribeForm">
    <h2>Subscribe to our mailing list</h2>
    <label for="mce-EMAIL">Email Address </label>
    <input type="email" value="" name="EMAIL" id="mce-EMAIL"/>
    <button type="button" id="btnSubscribe">Subscribe!</button>
    <button type="button" id="btnReset">Reset</button>
  </form>
</body>
</html>
```

Accessing form elements

JavaScript offers several ways to access form input fields and their values. These ways are not all created equal, however, and differences of opinion exist among JavaScript programmers as to which technique is the best. The following list presents the different techniques and their benefits and drawbacks:

>> **Use the index number of the form and of its input fields.** For example, to access the first input field in the first form, you could use the following code:

```
document.forms[0].elements[0]
```

WARNING

Avoid the preceding technique because it relies on the structure of the document and the order of the elements within the form not to change. As soon as someone decides that the email field should come before the first name field in the form, your whole script will break.

>> **Use the name of the form and the name of the input field.** For example:

```
document.myForm.firstName
```

This technique has the benefit of being easy to read and easy to use. It's supported by every browser (and has been since very early in the development of the DOM).

» **Use** `getElementById` **to select the form and the name of the input field to select the input.** For example:

```
document.getElementById("myForm").firstName
```

This technique requires you to assign an `id` attribute to the form of the element. For example, the preceding code would match an input field named `firstName` inside of the following `form` element.

```
<form id="myForm" action="myaction.php">
  ...
</form>
```

» **Use a unique** `id` **attribute value on the field to access the field directly.** For example:

```
document.getElementById("firstName")
```

Something to remember when using the preceding technique is that if you have multiple forms on your page, you need to make sure that each form field has a unique `id` attribute (`id` attribute values must be unique anyway, so it's not really an issue).

Getting and setting form element values

The DOM gives you access to form elements' names and values using the name and value properties.

Listing 12-4 demonstrates the getting and setting of form input fields using a simple calculator application.

LISTING 12-4: **A Calculator App Demonstrating the Getting and Setting of Form Input Fields**

```
<html>
  <head>
    <title>Math Fun</title>
    <script>
      function registerEvents() {
        document.mathWiz.operate.addEventListener('click',
doTheMath, false);
      }
```

(continued)

LISTING 12-4: *(continued)*

```
function doTheMath() {
  let first = parseInt(document.mathWiz.numberOne.value);
  let second = parseInt(document.mathWiz.numberTwo.value);
  let operator = document.mathWiz.operator.value;
  let answer;
  switch (operator) {
    case 'add':
      answer = first + second;
      break;
    case 'subtract':
      answer = first - second;
      break;
    case 'multiply':
      answer = first * second;
      break;
    case 'divide':
      answer = first / second;
      break;
  }
  document.mathWiz.theResult.value = answer;
}
    </script>
  </head>
  <body onload="registerEvents();">
    <form name="mathWiz">
      <label>First Number: <input type="number"
name="numberOne"/></label
      ><br/>
      <label>Second Number: <input type="number"
name="numberTwo"/></label
      ><br/>
      <label
        >Operator:
        <select name="operator">
          <option value="add">+</option>
          <option value="subtract">-</option>
          <option value="multiply">*</option>
          <option value="divide">/</option>
        </select>
      </label>
      <br/>
```

```
    <input type="button" name="operate" value="Do the
Math!"/><br/>
    <label>Result: <input type="number" name="theResult"/> </
label>
  </form>
 </body>
</html>
```

Validating user input

One of the most common uses for JavaScript is to check, or validate, form input before submitting user input to the server. JavaScript form validation provides an extra safeguard against bad or potentially unsafe data making its way into a web application. It also provides users with instant feedback about whether they've made a mistake.

Some of the most common JavaScript input validation tasks have been replaced by HTML attributes in HTML5. However, due to browser incompatibilities, it's still a good practice to validate user-submitted data using JavaScript.

In the calculator program in Listing 12-4, the input type was set to number for the operand units. This should cause the browser to prevent the user from submitting non-numeric values into these fields. Because the number input type is relatively new, you can't always count on the browsers to support it, so using JavaScript user input validation is important.

Listing 12-5 demonstrates an input validation script. The important thing to notice here is that the action of the form has been set to the input validation function. The submit method of the form runs only after the tests in the input validation function have finished.

The line in the preceding code that does the real magic is this strange-looking one inside of the validate function:

```
if (/^\d+$/.test(first) && /^\d+$/.test(second)) {
```

The characters between / and / make up what's called a *regular expression*. A regular expression is a search pattern made up of symbols that represent groups of other symbols. In this case, we're using a regular expression to check whether the values the user entered are both numeric.

TIP

Input validation is such a common use for JavaScript that many different techniques have been created for doing it. Before you reinvent the wheel for your particular JavaScript application, do a search for *open source JavaScript input validation* and see whether any existing libraries of code can save you some time and give you more functionality.

LISTING 12-5: Performing Input Validation with JavaScript

```
<html>
  <head>
    <title>Math Fun</title>
    <script>
      function registerEvents() {
        document.mathWiz.operate.addEventListener('click', validate, false);
      }
      function validate() {
        let first = document.mathWiz.numberOne.value;
        let second = document.mathWiz.numberTwo.value;
        let operator = document.mathWiz.operator.value;
        let answer;
        if (/^\d+$/.test(first) && /^\d+$/.test(second)) {
          doTheMath();
        } else {
          alert('Error: Both numbers must be numeric');
        }
      }
      function doTheMath() {
        let first = parseInt(document.mathWiz.numberOne.value);
        let second = parseInt(document.mathWiz.numberTwo.value);
        let operator = document.mathWiz.operator.value;
        switch (operator) {
          case 'add':
            answer = first + second;
            break;
          case 'subtract':
            answer = first - second;
            break;
          case 'multiply':
            answer = first * second;
            break;
          case 'divide':
            answer = first / second;
            break;
        }
        document.mathWiz.theResult.value = answer;
      }
```

```
      </script>
   </head>
   <body onload="registerEvents();">
     <div id="formErrors"></div>
     <form name="mathWiz">
       <label>First Number: <input type="text" name="numberOne"/></label><br/>
       <label>Second Number: <input type="text" name="numberTwo"/></label><br/>
       <label
         >Operator:
         <select name="operator">
           <option value="add">+</option>
           <option value="subtract">-</option>
           <option value="multiply">*</option>
           <option value="divide">/</option>
         </select>
       </label>
       <br/>
       <input type="button" name="operate" value="Do the Math!"/><br/>
       <label>Result: <input type="number" name="theResult"/> </label>
     </form>
   </body>
</html>
```

Chapter **13**

Understanding Callbacks and Closures

"O, call back yesterday, bid time return."

— EARL OF SALISBURY, RICHARD II

Callbacks and closures are two of the most useful and widely used techniques in JavaScript. In this chapter, you find out how and why to pass functions as arguments to other functions.

What Are Callbacks?

REMEMBER

JavaScript functions are objects. This statement is the key to understanding many of the more advanced JavaScript topics, including callback functions.

Functions, like any other object, can be assigned to variables, be passed as arguments to other functions, and created within and returned from functions.

Passing functions as arguments

A *callback function* is a function that is passed as an argument to another function. Callback functions are a technique that's possible in JavaScript because of the fact that functions are objects.

Function objects contain a string with the code of the function. When you call a function by naming the function, followed by ( ), you're telling the function to execute its code. When you name a function or pass a function without the ( ), the function does not execute.

Here is an example of a callback function using the addEventListener method:

```
document.addEventListener('click',doSomething,false);
```

This method takes an event (click) and a Function object (doSomething) as arguments. The callback function doesn't execute right away. Instead, the addEventListener method executes the function when the event occurs.

Writing functions with callbacks

Here's a simple example function, doMath, that accepts a callback function as an argument:

```
function doMath(number1,number2,callback) {
  let result = callback(number1,number2);
  document.write ('The result is: ' + result);
}
```

This is a generic function for returning the result of any math operation involving two operands. The callback function that you pass to it specifies what actual operations will be done.

To call the doMath function, pass two number arguments and then a function as the third argument:

```
doMath(5,2,function(number1,number2){
  let calculation = number1 * number2 / 6;
  return calculation;
});
```

Listing 13-1 is a complete web page that contains the doMath function and then invokes it several times with different callback functions.

LISTING 13-1: Calling a Function with Different Callback Functions

```
<html>
  <head>
    <title>Introducing the doMath function</title>
    <script>
      function doMath(number1, number2, callback) {
        let result = callback(number1, number2);
        document.getElementById('theResult').innerHTML +=
          'The result is: ' + result + '<br>';
      }

      document.addEventListener(
        'DOMContentLoaded',
        function () {
          doMath(5, 2, function (number1, number2) {
            let calculation = number1 * number2;
            return calculation;
          });
          doMath(10, 3, function (number1, number2) {
            let calculation = number1 / number2;
            return calculation;
          });
          doMath(81, 9, function (number1, number2) {
            let calculation = number1 % number2;
            return calculation;
          });
        },
        false
      );
    </script>
  </head>
  <body>
    <h1>Do the Math</h1>
    <div id="theResult"></div>
  </body>
</html>
```

The result of running Listing 13-1 in a browser is shown in Figure 13-1.

Using named callback functions

In the examples in the preceding section, the callback functions were all written as anonymous functions. It's also possible to define named functions and then pass the name of the function as a callback function.

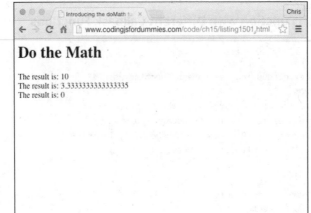

FIGURE 13-1:
Doing
calculations
using callbacks.

© John Wiley & Sons

REMEMBER

Anonymous functions are functions that you create without giving them names.

Using named functions as callbacks can reduce the visual code clutter that can come with using anonymous functions. Listing 13-2 shows an example of how to use a named function as a callback. This example also features the following two improvements over Listing 13-1:

>> A test has been added to the doMath function to make sure that the callback argument is actually a function.

>> It prints the code of the callback function before displaying the result of running it.

LISTING 13-2: **Using Named Functions as Callbacks**

```html
<html>
  <head>
    <title>doMath with Named Functions</title>
    <script>
      function doMath(number1, number2, callback) {
        if (typeof callback === 'function') {
          let result = callback(number1, number2);
          document.getElementById('theResult').innerHTML +=
            callback.toString() +
            '<br><br>The result is: ' +
            result +
            '<br><br>';
        }
      }
```

```
      function multiplyThem(number1, number2) {
        let calculation = number1 * number2;
        return calculation;
      }
      function divideThem(number1, number2) {
        let calculation = number1 / number2;
        return calculation;
      }
      function modThem(number1, number2) {
        let calculation = number1 % number2;
        return calculation;
      }
      document.addEventListener(
        'DOMContentLoaded',
        function () {
          doMath(5, 2, multiplyThem);
          doMath(10, 3, divideThem);
          doMath(81, 9, modThem);
        },
        false
      );
    </script>
  </head>
  <body>
    <h1>Do the Math</h1>
    <div id="theResult"></div>
  </body>
</html>
```

The result of running Listing 13-2 in a browser is shown in Figure 13-2.

Using named functions for callbacks has two advantages over using anonymous functions for callbacks:

>> It makes your code easier to read.

>> Named functions are multipurpose and can be used on their own or as callbacks.

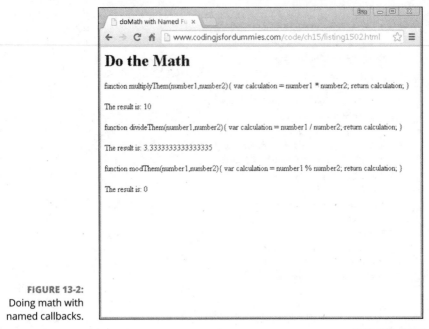

Do the Math

function multiplyThem(number1,number2){ var calculation = number1 * number2; return calculation; }

The result is: 10

function divideThem(number1,number2){ var calculation = number1 / number2; return calculation; }

The result is: 3.3333333333333335

function modThem(number1,number2){ var calculation = number1 % number2; return calculation; }

The result is: 0

© John Wiley & Sons

FIGURE 13-2:
Doing math with named callbacks.

Understanding Closures

A *closure* is the local variable for a function, kept alive after the function has returned.

Take a look at the example in Listing 13-3. In this example, an inner function is defined within an outer function. When the outer function returns a reference to the inner function, the returned reference can still access the local data from the outer function.

In Listing 13-3, the greetVisitor function returns a function that is created within it called sayWelcome. Notice that the return statement doesn't use ( ) after sayWelcome. That's because you don't want to return the value of running the function, but rather the code of the actual function.

LISTING 13-3: **Creating a Function Using a Function**

```
function greetVisitor(phrase) {
  let welcome = phrase + '. Great to see you!'; // Local variable
  let sayWelcome = function () {
    alert(welcome);
  };
```

```
    return sayWelcome;
}
let personalGreeting = greetVisitor('Hola Amiga');
personalGreeting(); // alerts "Hola Amiga. Great to see you!"
```

The useful thing about Listing 13-3 is that it uses the greetVisitor function to create a new custom function called personalGreeting, which can still access the variables from the original function.

Normally, when a function has finished executing, the local variables within it are inaccessible. By returning a function reference (sayWelcome), however, the greetVisitor function's internal data becomes accessible to the outside world.

TIP

The keys to understanding closures are to understand variable scope in JavaScript and to understand the difference between executing a function and a function reference. By assigning the return value of the greetVisitor function to the new personalGreeting function, the program stores the code of the sayWelcome function. You can test this by using the toString method:

```
personalGreeting.toString()
```

If you add to Listing 13-3 an alert statement to output the toString() value of personalGreeting, you get the result shown in Figure 13-3.

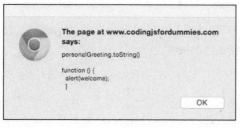

© John Wiley & Sons

FIGURE 13-3:
A closure includes the code of the returned inner function.

In Figure 13-3, the variable welcome is a copy of the variable welcome from the original greetVisitor function at the time that the closure was created.

In Listing 13-4, a new closure is created using a different argument to the greetVisitor function. Even though calling greetVisitor() changes the value of the welcome variable, the result of calling the first function (personalGreeting) remains the same.

LISTING 13-4: **Closures Contain Secret References to Outer Function Variables**

```html
<html>
<head>
  <title>Using Closures</title>
  <script>
    function greetVisitor(phrase) {
      let welcome = phrase + ". Great to see you!<br><br>"; // Local variable
      let sayWelcome = function() {
      document.getElementById("greeting").innerHTML += welcome;
      }
    return sayWelcome;
    }
    // wait until the document is loaded
    document.addEventListener('DOMContentLoaded', function() {
    // make a function
    let personalGreeting = greetVisitor("Hola Amiga");
    // make another function
    let anotherGreeting = greetVisitor("Howdy, Friend");
    // look at the code of the first function
    document.getElementById("greeting").innerHTML +=
    "personalGreeting.toString() <br>" + personalGreeting.toString() + "<br>";
    // run the  first function
    personalGreeting(); // alerts "Hola Amiga. Great to see you!""
    // look at the code of the 2nd function
    document.getElementById("greeting").innerHTML +=
    "anotherGreeting.toString() <br>" + anotherGreeting.toString() + "<br>";
    // run the 2nd function
    anotherGreeting(); // alerts "Howdy, Friend. Great to see you!"
    // check the first function
    personalGreeting(); // alerts "Hola Amiga. Great to see you!""
    // finish the addEventListener method
    }, false);
  </script>
</head>
<body>
  <p id="greeting"</p>
</body>
</html>
```

The result of running Listing 13-4 in a web browser is shown in Figure 13-4.

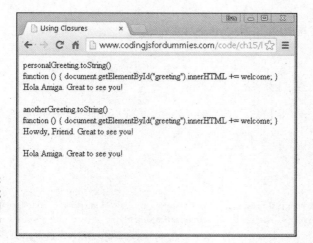

Using Closures

www.codingjsfordummies.com/code/ch15/1

```
personalGreeting.toString()
function () { document.getElementById("greeting").innerHTML += welcome; }
Hola Amiga. Great to see you!

anotherGreeting.toString()
function () { document.getElementById("greeting").innerHTML += welcome; }
Howdy, Friend. Great to see you!

Hola Amiga. Great to see you!
```

FIGURE 13-4:
Creating customized greetings with closures.

TIP

Closures are not hard to understand after you know the underlying concepts and have a need for them. Don't worry if you don't feel totally comfortable with them just yet. It's fully possible to code in JavaScript without using closures, but once you do understand them, they can be quite useful and will make you a better programmer.

Using Closures

A closure is like keeping a copy of the local variables of a function as they were when the closure was created.

In web programming, closures are frequently used to eliminate the duplication of effort within a program or to hold values that need to be reused throughout a program so that the program doesn't need to recalculate the value each time it's used.

Another use for closures is to create customized versions of functions for specific uses.

In Listing 13-5, closures are used to create functions with error messages specific to different problems that may occur in the program. All the error messages get created using the same function.

TECHNICAL STUFF

When a function's purpose is to create other functions, it's known as a *function factory.*

LISTING 13-5: **Using a Function to Create Functions**

```html
<html>
<head>
  <title>function factory</title>
  <script>
    function createMessageAlert(theMessage){
      return function() {
        alert (theMessage);
      }
    }

    let badEmailError = createMessageAlert("Unknown email address!");
    let wrongPasswordError = createMessageAlert("That's not your password!");

    window.addEventListener('load', loader, false);
    function loader(){
      document.login.yourEmail.addEventListener('change',badEmailError);
      document.login.yourPassword.addEventListener('change',wrongPasswordError);
    }
  </script>
</head>
<body>
    <form name="login" id="loginform">
      <p>
        <label>Enter Your Email Address:
          <input type="text" name="yourEmail">
        </label>
        </p>
      <p>
        <label>Enter Your Password:
          <input type="text" name="yourPassword">
</label>
        </p>
      <button>Submit</button>
</body>
</html>
```

The key to understanding Listing 13-5 is the function factory.

```
function createMessageAlert(theMessage){
    return function() {
      alert (theMessage);
    }
}
```

To use this function factory, assign its return value to a variable, as in the following statement:

```
let badEmailError = createMessageAlert("Unknown email address!");
```

The preceding statement creates a closure that can be used elsewhere in the program just by running badEmailError as a function, as in the following event handler:

```
document.login.yourEmail.addEventListener('change',badEmailError);
```

Chapter **14**

Embracing AJAX and JSON

"The Web does not just connect machines, it connects people."

— TIM BERNERS-LEE

A JAX is a technique for making web pages more dynamic by sending and receiving data in the background while the user interacts with the pages. JSON has become the standard data format used by AJAX applications. In this chapter, you find out how to use AJAX techniques to make your site sparkle!

Working behind the Scenes with AJAX

Asynchronous JavaScript + XML (AJAX) is a term that's used to describe a method of using JavaScript, the DOM, HTML, and the XMLHttpRequest object together to refresh parts of a web page with live data without needing to refresh the entire page.

TECHNICAL STUFF

AJAX was first implemented on a large scale by Google's Gmail in 2004 and then was given its name by Jesse James Garret in 2005.

The HTML DOM changes the page dynamically. The important innovation that AJAX made was to use the XMLHttpRequest object to retrieve data from the server asynchronously (in the background) without blocking the execution of the rest of the JavaScript on the web page.

Although AJAX originally relied on data formatted as XML (hence the X in the name), it's much more common today for AJAX applications to use a data format called JavaScript Object Notation (JSON). Most people still call applications that get JSON data asynchronously from a server AJAX, but a more technically accurate (but less memorable) acronym would be AJAJ.

AJAX examples

When web developers first started to use AJAX, it became one of the hallmarks of what was labeled Web 2.0. The most common way for web pages to show dynamic data prior to AJAX was by downloading a new web page from the server. For example, consider craigslist.org, shown in Figure 14-1.

To navigate through the categories of listings or search results on Craigslist, you click links that cause the entire page to refresh and reveal the content of the page you requested.

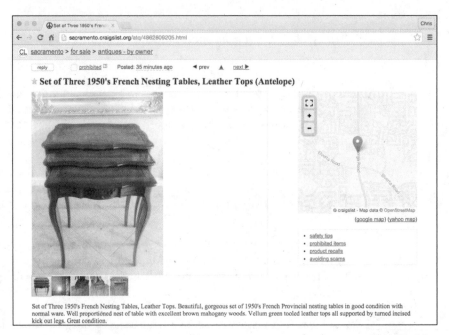

FIGURE 14-1: Craigslist.org was quite happy with Web 1.0, thank you very much.

© John Wiley & Sons

While still very common, refreshing the entire page to display new data in just part of the page is unnecessarily slow and can provide a less smooth user experience.

Compare the old Craigslist-style navigation with the application-like user interface of Google Slides, shown in Figure 14-2, which uses AJAX to load new content into part of the screen while the navigation bars remain static.

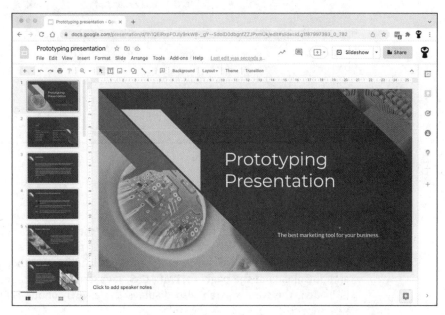

© John Wiley & Sons

FIGURE 14-2: Google Slides uses AJAX to provide a more modern user experience.

In addition to making web page navigation smoother, AJAX is also great for creating live data elements in a web page. Prior to AJAX, if you wanted to display live data, a chart, or an up-to-date view of an email inbox, you either needed to use a plug-in (such as Adobe Flash) or periodically cause the web page to automatically refresh.

With AJAX, it's possible to periodically refresh data through an asynchronous process that runs in the background and then update only the elements of the page that need to be modified.

Weather Underground's WunderMap, shown in Figure 14-3, shows a weather map with constantly changing and updating data overlays. The data for the map is retrieved from remote servers using AJAX.

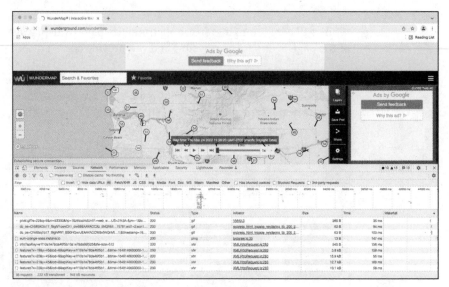

FIGURE 14-3:
WunderMap uses
AJAX to display
live weather data.

Viewing AJAX in action

In Figure 14-3, shown in the preceding section, the Chrome Developer Tools window is open to the Network tab. The Network tab shows all network activity involving the current web page. When a page is loading, this includes the requests and downloads of the page's HTML, CSS, JavaScript, and images. After the page is loaded, the Network tab also displays the asynchronous HTTP requests and responses that make AJAX possible.

Follow these steps to view AJAX requests and responses in Chrome:

1. **Open your Chrome web browser and navigate to** www.wunderground.com/ wundermap.

2. **Open your Chrome Developer Tools by using the Chrome menu or by pressing Cmd+Option+I (on Mac) or Ctrl+Shift+I (on Windows).**

3. **Open the Network tab.**

   Your Developer Tools window should now resemble Figure 14-4. You may want to drag the top border of the Developer Tools to make it larger at this point. Don't worry if this makes the content area of the browser too small to use. What's going on in the Developer Tools is the important thing right now.

   Notice that new items are periodically appearing in the Network tab. These are the AJAX requests and responses. Some of them are images returned from the server, and some are data for use by the client-side JavaScript.

4. **Click one of the rows in the Name column of the Networks tab.**

Additional data will be displayed about that particular item, as shown in Figure 14-5.

5. **Click through the tabs (Headers, Preview, Response and so on) in the detailed data pane and examine the data.**

The first tab, Headers, displays the HTTP request that was sent to the remote server. Take a look in particular at the Request URL. This is a standard website address that passes data to a remote server.

6. **Select and copy the value of the Request URL from one of the items you inspected.**

7. **Open a new tab in your browser and paste the entire Request URL into the address bar.**

A page containing data or an image opens, as in Figure 14-6.

8. **Compare the results of opening the Request URL in a new tab with the results shown in the Response tab in the Developer Tools.**

They should be similar, although they may not look identical because they weren't run at the same time.

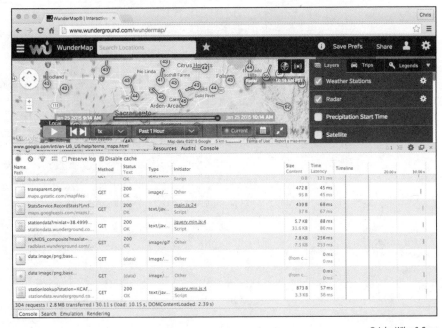

FIGURE 14-4:
The Network tab of the Developer Tools.

© John Wiley & Sons

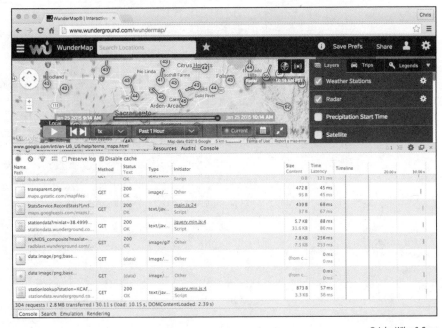

Embracing AJAX and JSON

FIGURE 14-5:
Viewing additional information about a particular record in the Network tab.

© John Wiley & Sons

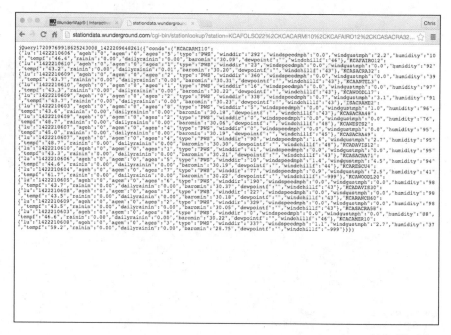

FIGURE 14-6:
The result of copying an HTTP Request URL from the Network tab.

© John Wiley & Sons

As you can see, there's really no magic to AJAX. The JavaScript on the web page is simply requesting and receiving data from a server. Everything that happens behind the scenes is open to inspection through the Chrome Developer Tools (or the similar tools that are available with most other web browsers today).

Using the XMLHttpRequest object

The XMLHttpRequest object provides a way for web browsers to request data from a URL without having to refresh the page.

The XMLHttpRequest object was created and implemented first by Microsoft in its Internet Explorer browser and has since become a web standard that has been adopted by every modern web browser.

You can use the methods and properties of the XMLHttpRequest object to retrieve data from a remote server or your local server. Despite its name, the XMLHttpRequest object can get other types of data besides XML, and it can even use different protocols to get data besides HTTP.

Listing 14-1 shows how you can use XMLHttpRequest to load the contents of an external text document containing HTML into the current HTML document.

LISTING 14-1: **Using XMLHttpRequest to Load External Data**

```
<html>
  <head>
    <title>Loading External Data</title>
    <script>
      window.addEventListener('load', init, false);
      function init(e) {
        document
          .getElementById('myButton')
          .addEventListener('click', documentLoader, false);
      }
      function reqListener() {
        console.log(this.responseText);
        document.getElementById('content').innerHTML = this.responseText;
      }
      function documentLoader() {
        let oReq = new XMLHttpRequest();
        oReq.onload = reqListener;
        oReq.open('get', 'loadme.txt', true);
        oReq.send();
      }
```

(continued)

LISTING 14-1: *(continued)*

```
    </script>
  </head>
  <body>
    <form id="myForm">
      <button id="myButton" type="button">Click to Load</button>
    </form>
    <div id="content"></div>
  </body>
</html>
```

The heart of this document is the documentLoader function:

```
function documentLoader(){
  var oReq = new XMLHttpRequest();
  oReq.onload = reqListener;
  oReq.open("get", "loadme.txt", true);
  oReq.send();
}
```

The first line of code inside the function creates the new XMLHttpRequest object and gives it the name of oReq:

```
var oReq = new XMLHttpRequest();
```

The methods and properties of the XMLHttpRequest object are accessible through the oReq object.

This second line assigns a function, reqListener, to the onload event of the oReq object. The purpose of this is to cause the reqListener function to be called when oReq loads a document:

```
oReq.onload = reqListener;
```

The third line uses the open method to create a request:

```
oReq.open("get", "loadme.txt", true);
```

In this case, the function uses the HTTP GET method to load the file called loadme. txt. The third parameter is the async argument. It specifies whether the request should be asynchronous. If it's set to false, the send method won't return until the request is complete. If it's set to true, notifications about the completion of the request will be provided through event listeners. Because the event listener is set to listen for the load event, an asynchronous request is what's desired.

WARNING

It's unlikely that you'll run into a situation where you'll want to set the `async` argument to `false`. In fact, some browsers have begun to just ignore this argument if it's set to `false` and to treat it as if it's `true` either way because of the bad effect on the user experience that synchronous requests have.

The last line in the `documentLoader` function sends the requests that you created with the `open` method:

```
oReq.send();
```

TECHNICAL STUFF

The `open` method will get the latest version of the requested file. So-called live-data applications often use loops to repeatedly request updated data from a server using AJAX.

Working with the same-origin policy

If you save the HTML document in Listing 14-1 to your computer and open it in a web browser, more than likely, you won't get the results that you'd expect. If you load the document from your computer and then open the Chrome Developer Tools JavaScript Console, you will see a couple of error messages similar to the errors shown in Figure 14-7.

FIGURE 14-7: Errors when trying to use XMLHttp Request on a local file.

The problem here is what's called the *same-origin policy*. In order to prevent web pages from causing users to unknowingly download code that may be malicious using `XMLHttpRequest`, browsers will return an error by default whenever a script tries to load an URL that doesn't have the same origin. If you load a web page from www.example.com and a script on that page tries to retrieve data from www.watzthis.com, the browser will prevent the request with a similar error to the one you see in Figure 14-7.

The same-origin policy also applies to files on your local computer. If it didn't, XMLHttpRequest could be used to compromise the security of your computer.

There's no reason to worry about the examples in this book negatively affecting your computer. However, in order for the examples in this chapter to work correctly on your computer, you need a way around the same-origin policy.

The first way around the same-origin policy is to put the HTML file containing the documentLoader function and the text file on the same web server.

The other way around the same-origin policy is to start your browser with the same-origin policy restrictions temporarily disabled.

WARNING

These instructions are to allow you to test your own files on your local computer only. Do not surf the web with the same-origin policy disabled. You may expose your computer to malicious code.

To disable the same-origin policy on macOS:

1. **If your Chrome browser is open, close it.**

2. **Open the Terminal app and launch Chrome using the following command:**

```
/Applications/Google\ Chrome.app/Contents/MacOS/Google\ Chrome
    --disable-web-security
```

To disable the same-origin policy on Windows:

1. **If your Chrome browser is open, close it.**

2. **Open the Command prompt and navigate to the folder where you installed Chrome.**

3. **Type the following command to launch the browser:**

```
Chrome.exe --disable-web-security
```

Once the browser starts up, you'll be able to run files containing AJAX requests locally until you close the browser. Once the browser is closed and reopened, the security restrictions will be re-enabled automatically.

Figure 14-8 shows the result of running Listing 14-1 in a browser without the same-origin policy errors.

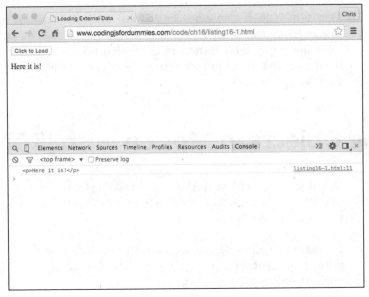

FIGURE 14-8:
Listing 14-1 run in a browser with the same-origin policy disabled.

Using CORS, the silver bullet for AJAX requests

It's quite common for a web application to make requests to a different server in order to retrieve data. For example, many websites and mobile apps use Google's Maps through the Google Maps Platform API.

In order for the transactions between servers to be secure, mechanisms have been created for browsers and servers to work out their differences and establish trust.

Currently, the best method for allowing and restricting access to resources between servers is the standard called *Cross-Origin Resource Sharing* (CORS).

To see CORS in action, visit the Weather Underground's WunderMap (www. wunderground.com/wundermap) using the Chrome web browser. When the page has loaded, right-click and select Inspect to open the Chrome Developer Tools, then select the Network tab. Click one of the requests where the Name starts with "stationdata?" and the Type is xhr.

Click the Headers tab, and you'll see the following text in the HTTP header:

```
Access-Control-Allow-Origin: *
```

This is the CORS response header that this particular server is configured to send. The asterisk value after the colon indicates that this server will accept requests from any origin. If the owners of wunderground.com wanted to restrict access to the data at this script to only specific servers or authenticated users, they could do so using CORS.

Putting Objects in Motion with JSON

In Listing 14-1, you use AJAX to open and display a text document containing a snippet of HTML. Another common use for AJAX is to request and receive data for processing by the browser.

For example, gasbuddy.com uses a map from Google along with data about gas prices to present a simple and up-to-date view of gas prices in different locations, as shown in Figure 14-9.

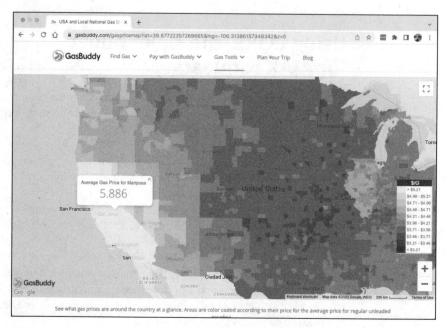

FIGURE 14-9: gasbuddy.com uses AJAX to display gas prices on a map.

© John Wiley & Sons

If you examine gasbuddy.com in the Network tab, you'll find that some requests have responses that look something like the code shown in Listing 14-2.

LISTING 14-2: **Part of a Response to an AJAX Request on gasbuddy.com**

```
([{id:"tuwtvtuvvvv",base:[351289344,822599680],zrange:[11,11],
layer:"m@288429816",features:[{
id:"17243857463485476481",a:[0,0],bb:[-8,-8,7,7,-47,7,48,22,-41,19,41,34],c:"{1:
    {title:\"Folsom Lake State Recreation Area\"},4:{type:1}}"}]},{id:"tuwtvtuvvvw",
    zrange:[11,11],layer:"m@288429816"},{id:"tuwtvtuvvwv",base:[351506432,824291328],
    zrange:[11,11],layer:"m@288429816",features:[{id:"8748558518353272790",a:[0,0],
    bb:[-8,-8,7,7,-41,7,41,22],c:"{1:{title:\"Deer Creek Hills\"},4:{type:1}}"}]},
    {id:"tuwtvtuvvww",zrange:[11,11],layer:"m@288429816"}])
```

If you take a small piece of data out of this block of code and reformat it, you get something like Listing 14-3, which should look more familiar to you.

LISTING 14-3: **gasbuddy.com Response Data, Reformatted**

```
{id:"tuwtvtuvvvv",
base:[351289344,822599680],
zrange:[11,11],
layer:"m@288429816",
features:[{
id:"17243857463485476481",
a:[0,0],
bb:[-8,-8,7,7,-47,7,48,22,-41,19,41,34],
c:"{
1:{title:\"Folsom Lake State Recreation Area\"},
4:{type:1}
}"}
]}
}
```

By looking at the format of the data, you can see that it looks suspiciously like the name:value format of a JavaScript object literal, also known as a comma-separated list of name-value pairs enclosed in curly braces.

The main reason JSON is so easy to use is because it's already in a format that JavaScript can work with, so no conversion is necessary. For example, Listing 14-4 shows a JSON file containing information about this book.

LISTING 14-4: **JSON Data Describing** *Coding All-in-One For Dummies*

```
{ "book_title": "Coding All-in-One For Dummies",
"book_author": "Chris Minnick",
"summary": "Everything beginners need to know to start coding.",
"isbn":"978-1119889564"
}
```

Listing 14-5 shows how this data can be loaded into a web page using JavaScript and then used to display its data in HTML.

LISTING 14-5: **Displaying JSON Data with JavaScript**

```html
<html>
  <head>
    <title>Displaying JSON Data</title>
    <script>
      window.addEventListener('load', init, false);
      function init(e) {
        document
          .getElementById('myButton')
          .addEventListener('click', documentLoader, false);
      }
      function reqListener() {
        // convert the string from the file to an object with JSON.parse
        var obj = JSON.parse(this.responseText);
        // display the object's data like any object
        document.getElementById('book_title').innerHTML = obj.book_title;
        document.getElementById('book_author').innerHTML = obj.book_author;
        document.getElementById('summary').innerHTML = obj.summary;
      }
      function documentLoader() {
        var oReq = new XMLHttpRequest();
        oReq.onload = reqListener;
        oReq.open('get', 'listing14-5.json', true);
        oReq.send();
      }
    </script>
  </head>
  <body>
    <form id="myForm">
      <button id="myButton" type="button">Click to Load</button>
    </form>
    <h1>Book Title</h1>
    <div id="book_title"></div>
```

```
      <h2>Authors</h2>
      <div id="book_author"></div>
      <h2>Summary</h2>
      <div id="summary"></div>
   </body>
</html>
```

The key to displaying any JSON data that's brought into a JavaScript document from an external source is to convert it from a string to an object using the `JSON.parse` method. After you do that, you can access the values within the JSON file using dot notation or bracket notation, as you would access the properties of any JavaScript object.

Figure 14-10 shows the results of running Listing 14-5 in a web browser and pressing the button to load the JSON data.

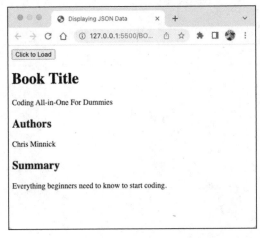

© John Wiley & Sons

FIGURE 14-10:
Displaying JSON data within an HTML page.

4
Creating Mobile Apps

Contents at a Glance

» What makes Flutter great

» Alternatives to Flutter

» Mobile app and Flutter terminology

Chapter **1**

What Is Flutter?

Before you learn how to program mobile apps with Flutter, it's important to understand the big picture and how mobile apps fit into it. No doubt about it: Mobile phones are complicated beasts. So how do they work? What makes them tick? What's going on inside each of those remarkable gadgets?

All About Hardware and Software

A mobile phone is really a small computer. And, like any computer, a mobile phone operates on several layers. Figure 1-1 shows you a few of those layers.

Hardware is the stuff you can touch. It's the bottom layer of the diagram in Figure 1-1. Hardware consists of items like circuitry, memory, and the battery.

Electrical signals that travel along the hardware's circuits make the hardware do what you want it to do. These signals encode instructions. Taken as a whole, these instructions are called *software*.

When people create software, they don't describe each electrical signal that travels through the hardware's circuitry. Instead, people write *source code* — instructions that look something like English-language instructions. One source code instruction can be shorthand for hundreds or thousands of electrical signals.

The User

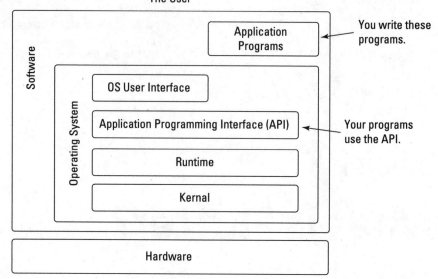

You write these programs.

Your programs use the API.

FIGURE 1-1:
A conceptual view of your mobile phone.

A collection of source code instructions that perform a particular task (word processing, web browsing, managing a smart thermostat, or whatever) is called a *program*. A person who writes these instructions is a *programmer* or — a fanciersounding term — a *developer*. The person who runs a program on their own device is a *user*.

Just as people communicate using many spoken languages, programmers write source code using many *programming languages*. If you create iPhone apps, you probably write code in either the Swift language or the Objective-C language. If you create Android apps, you're likely to write code in either Kotlin or Java.

When you create a Flutter app, you write code in the Dart programming language. Here's a complete Dart language program:

```
main() => print('Hello');
```

This program displays the word *Hello* on the screen. It's not very useful, but please be patient. This is only Chapter 1!

Figure 1-1 distinguishes between two kinds of software:

>> ***Operating system* (OS) software runs whenever the device is turned on.**

OS software manages the device and provides ways for the user to interact with the device. Devices made by Apple, such as iPhones and iPads, run the *iOS* operating system. Android phones and tablets run the *Android* operating system (of course).

>> ***Application programs* do the work that users want done.**

Apps to make phone calls, apps to read email, calendar apps, web browsers, and games are examples of application programs. As a Flutter developer, your job is to create application programs.

By one estimate, the popular operating system named Linux consists of nearly 28 million instructions. No one can deal with that much code, so operating systems are divided into layers of their own. Figure 1-1 shows only four of a typical operating system's many layers:

>> **A *kernel* performs the operating system's most fundamental tasks.**

The kernel schedules apps to be run, manages a device's memory and files, provides access to input and output, and does many other essential tasks.

>> **A *runtime* is a bunch of code that does extra work in the background while your application program runs.**

Runtimes come in many shapes and sizes. A runtime for the C programming language consists of a relatively small amount of code. In contrast, a Java language runtime (a *Java Virtual Machine,* or *JVM*) is a big piece of software with lots of moving parts.

When you run an iOS app, the app uses the *Objective-C runtime*. When you run an Android app, that app uses the *Android runtime*, also known as *ART*.

>> **An *application programming interface* (API) is a bunch of code that app developers use over and over again.**

For example, Android's API has something named toUpperCase. If you apply toUpperCase to "Flutter For Dummies", you get "FLUTTER FOR DUMMIES". You don't have to write your own code to change each of the letters. Android's API provides this functionality for you. All you have to do is tell Android's API to apply its toUpperCase feature, and then you're all set.

Here's some useful terminology: Rather than tell an API to "apply its toUpper Case feature," you *call* toUpperCase. This use of the word *call* dates back to the FORTRAN programming language of the 1950s.

Operating systems haven't cornered the market on APIs. All kinds of software come with APIs. Flutter and Dart have their own APIs.

Dart's API has general-purpose things, like `toUpperCase`, `isAtSameMomentAs`, and a bunch of others. Flutter's API has features that apply to visually oriented apps. For example, when you want to display a box where the user can type text, you don't have to describe every aspect of the box's appearance and behavior. Instead, you can call the API's `TextField` constructor and have Flutter do the hard work for you.

An API is sometimes referred to as a *library*. You borrow books from a public library, and you borrow existing code from the Dart and Flutter APIs.

TECHNICAL STUFF

In the Dart programming terminology, the word *library* has a slightly different meaning. You don't have to worry about that yet.

In this book, you'll learn about pieces of the Dart and Flutter APIs and then you'll use those pieces to create Flutter programs.

REMEMBER

A typical API has thousands of pieces. No one memorizes all of them. When you want to add an image to your app, you open Flutter's documentation and search for the word *Image*. The documentation's `Image` page tells you how to display an image, how to size an image, how to tile an image, and how to do all kinds of other good stuff.

>> **The *OS user interface* is the area that includes the home screen, the launch icons, a file explorer, and any other stuff users see when they're not working with a particular application program.**

On your laptop computer, you probably have a *desktop* instead of a home screen. One way or another, the OS presents options to help users launch application programs and perform other maintenance tasks. These options are part of the OS user interface.

Each layer in Figure 1-1 contains a collection of related components. This helps programmers focus on the components that concern them the most — for example:

>> **The API has code to help developers write application programs.**

A developer who's creating an online purchasing app looks for components in the API.

>> **The runtime layer has code to run programs efficiently.**

To make everyone's code run faster, engineers at Apple make improvements to the iOS Runtime layer.

In addition to separating parts of the code from one another, the layers form organized paths of communication among parts of the system. In general, a layer's code communicates only with the layers immediately above and below it.

For example, a user taps a button belonging to a weather app. The app responds by calling on functionality provided by the API. Communication works its way down the diagram in Figure 1-1 until it reaches the hardware, which responds by changing the pixels on the device's screen. A user never communicates directly with the API, and application programs have no direct access to the operating system's kernel.

When you create a Flutter app, you use the Dart programming language. Dart and Flutter have separate APIs:

>> **Dart's API deals with the tasks that every programming language should be able to do, no matter what programmers want to do with that language.**

For example, Dart's API helps programmers round a number, trim a string of characters, describe a time interval, reverse a list, and so on.

>> **Flutter's API deals with the presentation of components and images on a device's screen.**

One part of Flutter's API deals with buttons, text fields, checkboxes, and the like. Another part handles a user's gestures. Yet another covers animation.

Every Dart program, even the simplest one, calls on code in the Dart API, and every Flutter app calls on both the Dart and Flutter APIs. These APIs are both useful and formidable. They're useful because of all the things you can do with the API code. They're formidable because both APIs are extensive. No one memorizes all the features made available by the Dart and Flutter APIs. Programmers remember the features that they use often and look up the features that they need in a pinch. They look up these features on a website called the *Flutter API reference documentation*.

The API documentation (see `https://api.flutter.dev`) describes the features in both the Dart and Flutter APIs. As a Flutter developer, you consult this API documentation on a daily basis. You can bookmark the website and revisit the site whenever you need to look up something.

Where Does Flutter Fit In?

The heart of Flutter is an API for creating apps. Most Flutter apps run on mobile devices, but Flutter apps can run on laptop and desktop computers, too. Flutter certainly wasn't the first API for mobile devices, so why should anyone consider using Flutter to create apps?

Cross-platform development

People throw around the word *platform* as if the word means everything and nothing. A simple definition of a *platform* is a particular operating system along with the hardware the OS runs on.

What makes the Android platform different from its iOS counterpart? To create radio buttons in Android's API, you write code of the following kind:

```
<RadioGroup>

    <RadioButton
        android:id="@+id/radioButton1"
        android:text="Red"
        android:onClick="onRadioButtonClicked"/>

    <RadioButton
        android:id="@+id/radioButton2"
        android:text="Yellow"
        android:onClick="onRadioButtonClicked"/>

    <RadioButton
        android:id="@+id/radioButton3"
        android:text="Green"
        android:onClick="onRadioButtonClicked"/>

</RadioGroup>
```

Try converting that code to work on an iPhone. The iOS API doesn't have radio buttons, so, to adapt an Android app with radio buttons for iOS, you write code to make things that look like radio buttons. You also code rules for the radio buttons to follow — rules like "only one button at a time can be selected." If you don't want to create radio buttons from scratch, you can replace Android's radio buttons with an iOS picker component, a thing that looks like an old automobile odometer. One way or another, replacing an app's components takes time and costs money.

Some companies give up and create apps for only one platform — iPhone or Android. Other companies hire two teams of programmers — one for iPhone development and another for Android development. Still other companies have one team of programmers that work on both versions of the code. For the companies' managers, the problem is exasperating. Why spend nearly twice the money and create two apps that do almost the same things?

The developer community has names for this ugly situation:

>> Software written for one platform isn't *compatible* with other platforms.

>> The mobile phone arena suffers from *fragmentation*: The market is divided between two different operating systems, and the Android half is divided among many vendors' phones.

A program that makes direct use of either the Android or iOS API is called *native code*, and native code written for Android can't run on an iOS device. In the same way, native code written for iOS is meaningless to an Android device. What's a developer to do?

A framework is a second-level API. What the heck does that mean? A *framework* is an API that serves as an intermediary between the developer and some other API. If direct use of the Android or iOS API is problematic, you switch to a framework's API. The framework's API deals head-on with Android's and iOS's problems.

Frameworks like Flutter offer an alternative to native app development. When you write a Flutter program, you don't write code specifically for Android or iOS. Instead, you write code that can be translated into either system's API calls. Here's how you create radio buttons in the Flutter framework:

```
Radio(
  value: TrafficLight.Red,
  groupValue: _trafficLightValue,
  onChanged: _updateTrafficLight,
),
Radio(
  value: TrafficLight.Yellow,
  groupValue: _trafficLightValue,
  onChanged: _updateTrafficLight,
),
Radio(
  value: TrafficLight.Green,
  groupValue: _trafficLightValue,
  onChanged: _updateTrafficLight,
)
```

Your computer translates code of this kind into either Android API calls or iOS API calls — or both. That's cool!

A BRIEF HISTORY

130,000 years ago: Humans first walk the earth.

10,000 years ago: Humans begin farming.

1752: Ben Franklin discovers electricity.

1760: The Industrial Revolution begins.

March 10, 1876: Alexander Graham Bell makes the first telephone call.

April 3, 1973: Martin Cooper makes the first mobile phone call.

August 16, 1994: BellSouth Cellular releases IBM Simon — the first smartphone.

June 29, 2007: Apple releases the first iPhone.

November 5, 2007: Google releases the first public beta of Android.

Both the iOS and Android are native development technologies. With native development, the programmer makes calls directly to the system's API.

December 2007: Articles and blog posts about fragmentation in mobile phone technologies start appearing in large numbers.

March 13, 2009: Nitobi Software introduces a framework that uses HTML, CSS, and JavaScript to create mobile phone apps.

October 4, 2011: Adobe acquires Nitobi, rebrands its framework with the name PhoneGap, and spins off an open-source version that eventually becomes Apache Cordova.

Cordova and its cousins are hybrid app development frameworks. With *hybrid app development*, an app runs in a window that's essentially a web browser. Because web browser technology is standard across all platforms, a hybrid app can run on both Android and iOS devices, or even on a desktop computer.

What's "hybrid" about hybrid apps? The code to display text and images in a web browser doesn't vary much from one environment to another, so a browser page on an iPhone looks more or less like the same page on an Android phone. But communicating with hardware devices, such as the GPS receiver and vibration motor, is another story entirely.

Web pages aren't designed to talk directly to a device's hardware. In fact, you don't want to visit awfulwebsite.com and have the site's code quietly take pictures with your laptop's built-in camera. To make a hybrid app interact with hardware, you have to backpedal and make calls to the iPhone's API, the Android API, or whatever other API you can use. That's why frameworks like Apache Cordova have *plug-ins* — additional programs whose code is specific to either iOS or Android. The bottom line is, a typical hybrid app does some of its work in a web browser and the rest of its work with native API calls.

What's the downside with hybrid apps? Frameworks like Apache Cordova are like foreign language interpreters: While the app runs, the device must constantly translate web browser instructions into native code instructions. When you talk through an interpreter, the conversation can become sluggish. Hybrid apps aren't always as responsive as native apps. In addition, hybrid apps can't do all the things that native apps can do. It's the same when you talk through a foreign language interpreter. You can say most of the things you want to say, but some ideas simply can't be translated.

Returning to the history lesson . . .

Summer 2013: A hackathon for Facebook employees gives birth to *React Native* — a cross-platform framework based on the React.js JavaScript framework.

February 24, 2016: Microsoft acquires Xamarin — a cross-platform mobile development framework based indirectly on Microsoft's own .NET framework.

With a *cross-platform framework*, a programmer writes one program that targets neither iOS nor Android. When the programmer says, "Test this code," the framework translates the whole program into native code for either Android or iOS, whichever platform the programmer chooses. When the program is ready for public distribution, the framework translates it into two different native apps — one for iOS and the other for Android.

But why stop there? If you can translate code into both iOS and Android apps, you can translate the code into web pages and desktop apps. A developer can create one piece of code and have it run on all kinds of phones, tablets, PCs, Macs, watches, toasters, or whatever.

This brings us to the subject of this book:

December 4, 2018: Google announces Flutter 1.0 for cross-platform development.

(continued)

(continued)

Flutter differs from Xamarin and React Native in some significant ways. First and foremost, Xamarin isn't entirely free. Using Xamarin for professional projects costs between $300 and $1900 a year, depending on the size and scope of the projects under development.

In addition, Flutter's way of displaying components is different from the React Native and Xamarin way. When you run a React Native app on an iPhone, the app calls on the iOS API to create iOS buttons, text fields, and other visual components. The same is true for Android development. React Native gets the Android API to display Android-specific components. Components created by the iOS and Android APIs don't look alike. The two APIs use different shapes, different color palettes, and different navigation schemes. The differences can lead to unexpected results and can occasionally sabotage the whole cross-platform development effort.

Flutter doesn't call on the iOS or Android APIs to display an app's components. Instead, Flutter specifies all the tiny pixels required to draw a button or a text field and calls on the iOS or Android API to paint those pixels. If you want an app to look the same on both iOS and Android devices, Flutter is your natural choice.

What if you want your app to have that special, iPhone look when it runs on iOS devices? Can you do that with Flutter? Of course, you can. The Flutter framework has two special libraries — one for Android and another for iOS. Flutter's Material Design library draws things that look like Android components, and Flutter's Cupertino library makes objects look like iOS components. This book emphasizes the Material library, but almost everything in it has a Cupertino counterpart.

A quick-and-easy development cycle

Here's what happens when you create an app for mobile devices:

1. **You write some code, or you modify some existing code.**

REMEMBER

   You don't write Android or iOS code on a phone of any kind. Phones aren't powerful enough for all the editing and other stuff you need to do. Instead, you create an app's code on a laptop or desktop computer. This laptop or desktop computer is called your *development computer*.

2. **You issue a command for your development computer to build the code.**

   Building the code takes place in several stages, one of which is called *compiling*. *Compiling* means automatically translating your program from the source code you wrote to detailed object code instructions. Think of object code as a bunch of zeros and ones. It's very detailed and extremely unintuitive. Humans hardly ever read or write object code but, at the heart of things, processors respond only to object code instructions. For a detailed look at compiling code, see this section's "What is a compiler?" sidebar.

In addition to the translation step, the build process connects the program you wrote with additional code that your program needs in order to run. For example, if your program accesses the Internet, the build process integrates your code with existing network code.

3. **The development computer *deploys* your code to a target device.**

   This so-called "device" may be a real phone connected to your computer or a program that simulates a phone on your computer's screen. One way or another, your program starts running.

4. **You press buttons, type text, and otherwise test your app to find out whether it's doing the things you want it to do.**

   Of course, it's not doing all those things. So you return to Step 1 and keep trying.

Steps 2 and 3 can be painfully slow. For some simple iPhone and Android apps, it's common to watch for several minutes as the computer prepares code for the program's next run. This sluggishness reduces a developer's productivity considerably.

But along with Flutter comes some good news. Flutter uses the Dart programming language, and Dart comes with these two (count 'em — two) compilers:

>> **Ahead-of-time (AOT) compiler**

With an *AOT compiler*, your development computer translates an entire program and makes the translated code available for devices to run. No further translation takes place when the devices run your program. Each target device devotes its processing power to the efficient running of your code.

An app running on AOT-compiled code runs smoothly and efficiently.

>> **Just-in-time (JIT) compiler**

With a *JIT compiler*, your development computer translates enough code to start the app running. It feeds this code to a test device and continues translating while the test device runs the app. If the developer presses a button on the test device's screen, the JIT compiler hurries to translate that button's code.

An app running on a JIT compiler may appear to be sluggish because the compiler translates code while the app runs. But using a JIT compiler is a great way to test an app.

Here's what happens when you develop a Flutter app:

REMEMBER

1. **You write some code.**

2. **You issue a command for your development computer to build the code.**

   The first time around, building code can take some time.

3. **The development computer deploys your code to a target device.**

   Again, you face a noticeable time lag.

4. **In testing your code, you find out that it's not doing all the things you want it to do.**

5. **You modify your existing code, and then . . .**

6. **You issue a command for your development computer to rebuild the code.**

   Here's where Flutter's magic happens. Dart's JIT compiler recompiles only the part of the app that you've modified and sends the change straight to the target device. The modified code starts running in a fraction of a second. You save hours of time every day because you're not waiting for code changes to take effect.

Flutter gives you two ways to apply changes to a running app:

>> With *hot restart*, the app begins its run anew, removing any data that you've entered during the most recent test, displaying the app as if you're running it for the first time.

>> With *hot reload*, the app takes up from where it left off, with the data you last entered intact, if possible. The only changes are the ones dictated by your modifications to the code.

Flutter's hot restart and hot reload are both blazingly fast. They turn the app development cycle into a pleasure rather than a chore. Book 4, Chapter 2 tells you more about building, testing, and rerunning apps.

A great way to think about app development

You may have heard the all-encompassing mantra of Flutter app development:

In Flutter, almost everything is a widget.

WHAT IS A COMPILER?

You're a human being. (Sure, every rule has exceptions. But if you're reading this book, you're probably human.) Anyway, humans can write and comprehend the following Flutter source code:

```
import 'package:flutter/widgets.dart';
main() => runApp(SizedBox());
```

When you paraphrase the source code in English, here's what you get:

Get some code (code from the Flutter API) named widgets.dart.
Run an application whose only component is a box widget.

If you don't see the similarities between the Flutter code and its English equivalent, don't worry. Like most human beings, you can learn to read and write the Flutter code. In case you're wondering, this source code contains the world's simplest and most useless Flutter app. When the app runs, you see a completely black screen. It's not what you'd call a "killer app."

Source code is nice, but source code isn't for everyone and everything. The processors in computers and mobile devices aren't human beings. Processors don't follow source code instructions. Instead, they follow cryptic instructions of the following kind:

```
1100100 1100101 1111000 00001010 00110000 00110011 00110101 00000000
    10000100
```

These zeros and ones are, in fact, the first few words in an Android phone's version of the Black Screen app's code. Here's the Black Screen app after a processor interprets the zeros and ones:

```
.class public com/allmycode/dexperiment/MainActivity
.super io/flutter/embedding/android/FlutterActivity
.source MainActivity.java


.method public <init>()V
.limit registers 1
; this: v0 (Lcom/allmycode/dexperiment/MainActivity;)
.line 8
      invoke-direct     {v0},io/flutter/embedding/android/
    FlutterActivity/<init>
      ; <init>()V
      return-void
.end method
```

(continued)

(continued)

What a mess! Humans don't want to read or write instructions of this kind. These instructions aren't Dart source code instructions. They're *Dalvik bytecode* instructions. When you write a Flutter program, you write Dart source code instructions. If you test your program on an Android device, your development computer translates the source code into bytecode. If you test your program on an iPhone, the computer translates your source code into something that's even more obscure than bytecode.

The tool that performs the translation is a compiler. The *compiler* takes code that you can write and understand and translates it into code that a processor has a fighting chance of carrying out.

You might put your source code in a file named `main.dart`. To run your app on Android devices, the compiler creates other files named `MainActivity.dex` and `app.apk`. Normally, you don't bother looking at these compiled files. You can't even examine `.dex` files or `.apk` files with an ordinary editor. If you try to open `MainActivity.dex` with Notepad, TextEdit, or even Microsoft Word, you'll see nothing but dots, squiggles, and other gobbledygook.

No one (except for a few crazy programmers in some isolated labs in faraway places) writes Dalvik bytecode or any other kind of code that processors actually understand. When you ask your development computer to run your code, the computer uses its own software (a compiler) to create processor-friendly instructions. The only reason to look at the bytecode in this sidebar is to understand what a hard worker your development computer is.

And what is a widget? In a mobile app, every button is one of the app's widgets. Every text field is a widget. The app itself is a widget. The positioning of buttons and text fields is a widget. The animating of objects from one part of the screen to another is a widget. When you create a Flutter app, you put widgets inside of other widgets, which in turn are inside even more widgets. Listing 1-1 has some fake code that illustrates the point:

LISTING 1-1: **Like a Wheel within a Wheel**

```
// This isn't real Flutter code!
Application(
  Background(
    CenterWhateverIsInsideThis(
      Button(
        onPressed: print("I've been clicked."),
        Padding(
          Text(
```

```
        "Click Me"
      ),
    ),
   ),
  ),
 ),
)
```

Listing 1-1 has a Text widget inside of a Padding widget, which is inside of a Button **widget inside a** CenterWhateverIsInsideThis **widget. That** Center WhateverIsInsideThis **widget is inside a** Background **widget, which is inside an** Application **widget. Listing 1-1 is modeled after real Flutter code. The real Flutter code creates the app shown in Figure 1-2. When the user presses the** Button **in Figure 1-2, the words** *I've been clicked* **appear.**

FIGURE 1-2:
An app with
a button.

Compare Figures 1-2 and 1-3. Figure 1-2 shows the app as the user sees it. Figure 1-3 shows the same app as the Flutter developer codes it.

If you're not already a Flutter developer, the word *widget* might suggest a visible component, such as a button, a slider, an icon, or some other such thing. But in Flutter, things that aren't really visible are also widgets. For example, in Listing 1-1, CenterWhateverIsInsideThis is a widget. Having layout features like CenterWhateverIsInsideThis be widgets is a powerful idea. It means that Flutter developers can focus their attention on one overarching task — stuffing widgets inside other widgets. Flutter has a certain simplicity and elegance that other app development frameworks don't have.

TIP

Flutter has no built-in widget named CenterWhateverIsInsideThis. But don't be disappointed. Flutter's Center widget does what the fictitious CenterWhatever IsInsideThis widget is supposed to do.

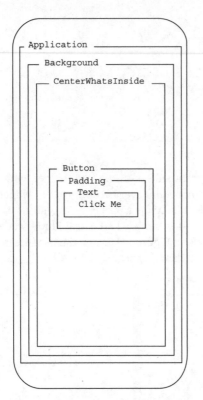

FIGURE 1-3:
Widgets within
widgets.

Enough New Terminology! What's Next?

You may have read this chapter from start to finish but not one word in the chapter prompted you to touch your computer keyboard. What a shame! The next chapter will rectify that awful omission.

Chapter **2**

Setting Up Your Computer for Mobile App Development

Tools don't directly do the things you want done. You can't eat a tool, read a good tool, hear a tool's happy song, or dance the jig with a tool. But you can use tools to make food, books, musical instruments, and dance floors.

This chapter is all about tools — the tools you use to make great mobile apps.

The Stuff You Need

This book tells you how to create apps using Flutter. Before you can create apps, you need some software tools. Here's a list of the tools you need:

> » **The Flutter Software Development Kit (SDK)**
>
> The Flutter SDK includes lots and lots of prewritten, reusable Flutter code and a bunch of software tools for running and testing Flutter apps. The SDK has

the official Flutter code libraries, Dart code libraries, documentation, and even some sample apps.

» An integrated development environment

You can create Flutter apps by using geeky, keyboard-only tools, but eventually you'll tire of typing and retyping commands. An *integrated development environment (IDE),* on the other hand, is a little like a word processor. A word processor helps you compose documents (memos, poems, and other works of fine literature); in contrast, an IDE helps you compose instructions for processors.

One way to compose Flutter apps is by using the Android Studio IDE. Don't be fooled by the word *Android* in the IDE's name. Using Android Studio, you can create iPhone apps, web apps, and other kinds of apps.

» Some sample Flutter apps, to help you get started

All examples in this book are available for download here:

```
www.dummies.com/go/codingallinonefd2e
```

» A device for testing your Flutter code

You write some code, and then you run it to see whether it works correctly. Usually, it doesn't work correctly until you make some changes. Most often, it doesn't work correctly until you make *lots* of changes.

This book emphasizes the creation of apps for iPhones and Android phones. You can run your code on your own phone, but you can also run it on your computer. To run a mobile app on your computer, you need software that displays a phone on your screen and runs your app within that display.

In the iPhone world, this type of software is called a *simulator*, and Android calls its software an *emulator*. Simulators and emulators are examples of *virtual devices*. In contrast, an actual iPhone or Android phone is called a *physical device* (also called a real device).

TECHNICAL STUFF

An emulator isn't quite the same thing as a simulator. An emulator is software that behaves, to a large extent, like the hardware of a real, physical phone. A simulator is software that runs a phone's apps without really behaving too much like the phone's hardware. Fortunately, when you run this book's apps, you can ignore this subtle difference.

All these tools run on the *development computer* — the laptop or desktop computer you use to develop Flutter apps. Later, when you publish your app, users run the app on their *target devices* — physical devices such as iPhones, Android phones, and (someday soon) smart toasters.

Here's good news: You can download for free all the software you need to run this book's examples. The software is separated into four downloads:

» When you visit https://flutter.dev/docs/get-started/install, you can click a button to install the Flutter SDK.

» A button at the page http://developer.android.com/studio gives you the Android Studio IDE download. Along with this download comes the Android emulator.

» This book's website has a link to all of the book's code.

» The iPhone simulator, as well as all the code you need for generating iPhone apps, comes with the installation of Xcode on your Mac. Xcode is available from the Macintosh App Store. (Unfortunately, you can't develop for iPhone on a Windows PC.)

WARNING

In the world of mobile app development, things change very quickly. The creators of Flutter are always creating new features and new tools. The old tools stop working, and the old instructions no longer apply. If you see something on your screen that doesn't look like one of the screenshots in this book, don't despair. It might be something very new, or you might have reached a corner of the software that isn't described in this book. Visit the book's website to find out about late-breaking changes, to report a bug, or to ask a question.

What to Do

It's an old, familiar refrain. First you get some software. Then you run the software.

Getting and installing the stuff

1. **Visit the book's website (www.dummies.com/go/codingallinonefd2e) and download the BOOK_4_CREATING_MOBILE_APPS.zip file, which contains all the program examples in this book.**

The downloaded file is a .zip archive file. (Refer to the later sidebars "Those pesky filename extensions" and "Compressed archive files.")

TIP

Most web browsers save files to the Downloads directory on the computer's hard drive. But your browser may be configured a bit differently. One way or another, make note of the folder containing the downloaded file BOOK_4_CREATING_MOBILE_APPS.zip.

2. **Extract the contents of the downloaded file to a place on your computer's hard drive.**

3. **Visit** `https://flutter.dev/docs/get-started/install` **and download the Flutter SDK.**

   Choose a version of the software that matches your operating system (Windows, Macintosh, or whatever).

4. **Extract the contents of the downloaded file to a place on your computer's hard drive.**

   The aforementioned *contents* is actually a directory full of stuff. The directory's name is `flutter`. Put your new `flutter` directory in a place that isn't protected with special privileges. For example, if you try extracting the `flutter` directory inside the `c:\program files` directory, Windows displays its User Account Control dialog box and asks for confirmation. Don't put the `flutter` directory inside a place like that.

   TIP

   You say "folder." I say "directory." To not-quite-quote Gershwin, let's call the whole thing off because, in this book, these two words are used interchangeably.

   A good place to put the `flutter` directory is inside your home directory. For example, your computer probably has a directory named `Users`, and inside that `Users` directory is a directory with your name on it. That directory is your home directory. This *home directory* contains the `Documents` directory, the `Downloads` directory, and lots of other stuff. After you extract the downloaded file's content, your home directory has a brand-new `flutter` directory.

   You don't have to extract the `flutter` directory right inside your home directory, but it's the simplest, most reliable thing to do.

5. **Make a note of the place on your hard drive where the new** `flutter` **directory lives.**

   For example, if you copied the `.zip` file's contents to your `/Users/janeqreader` directory, make a note of the `/Users/janeqreader/flutter` directory. That's your *Flutter SDK path*.

   TIP

   To make sure that you've extracted the downloaded file's contents correctly, look inside the `flutter` directory for a subdirectory named `bin`. The `flutter` directory has other subdirectories, named `dev`, `examples`, and `packages`. Your mileage may vary, depending on when you download the Flutter SDK.

6. **Visit** `http://developer.android.com/studio` **and download the Android Studio IDE.**

   The download is an `.exe` file, a `.dmg` file, or maybe something else.

7. **Install the software that you downloaded in Step 6.**

   During the installation, a dialog box may offer the option of installing an Android virtual device (AVD). If so, accept the option.

For other details about installing Android Studio, see this chapter's later section "On installing Android Studio."

TIP

Android Studio isn't the only IDE that has features for creating Flutter apps. Some developers prefer Virtual Studio Code (known affectionately as VS Code), which is available for Windows, Macintosh, and Linux. And if you enjoy roughing it, you can do without an IDE and use the command line along with your favorite text editor — Emacs, vi, or Notepad. In this book, I focus on Android Studio, but you can find plenty of alternatives.

To learn more about Visual Studio Code, visit `https://code.visualstudio.com`.

TIP

While you're visiting any software download site, check the requirements for downloading, installing, and running that software. Make sure you have enough memory and an operating system that's sufficiently up to date.

THOSE PESKY FILENAME EXTENSIONS

The filenames displayed in File Explorer or in a Finder window can be misleading. You may browse a directory and see the name `android-studio-ide` or `flutter_win-dows`. The file's real name might be `android-studio-ide.exe`, `flutter_windows.zip`, or plain old `flutter_windows`. Filename endings such as `.zip`, `.exe`, `.dmg`, `.app`, and `.dart` are *filename extensions*.

The ugly truth is that, by default, Windows and the Mac hide many filename extensions. This awful feature tends to confuse people. If you don't want to be confused, change your computer's system-wide settings. Here's how to do it:

- **In Windows 7:** Choose Start ⇨ Control Panel ⇨ Appearance and Personalization ⇨ Folder Options. Then skip to the third bullet.

- **In Windows 8:** On the Charms bar, choose Settings ⇨ Control Panel. In the Control Panel, choose Appearance and Personalization ⇨ Folder Options. Then proceed to the following bullet.

- **In Windows 7 or 8:** Follow the instructions in one of the preceding bullets. Then, in the Folder Options dialog box, click the View tab. Look for the Hide File Extensions for Known File Types option. Make sure that this checkbox is *not* selected.

- **In Windows 10:** On the File Explorer's main menu, select View. On the ribbon that appears, put a check mark next to File Name Extensions.

- **In macOS:** On the Finder application's menu, select Preferences. In the resulting dialog box, select the Advanced tab and look for the Show All File Extensions option. Make sure that this checkbox *is* selected.

COMPRESSED ARCHIVE FILES

When you visit this book's website and download the examples, you download a file named BOOK_4_CREATING_MOBILE_APPS.zip. A ZIP file is a single file that encodes a bunch of smaller files. The BOOK_4_CREATING_MOBILE_APPS.zip file encodes files with names such as app0301.dart, app0302.dart, and app0401.dart. The app0301.dart file contains the code in Listing 3-1 — the first listing in Book 4, Chapter 3. Likewise, app0302.dart and app0401.dart have the code in Listings 3-2 and 4-1.

The BOOK_4_CREATING_MOBILE_APPS.zip file also encodes a folder named assets. This folder contains copies of the images that appear in the book's apps.

A .zip file is an example of a *compressed archive* file. Other examples of compressed archives include .tar.gz files, .rar files, and .sparsebundle files. When you *uncompress* a file, you extract the original files and folders stored inside the larger archive file. (For a .zip file, another word for uncompressing is *unzipping*.)

When you download BOOK_4_CREATING_MOBILE_APPS.zip, the web browser may uncompress the file automatically for you. If not, you can get your computer to uncompress the file. Here's how:

- **On a Windows computer,** double-click the .zip file's icon. When you do this, Windows File Explorer shows you the files and folders inside the compressed .zip archive. Drag all these files and folders to another place on your computer's hard drive (a place that's not inside the archive file).

- **On a Mac,** double-click the .zip file's icon. When you do this, the Mac extracts the contents of the archive file and shows you the extracted contents in a Finder window.

For Mac users only

If you have a Mac and you want to create iPhone apps, follow these steps:

1. **Select App Store from the Apple menu.**

2. **In the store's search field, type Xcode and then press Enter.**

   The App Store's search finds dozens of apps, but only one has the simple name Xcode.

3. **Click the Xcode app's Get button.**

   As a result, the App Store installs Xcode on your computer.

4. **Launch the Xcode application.**

   The first time you run Xcode, your Mac installs some additional components. If you
   want your apps to run on Apple devices, you need those additional components.

Configuring Android Studio

Android Studio doesn't come automatically with Flutter support, meaning you
have to add Flutter support the first time you run the IDE. Here's what you do.

1. **Launch the Android Studio application.**

   The first time you run a fresh, new copy of Android Studio, you see the
   Welcome screen.

2. **Select Plugins on the Welcome screen.**

   You'll find the Plugins link on the left side of the Welcome screen. (See
   Figure 2-1.)

3. **Search for a plugin named Flutter. Install that plugin.**

   If Android Studio offers the option of installing Dart as well, accept the option.

   After installing the plugin, Android Studio may want to be restarted. Of course,
   you should restart it. When you do, you see the Welcome screen again. Now the
   Welcome screen includes the New Flutter Project option. (See Figure 2-2.)

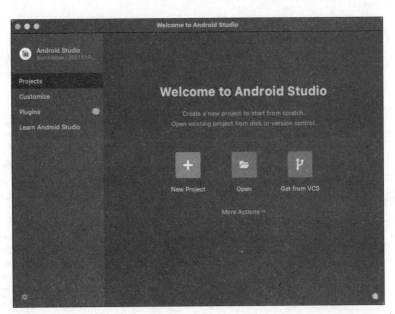

FIGURE 2-1:
Android Studio's
default Welcome
screen.

© John Wiley & Sons

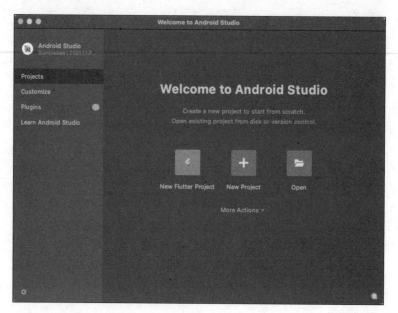

© John Wiley & Sons

FIGURE 2-2:
You've installed
the Flutter plugin.

Running your first app

You've installed Android Studio, added Android Studio's Flutter plugin, and then restarted Android Studio. Now you're staring at Android Studio's Welcome screen. What do you do next?

1. **Connect to the Internet.**

During the run of your very first app, Android Studio downloads some additional software.

2. **Select the New Flutter Project option. (Refer to Figure 2-2.)**

On your phone, an app is an app, and that's all there is to it. But on your development computer, all your work is divided into projects. For professional purposes, you're not absolutely correct if you think of one app as equaling one project. But, for the examples in this book, the "one project equals one app" model works just fine.

TIP

If you don't see the New Flutter Project option, you may not have installed the Flutter plugin correctly. Double-check the instructions in the "Configuring Android Studio" section, earlier in this chapter.

Having selected New Flutter Project, you'll see three dialog boxes, one after another. The first asks for the path to the Flutter SDK, the second asks for the new app's name and other details, and the third creates something called a package.

3. **In the first step, enter the Flutter SDK path that you noted earlier. (See Figure 2-3.) Click Next and the second dialog box will appear.**

The second dialog box has several fields for you to fill out: Project Name, Project Location, Description, Project Type, Organization, and information about the languages and platforms the app should use and support. (See Figure 2-4.)

4. **Select a name that has only lowercase letters and, if you want, underscore (_) characters.**

Flutter project names cannot contain uppercase letters, blank spaces, or punctuation characters other than the underscore.

REMEMBER

TIP

If you create many apps, keeping track of them all can drive you crazy. So, it helps if you decide on a formula for naming your apps and then stick to that formula as closely as you can. Later on, when you start marketing your apps, you can abandon the formula, and use clever names that attract peoples' attention.

5. **Don't change the Project Location option unless you have a specific reason for doing so.**

You don't have to specify a new directory for each of your projects. Android Studio does that for you automatically with this project location as the starting point.

6. **For the description, type something that's silly and off the wall.**

Do it now, while you still can. When you create apps professionally, you have to be more serious.

7. **If your company has a domain name, or if you have your own domain name, type it in the Organization field. If not, type anything at all or leave the default text alone.**

A *package* is a collection of closely related pieces of code, and each Flutter app belongs to its own package. In the Flutter world, it's customary to start a package's name with the reverse of a domain name. For example, if your company's domain name is wiley.com, the app is usually in a package named com.wiley.*somethingorother*. The *somethingorother* part will be unique to each of your apps.

When you create your first project, the Organization field's default text is probably example.com. Several years ago, the Internet Corporation for Assigned Names and Numbers (ICANN) set this name aside for anyone to use.

8. **Under the Organization field are some buttons for selecting the Android and iOS languages and the platforms you want to enable support for. Leave these settings as they are for now.**

9. **Click Finish.**

As if by magic, Android Studio's main window appears. (See Figure 2-5.) The main window has all the tools you need for developing top-notch Flutter applications. It even has a sample starter application, which you run in the next few steps.

Android Studio's main window may look overwhelming at first. The main window's parts are described in this chapter's "Using Android Studio" section, later in this chapter.

In Figure 2-6, notice two important items near the top of Android Studio's main window:

- The *Target Selector* displays the text <no devices>.

- The *Run icon* is a little right-pointing green arrow.

10. What you do next depends on your development computer and your development goals.

If you have a Mac and you want to run an iPhone simulator, select Open iOS Simulator in the Target Selector drop-down list.

If you don't have a Mac, or if you want to run an Android emulator, select Tools ⇨ AVD Manager on Android Studio's main menu bar. In the resulting dialog box, look for a Green Arrow icon on the right side of the dialog box. Click that Green Arrow icon. (See Figure 2-7.)

If the AVD manager is empty — that is to say, if it's not like the manager shown in Figure 2-7, which shows a virtual device labeled Pixel API 28 — you have to create an Android Virtual Device. See the section "Running apps on an Android device," later in this chapter, for details.

WARNING

Android Virtual Devices don't always start quickly. For a computer with 16 gigabytes of RAM, the start-up time may be two to three minutes. On a computer with only 4 gigabytes of RAM, the AVD might never start up. Apple's iPhone simulator tends to be a bit snappier, but you never know. Two later sections of this chapter are devoted to Android emulator and iPhone simulator tricks — "On adding virtual devices" and "Divisiveness Among Devices."

When your virtual device's home screen appears on the screen, you're ready to run the sample Flutter app.

11. **Click the Run icon on Android Studio's toolbar. (Refer to Figure 2-6.)**

As a result, Android Studio's Run tool window appears in the lower portion of the main window. A few messages appear while you wait impatiently for the app to start running. When the app starts running, the virtual device (the simulator or emulator) sports a handsome display. (See Figure 2-8.)

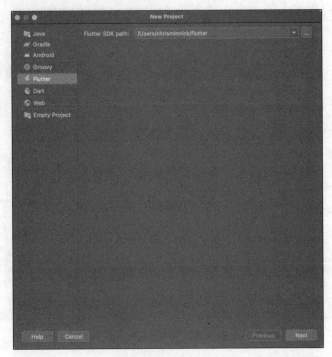

FIGURE 2-3:
Enter the Flutter
SDK path.

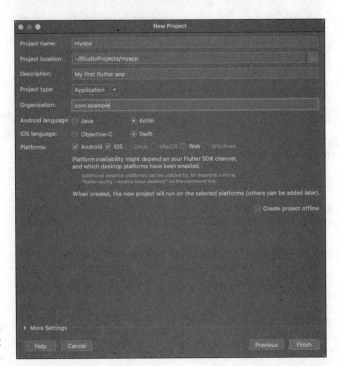

FIGURE 2-4:
Details about
your new app.

CHAPTER 2 **Setting Up Your Computer for Mobile App Development** 411

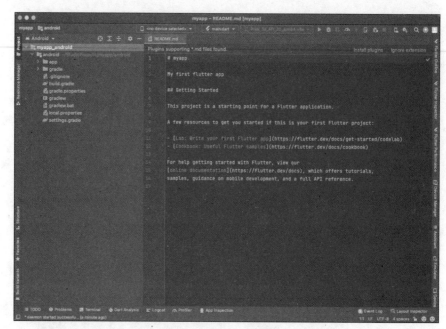

FIGURE 2-5:
Android Studio's
main window.

Target selector   Run icon

FIGURE 2-6:
Android Studio's
toolbar.

FIGURE 2-7:
Start running
an Android
Virtual Device.

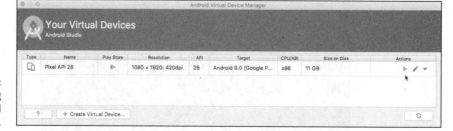

FIGURE 2-8:
Isn't it wonderful?

© John Wiley & Sons

Congratulations! Your first app is running. You can try out the app by clicking the mouse on the app's floating action button (the circular item in the lower-right corner of the virtual device's screen). The message in the middle tells you how many times you've clicked the button. It's not the world's most useful app, but it's a good start.

For details about any of these steps, see the next several sections.

Dealing with the Devil's Details

In earlier sections, you learned the basic steps for setting up your computer and running your first Flutter app. Basic steps are nice, but they don't work for everyone. That's why, in this section, you'll delve a bit deeper.

WARNING

In the world of mobile app development, things change very quickly. The creators of Flutter are always creating new features and new tools. The old tools stop working, and the old instructions no longer apply. If you see something on your screen that doesn't look like one of my screenshots, don't despair. It might be something very new, or you might have reached a corner of the software that's not described in this book. If you get stuck, check this book's website for the latest updates and to get additional help.

On installing Android Studio

What you do to install Android Studio depends on your operating system:

» **In Windows:** The downloaded file is probably an .exe file. Double-click the .exe file's icon.

When you double-click the .exe file's icon, a wizard guides you through the installation.

» **On a Mac:** The downloaded file is probably a .dmg file. Double-click the .dmg file's icon.

When you double-click the .dmg file's icon, you see the Android Studio icon (also known as the Android Studio.app icon). Drag the Android Studio icon to your Applications folder.

For more information on topics like .exe and .dmg, refer to the earlier sidebar "Those pesky filename extensions." And, if you need help with .zip files, see the earlier sidebar "Compressed archive files."

On launching Android Studio for the first time

Is it time to launch Android Studio? This section has a few small details.

» **In Windows:** Click the Start button and look for the Android Studio entry.

» **On a Mac:** Press Command-space to make the Spotlight appear. In the Spotlight's search field, start typing *Android Studio*. When your Mac makes the full name *Android Studio* appear in the Spotlight's search field, press Enter.

When you launch Android Studio for the first time, you might see a dialog box offering to import settings from a previous Android Studio installation. Chances are, you don't have a previous Android Studio installation, so you should firmly but politely decline this offer.

When the dust settles, Android Studio displays the Welcome screen. The Welcome screen has options such as Start a New Android Studio Project, Open an Existing Android Studio Project, Configure, and Get Help. (Refer to Figures 2-1 and 2-2.)

You see this Welcome screen again and again. Stated informally, the Welcome screen says, "At the moment, you're not working on any particular project (any particular Flutter app). So, what do you want to do next?"

On adding virtual devices

When it comes to installing virtual devices, the stories for iPhone and Android are a bit different.

>> With an Apple, Windows, or Linux computer, you can download Android Studio and get the Android emulator that comes with it. You might have to do a bit of work to install an Android Virtual Device (AVD), but that's not a big deal.

>> If you have an Apple computer, you get an iPhone simulator by downloading Apple's Xcode software.

WARNING

If you don't have an Apple computer, you can find third-party simulators by searching the Web, but keep in mind that creating iPhone apps on anything other than a Mac is difficult. Depending on the way you do it, the process might even be illegal.

Android makes a distinction between an emulator and an Android Virtual Device (AVD). Here's the scoop:

>> When you install Android Studio, you get the Android phone emulator automatically. This emulator can bridge the gap between your development computer's hardware and a mock-up of a phone's hardware. But which phone's hardware is it mocking? Is it a Samsung Galaxy or a Sony Xperia? How big is the phone's screen? What kind of camera does the phone have?

>> An *Android Virtual Device* is a description of a phone's hardware. The emulator doesn't work unless you create an AVD for the emulator to emulate. When you install Android Studio, you may or may not see an option to install an AVD. If you do, accept the option. If you don't, that's okay. You'll be able to create a bunch of AVDs when you get Android Studio running.

When you install Android Studio, the installer may offer you the option to create an AVD for you to use. If you weren't offered this option, or if you skipped the option, you can create an AVD using the AVD Manager tool. In fact, you can create several additional AVDs and use several different AVDs to run and test your Flutter apps on Android's emulator.

To open the AVD Manager, go to Android Studio's main menu bar and choose Tools ⇨ AVD Manager.

MIMICKING AN ANDROID PHYSICAL DEVICE

Android's emulated device is really three pieces of software rolled into one:

- **A *system image* is a copy of one version of the Android operating system.**

  For example, a particular system image might be for Android Pie (API Level 28) running on an Intel x86_64 processor.

- **An *emulator* bridges the gap between the system image and the processor on your development computer.**

  You might have a system image for an Atom_64 processor, but your development computer runs a Core i5 processor. The emulator translates instructions for the Atom_64 processor into instructions that the Core i5 processor can execute.

- **An Android Virtual Device (AVD) is a piece of software that describes a device's hardware.**

  An AVD contains a bunch of settings, telling the emulator all the details about the device to be emulated. What's the screen resolution of the device? Does the device have a physical keyboard? Does it have a camera? How much memory does it have? Does it have an SD card? All these choices belong to a particular AVD.

Android Studio's menus and dialog boxes make it easy to confuse these three items. When you create a new AVD, you create a new system image to go with that AVD. But Android Studio's dialog boxes blur the distinction between the AVD and the system image. You also see the word *emulator,* when the correct term is *AVD*. If the subtle differences between system images, emulators, and AVDs don't bother you, don't worry about them.

A seasoned Android developer typically has several system images and several AVDs on the development computer, but only one Android emulator program.

On installing Flutter

If you're having trouble running apps, and you think your Flutter installation is sick, you can take Flutter to the doctor. Here's how:

1. **In Android Studio, start a new Flutter project or open an existing project.**

   For help with that, refer to this chapter's "Running your first app" section.

2. **In Android Studio's main menu bar, select Tools ⇨ Flutter ⇨ Flutter Doctor.**

   As a result, the computer reports to you on the health of your Flutter installation.

YOUR FRIEND, THE COMMAND LINE

Most of the instructions in this book require pointing and clicking. But some tasks still require long, cryptic typewritten commands, and some people prefer typing commands over clicking buttons. To help you survive the unimaginable misery of typing error-prone, enigmatic commands, here are a few tips:

- You can't type commands just anywhere. To communicate directly with your computer, you must first open your computer's Terminal (as it's known in the Mac world) or Command Prompt (as it's known to Windows users).

  If Android Studio is running, you can open Mac's Terminal or the Windows Command Prompt by clicking the little Terminal tool button near the bottom of Android Studio's window.

- On a Mac, you can always open Mac's Terminal by pressing Command+space, typing **Terminal**, and then pressing Enter.

  On Windows, you can always open the Command Prompt by pressing Start, typing **cmd**, and then pressing Enter.

- At any moment, a Terminal or Command Prompt window has a *working directory*. For example, if the working directory is /Users/isaacnewton/Documents, and you type myfile.txt, the computer looks in the /Users/isaacnewton/ Documents directory for a file named myfile.txt. If the /Users/isaacnewton/ Documents directory has a file named myfile.txt, the computer displays the contents of myfile.txt in page-size chunks.

  (On Windows): To find out which directory is the working directory, look at the prompt or type **cd**. To change the working directory, type **cd** followed by the new directory's name.

  ```
  c:\Users\isaacnewton\Documents>cd
  c:\Users\isaacnewton\Documents
  c:\Users\isaacnewton\Documents>cd c:\Users\isaacnewton
  c:\Users\isaacnewton>cd
  c:\Users\isaacnewton
  ```

- **(On a Mac):** To find out which directory is the working directory, type pwd. To change the working directory, type **cd** followed by the new directory's name.

  ```
  Isaacs-Air:Documents isaacnewton$ pwd
  /Users/isaacnewton/Documents
  Isaacs-Air:Documents isaacnewton$ cd /Users/isaacnewton
  Isaacs-Air:~ isaacnewton$ pwd
  /Users/isaacnewton
  ```

The report from Flutter Doctor isn't always helpful. Some of the report's findings may be false alarms. Others may be difficult to interpret. If you see something that looks like a useful diagnosis, give it a try. Many of the doctor's hints involve opening up a Terminal or Command Prompt window. You'll find advice about that in the "Your friend, the command line" sidebar.

Divisiveness Among Devices

If your development computer has enough horsepower, you can run a few Android Virtual Devices simultaneously. On a Mac, you can run an iPhone simulator while your Android Virtual Devices are running. But using your virtual and physical devices can be tricky. This section gives you some tips.

Running apps on an Android device

The emulator that comes with Android Studio swallows up lots of resources on your development computer. If you don't have the latest, most powerful hardware, you may have trouble running apps in the emulator. Maybe you don't see Android's home screen or you don't see your app running five minutes or so after the emulator starts running. If so, here are several things you can try:

>> **Lather, rinse, repeat.**

Close the emulator and launch your application again. Sometimes, the second or third time's a charm. On rare occasions, the first three attempts fail, but the fourth attempt succeeds.

>> **If you have access to a computer with more RAM, try running your app on it.**

Horsepower matters.

>> **If you don't have access to a computer with more RAM, close all non-essential programs on your development computer and try running your app again.**

>> **Try a different AVD.**

The "On adding virtual devices" section, earlier in this chapter, tells you how to add a new AVD to your system. An AVD with an x86 system image is better than an AVD with an armeabi image. (Fortunately, when a dialog box lets you choose between x86 and armeabi, you don't have to know what *x86* or *armeabi* means.)

>> **Wrestle with virtualization technology.**

You might not want to start down this rabbit hole.

When it runs on an Intel x86 processor, Android's emulator tries to use something called Intel Virtualization Technology (VT) with the Intel Hardware Accelerated Execution Manager (HAXM). If your computer isn't completely comfortable with a VT-and-HAXM configuration, you're likely to have trouble using Android's emulator.

Don't despair! Try installing an armeabi system image.

The previous bulleted list describes a few remedies for problems with Android Studio's emulator. Unfortunately, none of the bullets in this list is a silver bullet. If you've tried these tricks and you're still having trouble, you might try abandoning the emulator that comes with Android Studio and running apps on a "real" device.

Testing apps on a physical device

You can bypass virtual devices and test your apps on a physical phone, a tablet device, or maybe even a smart coffee pot. To do so, you have to prepare the physical device, prepare your development computer, and then hook together the two. It's quite a chore, but after you do it the first time, it becomes much easier. This section describes an outline of the steps you must follow. For more details, visit these pages:

>> `https://flutter.dev/docs/get-started/install/macos` – deploy-to-ios-devices

>> `https://flutter.dev/docs/get-started/install/windows` – set-up-your-android-device

Preparing to test on an Android physical device

To test your app on an Android device, follow these steps:

1. **On your Android device, enable Developer Options.**

   On many Android devices, you do this by choosing Settings ⇨ About. In the About list, tap the Build Number item seven times. (Yes, seven times.) Then press the Back button to return to the Settings list. In the Settings list, tap System ⇨ Developer Options.

2. **In the Developer Options list, turn on USB debugging.**

You may see a message similar to the following:

```
USB debugging is intended for development purposes.
Use it to copy data between your computer and your device,
install apps on your device without notification, and read log data.
```

The stewards of Android are warning you that the USB Debugging option can expose your device to malware.

Many developers keep USB Debugging on all the time with no problems. But if you're nervous about security, turn off USB Debugging when you're not using the device to develop apps.

3. **(For Windows users only) Visit** `https://developer.android.com/studio/run/oem-usb.html` **to download your Android device's Windows USB driver. Install the driver on your Windows development computer.**

While you follow the next step, keep an eye on your Android device's screen.

4. **With a USB cable, connect the device to the development computer.**

TIP

Not all USB cables are created equal. Some cables, called *data cables*, have wires and metal in places where other cables, called *charging cables*, have nothing except plastic. Try to use whatever USB cable came with your device. If you can't find the cable that came with your device or you don't know which cable came with your device, try more than one cable. When you find a cable that works, label that cable.

When you plug in the cable, you see a popup dialog box on the Android device's screen. The popup asks whether you want to allow USB debugging.

5. **Yes, allow USB debugging.**

If you're not looking for it, you can miss the popup to allow USB debugging. Be sure to look for this popup when you plug in your device. If you definitely don't see the popup, you might be okay anyway. But if the message appears and you don't respond to it, you definitely won't be okay.

CHECKING THE CONNECTION AND BREAKING THE CONNECTION

To find out whether your Android phone is properly connected to your development computer, follow these steps:

1. **Open the Terminal on a Mac or the Command Prompt on Windows.**

   For details, refer to the earlier sidebar "Your friend, the command line."

2. **Use the `cd` command to navigate to Android's `platform-tools` directory.**

   On Windows, the command to do this looks like this:

   ```
   cd %HOMEDRIVE%%HOMEPATH%\AppData\Local\Android\Sdk\platform-tools
   ```

   On macOS, you can use the following command:

   ```
   cd ~/Library/Android/sdk/platform-tools/
   ```

3. **Type `adb devices`. (On a Mac, type `./adb devices`.)**

   If your computer's response includes a very long hexadecimal number (such as 2885046445FF097), that number represents your connected device. For example, with one particular phone connected, you might get a response such as this:

   ```
   emulator-5554 device
   emulator-5556 device
   2885046445FF097 device
   ```

   If you see the word *unauthorized* next to the long hexadecimal number, you probably didn't answer OK to the question "Allow USB debugging?" in Step 5 of the earlier section "Preparing to test on an Android physical device."

   If your computer's response doesn't include a long hexadecimal number, you might have missed one of the other steps in that earlier section.

Eventually, you'll want to disconnect your device from the development computer. Look for some reference to the device in File Explorer or the Finder.

- If you don't see a reference, you can probably yank the device's USB cable from your computer.

- If you see a reference, try to eject the device.

(continued)

(continued)

If you try to eject the device, and you see the dreaded Not Safe to Remove Device message, start by following Steps 1 and 2 in this sidebar. Then do one of the following:

- On a Mac, type the following and press Enter:

    ```
    ./adb kill-server
    ```

- On Windows, type the following and press Enter

    ```
    adb kill-server
    ```

After that, you see the friendly Safe to Remove Hardware message.

Preparing to test on an iPhone

To test your app on an iPhone (or even an iPad), you must be using an Apple computer. If you have a Mac, follow these steps:

1. **Visit `https://brew.sh` and follow the instructions to install Homebrew on your computer.**

    Homebrew is a third-party software package manager for macOS and Linux. You can use it to install all kinds of software, not just iPhone development tools.

2. **Open your Mac's Terminal application.**

3. **In the Terminal application window, type the following commands, one after another:**

    ```
    brew update
    brew install --HEAD libusbmuxd
    brew link libusbmuxd
    brew install --HEAD libimobiledevice
    brew install ideviceinstaller ios-deploy cocoapods
    pod setup
    ```

    Wasn't that fun? It takes a long time to get responses, and you probably see scary warning messages along the way.

4. **Visit `developer.apple.com` and sign up for membership in Apple's developer program.**

After these three steps, your development computer is ready to go. Follow these steps whenever you want to test a new Flutter app on a physical iPhone:

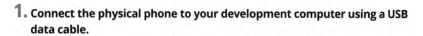

1. **Connect the physical phone to your development computer using a USB data cable.**

REMEMBER

Not all cables are alike. Apple puts a proprietary chip in each of its iPhone cables. If you buy your cable from a third-party vendor, you might not be able to use it to transfer an app to your phone.

2. **In Android Studio, open your new Flutter project.**

3. **Look for the Project tool window — the panel displaying a tree of files and folders.**

You find the Project tool window along the left side of Android Studio's main window. If you have trouble finding it, skip ahead to the section entitled "The Project tool window" in this chapter.

4. **Expand one of the tree's topmost branches to find a subbranch named** iOS.

5. **Right-click the** iOS **subbranch. In the resulting context menu, select Flutter ⇨ Open iOS Module in Xcode.**

As a result, Xcode starts up. There's a tree of files and folders on the left side of the Xcode window.

TIP

Throughout this chapter, I write *right-click* as though everyone has a mouse with two or more buttons. If you're a Mac user and your mouse has only one button, you can use Control+click wherever you see the term *right-click*.

6. **In the tree of files and folders, select Runner. (See Figure 2-9.)**

7. **Select the Signing & Capabilities tab near the top of the Xcode window. (Again, refer to Figure 2-9.)**

The Signing & Capabilities tab has a Team drop-down list.

8. **In the Team drop-down list, select Add an Account.**

As a result, an Accounts dialog box appears. With your Apple ID, you automatically belong to a team of developers — your personal team with you as its only member.

9. **Do whatever you have to do in the Accounts dialog box and then dismiss the dialog box.**

As a result, you return to the Signing & Capabilities tab.

10. **In the Team drop-down list, select your very own team.**

11. **Close Xcode.**

You're good to go.

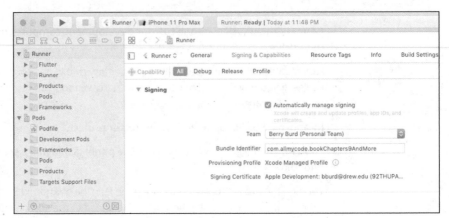

FIGURE 2-9:
Who's Berry
Burd?

Testing on any physical device (Android or iPhone)

When you're ready to test your app on a physical device, and you've connected the device to your development computer, look at the Target Selector drop-down list on Android Studio's toolbar. When your development computer is communicating properly with the physical device, the device's name appears as one of this drop-down list's items. (See Figure 2-10.) Select this item and then click the Run icon.

FIGURE 2-10:
iPhone is
connected!

Using Android Studio

Android Studio is a customized version of IntelliJ IDEA — a general-purpose IDE with tools for Java development, C/C++ development, PHP development, modeling, project management, testing, debugging, and much more.

In this section, you get an overview of Android Studio's main window and of the most useful features that help you build Flutter apps.

Starting up

Each Flutter app belongs to a project. You can have dozens of projects on your computer's hard drive. When you run Android Studio, each of your projects is either open or closed. An *open* project appears in a window (its own window) on your computer screen. A *closed* project doesn't appear in a window.

Several of your projects can be open at the same time. You can switch between projects by moving from window to window.

If Android Studio is running and no projects are open, Android Studio displays its Welcome screen. (Refer to Figure 2-2.) The Welcome screen may display some recently closed projects. If so, you can open a project by clicking its name on the Welcome screen. For an existing app that's not on the Recent Projects list, you can click the Welcome screen's Open an Existing Android Studio Project option.

If you have any open projects, Android Studio doesn't display the Welcome screen. In that case, you can open another project by choosing File➪Open or File➪Open Recent in an open project's window. To close a project, you can choose File➪Close Project, or you can do whatever you normally do to close one of the windows on your computer. (On a PC, click the X in the window's upper-right corner. On a Mac, click the little red button in the window's upper left corner.)

TIP

Android Studio remembers which projects were open from one run to the next. If any projects are open when you quit Android Studio, those projects open again the next time you launch Android Studio. You can override this behavior (so that only the Welcome screen appears each time you launch Android Studio). In Android Studio on a Windows computer, start by choosing File➪Settings➪Appearance and Behavior➪System Settings. In Android Studio on a Mac, choose Android Studio➪Preferences➪Appearance and Behavior➪System Settings. In either case, uncheck the Reopen Last Project on Startup checkbox.

The main window

Android Studio's main window is divided into several areas. Some of these areas can appear and disappear on your command. What comes next is a description of the areas in Figure 2-11, moving from the top of the main window to the bottom.

REMEMBER

The areas that you see on your computer screen may be different from the areas in Figure 2-11. Usually, that's okay. You can make areas come and go by choosing certain menu options, including the View option on Android Studio's main menu bar. You can also click the little tool buttons on the edges of the main window.

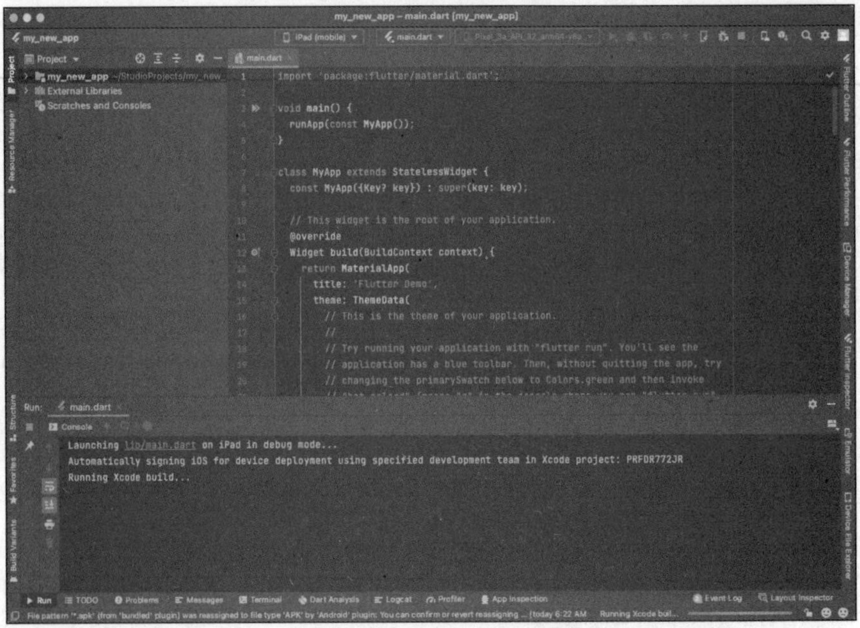

FIGURE 2-11:
The main window
has several areas.

The top of the main window

The topmost area contains the toolbar and the navigation bar.

>> **The *toolbar* contains action buttons, such as Open and Save All. It also contains the Target Selector and the Run icon.**

   The Target Selector is the drop-down list whose default option is <no devices>. In Figure 2-11, the Target Selector displays the name *iPad (mobile)*.

   The Run icon is the thing that looks like a green Play button.

   You can read more about these items earlier, in this chapter's "Running your first app" section.

>> **The navigation bar displays the path to one of the files in your Flutter project.**

   A Flutter project contains many files, and, at any particular moment, you work on one of these files. The navigation bar points to that file.

The Project tool window

Below the main menu and the toolbars, you see two different areas. The area on the left contains the *Project tool window*, which you use to navigate from one file to another within your Android app.

At any given moment, the Project tool window displays one of several possible views. For example, back in Figure 2-11, the Project tool window displays its *Project view*. In Figure 2-12, the Packages view is displayed.

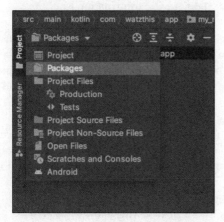

FIGURE 2-12:
Selecting
Packages view.

© John Wiley & Sons

Packages view displays many of the same files as Project view, but in Packages view, the files are grouped differently. In this book, you'll primarily be using the Project view.

REMEMBER

If Android Studio doesn't display the Project tool window, look for the Project tool button — the little button displaying the word *Project* on the left edge of the main window. Click that Project tool button. (But wait! What if you can't find the little Project button? In that case, go to Android Studio's main menu and select Window⇨Restore Default Layout.)

The Editor area

The area to the right of the Project tool window is the *Editor area*. When you edit a Dart program file, the editor displays the file's text. (Refer to Figure 2-11.) You can type, cut, copy, and paste text as you would in other text editors.

The Editor area can have several tabs. Each tab contains a file that's open for editing. To open a file for editing, double-click the file's branch in the Project tool window. To close the file, click the little x next to the file's name on the Editor tab.

The lower area

Below the Project tool window and the Editor area is another area that contains several tool windows. When you're not using any of these tool windows, you might not see this lower area.

In the lower area, the tool window that you'll use most often is the Run tool window. (Refer to the lower portion of Figure 2-11.) The Run tool window appears automatically when you click the Run icon. This tool window displays information about the run of a Flutter app. If your app isn't running correctly, the Run tool window may contain useful diagnostic information.

You can force other tool windows to appear in the lower area by clicking tool buttons near the bottom of the Android Studio window. For example, when you click the Terminal tool button, Android Studio displays the Windows Command Prompt, the Mac Terminal app, or another text-based command screen that you specify. For details, refer to the earlier sidebar "Your friend, the command line."

A particular tool button might not appear when there's nothing you can do with it. For example, the Run tool button might not appear until you press the Run icon. Don't worry about that. The tool button shows up whenever you need it.

Finishing your tour of the areas in Figure 2-11.

The status bar

The status bar is at the bottom of Android Studio's window.

The status bar tells you what's happening now. For example, if the cursor is on the 37th character of the 11th line in the editor, you see $11:37$ somewhere on the status line. When you tell Android Studio to run your app, the status bar contains the Run tool window's most recent message.

The kitchen sink

In addition to the areas that I mention in this section, other areas might pop up as the need arises. You can dismiss an area by clicking the area's Hide icon. (See Figure 2-13.)

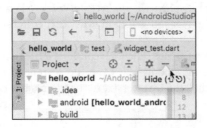

FIGURE 2-13:
Hiding the Project tool window area.

© John Wiley & Sons

Running This Book's Sample Programs

This book has dozens of sample Flutter apps, and they're all available for download from the book's website. You can run any of these programs as part of an Android Studio Flutter app. This section has all the details.

REMEMBER

1. **Launch Android Studio.**

   For the run of your first app, you need an Internet connection.

   What you do next depends on what you see when you launch Android Studio.

2. **If you see Android Studio's Welcome screen (refer to Figure 2-2), select Start a New Flutter Project. If you see another Android Studio window with a File option on the main menu bar, choose File ⇨ New ⇨ New Flutter Project on the main menu bar.**

   Either way, the first dialog box for creating a new Flutter project appears.

3. **Create a new Flutter project by following Steps 3 through 9 in this chapter's earlier section "Running your first app."**

4. **In Android Studio's Project tool window, look for a folder named** lib.

   If you need help finding that tool window, refer to the "The Project tool window" section earlier in this chapter.

   The Project tool window contains a tree of folders and files. Expand one of the tree's topmost branches to find the lib folder. This lib folder contains your project's Dart code.

5. **Right-click the tree's** main.dart **branch and then select Delete.**

   A window will pop up asking you if you want to do a "Safe delete." Uncheck the box next to Safe delete (which will also cause the other checkbox to become unchecked.)

6. **Make sure that you've uncompressed the** BOOK_4_CREATING_MOBILE_APPS.zip **file.**

   For details, refer to the earlier sidebar "Compressed archive files."

TIP

   If you're unsure where to find the BOOK_4_CREATING_MOBILE_APPS.zip file, look first in a folder named Downloads. Most web browsers put stuff inside Downloads by default.

   Safari on a Mac generally uncompresses .zip archives automatically, and Windows browsers (Internet Explorer, Firefox, Chrome, and others) do not uncompress .zip archives automatically. For the complete scoop on archive files, see the earlier sidebar "Compressed archive files."

7. **In File Explorer or the Finder, navigate to the uncompressed** BOOK_4_ CREATING_MOBILE_APPS **folder. Inside that folder, look for the example that you want to run.**

If you look inside the uncompressed download, you notice files named app0301.dart, app0302.dart, and so on. With a few exceptions, the numbers in these file names are chapter numbers followed by listing numbers. For example, in the name app0602.dart, the 06 stands for Chapter 6, and the 02 stands for the second code listing in that chapter.

For this experiment, I suggest that you look for the app0201.dart file. (No code is listed anywhere in this chapter. So, in this unusual case, 0201 doesn't refer to a project whose code is in something called Listing 2-1.)

8. **Right-click the chosen** app####.dart **file. Then, from the resulting context menu, select Copy.**

9. **Right-click the new project's empty** lib **folder. From the resulting context menu, select Paste.**

If Android Studio displays a dialog box offering to paste to a particular directory, check to make sure that the directory's full name ends in lib. Then, press OK.

10. **Look near the top of the Android Studio window for a drop-down list with the name** main.dart **in it (see Figure 2-14).**

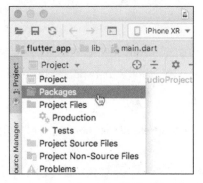

FIGURE 2-14: Opening the Edit Run/Debug Configurations dialog.

© John Wiley & Sons

11. **In the drop-down list, select Edit Configuration. The Edit Run/Debug Configurations dialog box will appear, as shown in Figure 2-15.**

12. **Change the entry point from** main.dart **to the name of the file you copied into the** lib **directory.**

Now you're ready to run one of this book's examples. Go for it!

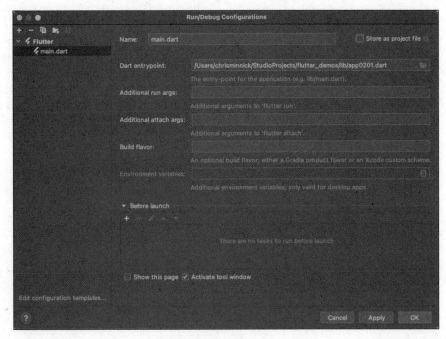

FIGURE 2-15:
Changing the
Dart entry
point in the
Edit Run/Debug
Configurations
dialog.

WARNING

On occasion, you may have more than one file in your project's `lib` folder and more than one app in your project. If you do, pressing the Run icon might not run the app that appears in Android Studio's editor area. To run the app that's showing in the editor area, look for that app's tab along the top of the editor area. When you right-click that tab, you see an option such as Run 'app0201.dart'. Select that option and watch the program run.

Enjoying reruns

The second time you run a particular example from this book, you don't have to follow all the steps in the previous section. It's easy to run an example over and over again. You can make changes to the code and then click the Run icon again. That's all you have to do.

If you've closed a project and you want to run it again, simply reopen the project in Android Studio and click the Run icon. For details, refer to this chapter's "Starting up" section.

If you're finicky . . .

After following the steps in the previous section, you may see some error markers (squiggly, red underlines) in the Project tool window. Android Studio's sample Flutter project describes something named MyApp, but the code that you copied into the lib folder makes no mention of MyApp. You can run this project over and over again without fixing the squiggly, red underlines. But if you want to fix them, simply follow these steps:

1. **In the Project tool window, expand the branch labeled** test.

   Inside that branch, you find a file named widget_test.dart.

2. **Delete the** widget_test.dart **file.**

   The squiggly, red underlines are gone. Problem solved!

WARNING

The apps in this book are practice apps. No one runs these apps to get real work done. When you develop a real app, you must never ignore code in the test folder. Testing is an essential part of the software development process. Thorough testing is what makes programs work reliably.

TIP

Another way to get rid of the squiggly, red underlines is to jump into a time machine and redo instructions in the "Running This Book's Sample Programs" section. If you disregard Step 5 and don't delete main.dart, you won't get those red underlines. But you may have to deal with two other issues. The Run icon's behavior may become a bit confusing.

Chapter **3**

"Hello" from Flutter

♪ *"Hello, I Must Be Going"* ♪

BERT KALMAR AND HARRY RUBY, SUNG BY GROUCHO MARX, IN
ANIMAL CRACKERS, 1930

Accxording to legend, the first computer program to print nothing but "Hello world!" was written by Brian Kernighan, as part of the BCPL programming language documentation. The first public appearance of such a program was in Kernighan and Ritchie's 1972 book, *The C Programming Language*. Nowadays, the term *Hello world program*, or simply *Hello program*, applies to any dirt-simple code for someone's first exposure to a new language or new framework.

This chapter features a simple "Hello world" Flutter program and several embellishments. You can run the code, dissect it, change it, and have fun with it.

First Things First: Creating a Flutter Project

Listing 3-1 contains your first Flutter app.

LISTING 3-1:	Ahoy, Maties!

```dart
import 'package:flutter/material.dart';

main() => runApp(App0301());

class App0301 extends StatelessWidget {
  Widget build(BuildContext context) {
    return MaterialApp(
      home: Material(
        child: Text("Hello world!"),
      ),
    );
  }
}
```

Follow these steps to run this code in a Flutter project:

1. **Create a new Flutter project.**

   Refer to Book 4, Chapter 2. As usual, Android Studio creates a file full of Dart code for you. The file's name is main.dart.

2. **Make sure that the main.dart code appears in Android Studio's editor.**

   Android Studio opens the directory named android in the Project tool window by default. To get to the main project directory (where the lib directory containing main.dart is), click the drop-down at the top of the Project tool window (which will say Android) and select Project. Expand the tree in the Project tool window on the left side of Android Studio's main window. Look for lib branch and, within the lib branch, the main.dart branch. Double-click that main.dart branch.

3. **In Android Studio's editor, delete all the main.dart code.**

   How liberating!

4. **In Android Studio's editor, type the code that you see in Listing 3-1.**

WARNING

tHE dART PROGRAMMING LANGUAGE IS cASe-sEnsITiVE. If you change a lowercase letter in a word to an UpperCase letter, you can change the word's meaning. cHANGING the case can make the entire word go from being meaningful to being meaningless. In the first line of Listing 3-1, you can't replace `import` with `Import`. iF YOU DO, THE WHOLE PROGRAM STOPS WORKING. Try it and see for yourself!

Figure 3-1 shows you the finished product.

```
main.dart ×
1       import 'package:flutter/material.dart';
2
3       main() => runApp(App0301());
4
5       class App0301 extends StatelessWidget {
6         Widget build(BuildContext context) {
7           return MaterialApp(
8             home: Material(
9               child: Text("Hello world!"),
10            ),
11          );
12        }
13      }
14
```

FIGURE 3-1:
A Flutter app is
ready to run.

© John Wiley & Sons

5. **Run your new app.**

For detailed instructions about initiating a run, refer to Book 4, Chapter 2.

Figure 3-2 shows you what you see when you run the Flutter app in Listing 3-1. The app looks pretty bad, but at least you can see the little *Hello world!* in the upper-left corner of the screen. You'll tend to the app's cosmetic aspects later in this chapter.

FIGURE 3-2:
Running the code
in Listing 3-1.

© John Wiley & Sons

TIP

You may see red markers in Android Studio's editor. If you do, hover over a marker and read the explanation that appears. Some explanations are easy to understand; others aren't. The more practice you have in interpreting these messages, the more skilled you become at fixing the problems.

Another thing you can try is to select the Dart Analysis tab at the bottom of Android Studio's main window. This tab lists many of the spots in your project that contain questionable code. For any item in the list, a red icon indicates an error — something that must be fixed. (If you don't fix it, your app can't run.) Any other color icon indicates a warning — something that won't prevent your code from running but might be worth considering.

Often times, Android Studio will underline code with a green squiggly line. This indicates a warning or a hint for how your code could be better. If you hover over the underlined code, you'll get a description of the improvement you could make. At this point, these hints may not make much sense. However, at the bottom of the popup window will be a suggested action (such as Add 'key' to constructors), as shown in Figure 3-3.

FIGURE 3-3:
Can you take
a hint?

© John Wiley & Sons

If you click the hint text in the popup window, Android Studio will magically make the fix for you and the green squiggly line will be gone! Most of the fixes that are suggested this way won't affect how your app runs, but they're good practices, which you'll learn about as you become more familiar with Dart.

TECHNICAL STUFF

If you look at the code listings you downloaded from this book's website, you'll see that many of the suggested fixes have been implemented there, even if the book lists the shorter syntax that accomplishes the same thing. This was done in the interest of keeping the code listings shorter in the book and saving a few trees.

In the next several sections, you'll take apart the code in Listing 3-1 and explore it from many points of view. In the process, you'll learn what the code does, why it does what it does, and what it might do differently.

What's it all about?

When you look at Listing 3-1, you may see words, punctuation, and indentation, but that's not what experienced Flutter developers see. They see the broad outline. They see big ideas in complete sentences. Figure 3-4 shows you what Listing 3-1 looks like to an experienced developer.

```
import 'package:flutter/material.dart';

main() => runApp(App0301());

class App0301 extends StatelessWidget {
  Widget build(BuildContext context) {
    return MaterialApp (
      home: Material(
        child: Text("Hello world!"),
      ),
    );
  }
}
```

> This Flutter app is a Material Design app. *Material Design* is a set of specifications describing the way an app looks.

> An app's home is the app's starting screen—the initial page of the app. This app's home is something that looks like a piece of Material.

> The piece of Material has one thing on it—one child. That Child is a bunch of Text. It's the words Hello world!

FIGURE 3-4:
The big picture.

A Flutter program is like a set of Russian matryoshka dolls. It's a thing within a thing within another thing, and so on, until you reach an endpoint. (See Figure 3-5.)

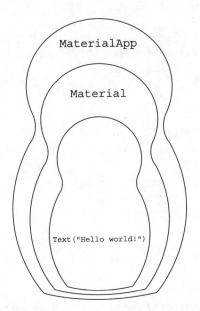

FIGURE 3-5:
The layered look.

Listing 3-1 has some Text inside a piece of Material which is, in turn, inside a MaterialApp. The words Text, Material, and MaterialApp begin commands to construct things. In Dart language terminology, the words Text, Material, and MaterialApp are the names of *constructor calls*. Here's the inside story:

>> The code

```
Text("Hello world!")
```

>> is a *constructor call*. When Flutter executes this code, it constructs a Text object. That Text object contains the words Hello world!

>> The code

```
Material(
    child: Text("Hello world!"),
)
```

is another constructor call. When Flutter executes this code, it constructs a Material object. That Material object contains the aforementioned Text object. (See Figure 3-6.)

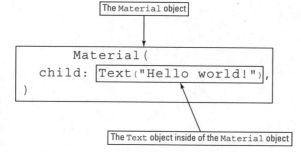

FIGURE 3-6:
Each constructor call creates an object.

A Material object has some of the characteristics that physical material, such as a piece of fabric, might have. It has a certain shape. It may be elevated from the surface below it. You can move it or pinch it. Granted, the background in Figure 3-2 doesn't look much like a piece of fabric. But imitating the texture of cloth isn't Material Design's goal. The point of Material Design is to create a language for describing the status of the components on a user's screen, and to describe how these components relate to one another. For the scoop on Material Design, visit https://material.io/.

» The code

```
MaterialApp(
  home: Material(
    child: Text("Hello world!"),
  ),
)
```

» is yet another constructor call. When Flutter executes this code, it constructs a MaterialApp whose starting screen is the Material object. (Refer to Figure 3-4.)

Here's a way to sum it all up:

In Listing 3-1, the MaterialApp object **has a** Material object, and the Material object **has a** Text object.

In that sentence, the seemingly innocent use of the words "has a" is important. For more details, see the later section "A brief treatise on 'within-ness'."

TIP

To understand the code in Listing 3-1, you have to know where pairs of parentheses begin and end. But finding the matches between open and close parentheses isn't always easy. To help with this problem, Android Studio has a few tricks up its virtual sleeve. If you place the cursor near a parenthesis character, Android Studio highlights the matching parenthesis. In addition, you can visit Android Studio's Settings or Preferences dialog box. (On Windows, select File↔Settings. On a Mac, select Android Studio↔Preferences.) In that dialog box, select Editor↔General↔Appearance and put a check mark in the Show Closing Labels in Dart Source Code checkbox. After you dismiss the dialog box, Android Studio displays comments marking the ends of many constructor calls. (Notice the labels // Material and // MaterialApp in Figure 3-7.)

```
main.dart ×
1   import 'package:flutter/material.dart';
2
3   main() => runApp(App0301());
4
5   class App0301 extends StatelessWidget {
6     Widget build(BuildContext context) {
7       return MaterialApp(
8         home: Material(
9           child: Text("Hello world!"),
10        ), // Material
11      ); // MaterialApp
12    }
13  }
```

FIGURE 3-7: Helpful closing labels.

© John Wiley & Sons

A constructor's parameters

Every constructor call has a list of *parameters* (usually called a *parameter list*). In Listing 3-1, each constructor's parameter list has only one parameter in it. (See Figure 3-8.)

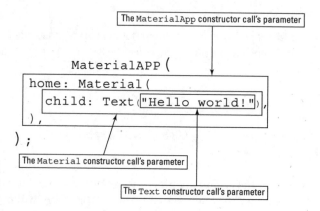

FIGURE 3-8:
Constructor calls
have parameters.

Constructor calls can have many parameters, or have no parameters. Take, for example, the Text call in Listing 3-1. In that code, the parameter "Hello world!" supplies information to Dart — information that's specific to the Text widget that Dart is constructing. Try changing Text("Hello world!") to Text("Hello world!", textScaleFactor: 4.0). When you save the new code, Android Studio does a hot restart that changes the look of the app in your emulator. (See Figure 3-9.)

FIGURE 3-9:
An ugly app to
illustrate the
textScale
Factor
parameter's
effect.

Book 4, Chapter 1 describes the difference between Flutter's hot restart and hot reload features. Both features apply updates to an app while the app is running. To do a hot restart, simply save your code. To do a hot reload, press the Run icon near the top of Android Studio's main window.

TIP

The constructor call

```
Text("Hello world!", textScaleFactor: 4.0)
```

contains two kinds of parameters:

» **"Hello world!" is a positional parameter.**

A *positional parameter* is a parameter whose meaning depends on its position in the parameter list. When you create a new Text object, the characters to be displayed must always come first in the list. You can see this for yourself by changing the constructor call to the following, invalid code:

```
Text(textScaleFactor: 4.0, "Hello world!")  // Bad code!!
```

» In this code, the positional "Hello world!" parameter doesn't come first in the list. So, if you type this line in Android Studio's editor, the editor marks this line with an ugly red error indicator. Quick! Change it back so that the "Hello world!" parameter comes first! You don't want Android Studio to form a bad impression of you!

» **textScaleFactor: 4.0 is a named parameter.**

A *named parameter* is a parameter whose meaning depends on the word before the colon. A Text constructor call can have many different named parameters, such as textScaleFactor, style, and maxLines. You can write the named parameters in any order as long as they come after any of the positional parameters.

When you supply a textScaleFactor parameter, the parameter tells Flutter how large the text should be. (Refer to Figure 3-9.) When you don't supply a textScaleFactor parameter, Flutter uses the default 1.0 factor.

The size of the text depends on a few things, such as the textScaleFactor and a style parameter's font size. For example, the following code makes Hello world! twice as large as it is in Figure 3-9.

```
Text("Hello world!", textScaleFactor: 4.0,
    style: TextStyle(fontSize: 28.0))
```

TECHNICAL STUFF

» The app shown in Figure 3-9 already has textScaleFactor 4.0. But it has the default font size, which is 14.0. Because 28.0 is two times 14.0, the fontSize: 28.0 parameter doubles the size of the text.

A note about punctuation

In Dart, you use commas to separate a constructor's parameters from one another. And, for all but the simplest parameter lists, you end the list with a *trailing comma*.

```
return MaterialApp(
  home: Material(
    child: Text("Hello world!"), // Trailing comma after the child parameter
  ),                             // Trailing comma after the home parameter
);
```

Without trailing commas, your code runs as expected. But the next section tells you how you can get Android Studio to make your code look good. And, without trailing commas, Android Studio doesn't do its best. A pair of slashes (//) has a special meaning in Dart. (To find out what it is, see Book 4, Chapter 4.)

Don't relent — simply indent

Take another look at Listing 3-1 and notice how some of the lines are indented. As a general rule, if one thing is subordinate to some other thing, its line of code is indented more than that other thing. For example, in Listing 3-1, the MaterialApp object contains the Material object, so the home: Material line is indented more than the return MaterialApp line.

Here are two facts to keep in mind:

>> In a Dart program, indentation *isn't* necessary.

>> In a Dart program, indentation *is* necessary.

Wait! What are those two facts again?

If you change the indentation in a Dart program, the program still runs. Here's a valid reworking of the code in Listing 3-1.

```
// Don't do this. It's poorly indented code.
  import 'package:flutter/material.dart';

main() => runApp(App0301());

class App0301 extends StatelessWidget {
Widget build(BuildContext context) {
return MaterialApp(
```

```
home: Material(
child: Text("Hello world!"),
  ),
    );
    }
      }
```

When you ask Android Studio to run this poorly indented code, it works. Android Studio dutifully runs the code on your virtual or physical device. But having this code run isn't good enough. *This poorly indented code is hideous. It's almost impossible to read.* The indentation, or lack thereof, gives you no indication of the program's structure. You have to wade through the words to discover that the `Material` widget is inside the `MaterialApp` widget. Instead of showing you the app's structure at a glance, this code makes your eyes wander aimlessly in a sea of seemingly unrelated commands.

The good news is, you don't have to learn how to indent your code. Android Studio can do the indentation for you. Here's how:

1. **Open Android Studio's Settings or Preferences dialog box.**

   On Windows, select File⇨Settings.

   On a Mac, select Android Studio⇨Preferences.

2. **In that dialog box, select Languages & Frameworks⇨Flutter and then put a check mark in the Format Code on Save checkbox.**

   The check mark tells Android Studio to fix your code's indentation whenever you save your work.

   While you're at it, you might as well put a check mark in the next checkbox — the Organize Imports on Save checkbox.

3. **Select OK to dismiss the dialog box.**

   Hazzah! When you run the code — or simply save the code — Android Studio fixes the code's indentation.

If you want more control over Android Studio's behavior, don't fiddle with the Settings or Preferences dialog box. Instead, whenever you want indentation to be fixed, put the cursor in the Editor panel, and then choose Code⇨Reformat Code from Android Studio's main menu.

One way or another, please indent your code properly.

Classes, Objects, and Widgets

Dart is an object-oriented language, so Dart has things called objects and classes. Listing 3-1 contains the names of many classes, such as App0301, Stateless Widget, Widget, BuildContext, MaterialApp, Material, and Text. It's fair to say that almost every word in Listing 3-1 that starts with an uppercase letter is the name of a class.

You don't have to know a lot about object-oriented programming to understand the role of these words in Listing 3-1, but it helps to keep a few facts in mind:

>> **An object is a thing of some kind. Each object belongs to a particular class of things.**

The word Text is the name of a class of things — things that contain characters to be displayed on the screen. On its own, a class doesn't do much. The fact that Flutter has a Text class doesn't mean anything for an app that displays images and no characters.

In contrast, the constructor call Text("Hello world!") constructs an actual object. That object appears on the user's screen. For example, a Text object containing the words Hello world! appears in Figure 3-2. You can refer to that object as an *instance* of the Text class.

In any particular app, you can construct no Text instances, one Text instance, or many Text instances. The same is true of classes such as Widget and Material and almost every other class.

>> **Being an instance of one class might make you automatically be an instance of a bigger class.**

Every instance of the Cat class is, by definition, an instance of the Animal class. (If that weren't true, millions of YouTube videos wouldn't exist.) And what about the Animal class? Every instance of the Animal class is an instance of the LivingThing class. (See Figure 3-10.)

In the same way, every instance of Flutter's Text class is, by definition, an instance of Flutter's StatelessWidget class. And, in turn, every instance of the StatelessWidget class is an instance of Flutter's Widget class. So every Text instance is also a Widget instance. (Refer to Figure 3-10.)

>> **In Flutter, almost every object is, in one way or another, an instance of the Widget class.**

Informally, a widget is a component on a user's screen. Flutter takes this idea to another level, with each part of the user interface (the Text instance, the Material instance, and even the MaterialApp instance) being a widget in its own right.

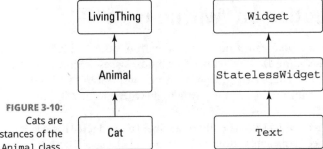

FIGURE 3-10:
Cats are
instances of the
Animal class.

In Listing 3-1, App0301 is the name of a class. In the line

```
main() => runApp(App0301());
```

the term App0301() is yet another constructor call. This call constructs an instance of the App0301 class.

The line

```
class App0301 extends StatelessWidget
```

» and all the code below it is the *declaration* of the App0301 class. The declaration tells Dart what kind of class it is and what kinds of things you can do with the class. In particular, the word extends in that first line makes any instance of the App0301 class be an instance of the StatelessWidget class. That's all you have to do to make App0301 instances be instances of the StatelessWidget class.

Now you have several terms with subtly different meanings — *class*, *object*, *instance*, and *widget*. In Listing 3-1, the code Text("Hello world!") constructs something, but exactly what kind of thing does that code construct?

» **From the Dart language's point of view, Text("Hello world!") constructs an object.**

In Dart terminology, you call it an instance of the Text class.

» **From the Flutter point of view, Text("Hello world!") creates a widget.**

It's an instance of the Text class and therefore an instance of the StatelessWidget class and an instance of the Widget class. For more of about objects, classes, and widgets, see Book 4, Chapter 7.

A brief treatise on "within-ness"

In a Dart program, you can find widgets within other widgets. (Refer to Figure 3-5.) In the same Dart program, you find classes within other classes. (Refer to Figure 3-10.) These two kinds of "within-ness" aren't the same. In fact, these two kinds of "within-ness" have little to do with one another.

In Figure 3-4, a Text widget is the child of a Material widget. This *doesn't* mean that a Text instance is also an instance of the Material class. To understand the difference, think about two kinds of relationships: "is a" relationships and "has a" relationships.

>> **The relationships described in the "What's it all about?" section are "has a" relationships.**

In Listing 3-1, the MaterialApp object has a Material object inside of it, and the Material object has a Text object inside of it.

There's nothing special about "has a" relationships. There can be "has a" relationships in a barnyard. A Cat has a Mouse, and the Mouse has a PieceOfCheese.

>> **The relationships described in the earlier "Classes, Objects, and Widgets" section are "is a" relationships.**

In every Flutter program, each Text object is a StatelessWidget object and, in turn, each StatelessWidget object is a Widget object.

In a barnyard, each Cat is an Animal and, in turn, each Animal is a LivingThing.

It wouldn't make sense to say that a Cat is a Mouse, or that a Material object is a Text object. In the same way, it's not correct to say that every Cat has an Animal, or that every Text object has a StatelessWidget object. The two kinds of relationships — "has a" and "is a" — are quite different.

If you're hungering for terminology that's more formal than "has a" and "is a," I have some for you:

>> **A chain of things connected by the "has a" relationship is called a *composition hierarchy*.**

Frivolous as it may be, the diagram in Figure 3-5 illustrates a composition hierarchy.

>> **The chain of things connected by the "is a" relationship is called the *inheritance hierarchy*.**

The diagrams in Figure 3-10 are part of Flutter's class hierarchy.

Don't you feel better now that you have these fancy terms to fling around?

REMEMBER

In Flutter, almost everything is called a "widget." Many classes are widgets. When a class is a widget, the class's instances (any objects constructed from that class) are also called widgets.

The documentation is your friend

You may be asking yourself how you're going to memorize all these names: `Text`, `StatelessWidget`, `MaterialApp`, and probably thousands more. Sorry to say, you're asking the wrong question. You don't memorize anything. When you use a name often enough, you remember it naturally. When you don't remember a name, you look it up in the online Flutter docs. (Sometimes, you're not sure where to look for the name you want. In that case, you have to poke around a bit.)

For example, point your web browser to `https://api.flutter.dev/flutter/widgets/Text-class.html`. When you do, you see a page with information about the `Text` class, some sample code, and some other stuff. (See Figure 3-11.)

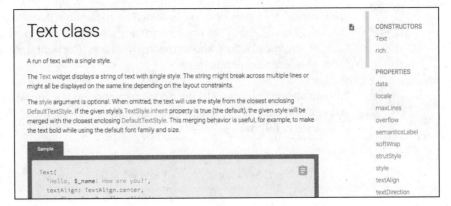

FIGURE 3-11:
Useful info about the Text class.

In the page's upper-right corner, you find a list of `Text` constructors. In Figure 3-11, there are two possibilities: `Text` and `rich`. If you select the `Text` link, you see a page describing the `Text` constructor call. (See Figure 3-12.)

This page lists the parameters in the constructor call and provides other helpful information.

Text constructor

```
const Text(
    String data, {
    Key key,
    TextStyle style,
    StrutStyle strutStyle,
    TextAlign textAlign,
    TextDirection textDirection,
    Locale locale,
    bool softWrap,
    TextOverflow overflow,
    double textScaleFactor,
    int maxLines,
    String semanticsLabel,
    TextWidthBasis textWidthBasis
})
```

Creates a text widget.

If the style argument is null, the text will use the style from

The data parameter must not be null.

Implementation

FIGURE 3-12:
The Text
constructor call.

TIP

On the page in Figure 3-12, notice how all but one of the constructor's parameters are enclosed in a pair of curly braces. The parameter that's not in curly braces (namely, String data) is the constructor's one and only positional parameter. Each of the parameters inside the curly braces (including double textScale Factor) is a named parameter.

REMEMBER

You can always count on Flutter's documentation to tell you what kinds of objects you can and cannot put inside of other objects. For example, the following code is doomed to failure:

```
return MaterialApp(
    child: Text("Hello world!"), // Don't do this!
);
```

It's doomed because, according to the Flutter docs, the MaterialApp constructor has no parameter named child.

Making Things Look Nicer

The app shown in Figure 3-2 looks pretty bad. The words *Hello world!* are tucked up against the screen's upper-left corner. Fortunately, Flutter offers an easy way to fix this: You surround the Text widget with a Center widget. As its name suggests, the Center widget centers whatever is inside of it.

REMEMBER

The word Center is the name of a class, so any object constructed from that class is called an instance of that class. In a term such as "Center widget," the word *widget* suggests that something like Center (something to help manage the screen's layout) is a component of some kind. A piece of Text on the screen is a component, a piece of Material on the screen is a component, and a Center object is also a component. Even though a Center widget doesn't light up somewhere on the screen, a Center widget is still a component. Part of Flutter's great strength is that Flutter treats all things the same way. When so many things are widgets, so many things can serve as parameters in the constructors of other things. The people who make up names for programming features call this the *composability* feature, and composability is a very nice feature to have.

You have a few ways to surround a Text widget's code with a Center widget's code. One way is to poke the cursor somewhere inside Android Studio's editor, start typing, and hope that you navigate the thicket of parentheses correctly. A better way is to do the following:

1. **Place the cursor on the word Text in the editor.**

2. **Press Alt+Enter (on Windows) or Opt+Return (on macOS).**

   As a result, a drop-down list appears.

3. **In the drop-down list, select Center Widget.**

   Listing 3-2 shows you what you get.

LISTING 3-2: **Centering the Text**

```
import 'package:flutter/material.dart';

main() => runApp(App0302());

class App0302 extends StatelessWidget {
  Widget build(BuildContext context) {
    return MaterialApp(
      home: Material(
        child: Center(
          child: Text("Hello world!"),
        ),
      ),
    );
  }
}
```

In Listing 3-2, the Material widget has a Center widget child, which, in turn, has a Text widget child. You can think of the Text widget as the grandchild of the Material widget.

Flutter supports hot restarting. After adding the Center code to the program in Android Studio's editor, save the changes by pressing Ctrl+S (on Windows) or Cmd+S (on a Mac). If the program from Listing 3-1 was already running, Flutter applies your changes and updates the emulator screen almost immediately.

In some situations, hot restart doesn't work. Instead of updating your app, Android Studio displays an error message. If that happens, try a hot reload. (Press the Run icon near the top of Android Studio's main window.) And what if hot reload fails? In that case, press the Stop icon — the red square icon that's in the same row as the Run icon. When you press the Stop icon, the run of your app ends completely. Pressing the Run icon to start afresh may fix the problem.

Figure 3-13 shows what you get when you run the code in Listing 3-2.

FIGURE 3-13:
Yes, you've centered the text.

© John Wiley & Sons

Creating a scaffold

The Text widget in Figure 3-13 looks so lonely. Let's add some fanfare to the basic app. Listing 3-3 has the code; Figures 3-14 and 3-15 show you the new screen.

LISTING 3-3: **Using a Scaffold**

```
import 'package:flutter/material.dart';

main() => runApp(App0303());

class App0303 extends StatelessWidget {
  Widget build(BuildContext context) {
    return MaterialApp(
      home: Scaffold(
        appBar: AppBar(
          title: Text("My First Scaffold"),
        ),
        body: Center(
          child: Text("Hello world!"),
        ),
        drawer: Drawer(
          child: Center(
            child: Text("I'm a drawer."),
          ),
        ),
      ),
    );
  }
}
```

The home for a MaterialApp doesn't have to be a Material widget. In Listing 3-3, the home is a Scaffold. When companies build skyscrapers, they create scaffolds — temporary wooden structures to support workers in high places. In programming, a *scaffold* is a structure that provides basic, often-used functionality.

The Scaffold constructor in Listing 3-3 has three parameters — an appBar, a body, and a drawer. In Figures 3-14 and 3-15, the appBar is the dark region at the top of the screen. The body is the large white region containing the Center with its Text widget. In Figure 3-15, the drawer is the big white area that appears when the user swipes from the left edge of the screen. The drawer also appears when the user presses the "hamburger" icon — three horizontal lines near the screen's top-left corner.

FIGURE 3-14:
Behold! A
scaffold!

© John Wiley & Sons

FIGURE 3-15:
Pulling out a
drawer.

© John Wiley & Sons

The body is nothing special. It's very much like the entire screen in the earlier examples. But the appBar and drawer are new. The appBar and drawer are two of the things you can have when you create a Scaffold. Other things made available by Scaffold widgets include navigation bars, floating buttons, bottom sheets, footer buttons, and more.

WARNING

In this chapter, Listings 3-1 and 3-2 have Material widgets, and Listing 3-3 has a Scaffold. These widgets form the backgrounds for their respective apps. If you remove the Material widget from Listing 3-1 or 3-2, your app's screen becomes an ugly mess. You get large red letters with yellow underlines against a black background. The same thing happens when you remove the `Scaffold` from Listing 3-3. There are other widgets that can provide backgrounds for your apps, but `Material` and `Scaffold` are the most commonly used.

Adding visual tweaks

Try this experiment: Change the `appBar` parameter from Listing 3-3 to the code snippet in Listing 3-4.

LISTING 3-4: **A Slight Change for the Code from Listing 3-3**

```
appBar: AppBar(
  title: Text("My First Scaffold"),
  elevation: 100,
  systemOverlayStyle: SystemUiOverlayStyle.dark,
)
```

Figure 3-16 shows the effect of adding the `elevation` and `systemOverlayStyle` parameters to the `AppBar` constructor call. The effect of the `elevation` parameter is subtle, but it's details like this that can make a big difference in the overall appearance of an app.

FIGURE 3-16:
A slight change
from the screen
in Figure 3-14.

© John Wiley & Sons

In Google's Material Design language, you imagine that the background rests on some flat surface, and that other components are elevated off the background by some number of pixels. For an `AppBar`, the default elevation is 4, but you can change a bar's elevation with . . . wait for it . . . the `elevation` parameter.

A component's elevation affects several aspects of the component's appearance. But in this section, the most obvious change is probably the shadow beneath the AppBar. You might not be able to see the difference between the shadows in Figures 3-14 and 3-16, but when you run the code on a virtual or physical device, an AppBar with elevation: 100 casts quite a large shadow.

You may be wondering what the 100 in elevation: 100 means. Is it millimeters, pixels, points, or light-years? In truth, it means "100 density-independent pixels" — or "100 dps," for short. No matter what screen the user has, one dp is 1/160 of an inch. So elevation: 100 means 100/160 of an inch (better known as five-eighths of an inch). For all the details about Material Design's elevation property, visit https://material.io/design/environment/elevation.html.

An AppBar widget's systemOverlayStyle parameter is yet another matter. The effect of adding systemOverlayStyle: SystemUiOverlayStyle.dark is to tell Flutter that, because the AppBar is light, the text and icons at the top of the AppBar should be dark. (Compare Figures 3-14 and 3-16.) The dark text and icons are easy to see against what is considered to be a light AppBar.

Dart's enum feature

An interesting feature of the Dart programming language is hiding inside Listing 3-4. The name SystemUiOverlayStyle refers to something called an *enum* (pronounced "ee-noom"). The word enum is short for *enumeration.* An enum is a bunch of values, like SystemUiOverlayStyle.light and SystemUiOverlayStyle.dark.

In Listing 3-4, notice how you refer to an enum's value. You don't use a constructor call. Instead, you use the name of the enum (such as SystemUiOverlayStyle), followed by a period, followed by the unique part of the value's name (such as light or dark).

Flutter has many other built-in enums. For example, the Orientation enum has values Orientation.portrait and Orientation.landscape. The Animation Status enum has values AnimationStatus.forward, AnimationStatus.reverse, AnimationStatus.completed, and AnimationStatus.dismissed. To find out how to create a new enum, see Book 4, Chapter 7.

Hello from sunny California!

Google announced Material Design at its developer conference in 2014. The first version of this design language dealt mostly with Android devices, but Version 2 embraced custom branding for iPhones and other iOS devices. Flutter's Material widget runs on iPhones with automatic platform-specific adaptations. You can run any of this book's MaterialApp examples on iPhones as well as Android phones, but if you want an iPhone-first design strategy, you can use Flutter's Cupertino widget collection. Listing 3-5 has an example.

LISTING 3-5:	How to Look Like an iPhone App

```
import 'package:flutter/cupertino.dart';

void main() => runApp(App0305());

class App0305 extends StatelessWidget {
  Widget build(BuildContext context) {
    return CupertinoApp(
      home: CupertinoPageScaffold(
        navigationBar: CupertinoNavigationBar(),
        child: Center(
          child: Text("Hello world!"),
        ),
      ),
    );
  }
}
```

Listing 3-5 is very much like its Material Design cousin, Listing 3-3. But instead of having `MaterialApp`, `Scaffold` and `AppBar` widgets, Listing 3-5 has the `CupertinoApp`, `CupertinoPageScaffold`, and `CupertinoNavigationBar` widgets. Instead of importing `'package:flutter/material.dart'`, Listing 3-5 imports `'package:flutter/cupertino.dart'`. (This `import` declaration makes Flutter's Cupertino widget library available for use by the rest of the listing's code.)

WARNING

Flutter's Material Design and Cupertino widgets aren't completely parallel with one another. For example, the `Scaffold` constructor call in Listing 3-3 has a body parameter. In place of that parameter, the `CupertinoPageScaffold` constructor call in Listing 3-5 has a `child` parameter. When in doubt, check the official Flutter documentation pages to find out which parameter names belong to which widgets' constructor calls.

TECHNICAL STUFF

You can mix and match Material Design and Cupertino widgets in the same app. You can even tailor your app's design style for different kinds of phones. You can even put code of the following kind in your app:

```
if (Platform.isAndroid) {
  // Do Android-specific stuff
}
if (Platform.isIOS) {
  // Do iOS-specific stuff
}
```

For more information, visit `https://pub.dev/packages/device_info_plus`.

Adding another widget

Relationships between widgets can be described in terms that are similar to a family tree. In the previous examples, the Text widget is a child of the Center widget and the Center widget is a child of the body. In both cases, the widgets are only children.

How do you put two children on a scaffold's body? You might be tempted to try this:

```
// DON'T DO THIS:
body: Center(
  child: Text("Hello world!"),
  child: AnotherWidget(...)
)
```

But a constructor call can't have two parameters with the same name. So, what can you do?

Flutter has a Column widget. The Column widget's constructor has a children parameter. The Column widget's children line up, one under another, on the screen. That sounds promising! Listing 3-6 has some code, and Figure 3-17 has the resulting display.

LISTING 3-6: **More Widgets, Please!**

```
import 'package:flutter/material.dart';

main() => runApp(App0306());

class App0306 extends StatelessWidget {
  Widget build(BuildContext context) {
    return MaterialApp(
      home: Scaffold(
        appBar: AppBar(
          title: Text("Adding Widgets"),
        ),
        body: Column(
          children: [
            Text(
              "Hello world!",
              textScaleFactor: 2.0,
            ),
            Text("It's lonely for me inside this phone.")
          ],
```

```
      ),
    ),
  );
}
}
```

FIGURE 3-17:
Who's in there?

© John Wiley & Sons

A `Column` constructor call has a `children` parameter, and the `children` parameter's value is a list. In the Dart programming language, a *list* is a bunch of objects. Each object's position in the list is called an *index*. The index values start from 0 and work their way upward.

One way to create a list is to enclose objects in square brackets. For example, Listing 3-6 contains a list with two objects. (See Figure 3-18.)

REMEMBER

A list's indices don't begin with 1. They begin with 0.

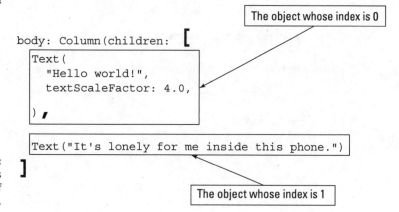

```
body: Column(children: [
    Text(
        "Hello world!",
        textScaleFactor: 4.0,
    ),
    Text("It's lonely for me inside this phone.")
]
```

The object whose index is 0

The object whose index is 1

FIGURE 3-18:
Square brackets
create lists of
things.

STRING THINGS

In the Dart programming language (and in JavaScript and other programming languages), the stuff that you surround with quotation marks (as in "Hello world!") is called a *string*. It's a bunch of characters, one after another. Here are some handy facts about strings:

- **To create a string, you can use double quotation marks or single quotation marks.**

  In other words, `'Hello world!'` is the same as `"Hello world!"`.

- **It's easy to put a single quotation mark inside a double quoted string.**

  Refer to this string in Listing 3-6:

  ```
  "It's lonely for me inside this phone."
  ```

- **It's easy to put a double quotation mark inside a single quoted string.**

  For example, the following is a valid string:

  ```
  '"Yikes!" she said.'
  ```

- **Using backslash characters (\), you can put either kind of quotation mark inside either kind of string.**

  Here are two examples:

  ```
  'It\'s lonely for me inside this phone.'
  "\"Yikes!\" she said."
  ```

- **A string can straddle several lines if you use triple quotation marks.**

  Both of these examples are valid Dart code:

  ```
  '''And the winner is ...
                  Charles Van Doren!'''
  """And the winner is ...
                  Charles Van Doren!"""
  ```

- **To paste strings one after another, use a plus sign (+) or some blank spaces.**

  Both of these examples are valid Dart code:

  ```
  "Hello" + " world!"

  "Hello" " world!"
  ```

For some other things you can do with strings, see Book 4, Chapter 4.

Centering the text (Part 1)

Figure 3-17 looks strange because the words are tucked up against the upper-left corner. In this section, you'll walk through some steps to diagnose this problem and fix it.

1. **While the app in Listing 3-6 runs, look on the right edge of Android Studio's window for a toolbar button with the words *Flutter Inspector* on it. Click that toolbar button.**

    As a result, the Flutter Inspector appears. (See Figure 3-19.)

FIGURE 3-19: The Flutter Inspector.

© John Wiley & Sons

2. **In the upper-left corner of the Flutter Inspector, look for the Toggle Select Widget Mode icon. (Refer to Figure 3-19.) Click that icon.**

3. **In the tree of widgets, select Column. (See Figure 3-20.)**

FIGURE 3-20: Selecting a branch of the Flutter Inspector's tree.

© John Wiley & Sons

As a result, the device that's running your app adds highlighting and a little label to the Column widget on the screen. (See Figure 3-21.)

© John Wiley & Sons

FIGURE 3-21:
Widget Select
mode is really
useful!

4. **Just for fun, select a few other branches in the Flutter Inspector's tree of widgets.**

   You can determine the boundaries of almost any of your widgets by using this technique.

The graphic in Figure 3-21 tells you that the Column widget isn't centered inside of its parent Scaffold widget, and it's not wide enough to fill the entire Scaffold widget. To fix this, put the Column widget inside of a Center widget. Put the cursor on the word Column in Android Studio's editor, and then follow the instructions at the start of the earlier "Making Things Look Nicer" section. Listing 3-7 shows you what you get.

LISTING 3-7: **Centering the Column Widget**

```
import 'package:flutter/material.dart';

main() => runApp(App0307());

class App0307 extends StatelessWidget {
  Widget build(BuildContext context) {
    return MaterialApp(
      home: Scaffold(
        appBar: AppBar(
          title: Text("Adding Widgets"),
        ),
        body: Center(
          child: Column(
```

```
      children: [
        Text(
          "Hello world!",
          textScaleFactor: 2.0,
        ),
        Text("It's lonely for me inside this phone.")
      ],
    ),
  ),
);
}
}
```

When you save your changes, Android Studio does a hot restart and you see the new-and-improved display in Figure 3-22.

FIGURE 3-22: The Column widget is centered.

Centering the text (Part 2)

The Text widgets in Figure 3-22 are centered horizontally, but they're not centered vertically. To center them vertically, you can fiddle with Flutter's Center widget, but there's a much easier way.

1. **In Android Studio's Flutter Inspector, hover your mouse pointer over the Column widget.**

The Flutter Inspector displays all the properties of whatever widget you're hovering over in a popup.

Wait! What's a "property"? Every object has *properties*, and each property of each object has a *value*. For example, every instance of Flutter's Text class has a textScaleFactor property. In Listing 3-7, a constructor call sets a Text instance's textScaleFactor property to the value 2.0.

Constructor calls aren't the only way of setting the properties of objects. In Figure 3-23, the Flutter Inspector shows the values of the Column widget's direction property, its mainAxisAlignment property, and many other properties.

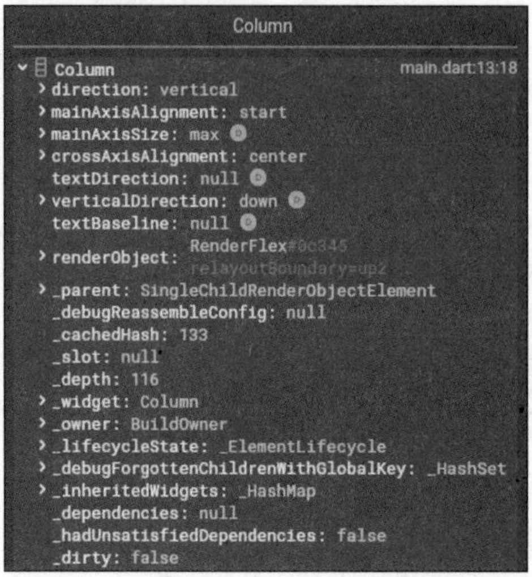

© John Wiley & Sons

FIGURE 3-23: Properties of the Column (the Column widget that's constructed in Listing 3-7).

A column's *main axis* is an invisible line going from the column's top to its bottom. You can replace start with any of the values end, center, spaceBetween, spaceAround, or spaceEvenly.

2. **In Android Studio's editor, add a mainAxisAlignment parameter to the Column widget's constructor. (See Listing 3-8.)**

LISTING 3-8: **Time for an Alignment**

```
import 'package:flutter/material.dart';

main() => runApp(App0308());

class App0308 extends StatelessWidget {
  Widget build(BuildContext context) {
    return MaterialApp(
      home: Scaffold(
        appBar: AppBar(
```

```
        title: Text("Adding Widgets"),
      ),
      body: Center(
        child: Column(
          mainAxisAlignment: MainAxisAlignment.center,
          children: [
            Text(
              "Hello world!",
              textScaleFactor: 2.0,
            ),
            Text("It's lonely for me inside this phone.")
          ],
        ),
      ),
    ),
  );
  }
}
```

In Listing 3-8, mainAxisAlignment is the name of a parameter, MainAxisAlignment is the name of an enum, and MainAxisAlignment. center is one of the enum's values.

For another look at Dart's enum feature, refer to the "Dart's enum feature" section earlier in this chapter. And if you hunger for even more, see Book 4, Chapter 7.

3. **Save your editor changes to do a hot restart.**

   On the device that's running your app, the Text widgets are now centered horizontally and vertically. (See Figure 3-24.)

This section's example illustrates aspects of Flutter's Column widget, which displays things from top to bottom. It should come as no surprise that Flutter has a Row widget, which displays things from side to side. Most facts about the Column widget are also true of the Row widget. (Well, they're true when you're lying down instead of sitting upright.)

In addition, Flutter has a ListView widget. The ListView widget displays things either way — from top to bottom or from side to side. In addition, the ListView widget has its own scrolling feature. You can put 100 items on a ListView even though only 20 items fit on the screen. When the user scrolls the screen, items move off the screen while other items move on. To read about Flutter's ListView widget, see Book 4, Chapter 8.

FIGURE 3-24:
How lovely!

© John Wiley & Sons

Displaying an image

Words are nice, but pictures are prettier. In this section, you put an image on your Flutter app screen.

1. **In Android Studio, start a new Flutter project.**

   This project is named app0308 in the following screenshots, but you don't have to use that name.

2. **In Android Studio's Project Tool window, right-click the project's name.**

   As a result, a contextual menu appears. (See Figure 3-25.)

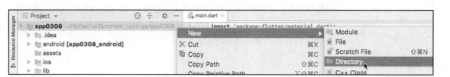

FIGURE 3-25:
Right-clicking the
app0308 branch.

© John Wiley & Sons

3. **On the contextual menu, choose New⇨Directory. (Refer to Figure 3-25.)**

   As a result, the New Directory dialog box appears. How convenient!

4. **In the dialog box, type the name** assets **and then press Enter.**

   To be honest, you can name this new directory almost anything you want. But if you don't name it assets, you'll confuse other Flutter developers.

5. **Check the Project Tool window to make sure that the project tree has a new assets branch. (See Figure 3-26.)**

   Seasoned Flutter developers create an images subdirectory of the new assets directory. I won't bother with that right now.

TECHNICAL STUFF

FIGURE 3-26:
The assets
directory is a
subdirectory
of the app0308
directory.

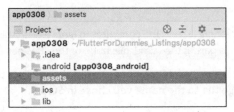

© John Wiley & Sons

6. **Find an image file.**

   Search your development computer's hard drive for an image file. Look for filenames ending in .png, .jpg, .jpeg, or .gif.

   If your File Explorer or Finder doesn't show filename extensions (such as .png, .jpg, .jpeg, or .gif for image files), refer to the sidebar in Book 4, Chapter 2 that talks about those pesky filename extensions.

7. **In your development computer's File Explorer or Finder, copy the image file.**

   That is, right-click the image file's name. On the contextual menu that appears, select Copy.

8. **Using Android Studio's Project Tool window, paste the image file into the assets directory.**

   That is, right-click the assets branch. On the resulting contextual menu, choose Paste. In the resulting dialog box, type a name for your image file, and then press Enter.

9. **Open your project's** pubspec.yaml **file.**

   More specifically, double-click the pubspec.yaml branch in the Project Tool window's tree.

   Here's a fun fact: The extension .yaml stands for Yet Another Markup Language.

10. **In the** pubspec.yaml **file, look for advice about adding assets to your project.**

The advice might look something like this:

```
# To add assets to your application,
# add an assets section, like this:
# assets:
#   - images/a_dot_burr.jpeg
#   - images/a_dot_ham.jpeg
```

(In case you're wondering, the filenames a_dot_burr.jpeg and a_dot_ham.jpeg refer to Aaron Burr and Alexander Hamilton. These file names occur many times in Flutter's official documentation. Flutter is the technology behind the mobile app for the Broadway musical *Hamilton*.)

In a .yaml file, a hashtag (#) tells the computer to ignore everything on the rest of the line. So, in this part of the .yaml file, none of the lines has any effect.

11. **Delete the hashtags on two of the lines. On the second line, change the name of the image file to the name you chose in Step 8.**

When I do this, my pubspec.yaml file contains the following text:

REMEMBER

```
# To add assets to your application,
# add an assets section, like this:
assets:
  - MyImage.png
#   - images/a_dot_ham.jpeg
```

It's common to forget to make the necessary changes in the pubspec.yaml file. Try not to forget this step. When you do forget (and almost everyone does), go back and edit the project's pubspec.yaml file.

12. **Replace all the code in the** main.dart **file with the code in Listing 3-9.**

Use your own class name and filename instead of my App0309 and MyImage.png names.

LISTING 3-9: **Displaying an Image**

```
import 'package:flutter/material.dart';

main() => runApp(App0309());

class App0309 extends StatelessWidget {
  Widget build(BuildContext context) {
```

```
    return MaterialApp(
      home: Scaffold(
        appBar: AppBar(
          title: Text("My First Image"),
        ),
        body: Center(
          child: Image.asset('MyImage.png'),
        ),
      ),
    );
  }
}
```

13. **Let 'er rip.**

That is, run the code on a virtual or physical device. The display on the device's screen looks something like the result in Figure 3-27.

FIGURE 3-27:
It's a robot!

© John Wiley & Sons

Flutter has an Image class, and the Image class has several different constructors. The Image.asset constructor in Listing 3-9 grabs a file from a place inside your Flutter project's directory. To grab an image off the Internet, you call a different constructor — the Image.network constructor. To get an image from somewhere on your hard drive (somewhere outside of your Flutter project's directory), you can call the Image.file constructor. Each of these constructors is called a *named constructor*. In each case, the stuff after the dot (.asset, .network, and .file) is that particular constructor's *name*.

Hey, Wait a Minute . . .

This chapter covers some fundamental ideas in Dart and Flutter app development. You start with a Hello World program and make several changes to it. While you do all that, you build up a vocabulary of useful concepts — concepts like classes, constructors, enums, and widgets.

But, what do the first four lines of the Hello World program do? Why do you return something when you construct a MaterialApp?

The answers to these questions, and others like them, are in the next chapter. What are you waiting for? Read on!

Chapter **4**

Hello Again

♪ *"Hello, hello again, sh-boom and hopin' we'll meet again."* ♪

—JAMES KEYES, CLAUDE FEASTER, CARL FEASTER, FLOYD F. MCRAE,
AND JAMES EDWARDS, SUNG BY THE CHORDS, THE CREW-CUTS,
STAN FREBERG, AND OTHERS, 1954

Chapter 3 is all about a simple Hello World program. Listing 4-1 shows one version of the code.

LISTING 4-1: **Yet Another Look at the First Hello Program**

```dart
import 'package:flutter/material.dart';

main() => runApp(App0401());

class App0401 extends StatelessWidget {
  Widget build(BuildContext context) {
    return MaterialApp(
      home: Material(
        child: Center(child: Text("Hello world!")),
      ),
    );
  }
}
```

In Chapter 3, you focused on the middle of the program — the MaterialApp and all the stuff inside it — while ignoring anything having to do with things called "functions." This chapter continues the tour of a Hello World program and sets its sites on those "function" things.

Creating and Using a Function

Here's an experiment: Run the app whose code is shown in Listing 4-2.

Words, Words, Words

```
import 'package:flutter/material.dart';

main() => runApp(App0402());

class App0402 extends StatelessWidget {
  Widget build(BuildContext context) {
    return MaterialApp(
      home: Material(
        child: Center(child: Text(highlight("Look at me"))),
      ),
    );
  }
}

highlight(words) {
  return "*** " + words + " ***";
}
```

Figure 4-1 shows you the output of the app in Listing 4-2.

FIGURE 4-1:
Another exciting
Flutter app.

*** Look at me ***

Listing 4-2 contains a function declaration and a function call. (See Figure 4-2.)

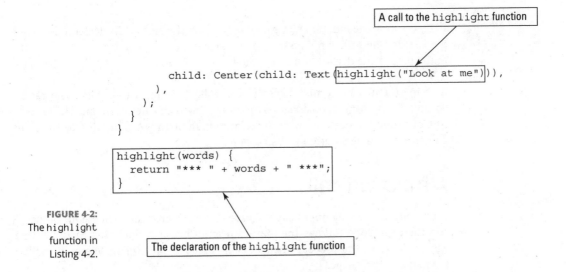

```
            child: Center(child: Text(highlight("Look at me")))),
        ),
    );
  }
}

highlight(words) {
  return "*** " + words + " ***";
}
```

A call to the highlight function

The declaration of the highlight function

FIGURE 4-2:
The highlight function in Listing 4-2.

The function declaration

Think about a recipe — a set of instructions for preparing a particular meal. A function declaration is like a recipe: It's a set of instructions for performing a particular task. In Listing 4-2, this set of instructions says, "Form the string containing asterisks followed by some words followed by more asterisks and return that string somewhere."

Most recipes have names, like Macaroni and Cheese or Triple Chocolate Cake. The function at the bottom of Listing 4-2 also has a name: Its name is highlight. (See Figure 4-3.) There's nothing special about the name highlight. It could have just as easily been called makeItFancy or tacos (although, calling it tacos might not be the best choice in terms of making your code understandable to other programmers).

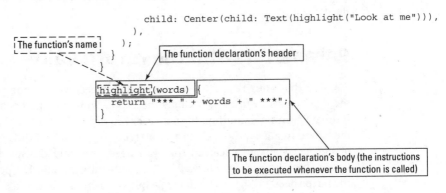

```
            child: Center(child: Text(highlight("Look at me"))),
        ),
    );
  }
}

highlight(words) {
  return "*** " + words + " ***";
}
```

The function's name

The function declaration's header

The function declaration's body (the instructions to be executed whenever the function is called)

FIGURE 4-3:
A header and a body.

TIP

In Figure 4-3, the function name `highlight` is in the part of the declaration called the *header*. The function's instructions (`return "*** " + words + " ***"`) are in the part of the declaration called the *body*.

A recipe for macaroni and cheese sits in a book or on a web page. The recipe doesn't do anything. If no one uses the recipe, the recipe lies dormant. The same is true of a function declaration. The declaration in Listing 4-2 doesn't do anything on its own. The declaration just sits there.

A function call

Eventually, somebody might say, "Please make macaroni and cheese for dinner," and then someone follows the Macaroni and Cheese recipe's instructions. One way or another, the process begins when someone says (or maybe only thinks) the name of the recipe.

A *function call* is code that says, "Please execute a particular function declaration's instructions." Imagine a phone or another device that's running the code in Listing 4-2. When the phone encounters the function call `highlight("Look at me")`, the phone is diverted from its primary task — the task of constructing an app with its `Material`, `Center`, and `Text` widgets. The phone takes a detour to execute the instructions in the `highlight` function's body. After figuring out that it should create `"*** Look at me ***"`, the phone returns to its primary task, adding the `Text` widget with `"*** Look at me ***"` to the `Center` widget, adding the `Center` widget to the `Material` widget, and so on.

A function call consists of a function's name (such as the name `highlight` in Listing 4-2), followed by some last-minute information (such as `"Look at me"` in Listing 4-2).

Wait! In the previous sentence, what does *some last-minute information* mean? Read on.

Parameters and the return value

Suppose that your recipe for macaroni and cheese serves one person and calls for two ounces of uncooked elbow macaroni. You've invited 100 people to your intimate evening gathering. In that case, you need 200 ounces of uncooked elbow macaroni. In a way, the recipe says the following: "To find the number of ounces of uncooked elbow macaroni that you need, multiply the number of servings by 2." That number of servings is last-minute information. The person who wrote the recipe doesn't know how many people you'll be serving. You provide a number of servings when you start preparing the mac-and-cheese. All the recipe says is to multiply that number by 2.

In a similar way, the `highlight` function declaration in Listing 4-2 says, "To find the value that this function returns, combine asterisks followed by the `words` that you want to be highlighted followed by more asterisks."

A function declaration is like a black box. You give it some values. The function does something with those values to calculate a new value. Then the function returns that new value. (See Figures 4-4 and 4-5.)

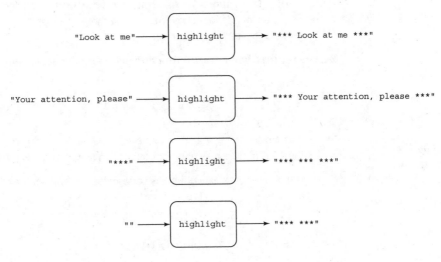

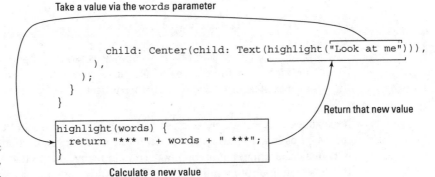

FIGURE 4-4: Good stuff in, good stuff out.

FIGURE 4-5: In with the old, out with the new.

Figures 4-4 and 4-5 show what it means to give values to a function, and for a function to return a value.

>> **You give values to a function with the function's parameter list.**

Like any constructor call, every function call has a parameter list. Each parameter feeds a piece of information for the function to use. In Figure 4-5, the function call highlight("Look at me") passes the value "Look at me" to the highlight function's declaration. Inside the function declaration, the name words stands for "Look at me", so the expression "*** " + words + " ***" stands for "*** Look at me ***".

>> **You return a value from a function with a return statement.**

In Listing 4-2, the line

```
return "*** " + words + " ***";
```

>> is a *return statement*. Again, imagine a phone that's running the code in Listing 4-2. With the execution of this return statement, this is what happens:

- The phone stops executing any code inside the body of the highlight function.

- The phone replaces the entire function call with the returned value so that

```
Center(child: Text(highlight("Look at me")))
```

- effectively becomes

```
Center(child: Text("*** Look at me ***"))
```

- It continues to execute whatever code it was executing before it became diverted by the function call. It takes up where it left off, constructing the Center, Material, and MaterialApp widgets.

A cookbook may have only one recipe for chicken fricassee, but you can follow the recipe as many times as you want. In the same way, a particular function has only one declaration, but an app may contain many calls to that function. To see this in action, look at Listing 4-2 and change the code's child parameter, like so:

```
child: Column(mainAxisAlignment: MainAxisAlignment.center, children: [
  Text(highlight("Look at me")),
  Text(highlight("Your attention, please"))
])
```

The new child contains two calls to the highlight function, each with its own parameter value. The resulting app is what you see in Figure 4-6.

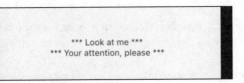

FIGURE 4-6:
Two Text
widgets.

A `return` statement is only one of several kinds of statements in the Dart programming language. For more about this topic, see the section "Statements and declarations," later in this chapter.

Programming in Dart: The Small Stuff

"Dart is boring." That's what Faisal Abid said during a presentation at DevFest NYC 2017. He wasn't talking trash about Dart. He was merely explaining that Dart is much like many other programming languages. If you've written some programs in Java, C++, or JavaScript, you find Dart's features to be quite familiar. You encounter a few surprises, but not too many. When you're learning to create Flutter apps, you don't want a new, complicated programming language to get in your way. So, a boring language like Dart is just what you need.

This section presents some facts about the Dart programming language. Some of it may look quite similar to other languages you've learned. Other parts are unique to Dart.

Statements and declarations

A *statement* is a piece of code that commands Dart to do something. If you think this definition is vague, that's okay for now. Anyway, in Listing 4-2, the line

```
return "*** " + words + " ***";
```

is a statement because it commands Dart to return a value from the execution of the `highlight` function.

Unlike a statement, a *declaration's* primary purpose is to define something. For example, the `highlight` function declaration in Listing 4-2 defines what should happen if and when the `highlight` function is called.

Statements and declarations aren't completely separate from one another. In Listing 4-2, the `highlight` function declaration contains one statement — a return statement. A function declaration may contain several statements. For example, the following declaration contains three statements:

```
highlight2(words) {
  print("Wha' da' ya' know!");
  print("You've just called the highlight2 function!");
  return "*** " + words + " ***";
}
```

The first two statements (calls to Dart's print function) send text to Android Studio's Run tool window. The third statement (the return statement) makes highlight("Look at me") have the value "*** Look at me ***".

REMEMBER

Use Dart's print function *only* for testing your code. Remove all calls to print before publishing an app. If you don't, you might face some trouble. At best, the calls serve no purpose and can slow down the run of your app. At worst, you may print sensitive data and show it to malicious hackers.

Dart's typing feature

What does "five" mean? You can have five children, but you can also be five feet tall. With five children, you know exactly how many kids you have. (Unlike the average American family, you can't have 2.5 kids.) But if you're five feet tall, you might really be five feet and half an inch tall. Or you might be four feet eleven-and-three-quarter inches tall, and no one would argue about it.

What else can "five" mean? Nuclear power plants can undergo fire-induced vulnerability evaluation, also known as *five*. In this case, "five" has nothing to do with a number. It's just f-i-v-e.

A value's meaning depends on the value's *type.* Consider three of the Dart language's built-in types: int, double, and String.

>> **An int is a whole number, with no digits to the right of the decimal point.**

If you write

```
int howManyChildren = 5;
```

>> in a Dart program, the 5 means "exactly five."

>> **A double is a fractional number, with digits to the right of the decimal point.**

If you write

```
double height = 5;
```

>> in a Dart program, the 5 means "as close to five as you care to measure."

>> A String **is a bunch of characters.**

If you use single quotes (or double quotes) and write

```
String keystroke = '5';
```

>> in a Dart program, the '5' means "the character that looks like an uppercase letter *S* but whose upper half has pointy turns."

A value's type determines what you can do with that value. Consider the values 86 and "86".

>> **The first one,** 86, **is a number. You can add another number to it.**

86 + 1 is 87

>> **The second one,** "86", **is a string. You can't add a number to it, but you can add another string to it.**

"86" + "1" is "861"

REMEMBER

In some languages (such as JavaScript, for example), you can combine any value with any other value and usually produce some kind of a result. You can't do that in Dart. The Dart programming language is *type safe.*

Literals, variables, and expressions

The Dart language has literals and variables. The value of a *literal* is the same in every Dart program. For example, 1.5 is a literal because 1.5 means "one-and-a-half" in every Dart program. Likewise, "Hello world!" in Listing 4-1 is a literal because "Hello world!" stands for the same string of 12 characters in every Dart program. (Yes, the blank space counts as one of the characters.)

TECHNICAL STUFF

Fun fact: In early versions of FORTRAN (circa 1956), you could change the meaning of the literal 5 so that it stood for something else, like the number 6. Talk about confusing!

The value of a *variable* is not the same in every Dart program. In fact, the value of a variable may not be the same from one part of a Dart program to another. Take, for example, the following line of code:

```
int howManyChildren = 5;
```

This line is called a *variable declaration*. The line defines a variable named howManyChildren whose type is int. The line *initializes* that variable with the value 5. When Dart encounters this line, howManyChildren stands for the number 5.

Later, in the same program, Dart may execute the following line:

```
howManyChildren = 6;
```

This line is called an *assignment statement*. The line makes howManyChildren refer to 6 instead of 5. Congratulations on the birth of a new child! Is it a girl or a boy?

An *expression* is a part of a Dart program that stands for a value. Imagine that your code contains the following variable declarations:

```
int numberOfApples = 7;
int numberOfOranges = 10;
```

If you start with these two declarations, each entry in the left column of Table 4-1 is an expression.

In the last row of Table 4-1, do you really need the toString() part? Yes, you do. If you write '9' + numberOfApples, you get an error message because '9' is a String and numberOfApples is an int. You can't add an int value to a String value.

REMEMBER

The Dart language has statements and expressions. A *statement* is a command to do something; an *expression* is code that has a value. For example, the statement print("Hello"); does something. (It displays Hello in Android Studio's Run tool window.) The expression 3 + 7 * 21 has a value. (Its value is 150.)

You can apply Dart's toString to any expression. For some examples, see Book 4, Chapter 7.

TABLE 4-1 **Fruitful Expressions**

Expression	Value	Type	Notes
7	7	int	
7.1	7.1	double	
7.0	7.0	double	Even with .0, you get a double.
7.1 + 8	15.1	double	A double plus an int is a double.
0.1 + 0.1 + 0.1	0.30000000000000004	double	Arithmetic on double values isn't always accurate.
numberOfApples	7	int	
numberOfOranges	10	int	
numberOfApples + numberOfOranges	17	int	Who says you can't add apples and oranges?
8 + numberOfApples	15	int	
numberOfOranges * 10	100		An asterisk (*) stands for multiplication.
20 / 7	2.857142857142857	double	A slash (/) performs division and produces a double.
20.0 ~/ 7.0	2	int	The ~/ combination performs division and produces an int. It *always* rounds down.
(20 / 7).round()	3	int	This is how you round up or down to the nearest int value.
20 % 7	6	int	When you divide 20 by 7, you get 2 with a remainder of 6.
highlight("Look at me")	"*** Look at me ***"	String	Assuming that you've declared highlight as in Listing 4-2, the function returns a Striing.
'9' + numberOfApples. toString()	'97'	String	numberOfApples.toString() is a String. Its value is '7'.

TIP

Dart provides a quick way to determine the type of a particular expression. To see this, change the `highlight` function declaration in Listing 4-2 as follows:

```
highlight(words) {
  print(20 / 7);
  print((20 / 7).runtimeType);
  return "*** " + words + " ***";
}
```

When you run the app, the following lines appear in Android Studio's Run tool window:

```
flutter: 2.857142857142857
flutter: double
```

The value of `20 /7` is `2.857142857142857`, and the value of `(20 / 7).runtimeType` is `double`.

Two for the price of one

In Dart, some statements do double duty as both statements and expressions. As an experiment, change the `highlight` function in Listing 4-2 so that it looks like this:

```
highlight(words) {
  int numberOfKazoos;
  print(numberOfKazoos);
  print(numberOfKazoos = 94);
  return "*** " + words + " ***";
}
```

Android Studio reports an error that the `numberOfKazoos` must be defined before it's used. Dart variables are non-nullable by default. What this means is that, unless you specifically say that a variable can be null (which is the value of a Dart variable before it's initialized), Dart will enforce what's called "null safety" and refuse to run programs with variables that aren't initialized to a non-null value.

Null safety is one of the things that makes Dart fast. It also decreases the chances of programs having errors. If you want to let a variable be null, you can use the "nullable" type operator, which is a question mark. For example, the preceding example can be written like this and it will run just fine:

```
highlight(words) {
  int? numberOfKazoos;
  print(numberOfKazoos);
  print(numberOfKazoos = 94);
```

```
    return "*** " + words + " ***";
  }
```

Here's what you see in Android Studio's Run tool window when you run this code:

```
flutter: null
flutter: 94
```

The line int? numberOfKazoos; is a variable declaration without an initialization. That's fair game in the Dart programming language, as long as you use the nullable type operator.

When Dart executes print(numberOfKazoos); you see flutter: null in the Run tool window. Roughly speaking, null means "nothing." At this point in the program, the variable numberOfKazoos has been declared but hasn't yet been given a value, so numberOfKazoos is still null.

Finally, when Dart executes print(numberOfKazoos = 94); you see flutter: 94 in the Run tool window. Aha! The code numberOfKazoos = 94 is both a statement and an expression! Here's why:

>> **As a statement,** numberOfKazoos = 94 **makes the value of** number OfKazoos **be** 94.

>> **As an expression, the value of** numberOfKazoos = 94 **is** 94.

Of these two facts, the second is more difficult for people to digest. (I've known some experienced programmers who think about this the wrong way.) To execute print(numberOfKazoos = 94); Dart covertly substitutes 94 for the expression numberOfKazoos = 94, as shown in Figure 4-7.

```
              94
print(numberOfKazoos = 94);


numberOfKazoos = 100;
                   100
print(numberOfKazoos);
                   100
print(numberOfKazoos++);
                   101
print(numberOfKazoos);
```

FIGURE 4-7:
Dart's innermost
thoughts.

In other words, the value numberOfKazoos = 94 is 94. So, in addition to doing something, the code numberOfKazoos = 94 also has a value. That's why numberOfKazoos = 94 is both a statement and an expression.

Simple assignment statements aren't the only things that double as expressions. Try this code out for size:

```
int numberOfKazoos = 100;
print(numberOfKazoos);
print(numberOfKazoos++);
print(numberOfKazoos);
```

The code's output is

```
flutter: 100
flutter: 100
flutter: 101
```

If the middle line of output surprises you, you're not alone. As a statement, numberOfKazoos++ adds 1 to the value of numberOfKazoos, changing the value from 100 to 101. But, as an expression, the value of numberOfKazoos++ is 100, not 101. (Refer to Figure 4-7.)

Here's a comforting thought. By the time Dart executes the last print (numberOfKazoos) statement, the value of numberOfKazoos has already changed to 101. Whew!

TIP

As a statement, ++numberOfKazoos (with the plus signs in front) does the same thing that numberOfKazoos++ does: It adds 1 to the value of numberOfKazoos. But, as an expression, the value of ++numberOfKazoos isn't the same as the value of numberOfKazoos++. Try it. You'll see.

Dart has some other statements whose values are expressions. For example, the following code prints flutter: 15 twice:

```
int howManyGiraffes = 10;
print(howManyGiraffes += 5);
print(howManyGiraffes);
```

And the following code prints flutter: 5000 twice:

```
int rabbitCount = 500;
print(rabbitCount *= 10);
print(rabbitCount);
```

For more info about topics like += and *=, visit this page:

```
https://dart.dev/guides/language/language-tour#operators
```

Dart's var keyword

On occasion, you might want to create a variable whose type can change. To do so, declare the variable using Dart's var keyword and leave out an initialization in the declaration. For example, the following code won't work:

```
int x = 7;
print(x);
x = "Someone's trying to turn me into a String"; // You can't do this
print(x);
```

But the following code works just fine:

```
var x;
x = 7;
print(x);
x = "I've been turned into a String"; // Dart is happy to oblige
print(x);
```

Another reason for using var is to avoid long, complicated type names. For an example, see this chapter's "Built-in types" section.

WE PAUSE FOR A FEW COMMENTS

You may have noticed some stuff beginning with two slashes (//) in some of the chapter's code examples. Two slashes signal the beginning of a comment.

A *comment* is part of a program's text. But unlike declarations, constructor calls, and other such elements, a comment's purpose is to help people understand your code. A comment is part of a good program's documentation.

The Dart programming language has three kinds of comments:

- **End-of-line comments**

  An *end-of-line comment* starts with two slashes and goes to the end of a line of type. So, in the following code snippet, the text // Dart is happy to oblige is an end-of-line comment:

  ```
  x = "I've been turned into a String"; // Dart is happy to oblige
  ```

  All the text in an end-of-line comment is for human eyes only. No information from the two slashes to the end of the line is translated by Dart's compiler.

(continued)

(continued)

- **Block comments**

  A *block comment* begins with /∗ and ends with ∗/.

  A block comment can span across several lines. For example, the following code is a block comment:

  ```
  /* Temporarily commenting out this code.
     That is, omitting these statements to see what happens:
     x = "Someone's trying to turn me into a String";
     print(x); */
  ```

  Once again, no information between /∗ and ∗/ gets translated by the compiler.

- **Doc comments**

  An *end-of-line doc comment* begins with three slashes (///). A *block doc comment* begins with /∗∗ and ends with ∗/.

  A doc comment is meant to be read by people who never even look at the Dart code. But that doesn't make sense. How can you see a doc comment if you never look at the code?

  Well, a certain program called dartdoc (what else?) can find any doc comments in a program and turn these comments into a nice-looking web page. (For an example of such a page, visit https://api.flutter.dev/flutter/widgets/Widget-class.html.)

One more thought about comments in general: Book 4, Chapter 3 describes a way to display closing labels in Android Studio's editor.

```
home: Material(
  child: Text("Hello world!"),
), // Material
```

Does that final // Material look like a comment to you? Well, it's not really a comment. (Sorry about that.) Closing labels belong to a broader category of items called *code decoration*. When Android Studio creates code decoration, it doesn't add the decoration to the program's text. It only displays that decoration in the editor. If you examine a program's text using Notepad or TextEdit, you don't see the code decoration.

Built-in types

In a Dart program, every value has a *type*. Dart has ten built-in types. (See Table 4-2.)

TABLE 4-2   **Dart's Built-In Types**

Type Name	What Literals Look Like	Useful Info About the Type
Number types		
int	42	Numbers with no digits to the right of the decimal point — typically, from –9007199254740992 to 9007199254740991.
double	42.0 42.1	Numbers with digits to the right of the decimal point (possibly, all zero digits).
num	42 42.0 42.1	A number of some kind. Every int value, and every double value, is an example of a num value.
Collection Types		
List	[2, 4, –9, 25, 18] ["Hello", "Goodbye", 86] [] <int>[]	A bunch of values. The initial value is the 0th, the next value is the 1st, the next value is the 2nd, and so on. (With [], the bunch has no values in it.)
Set	{2, 4, –9, 25, 18} {"Hello", "Goodbye", 86} {} <int>{}	A bunch of values with no duplicates in no particular order. (With {}, the bunch has no values in it.)
Map	{ 'one' : 1, 'two' : 2 , 'three' : 3, 'many': 99} <String, int>{}	A bunch of pairs, each pair consisting of a *key* (such as 'one', 'two', 'three', or 'many') and a *value* (such as 1, 2, 3, or 99). (With {}, the bunch has no pairs in it.)
Other Types		
String	'Dart is boring' "" """The previous string is empty."""	A sequence of characters.
bool	true, false	A logical value. A variable of this type has one of only two possible values: true and false.
Runes	Runes('I ' '\u2665' ' you')	A string of Unicode characters. For example, '\u2665' is a heart character (♥).
Symbol	(Not applicable)	Turns an identifier in a Dart program into a value in a Dart program. (Don't worry about it!)

You can combine types to create new types. One way to do this is to put types inside of collection types. For example, in the following declaration, the variable amounts is a List containing only int values.

```
List<int> amounts = [7, 3, 8, 2];
```

Of course, you can go crazy layering types within types within other types:

```
Map<String, Map<String, List<int>>> values = {
  "Size": {
    "Small": [1, 2, 3],
  },
};
```

In cases like that, your best bet is to use the var keyword. Dart can usually figure things out by looking at the rest of the code.

```
var values = {
  "Size": {
    "Small": [1, 2, 3],
  },
};
```

Types that aren't built-in

In addition to the types in Table 4-2, every class is a type. For example, in Listing 4-1, App0401 is the name of a type. It's a type that's defined in Listing 4-1. You can add a line to Listing 4-1 that makes a variable refer to an instance of the App0401 class. Here's one such line:

```
App0401 myApp = App0401();
```

Like many other variable declarations, this line has a type name (App0401), followed by a new variable name (myApp), followed by an initialization. The initialization makes myApp refer to a newly constructed App0401 instance.

The Dart language comes with a library full of standard, reusable code. The formal name for such as library is an *application programming interface* (API). Dart's API has declarations of many classes. For example, instances of Dart's DateTime class are moments in time, and instances of the Duration class are time intervals.

Similarly, the Flutter toolkit comes with a feature-rich API. In Listing 4-1, Widget, StatelessWidget, BuildContext, MaterialApp, Material, Center, and Text are the names of classes in the Flutter API.

Using import declarations

Woe is me! I can't read the new book by my favorite author unless I go to my local library and check out a copy. The same is true of Dart's and Flutter's library classes (well, almost). You can't use Flutter's `MaterialApp` or `Material` classes unless you start your program with

```
import 'package:flutter/material.dart';
```

If you delete this line, you can't even use any of Flutter's `Widget` classes (`StatelessWidget`, `Widget`, `Center`, and `Text`, to name a few). That's because, when you import `'package:flutter/material.dart'`, you automatically import `'package:flutter/widgets.dart'` also.

A relatively small number of Dart's API classes, like the aforementioned `DateTime` class, belong to a package named `dart.core`. You can start your program with the line

```
import 'dart:core';
```

but it won't do you any good. Classes from the `dart.core` package are always imported, whether you ask for it or not.

REMEMBER

No one memorizes the names of all the classes in the Dart or Flutter libraries. When you need to know about a class, look it up by visiting `https://api.flutter.dev`.

Creating Function Declaration Variations

This section shows some alternative ways of creating function declarations. Listing 4-3 has the first example.

LISTING 4-3: **Messing with Function Declarations**

```
import 'package:flutter/material.dart';

main() {
  runApp(App0403());
}

class App0403 extends StatelessWidget {
  Widget build(BuildContext context) {
```

(continued)

(continued)

```
        return MaterialApp(
          home: Material(
            child: Center(child: Text(highlight("Look at me")))),
          ),
        );
      }
    }

    highlight(words) => "*** $words ***";
```

To read all about the dollar sign ($) on the last line of Listing 4-3, see the nearby "Bling your string" sidebar.

BLING YOUR STRING

Listing 4-2 contains the following code:

```
"*** " + words + " ***"
```

The juxtaposition of plus signs and quotation marks can make code difficult to read. To make your life easier, Dart has string interpolation. With *string interpolation*, a dollar sign ($) means, "Temporarily ignore the surrounding quotation marks and find the value of the following variable." That's why, in Listing 4-3, the expression "*** $words ***" stands for "*** Look at me ***" — the same string you get in Listing 4-2.

Not impressed with string interpolation? Look over the following function and see what you think of it:

```
// The function call
getInstructions1(8, "+", ";", "'")

// The function's declaration
getInstructions1(howMany, char1, char2, char3) {
  return "Password: " +
      howMany.toString() +
      " characters; Don't use " +
      char1 +
      " " +
      char2 +
      " or " +
      char3;
}
```

Quite a mess, isn't it? The value that the getInstructions1 function returns is

```
Password: 8 characters; Don't use + ; or '
```

It's easy to forget to include some blank spaces, quotation marks, or other items in this sort of code. Here's how you get the same return value using string interpolation:

```
// The function call
Text(getInstructions2(8, "+", ";", "'"))

// The function's declaration
getInstructions2(howMany, char1, char2, char3) {
  return "Password: $howMany characters; Don't use $char1 $char2 or
    $char3";
}
```

This new function, getInstructions2, is easier to create and understand than getInstructions1.

When you use string interpolation, you can go a step further. Here's what you can do when you add curly braces to the mix:

```
// The function call
getInstructions3(8, "+", ";", "'")

// The function's declaration
getInstructions3(howMany, char1, char2, char3) {
  return "Password: ${howMany + 1} characters; Don't use $char1 $char2
    or $char3";
}
```

This new getInstructions3 function returns

```
Password: 9 characters; Don't use + ; or '
```

String interpolation can handle all kinds of expressions — arithmetic expressions, logical expressions, and others.

A run of the code in Listing 4-3 is the same as that of Listing 4-2. (Refer to Figure 4-1.) In a sense, Listing 4-3 contains the same program as Listing 4-2. The notation for things is slightly different, but the things themselves are the same.

In Listing 4-3, the highlight function declaration

```
highlight(words) => "*** $words ***";
```

is shorthand for the more long-winded highlight declaration in Listing 4-2. When the body of a function declaration contains only one statement, you can use this quick-and-easy *fat arrow* (=>) notation.

REMEMBER

In a fat arrow function declaration, you never use the return keyword.

Every Dart program has a function named main. When you start running a program, Dart looks for the program's main function declaration and starts executing whatever statements are in the declaration's body. In a Flutter app, a statement like

```
runApp(App0403());
```

tells Dart to construct an instance of App0403 and then run that instance. The runApp function is part of Flutter's API.

Type names in function declarations

Listing 4-4 adds some type names to the code from Listing 4-2.

LISTING 4-4: **Better Safe than Sorry**

```
import 'package:flutter/material.dart';

void main() => runApp(App0404());

class App0404 extends StatelessWidget {
  Widget build(BuildContext context) {
    return MaterialApp(
      home: Material(
        child: Center(child: Text(highlight("Look at me"))),
      ),
    );
  }
}

String highlight(String words) {
  return "*** $words ***";
}
```

In Listing 4-4, String and void add some welcome redundancy to the code. The occurrence of String in (String words) tells Dart that, in any call to the highlight function, the words parameter must have type String. Armed with this extra String information, Dart will cough up and spit out a bad function call such as

```
highlight(19)
```

This is bad because 19 is a number, not a String. You may argue and say, "I'll never make the mistake of putting a number in a call to the highlight function."

Yes you will, and so will every other programmer on earth. When you're writing code, mistakes are inevitable. The trick is to catch them sooner rather than later.

Near the end of Listing 4-4, `String highlight` tells Dart that the value returned by the `highlight` function must be a `String`. If you accidentally write the following code, Dart will complain like nobody's business:

```
String highlight(String words) {
  return 99;                     //Bad code!
}
```

Sorry, chief. The value 99 isn't a `String`.

Continuing our journey through Listing 4-4, `void main` doesn't quite mean, "The `main` function must return a value of type `void`." Why not? It's okay to put a type name in front of a fat arrow declaration. So, what's different about `void main`?

Simply stated, `void` isn't a type. In a way, `void` means "no type." The word `void` reminds Dart that this `main` function isn't supposed to return anything useful. Try declaring `void main` and putting a `return` statement in the declaration's body:

```
void main() {
  runApp(App0404());
  return 0;         // Bad
}
```

If you do this, Android Studio's editor adds red marks to your code. Dart is saying, "Sorry, Bud. You can't do that."

Naming your parameters

Book 4, Chapter 3 distinguishes between constructors' positional parameters and named parameters. All that fuss about the kinds of parameters applies to functions as well. For example, the highlight function in Listing 4-4 has one parameter — a positional parameter.

```
highlight("Look at me")                // A function call

String highlight(String words) {       // The function declaration
  return "*** $words ***";
}
```

If you want, you can turn `words` into a named parameter. Simply surround the parameter with curly braces:

```
highlight(words: "Look at me")          // A function call

String highlight({String words}) {      // The function declaration
  return "*** " + words + " ***";
}
```

You can even have a function with both positional and named parameters. In the parameter list, all the positional parameters must come before any of the named parameters. For example, the following code displays +++Look at me!+++.

```
highlight(                              // A function call
  "Look at me",
  punctuation: "!",
  symbols: "+++",
)

String highlight(                       // The function declaration
  String words, {
  String punctuation,
  String symbols,
}) {
  return symbols + words + punctuation + symbols;
}
```

What about the build function?

Listing 4-4 contains some familiar-looking code:

```
class App0404 extends StatelessWidget {
  Widget build(BuildContext context) {
    return MaterialApp(
```

Here are some facts:

>> **In this code, `build` is the name of a function, and**

```
Widget build(BuildContext context)
```

is the function declaration's header.

The `build` function does exactly what its name suggests. It builds something. To be precise, it builds the widget whose content is the entire Flutter app.

>> **The** `build` **function returns a value of type** `Widget`.

Quoting from Book 4, Chapter 3, "Being an instance of one class might make you automatically be an instance of a bigger class." In fact, every instance of the `MaterialApp` class is automatically an instance of the `StatefulWidget` class, which, in turn, is automatically an instance of the `Widget` class. So there you have it — every `MaterialApp` is a `Widget`. That's why it's okay for the `build` function's `return` statement to return a `MaterialApp` object.

>> **The function's one-and-only parameter has the type** `BuildContext`.

When Dart builds a widget, Dart creates a `BuildContext` object and passes that to the widget's `build` function. A `BuildContext` object contains information about the widget and the widget's relationship to other widgets in the program. For more info, see Book 4, Chapter 6.

In Listing 4-4, the `build` function's declaration is inside the `class App0404` definition, but the `highlight` function declaration isn't inside *any* class definition. In a sense, this `build` function "belongs to" instances of the `App0404` class.

A function that belongs to a class, or to the class's instances, has a special name. It's called a *method*. More on this in Book 4, Chapter 5.

More Fun to Come!

What happens if a user taps the screen and wants a response from the app in Listing 4-4? Absolutely nothing.

Let's fix that. Turn the page to see what's in Chapter 5.

♪ *"Goodbye from us to you."* ♪

—*BUFFALO BOB ON "THE HOWDY DOODY SHOW,"* 1947–1960

Chapter **5**

Making Things Happen

U ntil now, you've only used Flutter to build static apps. A static app always does the same thing. Through building these static apps, you've learned about Flutter's programming strategies, constructors, functions, and other good stuff. But here in Chapter 5, you're going to learn to make more interesting apps. An app that always displays the same text is boring, and users will rate the app with zero stars. An interesting app interacts with the user. The app's screen changes when the user enters text, taps a button, moves a slider, or does something else to get a useful response from the app. Making things happen is essential for any kind of mobile app development. So, in this chapter, you begin learning how to make things happen.

Let's All Press a Floating Action Button

When you create a new Flutter project, Android Studio makes a main.dart file for you. The main.dart file contains a cute little starter app. Listing 5-1 has a scaled-down version of that starter app.

LISTING 5-1: **Press a Button; Change the Screen**

```dart
import 'package:flutter/material.dart';

void main() => runApp(App0501());

class App0501 extends StatelessWidget {
  Widget build(BuildContext context) {
    return MaterialApp(
      home: MyHomePage(),
    );
  }
}

class MyHomePage extends StatefulWidget {
  _MyHomePageState createState() => _MyHomePageState();
}

class _MyHomePageState extends State {
  String _pressedOrNot = "You haven't pressed the button.";

  void _changeText() {
    setState(_getNewText);
  }

  void _getNewText() {
    _pressedOrNot = "You've pressed the button.";
  }

  Widget build(BuildContext context) {
    return Scaffold(
        body: Center(
          child: Text(
            _pressedOrNot,
          ),
        ),
        floatingActionButton: FloatingActionButton(
          onPressed: _changeText,
        ));
  }
}
```

WARNING

The code in Listing 5-1 captures the essence of the starter app in the February 2022 version of Android Studio. By the time you read this book, the creators of Flutter may have completely changed the starter app. If the stuff in Listing 5-1 bears little resemblance to the starter app you get when you create a new project, don't worry. Just do what you've been doing. That is, delete all of Android Studio's `main.dart` code and replace it with the code in Listing 5-1.

When you launch the app in Listing 5-1, you see the text "You haven't pressed the button" and, in the screen's lower-right corner, a blue circle. (See Figure 5-1.)

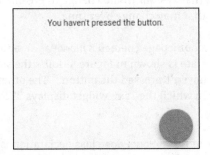

FIGURE 5-1:
Before pressing
the button.

That blue circle is called a *floating action button*. It's one of the widgets that you can add to a `Scaffold`. When you click this app's floating action button, the words on the screen change to "You've pressed the button." (See Figure 5-2.)

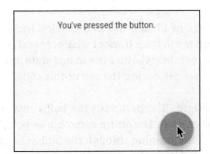

FIGURE 5-2:
After pressing
the button.

At last! A Flutter app is making something happen!

To understand what's going on, you have to know about two kinds of widgets. To learn their names, read the next section's title.

Stateless widgets and stateful widgets

Some systems have properties that can change over time. Take, for example, your common, everyday traffic light. If it's functioning properly, it's red, yellow, or green. Imagine that you're hurrying to get to work and you stop for a red light. Under your breath, you may grumble, "I'm annoyed that this traffic light's state is red. I wish that the state of that system would change to green." A system's *state* is a property of the system that may change over time.

The app in Listing 5-1 has a homepage (named `MyHomePage`), and that homepage is in one of two states. One state is shown in Figure 5-1. It's the state in which the `Text` widget displays "You haven't pressed the button." The other state is shown in Figure 5-2. It's the state in which the `Text` widget displays "You've pressed the button."

In Listing 5-1, the first line of the `MyHomePage` class declaration is

```
class MyHomePage extends StatefulWidget
```

You want the look of the `MyHomePage` widget to be able to change itself nimbly, so you declare `MyHomePage` objects to be *stateful widgets*. Each `MyHomePage` instance has a state — something about it that may change over time.

In contrast, the `App0501` class in Listing 5-1 is a *stateless widget*. The app itself (`App0501`) relies on its homepage to keep track of whatever text is being displayed. So, the app has no need to remember whether it's in one state or another. Nothing about an `App0501` instance changes during the run of this code.

Think again about a traffic light. The part with the bulbs rests on a pole that's fastened permanently to the ground. The entire assembly — pole, bulbs and all — doesn't change. But the currents running through the bulbs change every 30 seconds or so. There you have it. The entire assembly is unchanging and stateless, but a part of that assembly — the part that's responsible for showing colors — is changing and stateful. (See Figure 5-3.)

Widgets have methods

In Listing 5-1, the declaration of the `App0501` class contains a function named `build`. A function that's defined inside of a class declaration is called a *method*. The `App0501` class has a `build` method. That's good because there's some fine print in the code for `StatelessWidget`. According to that fine print, every class that extends `StatelessWidget` must contain the declaration of a `build` method.

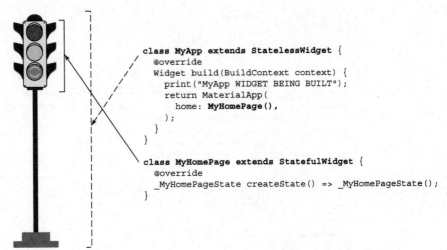

```
class MyApp extends StatelessWidget {
  @override
  Widget build(BuildContext context) {
    print("MyApp WIDGET BEING BUILT");
    return MaterialApp(
      home: MyHomePage(),
    );
  }
}

class MyHomePage extends StatefulWidget {
  @override
  _MyHomePageState createState() => _MyHomePageState();
}
```

FIGURE 5-3:
A riddle: How is a
Flutter program
like a traffic light?

A stateless widget's `build` method tells Flutter how to build the widget. Among other things, the method describes the widget's look and behavior. Whenever you launch the program in Listing 5-1, Flutter calls the `App0501` class's `build` method. That `build` method constructs a `MaterialApp` instance, which, in turn, constructs a `MyHomePage` instance. And so on. From that point onward, the `MaterialApp` instance doesn't change. Yes, things inside the `MaterialApp` instance change, but the instance itself doesn't change.

How often does your town build a new traffic light assembly? Perhaps you might see one going up every two years or so. The metal part of a traffic light isn't designed to change regularly. The town planners call the traffic light assembly's `build` method only when they construct a new light. The same is true of stateless widgets in Flutter. A stateless widget isn't designed to be changed. When a stateless widget requires changing, Flutter replaces the widget.

What about stateful widgets? Do they have `build` methods? Well, they do and they don't. Every stateful widget has to have a `createState` method. The `createState` method makes an instance of Flutter's `State` class, and every `State` class has its own `build` method. In other words, a stateful widget doesn't build itself. Instead, a stateful widget creates a state, and the state builds itself. (See Figure 5-4.)

A typical traffic light's state changes every 30 seconds or every few minutes, and thus, the state of the light gets rebuilt. In the same way, the `build` method that belongs (indirectly) to a stateful widget gets called over and over again during the run of a program. That's what stateful widgets are for. They're nimble things whose appearance can easily change. In contrast, a stateless widget is like the pole of a traffic light. It's a rigid structure meant for one-time use.

```
class MyApp extends StatelessWidget {
  @override
  Widget build(BuildContext context) {
    return MaterialApp(
      home: MyHomePage(),
    );
  )
}

class MyHomePage extends StatefulWidget {
  @override
  _MyHomePageState createState() => _MyHomePageState();
)

class _MyHomePageState extends State<MyHomePage> {
  String _pressedOrNot = "You haven't pressed the button.";

  void _changeText() {
    setState(() {
      _pressedOrNot = "You've pressed the button.";
    });
  }

  @override
  Widget build(BuildContext context) {
    return Scaffold(
        body: Center(
          child: Text(
            _pressedOrNot,
          ),
        ),
        floatingActionButton: FloatingActionButton(
          onPressed: _changeText,
        ));
  }
}
```

A stateless widget builds itself.

A stateful widget creates a state, and ...

... the state builds itself.

FIGURE 5-4:
Stateful widgets
weren't built
in a day.

Pay no attention to the framework behind the curtain

A program that displays buttons and other nice-looking things has a *graphical user interface*. Such an interface is commonly called a *GUI* (pronounced "goo-ey," as in "This peanut butter is really gooey"). In many GUI programs, things happen behind the scenes. While your app's code runs, lots of other code runs in the background. When you run a Flutter app, code that was written by the creators of Flutter runs constantly to support your own app's code. This background support code belongs to the *Flutter framework*.

Listing 5-1 has declarations for functions named main, build, createState, _getNewText, and _changeText, but the code in Listing 5-1 doesn't call any of these functions. Instead, Flutter's framework code calls these functions when a device runs the app.

TIP

"I'M TALKING TO YOU, STATELESS WIDGET — YOU MUST HAVE A BUILD METHOD!"

Every class that extends StatelessWidget must have a build method. Flutter's API enforces that rule.

But don't take my word for it. Temporarily comment out the build method declaration in Listing 5-1. That is, change the declaration of App0501 so that it looks like this:

```
class App0501 extends StatelessWidget {
//  Widget build(BuildContext context) {
//    return MaterialApp(
//      home: MyHomePage(),
//    );
//  }
}
```

When you do, you'll see some red marks in Android Studio's editor. The red marks indicate that the program contains an error; namely, that App0501 doesn't have its own build method.

To quickly comment out several lines of code, drag the mouse so that the highlight touches each of those lines. Then, if you're using Windows, press Ctrl-/. If you're using a Mac, press Cmd-/.

How does Dart enforce its build method requirement? As a novice developer, you don't have to know the answer. You can skip the rest of this sidebar and go merrily on your way. But if you're curious, and you don't mind taking a little detour in your learning, try this:

In Android Studio's editor, right-click on the word StatelessWidget. On the resulting context menu, select Go To⇨Declaration. *Et voila!* A new tab containing the StatelessWidget class declaration opens up in the editor. If you ignore most of the code in the StatelessWidget class declaration, you see something like this:

```
abstract class StatelessWidget extends Widget {
    // A bunch of code that you don't have to worry about, followed by ...

    Widget build(BuildContext context);
}
```

The first word, abstract, warns Dart that this class declaration contains methods (that is, functions) with no bodies. And, indeed, the line

```
Widget build(BuildContext context);
```

(continued)

(continued)

is a method header with no body. In place of a body, there's only a semicolon.

You might not be surprised to learn that StatelessWidget is an example of an *abstract class* and that the class's build method is an *abstract method*. With that in mind, I offer you these two facts:

- **You can't make a constructor call for an abstract class.**

  You can construct a Text widget by writing Text("Hello") because the Text class isn't abstract. But you can't construct a StatelessWidget by writing StatelessWidget(). That makes sense because, in the declaration of StatelessWidget, the build method isn't fully defined.

- **If you extend an abstract class, you have to provide a full declaration for each of the class's abstract methods.**

  The StatelessWidget class declaration contains the following line:
      Widget build(BuildContext context);

Because of this, the App0501 class in Listing 5-1 must contain a full build method declaration. What's more, the declaration must specify a parameter of type BuildContext. Sure enough, the build method belonging to App0501 does the job:

```
Widget build(BuildContext context) {
  return MaterialApp(
    home: MyHomePage(),
  );
}
```

With a fully defined build method, the App0501 class isn't abstract. That's good because, near the top of Listing 5-1, there's a line containing an App0501() constructor call.

Here's a blow-by-blow description:

- » **The Dart language calls the main function when the code in Listing 5-1 starts running.**

  The main function constructs an instance of App0501 and calls runApp to get things going. Then . . .

- » **The Flutter framework calls the App0501 instance's build function.**

  The build function constructs an instance of MyHomePage. Then . . .

- » **The Flutter framework calls the MyHomePage instance's createState function.**

The createState function constructs an instance of _myHomePageState. Then . . .

>> **The Flutter framework calls the _myHomePageState instance's build function.**

The build function constructs a Scaffold containing a Center with a Text widget and a FloatingActionButton widget.

To understand the Text widget's constructor, look at a few lines of code:

```
String _pressedOrNot = "You haven't pressed the button.";

// Later in the listing ...

    child: Text(
      _pressedOrNot,
    ),
```

Initially, the value of the _pressedOrNot variable is "You haven't pressed the button." So, when the app starts running, the Text widget obediently displays "You haven't pressed the button."

But the floating action button's code is a different story.

```
void _changeText() {
  setState(_getNewText);
}

void _getNewText() {
  _pressedOrNot = "You've pressed the button.";
}

// Later in the listing ...

    floatingActionButton: FloatingActionButton(
      onPressed: _changeText,
    )
```

The constructor for the FloatingActionButton has an onPressed parameter, and the value of that parameter is _changeText. What's that all about?

The onPressed parameter tells Flutter "If and when the user presses the button, have the device call the _changeText function." In fact, a lot of stuff happens when the user presses the floating action button. In the next few sections, you see some of the details.

The big event

In GUI programming, an *event* is something that happens — something that may require a response of some kind. The press of a button is an example of an event. Other examples of events include an incoming phone call, the movement of a device to a new GPS location, or the fact that one app needs information from another app.

An *event handler* is a function that's called when an event occurs. In Listing 5-1, the _changeText function is a handler for the button's onPressed event. In and of itself, the code onPressed: _changeText doesn't call the _changeText function. Instead, that code *registers the function _changeText as the official handler for floating action button presses.*

REMEMBER

A call to the _changeText function would look like this: _changeText(). The call would end with open and closed parentheses. The code onPressed: _changeText, with no parentheses, doesn't call the _changeText function. That code tells the device to remember that the name of the button's onPressed event handler is _changeText. The device uses this information when, and only when, the user presses the button.

Call me back

The functions _changeText and _getNewText in Listing 5-1 are *callback functions.* The line

```
onPressed: _changeText
```

tells the framework, "When the button is pressed, call my _changeText function." And the line

```
setState(_getNewText)
```

tells the framework "Set the state by calling my _getNewText function."

A callback function is simply a function that's passed to another function as an argument and is invoked by the function it's passed to.

Callbacks are useful

You may have written programs that have no callbacks. When your program starts running, the system executes the first line of code and keeps executing instructions until it reaches the last line of code. Everything runs as planned from start to finish. (Well, in the best of circumstances, everything runs as planned.)

A callback adds an element of uncertainty to a program. When will an event take place? When will a function be called? Where's the code that calls the function?

Programs with callbacks are more difficult to understand than programs with no callbacks.

Why do you need callbacks? Can you get away without having them? To help answer this question, think about your common, everyday alarm clock. Before going to sleep, you tell the alarm clock to send sound to your ears (a callback) when the 9 A.M. event happens:

```
on9am: _rattleMyEarDrums,
```

If you didn't rely on a callback, you'd have to keep track of the time all night on your own. Like Bart and Lisa Simpson in the back seat of a car, you'd repeatedly be asking, "Is it 9 A.M. yet? Is it 9 A.M. yet? Is it 9 A.M. yet?" You certainly wouldn't get a good night's sleep. By the same token, if a Flutter program had to check every hundred milliseconds for a recent press of the button, there wouldn't be much time for the program to get anything else done. That's why you need callbacks in Flutter programs.

TECHNICAL STUFF

Programming with callbacks is called *event driven programming*. If a program doesn't use callbacks and, instead, repeatedly checks for button presses and other such things, that program is *polling*. In some situations, polling is unavoidable. But when event driven programming is possible, it's far superior to polling.

The outline of the code

One good way to look at code is to squint so that most of it is blurry and unreadable. The part that you can still read is the important part. Figure 5-5 contains my mostly blurry version of some code in Listing 5-1.

```
class MyHomePageState extends State {
  String _pressedOrNot = "You haven't pressed the button.";

  void _changeText() {                          ──── ② _changeText calls setState.
    setState(_getNewText);  ◄────────────────────     Behind the scenes, setState calls _getNewText.
  }

  void _getNewText() {  ◄──────────────────────  ──── ③ _getNewText changes something
    _pressedOrNot = "You've pressed the button.";      about the home page's state.
  }

  Widget build(BuildContext context) {  ◄──────  ──── ④ Behind the scenes, setState calls
    return Scaffold(                                   build which redraws the home page.
      body: Center(
        child: Text(
          _pressedOrNot,
        ),
      ),
      floatingActionButton: FloatingActionButton(
        onPressed: _changeText,  ◄─────────────  ──── ① This line registers _changeText as the
      ));                                              callback function for a button press event.
  }
}
```

FIGURE 5-5:
What to look for in Listing 5-1.

According to Figure 5-5, this is the state management strategy in Listing 5-1:

1. Register _changeText as a callback function and wait for the user to press the floating action button.

When, at last, the user presses the floating action button, . . .

2. Have _changeText call setState and pass _getNewText as the one-and-only parameter in the setState function call.

The setState function calls _getNewText. When it does, . . .

3. The _getNewText function does whatever it has to do with some text.

The setState function also gets the Flutter framework to call build. When it does, . . .

4. The stuff on the user's screen is rebuilt.

The rebuilt screen displays the new text.

There's nothing special about the state management strategy in Listing 5-1. You can copy-and-paste this strategy into many other programs. Figure 5-6 shows you the general idea.

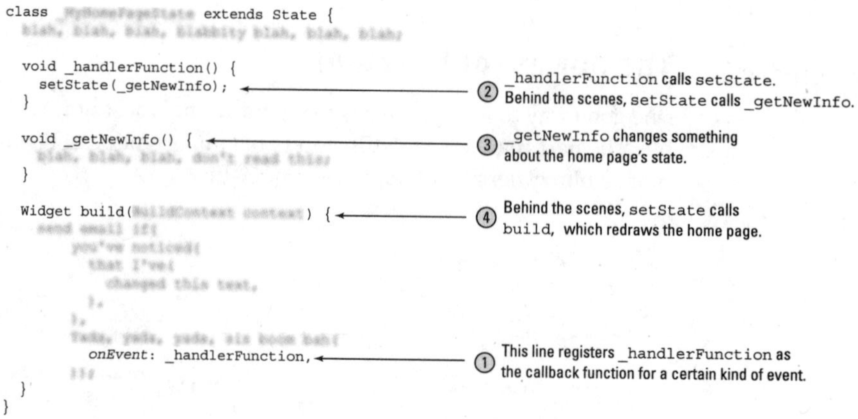

FIGURE 5-6:
What to look for
in many Flutter
programs.

According to Figure 5-6, these steps form a state management strategy:

1. Register a function as a callback function for an event and wait for that event to take place.

In Figure 5-6, the name of the callback function is _handlerFunction. Like all such functions, the _handlerFunction takes no parameters and returns void.

When, at last, the event takes place, . . .

2. Have the callback function call setState and pass another function as the one-and-only parameter in the setState function call.

In Figure 5-6, the name of this other function is _getNewInfo. Like all such functions, the _getNewInfo function takes no parameters and returns void.

The setState function calls _getNewInfo (or whatever name you've used, other than _getNewInfo). When it does, . . .

3. The _getNewInfo function changes something about the state of a widget.

The setState function also gets the Flutter framework to call build. When it does, . . .

4. The stuff on the user's screen is rebuilt.

The rebuilt screen displays the widget in its new state.

And so it goes.

C'mon, what really happens?

When you run a program that has a graphical user interface, lots of stuff happens behind the scenes. If you want, you can look at the framework's code, but that code can be quite complex. Besides, with any decent framework, you shouldn't have to read the framework's own code. You should be able to call the framework's functions and constructors by knowing only the stuff in the framework's documentation.

You can be sure that when Listing 5-1 runs, the setState call results in a call to _getNewText. You know this because, if you comment out the setState call, the text doesn't change. But, it's often helpful to get some sense of the framework's inner mechanisms, even if it's only a rough outline.

To that end, take a look at Figure 5-7. The figure summarizes the description of event handling in the previous few sections. It illustrates some of the action in Listing 5-1, including a capsule summary of the code in the setState function. Make no mistake: Figure 5-7 is an oversimplified view of what happens when Flutter handles an event, but you might find the figure useful.

Listing 5-1 | Inside the Flutter Framework

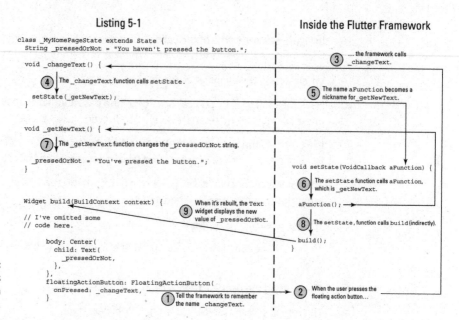

FIGURE 5-7:
Flutter responds to the press of a button.

WHAT TO DO WHEN YOU CALL SETSTATE

Try this experiment: Modify the _changeText function in Listing 5-1 this way:

```
void _changeText() {
  _getNewText();
  setState(_doNothing);
}


void _doNothing() {}
```

Move the reference to _getNewText outside of the setState function. After this move, the change of text happens before the call to setState, so setState doesn't have to call _getNewText. Of course, you still have to feed setState a function to call, so you feed it the _doNothing function. That _doNothing function keeps setState busy while it prepares to call the build method.

Does the modified code work? In this chapter's example, it does. But, in general, a change of this kind is a bad idea. Putting _getNewText inside the setState call ensures that the assignment to _pressedOrNot and the call to build happen together. In a more complicated program, the call to build might be delayed, and the results can be *strange*.

Here's another thing to consider: In Listing 5-1, the _getNewText function contains one simple assignment statement. But imagine an app that does a long, time-consuming calculation before displaying that calculation's result. The update of the screen comes in these three parts:

1. Do the calculation.

2. Change the text to be displayed so that it contains the calculation's result.

3. Have the framework call build to refresh the display.

In that case, Flutter experts recommend the following division of labor:

- Do the long, time-consuming calculation before the call to setState.

- Do the change of text in a parameter when you call setState.

In other words, keep the code that does heavy lifting outside the setState call, but put the code that changes the state's values inside the setState call. That's good advice.

Enhancing Your App

The code in Listing 5-1 is a simplified version of Android Studio's starter app. That's nice, but maybe you want to know more about the starter app. To that end, Listing 5-2 includes a few more features — features that enhance the look and behavior of the simple Flutter demo program.

LISTING 5-2: **Inching Toward Android Studio's Starter App**

```
import 'package:flutter/material.dart';

void main() => runApp(App0502());

class App0502 extends StatelessWidget {
  @override
  Widget build(BuildContext context) {
    return MaterialApp(
      title: 'Flutter Demo',
      theme: ThemeData(
        primarySwatch: Colors.blue,
      ),
      home: MyHomePage(),
    );
```

(continued)

(continued)

```
      }
    }

class MyHomePage extends StatefulWidget {
  @override
  _MyHomePageState createState() => _MyHomePageState();
}

class _MyHomePageState extends State {
  int _counter = 0;

  void _incrementCounter() {
    setState(() {
      _counter++;
    });
  }

  @override
  Widget build(BuildContext context) {
    return Scaffold(
      appBar: AppBar(
        title: Text("Listing 5-2"),
      ),
      body: Center(
        child: Column(
          mainAxisAlignment: MainAxisAlignment.center,
          children: <Widget>[
            Text(
              'You have pushed the button this many times:',
            ),
            Text(
              '$_counter',
              style: Theme.of(context).textTheme.titleLarge,
            ),
          ],
        ),
      ),
      floatingActionButton: FloatingActionButton(
        onPressed: _incrementCounter,
        tooltip: 'Increment',
        child: Icon(Icons.add),
      ),
    );
  }
}
```

Figures 5-8 and 5-9 show a run of the code in Listing 5-2. Figure 5-8 is what you see when the app starts running, and Figure 5-9 is what you see after one click of the floating action button. On subsequent clicks, you see the numbers 2, 3, 4, and so on.

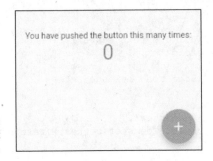

FIGURE 5-8:
Before the first button press.

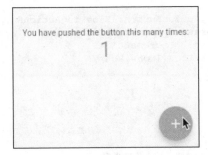

FIGURE 5-9:
After the first button press.

Whenever the user clicks the floating action button, the number on the screen increases by 1. To make this happen, Listing 5-2 has three references to the variable named _counter. Figure 5-10 illustrates the role of the _counter variable in the running of the app.

The app's Text widget displays the value of the _counter variable. So, when the app starts running, the Text widget displays 0. When the user first presses the floating action button and the Flutter framework calls setState, the _counter variable becomes 1. So, the number 1 appears in the center of the app's screen. When the user presses the action button again, _counter becomes 2, and so on.

```
class _MyHomePageState extends State {
  int _counter = 0;

  void _incrementCounter() {
    setState(() {
      _counter++;
    ));
  }

  @override
  Widget build(BuildContext context) {
    return Scaffold(

      // Some code belongs here

      Text(
        '$_counter',
        style: Theme.of(context).textTheme.display1,
      ),
    ),
  ),
),
      floatingActionButton: FloatingActionButton(
        onPressed: _incrementCounter,
        tooltip: 'Increment'
        child: Icon(Icons.add),
      ),
    );
  }
}
```

0   1 2 3 ... Etc.

FIGURE 5-10:
Updating the
Text widget.

More parameters, please

Listing 5-2 introduces some tried-and-true constructor parameters. For example, the MaterialApp constructor has title and theme parameters.

» The title (in this example, Flutter Demo) appears only on Android phones, and only when the user conjures up the Recent Apps list.

» The value of theme is a ThemeData instance (thus, the use of the ThemeData constructor in Listing 5-2).

In the world of app design, themes are vitally important. A *theme* is a bunch of choices that apply to all parts of an app. For example, "Use the Roboto font for all elements that aren't related to accessibility" is a choice, and that choice can be part of a theme.

The choice made in Listing 5-2 is "Use the blue color swatch throughout the app." A *swatch* is a bunch of similar colors — variations on a single color that can be used throughout the app. The Colors.blue swatch contains ten shades of blue, ranging from very light to very dark. (For a look at some pretty swatches, see https://api.flutter.dev/flutter/material/Colors-class.html.)

As an experiment, run the code in Listing 5-2 and then change Colors.blue to Colors.deepOrange or Colors.blueGrey. When you save the change, all elements in the app suddenly look different. That's cool! You don't have to specify each widget's color. The theme maintains a consistent look among all widgets on the screen. For a big app with more than one page, the theme maintains a consistent look from one page to another. This helps the user understand the flow of elements in the app.

In Listing 5-2, a Text widget's style parameter uses a roundabout way to get a TextStyle instance. The code Theme.of(context).textTheme.titleLarge represents a TextStyle with large text size. Figure 5-11 shows you the options that are available when you use Theme.of(context).textTheme.

FIGURE 5-11:
Flutter's
TextTheme styles.

As it is with the MaterialApp theme, the notion of a text theme is mighty handy. When you rely on Flutter's Theme.of(context).textTheme values, you provide a uniform look for all the text elements in your app. You can also take comfort in the fact that you're using standard values — nice-looking values chosen by professional app designers.

Finally, the floating action button in Listing 5-2 has `tooltip` and `child` parameters.

>> **The `tooltip` string shows up when a user long-presses the button.**

When you touch the screen and keep your finger in the same place for a second or two, you're *long-pressing* that part of the screen. The app in Listing 5-2 displays the word `Increment` whenever the user long-presses the floating action button.

>> **For the button's `child`, you construct an `Icon` instance.**

The `Icon` instance displays a tiny image from Flutter's `Icons` class; namely, the `Icons.add` image. Sure enough, that image is a plus sign. (Refer to Figures 5-8 and 5-9.)

For a list of images in Flutter's `Icons` class, visit

```
https://api.flutter.dev/flutter/material/Icons-class.html
```

You can read more about parameters in Listing 5-2 and discover other useful parameters by visiting Flutter's documentation pages. For a brief introduction to those pages, refer to Book 4, Chapter 3.

The override annotation

The line `@override`, which appears several times in Listing 5-2, is called an *annotation*. In Dart, an annotation begins with the at sign (@).

A statement, such as `_pressedOrNot = "You've pressed the button."`, tells Dart what to do during the run of a program. But an annotation is different. An annotation tells Dart something *about* part of a Dart program. An `@override` annotation reminds Dart that the class you're extending has a matching declaration.

For example, consider the following code in Listing 5-2:

```
class App0502 extends StatelessWidget {
  @override
  Widget build(BuildContext context) {
```

The line `@override` says "The `StatelessWidget` class, which this `App0502` class extends, has its own `build(BuildContext context)` method declaration." And indeed, according to this chapter's earlier sidebar ("I'm talking to you, stateless widget — you must have a build method!") the `StatelessWidget` class in the

Flutter API code has a `build(BuildContext context)` method with no body. It all works out nicely.

Listing 5-2 has `@override` annotations, but Listing 5-1 doesn't. Look at that! You can get away without having `@override` annotations! So, why bother having them?

The answer is "safety." The more information you give Dart about your code, the less likely it is that Dart will let you do something wrong. If you make a mistake and declare your `build` method incorrectly, Dart might warn you. "Hey! You said that you intend to override the `build` method that's declared in the `StatelessWidget` class, but your new `build` method doesn't do that correctly. Fix it, my friend!"

You can make Dart warn you about methods that don't match with their `@override` annotations. For details, visit `https://dart.dev/guides/language/analysis-options`.

What does <Widget> mean?

In Listing 5-2, the column's list of children starts with some extra stuff:

```
children: <Widget>[
  Text(
    'You have pushed the button this many times:',
  ),
  Text(
    '$_counter',
    style: Theme.of(context).textTheme.display1,
  ),
]
```

The `<Widget>` word, with its surrounding angle brackets, is called a *generic*, and a list that starts with a generic is called a *parameterized list*. In Listing 5-2, the `<Widget>` generic tells Dart that each of the list's values is, in one way or another, a `Widget`. According to Book 4, Chapter 3, every instance of the `Text` class is an instance of the `Widget` class, so the `<Widget>` generic isn't lying.

In many situations, the use of generics is a safety issue. Consider the following two lines of code:

```
var words1 = ["Hello", "Goodbye", 1108];          // No error message
var words2 = <String>["Hello", "Goodbye", 1108];  // Error message!
```

You may plan to fill your list with String values, but when you declare words1 and words2, you accidentally include the int value 1108. The words1 list isn't parameterized, so Dart doesn't catch the error. But the words2 list is parameterized with the <String> generic, so Dart catches the mistake and refuses to run the code. An error message says The element type 'int' can't be assigned to the list type 'String'. To this, you should respond, "Good catch, Dart. Thank you very much."

Anonymous functions

In the Dart programming language, some functions don't have names. Take a look at the following code:

```
void _incrementCounter() {
  setState(_addOne);
}

void _addOne() {
  _counter++;
}
```

Imagine that your app contains no other references to _addOne. In that case, you've made up the name _addOne and used the name only once in your app. Why bother giving something a name if you'll be using the name only once? "Let's give this ear of corn the name 'sinkadillie'. And now, let's eat sinkadillie."

To create a function with no name, you remove the name. If the function's header has a return type, you remove that too. So, for example,

```
void _addOne() {
  _counter++;
}
```

becomes

```
        () {
  _counter++;
}
```

When you make this be the parameter for the setState function call, it looks like this:

```
void _incrementCounter() {
  setState(() {
```

```
      _counter++;
   });
 }
```

That's what you have in Listing 5-2.

A function with no name is called an *anonymous function*. When an anonymous function contains more than one statement, those statements must be enclosed in curly braces. But if the function contains only one statement, you can use fat arrow notation. For example, in Listing 5-2, the following code would work just fine:

```
void _incrementCounter() {
   setState(() => _counter++);
 }
```

CONFRONTING THE GREAT VOID

Take a nostalgic look at some code from the beginning of this chapter. It's in Listing 5-1.

```
void _changeText() {
   setState(_getNewText);
 }
```

And later, in Listing 5-1:

```
floatingActionButton: FloatingActionButton(
    onPressed: _changeText,
 ))
```

The button press triggers a call to _changeText, and the _changeText function calls setState(_getNewText). Why not eliminate the middleman and have onPressed point directly to setState(_getNewText)? The resulting code would look something like this:

```
floatingActionButton: FloatingActionButton(
    onPressed: setState(_getNewText),          // This doesn't work.
 ))
```

When you write this code, an error message says, "The expression here has a type of 'void' and therefore can't be used." Flutter wants the onPressed parameter to be a function, but the expression setState(_getNewText) isn't a function. It's a call to setState, and a call to setState returns void. (See this sidebar's first figure.)

(continued)

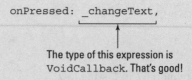

The type of this expression is
VoidCallback. That's good!

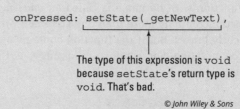

The type of this expression is void
because setState's return type is
void. That's bad.

© John Wiley & Sons

A VoidCallback function is a function that takes no arguments and has the return type void. A common reason for creating a VoidCallback function is . . . well . . . to call a function back. Flutter wants the onPressed parameter to be a VoidCallback function, and the _changeText function fulfills the criteria for being a VoidCallback function. So, in Listing 5-1, the code onPressed: _changeText is fine and dandy.

But setState(_getNewText) isn't a VoidCallback. No, setState(_getNewText) is a plain old void. So the code onPressed: setState(_getNewText) falls flat on its face.

How can you fix the problem? You can revert to the original Listing 5-1 code, or you can save the day by using yet another anonymous function. All you do is add () => before the reference to setState, like so:

```
floatingActionButton: FloatingActionButton(
  onPressed: () => setState(_getNewText),
)
```

This sidebar's second figure describes the miraculous change that takes place when you add a few characters to your code. What was formerly a call to setState becomes a VoidCallback, and everyone is happy. Most importantly, Dart is happy. Your program runs correctly.

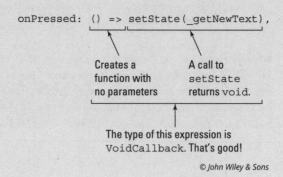

Creates a
function with
no parameters

A call to
setState
returns void.

The type of this expression is
VoidCallback. That's good!

© John Wiley & Sons

What belongs where

In Listing 5-2, the _counter variable's declaration is inside the _MyHomePage State class but outside of that class's _incrementCounter and build methods. A variable of this kind is called an *instance variable* or a *field*. (It depends on whom you ask.)

Why did I declare the _counter variable in that particular place? Why not put the declaration somewhere else in the code? A whole chapter could be written to answer the question in detail, but you don't want to read all that. Instead, here's an experiment for you to try:

1. **Starting with the code in Listing 5-2, add a reference to _counter inside the MyHomePage class. (See Figure 5-12.)**

```
void main() => runApp(App0502());

class App0502 extends StatelessWidget {
  // Blah, blah, blah ...
}

class MyHomePage extends StatefulWidget {
  @override
  _MyHomePageState createState() => _MyHomePageState();
  _counter = 86;  // This line is incorrect.
}

class _MyHomePageState extends State {
  int _counter = 0;

  void _incrementCounter() {
    setState(() {
      _counter++;
    });
  }

  @override
  Widget build(BuildContext context) {
    // Yada, yada ...
  }
}
```

FIGURE 5-12:
References to the boldface _counter variable are valid only inside the gray box.

Android Studio marks this new reference with a jagged red underline. The underline shames you into admitting that this additional reference was a bad idea. You've declared the _counter variable in the _MyHomePageState class, but you're trying to reference the variable in a different class; namely, the MyHomePage class.

Whenever you declare a variable inside of a class, that variable is *local* to the class. You can't refer to that variable outside the class. In particular, you can't refer to that variable inside a different class.

Don't you hate it when authors contradict themselves? There *is* a way to refer to a variable outside of its class's code. It's covered in detail in Book 4, Chapter 7.

2. **Remove the reference to `_counter` that you added in Step 1. Then move the declaration of `_counter` to the end of the `_MyHomePageState` class. (See Figure 5-13.)**

```
void main() => runApp(App0502());

class App0502 extends StatelessWidget {
  // Blah, blah, blah ...
}

class MyHomePage extends StatefulWidget {
  // Yada, yada ...
}

class _MyHomePageState extends State {
  void _incrementCounter() {
    setState(() {
      _counter++;
    });
  }

  @override
  Widget build(BuildContext context) {
    // Whatever ...
  }

  int _counter = 0;
}
```

FIGURE 5-13: References to the boldface _counter variable are valid inside the gray box.

Near the start of the _MyHomePageState class, you do _counter++. But you don't declare the _counter variable until the end of the _MyHomePageState class. Nevertheless, the program runs correctly. The moral of this story is, you don't have to declare a variable before you refer to that variable. Nice!

3. **Move the declaration of `_counter` so that it's inside the body of the `_incrementCounter` function. (See Figure 5-14.)**

When you do, you see an error marker on the occurrence of _counter in the build function. You've declared the _counter variable inside the _incrementCounter function, but you're trying to reference that variable in a different function; namely, the build function.

```
void main() => runApp(App0502());

class App0502 extends StatelessWidget {
  // Blah, blah, blah ...
}

class MyHomePage extends StatefulWidget {
  // Yada, yada ...
}

class _MyHomePageState extends State {

  void _incrementCounter() {
    int _counter = 0;
    setState(() {
      _counter++;
    });
  }

  @override
  Widget build(BuildContext context) {
    // Whatever ...
    Test{
      '$_counter',
    }
  }
}
```

FIGURE 5-14:
References to
the boldface
_counter
variable are valid
only inside the
gray box.

Whenever you declare a variable inside a function, that variable is local to the function. You can't refer to that variable outside the function. In particular, you can't refer to that variable inside a different function.

4. **Keep the declaration of `_counter` inside the `_incrementCounter` function and add another `_counter` declaration inside the `build` function. Initialize the `build` function's `_counter` variable to 99. (See Figure 5-15.)**

When you do this, the error message from Step 3 goes away. So the code is correct. Right?

No! The code isn't correct. When you run the code, the number in the center of the device is 99, and its value never changes. Pressing the floating action button has no effect. What's going on?

With this revised code, you have two different _counter variables — one that's local to the `_incrementCounter` function and another that's local to the `build` function. The statement _counter++ adds 1 to one of these _counter variables, but it doesn't add 1 to the other _counter variable. It's like having two people named Barry Burd — one living in New Jersey and the other in California. If you add a dollar to one of their bank accounts, the other person doesn't automatically get an additional dollar.

5. **Include only one `_counter` declaration. Put it just before the start of the `_MyHomePageState` class. (See Figure 5-16.)**

```
void main() => runApp(App0502());

class App0502 extends StatelessWidget {
  // Blah, blah, blah ...
}

class MyHomePage extends StatefulWidget {
  // Yada, yada ...
}

class _MyHomePageState extends State {

  void _incrementCounter() {
    int _counter = 0;
    setState(() {
      _counter++;
    });
  }

  @override
  Widget build(BuildContext context) {
    int _counter = 99;
    // Whatever ...
  }
}
```

0

99

FIGURE 5-15:
You can refer to one _counter variable only in the upper gray region; you can refer to the other _counter variable only in the lower gray region.

```
void main() => runApp(App0502());

class App0502 extends StatelessWidget {
  // Blah, blah, blah ...
}

class MyHomePage extends StatefulWidget {
  // Yada, yada ...
}

int _counter = 0;

class _MyHomePageState extends State {

  void _incrementCounter() {
    setState(() {
      _counter++;
    });
  }

  @override
  Widget build(BuildContext context) {
    // Whatever ...
  }
}
```

FIGURE 5-16:
Use a top-level name anywhere in your .dart file.

After making this change, the editor doesn't display any error markers. Maybe you click the Run icon, anticipating bad news. Either the app doesn't run, or it runs and behaves badly. But, lo and behold, the app runs correctly!

A declaration that's not inside a class or a function is called a *top-level* declaration, and a top-level name can be referenced anywhere in your program. (Well, almost anywhere. There are some limits. In particular, see the later section "Names that start with an underscore.")

6. **Include two _counter variable declarations — one at the top level, and another inside the _MyHomePageState class. Initialize the top-level _counter to 2873 and the latter _counter to 0. (See Figure 5-17.)**

```
void main() => runApp(App0502());

class App0502 extends StatelessWidget {
  // Blah, blah, blah ...
}                                                     2873

class MyHomePage extends StatefulWidget {
  // Yada, yada ...
}

int _counter = 2873;

class _MyHomePageState extends State {
  int _counter = 0;

  void _incrementCounter() {
    setState(() {
      _counter++;
    });
  }                                                   0

  @override
  Widget build(BuildContext context) {
    // Whatever  ...
  }
}

// What if there's more code after the              2873
//   _MyHomePageState class declaration?
```

FIGURE 5-17: The Shadow knows!

Before testing this version of the code, end the run of any other version. Start this version of the code afresh.

When this modified app starts running, the number in the center of the screen is 0, not 2873. The top-level declaration of _counter has no effect because it's shadowed by the declaration in the _MyHomePageState class.

The _counter declaration in the _MyHomePageState class applies to the code inside the _MyHomePageState class. The top-level _counter declaration applies everywhere else in this file's code.

This section is all about classes, methods, and variables. The section describes an instance variable as a variable whose declaration is inside of a class, but not inside any of the class's methods. That's *almost* a correct description of an instance variable. To be precise, an instance variable's declaration is one that doesn't contain the word static — a word that you encounter in Book 4, Chapters 7 and 8. Until you read Chapters 7 and 8, don't worry about it.

Names that start with an underscore

Someday soon, when you're a big-shot Flutter developer, you'll create a large, complicated app that involves several different .dart files. A file's import statements will make code from one file available for use in another file. But how does this work? Are there any restrictions? Figure 5-18 says it all.

TOP-LEVEL NAMES AREN'T ALWAYS BEST

In Step 5 of this section's instructions, you declare _counter at the top level and the program runs without a hitch. If it's okay to declare _counter at the top level, why don't you do that in Listing 5-2? Well, you should expect more from a program than that it simply runs correctly. In addition to running correctly, a good program is sturdy. The program doesn't break when someone changes a bit of code.

In Listing 5-2, the only use of the _counter variable is inside the _MyHomePageState class. A programmer who's working on the _MyHomePageState class's code should be able to mess with the _counter variable. But other programmers, those who work on other parts of the app, have no need to reference the _counter variable. By keeping access to _counter inside the _MyHomePageState class, you're protecting the variable from accidental misuse by programmers who don't need to reference it. (Object-oriented programmers call this *encapsulation*.)

The program in Listing 5-2 isn't a large, industrial-strength app. So, in that program, anyone who writes code outside the _MyHomePageState class is likely to know all about the code inside the _MyHomePageState class. But for real-life applications in which teams of programmers work on different parts of the code, protecting one part of the code from the other parts is important. No, it's not important. It's absolutely essential.

In any program that you write, limit access to variable names and other names as much as you can. Don't declare them at the top level if you don't have to. It's safer that way.

FIGURE 5-18:
"I got plenty
numbers left."
(Google it.)

```
one_file.dart ×                                          another_file.dart ×
1    import 'package:flutter/material.dart'; ✓       1    import 'one_file.dart';
2                                                    2
3    void main() => runApp(MyApp());                 3
4                                                    4
5    var _number = 50;                               5    var num = _number;
6    var amount = 10;                                6    var amnt = amount;
7                                                    7
8    class MyApp extends StatelessWidget {
9      @override
10     Widget build(BuildContext context) {
11       return MaterialApp(
```

A variable or function whose name begins with an underscore (_) is local to
the file in which it's declared and can't be referenced in other .dart files. All
other names can be imported and shared among all the files in an application. In
Figure 5-18, the _number variable can be used only in one_file.dart. But, because
of an import statement, the amount variable is available in both one_file.dart
and another_file.dart.

TECHNICAL STUFF

If you're used to writing code in languages like Java, forget about access modifiers
such as public and private. The Dart language doesn't have those things.

Whew!

This is a heavy-duty chapter. If you've spent the evening reading every word of it,
you're probably a bit tired. But that's okay. Take a breather. Make yourself a cup
of tea. Sit in your easy chair and relax with a performance of *The Well-Tempered
Clavier* (Praeludium 1, BWV 846).

Chapter 6 continues the theme of widgets responding to user actions. In that
chapter, you slide sliders, switch switches, drop drop-down lists, and do other
fun things. Go for it (but don't forget to unwind a bit first)!

Chapter **6**

Laying Things Out

I n a Flutter layout, widgets are nested inside of other widgets. The outer widget sends a constraint to the inner widget:

"You can be as wide as you want, as long as your width is between 0 and 400 density-independent pixels."

Later on, the inner widget sends its exact height to the outer widget:

"I'm 200 density-independent pixels wide."

The outer widget uses that information to position the inner widget:

"Because you're 200 density-independent pixels wide, I'll position your left edge 100 pixels from my left edge."

Of course, this is a simplified version of the true scenario. But it's a useful starting point for understanding the way Flutter layouts work. Most importantly, this outer/inner communication works its way all along an app's widget chain.

Imagine having four widgets. Starting from the outermost widget (such as the Material widget), call these widgets "great-grandmother", "grandmother", "mother", and "Elsie." Here's how Flutter decides how to draw these widgets:

1. Great-grandmother tells grandmother how big she (grandmother) can be.

2. Grandmother tells mother how big she (mother) can be.

3. Mother tells Elsie how big she (Elsie) can be.

4. Elsie decides how big she is and tells mother.

5. Mother determines Elsie's position, decides how big she (mother) is, and then tells grandmother.

6. Grandmother determines mother's position, decides how big she (grand-mother) is, and then tells great-grandmother.

7. Great-grandmother determines mother's position and then decides how big she (great-grandmother is).

Yes, the details are fuzzy. But it helps to keep this pattern in mind as you read about Flutter layouts.

Understanding the Big Picture

Listings 6-1 and 6-2 introduce a handful of Flutter layout concepts, and Figure 6-1 shows what you see when you run these listings together.

LISTING 6-1: **Reuse This Code**

```
// app06main.dart

import 'package:flutter/material.dart';

import 'app0602.dart'; // Change this line to app0605, app0606, and so on.

void main() => runApp(App06Main());

class App06Main extends StatelessWidget {
  @override
  Widget build(BuildContext context) {
    return MaterialApp(
      home: _MyHomePage(),
    );
  }
}
```

```
class _MyHomePage extends StatelessWidget {
  @override
  Widget build(BuildContext context) {
    return Material(
      color: Colors.grey[400],
      child: Padding(
        padding: const EdgeInsets.symmetric(
          horizontal: 20.0,
        ),
        child: buildColumn(context),
      ),
    );
  }
}

Widget buildTitleText() {
  return Text(
    "My Pet Shop",
    textScaleFactor: 3.0,
    textAlign: TextAlign.center,
  );
}

Widget buildRoundedBox(
  String label, {
  double height = 88.0,
}) {
  return Container(
    height: height,
    width: 88.0,
    alignment: Alignment(0.0, 0.0),
    decoration: BoxDecoration(
      color: Colors.white,
      border: Border.all(color: Colors.black),
      borderRadius: BorderRadius.all(
        Radius.circular(10.0),
      ),
    ),
    child: Text(
      label,
      textAlign: TextAlign.center,
    ),
  );
}
```

LISTING 6-2: **A Very Simple Layout**

```dart
// app0602.dart

import 'package:flutter/material.dart';

import 'app06main.dart';

Widget buildColumn(BuildContext context) {
  return Column(
    mainAxisAlignment: MainAxisAlignment.center,
    crossAxisAlignment: CrossAxisAlignment.stretch,
    children: <Widget>[
      buildTitleText(),
      SizedBox(height: 20.0),
      buildRoundedBox(
        "Sale Today",
        height: 150.0,
      ),
    ],
  );
}
```

FIGURE 6-1:
A sale at
My Pet Shop.

The code in Listing 6-1 refers to code in Listing 6-2, and vice versa. As long as these two files are in the same Android Studio project, running the app in Listing 6-1 automatically uses code from Listing 6-2. This works because of the import declarations near the top of each of the listings. For info about import declarations, refer to Book 4, Chapter 4.

Listings 6-1 and 6-2 illustrate some coding concepts along with a bunch of useful Flutter features that will be covered in the next several sections.

Creating bite-size pieces of code

In Listings 6-1 and 6-2, method calls create some of the widgets.

```
child: buildColumn(context),

// ... And elsewhere, ...

Column(
  // ... Blah, blah, ...
  children: <Widget>[
    buildTitleText(),
    SizedBox(height: 20.0),
    buildRoundedBox(
    // ... Etc.
```

Each method call takes the place of a longer piece of code — one that describes a particular widget in detail. These methods makes the code easier to read and digest. With a glance at Listing 6-2, you can tell that the Column consists of title text, a sized box, and a rounded box. You don't know any of the details until you look at the buildTitleText and buildRoundedBox method declarations in Listing 6-1, but that's okay. With the code divided into methods this way, you don't lose sight of the app's overall outline.

In the design of good software, planning is essential. But sometimes your plans change. Imagine this scenario: You start writing some code that you believe will be fairly simple. After several minutes (or, sometimes, several hours), you realize that the code has become large and unwieldy. So you decide to divide the code into methods. To do this, you can take advantage of one of Android Studio's handy refactoring features. Here's how it works:

1. **Start with a constructor call that you want to replace with your own method call.**

   For example, you want to replace the Text constructor call in the following code snippet:

```
children: <Widget>[
  Text(
    "My Pet Shop",
    textScaleFactor: 3.0,
    textAlign: TextAlign.center,
  ),
  SizedBox(height: 20.0),
```

2. Place the mouse cursor on the constructor call's name.

For the snippet in Step 1, click on the word Text.

3. On Android Studio's main menu, select Refactor⇨Extract⇨Method.

As a result, Android Studio displays the Extract Method dialog box.

4. In the Extract Method dialog box, type a name for your new method.

For a constructor named Text, Android Studio suggests the method name buildText. But, to create Listings 6-1 and 6-2, I made up the name buildTitleText.

5. In the Extract Method dialog box, choose Refactor.

As if by magic, Android Studio adds a new method declaration to your code and replaces the original widget constructor with a call to the method.

The new method's return type is whatever kind of widget your code is trying to construct. For example, starting with the code in Step 1, the method's first two lines might look like this:

```
Text buildTitleText() {
  return Text(
```

6. Do yourself a favor and change the type in the method's header to Widget.

```
Widget buildTitleText() {
  return Text(
```

Every instance of the Text class is an instance of the Widget class, so this change doesn't do any harm. In addition, the change adds a tiny bit of flexibility that may eventually save you some mental energy. Maybe later, you'll decide to surround the method's Text widget with a Center widget.

```
Text buildTitleText() {
  return Center(
    child: Text(
```

After you make this change, your code is messed up because the header's return type is inaccurate. Yes, every instance of the Text class is an instance of the Widget class. But, no, an instance of the Center class isn't an instance of the Text class. Your method returns an instance of Center, but the method's header expects the method to return an instance of Text. Don't you wish you had changed the first word in the header to Widget? Do it sooner rather than later. That way, you won't be distracted when you're concentrating on making changes in the method's body.

Creating a parameter list

In Listing 6-1, the header of the `buildRoundedBox` declaration looks like this:

```
Widget buildRoundedBox(
  String label, {
  double height = 88.0,
})
```

The method has two parameters: `label` and `height`.

>> **The `label` parameter is a positional parameter.**

It's a positional parameter because it's not surrounded by curly braces. In a header, all the positional parameters must come before any of the named parameters.

>> **The `height` parameter is a named parameter.**

It's a named parameter because it's surrounded by curly braces. In a call to this method, you can omit the `height` parameter. When you do, the parameter's default value is 88.0.

With these facts in mind, the following calls to `buildRoundedBox` are both valid:

```
buildRoundedBox(           // Flutter style guidelines recommend having a
  "Flutter",               //   trailing comma at the end of every list.
  height: 1000.0,          //   It's the comma after the height parameter.
)

buildRoundedBox("Flutter") // In the method header, the height parameter
                           //   has the default value 88.0.
```

Here are some calls that aren't valid:

```
buildRoundedBox(           // In a function call, all positional parameters
  height: 1000.0,          //   must come before any named parameters.
  "Flutter",
)

buildRoundedBox(
  label: "Flutter",        // The label parameter is a positional parameter,
  height: 1000.0,          //   not a named parameter.
)
```

```
buildRoundedBox(            // The height parameter is a named parameter,
  "Flutter",                //   not a positional parameter.
  1000.0,
)

buildRoundedBox()           // You can't omit the label parameter, because
                            //   the label parameter has no default value.
```

For info about positional parameters and named parameters, refer to Book 4, Chapter 3. For the basics on declaring functions, refer to Book 4, Chapter 4.

In Listing 6-2, the declaration of buildColumn has a BuildContext parameter. You may ask, "What good is this BuildContext parameter? The body of the buildColumn method makes no reference to this parameter's value." For an answer, see the last section of this chapter.

Living color

Book 4, Chapter 5 introduces Flutter's Colors class with basic things like Colors. grey and Colors.black. In fact, the Colors class provides 12 different shades of gray, 7 shades of black, 28 shades of blue, and a similar variety for other colors. For example, the shades of grey are named Colors.grey[50] (the lightest), Colors.grey[100], Colors.grey[200], Colors.grey[300], and so on, up to Colors.grey[900] (the darkest). You can't put arbitrary numbers inside the brackets, so things like Colors.grey[101] and Colors.grey[350] simply don't exist. But one shade — Colors.grey[500] — is special. You can abbreviate Colors.grey[500] by writing Colors.grey without having a number in brackets.

If you want extra-fine control over the look of your app, you can use Flutter's Color.fromRGBO constructor. (That's Color singular, as opposed to Colors plural.) The letters RGBO stand for Red, Green, Blue, and Opacity. In the constructor, the values of Red, Green, and Blue range from 0 to 255, and the value of Opacity ranges from 0.0 to 1.0. For example, Color.fromRGBO(255, 0, 0, 1.0) stands for completely opaque Red. Table 6-1 has some other examples.

To find out about other options for describing colors, visit Flutter's Color class documentation page:

```
https://api.flutter.dev/flutter/dart-ui/Color-class.html
```

TABLE 6-1 ## Sample Parameters for the Color.fromRGBO Constructor

Parameter List	What the Parameter List Means
(0, 255, 0, 1.0)	Green
(0, 0, 255, 1.0)	Blue
(255, 0, 255, 1.0)	Purple (equal amounts of Red and Blue)
(0, 0, 0, 1.0)	Black
(255, 255, 255, 1.0)	White
(190, 190, 190, 1.0)	Gray (approximately 75% whiteness)
(255, 0, 0, 0.5)	50% transparent Red
(255, 0, 0, 0.0)	Nothing (complete transparency, no matter what the Red, Green, and Blue values are)

Adding padding

Flutter's Padding widget puts some empty space between its outermost edge and its child. In Listing 6-1, the code

```
Padding(
  padding: const EdgeInsets.symmetric(
    horizontal: 20.0,
  ),
  child: buildColumn(context),
```

surrounds the buildColumn call with 20.0 units of empty space on the left and the right. (Refer to Figure 6-1.) With no padding, the column would touch the left and right edges of the user's screen, and so would the white Sale Today box inside the column. That wouldn't look nice.

In Flutter, a line such as horizontal: 20.0 stands for 20.0 density-independent pixels. A *density-independent pixel* (dp) has no fixed size. Instead, the size of a density-independent pixel depends on the user's hardware. In particular, every inch of the user's screen is roughly 96 dp long. That makes every centimeter approximately 38 pixels long. According to Flutter's official documentation, the rule about having 96 dp per inch "may be inaccurate, sometimes by a significant margin." Run this section's app on your own phone and you'll see what they mean.

In Flutter, you describe padding of any kind by constructing an EdgeInsets object. The EdgeInsets.symmetric constructor in Listing 6-1 has one parameter — a horizontal parameter. In addition to the horizontal parameter, an EdgeInsets.symmetric constructor can have a vertical parameter, like so:

```
Padding(
  padding: const EdgeInsets.symmetric(
    horizontal: 20.0,
    vertical: 10.0,
  )
```

A vertical parameter adds empty space to the top and bottom of the child widget. Table 6-2 lists some alternatives to the EdgeInsets.symmetric constructor.

TABLE 6-2

EdgeInsets Constructor Calls

Constructor Call	How Much Blank Space Surrounds the Child Widget
EdgeInsets.all(20.0)	20.0 dp on all four sides
EdgeInsets.only(left: 15.0, top: 10.0,)	15.0 dp on the left 10.0 dp on top
EdgeInsets.only(top: 10.0, right: 15.0, bottom: 15.0,)	10.0 dp on top 15.0 dp on the right 15.0 dp on the bottom
EdgeInsets.fromLTRB(5.0, 10.0, 3.0, 2.0,)	5.0 dp on the left 10.0 dp on top 3.0 dp on the right 2.0 dp on the bottom

REMEMBER

The `Padding` widget adds blank space inside of itself. To add space outside of a widget, see the section "Your friend, the Container widget," later in this chapter.

Your humble servant, the Column widget

Think about it: Without Flutter's `Column` widget, you wouldn't be able to position one widget above another. Everything on a user's screen would be squished into one place. The screen would be unreadable, and no one would use Flutter. You wouldn't be reading this book. What an awful world it would be!

The `Column` widget in Listing 6-2 has two properties related to alignment:

```
Column(
    mainAxisAlignment: MainAxisAlignment.center,
    crossAxisAlignment: CrossAxisAlignment.stretch,
    // ... And so on.
```

The `mainAxisAlignment` property comes up in Book 4, Chapter 3. It describes the way children are positioned from the top to the bottom of the column. With `MainAxisAlignment.center`, children gather about halfway down from the top of the screen. (Refer to Figure 6-1.) In contrast, the `crossAxisAlignment` describes how children are situated from side to side within the column. (See Figure 6-2.)

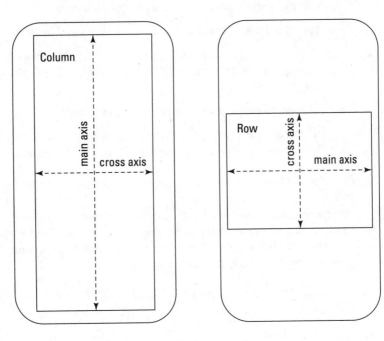

FIGURE 6-2:
Every Flutter book contains a drawing like this.

A column's `crossAxisAlignment` can make a big difference in the way the column's children appear on the screen. For example, if you comment out the `crossAxisAlignment` line in Listing 6-2, you see the screen shown in Figure 6-3.

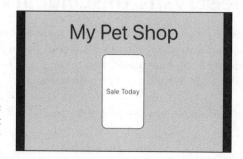

FIGURE 6-3:
When you don't
stretch the Sale
Today box.

In Listing 6-2, the `CrossAxisAlignment.stretch` value tells the column that its children should fill the entire cross axis. This means that, regardless of the children's explicit width values, children shrink or widen so that they run across the entire column. If you don't believe me, try the following experiment:

1. **Run the code in Listing 6-1.**

   Use the iPhone simulator, the Android emulator, or a real physical phone. Start with the device in portrait mode, as in Figure 6-1.

2. **Turn the device sideways so that it is in landscape mode.**

   If you're running a virtual device, press Command-right arrow (on a Mac) or Ctrl+right arrow (on Windows). If you're running a physical device, turn the darn thing sideways.

3. **Observe the change in the size of the Sale Today box.**

   No matter how wide the screen is, the Sale Today box stretches almost all the way across. The `width: 88.0` setting in Listing 6-1 has no effect.

You can read more about axis alignments in the sections that follow.

TIP

When you turn a device sideways, the device might not switch between portrait and landscape modes. This is true for both physical devices (real phones and tablets) and virtual devices (emulators and simulators). If your device's orientation refuses to change, try this:

» On an Android device, in Settings⇨Display, turn on Auto Rotate Screen.

» On an iPhone or iPad, swipe up from the bottom of the screen and press the button that displays a lock and a circular arrow.

The SizedBox widget

If you plan to live on a desert island and can bring only seven widgets with you, those seven widgets should be Column, Row, SizedBox, Container, Expanded, Spacer, and Padding.

A SizedBox is a rectangle that developers use for taking up space. A SizedBox has a width, a height, and possibly a child. Very often, only the width or the height matters.

Listing 6-2 has a SizedBox of height 20.0 sitting between the title text and the rounded box. Without the SizedBox, there would be no space between the title text and the rounded box.

TIP

A Spacer is like a SizedBox, except that a Spacer uses flex instead of explicit height and width parameters. For a look at Flutter's flex property, see the section "Flexing some muscles," later in this chapter.

Your friend, the Container widget

In Listing 6-2, the box displaying the words *Sale Today* uses a Container widget. A Container is a widget that contains something. (That's not surprising.) While the widget is containing something, it has properties like height, width, alignment, decoration, padding, and margin.

The height and width parameters

You might be curious about a particular line in Listing 6-1:

```
return Container(
  height: height,
```

What could height: height possibly mean? The height is what it is? The height is the height is the height?

To find out what's going on, place the cursor on the second occurrence of the word height — the one after the colon. When you do, Android Studio highlights that occurrence along with one other. (See Figure 6-4.)

FIGURE 6-4:
Selecting a
name in Android
Studio's editor.

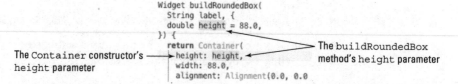

```
Widget buildRoundedBox(
    String label, {
    double height = 88.0,
}) {
    return Container(
        height: height,
        width: 88.0,
        alignment: Alignment(0.0, 0.0
```

The Container constructor's
height parameter

The buildRoundedBox
method's height parameter

Noticeably absent is any highlight on the `height` that's immediately before the colon. Listing 6-1 has two variables named `height`. One is a parameter of `build RoundedBox`; the other is a parameter of the `Container` constructor. The line

```
height: height,
```

makes the `Container` parameter have the same value as the `buildRounded Box` parameter. (The `buildRoundedBox` parameter gets its value from the call in Listing 6-2.)

WARNING

In a `Container` constructor call, the `height` and `width` parameters are suggestions — not absolute sizes. For details, refer to the section "Your humble servant, the Column widget," earlier in this chapter. And, while you're at it, check out the section "Using the Expanded Widget," later in this chapter.

The alignment parameter

To align a child within a `Container` widget, you don't use `mainAxisAlignment` or `crossAxisAlignment`. Instead, you use the plain old `alignment` parameter. In Listing 6-1, the line

```
alignment: Alignment(0.0, 0.0)
```

tells Flutter to put the child of the container in the center of the container. Figure 6-5 illustrates the secrets behind the `Alignment` class.

The decoration parameter

As the name suggests, `decoration` is something that livens up an otherwise dull-looking widget. In Listing 6-1, the `BoxDecoration` constructor has three parameters of its own:

» `color`: **The widget's fill color.**

This property fills the Sale Today box in Figure 6-1 with white.

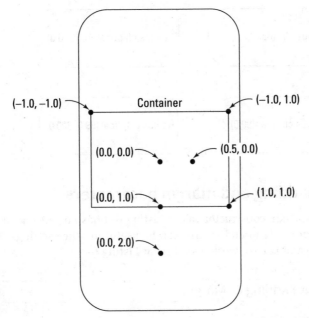

FIGURE 6-5:
Using a
container's
alignment
parameter.

WARNING

Both the Container and BoxDecoration constructors have color parameters. When you put a BoxDecoration inside of a Container, have a color parameter for the BoxDecoration, not the Container. If you have both, your program may crash.

» **border: The outline surrounding the widget.**

Listing 6-1 uses the Border.all constructor, which describes a border on all four sides of the Sale Today box.

To create a border whose sides aren't all the same, use Flutter's Border constructor (without the .all part). Here's an example:

```
Border(
    top: BorderSide(width: 5.0, color: Colors.black),
    bottom: BorderSide(width: 5.0, color: Colors.black),
    left: BorderSide(width: 3.0, color: Colors.blue),
    right: BorderSide(width: 3.0, color: Colors.blue),
)
```

» **borderRadius: The amount of curvature of the widget's border.**

Figure 6-6 shows what happens when you use different values for the borderRadius parameter.

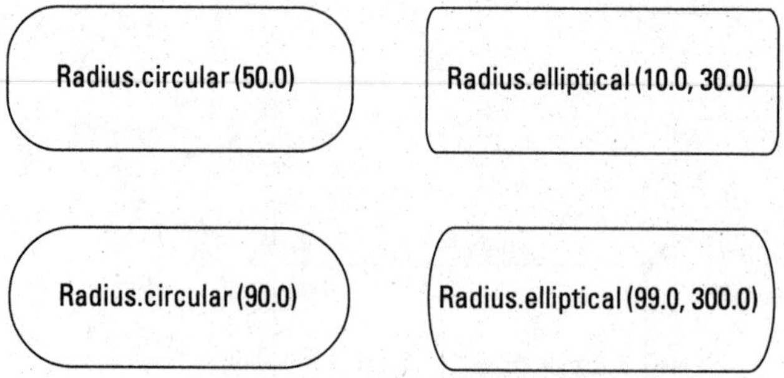

Radius.circular (50.0)

Radius.elliptical (10.0, 30.0)

Radius.circular (90.0)

Radius.elliptical (99.0, 300.0)

FIGURE 6-6:
Experiments with
a border radius.

The padding and margin parameters

The Container constructor call in Listing 6-1 has no padding or margin parameters, but padding and margin can be useful in other settings. To find out how
padding and margin work, look first at Listing 6-3.

LISTING 6-3: **Without Padding or Margin**

```
// app0603.dart

import 'package:flutter/material.dart';

void main() => runApp(App0602());

class App0602 extends StatelessWidget {
  @override
  Widget build(BuildContext context) {
    return MaterialApp(
      home: Material(
        color: Colors.grey[50],
        child: Container(
          color: Colors.grey[500],
          child: Container(
            color: Colors.grey[700],
          ),
        ),
      ),
    );
  }
}
```

Listing 6-3 has a container within another container that's within a `Material` widget. The inner container is `grey[700]`, which is fairly dark gray. The outer container is a lighter gray, and the `Material` widget background is `grey[50]`, which is almost white.

When you run the app in Listing 6-3, the inner container completely covers the outer container, which, in turn, completely covers the `Material` widget. Each of these widgets expands to fill its parent, so each of the three widgets takes up the entire screen. The only widget you can see is the innermost, dark gray container. What a waste!

To remedy this situation, Listing 6-4 uses both `padding` and `margin`. Figure 6-7 shows you the result.

LISTING 6-4: **With Padding and Margin**

```
// app0604.dart

import 'package:flutter/material.dart';

void main() => runApp(App0604());

class App0604 extends StatelessWidget {
  @override
  Widget build(BuildContext context) {
    return MaterialApp(
      home: SafeArea(
        child: Material(
          color: Colors.grey[50],
          child: Container(
            color: Colors.grey[500],
            padding: EdgeInsets.all(80.0),
            margin: EdgeInsets.all(40.0),
            child: Container(
              color: Colors.grey[700],
            ),
          ),
        ),
      ),
    );
  }
}
```

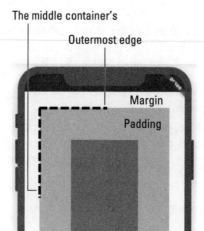

The middle container's

Outermost edge

Margin

Padding

FIGURE 6-7:
Padding versus
margin.

Listing 6-4 is all about the middle container — the one whose color is a medium shade of gray. I've marked up Figure 6-7 to make the result crystal-clear. The general rules are as follows:

>> *Padding* **is the space between a widget's outermost edges and the widget's child.**

In Figure 6-7, the medium gray stuff is padding.

>> **A** *margin* **is the space between a widget's outermost edges and the widget's parent.**

In Figure 6-7, the white (or nearly white) stuff is the margin.

REMEMBER

You can add padding to almost any widget without putting that widget inside a Container. To do so, simply put the widget inside of a Padding widget. For an example, look for the Padding widget in Listing 6-1.

When you think about a mobile device, you probably imagine a rectangular screen. Does this mean that an entire rectangle is available for use by your app? It doesn't. The top of the rectangle may have a notch. The corners of the rectangle may be rounded instead of square. The operating system (iOS or Android) may consume parts of the screen with an Action Bar or other junk.

To avoid items in this obstacle course, Flutter has a SafeArea widget. The SafeArea is the part of the screen that's available for the free, unencumbered use by your app. In Listing 6-4, a SafeArea helps me show the padding and margin in all their glory. Without that SafeArea, the top part of the margin might be covered by stuff that's not part of my app.

Nesting Rows and Columns

You hardly ever see an app with only one column of widgets. Most of the time, you see widgets alongside other widgets, widgets arranged in grids, widgets at angles to other widgets, and so on. The most straightforward way to arrange Flutter widgets is to put columns inside of rows and rows inside of columns. Listing 6-5 has an example, and Figure 6-8 shows you the results.

LISTING 6-5: **A Row within a Column**

```
// app0605.dart

import 'package:flutter/material.dart';

import 'app06main.dart';

Widget buildColumn(BuildContext context) {
  return Column(
    mainAxisAlignment: MainAxisAlignment.center,
    crossAxisAlignment: CrossAxisAlignment.stretch,
    children: <Widget>[
      buildTitleText(),
      SizedBox(height: 20.0),
      _buildRowOfThree(),
    ],
  );
}

Widget _buildRowOfThree() {
  return Row(
    mainAxisAlignment: MainAxisAlignment.spaceBetween,
    children: <Widget>[
      buildRoundedBox("Cat"),
      buildRoundedBox("Dog"),
      buildRoundedBox("Ape"),
    ],
  );
}
```

In Listing 6-1, the Column widget's crossAxisAlignment property forces the Sale Today box to be as wide as it could possibly be. That happens because the Sale Today box is one of the Column widget's children. But in Listing 6-5, the Cat, Dog, and Ape boxes aren't children of the Column widget. Instead, they're *grandchildren* of the Column widget. So, for Listing 6-5, the major factor positioning the Cat, Dog, and Ape boxes is the Row widget's mainAxisAlignment property.

To see this in action, change these lines in Listing 6-5:

```
return Row(
    mainAxisAlignment: MainAxisAlignment.spaceBetween,
```

To the following lines:

```
return Row(
    mainAxisAlignment: MainAxisAlignment.center,
```

When you do, you see the arrangement shown in Figure 6-9.

To find out about values you can give to a `mainAxisAlignment` property, refer to Book 4, Chapter 3.

Introducing More Levels of Nesting

Yes, you can create a row within a column within a row within a column within a row. You can go on like that for a very long time. This section has two modest examples. The first example (Listing 6-6) has a row of captioned boxes.

LISTING 6-6: **Adding Captions to the Boxes**

```
// app0606.dart

import 'package:flutter/material.dart';

import 'app06main.dart';

Widget buildColumn(BuildContext context) {
  return Column(
    mainAxisAlignment: MainAxisAlignment.center,
    crossAxisAlignment: CrossAxisAlignment.stretch,
    children: <Widget>[
      buildTitleText(),
      SizedBox(height: 20.0),
      _buildCaptionedRow(),
    ],
  );
}

Widget _buildCaptionedRow() {
  return Row(
    mainAxisAlignment: MainAxisAlignment.spaceBetween,
    children: <Widget>[
      _buildCaptionedItem(
        "Cat",
        caption: "Meow",
      ),
      _buildCaptionedItem(
        "Dog",
        caption: "Woof",
      ),
      _buildCaptionedItem(
        "Ape",
        caption: "Chatter",
      ),
    ],
  );
}

Column _buildCaptionedItem(String label, {required String caption}) {
  return Column(
    children: <Widget>[
      buildRoundedBox(label),
      SizedBox(
        height: 5.0,
      ),
```

(continued)

LISTING 6-6: (continued)

```
      Text(
        caption,
        textScaleFactor: 1.25,
      ),
    ],
  );
}
```

Figure 6-10 shows a run of the code from Listing 6-6.

FIGURE 6-10:
Noisy animals
for sale.

The next example, Listing 6-7, does something a bit different. In Listing 6-7, two boxes share the space where one box might be.

LISTING 6-7: **More Widget Nesting**

```
// app0607.dart

import 'package:flutter/material.dart';

import 'app06main.dart';

Widget buildColumn(BuildContext context) {
  return Column(
    mainAxisAlignment: MainAxisAlignment.center,
    crossAxisAlignment: CrossAxisAlignment.stretch,
    children: <Widget>[
      buildTitleText(),
      SizedBox(height: 20.0),
      _buildColumnWithinRow(),
    ],
  );
}
```

```
Widget _buildColumnWithinRow() {
  return Row(
    mainAxisAlignment: MainAxisAlignment.spaceBetween,
    children: <Widget>[
      buildRoundedBox("Cat"),
      SizedBox(width: 20.0),
      buildRoundedBox("Dog"),
      SizedBox(width: 20.0),
      Column(
        children: <Widget>[
          buildRoundedBox(
            "Big ox",
            height: 36.0,
          ),
          SizedBox(height: 16.0),
          buildRoundedBox(
            "Small ox",
            height: 36.0,
          ),
        ],
      ),
    ],
  );
}
```

Figure 6-11 shows a run of the code from Listing 6-7.

FIGURE 6-11:
A multilevel
arrangement.

Using the Expanded Widget

Start with the code in Listing 6-5 and add two more boxes to the row:

```
Widget _buildRowOfFive() {
  return Row(
    mainAxisAlignment: MainAxisAlignment.spaceBetween,
    children: <Widget>[
```

```
      buildRoundedBox("Cat"),
      buildRoundedBox("Dog"),
      buildRoundedBox("Ape"),
      buildRoundedBox("Ox"),
      buildRoundedBox("Gnu"),
    ],
  );
}
```

When you run this modified code on a not-too-large phone in portrait mode, you see the ugly display in Figure 6-12. (If your phone is too large to see the ugliness, add more buildRoundedBox calls.)

The segment on the right side of Figure 6-12 (the stuff that looks like barricade tape) indicates *overflow*. The row is trying to be wider than the phone's screen. Look near the top of Android Studio's Run tool window and you see the following message:

```
A RenderFlex overflowed by 67 pixels on the right.
```

When you line up too many boxes side-by-side, the screen becomes overcrowded. That's not surprising. But some layout situations aren't so obvious. You can stumble into an overflow problem when you least expect it.

What can you do when your app overflows? Here's an off-the-wall suggestion: Tell each of the boxes to expand. (You read that correctly: Tell them to expand!) Listing 6-8 has the code, and Figure 6-13 shows you the results.

LISTING 6-8: **Expanding Your Widgets**

```
// app0608.dart

import 'package:flutter/material.dart';
```

```
import 'app06main.dart';

Widget buildColumn(BuildContext context) {
  return Column(
    mainAxisAlignment: MainAxisAlignment.center,
    crossAxisAlignment: CrossAxisAlignment.stretch,
    children: <Widget>[
      buildTitleText(),
      SizedBox(height: 20.0),
      _buildRowOfFive(),
    ],
  );
}

Widget _buildRowOfFive() {
  return Row(
    mainAxisAlignment: MainAxisAlignment.spaceBetween,
    children: <Widget>[
      _buildExpandedBox("Cat"),
      _buildExpandedBox("Dog"),
      _buildExpandedBox("Ape"),
      _buildExpandedBox("Ox"),
      _buildExpandedBox("Gnu"),
    ],
  );
}

Widget _buildExpandedBox(
  String label, {
  double height = 88.0,
}) {
  return Expanded(
    child: buildRoundedBox(
      label,
      height: height,
    ),
  );
}
```

FIGURE 6-13:
A nice row of five.

To quote from the official Flutter documentation (https://api.flutter.dev/flutter/widgets/Expanded-class.html):

> "A widget that expands a child of a Row, Column, or Flex so that the child fills the available space.
>
> Using an Expanded widget makes a child of a Row, Column, or Flex expand to fill the available space along the main axis (horizontally for a Row or vertically for a Column). If multiple children are expanded, the available space is divided among them according to the flex factor."

In spite of its name, the Expanded widget doesn't necessarily make its child bigger. Instead, the Expanded widget makes its child fill the available space along with any other widgets that are competing for that space. If that available space differs from the code's explicit height or width value, so be it. Listing 6-8 inherits the line

```
width: 88.0,
```

to describe the width of each rounded box. But, in Figure 6-13, none of the boxes is 88.0 dp wide. On an iPhone 11 Pro Max, each box is only 74.8 dp wide.

Expanded versus unexpanded

The code in the previous section surrounds each of a row's boxes with the Expanded widget. In this section, Listing 6-9 shows you what happens when you use Expanded more sparingly.

LISTING 6-9:   Expanding One of Three Widgets

```
// app0609.dart

import 'package:flutter/material.dart';

import 'app06main.dart';

Widget buildColumn(BuildContext context) {
  return Column(
    mainAxisAlignment: MainAxisAlignment.center,
    crossAxisAlignment: CrossAxisAlignment.stretch,
    children: <Widget>[
      buildTitleText(),
      SizedBox(height: 20.0),
      _buildRowOfThree(),
    ],
  );
}
```

```
Widget _buildRowOfThree() {
  return Row(
    mainAxisAlignment: MainAxisAlignment.spaceBetween,
    children: <Widget>[
      buildRoundedBox(
        "Giraffe",
        height: 150.0,
      ),
      SizedBox(width: 10.0),
      buildRoundedBox(
        "Wombat",
        height: 36.0,
      ),
      SizedBox(width: 10.0),
      _buildExpandedBox(
        "Store Manager",
        height: 36.0,
      ),
    ],
  );
}

Widget _buildExpandedBox(
  String label, {
  double height = 88.0,
}) {
  return Expanded(
    child: buildRoundedBox(
      label,
      height: height,
    ),
  );
}
```

The code in Listing 6-9 surrounds only one box — the Store Manager box — with an Expanded widget. Here's what happens:

» The code gets width: 88.0 from the buildRoundedBox method in Listing 6-1, so the Giraffe and Wombat boxes are 88.0 dp wide each.

» Two SizedBox widgets are 10.0 dp wide each.

  So far, the total is 196.0 dp.

» Because the Store Manager box sits inside an Expanded widget, the remaining screen width goes to the Store Manager box. (See Figure 6-14.)

FIGURE 6-14:
The store
manager takes
up space.

Use of the Expanded widget affects a widget's size along its parent's main axis, but not along its parent's cross axis. So, in Figure 6-14, the Store Manager box grows from side to side (along the row's main axis) but doesn't grow from top to bottom (along the row's cross axis). In fact, only the numbers 150.0, 36.0, and 36.0 in the _buildRowOfThree method (see Listing 6-9) have any influence on the heights of the boxes.

With a bit of tweaking, the code in Listing 6-9 can provide more evidence that an Expanded widget isn't necessarily a large widget. Try these two experiments:

1. **Rerun the code from Listings 6-1 and 6-9. But, in the** buildRoundedBox
   method declaration, change width: 88.0 **to** width: 130.0.

   On an iPhone simulator, the widths of the Giraffe and Wombat boxes are 130.0
   dp each. But the width of the Expanded Store Manager box is only 94.0 dp. The
   Giraffe and Wombat boxes are quite large. So, when the Store Manager box
   fills the remaining available space, that space is only 94.0 dp wide. (See
   Figure 6-15.)

FIGURE 6-15:
Expanding to
fit into a
small space.

2. In the `buildRoundedBox` method declaration, change `width` from its value in Step 1 (`width: 130.0`) to `width: 180.0`.

With the Giraffe and Wombat boxes and the `SizedBox` widgets taking up 380.0 dp, there's no room left on the iPhone simulator for the Store Manager box and you'll see the black-and-yellow stripe, indicating RenderBox overflow. (See Figure 6-16.) The `Expanded` widget isn't a miracle worker. It doesn't help solve every problem.

FIGURE 6-16: More barricade tape.

Expanded widget saves the day

Listings 6-10 and 6-11 illustrate a nasty situation that may arise when you mix rows and columns at various levels.

LISTING 6-10: **A Listing That's Doomed to Failure**

```
// app0610.dart -- BAD CODE

import 'package:flutter/material.dart';

import 'app06main.dart';
import 'constraints_logger.dart';

Widget buildColumn(BuildContext context) {
  return Row(
    children: [
      _buildRowOfThree(),
    ],
  );
}

Widget _buildRowOfThree() {
  return ConstraintsLogger(
    comment: 'In _buildRowOfThree',
```

(continued)

LISTING 6-10: *(continued)*

```
        child: Row(
          children: <Widget>[
            _buildExpandedBox("Cat"),
            _buildExpandedBox("Dog"),
            _buildExpandedBox("Ape"),
          ],
        ),
      );
    }

  Widget _buildExpandedBox(
    String label, {
    double height = 88.0,
  }) {
    return Expanded(
      child: buildRoundedBox(
        label,
        height: height,
      ),
    );
  }
```

LISTING 6-11: ## An Aid for Debugging

```
// constraints_logger.dart

import 'package:flutter/material.dart';

class ConstraintsLogger extends StatelessWidget {
  final String comment;
  final Widget child;

  ConstraintsLogger({
    this.comment = "",
    required this.child,
  }) : assert(comment != null);

  Widget build(BuildContext context) {
    return LayoutBuilder(
      builder: (BuildContext context, BoxConstraints constraints) {
        print('$comment: $constraints to ${child.runtimeType}');
        return child;
      },
    );
  }
}
```

When you run the code in Listings 6-10 and 6-11, three things happen:

» **Nothing appears on your device's screen except maybe a dull, gray background.**

» **In Android Studio's Run tool window, you see the following error message:**

```
RenderFlex children have non-zero flex but incoming width
constraints are unbounded.
```

Flutter developers start groaning when they see this message.

Later on, in the Run tool window . . .

```
If a parent is to shrink-wrap its child, the child
cannot simultaneously expand to fit its parent.
```

» **Also, in the Run tool window, you see a message like this one:**

```
I/flutter ( 5317): In _buildRowOfThree:
BoxConstraints(0.0<=w<=Infinity, 0.0<=h<=683.4) to Row
```

» This I/flutter message tells you that the layout's inner row is being handed a width constraint that has something to do with Infinity. This informative 0.0<=w<=Infinity message comes to you courtesy of the code in Listing 6-11.

What do all these messages mean? In a Flutter app, your widgets form a tree. Figure 6-17 shows a tree of widgets as it's depicted in Android Studio's Flutter Inspector.

To display your widgets, Flutter travels in two directions:

» **Along the tree from top to bottom**

During this travel, each widget tells its children what sizes they can be. In Flutter terminology, each parent widget *passes constraints* to its children.

For example, a Run tool window message says that, in Listing 6-11, the outer row passes the width constraint of 0.0<=w<=Infinity to the inner row. Because of the word Infinity, this constraint is called an *unbounded constraint*.

If you're looking for an example of a *bounded constraint*, look at the same Run tool window message. The outer row passes the height constraint of 0.0<=h<=683.4 to the inner row. That constraint is bounded by the value 683.4 dp.

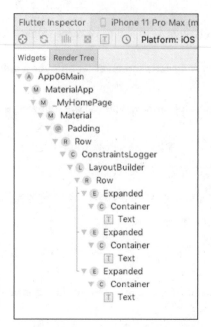

Eventually, Flutter reaches the bottom of your app's widget tree. At that point . . .

» Along the tree again — this time, from bottom to top

During this travel, each child widget tells its parent exactly what size it wants to be. The parent collects this information from each of its children and uses the information to assign positions to the children.

Sometimes this works well, but in Listing 6-11, it fails miserably.

In Listing 6-11, because each animal box is inside an Expanded widget, the inner row doesn't know how large it should be. The inner row needs to be given a width in order to divide up the space among the animal boxes. But the outer row has given an unbounded constraint to the inner row. Instead of telling the inner row its width, the outer row is asking the inner row for its width. Nobody wants to take responsibility, so Flutter doesn't know what to do. (See Figure 6-18.)

How can you fix this unpleasant problem? Oddly enough, another Expanded widget comes to the rescue.

```
Widget _buildRowOfThree() {
  return Expanded(
    child: ConstraintsLogger(
```

FIGURE 6-17:
The tree created
by Listings 6-10
and 6-11.

```
      comment: 'In _buildRowOfThree',
      child: Row(
        children: <Widget>[
          _buildExpandedBox("Cat"),
          _buildExpandedBox("Dog"),
          _buildExpandedBox("Ape"),
        ],
      ),
    ),
  );
}
```

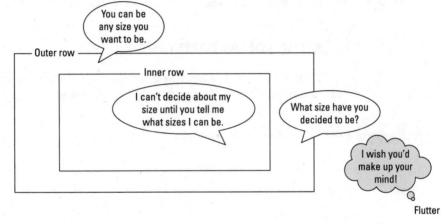

FIGURE 6-18:
Someone needs
to make a
decision!

This new Expanded widget passes bounded constraints down the widget tree, as you can see from this new message in the Run tool window:

```
I/flutter ( 5317): In _buildRowOfThree:
BoxConstraints(w=371.4, 0.0<=h<=683.4) to Row
```

The new Expanded widget tells the inner row that its width must be exactly 371.4 dp, so the confusion that's illustrated in Figure 6-18 goes away. Flutter knows how to display the app's widgets, and you see three nicely arranged animal boxes on your device's screen. Problem solved!

TECHNICAL STUFF

The constraint w=371.4 is called a *tight constraint* because it gives the row an exact size with no leeway whatsoever. In contrast, the constraint 0.0<=h<=683.4 is called a *loose constraint*. The loose constraint says, "Be as short as 0.0 dp high and as tall as 683.4 dp high. See if I care."

This business with constraints and sizes may seem overly complicated. But the process of scanning down the tree and then up the tree is an important part of the Flutter framework. The two-scan approach makes for efficient rebuilding of stateful widgets. And the rebuilding of stateful widgets is fundamental to the way Flutter apps are designed.

Some layout schemes work well with small numbers of components but start slowing down when the number of components becomes large. Flutter's layout scheme works well with only a few widgets and scales nicely for complicated layouts with large numbers of widgets.

The ConstraintsLogger widget is for debugging purposes only. Before publishing an app, remove all uses of the ConstraintsLogger from your code.

Flexing some muscles

Using Flutter's Expanded widget, you can specify the relative sizes of the children inside a column or a row. Listing 6-12 has an example.

LISTING 6-12: **How to Specify Relative Sizes**

```
// app0612.dart

import 'package:flutter/material.dart';

import 'app06main.dart';

Widget buildColumn(BuildContext context) {
  return Column(
    mainAxisAlignment: MainAxisAlignment.center,
    crossAxisAlignment: CrossAxisAlignment.stretch,
    children: <Widget>[
      buildTitleText(),
      SizedBox(height: 20.0),
      _buildRowOfThree(),
    ],
  );
}

Widget _buildRowOfThree() {
  return Row(
    mainAxisAlignment: MainAxisAlignment.spaceBetween,
    children: <Widget>[
      _buildExpandedBox(
        "Moose",
```

```
    ),
    _buildExpandedBox(
      "Squirrel",
      flex: 1,
    ),
    _buildExpandedBox(
      "Dinosaur",
      flex: 3,
    ),
  ],
);
}

Widget _buildExpandedBox(
  String label, {
  double height = 88.0,
  int flex = 1,
}) {
  return Expanded(
    flex: flex,
    child: buildRoundedBox(
      label,
      height: height,
    ),
  );
}
```

What will happen to our heroes, the Moose and the Squirrel, in Listing 6-12? To find out, see Figure 6-19.

FIGURE 6-19:
The squirrel is small; the dinosaur is big.

Notice the frequent use of the word flex in Listing 6-12. An Expanded widget can have a flex value, also known as a flex factor. A *flex factor* decides how much space the widget consumes relative to the other widgets in the row or column.

Listing 6-12 has three boxes:

>> Moose, with no flex value (so it gets the value of 1 set when flex is initiated)

>> Squirrel, with flex value 1

>> Dinosaur, with flex value 3

Here's the lowdown on the resulting size of each box:

Because the Moose box has a null flex value, the Moose box has whatever width comes explicitly from the _buildExpandedBox method.

Both the Squirrel and Dinosaur boxes have non-null, non-zero flex values. So those two boxes share the space that remains after the Moose box is in place. With flex values of Squirrel: 1, Dinosaur: 3, the Dinosaur box is three times the width of the Squirrel box. On a Pixel 2 emulator, the Squirrel box is 70.9 dp wide, and the Dinosaur box is 212.5 dp wide. That's the way flex values work.

TECHNICAL STUFF

In addition to the Expanded widget's flex property, Flutter has classes named Flex and Flexible. It's easy to confuse the three of them. Every Flex instance is either a Row instance or a Column instance. And every Expanded instance is an instance of the Flexible class. A Flexible instance can have a flex value, but a Flexible instance doesn't force its child to fill the available space. How about that!

How Big Is My Device?

The title of this section is a question, and the answer is "You don't know." A Flutter app can run on a small iPhone 6, or in a web page on a 50-inch screen. You want your app to look good no matter what size your device happens to be. How can you do that? Listing 6-13 has an answer.

LISTING 6-13: **Checking Device Orientation**

```
// app0613.dart

import 'package:flutter/material.dart';

import 'app06main.dart';

Widget buildColumn(context) {
  if (MediaQuery.of(context).orientation == Orientation.landscape) {
    return _buildOneLargeRow();
  } else {
```

```dart
    return _buildTwoSmallRows();
  }
}

Widget _buildOneLargeRow() {
  return Column(
    mainAxisAlignment: MainAxisAlignment.center,
    children: <Widget>[
      Row(
        mainAxisAlignment: MainAxisAlignment.spaceEvenly,
        children: <Widget>[
          buildRoundedBox("Aardvark"),
          buildRoundedBox("Baboon"),
          buildRoundedBox("Unicorn"),
          buildRoundedBox("Eel"),
          buildRoundedBox("Emu"),
          buildRoundedBox("Platypus"),
        ],
      ),
    ],
  );
}

Widget _buildTwoSmallRows() {
  return Column(
    mainAxisAlignment: MainAxisAlignment.center,
    children: [
      Row(
        mainAxisAlignment: MainAxisAlignment.spaceEvenly,
        children: [
          buildRoundedBox("Aardvark"),
          buildRoundedBox("Baboon"),
          buildRoundedBox("Unicorn"),
        ],
      ),
      SizedBox(
        height: 30.0,
      ),
      Row(
        mainAxisAlignment: MainAxisAlignment.spaceEvenly,
        children: [
          buildRoundedBox("Eel"),
          buildRoundedBox("Emu"),
          buildRoundedBox("Platypus"),
        ],
      ),
    ],
  );
}
```

Figures 6-20 and 6-21 show what happens when you run the code in Listing 6-13. When the device is in portrait mode, you see two rows, with three boxes on each row. But when the device is in landscape mode, you see only one row, with six boxes.

FIGURE 6-20:
Listing 6-13 in portrait mode.

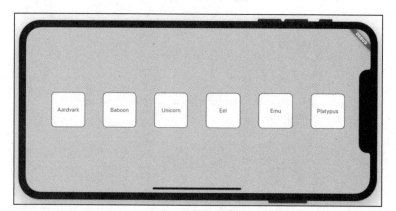

FIGURE 6-21:
Listing 6-13 in landscape mode.

The difference comes about because of the `if` statement in Listing 6-13.

```
if (MediaQuery.of(context).orientation == Orientation.landscape) {
  return _buildOneLargeRow();
} else {
  return _buildTwoSmallRows();
}
```

Yes, the Dart programming language has an `if` statement. It works the same way that `if` statements work in other programming languages.

```
if (a certain condition is true) {
  Do this stuff;
} otherwise {
  Do this other stuff;
}
```

In the name `MediaQuery`, the word `Media` refers to the screen that runs your app. When you call `MediaQuery.of(context)`, you get back a treasure trove of information about that screen, such as

>> `orientation`: Whether the device is in portrait mode or landscape mode

>> `size.height` and `size.width`: The number of dp units from top to bottom and across the device's screen

>> `size.longestSide` and `size.shortestSide`: The larger and smaller screen size values, regardless of which is the height and which is the width

>> `size.aspectRatio`: The screen's width divided by its height

>> `devicePixelRatio`: The number of physical pixels for each dp unit

>> `padding`, `viewInsets`, and `viewPadding`: The parts of the display that aren't available to the Flutter app developer, such as the parts covered up by the phone's notch or (at times) the soft keyboard

>> `alwaysUse24HourFormat`: The device's time display setting

>> `platformBrightness`: The device's current brightness setting

>> . . . and many more

For example, a Pixel C tablet with 2560-by-1800 dp is big enough to display a row of six animal boxes in either portrait or landscape mode. To prepare for your app to run on such a device, you may not want to rely on the device's `orientation` property. In that case, you can replace the condition in Listing 6-13 with something like the following:

```
if (MediaQuery.of(context).size.width >= 500.0) {
  return _buildOneLargeRow();
} else {
  return _buildTwoSmallRows();
}
```

Notice the word context in the code MediaQuery.of(context). In order to query media, Flutter has to know the context in which the app is running. That's why, starting with this chapter's very first listing, the _MyHomePage class's build method has a BuildContext context parameter. Listing 6-1 has this method call:

```
buildColumn(context)
```

And other listings have method declarations with this header:

```
Widget buildColumn(BuildContext context)
```

Listings 6-2 to 6-12 make no use of that context parameter. But what if, in Listing 6-1, you omit the method's context parameter, like so:

```
buildColumn()
```

Then everything is hunky-dory until Listing 6-13, which would have no access to the context and would be unable to call MediaQuery.of(context). Including the context parameter in Listings 6-1 to 6-12 was unnecessary, except that it would eventually be used when you got up to Listing 6-13.

Chapter **7**

Interacting with the User

ove is in the air! The sun is shining. The birds are singing. Hearts are all a-Flutter. (Pun intended.)

Doris D. Developer wants to find a mate, and she has two important criteria. First, she wants someone who's 18 or older. Second, she's looking for someone who loves developing Flutter apps. What better way for Doris to achieve her goal than for her to write her own dating app?

This chapter covers Doris's outstanding work. To create the app, Doris uses several kinds of widgets: a text field, a slider, a drop-down button, and some others. A widget of this kind — one that the user sees and interacts with — is called a *control element*, or simply a *control*.

Doris's app also has some layout widgets, such as `Center`, `Row`, and `Column`, but these layout widgets aren't called *controls*. The user doesn't really see them and certainly doesn't interact with them. This chapter's emphasis is on the controls, not on the layout widgets or the app's other assorted parts.

Doris's final dating app isn't full-featured by commercial standards, but the code for the app is a few hundred lines long. That's why Doris develops the app in small pieces — first one control, and then another, and another, and so on. Each piece is a small, free-standing practice app.

The first practice app deals with a simple question: Is the prospective mate at least 18 years old?

A Simple Switch

A Switch is a control that's in one of two possible states: on or off, yes or no, true or false, happy or sad, over 18 or not. Listing 7-1 has the code for the practice Switch app.

LISTING 7-1: **How Old Are You?**

```
import 'package:flutter/material.dart';

void main() => runApp(app0701());

class App0701 extends StatelessWidget {
  @override
  Widget build(BuildContext context) {
    return MaterialApp(
      home: MyHomePage(),
    );
  }
}

class MyHomePage extends StatefulWidget {
  @override
  _MyHomePageState createState() => _MyHomePageState();
}

const _youAre = 'You are';
const _compatible = 'compatible with\nDoris D. Developer.';

class _MyHomePageState extends State<MyHomePage> {
  bool _ageSwitchValue = false;
  String _messageToUser = "$_youAre NOT $_compatible";

  /// State

  @override
  Widget build(BuildContext context) {
    return Scaffold(
      appBar: AppBar(
        title: Text("Are you compatible with Doris?"),
      ),
      body: Padding(
```

```
        padding: const EdgeInsets.all(8.0),
        child: Column(
          children: <Widget>[
            _buildAgeSwitch(),
            _buildResultArea(),
          ],
        ),
      ),
    );
}


/// Build

Widget _buildAgeSwitch() {
  return Row(
    children: <Widget>[
      Text("Are you 18 or older?"),
      Switch(
        value: _ageSwitchValue,
        onChanged: _updateAgeSwitch,
      ),
    ],
  );
}


Widget _buildResultArea() {
  return Text(_messageToUser, textAlign: TextAlign.center);
}


/// Actions

void _updateAgeSwitch(bool newValue) {
  setState(() {
    _ageSwitchValue = newValue;
    _messageToUser =
        _youAre + (_ageSwitchValue ? " " : " NOT ") + _compatible;
  });
}
}
```

Figures 7-1 and 7-2 show the app in its two possible states.

TECHNICAL STUFF

This chapter's listings are practice apps. They're bite-size samples of Doris's completed dating app. But even "bite-size" programs can be long and complicated. To keep this chapter's listings short, code is reused from one listing to another. You can download the entire dating app from this book's website.

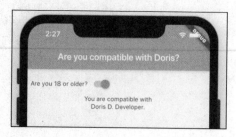

FIGURE 7-1:
The user turns on the switch.

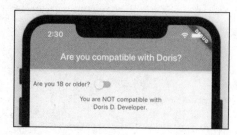

FIGURE 7-2:
The user turns off the switch.

The code in Listing 7-1 isn't much different from the code in Book 4, Chapter 5. In Chapter 5, the floating action button has an onPressed parameter. In Listing 7-1, the Switch widget has something similar. Listing 7-1 has an onChanged parameter. The onChanged parameter's value is a function; namely, the _updateAgeSwitch function. When the user flips the switch, that flip triggers the switch's onChanged event, causing the Flutter framework to call the _updateAgeSwitch function.

Unlike the event handling functions in Book 4, Chapter 5, the _updateAgeSwitch function in Listing 7-1 isn't a VoidCallback. A VoidCallback function takes no parameters, but the _updateAgeSwitch function has a parameter. The parameter's name is newValue:

```
void _updateAgeSwitch(bool newValue)
```

When the Flutter framework calls _updateAgeSwitch, the framework passes the Switch widget's new position (off or on) to the newValue parameter. Because the type of newValue is bool, newValue is either false or true. It's false when the switch is off and true when the switch is on.

If _updateAgeSwitch isn't a VoidCallback, what is it? The _updateAgeSwitch function is of type ValueChanged<bool>. A ValueChanged function takes one parameter and returns void. The function's parameter can be of any type, but a ValueChanged<bool> function's parameter must be of type bool. In the same way, a `ValueChanged<double>` function's parameter must be of type `double`. And so on.

Make no mistake about it: Even though the term `ValueChanged<bool>` doesn't have the word `Callback` in it, the `_updateAgeSwitch` function is a callback. When the user flips the `Switch` widget, the Flutter framework calls your code back. Yes, the `_updateAgeSwitch` function is a callback. It's just not a `VoidCallback`.

With many controls, nothing much happens if you don't change the control's value and call `setState`. To illustrate, try commenting out the `setState` call in the body of the `_updateAgeSwitch` function in Listing 7-1:

```
void _updateAgeSwitch(bool newValue) {
  // setState(() {
  _ageSwitchValue = newValue;
  _messageToUser = _youAre + (_ageSwitchValue ? " " : " NOT ") + _compatible;
  // });
}
```

Then uncomment the `setState` call and comment out the assignment statements:

```
void _updateAgeSwitch(bool newValue) {
  setState(() {
//      _ageSwitchValue = newValue;
//      _messageToUser =
//          _youAre + (_ageSwitchValue ? " " : " NOT ") + _compatible;
  });
}
```

In both cases, when you restart the program and tap on the switch, the `_messageToUser` refuses to change and the switch won't even budge. That settles it! The look of the switch is completely dependent on the `_ageSwitchValue` variable and the call to `setState`. If you don't assign anything to `_ageSwitchValue` or you don't call `setState`, the switch is completely unresponsive.

Dart's const keyword

In app development, the issue of change is very important. The term *variable* comes from the word *vary*, which means "change." But some things shouldn't change. Listing 7-1 refers to the strings `'You are'` and `'compatible with\nDoris D. Developer'` more than once, so Doris created the names `_youAre` and `_compatible` for these strings. That way, she didn't have to type things like `'compatible with\nDoris D. Developer'` more than once.

Doris wanted to make sure that the value of _youAre wouldn't change throughout the run of the program. That's why, in Listing 7-1, she declared _youAre with the word const. Dart's const keyword is short for *constant*. As a constant, the value of _youAre cannot change. The same holds true for the declaration of _compatible in Listing 7-1. The use of Dart's const keyword is a safety measure, and it's a darn good one!

TECHNICAL STUFF

In case you're wondering, \n in 'compatible with\nDoris D. Developer' tells Dart to go to a new line of text. That way, Doris D. Developer appears on a line of its own. (See Figures 7-1 and 7-2.) The character combination \n is called an *escape sequence*.

TIP

Referring to the code in Listing 7-1, an experienced developer might say, "the _youAre constant" or "the _youAre variable." The former is more accurate, but the latter is acceptable.

TECHNICAL STUFF

Dart has two keywords to indicate that certain things shouldn't change: const and final. The const keyword says, "Don't change this value at any time during a run of the app." The final keyword says, "Don't change this value unless you encounter this declaration again." The difference between const and final has many subtle consequences, but the important thing to know is that programs with const may run a bit faster than programs with final. You can put any old const declaration at the top level of your code or inside a function declaration. But, for a const at the start of a class, the story is different. The following code is illegal:

```
// Don't do this:
class _MyHomePageState extends State<MyHomePage> {
  const _youAre = 'You are';
```

But this code is just fine:

```
// Do this instead:
class _MyHomePageState extends State<MyHomePage> {
  static const _youAre = 'You are';
```

For the real scoop on Dart's static keyword, see the "Callout 4" section, later in this chapter.

Compatible or NOT?

For some users, the dating app should say, "You are compatible with Doris D. Developer." For other users, the app should add *NOT* to its message. That's why Listing 7-1 contains the following code:

```
_messageToUser =
    _youAre + (_ageSwitchValue ? " " : " NOT ") + _compatible;
```

The expression _ageSwitchValue ? " " : " NOT " is a *conditional expression*, and the combination of ? and : in that expression is Dart's *conditional operator*. Figure 7-3 shows you how Dart evaluates a conditional expression.

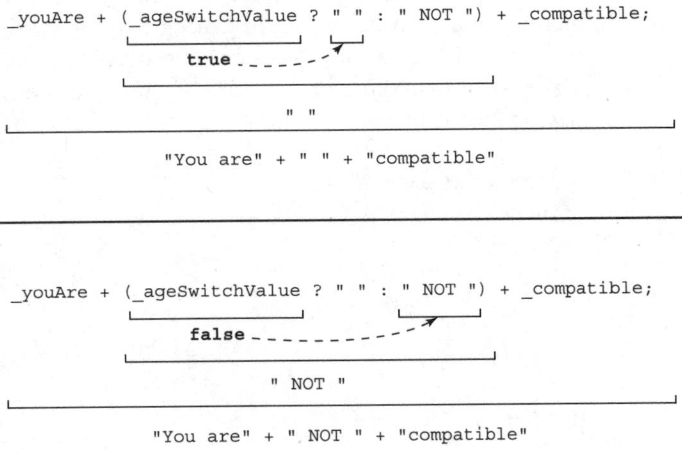

FIGURE 7-3:
Evaluating a
conditional
expression.

A conditional expression looks like this:

```
condition ? expression1 : expression2
```

When the `condition` is `true`, the value of the whole expression is whatever you find in the `expression1` part. But, when the `condition` is `false`, the value of the whole expression is whatever you find in the `expression2` part.

In addition to its conditional expressions, Dart has `if` statements. A conditional expression is like an `if` statement but, unlike an `if` statement, a conditional expression has a value. That value can be assigned to a variable.

To illustrate the point, here's an `if` statement whose effect is the same as the conditional expression in Listing 7-1:

```
if (_ageSwitchValue) {
  _messageToUser = _youAre + " " + _compatible;
} else {
  _messageToUser = _youAre + " NOT " + _compatible;
}
```

Translated into plain English, this `if` statement says:

```
If the bool variable _ageSwitchValue has the value true,
  _messageToUser = _youAre + " " + _compatible;
otherwise
  _messageToUser = _youAre + " NOT " + _compatible;
```

In some situations, choosing between an `if` statement and a conditional expression is a matter of taste. But in Listing 7-1, the conditional expression is a clear winner. After all, an `if` statement doesn't have a value. You can't assign an `if` statement to anything or add an `if` statement to anything. So, code of the following kind is illegal:

```
// THIS CODE IS INVALID.
_messageToUser =
  _youAre +

  if (_ageSwitchValue) {
    " ";
  } else {
    " NOT ";
  } +

_compatible;
```

Another name for Dart's conditional operator is the *ternary operator*. The word *ternary* means "three," and the operator has three parts: one before the question mark, a second between the question mark and the colon, and a third after the colon.

Wait For It!

Today's users are impatient. They want instant feedback. However, sometimes it can be useful to require an app's users to stop and think for a moment. In Doris's app, she wants to have at least two questions that a person needs to answer which will be used to determine the final result. She also wants to give the person using the app a chance to change their mind about their answers before they learn the final result. She decides she needs a Submit button that must be pressed after the users are happy with their responses to the questions.

To make a button, you can use the `ElevatedButton` widget. A button isn't much. You press it, and something happens. You press it again, and something may or may not happen.

This section's example shuns the quick response of the app in Listing 7-1. When the user flicks a switch, the switch simply moves. The app doesn't say, "You're compatible" or "You're not compatible" until the user presses the button. The code is in Listing 7-2.

LISTING 7-2: **Responding to a Button Press**

```
// Copy the code up to and including the _buildAgeSwitch
// method from Listing 7-1 here.

  Widget _buildResultArea() {
    return Row(
      children: <Widget>[
        ElevatedButton(
          child: Text("Submit"),
          onPressed: _updateResults,
        ),
        SizedBox(
          width: 15.0,
        ),
        Text(_messageToUser, textAlign: TextAlign.center),
      ],
    );
  }


  /// Actions

  void _updateAgeSwitch(bool newValue) {
    setState(() {
      _ageSwitchValue = newValue;
    });
  }


  void _updateResults() {
    setState(() {
      _messageToUser = _youAre +
        (_ageSwitchValue ? " " : " NOT ") +
        _compatible;
    });
  }
}
```

Figure 7-4 shows a snapshot from a run of the code in Listing 7-2.

FIGURE 7-4:
Good news!

When it's combined with some code from Listing 7-1, the app in Listing 7-2 has both onPressed and onChanged event handlers. In particular:

>> **The function _updateAgeSwitch handles** onChanged **events for the switch.**

When the user taps the switch, the appearance of the switch changes from off to on or from on to off.

>> **The function _updateResults handles** onPressed **events for the button.**

When the user presses the button, the app's message catches up with the switch's status. If the switch is on, the message becomes, "You are compatible." If the switch is off, the message becomes "You are NOT compatible."

Between the moment when the user flicks the switch and the time when the user presses the button, the message on the screen might be inconsistent with the switch's state. In an online form with several questions, that's not a problem. The user doesn't expect to see a result until after the concluding button press. But in this chapter's practice apps, each with only one question for the user, the lack of coordination between the user's answer and the message that's displayed is problematic. These practice apps don't win any user experience awards.

Fortunately, Doris doesn't publish her practice apps. Instead, she publishes an app that combines all the controls from her practice apps and more.

So, what's next? How about a slider?

How Much Do You Love Flutter?

Doris the Developer wants to meet someone who loves to create Flutter apps. Her homemade dating app includes a slider with values from 1 to 10. Scores of 8 and above are acceptable. Anyone with a response of 7 or below can take a hike. Listing 7-3 contains Doris's practice slider app.

LISTING 7-3:

For the Love of Flutter

```dart
import 'package:flutter/material.dart';

void main() => runApp(app0703());

class App0703 extends StatelessWidget {
  @override
  Widget build(BuildContext context) {
    return MaterialApp(
      home: MyHomePage(),
    );
  }
}

class MyHomePage extends StatefulWidget {
  @override
  _MyHomePageState createState() => _MyHomePageState();
}

const _youAre = 'You are';
const _compatible = 'compatible with\nDoris D. Developer.';

class _MyHomePageState extends State<MyHomePage> {
  double _loveFlutterSliderValue = 1.0;
  String _messageToUser = "";

  /// State

  @override
  Widget build(BuildContext context) {
    return Scaffold(
      appBar: AppBar(
        title: Text("Are you compatible with Doris?"),
      ),
      body: Padding(
        padding: const EdgeInsets.all(8.0),
        child: Column(
          children: <Widget>[
            _buildLoveFlutterSlider(),
            _buildResultArea(),
          ],
        ),
      ),
    );
  }
```

(continued)

LISTING 7-3: *(continued)*

```
/// Build

Widget _buildLoveFlutterSlider() {
  return Column(
    children: <Widget>[
      SizedBox(
        height: 10.0,
      ),
      Text("On a scale of 1 to 10, "
          "how much do you love developing Flutter apps?"),
      Slider(
        min: 1.0,
        max: 10.0,
        divisions: 9,
        value: _loveFlutterSliderValue,
        onChanged: _updateLoveFlutterSlider,
        label: '${_loveFlutterSliderValue.toInt()}',
      ),
    ],
  );
}

Widget _buildResultArea() {
  return Row(
    children: <Widget>[
      ElevatedButton(
        child: Text("Submit"),
        onPressed: _updateResults,
      ),
      SizedBox(
        width: 15.0,
      ),
      Text(_messageToUser, textAlign: TextAlign.center),
    ],
  );
}

/// Actions

void _updateLoveFlutterSlider(double newValue) {
  setState(() {
    _loveFlutterSliderValue = newValue;
  });
}

void _updateResults() {
  setState(() {
```

```
        _messageToUser = _youAre +
            (_loveFlutterSliderValue >= 8 ? " " : " NOT ") +
            _compatible;
    });
  }
}
```

Figure 7-5 shows a run of the slider app with the slider set all the way to 10.

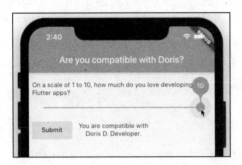

FIGURE 7-5:
Love at first byte.

The `Slider` constructor call in Listing 7-3 has these six parameters:

>> `min`: The slider's smallest value.

The little gizmo that moves from left to right along a slider is called a *thumb*. The position of the thumb determines the slider's *value*. So `min` is the value of the slider when the slider's thumb is at the leftmost point. The `min` parameter has type `double`.

>> `max`: The slider's largest value. This is the value of the slider (again, a `double`) when the thumb is at the rightmost point.

TECHNICAL
STUFF

A slider's values may increase going from left to right or from right to left. Before displaying a slider, Flutter checks a `textDirection` property. If the value is `TextDirection.ltr`, the slider's minimum value is on the left. But if the `textDirection` property's value is `TextDirection.rtl`, the slider's minimum value is on the right. Apps written for speakers of Arabic, Farsi, Hebrew, Pashto, and Urdu use `TextDirection.rtl`. Other apps use `TextDirection.ltr`.

>> `divisions`: The number of spaces between points where the thumb can be placed. (See Figure 7-6.)

FIGURE 7-6:
Why the number
of divisions is 9 in
Listing 7-3.

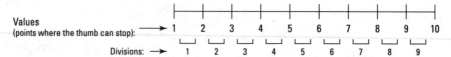

The slider in Listing 7-3 can be placed at values 1.0, 2.0, 3.0, and so on, up to 10.0.

If you omit the `divisions` parameter, or if you set that parameter to `null`, the thumb can be placed anywhere along the slider. For example, with the following constructor, the slider's value can be 0.0, 0.20571428571428554, 0.917142857142857, 1.0, or almost any other number between 0 and 1.

```
Slider(
  min: 0.0,
  max: 1.0,
  value: _loveFlutterSliderValue,
  onChanged: _updateLoveFlutterSlider,
)
```

>> `value`: A number in the range from `min` to `max`. This parameter determines the thumb's position.

>> `onChanged`: The event handling function for changes to the slider. When the user moves the slider's thumb, the Flutter framework calls this function.

>> `label`: The widget that's displayed on the slider's value indicator.

As the user moves the thumb, an additional shape appears. That shape is the slider's *value indicator*. In Figure 7-5, the bubble with the number 10 on it is the slider's value indicator.

Despite its name, the value indicator doesn't necessarily display a `Text` widget showing the slider's value. In fact, the value indicator can display anything you want it to display. (Well, almost anything.)

Luckily for us, the widget on the slider in Listing 7-3 displays `_loveFlutter SliderValue` — the slider's very own value. But remember: If you don't want numbers like 0.20571428571428554 to appear in the value indicator, you have to convert the slider's `double` values into `int` values. That's why, in Listing 7-3, the widget on the slider's value indicator displays `_loveFlutter SliderValue.toInt()`, not plain old `_loveFlutterSliderValue`.

If you don't specify a `label` parameter, or if you specify a `label` but make it `null`, the value indicator never appears.

TIP

Dealing with Text Fields

In this section, you'll meet Doris's friend Irving. Unlike Doris, Irving wants a companion with lots of money. To this end, Irving asks Doris to create a variation on her dating app. Irving's custom-made app has two text fields — one for a user's name and another for the user's income. If the user's income is $100,000 or more, the app reports "compatible." Otherwise, the app reports "incompatible." Figure 7-7 has an illustrated version of the app's _MyHomePageState class. To see the rest of Irving's app, look for the App0704 project in the download from this book's website.

TECHNICAL STUFF

To keep the size of Figure 7-7 manageable, I omitted the declaration of _build-Decoration. In case you're wondering, here's that method's code:

```
InputDecoration _buildDecoration(String label) {
  return InputDecoration(
    labelText: label,
    border: OutlineInputBorder(
      borderRadius: BorderRadius.all(Radius.circular(10.0)),
    ),
  );
}
```

Figure 7-8 shows Pat's attempt to be deemed compatible with Irving. With an income of $61,937, Pat doesn't have a chance.

Text fields have the same kinds of event handlers that switches and sliders have. In particular, a TextField constructor can have an onChanged event handler — a function that looks like this:

```
void _updateStuff(String newValue) {
  // When the user types a character, do something with
  // the characters inside the text field (the newValue).
}
```

But what about the press of a button? Is there a nice way to find out what's in a text field when the field's characters aren't changing? Yes, there is. It's the TextEditingController — a stand-out feature in Figure 7-7.

In fact, Figure 7-7 has two TextEditingController objects — one for the Your Name field and another for the Your Income field. The next several paragraphs add details to the numbered callouts in Figure 7-7.

```
class _MyHomePageState extends State<MyHomePage> {
  late TextEditingController _nameFieldController, _incomeFieldController;
  late String _messageToUser;


  @override
  void initState() {
    super.initState();
    _nameFieldController = TextEditingController();
    _incomeFieldController = TextEditingController();
    _messageToUser = "";
  }

  // Later in the code ...

  Widget _buildNameTextField() {
    return Container(
      padding: EdgeInsets.symmetric(vertical: 4.0, horizontal: 8.0),
      child: TextField(
        controller: _nameFieldController,
        decoration: _buildDecoration("Your name:"),
      ),
    );
  }

  Widget _buildIncomeTextField() {
    return Container(
      padding: EdgeInsets.symmetric(vertical: 4.0, horizontal: 8.0),
      child: TextField(
        controller: _incomeFieldController,
        decoration: _buildDecoration("Your income:"),
        keyboardType: TextInputType.number,
      ),
    );
  }

  // Later in the code ...

  void _updateResults() {
    bool _richUser = int.parse(_incomeFieldController.text) >= 1000000;
    setState(() {
      _messageToUser = _nameFieldController.text +
          "\n" +
          _youAre +
          (_richUser ? " " : " NOT ") +
          _compatible;
    });
  }

  @override
  void dispose() {
    _nameFieldController.dispose();
    _incomeFieldController.dispose();
    super.dispose();
  }
}
```

(1) Reserve the names _nameFieldController and _incomeFieldController to refer to instances of the TextEditingController class.

(2) When you initialize this _MyHomePageState, create two TextEditingController objects.

(3) Associate _nameFieldController with the name text field and _incomeFieldController with the income text field.

(4) The expressions _nameFieldController.text and _incomeFieldController.text stand for the characters in the two text fields.

(5) When the Flutter framework disposes of the _MyHomePageState instance, call each controller's own dispose method.

FIGURE 7-7:
How much do you earn?

Callouts 1 and 2

In a Flutter program, constructor calls rule the roost. You get a Text widget with a constructor call like Text("Hello"). You get a Column and two Text widgets with code like Column(children: [Text('a'), Text('b')]).

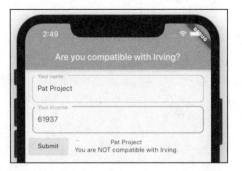

FIGURE 7-8:
Bad news for Pat.

When you issue a constructor call, the call itself stands for an object. For example, the call `Text("Hello")` stands for a particular `Text` widget — an instance of the `Text` class. You can assign the call to a variable and use that variable elsewhere in your code:

```
@override
Widget build(BuildContext context) {
  Text myTextInstance = Text("I'm reusable");
  return Scaffold(
    appBar: AppBar(
      title: myTextInstance,
    ),
    body: Column(
      children: <Widget>[
        myTextInstance,
      ],
    ),
  );
}
```

In many cases, you can separate the variable declaration from the call:

```
Text myTextInstance;

// More code here, and elsewhere ...

myTextInstance = Text("I'm reusable");
```

In Figure 7-7, the declaration of the two controller variables (`_nameField Controller` and `_incomeFieldController`) is separate from the corresponding `TextEditingController` constructor calls. This was done to introduce Flutter's `initState` and `dispose` methods.

NULL POUR LES NULS

You can declare a variable name without assigning anything to that variable. If you do, the variable's starting value is null, which means "absolutely nothing." In many cases, that's exactly what you want to do. However, in many cases, Flutter will refuse to run your program if a variable has the potential to be null.

That's because an unwanted null value can be dangerous. For example, the following code crashes like a reckless car on the New Jersey Turnpike:

```
main() {
  int quantity;
  print(quantity.isEven);  // null.isEven -- You can't do this
}
```

On the other hand, if you assign something to the quantity variable, the code runs without a hitch:

```
main() {
  int quantity = 22;
  print(quantity.isEven);  // Outputs the word "true" (without quotes)
}
```

A frequent mistake in programming is to create a variable declaration that doesn't assign a value to its variable and then to forget to assign a value to that variable elsewhere in the code. Oops! Your code crashes. Try not to make that mistake. If you need to declare variables for later use, one way is to use the late keyword. The late keyword lets you declare a variable and then give it a value (aka "initialize" it) later.

A State object is like anything else in the world — it comes into being and, eventually, it goes away. Flutter calls initState when a State instance comes into being and calls dispose when the State instance goes away.

It may not be obvious, but the code in Figure 7-7 refers to two different initState methods. The declaration that begins with void initState() describes a method that belongs to the _MyHomePageState class. But the _MyHomePageState class extends Flutter's own State class, and that State class has its own initState declaration. (See Figure 7-9.)

When you have two methods named initState, how do you distinguish one from another? Well, what if you meet a woman named Mary, whose child is also named Mary? Chances are, the child doesn't call her mother "Mary." Instead, the child calls her mother "Mom" or something like that. For her mother's birthday, she buys a souvenir mug displaying the words *Super Mom,* and her mother smiles politely on receiving another mug as a gift.

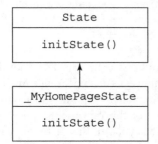

FIGURE 7-9: Overriding an extended class's initState method.

The same kind of thing happens when two classes — a parent and its child — have methods named initState. The child class (_MyHomePageState) has to call the initState method belonging to its parent class (Flutter's State class). To do so, the child class calls super.initState(). Unlike the Mary situation, the use of the keyword super isn't meant to be flattering. It's simply a reference to the init-State method that's defined in the parent class.

To stretch the mother/daughter metaphor a bit further, imagine that Super Mom Mary is a real estate agent. In that case, the child can't buy a house without first consulting her mother. The child's decideWhichHouse method must include a call to the mother's decideWhichHouse method, like so:

```
// The child's method declaration:
@override
void decideWhichHouse() {
  super.decideWhichHouse();
  // Etc.
}
```

That may be the situation when your code overrides Flutter's initState method. In some versions of Flutter, if you don't call super.initState(), your code won't run.

Callout 3

Each TextField constructor can have its own controller parameter. A text field's controller mediates the flow of information between the text field and other parts of the app. (For details, jump to the later section "Callout 4.")

Elsewhere in the `TextField` constructor call, the `TextInputType.number` parameter in the income text field's constructor tells a device to display a soft keyboard with only digits on the keys. Alternatives include `TextInputType.phone`, `TextInputType.emailAdress`, `TextInputType.datetime`, and others. For an authoritative list of `TextInputType` choices, visit `https://api.flutter.dev/flutter/services/TextInputType-class.html`.

TIP

This tip applies while you develop and test your app. The Android emulator and iPhone simulator have options to suppress the appearance of the soft keyboard, allowing input with only your development computer's keyboard. If that option is turned on, you don't see the effect of the `TextInputType.number` parameter. If you type a letter on your computer keyboard, that letter appears in your app's text field.

TIP

If you plan to run your app on a real, physical phone, you should test the app with the virtual device's soft keyboard enabled. When you do, you might see some troublesome effects that you weren't expecting. For example, when you move from a text field to another kind of control, the soft keyboard doesn't go away. To make the soft keyboard go away automatically, enclose the scaffold in a gesture detector. Here's how you do it:

```
Widget build(BuildContext context) {
  return GestureDetector(
    onTap: () {
      final currentFocus = FocusScope.of(context);
      if (!currentFocus.hasPrimaryFocus) {
        currentFocus.unfocus();
      }
    },
    child: Scaffold(
    // ... Etc.
```

For more chitchat about the `GestureDetector`, see Book 4, Chapter 9.

Callout 4

In Figure 7-7, the expression `_nameFieldController.text` stands for the characters that appear in the Name text field, and `_incomeFieldController.text` stands for the characters in the Income text field. If the code included the statement

```
_nameFieldController.text = "May I. Havanother";
```

execution of that statement would change whatever was already in the Name text field to *May I. Havanother*.

In Figure 7-7, the expression _nameFieldController.text adds the user's name to the outgoing message. The expression _incomeFieldController.text stands for whatever characters the user has entered in the app's Income field, but those characters come with a slight catch. The stuff in a text field is always a String value, never a numeric value. In Figure 7-8, Pat enters 61937 in the Income text field, so the value of _incomeFieldController.text is "61937" (the String), not 61937 (the number).

Luckily, Dart's int class has a parse method. If the value of _incomeField Controller.text is "61937" (the String), the value of int.parse(_incomeField Controller.text) is 61937 (the int number value). In Figure 7-7, the code

```
int.parse(_incomeFieldController.text) >= 1000000
```

compares a number like 61937 to Irving's high-demand number of 1000000. The result of the comparison is true or false, so the value of _richUser becomes true or false.

WHAT DOES A DARN DOT DO?

In object-oriented programming, an object can have certain things called *properties*. Using dot notation, you can refer to each of those properties.

Here are a few examples:

- **Every String instance has length and isEmpty properties.**

  The value of "Dart".length is 4, and the value of "".isEmpty is true.

- **Every int value has isEven, isNegative, and bitLength properties.**

  The value of 44.isEven is true, and the value of 99.isNegative is false. The value of 99.bitLength is 7 because the binary representation of 99 is 1100011, which has 7 bits.

- **Every TextEditingController instance has a text property.**

  In Figure 7-7, the value of _nameFieldController.text is whatever string of characters appears in the Name text field.

You can apply dot notation to expressions of all kinds. For example, the value of (29 + 10).isEven is false. With phrase = "I like Dart", the value of phrase. length is 11.

(continued)

(continued)

Properties are examples of things called *members*. A class's members also include the class's variables and methods. Consider the following:

- **Every** `String` **instance has methods named** `toUpperCase`, `endsWith`, `split`, `trim`, **and many others.**

  The value of `"Attention!".toUpperCase()` is `"ATTENTION!"`.

  The value of `"  Holy moly!  ".trim()` is `"Holy moly!"`.

- **Every** `int` **value has methods named** `abs`, `toRadixString`, **and several others.**

  The value of `(-182).abs()` is 182 because 182 is the absolute value of –182. The value of `99.toRadixString(2)` is 1100011 because the binary (base 2) representation of 99 is 1100011.

There's nothing mysterious about the members of a class. Here's a class named Account and a main function that calls the Account class's constructor:

```
class Account {
  // Two member variables:
  String customerName;
  int balance;

  // A member method:
  void deposit({int amount}) {
    balance += amount;
  }
}

void main() {
  // A call to the Account class's constructor:
  Account myAccount = Account();

  // References to the Account class's members:
  myAccount.customerName = "Barry Burd";
  myAccount.balance = 100;
  myAccount.deposit(amount: 20);
  print(myAccount.customerName);
  print(myAccount.balance);
}

/*
 * Output:
 * Barry Burd
 * 120
 */
```

The classes in this book's Flutter listings have members too. For example, the class in Figure 7-7 has several members, including _nameFieldController, _income FieldController, _messageToUser, initState, and build.

Some classes have things called *static members*. A static member belongs to an entire class, not to any of the class's instances. For example, the int class has a static method named parse. Because the parse method is static, you put the name of the class (the word int) before the dot. You *don't* put any particular int value before the dot. Here are some examples:

- **The value of int.parse("1951") is the number 1951.**

- **Expressions such as 1951.parse("1951"), 1951.parse() and 1951.parse are invalid.**

  None of these works because, in each case, the value before the dot isn't the class name int. Instead, the value before the dot is an object — an instance of the int class.

- **Putting any expression with an int value before .parse is invalid.**

  For example, the following code breaks your program:

```
int numberOfClowns;
int otherNumber = numberOfClowns.parse("2020");
```

Creating a static member is no big deal. Simply add the word static to your member declaration, like so:

```
class Automobile {
  static int numberOfWheels = 4;
}

void main() {
  Automobile jalopy = Automobile();
  // print(jalopy.numberOfWheels);  This is incorrect.
  print(Automobile.numberOfWheels);
}

/*
 * Output:
 * 4
 */
```

TIP

Figure 7-7 calls Dart's `int.parse` method — a handy method indeed! But Dart has an even better method. It's called `int.tryParse`. It's a lot like `int.parse`, but it's safer to use. When you call `int.tryParse('This is not a number')`, the app doesn't blow up in your face.

Callout 5

Much of the fuss in earlier paragraphs about the `initState` method applies equally to Flutter's `dispose` method. Before a `State` class gets the heave-ho, the Flutter framework calls the code's `dispose` method. In Figure 7-7, the `dispose` method does these three things:

» **It calls the `dispose` method belonging to the `_nameFieldController`.**

The `dispose` method for `_nameFieldController` trashes that controller, freeing up any resources that the controller happens to be hogging.

» **It calls the `dispose` method belonging to the `_incomeFieldController`.**

Goodbye, `_incomeFieldController`. Glad to see that your resources are being freed up.

» **It calls the `State` class's `dispose` method.**

The `State` class's `dispose` method, built solidly into the Flutter framework, cleans up any other stuff having to do with `_MyHomePageState`. As it is with `initState`, your own code's `dispose` method must call `super.dispose()`.

Creating Radio Buttons

Every dating app has a question about the user's gender. For this question, Doris decides on a group of radio buttons. Listing 7-4 includes much of Doris's radio button code.

For the rest of Doris's practice app with radio buttons, see `App0705` in the files that you download from this book's website.

LISTING 7-4: **How Do You Identify?**

```
// This is not a complete program.

enum Gender { Female, Male, Other, NoSelection }
```

```dart
String shorten(Gender gender) => gender.toString().replaceAll("Gender.", "");

class _MyHomePageState extends State<MyHomePage> {
  String _messageToUser = "";
  Gender _genderRadioValue = Gender.NoSelection;

// And later ...

  Widget _buildGenderRadio() {
    return Row(
      children: <Widget>[
        Text(shorten(Gender.Female)),
        Radio(
          value: Gender.Female,
          groupValue: _genderRadioValue,
          onChanged: _updateGenderRadio,
        ),
        SizedBox(width: 25.0),
        Text(shorten(Gender.Male)),
        Radio(
          value: Gender.Male,
          groupValue: _genderRadioValue,
          onChanged: _updateGenderRadio,
        ),
        SizedBox(width: 25.0),
        Text(shorten(Gender.Other)),
        Radio(
          value: Gender.Other,
          groupValue: _genderRadioValue,
          onChanged: _updateGenderRadio,
        ),
      ],
    );
  }

  Widget _buildResultArea() {
    return Row(
      children: <Widget>[
        ElevatedButton(
          child: Text("Submit"),
          onPressed: _genderRadioValue != null ? _updateResults : null,
        ),
        SizedBox(
          width: 15.0,
        ),
        Text(
          _messageToUser,
          textAlign: TextAlign.center,
```

(continued)

LISTING 7-4: *(continued)*

```
      ),
    ],
  );
}

/// Actions

void _updateGenderRadio(Gender? newValue) {
  setState(() {
    _genderRadioValue = newValue!;
  });
}

void _updateResults() {
  setState(() {
    _messageToUser =
        "You selected ${shorten(_genderRadioValue)}.";
  });
}
}
```

Figures 7-10 and 7-11 show snapshots from a run of the code in Listing 7-4.

FIGURE 7-10:
Before selecting a
radio button.

© John Wiley & Sons

FIGURE 7-11:
After selecting a
radio button and
pressing Submit.

© John Wiley & Sons

Creating an enum

Book 4, Chapter 3 introduces Flutter's built-in systemOverlayStyle enum with its values SystemUiOverlayStyle.light and SystemUiOverlayStyle.dark. That's nice, but why let the creators of Flutter have all the fun? You can define your own enum by doing what you see in Listing 7-4.

```
enum Gender { Female, Male, Other, NoSelection }
```

With this declaration, your code has four new values; namely, Gender.Female, Gender.Male, Gender.Other, and Gender.NoSelection. You can use these values in the rest of the app's code.

Building the radio group

The code in Listing 7-4 has three radio buttons. Each radio button has its own value but, taken together, all three buttons have only one groupValue. In fact, the common groupValue is what ties the three buttons together. When a user selects the button with value Gender.Female, the groupValue of all three becomes Gender.Female. It's as if part of the code suddenly looked like this:

```
// Don't try this at home. This is fake code.
Radio(
  value: Gender.Female,
  groupValue: Gender.Female,
),
Radio(
  value: Gender.Male,
  groupValue: Gender.Male,
),
Radio(
  value: Gender.Other,
  groupValue: Gender.Other,
),
Radio(
  value: Gender.NoSelection,
  groupValue: Gender.NoSelection,
),
```

Each radio button has its own onChanged parameter. In Listing 7-4, the function that handles onChanged events (the _updateGenderRadio function) does exactly what you would expect — it changes the radio buttons' groupValue to whatever value the user has selected.

WHY BOTHER?

A reader from Minnesota asks, "What good is the enum declaration in Listing 7-4? Why can't I assign the `String` values `"Female"`, `"Male"`, and `"Other"` directly to the three radio buttons?"

Good question, reader! Thanks for asking. The answer is, "You can assign `String` values to the radio buttons." You don't really need an enum to create a group of radio buttons. The following code with no enum is valid:

```
String _genderRadioValue;

// And later ...

Radio(
  value: "Female",
  groupValue: _genderRadioValue,
  onChanged: _updateGenderRadio,
),
Radio(
  value: "Male",
  groupValue: _genderRadioValue,
  onChanged: _updateGenderRadio,
),
Radio(
  value: "Other",
  groupValue: _genderRadioValue,
  onChanged: _updateGenderRadio,
),
Radio(
  value: "NoSelection",
  groupValue: _genderRadioValue,
  onChanged: _updateGenderRadio,
),


// And later ...

void _updateGenderRadio(String newValue) {
  setState(() {
    _genderRadioValue = newValue;
  });
}

void _updateResults() {
```

```
        setState(() {
          _messageToUser = "You selected $_genderRadioValue.";
        });
      }
```

So, in Listing 7-4, why should you bother creating the Gender enum? And the answer is, genders aren't strings. Being male doesn't mean that a person carries around the four letters *m*, then *a*, then *l*, and then *e*. Instead, maleness is one of several possibilities, another possibility being femaleness. The best way to represent genders in the code is to enumerate the alternatives, not to use a few strings and hope that no one misspells them.

Consider this code that uses the String type:

```
String _genderRadioValue = "Femail";
```

The code is incorrect but, as far as the Dart language is concerned, the code is peachy keen.

Now, consider this code that uses an enum type:

```
enum Gender { Female, Male, Other, NoSelection }
Gender _genderRadioValue = Gender.Femail;
```

The code is incorrect, and Dart refuses to accept it. With the declaration of the Gender enum, the programmer guarantees that the only possible values of _gender RadioValue are Gender.Female, Gender.Male, Gender.Other, and Gender. NoSelection. That's good programming practice. Safety first!

Displaying the user's choice

The shorten method in Listing 7-4 is a workaround for a slightly annoying Dart language feature. In Dart, every enum value has a toString method which, in theory, gives you a useful way to display the value. The problem is that, when you apply the toString method, the result is always a verbose name. For example, Gender.Female.toString() is "Gender.Female" and that's not quite what you want to display. In Figure 7-10, the user sees the sentence *You selected Female* instead of the overly technical sentence *You selected Gender.Female* sentence.

Applying the replaceAll("Gender.", "") method call turns "Gender." into the empty string, so "Gender.Female" becomes plain old "Female". Problem solved!

Look at the declaration of _genderRadioValue in Listing 7-4:

```
Gender _genderRadioValue = 'noSelection;
```

This declaration assigns _genderRadioValue a value of 'noSelection'. Since none of the radio group's buttons has a value of Gender.noSelection, none of the radio group's buttons is checked. That's exactly what you want when the app starts running.

Creating a Drop-Down Button

As soon as word gets around about Doris's dating app, everyone wants a piece of the action. Doris's friend Hilda wants a drop-down button to gauge the potential mate's level of commitment. Hilda wants a committed relationship and possibly marriage. Listing 7-5 shows the code that Doris writes for Hilda. Figures 7-12 and 7-13 show the code in action.

LISTING 7-5: **What Are You Looking For?**

```
import 'package:flutter/material.dart';

void main() => runApp(App0706());

class App0706 extends StatelessWidget {
  @override
  Widget build(BuildContext context) {
    return MaterialApp(
      home: MyHomePage(),
    );
  }
}

class MyHomePage extends StatefulWidget {
  @override
  _MyHomePageState createState() => _MyHomePageState();
}

enum Relationship {
  None,
  Friend,
  OneDate,
  Ongoing,
  Committed,
  Marriage,
}
```

```
Map<Relationship, String> show = {
  Relationship.None: "None",
  Relationship.Friend: "Friend",
  Relationship.OneDate: "One date",
  Relationship.Ongoing: "Ongoing relationship",
  Relationship.Committed: "Committed relationship",
  Relationship.Marriage: "Marriage"
};

List<DropdownMenuItem<Relationship>> _relationshipsList = [
  DropdownMenuItem(
    value: Relationship.None,
    child: Text(show[Relationship.None]!),
  ),
  DropdownMenuItem(
    value: Relationship.Friend,
    child: Text(show[Relationship.Friend]!),
  ),
  DropdownMenuItem(
    value: Relationship.OneDate,
    child: Text(show[Relationship.OneDate]!),
  ),
  DropdownMenuItem(
    value: Relationship.Ongoing,
    child: Text(show[Relationship.Ongoing]!),
  ),
  DropdownMenuItem(
    value: Relationship.Committed,
    child: Text(show[Relationship.Committed]!),
  ),
  DropdownMenuItem(
    value: Relationship.Marriage,
    child: Text(show[Relationship.Marriage]!),
  ),
];

class _MyHomePageState extends State<MyHomePage> {
  Relationship _relationshipDropdownValue = Relationship.None;

  /// State

  @override
  Widget build(BuildContext context) {
    return Scaffold(
      appBar: AppBar(
        title: Text("Are you compatible with Hilda?"),
      ),
```

(continued)

LISTING 7-5: *(continued)*

```
      body: Padding(
        padding: const EdgeInsets.all(16.0),
        child: Column(
          children: <Widget>[
            SizedBox(
              height: 30.0,
            ),
            _buildRelationshipDropdown(),
            _buildResultsImage(),
          ],
        ),
      ),
    );
  }


  /// Build

  Widget _buildRelationshipDropdown() {
    return Column(
      crossAxisAlignment: CrossAxisAlignment.start,
      children: <Widget>[
        Text("What kind of relationship are you looking for?"),
        _buildDropdownButtonRow(),
      ],
    );
  }


  Widget _buildDropdownButtonRow() {
    return Row(
      mainAxisAlignment: MainAxisAlignment.start,
      children: <Widget>[
        DropdownButton<Relationship>(
          items: _relationshipsList,
          onChanged: _updateRelationshipDropdown,
          value: _relationshipDropdownValue,
        ),
        if (_relationshipDropdownValue != Relationship.None)
          TextButton(
            child: Text(
              "Reset",
              style: TextStyle(color: Colors.blue),
            ),
            onPressed: _reset,
          ),
      ],
```

```
    );
  }

  Widget _buildResultsImage() {
    if (_relationshipDropdownValue != Relationship.None) {
      return Icon(
        (_relationshipDropdownValue.index >= 3)
            ? Icons.favorite
            : Icons.sentiment_dissatisfied,
        size: 96,
        color: Colors.pink,
      );
    } else {
      return SizedBox();
    }
  }

  /// Actions

  void _reset() {
    setState(() {
      _relationshipDropdownValue = Relationship.None;
    });
  }

  void _updateRelationshipDropdown(Relationship? newValue) {
    setState(() {
      _relationshipDropdownValue = newValue!;
    });
  }
}
```

FIGURE 7-12:
A user with
cold feet.

© John Wiley & Sons

FIGURE 7-13:
A serious user.

Building the drop-down button

A `DropdownButton` constructor has several parameters, one of which is a list of `items`. Each item is an instance of the `DropdownMenuItem` class. Each such instance has a `value` and a `child`.

>> **An item's `value` is something that identifies that particular item.**

In Listing 7-5, the items' values are `Relationship.Friend`, `Relationship.OneDate`, and so on. They're all members of the `Relationship` enum. You don't want things like `Relationship.OneDate` appearing on the surface of a menu item, so . . .

>> **An item's `child` is the thing that's displayed on that item.**

In Listing 7-5, the items' children are all `Text` widgets, but you can display all kinds of things on the drop-down items. For example, an item's child can be a `Row` containing a `Text` widget and an `Icon` widget.

In addition to its list of `items`, the `DropdownButton` constructor has `onChanged` and `value` parameters.

>> **The `onChanged` parameter does what such parameters do in so many other constructors.**

The parameter refers to a function that handles the user's taps, presses, tweaks, and pokes.

>> **At any moment, the `value` parameter refers to whichever drop-down button item is selected.**

The little Reset button

The Reset button in Listing 7-5 is interesting for more than one reason. First, it's not an ElevatedButton. Instead, it's a TextButton. A TextButton is like an ElevatedButton except . . . well, a TextButton is flat.

Another reason to wallow in the Reset button's code is because of a peculiar Dart language feature — one that's available only from Dart 2.3 onward. Here's an abridged version of the _buildDropdownButtonRow method's code in Listing 7-5:

```
Widget _buildDropdownButtonRow() {
  return Row(

    children: <Widget>[
      DropdownButton<Relationship>(

      ),

      if (_relationshipDropdownValue != Relationship.None)
        TextButton(

        ),
    ],
  );
}
```

In this code, the Row widget's children parameter is a list, and the list consists of two items: a DropdownButton and something that looks like an if statement. But appearances can be deceiving. The thing in Listing 7-5 isn't an if statement. The thing in Listing 7-5 is a *collection if*. In Book 4, Chapter 4, I unceremoniously sneak in the word *collection* to describe Dart's List, Set, and Map types. A collection if helps you define an instance of one of those types.

In Listing 7-5, the meaning of the collection if is exactly what you'd guess. If _relationshipDropdownValue isn't Relationship.None, the list includes a TextButton. Otherwise, the list doesn't include a TextButton. That makes sense because, when _relationshipDropdownValue is Relationship.None, there's no sense in offering the user an option to make it be Relationship.None.

In addition to its collection if, the Dart programming language has a collection for. You can read about the collection for in Book 4, Chapter 8.

Making a map

Book 4, Chapter 4 introduces Dart's types, one of which is the `Map` type. A `Map` is a lot like a dictionary. To find the definition of a word, you look up the word in a dictionary. To find a user-friendly representation of the enum value `Relationship.OneDate`, you look up `Relationship.OneDate` in the `show` map.

To be a bit more precise, a `Map` is a bunch of pairs, each pair consisting of a key and a value. In Listing 7-5, the variable `show` refers to a map whose keys are `Relationship.Friend`, `Relationship.OneDate`, and so on. The map's values are `"None"`, `"Friend"`, `"One date"`, `"Ongoing relationship"`, and so on. See Table 7-1.

TABLE 7-1 ## The show Map

Key	Value	Index
Relationship.None	"None"	0
Relationship.Friend	"Friend"	1
Relationship.OneDate	"One date"	2
Relationship.Ongoing	"Ongoing relationship"	3
Relationship.Committed	"Committed relationship"	4
Relationship.Marriage	"Marriage"	5

In a Dart program, you use brackets to look up a value in a map. For example, in Listing 7-5, looking up `show[Relationship.OneDate]` gives you the string `"One date"`.

In addition to their keys and values, each map entry has an *index*. An entry's index is its position number in the declaration of the map, starting with position number 0. Doris's buddy Hilda wants a committed relationship and possibly marriage. So the code in Listing 7-5 checks this condition. When this condition is true, the app displays a heart to indicate a good match. Otherwise, the app displays a sad face. (Sorry, Hilda.)

Onward and Upward

Doris's work on the dating app has paid off in spades. Doris is now in a committed relationship with an equally geeky Flutter developer — one who's well over 18 and who earns just enough money to live comfortably. Doris and her mate will live happily ever after, or at least until Google changes the Dart language specification and breaks some of Doris's code.

The next chapter is about navigation. How can your app go from one page to another? When the user finishes using the new page, how can your app go back? With more than one page in your app, how can the pages share information? For the answers to these questions, simply turn the next page!

Chapter **8**

Navigation, Lists, and Other Goodies

Until now, every sample Flutter app you've built has been a single self-contained page. They have some interactivity in the form of buttons and drop-down menus, but they're each like tiny, deserted islands. Once you've walked from one edge of the island to the other, there's not much else to do and no way to get news from the outside world. Unlike Tom Hanks's character in Castaway, you can't even befriend a volleyball.

For the same reasons that being stuck on a deserted island isn't much fun, apps that are islands aren't in high demand. In this lesson, you'll learn to add more complexity and variety to your apps by having multiple screens and by pulling data in from the vast world outside.

Extending a Dart Class

As the example code gets more complex, the code listings in this book can become unbearably long. A simple example to illustrate one new concept may consume several pages. You'd need magic powers to find each listing's new and interesting code. To combat this difficulty, examples can be split between two files — one file containing boilerplate code and another file containing the section's new features.

This works fine until you try to split a particular class's code between two files. Imagine that you have two files. One file's name is ReuseMe.dart:

```
// This is ReuseMe.dart
import 'MoreCode.dart';
class ReuseMe {
int x = 229;
}


main() => ReuseMe().displayNicely();
```

The other file's name is MoreCode.dart.

```
// This is a bad version of MoreCode.dart
import 'ReuseMe.dart';
void displayNicely() {
print('The value of x is $x.');
}
```

What could possibly go wrong?

Here's what goes wrong: The declaration of displayNicely isn't inside the ReuseMe class. In this pair of files, displayNicely is a lonely function that sits outside of any particular class. This causes two problems:

>> The line ReuseMe().displayNicely() makes no sense.

>> The displayNicely function can't casually refer to the ReuseMe class's x variable.

This code is bogus. Throw it out!

But wait! A sneaky trick can rescue this example. Since Dart's 2.7 version, you can add methods to a class without putting them inside the class's code using Dart's extension keyword. Here's how you do it:

```
// This is a good version of MoreCode.dart
import 'ReuseMe.dart';
extension MyExtension on ReuseMe {
void displayNicely() {
print('The value of x is $x.');
  }
}
```

After making this change, the `displayNicely` function becomes a method belonging to the ReuseMe class. Dart behaves as if you had written the following code:

```
class ReuseMe {
int x = 229;
void displayNicely() {
print('The value of x is $x.');
  }
}
```

Inside the `displayNicely` method's body, the name x refers to the ReuseMe class's x variable. Every instance of the ReuseMe class has a `displayNicely` method, so the call ReuseMe().displayNicely() makes perfect sense.

Everything works. And, best of all, the MoreCode.dart file can be swapped for another version of the file at any time.

```
// Another good version of MoreCode.dart
import 'ReuseMe.dart';
extension MyExtension on ReuseMe {
void displayNicely() {
print('   * $x *   ');
print('  ** $x **  ');
print(' *** $x *** ');
print('**** $x ****');
  }
}
```

The `displayNicely` function can be changed without touching the file that contains the original ReuseMe class declaration. That's handy!

WARNING

Extensions aren't available in all versions of Dart. If Android Studio complains to you about your use of extensions, look for the environment section of your project's pubspec.yaml file. That environment section may look something like this:

```
environment:
sdk: ">=2.1.0 <3.0.0"
```

Change the lower Dart version number like so:

```
environment:
sdk: ">=2.6.0 <3.0.0"
```

The name of an extension distinguishes that extension from any other extensions on the same class. For example, imagine that I've defined MyExtension and you've defined YourExtension, both on the ReuseMe class:

```
extension YourExtension on ReuseMe {
void displayNicely() {
print('!!! $x !!!');
  }
}
```

With two extensions declaring displayNicely methods, the expression ReuseMe().displayNicely() is ambiguous. To clear up the confusion, name one of the extensions explicitly:

```
YourExtension(ReuseMe()).displayNicely()
```

Navigating from One Page to Another

You've probably used an app with a master-detail interface. A *master-detail interface* has two pages. The first page displays a list of items. When the user selects an item in the list, a second page displays details about that item. This chapter's first example (in Listings 8-1 and 8-2) has a stripped-down master-detail interface. And why do I say "stripped-down"? The master page's list consists of only one item — the name of a particular movie.

LISTING 8-1: **Reuse This Code**

```
// app08main.dart
import 'package:flutter/material.dart';
import 'app0802.dart'; // Change this line to app0803, app0804, and so on.
void main() => runApp(App08Main());
class App08Main extends StatelessWidget {
@override
Widget build(BuildContext context) {
return MaterialApp(
home: MovieTitlePage(),
    );
  }
}

class MovieTitlePage extends StatefulWidget {
```

```
@override
MovieTitlePageState createState() => MovieTitlePageState();
}

class MovieTitlePageState extends State<MovieTitlePage> {
@override
Widget build(BuildContext context) {
return Scaffold(
appBar: AppBar(
title: Text(
'Movie Title',
),
),
body: Padding(
padding: const EdgeInsets.all(16.0),
child: Center(
child: buildTitlePageCore(),
),
),
);
}
}

class DetailPage extends StatelessWidget {
final overview = '(From themoviedb.com) One day at work, unsuccessful '
'puppeteer Craig finds a portal into the head of actor John '
'Malkovich. The portal soon becomes a passion for anybody who '
'enters its mad and controlling world of overtaking another human '
'body.';
@override
Widget build(BuildContext context) {
return Scaffold(
appBar: AppBar(
title: Text(
'Details',
),
),
body: Padding(
padding: const EdgeInsets.all(16.0),
child: Center(
child: buildDetailPageCore(context),
),
),
);
}
}
```

LISTING 8-2: **Basic Navigation**

```dart
// app0802.dart
import 'package:flutter/material.dart';
import 'app08main.dart';
extension MoreMovieTitlePage on MovieTitlePageState {
goToDetailPage() {
Navigator.push(
context,
MaterialPageRoute(
builder: (context) => DetailPage(),
    ),
  );
 }


Widget buildTitlePageCore() {
return Column(
crossAxisAlignment: CrossAxisAlignment.center,
children: <Widget>[
Text(
'Being John Malkovich',
textScaleFactor: 1.5,
      ),
SizedBox(height: 16.0),
ElevatedButton.icon(
icon: Icon(Icons.arrow_forward),
label: Text('Details'),
onPressed: goToDetailPage,
      ),
    ],
  );
 }
}


extension MoreDetailPage on DetailPage {
Widget buildDetailPageCore(context) {
return Column(
crossAxisAlignment: CrossAxisAlignment.center,
children: <Widget>[
Text(
overview,
     ),
   ],
  );
 }
}
```

To run this chapter's first app, your project must contain both Listing 8-1 and Listing 8-2. Each of these listings depends on code from the other listing. In fact, many of this chapter's listings depend on the code from Listing 8-1.

Listings 8-1 and 8-2 must be in separate .dart files because both listings contain import declarations.

Listing 8-2 doesn't have a main method. So, to run the app in Listings 8-1 and 8-2, you look for the App08Main.dart tab above Android Studio's editor. You right-click that tab and then select Run 'App08Main.dart' from the menu that appears.

Figures 8-1 and 8-2 show the pages generated by the code in Listings 8-1 and 8-2.

FIGURE 8-1:
A very simple master page.

© John Wiley & Sons

FIGURE 8-2:
A very simple detail page.

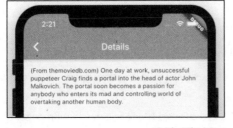

© John Wiley & Sons

Figure 8-1 shows the app's starting page — a page with an ElevatedButton on it. When the user presses this button, Flutter calls the goToDetailPage method in Listing 8-2. The goToDetailPage method calls the Navigator class's push method. The parameters of the push method point directly to the DetailPage class. So the app jumps to its second page — the DetailClass page in Figure 8-2.

The upper-left corner of Figure 8-2 has a little backward-pointing arrow. Flutter creates that arrow automatically whenever it navigates to a page that has an app bar. When the user presses that arrow, the app returns to the first page — the MovieTitlePage.

An icon on a button

For a tiny bit of cuteness, I add an icon (a little forward-pointing arrow) to the ElevatedButton in Figure 8-1. To make this happen, you use the word *icon* a bunch of times in Listing 8-2. Rather than call the ordinary ElevatedButton constructor, you call Flutter's ElevatedButton.icon constructor. Then, for the constructor's icon parameter, you write Icon(Icons.arrow_forward), which means, "Construct an actual Icon widget whose appearance is that of Flutter's built-in Icons.arrow_forward value."

Flutter has a whole bunch of built-in icons. Most of them are familiar user interface icons, like volume_up, warning, and signal_cellular_4_bar. But others are ones you don't expect to find. For example, Flutter has a pets icon (a picture of a paw), a casino icon (the face of a die), and an airline_seat_legroom_reduced icon (a person scrunched into a small space).

Pushing and popping

Here's some useful terminology:

>> A page that calls Navigator.push is a *source* page.

In Listings 8-1 and 8-2, the MovieTitlePage is a source page.

>> A page that the user sees as a result of a Navigator.push call is a *destination* page.

In Listings 8-1 and 8-2, the DetailPage is a destination page.

Some transitions go from a source page to a destination page; others go from a destination page back to a source page. In this section's example,

>> The user presses the ElevatedButton in Figure 8-1 to go from the source to the destination.

>> The user presses the app bar's Back button in Figure 8-2 to go from the destination to the source.

For the most part, a mobile app's transitions form a structure known as a *stack.* To create a stack, you pile each new page on top of all the existing pages. Then, when you're ready to remove a page, you remove the page that's at the top of the stack. It's like a seniority system for pages. The youngest page is the first to be removed. With this *Last-In-First-Out* (LIFO) rule, users form a clear mental image of their place among the app's pages.

Here's a bit more terminology:

>> When you add something to the top of a stack, you're *pushing* it onto the stack.

>> When you remove something from the top of a stack, you're *popping* it off the stack.

In Listing 8-2, the name `Navigator.push` suggests the pushing of a page onto a stack of pages. The most recent page obscures the older pages that lie below it. During a run of this chapter's first app, the `DetailPage` sits comfortably on top of the `MovieTitlePage`, completely obscuring the `MovieTitlePage` from the user's view.

In some situations, the notion of piling one page on top of another isn't appropriate. Maybe you don't want to push a destination page on top of a source page. Instead, you want to replace a source page with a destination page. To do this in Listing 8-2, you make one tiny change: You change the words `Navigator.push` to the words `Navigator.pushReplacement`. When you do, the `MovieTitlePage` looks as it does in Figure 8-1, but the `DetailPage` differs a bit from the image in Figure 8-2. In the new `DetailPage`, the app bar has no Back button.

In Flutter, screens and pages are called *routes*. That's why Listing 8-2 contains a `MaterialPageRoute` constructor call.

TECHNICAL STUFF

TIP

To make your app look like an iPhone app, use Flutter's Cupertino widgets instead of the Material Design widgets and construct a `CupertinoPageRoute` rather than a `MaterialPageRoute`. A `CupertinoPageRoute` makes page transitions look "Apple-like." For more on Flutter's Cupertino widgets, refer to Book 4, Chapter 3.

Passing Data from the Source to a Destination

Sometimes, you want to pass information from one page to another. The next example (see Listing 8-3) shows you how a source sends information to a destination.

REMEMBER

Before you try to run this section's app, change one of the import lines in Listing 8-1. Change 'App0802.dart' to 'App0803.dart'. Make similar changes to run Listings 8-3, 8-4, 8-5, 8-7, 8-8, and 8-10.

LISTING 8-3: ## From Movie Title Page to Detail Page

```
// App0803.dart
import 'package:flutter/material.dart';
import 'App08Main.dart';
extension MoreMovieTitlePage on MovieTitlePageState {
static bool _isFavorite = true; // You can change this to false.
goToDetailPage() {
Navigator.push(
context,
MaterialPageRoute(
builder: (context) => DetailPage(),
settings: RouteSettings(
arguments: _isFavorite,
    ),
   ),
  );
 }


Widget buildTitlePageCore() {
return Column(
crossAxisAlignment: CrossAxisAlignment.center,
children: <Widget>[
Text(
'Being John Malkovich',
textScaleFactor: 1.5,
    ),
SizedBox(height: 16.0),
ElevatedButton.icon(
icon: Icon(Icons.arrow_forward),
label: Text('Details'),
onPressed: goToDetailPage,
    ),
   ],
  );
 }
}

extension MoreDetailPage on DetailPage {
Widget buildDetailPageCore(context) {
return Column(
crossAxisAlignment: CrossAxisAlignment.center,
children: <Widget>[
Text(
```

```
    overview,
        ),
    Visibility(
    visible: ModalRoute.of(context)?.settings.arguments as bool,
    child: Icon(Icons.favorite),
        ),
      ],
    );
  }
}
```

Figure 8-3 shows you the `DetailPage` generated by the code in Listings 8-1 and 8-3. A little heart indicates that *Being John Malkovich* is a favorite movie.

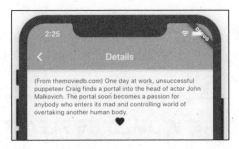
FIGURE 8-3:
The Favorite icon
on the detail
page.

Figure 8-4 illustrates the trip made by the `_isFavorite` variable's value in a run of this section's example.

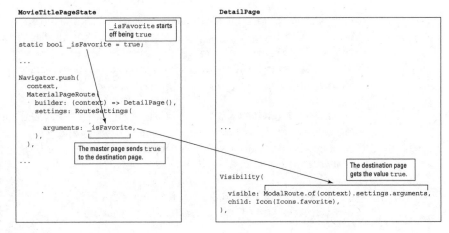

FIGURE 8-4:
Passing the value
of `_isFavorite`
from place to
place.

When Flutter displays the detail page, the value of

```
ModalRoute.of(context)?.settings.arguments
```

is `true`. It's as if the code near the bottom of Listing 8-3 looked like this:

```
// Remember, I said "as if" the code looked like this...
Visibility(
  visible: true,
  child: Icon(Icons.favorite),
),
```

A `Visibility` widget either shows or hides its child depending on the value of its `visible` parameter. So, in this example, Flutter's built-in `favorite` icon appears on the user's screen.

In Listing 8-3, you can change the declaration of `_isFavorite` like this:

```
static bool _isFavorite = false;
```

RUBE GOLDBERG WOULD BE PLEASED

You may be thinking at this point that you've never seen a more complicated way of making a tiny icon appear than the way it's done in Listing 8-3. But remember, passing information from one page to another is important, whether you're passing a simple `_isFavorite` value or a large chunk of medical data. Dividing an app into pages keeps the pages uncluttered. It also lends continuity to the flow of an app.

Book 4, Chapter 5 tells you that Dart has top-level variables — variables that aren't declared inside of a class. If you put all of your app's code in one file, all the code in your app can refer directly to those top-level variables. So why do you need this section's `arguments` feature? Why not let your master and detail pages share the values of top-level variables?

The answer is, top-level variables can be dangerous. While Mary withdraws funds on one page, another page processes an automatic payment and nearly empties Mary's account. As a result, Mary overdraws her account and owes a hefty fee to the bank. That's not good.

Use top-level variables sparingly. Don't use top-level variables to pass information between pages. Instead, use Flutter's `arguments` feature.

A STATIC VARIABLE

In Listing 8-3, the declaration of _isFavorite starts with the word static. Any variable that you declare in an extension, rather than inside any of the extension's methods, must be static. If you follow that rule blindly, you can understand Listing 8-3 without knowing what static means.

But, if you want to know what static means, consider this tiny bit of code from Book 4, Chapter 7:

```
... => _MyHomePageState();
// ... and later ...
class _MyHomePageState extends State<MyHomePage> {
bool _ageSwitchValue = false;
```

In the first line, a constructor call creates an instance of the _MyHomePageState class. A bit later on, the code gives _MyHomePageState an instance variable named _ageSwitchValue. The code doesn't have any other _MyHomePageState constructor calls, so you have only one _MyHomePageState instance, and only one _age SwitchValue variable.

In some programs, you may have occasion to call the _MyHomePageState constructor twice. If you do, you'll have two instances of _MyHomePageState, each with its own _ageSwitchValue variable. If you make an assignment such as _ageSwitchValue = true in one of the instances, it has no effect on the _ageSwitchValue variable in the other instance. That's the way instance variables work, but that's not the way static variables work.

In Listing 8-3, the _isFavorite variable is static. If you happen to declare two instances of MovieTitlePageState, both instances share one _isFavorite variable. If you make an assignment such as _isFavorite = true in one of the instances, it sets the _isFavorite value for both instances.

When you do, the movie title page passes false to the detail page. So, the Visibility widget's visible property becomes false, and the little favorite icon doesn't appear.

WARNING

In Listing 8-3, the variable _isFavorite is static. One consequence of this is that hot restarting the app doesn't work. If you change _isFavorite from true to false and then save your code, the little heart icon doesn't go away. To make that change in the value of _isFavorite take effect, stop the run of the app and then start it again.

In a RouteSettings constructor call, the parameter name arguments is a bit misleading. That parameter can have only one value at a time — a value such as _isFavorite. So why is the parameter name plural (arguments) instead of singular (argument)? It's plural because the single thing that you pass to another page can have several parts. For example, you can pass many values by making the one and only arguments value be a list:

```
settings: RouteSettings(
arguments: [_isFavorite, _isInTheaters, _isAComedy,],
),
```

Passing Data Back to the Source

In the previous section, the code uses Navigator.push to send a value from a source to a destination. That's cool, but how can the destination send values back to the source? Listing 8-4 has an answer.

LISTING 8-4: **From Detail Page to Movie Title Page**

```
import 'package:flutter/material.dart';
import 'App08Main.dart';
extension MoreMovieTitlePage on MovieTitlePageState {
static bool? _isFavorite;
goToDetailPage() async {
_isFavorite = await Navigator.push(
context,
MaterialPageRoute(
builder: (context) => DetailPage(),
),
);
setState(() {});
}

Widget buildTitlePageCore() {
return Column(
crossAxisAlignment: CrossAxisAlignment.center,
children: <Widget>[
Row(
mainAxisAlignment: MainAxisAlignment.center,
children: <Widget>[
Text(
'Being John Malkovich',
textScaleFactor: 1.5,
```

```
        ),
Visibility(
visible: _isFavorite ?? false,
child: Icon(Icons.favorite),
        ),
      ],
    ),
SizedBox(height: 16.0),
ElevatedButton.icon(
icon: Icon(Icons.arrow_forward),
label: Text('Details'),
onPressed: goToDetailPage,
      ),
    ],
  );
 }
}


extension MoreDetailPage on DetailPage {
Widget buildDetailPageCore(context) {
return Column(
crossAxisAlignment: CrossAxisAlignment.center,
children: <Widget>[
Text(
overview,
      ),
SizedBox(height: 16.0),
ElevatedButton(
child: Text(
'Make It a Favorite!',
        ),
onPressed: () {
Navigator.pop(context, true);
      },
    ),
  ],
 );
 }
}
```

Figure 8-5 illustrates the action that takes place during a run of this section's example.

The code in Listing 8-4 creates the DetailPage that you see in Figure 8-6.

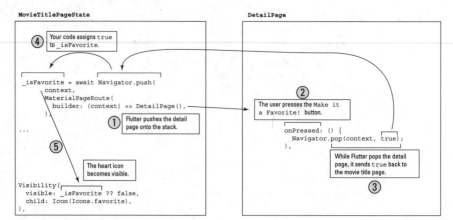

© John Wiley & Sons

The DetailPage has two buttons — one on the app bar (a Back button) and one beneath the movie's overview (the *Make It a Favorite!* button). If the user presses the app bar's Back button, nothing exciting happens. The app returns to a MovieTitlePage like the one in Figure 8-1. But, if the user presses the *Make It a Favorite!* button, Flutter executes the following statement:

```
Navigator.pop(context, true);
```

Flutter pops the DetailPage off of its stack and sends the value true back to the MovieTitlePage. In the MovieTitlePage, an assignment with a mysterious looking await word sets _isFavorite to true:

```
_isFavorite = await Navigator.push(
// ... Etc.
```

Finally, with _isFavorite set to true, the MovieTitlePage displays a little heart icon, as you see in Figure 8-7.

FIGURE 8-7:
A Favorite icon
on the movie title
page.

Dart's async and await keywords

A user launches the app in Listing 8-4, navigates from the `MovieTitlePage` to the `DetailPage`, and then pauses to have a cup of coffee. This user insists on having only the best coffee. With a smartphone displaying the `DetailPage`, this user takes an airplane to Vietnam, buys a fresh cup of Kopi Luwak, and then flies home. Finally, three days after having launched this section's app, the user presses the *Make It a Favorite!* button, which returns `true` to the app's `MovieTitlePage`.

You never know how long a user will linger on the app's `DetailPage`. That's why Flutter's `Navigator.push` method doesn't really get `true` back from the `DetailPage`. Instead, a call to `Navigator.push` returns an object of type `Future`.

A `Future` object is a callback of sorts. It's a box that may or may not contain a value like `true`. While our coffee-loving user is visiting Vietnam, the `Future` box has nothing inside of it. But later, when the user returns home and clicks the *Make It a Favorite!* button, the `Future` box contains the value `true`. This is how Flutter manages a "don't know when" navigation problem.

What would happen with the following code?

```
// Bad code because await is missing:
static bool _isFavorite;
// And elsewhere, ...
_isFavorite = Navigator.push(
// ... Etc.
```

In this erroneous code, the call to `Navigator.push` tries to hand a `Future` object to the `_isFavorite` variable. But the `_isFavorite` variable will have none of it because the `_isFavorite` variable's type is `bool`, not `Future`. What's a developer to do?

Listing 8-4 solves this problem using Dart's `await` keyword. An `await` keyword does two things:

» The `await` keyword tells Dart not to continue executing the current line until the `Future` box has something useful inside it. In Listing 8-4, Dart doesn't assign anything to `_isFavorite` until the `DetailPage` has been popped.

» When the `DetailPage` has been popped, the `await` keyword retrieves the useful value from the `Future` box.

In Listing 8-4, the call to `Navigator.push` is a `Future` value, but the expression `await Navigator.push( // ... etc` is a `bool` value. (See Figure 8-8.) The code assigns this `bool` value to `_isFavorite`, which, appropriately enough, is a `bool` variable.

```
static bool _isFavorite;

goToDetailPage() async {
    _isFavorite = await Navigator.push(...) ?? _isFavorite;
}
```

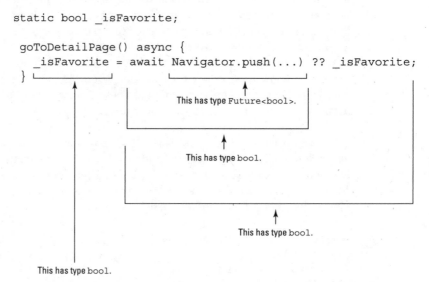

This has type `Future<bool>`.

This has type `bool`.

This has type `bool`.

This has type `bool`.

FIGURE 8-8:
The correct combination of types.

A function that contains the `await` keyword may take a long time to finish executing. If you're not careful, the entire app may come to a screeching halt while `await` does its awaiting. So, in addition to the `await` keyword, Dart has an `async` keyword and a rule to go along with this keyword:

If a function declaration contains the `await` keyword, that declaration must also include the `async` keyword.

(Refer to Listing 8-4.) The `async` keyword tells Dart that it's okay to execute some other code while this function sits there, doing nothing, executing its `await` keyword. That way, the app may continue whatever else it's doing while our friend, the Kopi Luwak coffee lover, visits Vietnam.

Taking control of the app bar's Back button

The app bar button in Figure 8-6 is a backward-pointing arrow. When the user clicks this button, your app returns to its source page. These two facts are true by default. But what if you don't like the defaults? Can you change them? Of course you can.

For example, you can change the button's appearance from a backward arrow to a red backspace button. To do so, add a `leading` parameter to an `AppBar` constructor call in Listing 8-1.

```
appBar: AppBar(
title: Text(
'Details',
  ),
leading: IconButton(
icon: new Icon(Icons.keyboard_backspace, color: Colors.red),
onPressed: () => Navigator.pop(context),
  ),
)
```

If you don't want a Back button to appear on the app bar, add an `automatically ImplyLeading` parameter to the `AppBar` constructor call.

```
appBar: AppBar(
automaticallyImplyLeading: false,
```

Changing the app bar button's behavior is trickier. In Listing 8-1, you surround the `Scaffold` constructor call with a `WillPopScope` call:

```
@override
Widget build(BuildContext context) {
return WillPopScope(
onWillPop: () => _onPop(context),
child: Scaffold(
```

In the `WillPopScope` constructor call, the `onWillPop` parameter is a function and, in keeping with the word `Will` in `onWillPop`, that function returns a `Future`. Here's a small example:

```
Future<bool> _onPop(BuildContext context) async {
return await showDialog(
```

```
context: context,
child: AlertDialog(
title: Text("The back button doesn't work"),
content: Text('Sorry about that, Chief.'),
actions: <Widget>[
new FlatButton(
onPressed: () => Navigator.pop(context, false),
child: Text('OK'),
          ),
        ],
      ),
    ) ??
false;
}
```

When the user clicks the Back button on the DetailPage app bar, Flutter displays a dialog box containing a FlatButton labeled OK. (See Figure 8-9.) When the user clicks the FlatButton, Flutter dismisses the dialog box.

FIGURE 8-9:
You Can't Go Home Again (Thomas Wolfe).

Passing Data in Both Directions

This section's example is a bit more realistic than examples in the previous sections. In this section, the source and destination pages pass information back and forth. The code is in Listing 8-5.

LISTING 8-5: **From Title Page to Detail Page and Back Again**

```
// app0805.dart
import 'package:flutter/material.dart';
import 'app08main.dart';
extension MoreMovieTitlePage on MovieTitlePageState {
static bool _isFavorite = false;
goToDetailPage() async {
_isFavorite = await Navigator.push(
```

```
context,
MaterialPageRoute(
builder: (context) => DetailPage(),
settings: RouteSettings(
arguments: _isFavorite,
        ),
      ),
    );
setState(() {});
  }


Widget buildTitlePageCore() {
return Column(
crossAxisAlignment: CrossAxisAlignment.center,
children: <Widget>[
Row(
mainAxisAlignment: MainAxisAlignment.center,
children: <Widget>[
Text(
'Being John Malkovich',
textScaleFactor: 1.5,
            ),
Visibility(
visible: _isFavorite,
child: Icon(Icons.favorite),
            ),
          ],
        ),
SizedBox(height: 16.0),
ElevatedButton.icon(
icon: Icon(Icons.arrow_forward),
label: Text('Details'),
onPressed: goToDetailPage,
        ),
      ],
    );
  }
}


extension MoreDetailPage on DetailPage {
Widget buildDetailPageCore(context) {
final bool _isFavoriteArgument =
ModalRoute.of(context)?.settings.arguments as bool;
return Column(
crossAxisAlignment: CrossAxisAlignment.center,
children: <Widget>[
Text(
overview,
```

(continued)

LISTING 8-5: *(continued)*

```
                ),
SizedBox(height: 16.0),
ElevatedButton(
child: Text(
_isFavoriteArgument == true
? 'Unfavorite this'
: 'Make It a Favorite!',
          ),
onPressed: () {
Navigator.pop(context, !_isFavoriteArgument);
          },
        ),
      ],
    );
  }
}
```

In this section's app, the `MainTitlePage` and `DetailPage` share the responsibility for the movie's "favorite" status. When the Favorite icon appears, it appears on the `MainTitlePage`, but the `DetailPage` has the button that switches between "favorite" and "not favorite."

Figure 8-10 describes the action of this section's app. In the next several paragraphs, I guide you through the numbered steps in that figure.

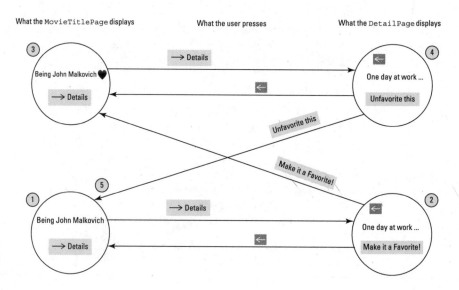

FIGURE 8-10: Moving from page to page.

1. When you launch this section's app, the value of _isFavorite becomes false. You see a page with a movie title and a Details button, but no Heart icon. To see that page as it appears on your phone, refer to Figure 8-1.

   When you press the Details button, the goToDetailPage method sends the value of _isFavorite to the DetailPage:

```
MaterialPageRoute(
builder: (context) => DetailPage(),
settings: RouteSettings(
arguments: _isFavorite,
  ),
),
```

2. The DetailPage receives the value coming from the MovieTitlePage. The DetailPage stores that value in its own _isFavoriteArgument variable:

```
final bool _isFavoriteArgument =
ModalRoute.of(context).settings.arguments as bool;
```

   Using this variable's value, the DetailPage decides what to display on the face of a button:

```
ElevatedButton(
child: Text(
_isFavoriteArgument ? 'Unfavorite this' : 'Make It a Favorite!',
  ),
```

   At this point in the app's run, _isFavoriteArgument is false. So the raised button displays the sentence *Make It a Favorite!* Figure 8-11 shows you the DetailPage that appears on your phone.

Navigation, Lists, and Other Goodies

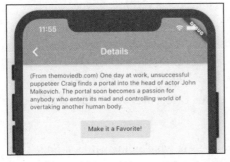

(From themoviedb.com) One day at work, unsuccessful puppeteer Craig finds a portal into the head of actor John Malkovich. The portal soon becomes a passion for anybody who enters its mad and controlling world of overtaking another human body.

Make it a Favorite!

FIGURE 8-11: You can make this movie a favorite.

© John Wiley & Sons

If you press the Make It a Favorite! button, Dart's exclamation point operator (!) prepares the opposite of _isFavoriteArgument to be sent back to the MovieTitlePage:

```
onPressed: () {
Navigator.pop(context, !_isFavoriteArgument);
},
```

Because _isFavoriteArgument is false, the DetailPage sends its opposite (true) back to the MovieTitlePage.

3. Upon receipt of the value true, the MovieTitlePage displays the Heart icon. Figure 8-12 shows you the MovieTitlePage that appears on your phone.

FIGURE 8-12:
This movie is a favorite.

When you press the Details button, the MovieTitlePage sends true to the DetailPage.

4. This time, the line

```
_isFavoriteArgument ? 'Unfavorite this' : 'Make It a Favorite!'
```

tells the DetailPage to display the Unfavorite This button. Figure 8-13 shows you the DetailPage that appears on your phone.

If you press the Unfavorite This button, Dart's exclamation point operator prepares the opposite of _isFavoriteArgument to be sent back to the MovieTitlePage. Because _isFavoriteArgument is true, the DetailPage sends its opposite (false) back to the MovieTitlePage.

5. Upon receipt of the value false, the MovieTitlePage doesn't display the Heart icon.

TECHNICAL STUFF

The drawing in Figure 8-10 is what is known as a *finite state machine* diagram. Diagrams of this kind help a lot when you want to organize your thoughts about an app's page transitions.

FIGURE 8-13:
You can unfavorite this movie.

Creating Named Routes

Navigation can be complicated. Here's an example:

> "Go where the user wants to go unless the user isn't logged in, in which case, go to the login page (but remember where the user wanted to go). If the user logs in correctly, go where the user wanted to go. Otherwise, go to the 'invalid login' page, where the user has the option to go to the 'forgot password' page. From the 'forget password' page . . ." And so on.

In Flutter, screens and pages are called *routes*, and Flutter lets you assign a name to each of your routes. This Named Routes feature makes your code a bit more concise. More importantly, the feature keeps you from going crazy, keeping track of the user's paths and detours. The code in Listing 8-6 doesn't display any movie data — only app bars and buttons. Even so, the listing shows you how named routes work.

LISTING 8-6: **Let's All Play "Name That Route"**

```
// app0806.dart
import 'package:flutter/material.dart';
void main() => runApp(App0806());
class App0806 extends StatelessWidget {
@override
Widget build(BuildContext context) {
return MaterialApp(
routes: {
'/': (context) => MovieTitlePage(),
'/details': (context) => DetailPage(),
'/details/cast': (context) => CastPage(),
'/details/reviews': (context) => ReviewsPage(),
    },
  );
```

(continued)

LISTING 8-6: *(continued)*

```
      }
    }

    class MovieTitlePage extends StatelessWidget {
    @override
    Widget build(BuildContext context) {
    return _buildEasyScaffold(
    appBarTitle: 'Movie Title Page',
    body: _buildEasyButton(
    context,
    label: 'Go to Detail Page',
    whichRoute: '/details',
        ),
      );
    }
  }

    class DetailPage extends StatelessWidget {
    @override
    Widget build(BuildContext context) {
    return _buildEasyScaffold(
    appBarTitle: 'Detail Page',
    body: Column(
    children: <Widget>[
    _buildEasyButton(
    context,
    label: 'Go to Cast Page',
    whichRoute: '/details/cast',
            ),
    _buildEasyButton(
    context,
    label: 'Go to Reviews Page',
    whichRoute: '/details/reviews',
          ),
        ],
      ),
    );
    }
  }

    class CastPage extends StatelessWidget {
    @override
    Widget build(BuildContext context) {
    return _buildEasyScaffold(
    appBarTitle: 'Cast Page',
    body: Container(),
      );
    }
  }
```

```dart
class ReviewsPage extends StatelessWidget {
@override
Widget build(BuildContext context) {
return _buildEasyScaffold(
appBarTitle: 'Reviews Page',
body: Container(),
    );
  }
}


Widget _buildEasyScaffold({required String appBarTitle, required Widget body}) {
return Scaffold(
appBar: AppBar(
title: Text(appBarTitle),
    ),
body: body,
  );
}


Widget _buildEasyButton(
BuildContext context, {
required String label,
required String whichRoute,
}) {
return ElevatedButton(
child: Text(label),
onPressed: () {
Navigator.pushNamed(
context,
whichRoute,
      );
    },
  );
}
```

REMEMBER

The code in Listing 8-6 doesn't depend on any other listing's code. Simply place this section's code in a .dart file, and then run it. Figure 8-14 shows the tops of the pages for the app in Listing 8-6.

Other listings in this chapter scatter their routing information willy-nilly throughout the code. But Listing 8-6 summarizes its routing information in the MaterialApp constructor's routes parameter. Notice the hierarchical naming of the routes in Figure 8-14. The more subordinate the route, the more slash characters (/) in the route's name.

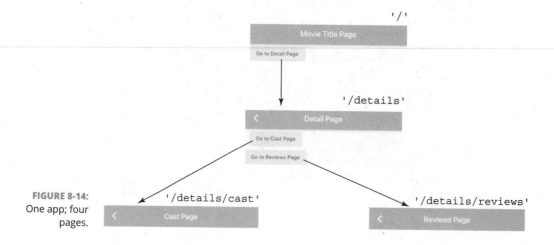

'/'

Movie Title Page

Go to Detail Page

'/details'

< Detail Page

Go to Cast Page

Go to Reviews Page

FIGURE 8-14:
One app; four
pages.

'/details/cast'

< Cast Page

'/details/reviews'

< Reviews Page

As an added bonus, the Navigator class's pushNamed method is a bit simpler than the class's plain old push method. With simpler code comes less anguish for you, the developer, and a better chance that the code is correct.

In Listing 8-6, the MaterialApp constructor call has no home parameter. That's okay because the constructor's routes parameter takes up the slack. By default, a route named '/' is the starting point for your app.

If you decide not to have a route named '/', or if you want to override the default, you can add the initialRoute parameter. For example, you can add one line to the code in Listing 8-6, like so:

```
Widget build(BuildContext context) {
return MaterialApp(
routes: {
'/': (context) => MovieTitlePage(),
'/details': (context) => DetailPage(),
'/details/cast': (context) => CastPage(),
'/details/reviews': (context) => ReviewsPage(),
    },
initialRoute: '/details/cast',
  );
}
```

When the app with this modified code starts running, the user sees the app's CastPage, and what happens next may or may not surprise you. When the user presses the app bar's Back button, Flutter navigates to the DetailPage. This happens because Flutter looks at the slashes in the route names. When you back away from a route named /details/cast, /details/reviews, or /details/whatever, Flutter takes you to the route named /details.

Creating a List

The beginning of this chapter describes the master-detail interface. It says, "The first page [in a master-detail interface] displays a *list* of items." You can't cram information about every item on the list into one page. So, for details about a particular item, the user clicks that item and navigates to a separate page.

This section shows you how to navigate between a list of items and a detail page. The new example is much more useful than the chapter's *Being John Malkovich* examples. The app in Listing 8-7 lists 25 films in Sylvester Stallone's *Rocky* franchise.

LISTING 8-7: **A Rather Long List**

```dart
// App0807.dart
import 'package:flutter/material.dart';
import 'App08Main.dart';
extension MoreMovieTitlePage on MovieTitlePageState {
goToDetailPage(int index) {
Navigator.push(
context,
MaterialPageRoute(
builder: (context) => DetailPage(),
settings: RouteSettings(
arguments: index,
),
),
);
}

Widget buildTitlePageCore() {
return ListView.builder(
itemCount: 25,
itemBuilder: (context, index) => ListTile(
title: Text('Rocky ${index + 1}'),
onTap: () => goToDetailPage(index + 1),
),
);
}
}

extension MoreDetailPage on DetailPage {
Widget buildDetailPageCore(context) {
final sequelNumber = ModalRoute.of(context)?.settings.arguments as int;
final overview =
'For the $sequelNumber${getSuffix(sequelNumber)} time, palooka '
'Rocky Balboa fights to be the world heavyweight boxing champion.';
```

(continued)

LISTING 8-7:   *(continued)*

```
return Column(
crossAxisAlignment: CrossAxisAlignment.center,
children: <Widget>[
Text(overview),
    ],
  );
  }

String getSuffix(int sequelNumber) {
String suffix;
switch (sequelNumber) {
case 1:
case 21:
suffix = 'st';
break;
case 2:
case 22:
suffix = 'nd';
break;
case 3:
case 23:
suffix = 'rd';
break;
default:
suffix = 'th';
    }
return suffix;
  }
}
```

REMEMBER

To run the app in Listing 8-7, your project must have at least two .dart files — one containing the code in Listing 8-7 and another containing the code in Listing 8-1.

When you run the code in Listing 8-7, you get two pages — a front page with a list of movie titles and, as usual, a detail page. Figure 8-15 shows you the page with the list of movie titles, and Figure 8-16 shows you a detail page.

The ListView widget

The essence of Listing 8-7 is a call to Flutter's ListView.builder constructor. The constructor takes two parameters: an itemCount and an itemBuilder.

FIGURE 8-15:
The start of a
long list.

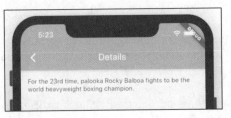

FIGURE 8-16:
The user taps the
23rd item in
the list.

The itemCount parameter

To no one's surprise, the `itemCount` tells Flutter how many items to display in the list. With the code in Listing 8-7, the list's last item is *Rocky 25*. But if you omit the `itemCount` parameter, the list never ends. The user can scroll for hours to see list items named *Rocky 1000* and *Rocky 10000*.

The secret behind `ListView` with its `itemCount` is the ability to scroll. In theory, the list has more items than the user sees on the device's screen. In reality, Flutter juggles list items and keeps only enough to fill the user's screen. When an item disappears off the edge of the screen, Flutter recycles that item by giving it a new *Rocky* number and displaying it at the other end of the screen. By recycling list items, Flutter saves memory space and processing time. So the scrolling of the list goes smoothly.

The itemBuilder parameter

An `itemBuilder` parameter's value is a function. In Listing 8-7, to create 25 items, Flutter starts by creating 25 indices with values 0, 1, 2, and so on, up to and including 24. Flutter plugs these values into the `itemBuilder` function, like so:

```
// This isn't real code. It's the way itemBuilder behaves.
(context, 0) => ListTile(
```

```
title: Text('Rocky ${0 + 1}'),
onTap: () => goToDetailPage(0 + 1),
)

(context, 1) => ListTile(
title: Text('Rocky ${1 + 1}'),
onTap: () => goToDetailPage(1 + 1),
)
(context, 2) => ListTile(
title: Text('Rocky ${2 + 1}'),
onTap: () => goToDetailPage(2 + 1),
)

// ...  and so on.
```

The result is a list containing 25 items. The *Rocky* number on each item's Text widget is one more than the index value. That way, the list doesn't start with a movie named *Rocky 0. (Rocky: The Prequel?)*

REMEMBER

In Dart, anything that counts automatically starts with 0, not 1. This includes things like the index of an itemBuilder, the position of a character in a String, and the default for the minimum value of a Slider.

In addition to its Text widget, each item has an onTap function. Each onTap function sends its own value (a number from 1 to 25) to the goToDetailPage function. If you keep following the trail, you find that the goToDetailPage function sends the number value onward as an argument to the app's DetailPage. And, in turn, the DetailPage uses that value to decide what information to display. In a real-life app, the DetailPage might use the value to look up the overview of a movie — maybe one of several thousand movies. But in Listing 8-7, the Detail-Page simply composes a fake overview. To see a way of getting real movie info, visit the later section "Fetching Data from the Internet."

By the way, you may notice that Listings 8-1 and 8-7 both have overview variables, and both of these variables live in the same DetailPage class. (The overview in Listing 8-1 is in the original DetailPage declaration. The overview in Listing 8-7 is in an extension of the DetailPage class.) This double-use of a variable name is okay. The overview in Listing 8-1 is an instance variable, and the overview in Listing 8-7 is local to the buildDetailPageCore method. So, when you run the code in Listing 8-7, the name overview stands for a sentence about Rocky Balboa. It's all good.

Are you unsure about the difference between instance variables and local variables? If so, refer to Book 4, Chapter 5.

PUTTING A LISTVIEW INSIDE A COLUMN

Some layouts — ones that you might think are okay — send Flutter into an unending, tail-chasing game. Book 4, Chapter 6 has a section about it. The game is especially frustrating when you try to put a list view inside a column. Here's some bad code:

```
// Don't do this:
Widget buildTitlePageCore() {
return Column(
children: <Widget>[
Text('Rocky Movies'),
ListView.builder(
itemCount: 25,
itemBuilder: (context, index) => ListTile(
title: Text('Rocky ${index + 1}'),
onTap: () => goToDetailPage(index + 1),
    ),
  ),
 ],
);
}
```

When you run this code, no list view appears. Among dozens of lines of diagnostics, Android Studio's Run tool window reports that Vertical viewport was given unbounded height. As it is in Book 4, Chapter 6, one widget (the Column widget) is sending an unbounded height constraint to its children, and one of the children (the ListView widget) can't handle all that freedom. The result is an impasse in which the ListView can't be displayed. To fix the problem, do the same thing that helps in Book 4, Chapter 6 — add an Expanded widget:

```
// Do this instead
return Column(
children: <Widget>[
Text('Rocky Movies'),
Expanded(
child: ListView.builder(
// ... etc.
```

The Expanded widget says, "Hey, Column. Figure out how tall the Text widget is and tell the ListView how much vertical space is left over." When the Column hands this information to the ListView, the ListView says, "Thanks. I'll use all of the left over space." The app displays itself correctly, and everyone's happy.

Dart's switch statement

In an early draft of Listing 8-7, the overview of *Rocky 3* reads:

> For the **3th** time, palooka Rocky Balboa fights to be the world heavyweight boxing champion.

That's completely unacceptable, so we need to enlist the help of our friend — the switch statement. A switch statement is like an if statement except that switch statements lend themselves to multiway branching.

The switch statement in Listing 8-7 says:

```
Look at the value of sequelNumber.
If that value is 1 or 21,
assign 'st' to suffix,
and then break out of the entire switch statement.
If you've reached this point and that value is 2 or 22,
assign 'nd' to suffix,
and then break out of the entire switch statement.
If you've reached this point and that value is 3 or 23,
assign 'rd' to suffix,
and then break out of the entire switch statement.
If you've reached this point,
assign 'th' to suffix.
```

Each break statement sends you out of the switch statement and onward to whatever code comes after the switch statement. What happens if you try to omit the break statements?

```
// Dart doesn't tolerate this ...
switch (sequelNumber) {
case 1:
case 21:
suffix = 'st';
case 2:
// ... and so on.
```

In Dart, this is a no-no. If you type this code in Android Studio's Dart editor, Android Studio complains immediately. Android Studio refuses to run your program.

TIP

If you're not fond of break statements, you can rewrite the getSuffix function using return statements:

```
String getSuffix(int sequelNumber) {
switch (sequelNumber) {
case 1:
case 21:
return 'st';
case 2:
case 22:
return 'nd';
case 3:
case 23:
return 'rd';
  }
return 'th';
}
```

This new version of getSuffix is much more concise than the one in Listing 8-7. In this version of getSuffix, each return statement jumps you entirely out of the getSuffix function. You don't even need a default clause, because you reach the return 'th' statement when none of the case clauses applies.

Even this new-and-improved getSuffix function falters if Sylvester Stallone makes *Rocky 31*. The movie's overview will be, "For the **31th** time, palooka Rocky Balboa . . ." That doesn't sound good.

There are dozens of ways to create more versatile versions of getSuffix, and it's fun to try to create one of your own. One of them looks like this:

```
String getSuffix(int sequelNumber) {
int onesDigit = sequelNumber % 10;
int tensDigit = sequelNumber ~/ 10 % 10;
Map<int, String> suffixes = {1: 'st', 2: 'nd', 3: 'rd'};
String suffix = suffixes[onesDigit] ?? 'th';
if (tensDigit == 1) suffix = 'th';
return suffix;
}
```

Creating list items one-by-one

From one row to another, the items in Figure 8-15 have no surprises. Each item displays the name *Rocky* and a number. Each item exhibits the same behavior when you tap on it. Because of this uniformity, you can create one itemBuilder that describes all 25 of the list's items.

SOME NEWS ABOUT SCROLLING

You don't need a ListView to create a scrolling screen. You can enclose all kinds of stuff inside a SingleChildScrollView. Here's some code:

```
return MaterialApp(
home: Material(
child: Column(
children: <Widget>[
SizedBox(height: 200, child: Text("You've")),
SizedBox(height: 200, child: Text("read")),
SizedBox(height: 200, child: Text("many")),
SizedBox(height: 200, child: Text("chapters")),
SizedBox(height: 200, child: Text("of")),
Icon(Icons.book),
SizedBox(height: 100, child: Text("Flutter For Dummies")),
Icon(Icons.thumb_up),
    ],
  ),
 ),
);
```

It's likely that your phone doesn't have enough room for all this stuff. So if you don't add some sort of scrolling, you'll see the dreaded black-and-yellow stripes along the bottom of the screen. To avoid seeing these stripes, enclose the widgets in a SingleChildScrollView:

```
return MaterialApp(
home: Material(
child: SingleChildScrollView(
child: Column(
children: <Widget>[
SizedBox(height: 200, child: Text("You've")),
// ... etc.
    ],
   ),
  ),
 ),
);
```

When you rerun the code, you'll see the topmost few widgets with the option to scroll and see others.

What do you do if there's little or no uniformity? What if there's some uniformity among the items but so few items that creating an `itemBuilder` isn't worth the effort?

In such cases, you describe the items one-by-one using Flutter's `ListView` constructor. Listing 8-8 has the code; Figures 8-17 and 8-18 show you some of the results.

LISTING 8-8: **A Small List**

```dart
// app0808.dart
import 'package:flutter/material.dart';
import 'app08main.dart';
const Map<String, String> synopses = { 'Casablanca':
'In Casablanca, Morocco in December 1941, a cynical American expatriate '
'meets a former lover, with unforeseen complications.',
'Citizen Kane':
'... Charles Foster Kane is taken from his mother as a boy ... '
'As a result, every well-meaning, tyrannical or '
'self-destructive move he makes for the rest of his life appears '
'in some way to be a reaction to that deeply wounding event.',
'Lawrence of Arabia':
"The story of British officer T.E. Lawrence's mission to aid the Arab "
"tribes in their revolt against the Ottoman Empire during the "
"First World War.",
};

extension MoreMovieTitlePage on MovieTitlePageState {
goToDetailPage(String movieName) {
Navigator.push(
context,
MaterialPageRoute(
builder: (context) => DetailPage(),
settings: RouteSettings(
arguments: movieName,
      ),
    ),
  );
  }

Widget buildTitlePageCore() {
return ListView(
children: [
ListTile(
title: Text('Casablanca'),
onTap: () => goToDetailPage('Casablanca'),
      ),
ListTile(
```

(continued)

LISTING 8-8: *(continued)*

```
      title: Text('Citizen Kane'),
      onTap: () => goToDetailPage('Citizen Kane'),
            ),
      ListTile(
      title: Text('Lawrence of Arabia'),
      onTap: () => goToDetailPage('Lawrence of Arabia'),
            ),
          ],
        );
      }
    }

    extension MoreDetailPage on DetailPage {
    Widget buildDetailPageCore(context) {
    final movieName = ModalRoute.of(context)?.settings.arguments;
    final overview = '(From themoviedb.com) ${synopses[movieName]}';
    return Column(
    crossAxisAlignment: CrossAxisAlignment.center,
    children: <Widget>[
    Text(overview),
          ],
        );
      }
    }
```

FIGURE 8-17:
Three movies.

© John Wiley & Sons

If you visit https://api.flutter.dev/flutter/widgets/ListView-class.html, you see the documentation for Flutter's ListView class. In the page's upper-right corner, you see the class's constructors, which include ListView and ListView. builder. Listing 8-7 calls the named ListView.builder constructor. But in the same place in Listing 8-8, you find the unnamed ListView constructor call. To read about Dart's named and unnamed constructors, refer to Book 4, Chapter 3.

FIGURE 8-18:
"Play it
again, Sam"
(misquoted).

Flutter's unnamed `ListView` constructor has a `children` parameter, and that `children` parameter's value is . . . wait for it . . . a Dart language `List`. A Dart language `List` is a bunch of objects inside a pair of square brackets, like this:

```
// A Dart language List:


    [
ListTile(...),
ListTile(...),
ListTile(...),
    ]
```

To read about Dart's `List` type, refer to Book 4, Chapter 4.

In Listing 8-8, the Dart `List` is actually a bunch of `ListTile` widgets. (They're like bathroom tiles with no grout between them.) But Flutter's `ListView` is versatile. The children don't have to be `ListTile` widgets. The children of a `ListView` may be a mixture of `Text` widgets, `SizedBox` widgets, `Image.asset` widgets, and any other kinds of widgets. It can be a big grab bag.

(If you're keeping score, Listing 8-8 contains a `ListView` which contains a Dart language `List` of `ListTile` widgets.)

Making loops with Dart

Most programming languages have statements that perform repetitive tasks. For example, languages such as Java, C/C++, and Dart have a thing called a `for` statement, also known as a `for` loop. Figure 8-19 shows you a tiny example.

The example in Figure 8-19 is a Dart program, but it's not a Flutter program. To run this program, there's no need to bother creating a Flutter project. Instead, you can visit `https://dartpad.dev`, type the code in the page's big editor window, and then press Run.

FIGURE 8-19:
Dart's for
statement in
action.

In Figure 8-19, the program's output is a column containing the numbers 1 through 5. That's because a `for` statement tells the device to repeat things over and over again. Figure 8-20 shows you an English language paraphrase of the `for` statement in Figure 8-19.

Initialize i once when the loop starts running.

```
Let i be 1.
Is i less than or equal to 5? If so,
    print(i), which is 1.
    Add 1 to i.
Is i less than or equal to 5? If so,
    print(i), which is 2.
    Add 1 to i.
Is i less than or equal to 5? If so,
    print(i), which is 3.
    Add 1 to i.
Is i less than or equal to 5? If so,
    print(i), which is 4.
    Add 1 to i.
Is i less than or equal to 5? If so,
    print(i), which is 5.
    Add 1 to i.
Is i less than or equal to 5? If not,
    leave the loop.
```

At the start of each iteration, check to see if i is less than or equal to 5.

At the end of each iteration, add 1 to i.

This is the fifth of five full *iterations*.

FIGURE 8-20:
Anatomy of a
for statement.

The fact that Dart has a `for` statement isn't newsworthy. Dart's `for` statement is almost exactly the same as the C language `for` statement, which was created in the early 1970s by Dennis Ritchie at Bell Labs. And the C language `for` statement is a direct descendant of FORTRAN's DO statement from the early 1960s. What's new and exciting in Dart is the idea that you can put a `for` construct inside a Dart language list. Listing 8-9 has an enlightening code snippet.

LISTING 8-9: **Interesting Code!**

```
Widget buildTitlePageCore() {
return ListView(
children: <Widget>[
for (int index = 0; index < 25; index++)
```

```
ListTile(
title: Text('Rocky ${index + 1}'),
onTap: () => goToDetailPage(index + 1),
        ),
    ],
  );
}
```

If you replace the `buildTitlePageCore` method in Listing 8-7 with the code in Listing 8-9, your app behaves exactly the same way. When Flutter encounters the code in Listing 8-9, it starts creating 25 `ListTile` widgets.

Listings 8-7 and 8-9 give you two ways to create a 25-item `ListView`. Which way is better? You can decide by asking, "Which way makes the code easier to read and understand?" Most people would agree that the new code (the code in Listing 8-9) is much clearer.

The stuff in Listing 8-9 looks like a `for` statement, but it's not really a `for` statement. It's a *collection for*. The name *collection for* comes from the fact that a `List` is one of Dart's collection types. (See Table 4-2, over in Book 4, Chapter 4, for more on collection types.) You can put a collection for inside any kind of collection — a `List`, a `Set`, or a `Map`. The following code does all three of these things:

```
main() {
List<int> myList = [for (int i = 1; i <= 5; i++) i];
Set<int> mySet = {for (int i = 1; i <= 5; i++) i};
Map<int; int> myMap = {for (int i = 1; i <= 5; i++) i: i + 100};
print(myList);
print(mySet);
print(myMap);
}
```

For some rollicking good fun, run this code at https://dartpad.dev. Compare Dart's collection `for` with its collection `if`. The collection `if` appears in Book 4, Chapter 7.

Dart's collection `for` is interesting because it's a new kind of programming language construct. The two pillars of programming languages are *statements* and *expressions*, but the collection `for` is neither a statement nor an expression. If you want to do some reading about all this geeky stuff, visit https://medium.com/dartlang/making-dart-a-better-language-for-ui-f1ccaf9f546c.

Fetching Data from the Internet

Do this chapter's examples remind you of movies that you've enjoyed? Would you like an app that displays facts about these movies? If so, look no further than Listing 8-10.

Accessing Online Data

```dart
// app0810.dart
import 'dart:convert';
import 'package:flutter/material.dart';
import 'package:http/http.dart';
import 'app08main.dart';
extension MoreMovieTitlePage on MovieTitlePageState {
goToDetailPage(String movieTitle) {
Navigator.push(
context,
MaterialPageRoute(
builder: (context) => DetailPage(),
settings: RouteSettings(
arguments: movieTitle,
  ),
 ),
 );
 }

Widget buildTitlePageCore() {
TextEditingController _controller = TextEditingController();
return Column(
crossAxisAlignment: CrossAxisAlignment.center,
children: <Widget>[
TextField(
decoration: InputDecoration(labelText: 'Movie title:'),
controller: _controller,
    ),
SizedBox(height: 16.0),
ElevatedButton.icon(
icon: Icon(Icons.arrow_forward),
label: Text('Details'),
onPressed: () => goToDetailPage(_controller.text),
    ),
   ],
  );
 }
}

extension MoreDetailPage on DetailPage {
Future<String> _getMovieData(String movieTitle) {
```

```
return updateOverview(
movieTitle: movieTitle,
api_key: "Parents: Don't let your sons and "
"daughters put api keys in their code.",
    );
  }

Widget buildDetailPageCore(context) {
final _movieTitle = ModalRoute.of(context)?.settings.arguments as String;
return Column(
crossAxisAlignment: CrossAxisAlignment.center,
children: <Widget>[
FutureBuilder<String>(
future: _getMovieData(_movieTitle),
builder: (context, snapshot) {
if (snapshot.hasData) {
return Text(snapshot.data as String);
          }
return CircularProgressIndicator();
        },
      ),
    ],
  );
  }

Future<String> updateOverview({required String api_key, required String
    movieTitle}) async {
final response = await get(Uri.parse(
'https://api.themoviedb.org/3/search/movie?api_key=' +
'$api_key&query="$movieTitle"'));
return json.decode(response.body)['results'][0]['overview'];
  }
}
```

Figures 8-21 and 8-22 show a run of the code in Listing 8-10.

There's a lot to unpack in Listing 8-10, so I divide it into parts.

Using a public API

Before creating Listing 8-10, I searched the web for a site that provides free access to movie information. Among the sites I found, the one I liked best was The Movie Database (www.themoviedb.org). Like many such sites, The Movie Database provides access through its own *application programming interface* (API). When you use the prescribed API code to send a query to themoviedb.org, the site spits back information about one or more movies.

FIGURE 8-21:
The user types a movie's name.

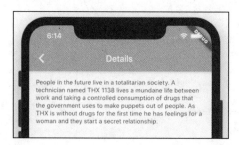

FIGURE 8-22:
The app displays info from The Movie Database.

For example, to get information about the movie *THX 1138*, you can try typing the following URL in a browser's address bar:

```
https://api.themoviedb.org/3/search/movie?api_key=XYZ&query="THX 1138"
```

When you do, the following message appears in your browser window:

```
Invalid API key: You must be granted a valid key.
```

Oops! Instead of typing XYZ, you should have typed a valid API key — a string of characters you get when you sign up on The Movie Database website. Everyone who signs up can get an API key by logging in and going to https://themoviedb.org/settings/api and then clicking the Request an API Key link.

The site will give you a choice between a Developer API key and a Professional API key. Select Developer, and then fill out the form on the next page, being sure to select Personal for the Type of Use. You can enter your own information into this form, or you can use the answers shown in Figure 8-23.

Once you get your own API key, replace XYZ with the API key and type the new URL into a web browser's address bar:

```
// Not a real API key ...
https://api.themoviedb.org/3/search/movie?api_key=4c23b2f8f&query="THX 1138"
```

FIGURE 8-23:
Requesting an
API key from the
moviedb.org.

When you do, you don't see an error message, and you don't get a fancy-looking
web page, either. Instead, you get code that looks something like the stuff in
Listing 8-11.

LISTING 8-11: **JSON Code**

```
{
"page": 1,
"total_results": 4,
"total_pages": 1,
"results": [
    {
"popularity": 8.126,

    .
    .
    .

"title": "THX 1138",
"vote_average": 6.6,
"overview": "People in the future live in a totalitarian ... ",
"release_date": "1971-03-11"
    },
    {
```

(continued)

LISTING 8-11: *(continued)*

```
"popularity": 3.11,
"id": 140979,

... and more ...
```

The text in Listing 8-11 isn't Dart code. It's JSON code. The acronym JSON stands for JavaScript Object Notation. The best way to understand JSON code is to realize that it describes a tree. Compare the code in Listing 8-11 with the upside-down tree in Figure 8-24.

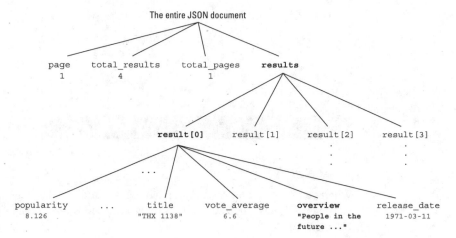

FIGURE 8-24:
A JSON document
describes a tree.

Sending an URL to a server and getting JSON code in return is an example of Representational State Transfer, also known as REST.

TECHNICAL STUFF

As an app developer, your job is to make your app do two things:

>> Send an URL to The Movie Database.

>> Make sense of the JSON code that comes back from The Movie Database.

Sending an URL to a server

One way to enable web server communication is to import Dart's `http` package. An `import` line near the top of Listing 8-10 does the trick. The only "gotcha" is that if you fail to add a line to your project's `pubspec.yaml` file, Flutter can't do the importing:

```
dependencies:
  flutter:
    sdk: flutter
  http: ^0.13.4
```

Of course, the strange looking version number ^0.13.4 is sure to be obsolete by the time you read this book. To find out what number you should be using, visit https://pub.dev/packages/http

REMEMBER

In a .yaml file, indentation matters. So, in your project's pubspec.yaml file, be sure to indent the http line the way you see it here. To find out about your project's pubspec.yaml file, refer to Book 4, Chapter 3.

In your app's Dart code, you use the package's get function to send an URL out onto the web:

```
final response = await get(
'https://api.themoviedb.org/3/search/movie?api_key=' +
'$api_key&query="$movieTitle"');
```

TIP

A simple function name like get doesn't scream out at you, "I'm part of the http package." To make your code more readable, do two things: Add some extra words to the http package's import declaration

```
import 'package:http/http.dart' as http;
```

and add a prefix to your get function call:

```
final response = await http.get(       // ... etc.
```

The need for await, async, and Future in Listing 8-10 comes from one undeniable fact: If you send a request to a web server, you don't know when you'll get a response. You don't want your Flutter app to freeze up while it waits for a response from who-knows-where. You want to entertain the user while a response makes its way along the Internet. That's why, in Listing 8-10, you display a CircularProgressIndicator widget until the response has arrived.

Making sense of a JSON response

In Listing 8-10, the updateOverview method awaits a response from The Movie Database. When a response arrives, the method assigns that response to its own variable named response. (How clever!) The response variable contains all kinds of information about HTTP headers and status codes, but it also contains a body, and that body looks like the JSON code in Listing 8-11.

But wait! How do you sift information out of all that JSON code? I'll tell you how. You call the json.decode function — one of the many functions in Dart's convert package. (Refer to code near the top and bottom of Listing 8-10.) The json.decode function turns the code in Listing 8-11 into a big Dart Map structure. Like all of Dart's maps, this map has keys and values, and some of the values can be lists. You use square brackets to get the values from maps and lists. (Refer to Book 4, Chapter 7.) So, to pull a movie's overview out of the code in Listing 8-11, write the following line:

```
return json.decode(response.body)['results'][0]['overview'];
```

Each pair of square brackets brings you closer to the bottom of the tree in Figure 8-24.

What's Next?

```
Navigator.push(
context,
MaterialPageRoute(
builder: (context) => Chapter_9(),
  ),
);
```

Chapter **9**

Moving Right Along . . .

This chapter is about animation — making things change right before the user's eyes. When I think about animation, I immediately think of movement, but Flutter provides a much broader definition of animation. With Flutter, you can change almost any property of a widget on almost any time scale.

Setting the Stage for Flutter Animation

This chapter's first listing has a bunch of reusable code. Subsequent listings contain code that works cooperatively with the code in the first listing. Thanks to Dart's extensions feature, each new listing can create methods belonging to the first listing's classes. You can read all about Dart extensions in Book 4, Chapter 8.

The code in Listing 9-1 can't do anything on its own. Instead, this code relies on declarations in the chapter's other listings.

LISTING 9-1: **Reuse This Code**

```
// app09main.dart

import 'package:flutter/material.dart';

import 'app0902.dart';  // Change to app0903, app0904, and so on.

void main() => runApp(App09Main());

class App09Main extends StatelessWidget {
  @override
  Widget build(BuildContext context) {
    return MaterialApp(
      home: MyHomePage(),
    );
  }
}

class MyHomePage extends StatefulWidget {
  @override
  MyHomePageState createState() => MyHomePageState();
}

class MyHomePageState extends State<MyHomePage>
    with SingleTickerProviderStateMixin {
  late Animation<double> animation;
  late AnimationController controller;

  @override
  void initState() {
    super.initState();
    controller =
        AnimationController(duration: const Duration(seconds: 3), vsync: this);
    animation = getAnimation(controller) as Animation<double>;
  }

  @override
  Widget build(BuildContext context) {
    return Material(
      child: SafeArea(
        child: Padding(
          padding: const EdgeInsets.all(8.0),
          child: Column(
            children: <Widget>[
              Expanded(
                child: Stack(
                  children: <Widget>[
                    buildPositionedWidget(),
```

```
              ],
            ),
          ),
          buildRowOfButtons(),
        ],
      ),
    ),
  ),
 );
}

Widget buildRowOfButtons() {
  return Row(
    mainAxisAlignment: MainAxisAlignment.center,
    children: <Widget>[
      ElevatedButton(
        onPressed: () => controller.forward(),
        child: Text('Forward'),
      ),
      SizedBox(
        width: 8.0,
      ),
      ElevatedButton(
        onPressed: () => controller.animateBack(0.0),
        child: Text('Backward'),
      ),
      SizedBox(
        width: 8.0,
      ),
      ElevatedButton(
        onPressed: () => controller.reset(),
        child: Text('Reset'),
      ),
    ],
  );
}

@override
void dispose() {
  controller.dispose();
  super.dispose();
}
}
```

Figure 9-1 illustrates the concepts that come together to make Flutter animation.

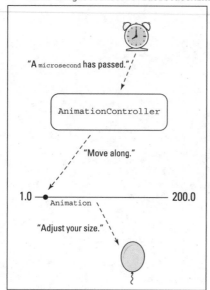

```
MyHomePageState
    with SingleTickerProviderStateMixin
```

"A microsecond has passed."

AnimationController

"Move along."

1.0 ———— Animation ———— 200.0

"Adjust your size."

FIGURE 9-1:
How Flutter
animation works.

You want something to change as the user looks on. To do this, you need four things: an `Animation`, an `AnimationController`, a ticker, and a feature of the app that changes. Here's how it all works:

>> **An `Animation` is a plan for changing a value.**

In Listing 9-1, the words `Animation<double>` indicate that the changing value is a number with digits beyond the decimal point — a number like `0.0`, `0.5`, or `0.75`. The plan in Figure 9-1 is to change a value in the range from 1.0 to 200.0.

The `Animation` itself isn't about movement of any kind. The value that goes from 1.0 to 200.0 may be a position, but it may also be a size, an amount of transparency, a degree of rotation, or whatever. For the animation variable in Listing 9-1, values like 1.0 and 200.0 are only numbers. Nothing else.

By the way, if you're looking in Listing 9-1 for a reference to an animation's `double` value, stop looking. The code in Listing 9-1 makes no reference to such a value. If you peek ahead to the next section's listing, you see `animation.value`. That's your tangible evidence that an `Animation` instance holds a value of some kind.

Flutter's Animation class is nice, but an Animation can't do much without an AnimationController. Here's why:

» **An AnimationController makes the animation start, stop, go forward, go backward, repeat, and so on.**

Calls such as controller.forward(), controller.animateBack(0.0), and controller.reset() push the animation in one direction or another.

In Listing 9-1, the AnimationController constructor call says that the animation lasts for three seconds. If seconds aren't good enough, you can use other parameters, such as microseconds, milliseconds, minutes, hours, and days. Each of the following constructors describes 51 hours:

```
Duration(hours: 51)

Duration(days: 1, hours: 27)

Duration(days: 2, hours: 3)

Duration(minutes: 3060)
```

» In addition to its duration, the AnimationController in Listing 9-1 has a vsync property. If you're wondering what that is, keep reading.

» **A *ticker* notifies the AnimationController when each time interval passes.**

The words with SingleTickerProviderStateMixin in Listing 9-1 make MyHomePageState into a ticker. The ticker wakes up repeatedly and says, "It's time to change a value."

But which value gets changed? What part of the code hears the ticker's announcement? Making MyHomePageState be a ticker doesn't connect MyHomePageState with a particular AnimationController.

To make that connection, the AnimationController in Listing 9-1 has a vsync: this parameter. That parameter tells Flutter that "this instance of MyHome PageState is the ticker for the newly constructed AnimationController."

In Listing 9-1, the name SingleTickerProviderStateMixin suggests that the Dart programming language has something called a mixin. A *mixin* is something like an extension, except that it's not the same as an extension. For a comparison, see the later sidebar "Another way to reuse code."

Here's the final ingredient in a Flutter animation:

>> **Some feature changes as a result of the change in the** `Animation` **value.**

In Figure 9-1, a balloon's size changes with an `Animation` instance's `double` value. But the code in Listing 9-1 makes no reference to a balloon's size, or to any other use of the `animation` variable's value. On this count, Listing 9-1 is somewhat lacking.

The code to make things change is in the `buildPositionedWidget` function, and that function's body is in Listings 9-2 through 9-6. Each of those listings does something different with the `Animation` object's `double` values.

Listing 9-1 has one more interesting feature: It has a place where widgets can move freely. Imagine making an icon the child of a `Center` widget. The `Center` widget determines the icon's position, and that's the end of the story. A `Center` widget's constructor has no parameters that let you wiggle its child in one direction or another. Don't bother trying to make a `Center` widget's child move. You have no vocabulary for moving it.

What you need is a widget that lets you mark its children's exact coordinates within the available space. For that, Flutter has a `Stack`.

A `Stack` is like a `Row` or a `Column`, but a `Stack` doesn't place its children in a straight line. Instead, a `Stack` has two kinds of children — `Positioned` widgets and all other kinds of widgets. Each `Positioned` widget can have `top`, `bottom`, `left`, and `right` properties, which determine the exact location of the `Positioned` widget's child. The other widgets (the ones that aren't `Positioned`) get stuffed into some default location.

Have a look at the following code:

```
Stack(
  children: <Widget>[
    Positioned(
      top: 100.0,
      left: 100.0,
      child: Container(
        width: 50.0,
        height: 50.0,
        color: Colors.black,
      ),
    ),
    Positioned(
      top: 120.0,
      left: 120.0,
```

```
      child: Container(
        width: 25.0,
        height: 25.0,
        color: Colors.white,
      ),
    ),
  ],
)
```

This code creates the drawing shown in Figure 9-2.

FIGURE 9-2:
Two containers
on a stack.

The drawing consists of two Container rectangles — one black and the other white. The white rectangle's width and height are half those of the black rectangle. But notice this: The two rectangles overlap because the rectangles' top and left edges are almost the same.

TIP

A Stack constructor has a children parameter, and that parameter's value is a list. The order of the widgets in the list matters. If two widgets overlap one another, the widget that comes later in the list appears to be on top. In the code accompanying Figure 9-2, you don't want to change the order of the two Positioned widgets in the list. If you do, the white rectangle becomes completely hidden behind the bigger black rectangle.

You can download and run the little Stack app shown in Figure 9-2. It's the project named app0900 in the files that you download from this book's website.

Moving Along a Straight Line

Listing 9-2 contains an extension for the code in Listing 9-1.

LISTING 9-2: **Going Downward**

```
// app0902.dart

import 'package:flutter/material.dart';

import 'app09main.dart';

extension MyHomePageStateExtension on MyHomePageState {
  Animation getAnimation(AnimationController controller) {
    Tween tween = Tween<double>(begin: 100.0, end: 500.0);
    Animation animation = tween.animate(controller);
    animation.addListener(() {
      setState(() {});
    });
    return animation;
  }

  Widget buildPositionedWidget() {
    return Positioned(
      left: 150.0,
      top: animation.value,
      child: Icon(
        Icons.music_note,
        size: 70.0,
      ),
    );
  }
}
```

Taken together, Listings 9-1 and 9-2 form a complete Flutter app. Figure 9-3 shows you what the app looks like when it starts running. The dotted line is my way of illustrating the movement of the app's Musical Note icon. (The dotted line doesn't actually appear as part of the app.)

Listing 9-2 has the buildPositionedWidget method declaration that's missing from Listing 9-1. In the method's body, a Positioned widget tells Flutter where its child (the Musical Note icon) should appear. When the app starts running, the numbers

```
left: 150,
top: animation.value,
```

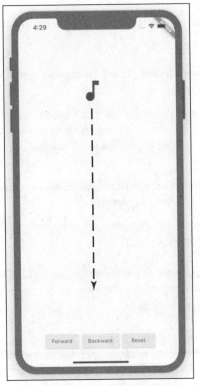

FIGURE 9-3:
Drop me a note.

© John Wiley & Sons

place the icon 150.0 dps from the left edge of the Stack, and 100.0 dps from the top of the Stack. The number 100.0 comes from the animation's begin value, which is declared near the start of Listing 9-2. As animation.value increases, the Musical Note icon moves downward. Recall from Book 4, Chapter 3 that *dps* means density-independent pixels.

Listing 9-2 also has a getAnimation method — a method that's called in Listing 9-1 but not declared in Listing 9-1. The getAnimation method in Listing 9-2 creates a Tween — a thing that comes from the world of animated cartoons. Imagine a cartoon character moving an arm from left to right. A cartoonist draws the arm's starting position and end position, and a computer creates the arm's "between" images. In the same way, an instance of Flutter's Tween class has begin and end values. When the animation moves forward, Flutter changes these values gradually from the begin value to the end value.

The rest of the `getAnimation` method's code connects the `Tween` with all the other puzzle pieces:

- » **The call to `tween.animate(controller)` creates an actual `Animation` instance.**

  The way I describe a `Tween`, you may think that a `Tween` is the same as an `Animation`. But it's not. Fortunately, if you've created a `Tween`, you can make an `Animation` from it. In Listing 9-2, the `tween.animate(controller)` call creates an `Animation` object. That's a step in the right direction.

- » **The call to `addListener` tells the `MyHomePageState` to rebuild itself whenever the animation's value changes.**

  In app development, a *listener* is a generic name for something that listens for events. The code in Listing 9-2 says,

  Create a function that redraws the screen by calling `setState`. Make that function listen for changes in the animation's value. That way, Flutter redraws the screen whenever the animation's value changes.

- » Each call to `setState` makes Flutter update the `left` and `top` values of the `Positioned` widget in Listing 9-2. Because `left` is always 150.0, the icon doesn't move sideways. But the `animation` object's `value` property changes from moment to moment, so the icon moves up and down along the screen.

The `AnimationController` in Listing 9-1 determines the icon's movement:

- » **When the user presses the app's Forward button, Listing 9-1 calls the `controller.forward` method.**

  The icon moves downward if it's not already at the bottom of its trajectory.

- » **When the user presses the app's Backward button, Listing 9-1 calls `controller.animateBack(0.0)`.**

  The icon moves upward if it's not already at the top.

  In the world of animations, numbers from 0.0 to 1.0 are very useful. In an `animateBack` call, the number `0.0` means "roll the animation backward until it reaches its `begin` value." To make the animation reach its midpoint, you'd call `controller.animateBack(0.5)`.

- » **When the user presses the app's Reset button, Listing 9-1 calls `controller.reset()`.**

  The icon jumps to its starting position. (If it's already at the starting position, it stays there.)

You may never see the code in Listing 9-2 in any other book. This book's version of the `getAnimation` method avoids a trick that Flutter developers commonly use. They summarize the entire method body in one statement:

```
return Tween<double>(begin: 100.0, end: 500.0).animate(controller)
  ..addListener(() {
    setState(() {});
  });
```

In this code, the pair of dots in front of `addListener` is Dart's *cascade* operator. The operator calls `addListener` on the `Animation` instance that's about to be returned. The use of this operator makes the code much more concise.

ANOTHER WAY TO REUSE CODE

Listing 9-2 has an extension, and Listing 9-1 has a mixin. Both extensions and mixins are ways to make use of code from outside sources. How do mixins differ from extensions?

When you create an extension, you name the class that you intend to extend.

```
extension MyHomePageStateExtension on MyHomePageState
```

This code from Listing 9-2 adds functionality to only one class — the `MyHomePageState` class in Listing 9-1. You can't use this extension in any other context.

On the other hand, you can add a mixin to almost any class. Here's the `SingleTickerProviderStateMixin` declaration from Flutter's API:

```
mixin SingleTickerProviderStateMixin<T extends StatefulWidget> on State<T>
    implements TickerProvider
```

The declaration says nothing about the `MyHomePageState` class or about any other such class, so any class can use this mixin. (Well, any class that's already a `StatefulWidget` can use this mixin.)

The good thing about mixins is that they spread the wealth. The stewards of Flutter write 75 lines of `SingleTickerProviderStateMixin` code and, as a result, anyone's `StatefulWidget` can become a ticker. How convenient!

Bouncing Around

The problem with a book chapter about animation is that the figures can't do justice to the apps they're supposed to illustrate. Figure 9-3 has a dotted line instead of real motion. Figure 9-4 is even worse because the dotted line isn't really accurate.

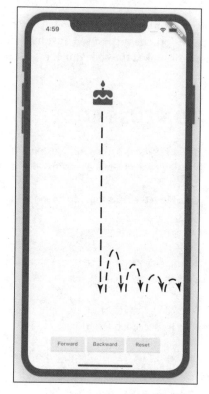

FIGURE 9-4:
A cake made of rubber?

In this section's app, the Cake icon doesn't move sideways. The dotted line in Figure 9-4 moves to the right only to show some up-and-down motion near the end of the animation. Even so, Flutter's API calls this motion a *curve*. The code for Figure 9-4 is shown in Listing 9-3.

LISTING 9-3: **Changing the Animation's Velocity**

```
// app0903.dart

import 'package:flutter/material.dart';
```

```
import 'app09main.dart';

extension MyHomePageStateExtension on MyHomePageState {
  Animation getAnimation(AnimationController controller) {
    return Tween<double>(begin: 100.0, end: 500.0).animate(
      CurvedAnimation(
        parent: controller,
        curve: Curves.bounceOut,
      ),
    )..addListener(() {
        setState(() {});
      });
  }

  Widget buildPositionedWidget() {
    return Positioned(
      left: 150.0,
      top: animation.value,
      child: Icon(
        Icons.cake,
        size: 70.0,
      ),
    );
  }
}
```

Once again, to change the properties of an object, you enclose that object inside of another object. It's a pattern that occurs over and over again in Flutter app development. Rather than call `animate(controller)` the way you do in Listing 9-2, you call

```
animate(
  CurvedAnimation(
    parent: controller,
    curve: Curves.bounceOut,
  )
```

You wrap the controller inside a `CurvedAnimation` object. In Listing 9-2, the object's `curve` property is `Curves.bounceOut`, which means "bounce as the animation ends." Table 9-1 lists some alternative `curve` values.

The Flutter API has many more `curve` values. Each value comes from a precise equation and describes its own, special pattern for timing the animation. You can see the whole list of ready-made `curve` values by visiting `https://api.flutter.dev/flutter/animation/Curves-class.html`.

TABLE 9-1   Some Constants of the Curves Class

Value	What It Does
Curves.bounceIn	Bounces as the animation begins
Curves.decelerate	Slows down as the animation progresses
Curves.slowMiddle	Moves normally, and then slowly, and then normally
Curves.fastOutSlowIn	Starts out fast and then eases into the end of the animation
Curve.ease	Speeds up quickly but ends slowly
Curve.elasticOut	Rushes in quickly enough to overshoot the end value and then settles in on the end value
Curve.linear	Doesn't change anything (used whenever you must use CurvedAnimation for some reason, but you don't want to apply a curve)

Animating Size and Color Changes

With Flutter's Animation class, you're not restricted to moving things. You can control the change of any value you think needs changing. This section's example changes an icon's size and color. The code is in Listing 9-4.

LISTING 9-4:   **Changing a Few Values**

```dart
// app0904.dart

import 'package:flutter/material.dart';

import 'app09main.dart';

extension MyHomePageStateExtension on MyHomePageState {
  Animation getAnimation(AnimationController controller) {
    return Tween<double>(begin: 50.0, end: 250.0).animate(controller)
      ..addListener(() {
        setState(() {});
      });
  }

  Widget buildPositionedWidget() {
    int intValue = animation.value.toInt();
    return Center(
      child: Icon(
        Icons.child_care,
```

```
      size: animation.value,
      color: Color.fromRGBO(
        intValue,
        0,
        255 - intValue,
        1.0,
      ),
    ),
  );
  }
}
```

When the app in Listing 9-4 starts running, a small, blue-colored baby face appears on the screen. (See Figure 9-5. If you're reading the printed version of this book, ignore the fact that you don't see the color.) When the user presses Forward, the baby face grows and turns color from red to blue. (See Figure 9-6.)

FIGURE 9-5:
Little baby.

FIGURE 9-6:
Big baby.

The icon in Listing 9-4 has two properties whose values can change.

> » **The `size` property changes along with `animation.value`.**
>
>   The icon grows from 50.0 dps to 250.0 dps.
>
> » **As the animation progresses, the `color` property's redness shrinks and its blueness grows.**
>
>   Book 4, Chapter 6 introduces Flutter's `Color.fromRGBO` constructor. The constructor's parameters are `int` values representing amounts of red, green, and blue and a double value that represents opacity. In Listing 9-4, the amount of red increases from 50 to 250, and the amount of blue decreases from 205 to 5.

This section is almost at an end. The lesson of this section is, an `Animation` instance's value can mean anything you want it to mean. In Listings 9-2 and 9-3, the animation's value controls an icon's position. But in Listing 9-4, the animation's value controls an icon's size and color.

What value would you like to animate? Rotation? Sound volume? Speed? Curvature? Shadow? Background color? Border shape? Mood? Be creative.

Moving Along a Curve

Life doesn't always move along a straight line. Sometimes, fate takes bends and turns. To make this happen in Flutter, you don't have to change anything about an animation. Instead, you change the way you use the animation's value.

The `Tween` constructor call in this section's example is almost identical to the calls in this chapter's other listings. What's different about this section's example is the `Positioned` widget's parameters. It's all in Listing 9-5.

LISTING 9-5: **Fancy Parabolic Motion**

```
// app0905.dart

import 'dart:math';

import 'package:flutter/material.dart';

import 'app09ain.dart';
```

```
extension MyHomePageStateExtension on MyHomePageState {
  Animation getAnimation(AnimationController controller) {
    return Tween<double>(begin: 0.0, end: 400.0).animate(controller)
      ..addListener(() {
        setState(() {});
      });
  }

  Widget buildPositionedWidget() {
    double newValue = animation.value;
    return Positioned(
      left: 15 * sqrt(newValue),
      top: newValue,
      child: Icon(
        Icons.hot_tub,
        size: 70,
      ),
    );
  }
}
```

In Figure 9-7, the dotted line shows the path taken by the Hot Tub icon when the animation moves forward.

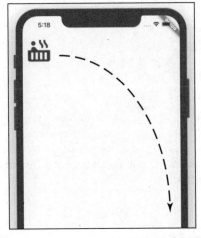

FIGURE 9-7: Since when do hot tubs move along a curve?

Have a look at the code in Listing 9-5. As the animation's value increases, both the icon's `left` and `top` parameter values change. The `top` parameter is the same as the animation's value, but the `left` parameter is 15 times the square root of the animation's value.

You can use Dart's `sqrt` function only if you import `dart.math`. When you forget to import `dart.math`, Android Studio says, `"Method 'sqrt' isn't defined."`

To illustrate the effect of using this formula, take a look at the values of `left` and `top` during a complete movement from the top left of the animation to the bottom right:

```
left:  top:
  0.0    0.0
  7.4   40.7
 22.1   70.5
 29.4   81.4
 41.2   96.2
 65.0  120.9
 71.8  127.1
 86.5  139.5
101.5  151.1
119.7  164.1
147.4  182.1
165.4  192.9
174.3  198.0
197.9  211.0
206.8  215.7
222.7  223.9
238.3  231.6
266.8  245.0
290.0  255.5
312.6  265.2
335.1  274.6
352.3  281.5
367.2  287.4
384.6  294.2
399.0  299.6
400.0  300.0
```

The `Positioned` widget's `left` and `top` values both change. But, because of the square root formula, the `left` and `top` values change at different rates. That's why the icon's movement forms a curve.

Dragging Things Around

In this section's app, the user drags a widget all around the screen. Since there's no way to show this in a figure, you have to use your imagination. Picture an icon that looks like the infinity symbol (∞). As the user moves a finger, the icon changes position.

But wait! Rather than imagine a user dragging an icon, you can run the code in Listing 9-6 and see it in action.

LISTING 9-6: **Exercise for a User's Index Finger**

```dart
// app0906.dart

import 'package:flutter/material.dart';

import 'app09main.dart';

double distanceFromLeft = 100;
double distanceFromTop = 100;

extension MyHomePageStateExtension on MyHomePageState {
  Animation getAnimation(AnimationController controller) {
    Animation animation = controller;
    return animation;
  }

  Widget buildPositionedWidget() {
    return Positioned(
      top: distanceFromTop,
      left: distanceFromLeft,
      child: GestureDetector(
        onPanUpdate: (details) {
          setState(() {
            distanceFromLeft += details.delta.dx;
            distanceFromTop += details.delta.dy;
          });
        },
        child: Icon(
          Icons.all_inclusive,
          size: 70,
        ),
      ),
    );
  }
}
```

Like other listings in this chapter, Listing 9-6 relies on the code in Listing 9-1. Because of that, the app that's generated by Listing 9-6 has Forward, Backward, and Reset buttons. Even so, pressing these buttons has no effect.

In the same way, Listing 9-6 has a getAnimation method. That's necessary because the code in Listing 9-1 calls a getAnimation method. But to make a widget move along with the user's finger, you don't need an Animation instance. In a

Moving Right Along . . .

sense, the user is the app's `AnimationController`, and the `Animation` instance is somewhere inside the user's mind. So, in Listing 9-6, the `getAnimation` method returns the same thing that's passed to it. In other words, it doesn't do anything.

So what part of the code makes the `all_inclusive` icon move? The icon lives inside of a `GestureDetector` — a widget that senses touches on the screen. A `GestureDetector` has tons of properties such as `onTap`, `onDoubleTap`, `onTapUp`, `onTapDown`, `onLongPress`, `onLongPressStart`, and `onLongPressEnd`. Other methods belonging to the `GestureDetector` class have names with less-than-obvious meanings. The following list has a few (somewhat oversimplified) examples:

>> `onSecondaryTapDown`: While holding one finger on the screen, the user places a second finger on the screen.

>> `onScaleUpdate`: With two fingers, the user pinches in or out.

>> `onHorizontalDragUpdate`: The user moves something sideways — a common gesture for dismissing an item.

>> `onPanUpdate`: The user moves a finger in one direction or another.

The `onPanUpdate` parameter's value is a method, and that method's parameter is a `DragUpdateDetails` object. In Listing 9-6, the `DragUpdateDetails` object goes by the name `details`:

```
onPanUpdate: (details) {
  setState(() {
    distanceFromLeft += details.delta.dx;
    distanceFromTop += details.delta.dy;
  });
```

When the user moves a finger along the screen, Flutter fills `details` with information about the movement and calls the `onPanUpdate` parameter's method.

The `details` variable contains some useful pieces of information:

>> `details.globalPosition`: The distance from the upper-left corner of the app screen to the current position of the user's finger

>> `details.localPosition`: The distance from the place where the user's finger first landed on the screen to the current position of the user's finger

>> `details.delta`: The distance from a finger's previous position to its current position

Each piece of information has two parts: `dx` (the horizontal distance) and `dy` (the vertical distance). The `Positioned` widget in Listing 9-6 places the app's `all_inclusive` icon at the points `distanceFromLeft` and `distanceFromTop`. When Flutter detects finger movement, the code changes the values of `distanceFromLeft` and `distanceFromTop` by adding the `details.delta` parameter's `dx` and `dy` values. That's what makes the icon move around. It's pretty clever!

TECHNICAL STUFF

The `GestureDectector` in Listing 9-6 has a child. But, for any old `Gesture Dectector` constructor call, the `child` parameter is optional. A `Gesture Detector` with no child grows to be as large as its parent widget. In contrast, a `GestureDetector` with a child shrinks to fit tightly around the child. With the app in Listing 9-6, the `GestureDetector` is about the same size as its child — the `all_inclusive` icon. To make the icon move, the user's finger must start right on the icon. Otherwise, nothing happens.

Tearing Things Up

You're near the end of this book, so maybe it's time to relax and have some raucous, carefree fun. Can destroying something be fun? Here are some ways to break Listing 9-6:

>> **Remove the `setState` call.**

```
// Bad code:
onPanUpdate: (details) {
  distanceFromLeft += details.delta.dx;
  distanceFromTop += details.delta.dy;
}
```

Removing a `setState` call is almost never a good idea. If you remove the call in Listing 9-6, the values of `distanceFromLeft` and `distanceFromTop` change, but Flutter doesn't redraw the screen. As a result, the icon doesn't budge.

>> **Move the `distanceFromLeft` and `distanceFromTop` declarations so that they're immediately before the `buildPositionedWidget` method.**

```
// More bad code:
Animation getAnimation(AnimationController controller) {
  return null;
}


double distanceFromLeft = 100;
double distanceFromTop = 100;
```

```
Widget buildPositionedWidget() {
  // ... etc.
```

If you do this, you can't even run the app. Dart's rules include one about declaring top-level variables inside of extensions. You're simply not allowed to do it. Book 4, Chapter 5 has some information about top-level variables.

» **Move the** `distanceFromLeft` **and** `distanceFromTop` **declarations so that they're inside the** `buildPositionedWidget` **method.**

```
// Even more bad code:
Widget buildPositionedWidget() {
  double distanceFromLeft = 100;
  double distanceFromTop = 100;
  return Positioned(
  // ... etc.
```

The program runs, but the icon never moves. This happens because the code sets `distanceFromLeft` and `distanceFromTop` to 100 whenever Flutter redraws the screen. (Actually, the icon moves a tiny bit but not enough for you to notice. You get a tiny bit of movement from the `details.delta` values, but not the kind of movement you want.)

» **Rather than add to the** `distanceFromLeft` **and** `distanceFromTop` **values, set them equal to the position of the user's finger:**

```
// You guessed it! Bad code!
onPanUpdate: (details) {
  setState(() {
    distanceFromLeft = details.globalPosition.dx;
    distanceFromTop = details.globalPosition.dy;
  });
}
```

The app runs, but the icon jumps when the user's finger starts moving. Throughout the dragging gesture, the icon stays half an inch away from the user's finger. This happens because Flutter doesn't use the middle of the icon as the `Positioned` widget's `top` and `left` points.

Similar things happen if you try to use `details.localPosition`.

Flutter's animation features don't end with simple movements and basic size changes. If you're interested in making objects move, be sure to check Flutter's `physics.dart` package. With that package, you can simulate springs, gravity, friction, and much more. You can get information about the package by visiting `https://api.flutter.dev/flutter/physics/physics-library.html`.

5
Getting Started with Python

Contents at a Glance

Chapter **1**

Wrapping Your Head around Python

I chose Python as a working title for the project, being in a slightly irreverent mood (and a big fan of Monty Python's Flying Circus).

— GUIDO VAN ROSSUM, CREATOR OF PYTHON

Python is a server-side language created by Guido van Rossum, a developer who was bored during the winter of 1989 and looking for a project to do. At the time, Van Rossum had already helped create one language, called ABC, and the experience had given him many ideas that he thought would appeal to programmers. Although ABC never achieved popularity with programmers, Python was a runaway success. Python is one of the world's most popular programming languages, used by beginners and professionals building heavy-duty applications.

In this chapter, you learn Python basics, including the design philosophy behind Python, how to write Python code to perform basic tasks, and steps to create your first Python program.

What Does Python Do?

Python is a general purpose programming language typically used for web development. Python allows for storing data after the user has navigated away from the page or closed the browser, unlike HTML, CSS, and JavaScript. Using Python commands you can create, update, store, and retrieve this data in a database. For example, imagine I wanted to create a local search and ratings site like Yelp.com. The reviews users write are stored in a central database. Any review author can exit the browser, turn off the computer, and come back to the website later to find their reviews. Additionally, when others search for venues, this same central database is queried, and the same review is displayed. Storing data in a database is a common task for Python developers, and existing Python libraries include prebuilt code to easily create and query databases.

TECHNICAL STUFF

SQLite is one free lightweight database commonly used by Python programmers to store data.

Many highly trafficked websites, such as YouTube, are created using Python. Other websites currently using Python include:

>> Quora for its community question and answer site.

>> Spotify for internal data analysis.

>> Dropbox for its desktop client software.

>> Reddit for generating crowd-sourced news.

>> Industrial Light & Magic and Disney Animation for creating film special effects.

From websites to software to special effects, Python is an extremely versatile language, powerful enough to support a range of applications. In addition, to help spread Python code, Python programmers create libraries, which are standalone pre-written code that does certain tasks, and make them publicly available for others to use and improve. For example, a library called Scrapy performs web scaping, while another library called SciPy performs math functions used by scientists and mathematicians. The Python community maintains thousands of libraries like these, and most are free and open-source software.

TIP

You can generally confirm the frontend programming language used by any major website with BuiltWith available at `www.builtwith.com`. After entering the website address in the search bar, look under the Frameworks section for Python. Note that websites may use Python for backend services not visible to BuiltWith.

Defining Python Structure

Python has its own set of design principles that guide how the rest of the language is structured. To implement these principles, every language has its own conventions, like curly braces in JavaScript or opening and closing tags in HTML. Python is no different, and we will cover both design principles and conventions so you can understand what Python code looks like, understand Python's style, and learn the special keywords and syntax that allow the computer to recognize what you are trying to do. Python, like Dart and JavaScript, can be very particular about syntax, and misspelling a keyword or forgetting a necessary character will result in the program not running.

Understanding the Zen of Python

There are 19 design principles that describe how the Python language is organized. Some of the most important principles include

>> **Readability counts:** This is possibly Python's most important design principle. Python code looks almost like English and even enforces certain formatting, such as indenting, to make the code easier to read. Highly readable code means that six months from now when you revisit your code to fix a bug or add a feature, you will be able to jump in without trying too hard to remember what you did. Readable code also means others can use your code or help debug your code with ease.

TECHNICAL STUFF

Reddit.com is a top-10-most-visited website in the United States, and a top-50-most-visited website in the world. Its co-founder, Steve Huffman, initially coded the website in Lisp and switched to Python because Python is "extremely readable, and extremely writeable."

>> **There should be one — and preferably *only* one — obvious way to do it:** In Python, two different programmers may approach the same problem and write two different programs, but the ideal is that the code will be similar and easy to read, adopt, and understand. Although Python does allow multiple ways to do a task — as, for example, when combining two strings — if an obvious and common option exists, it should be used.

>> **If the implementation is hard to explain, it's a bad idea:** Historically, programmers were known to write esoteric code to increase performance. However, Python was designed not to be the fastest language, and this principle reminds programmers that easy-to-understand implementations are preferable over faster but harder-to-explain ones.

You can access the full list by design principles, which is in the form of a poem, by typing `import this;` into any Python interpreter, or by visiting https://www.python.org/dev/peps/pep-0020. These principles, written by Tim Peters, a Python community member, were meant to describe the intentions of Python's creator, Van Rossum, who is also referred to as the Benevolent Dictator for Life (BDFL).

Styling and spacing

Python generally uses less punctuation than other programming languages you may have previously tried. Some sample code is included here:

```
first_name=input("What's your first name?")
first_name=first_name.upper()

if first_name=="NIK":
    print ("You may enter!")
else:
    print ("Nothing to see here.")
```

The examples in this book are written for Python 3. There are two popular version of Python currently in use — Python 2.7 and Python 3. Python 3 is the latest version of the language but it is not backward-compatible, so code written using Python 2.7 syntax does not work when using a Python 3 interpreter. Although there are still many programs that were written in Python 2.7, Python 2 officially reached its "end of life" on January 1, 2020. For more about the differences between versions see https://wiki.python.org/moin/Python2orPython3.

If you ran this code it would do the following:

>> Print a line asking for your first name.

>> Take user input (`input(What's your first name?)`) and save it to the `first_name` variable.

>> Transform any inputted text into uppercase.

>> Test the user input. If it equals "NIK," then it will `print` "You may enter!" Otherwise it will `print` "Nothing to see here."

Each of these statement types is covered in more detail later in this chapter. For now, as you look at the code, notice some of its styling characteristics:

>> **Less punctuation:** Unlike JavaScript, Python has no curly braces, and unlike HTML, no angle brackets.

>> **Whitespace matters:** Statements indented to the same level are grouped together. In the example, notice how the `if` and `else` align, and the `print` statements underneath each are indented the same amount. You can decide the amount of indentation, and whether to use tabs or spaces as long as you are consistent. Generally, four spaces from the left margin is considered the style norm.

TIP

See Python style suggestions on indentation, whitespaces, and commenting by visiting `https://www.python.org/dev/peps/pep-0008`.

>> **New lines indicate the end of statements:** Although you can use semicolons to put more than one statement on a line, the preferred and more common method is to put each statement on its own line.

>> **Colons separate code blocks:** New Python programmers sometimes ask why using colons to indicate code blocks, like the one at the end of the `if` statement, is necessary when new lines would suffice. Early user testing with and without the colons showed that beginner programmers better understood the code with the colon.

Coding Common Python Tasks and Commands

Python, as with other programming languages like Dart and JavaScript, can do everything from simple text manipulation to designing complex graphics in games. The following basic tasks are explained within a Python context, but they're foundational in understanding any programming language. Even experienced developers learning a new language, like Apple's Swift programming language, start by learning these foundational tasks.

TIP

Millions of people have learned Python before you, so it's easy to find answers to questions that might arise while learning simply by conducting an Internet search. The odds are in your favor that someone has asked your question before.

Defining data types and variables

Variables, like the ones in algebra, are keywords used to store data values for later use. Though the data stored in a variable may change, the variable name will always be the same. Think of a variable as a gym locker — what you store in the locker changes, but the locker number always stays the same.

Variables in Python are named using alphanumeric characters and the underscore (_) character, and they must start with a letter or an underscore. Table 1-1 lists some of the data types that Python can store.

TABLE 1-1

Data Stored by a Variable

Data Type	Description	Example
Numbers	Positive or negative numbers with or without decimals	101.96
Strings	Printable characters	Holly Novak
Boolean	Value can be true or false	true

To initially set or change a variable's value, write the variable name, a single equals sign, and the variable value, as shown in the following example:

```
myName = "Nik"
pizzaCost = 10
totalCost = pizzaCost * 2
```

TIP

Avoid starting your variable names with the number one (1), a lowercase "L" (l), or uppercase i (I). Depending on the font used these characters can all look the same, causing confusion for you or others later!

Variable names in Python are case sensitive, so when referring to a variable in your program remember that MyName is a different variable from myname. In general, give your variable a name that describes the data being stored.

Computing simple and advanced math

After you create variables, you may want to do some math on the numerical values stored in those variables. Simple math like addition, subtraction, multiplication, and division is done using operators you already know. Exponentiation (such as, for example, 2 to the power of 3) uses two asterisks, which is the same as JavaScript's exponentiation operator. Examples are shown here:

```
num1 = 1+1 #equals 2
num2 = 5-1 #equals 4
num3 = 3*4 #equals 12
num4 = 9/3 #equals 3
num5 = 2**3 #equals 8
```

TIP

The # symbol indicates a comment in Python.

TIP

Don't just read these commands, try them! Go to https://replit.com/new/python3 for a lightweight in-browser Python interpreter that you can use right in your browser without downloading or installing any software.

Advanced math like absolute value, rounding to the nearest decimal, rounding up, or rounding down can be performed using math functions. Python has some functions which are built-in pre-written code that can be referenced to make performing certain tasks easier. The general syntax to use Python math functions is to list the function name, followed by the variable name or value as an argument, as follows:

```
method(value)
method(variable)
```

The math functions for absolute value and rounding follow this syntax, but some math functions, like rounding up or rounding down are stored in a separate math module. To use these math functions you must:

» Write the statement import math just once in your code before using the math functions in the math module.

» Reference the math module, as follows: math.method(value) or math.method(variable).

See these math functions with examples in Table 1-2.

TABLE 1-2 ## Common Python Math Functions

Function Name	Description	Example	Result
abs(n)	Return the absolute value of a number (n)	abs(-99)	99
round (n, d)	Round a number (n) to a number of decimal points (d)	round (3.1415, 2)	3.14
math.floor(n)	Round down to the nearest integer	math.floor(4.7)	4.0
math.ceil(n)	Round up to the nearest integer	math.ceil(7.3)	8.0

TECHNICAL STUFF

Modules are separate files that contain Python code, and the module must be referenced or imported before any code from the module can be used.

TIP

See all the functions in the math module by visiting `https://docs.python.org/3/library/math.html`.

Using strings and special characters

Along with numbers, variables in Python can also store strings. To assign a value to a string, you can use single or double quotation marks, as follows:

```
firstname = "Travis"
lastname = 'Kalanick'
```

REMEMBER

Variables can also store numbers as strings instead of numbers. However, even though the string looks like a number, Python will not be able to add, subtract, or divide strings and numbers. For example, consider amountdue = "18" + 24 — running this code as is would result in an error. Python does multiply strings but in an interesting way — print ('Ha' * 3) results in 'HaHaHa'.

Including a single or double quote in your string can be problematic because the quotes inside your string will terminate the string definition prematurely. For example, if I want to store a string with the value 'I'm on my way home' Python will assume the ' after the first letter I is the end of the variable assignment, and the remaining characters will cause an error. The solution is to use special characters called *escape sequences* to indicate when you want to use characters like quotation marks, which normally signal the beginning or end of a string, or other non-printable characters like tabs. Table 1-3 shows some examples of escape sequences.

TABLE 1-3 **Common Python Escape Sequences**

Special Character	Description	Example	Result
\' or \"	Quotation marks	print ("You had me at \"Hello\"")	You had me at "Hello"
\t	Tab	print ("Item\tUnits \tPrice")	Item Units Price
\n	New line	print ("Anheuser?\nBusch? \nBueller? Bueller?")	Anheuser? Busch? Bueller? Bueller?

TIP

Escape sequences are interpreted only for strings with double quotation marks. For a full list of escape sequences see the table under Section 2.4, "Literals," at `https://docs.python.org/3/reference/lexical_analysis.html`.

Deciding with conditionals: if, elif, else

With data stored in a variable, one common task is to compare the variable's value to a fixed value or another variable's value, and then make a decision based on the comparison. If you previously read the chapters on JavaScript or Dart, the discussion and concepts here are very similar. The general syntax for an `if-elif-else` statement is as follows:

```
if conditional1:
    statement1 to execute if conditional1 is true
elif conditional2:
    statement2 to execute if conditional2 is true
else:
    statement3 to run if all previous conditional are false
```

TIP

Notice there are no curly brackets or semicolons, but don't forget the colons and to indent your statements!

The initial `if statement` will evaluate to `true` or `false`. When `conditional1` is `true`, then *statement1* is executed. This is the minimum necessary syntax needed for an `if-statement`, and the `elif` and `else` are optional. When present, the `elif` tests for an additional condition when `conditional1` is `false`. You can test for as many conditions as you like using `elif`. Specifying every condition to test for can become tedious, so having a "catch-all" is useful. When present, the `else` serves as the "catch-all," and it executes when all previous conditionals are `false`.

TIP

You cannot have an `elif` or an `else` by itself, without a preceding `if` statement. You can include many `elif` statements, but one and only one `else` statement.

The conditional in an `if` statement compares values using comparison operators, and common comparison operators are described in Table 1-4.

Here is an example `if` statement.

```
carSpeed=55
if carSpeed > 55:
    print ("You are over the speed limit!")
elif carSpeed == 55:
    print ("You are at the speed limit!")
else:
    print ("You are under the speed limit!")
```

TABLE 1-4   **Common Python Comparison Operators**

Type	Operator	Description	Example
Less than	<	Evaluates whether one value is less than another value	x < 55
Greater than	>	Evaluates whether one value is greater than another value	x > 55
Equality	==	Evaluates whether two values are equal	x == 55
Less than or equal to	<=	Evaluates whether one value is less than or equal to another value	x <= 55
Greater than or equal to	>=	Evaluates whether one value is greater than or equal to another value	x >= 55
Inequality	!=	Evaluates whether two values are not equal	x != 55

As the diagram in Figure 1-1 shows, there are two conditions, each signaled by the diamond, which are evaluated in sequence. In this example, carSpeed is equal to 55, so the first conditional (carSpeed > 55) is false, and the second conditional (carSpeed==55) is true. The statement executes by printing "You are at the speed limit!" When a conditional is true, the if statement stops executing, and the else is never reached.

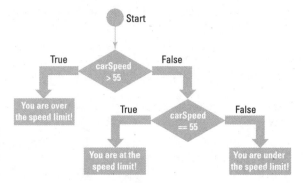

FIGURE 1-1:
An if–else
statement
with an elif.

Input and output

Python can collect input from the user and display output to the user. To collect user input use the input("Prompt") method, which stores the user input as a string. In the following example, the users enter their full name, which is stored in a variable called full_name.

```
full_name = input("What's your full name?")
```

Imagine that the users entered the name, "Eneyen González Samaniego." You can display the value of the variable using `print (full_name)` and you would see this:

```
Eneyen González Samaniego
```

At this point, you may feel like printing variables and values in a Python interpreter console window is very different from dynamically creating web pages with variables created in Python. Integrating Python into a web page to respond to user requests and generate HTML pages is typically done with a Python web framework, like Django or Flask, which have pre-written code to make the process easier. These frameworks typically require some installation and setup work, and they generally separate the data being displayed from templates used to display the page to the user.

Shaping Your Strings

Whenever you collect input from users, you need to clean the input to remove errors and inconsistencies. Here are some common data cleaning tasks:

>> Standardizing strings to have consistent upper- and lowercase

>> Removing whitespace from user input

>> Inserting a variable's value in strings displayed to the user

Python includes many built-in methods that make processing strings easy.

Dot notation with upper(), lower(), capitalize(), and strip()

Standardizing user input to have proper case and remove extra whitespace characters is often necessary to easily sort the data later. For example, imagine you are designing a website for the New York Knicks so fans can meet players after the game. The page asks for fans to enter their names, so that team security can later check fan names against this list before entry. Reviewing past fan entries, you see that fans enter the same name several ways like "Mark", "mark", "marK", and other similar variants that cause issues when the list is sorted alphabetically. To make the input and these names consistent, you could use the string functions described in Table 1-5.

TABLE 1-5   **Select Python String Functions**

Function Name	Description	Example	Result
`string.upper()`	Returns all uppercase characters	`"nY".upper()`	`"NY"`
`string.lower()`	Returns all lowercase characters	`"Hi".lower()`	`"hi"`
`string.capitalize()`	Capitalizes the first letter, lowercases the remaining letters	`"wake UP".capitalize()`	`"Wake up"`
`string.strip()`	Removes leading and trailing whitespaces	`" Ny ".strip()`	`"Ny"`

String formatting with %

To insert variable values into strings shown to the users, you can use the string format operator %. Inserted into the string definition, %d is used to specify integers, %s is used to specify strings, and the variables to format (mapping key) are specified in parentheses after the string is defined. See the example code and result that follow.

Code:

```
yearofbirth = 1990
pplinroom = 20
name = "Mary"
print ("Your year of birth is %d. Is this correct?" % (yearofbirth))
print ('Your year of birth is %d. Is this correct?' % (yearofbirth))
print ("There are %d women in the room born in %d and %s is one of them." %
    (pplinroom/2, yearofbirth, name))
```

Result:

```
Your year of birth is 1990. Is this correct?
Your year of birth is 1990. Is this correct?
There are 10 women in the room born in 1990 and Mary is one of them.
```

The first string used double quotes and the variable was inserted into the string and displayed to the user. The second string behaved just like the first string, because defining strings with single quotes does not affect the string formatting. The third string shows that code can be evaluated (`pplinroom / 2`) and inserted into the string.

TECHNICAL STUFF

The `string.format()` method is another way to format strings in Python.

IN THIS CHAPTER

» Determining which Python
distribution to use

» Performing a Linux, macOS X, and
Windows installation

» Obtaining the data sets and
example code

Chapter **2**

Installing a Python Distribution

Life is short (you need Python).

— BRUCE ECKEL

Before you can do too much with Python or use it to solve problems, you need a workable installation. In addition, you need access to the data sets and code used for this book. This chapter tells you how to perform the required Python setups and downloads. Downloading the sample code (found at www. dummies.com/go/codingallinonefd2e) and installing it on your system is the best way to get a good learning experience from the book.

REMEMBER

Using the downloadable source code doesn't prevent you from typing the examples on your own, following them using a debugger, expanding them, or working with the code in all sorts of ways. The downloadable source code is there to help you get a good start with your Python learning experience. After you see how the code works when it's correctly typed and configured, you can try to create the examples on your own. If you make a mistake, you can compare what you've typed with the downloadable source code and discover precisely where the error exists.

Using Anaconda

You can use a number of packages to write Python code. In fact, too many exist to discuss adequately in a single chapter. This book uses Anaconda for a number of reasons, as explained in the next section.

Getting Anaconda

The basic Anaconda package is a free download that you obtain at `https://www.anaconda.com/products/distribution`. Simply click Download to start the download of the most recent version. Anaconda supports the following platforms:

>> Windows 32-bit and 64-bit (the installer may offer you only the 64-bit or 32-bit version, depending on which version of Windows it detects)

>> Linux 64-bit (x86 and PowerPC 8/9 installers)

>> macOS X 64-bit (graphical and command-line installer)

The latest version at the time of this writing is Anaconda3-2021.11. To guarantee that the example code will work without modification, go to `https://repo.anaconda.com/archive/` and download the Anaconda3-2021.11 version for your operating system.

REMEMBER

Newer versions of Anaconda may work with the code in this book, but to guarantee the best and easiest experience, it's recommended that you download the Anaconda3-2021.11 version. If you want to upgrade at a later time, you can do so easily.

WARNING

The installation works best if you first remove previous versions of Anaconda from your system. Otherwise, one version of the product can interfere with other versions of the product. Anaconda provides a separate uninstall program in the Anaconda executable folder on your system, the location of which can vary. For example, to uninstall a previous version of Anaconda 3 on a Windows system, look in the `C:\Users\<UserName>\Anaconda3` folder on your system for `Uninstall Anaconda3.exe`. Execute this file to uninstall the product. In addition, this book doesn't support the use of the Miniconda installer described at `https://docs.conda.io/en/latest/miniconda.html`.

At the time of this writing, the default download version installs Python 3.9, which is the version used in this book. Both Windows and macOS X provide graphical installers. When using Linux, you rely on the `bash` utility.

Defining why Anaconda is used in this book

Anaconda isn't an Integrated Development Environment (IDE) like many other products out there. Rather, it's a centralized method of accessing a number of packages. This book uses Jupyter Notebook as an IDE because it supports literate programming techniques. However, you could just as easily use Spyder for development, and you might be happier with it because it provides a more traditional interface. You can see a comparison at `https://www.slant.co/versus/1246/15716/~spyder_vs_jupyter`. The point is that Anaconda helps you manage both IDEs, along with a wealth of other packages. In addition, you can create environments for using the IDEs in specific ways. For example, you could have an environment for using Jupyter Notebook for Python and an entirely different environment for using Jupyter Notebook for R.

So, it's important to know why this section emphasizes Jupyter Notebook when Anaconda provides access to a number of IDEs. Most IDEs look like fancy text editors, and that's precisely what they are. Yes, you get all sorts of intelligent features, hints, tips, code coloring, and so on, but at the end of the day, they're all text editors. Nothing is wrong with text editors, and this chapter isn't telling you anything of the sort. However, given that Python developers often focus on scientific applications that require something better than pure text presentation, using notebooks instead can be helpful.

REMEMBER

A *notebook* differs from a text editor in that it focuses on a technique called *literate programming,* advanced by Stanford computer scientist Donald Knuth. You use literate programming to create a kind of presentation of code, notes, math equations, and graphics. In short, you wind up with a scientist's notebook full of everything needed to understand the code completely. You commonly see literate programming techniques used in high-priced packages such as Mathematica and MATLAB. Notebook development excels at

>> Demonstration

>> Collaboration

>> Research

>> Teaching objectives

>> Presentation

This book uses the Anaconda tool collection because it provides you with a great Python coding experience but also helps you discover the enormous potential of literate programming techniques. If you spend a lot of time performing scientific tasks, Anaconda and products like it are essential. In addition, Anaconda is free, so you get the benefits of the literate programming style without the cost of other packages.

TIP

For more information about Anaconda and changes from previous editions, make sure to view the Release Notes at https://docs.anaconda.com/anaconda/reference/release-notes/. Most of the changes you find deal with bug fixes and updates.

Installing Anaconda on Linux

You use the command line to install Anaconda on Linux — there is no graphical installation option. The following procedure should work fine on any Linux system, whether you use the Intel or PowerPC version of Anaconda:

1. **Open a copy of Terminal.**

   The Terminal window appears.

2. **Change directories to the downloaded copy of Anaconda on your system.**

   The name of this file varies, but normally it appears as Anaconda3-2021.11-Linux-x86_64.sh for Intel systems and Anaconda3-2021.11-Linux-ppc64le.sh for PowerPC systems. The version number is embedded as part of the filename. In this case, the filename refers to version 3.2021.11, which is the version used for this book. If you use some other version, you may experience problems with the source code and need to make adjustments when working with it.

3. **Type** bash Anaconda3-2021.11-Linux-x86_64.sh **(for the Intel version) or** bash Anaconda3-2021.11-Linux-ppc64le.sh **(for the PowerPC version) and press Enter.**

   An installation wizard starts that asks you to accept the licensing terms for using Anaconda.

4. **Read the licensing agreement and accept the terms using the method required for your version of Linux.**

   The wizard asks you to provide an installation location for Anaconda. The book assumes that you use the default location for your platform. If you choose some other location, you may have to modify some procedures later in the book to work with your setup.

5. **Provide an installation location (if necessary) and press Enter (or click Next).**

   The application extraction process begins. The installer asks whether you want to initialize Anaconda3 using the conda init command.

6. **Type** yes **and press Enter or click Yes.**

   After the extraction is complete, you see a completion message.

7. **Add the installation path to your** PATH **statement using the method required for your version of Linux.**

   You're ready to begin using Anaconda.

Installing Anaconda on macOS X

The macOS X installation comes in only one form: 64-bit. The following steps help you install Anaconda 64-bit on a Mac system using the GUI method:

1. **Locate the downloaded copy of Anaconda on your system.**

   The name of this file varies, but normally it appears as Anaconda3–2021.11–MacOSX–x86_64.pkg. The version number is embedded as part of the filename. In this case, the filename refers to version 3.2021.11, which is the version used for this book. If you use some other version, you may experience problems with the source code and need to make adjustments when working with it.

2. **Double-click the installation file.**

   An introduction dialog box appears.

3. **Click Continue.**

   The wizard asks whether you want to review the Read Me materials. You can read these materials later. For now, you can safely skip the information.

4. **Click Continue.**

   The wizard displays a licensing agreement. Be sure to read through the licensing agreement so that you know the terms of usage.

5. **Click I Agree if you agree to the licensing agreement.**

   The wizard asks you to provide a destination for the installation. The destination controls whether the installation is for an individual user or a group.

6. **Click Continue.**

   This book assumes that you keep the default settings.

7. **Click Install.**

   The installation begins. A progress bar tells you how the installation process is progressing. When the installation is complete, you see a completion dialog box.

8. **Click Continue.**

   You're ready to begin using Anaconda.

Installing Anaconda on Windows

Anaconda comes with a graphical installation application for Windows, so getting a good install means using a wizard, as you would for any other installation. The following procedure should work fine on any Windows system, whether you use the 32-bit or the 64-bit version of Anaconda:

1. **Locate the downloaded copy of Anaconda on your system.**

   The name of this file varies, but normally it appears as Anaconda3–2021.11-Windows-x86.exe for 32-bit systems and Anaconda3–2021.11-Windows-x86_64.exe for 64-bit systems. The version number is embedded as part of the filename. In this case, the filename refers to version 3.2021.11, which is the version used for this book. If you use some other version, you may experience problems with the source code and need to make adjustments when working with it.

2. **Double-click the installation file.**

   You see a Welcome dialog box that tells you which version of Anaconda you have — 32-bit or 64-bit. Make sure you have the correct one.

3. **Click Next.**

   The wizard displays a licensing agreement. Be sure to read through the licensing agreement so that you know the terms of usage.

4. **Click I Agree if you agree to the licensing agreement.**

   You're asked what sort of installation type to perform, as shown in Figure 2-1. In most cases, you want to install the product just for yourself.

5. **Choose one of the installation types and then click Next.**

   The wizard asks where to install Anaconda on disk. The book assumes that you use the default location. If you choose some other location, you may have to modify some procedures later in the book to work with your setup.

6. **Choose an installation location (if necessary) and then click Next.**

   You see the Advanced Installation Options, shown in Figure 2-2.

7. **Leave the advanced options as they are and then click Install.**

   You see an Installing dialog box with a progress bar. The installation process can take a few minutes, so get yourself a cup of coffee and read the comics for a while. When the installation process is over, you see a Next button enabled.

8. **Click Next.**

   (If you see a page with a link for PyCharm, `https://www.jetbrains.com/pycharm/`, click Next again.) The wizard tells you that the installation is complete. This page includes options for the Anaconda tutorial and learning more about Anaconda. If you keep them selected, you see the appropriate pages loaded into your browser.

9. **Click Finish.**

   You're ready to begin using Anaconda.

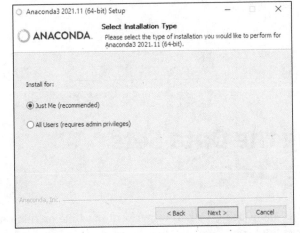

FIGURE 2-1:
Tell the wizard how to install Anaconda on your system.

© John Wiley & Sons

A WORD ABOUT THE SCREENSHOTS

As you work your way through the book, you use an IDE of your choice to open the Python and Python Notebook files containing the book's source code. Every screenshot that contains IDE-specific information relies on Anaconda because Anaconda runs on all three platforms supported by the book. The use of Anaconda doesn't imply that it's the best IDE; Anaconda simply works well as a demonstration product.

When you work with Anaconda, the name of the IDE, Jupyter Notebook, is precisely the same across all three platforms, and you won't even see any significant difference in the presentation. The differences that you do see are minor, and you should ignore them as you work through the book.

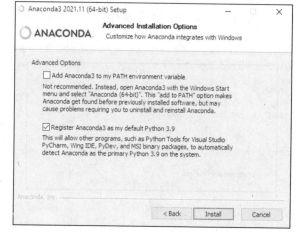

FIGURE 2-2:
Leave the advanced installation options as they are for now.

Downloading the Data Sets and Example Code

This book is about using Python to perform machine learning tasks. Of course, you can spend all your time creating the example code from scratch, debugging it, and only then discovering how it relates to machine learning, or you can take the easy way and download the pre-written code at www.dummies.com/go/codingallinonefd2e so that you can get right to work.

Likewise, creating data sets large enough for machine learning purposes would take quite a while. Fortunately, you can access standardized, precreated data sets quite easily using features provided in some of the data science libraries (which also work just fine for machine learning). The following sections help you download and use the example code and data sets so that you can save time and get right to work with data science–specific tasks.

Starting Anaconda Navigator

Find Anaconda Navigator in your Windows Start menu, your macOS Applications folder, or by opening a terminal window in Linux and typing anaconda-navigator. The main Anaconda Navigator screen will appear, as shown in Figure 2-3.

Using Jupyter Notebook

To make working with the relatively complex code in this book easier, you use Jupyter Notebook. This interface lets you easily create Python notebook files that can contain any number of examples, each of which can run individually. The program runs in your browser, so which platform you use for development doesn't matter; as long as it has a browser, you should be okay.

Starting Jupyter Notebook

You access Jupyter Notebook from Anaconda Navigator, which also provides centralized access to the various applications supported by a particular environment. The default environment or channel, base (root), supports Python development directly. Figure 2-3 shows the content of the base (root) channel.

TIP Notice that each entry tells which version of the product you'll access. For this book, you use Jupyter Notebook 6.4.8. If you don't see version 6.4.8, click the gear icon in the upper-right corner of the Jupyter Notebook entry and choose Install Specific Version ⇨ 6.4.8 from the menu. Anaconda Navigator will lead you through the installation process for the correct version.

To start Jupyter Notebook, simply click Launch in the Jupyter Notebook entry. Figure 2-4 shows how the interface looks when viewed in a Chrome browser. This is the homepage, where you do things like create a new folder to contain a project. The precise appearance on your system depends on the browser you use and the kind of platform you have installed.

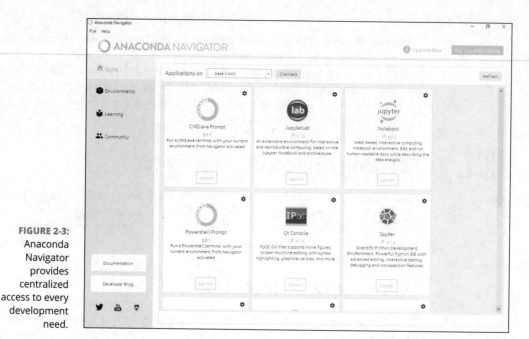

FIGURE 2-3:
Anaconda
Navigator
provides
centralized
access to every
development
need.

FIGURE 2-4:
Jupyter Notebook
provides an easy
method to create
machine learning
examples.

Stopping the Jupyter Notebook server

No matter how you start Jupyter Notebook (or just Notebook, as it appears in the remainder of the book), you need to click Quit in the upper-right corner of the client window to exit Notebook. Otherwise, the Notebook server remains running in the background and you leave your environment in an uncertain state, which could cause data loss in some situations. After you click Quit, you see a Server Stopped message box, which you can dismiss by clicking the X in the upper-right corner. Close the browser window.

If you're done working with Anaconda, you choose File⇨Quit in the Anaconda Navigator window. During the first (and possibly subsequent) shutdown, you see a Quit Application dialog box, where you must click Yes to end Anaconda Navigator. If you don't want to see this dialog box again, you can remove it by selecting Don't Show Again before you click Yes.

WARNING

Sometimes the server shutdown process takes longer than expected. In this case, Anaconda Navigator displays a message telling you that it's still working in the background. Allow it to complete whatever processes it needs to complete before you quit. You could also see this message if you didn't quit Jupyter Notebook correctly. In this case, you need to end Anaconda Navigator because the server will never stop.

Defining the code repository

The code you create and use in this book will reside in a repository on your hard drive. Think of a *repository* as a kind of filing cabinet where you put your code. Notebook opens a drawer, takes out the folder, and shows the code to you. You can modify it, run individual examples within the folder, add new examples, and simply interact with your code in a natural manner. The following sections get you started with Notebook so that you can see how this whole repository concept works.

Defining the book's folder

It pays to organize your files so that you can access them more easily later. This book keeps your Python files in the CAIO4D2E folder. The following steps show how to create the Python folder within Notebook.

1. **After launching Notebook, choose New ⇨ Folder.**

   Notebook creates a new folder named Untitled Folder, as shown in Figure 2-5. The file appears in alphanumeric order, so you may not initially see it. You must scroll down to the correct location.

2. **Select the box next to the Untitled Folder entry.**

3. **Click Rename at the top of the page.**

   You see a Rename Directory dialog box.

4. **Type** CAIO4D2E **and click the OK or RENAME button.**

   (This stands for *Coding All-in-One For Dummies, 2nd Edition*.) Notebook changes the name of the folder for you.

5. **Click the new** CAIO4D2E **entry in the list.**

   Notebook changes the location to the CAIO4D2E folder where you perform tasks related to the exercises in this book.

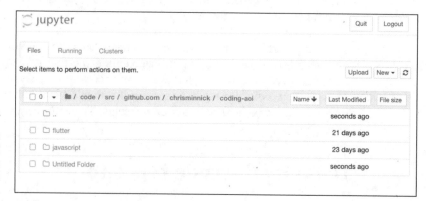

Creating a new notebook

Every new notebook is like a file folder. You can place individual examples within the file folder, just as you would sheets of paper into a physical file folder. Each example appears in a cell. You can put other sorts of things in the file folder, too, but you see how these things work as the book progresses. Use these steps to create a new notebook:

1. **Choose New ⇨ Python 3.**

   A new tab opens in the browser with the new notebook, as shown in Figure 2-6. Notice that the notebook contains a cell and that Notebook has highlighted the cell so that you can begin typing code in it. The title of the notebook is Untitled right now. That's not a particularly helpful title, so you need to change it.

2. **Click Untitled on the page.**

   Notebook asks what you want to use as a new name.

3. Type CAIO4D2E_Sample **and press Enter.**

The new name tells you that this is a file for *Coding All-In-One For Dummies,* 2nd Edition, Sample.ipynb. Using this naming convention will allow you to easily differentiate these files from other files in your repository.

FIGURE 2-6:
A notebook contains cells that you use to hold code.

© John Wiley & Sons

Of course, the Sample notebook doesn't contain anything just yet. Place the cursor in the cell and type the following code:

```
import sys
print('Python Version:\n', sys.version)

import os
result = os.popen('conda list anaconda$').read()
print('\nAnaconda Version:\n', result)
```

The first print() statement outputs the Python version number for your installation. The second print() statement prints the Anaconda version number for your installation. Both of these outputs depend on using external code using the import statement. The second call works directly with a command-line utility named conda that you see used several times in this book.

Click the Save and Checkpoint button (the button that looks like a floppy disk) to save your work.

Click the Run button (the button with the right-pointing arrow on the toolbar). You see the output shown in Figure 2-7. The version numbers for your setup should match the version numbers shown in Figure 2-7. The output is part of the same cell as the code. However, Notebook visually separates the output from the code so that you can tell them apart. Notebook automatically creates a new cell for you.

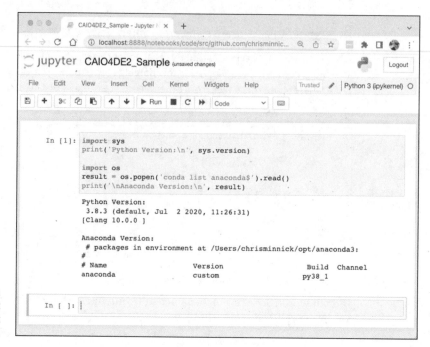

FIGURE 2-7:
The output of your first notebook.

When you finish working with a notebook, shutting it down is important. To close a notebook, choose File ⇨ Close and Halt. You return to the homepage, where you can see the notebook you just created added to the list.

Exporting a notebook

Creating notebooks and keeping them all to yourself isn't much fun. At some point, you want to share them with other people. To perform this task, you must export your notebook from the repository to a file. You can then send the file to someone else, who will import it into their repository.

The previous section shows how to create a notebook named CAIO4D2E_ Sample. You can open this notebook by clicking its entry in the repository list. The file reopens so that you can see your code again. To export this code, choose File ⇨ Download As ⇨ Notebook (.ipynb). What you see next depends on your browser, but you generally see some sort of dialog box for saving the notebook as a file. Use the same method for saving the IPython Notebook file as you use for any other file you save using your browser.

Removing a notebook

Sometimes notebooks get outdated or you simply don't need to work with them any longer. Rather than allow your repository to get clogged with files you don't need, you can remove these unwanted notebooks from the list. Use these steps to remove a notebook:

1. **Select the box next to the** `CAIO4D2E_Sample.ipynb` **entry.**

2. **Click the trash can icon (Delete) at the top of the page.**

   You see a Delete notebook warning message.

3. **Click Delete.**

   The file gets removed from the list.

Importing a notebook

To use the source code from this book, you must import the downloaded files into your repository. The source code comes in an archive file that you extract to a location on your hard drive. The archive contains a `.ipynb` (Notebook) file containing the source code for this book and the data files that you'll be using in subsequent chapters. The following steps explain how to import these files into your repository:

1. **Click Upload at the top of the page.**

   What you see depends on your browser. In most cases, you see some type of File Upload or Open dialog box that provides access to the files on your hard drive.

2. **Navigate to the directory containing the files that you want to import into Notebook.**

3. **Highlight one or more files to import and click the Open (or other, similar) button to begin the upload process.**

   You see the file added to an upload list, as shown in Figure 2-8. The file isn't part of the repository yet — you've simply selected it for upload.

4. **Click the Upload button next to each file.**

   Notebook places the files in the repository so that you can begin using them.

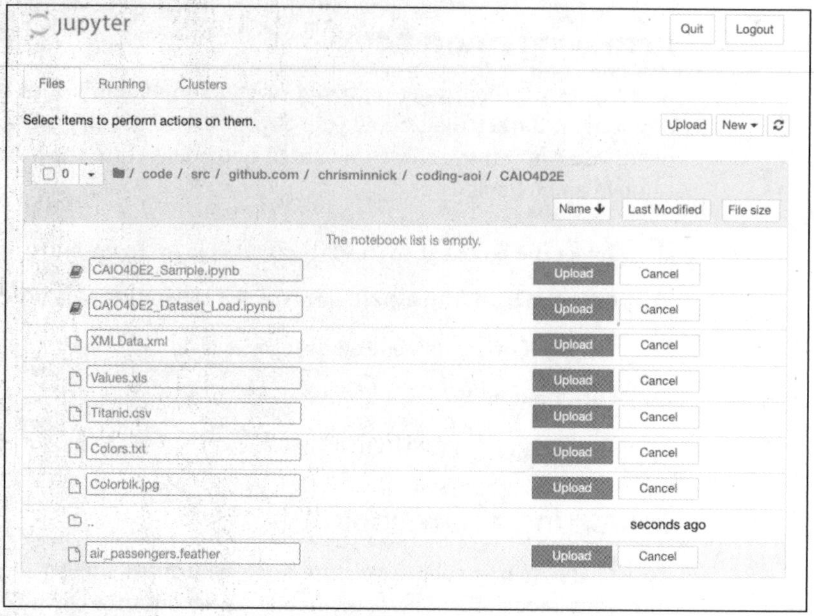

FIGURE 2-8:
The files that you want to add to the repository appear as part of an upload list.

© John Wiley & Sons

Understanding the data sets used in this book

Apart from the data sets offered by scikit-learn (`https://scikit-learn.org/stable/datasets/toy_dataset.html`), this book uses a number of data sets that you can access at `https://github.com/lmassaron/datasets`. These data sets demonstrate various ways in which you can interact with data, and you use them in the examples to perform a variety of tasks.

The technique for loading each of these data sets can vary according to the source. The following example shows how to load the Air Passengers data set, which is a `.csv` file containing the number of passengers on an example airline per month for 12 years starting in 1949. You can find the code in the `CAIO4D2E_Dataset_Load.ipynb` notebook.

The downloadable data sets are archived in the Apache Arrow-based Feather File Format (`https://arrow.apache.org/docs/python/feather.html`). To make this file format accessible in Notebook, open an Anaconda prompt in Windows (which is a separate program in your Program Files or Application folder) or a Terminal window in macOS or Linux and type the following command:

```
conda install feather-format -c conda-forge
```

The command takes a while to complete as it collects the package information and solves the environment (determines what to do to perform the installation). At some point, you'll need to type **y** and press Enter to complete the installation. To verify that you have a good installation, use this command:

```
conda list feather-format
```

After a few moments, you see output similar to this:

```
# packages in environment at C:\Users\John\anaconda3:
#
# Name          Version      Build         Channel
feather-format  0.4.1        pyh9f0ad1d_0  conda-forge
```

Now that you have the required library to use, you can load a data set from those supplied on the book's data set site. If you haven't already downloaded air_passengers.feather, which is one of the files available from this book's website, download it now and place it in folder you created for this book. (In later chapters, you see how to download the .feather files directly from the book's data set site, but performing the download now keeps things simple.)

Once you've downloaded the .feather file, go back to Jupyter Navigator and run CAIO4D2E_Dataset Load. Here is the code you use to load the Air Passengers data set as a data frame.

```
import pyarrow.feather as feather
read_df =
    feather.read_feather('air_passengers.feather')
print(read_df)
```

The result is a 144-row data frame containing the number of passengers per month. Figure 2-9 shows typical output.

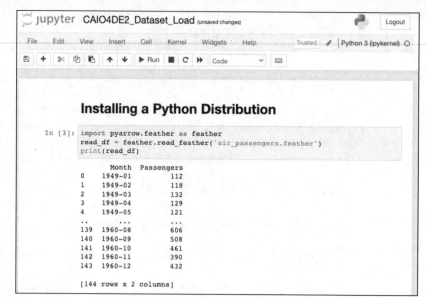

Installing a Python Distribution

```
In [3]: import pyarrow.feather as feather
        read_df = feather.read_feather('air_passengers.feather')
        print(read_df)

               Month  Passengers
        0    1949-01         112
        1    1949-02         118
        2    1949-03         132
        3    1949-04         129
        4    1949-05         121
        ..       ...         ...
        139  1960-08         606
        140  1960-09         508
        141  1960-10         461
        142  1960-11         390
        143  1960-12         432

        [144 rows x 2 columns]
```

FIGURE 2-9:
The read_df object contains the loaded data set as a data frame.

> » **Working with flat and unstructured files**
>
> » **Interacting with relational databases**
>
> » **Using NoSQL as a data source**
>
> » **Interacting with web-based data**

Chapter **3**

Working with Real Data

Data is the new oil.

— CLIVE HUMBY

Data science applications require data by definition. It would be nice if you could simply go to a data store somewhere, purchase the data you need in an easy-open package, and then write an application to access that data. However, data is messy. It appears in all sorts of places, in many different forms, and you can interpret it in many different ways. Every organization has a different method of viewing data and stores it in a different manner as well. Even when the data management system used by one company is the same as the data management system used by another company, the chances are slim that the data will appear in the same format or even use the same data types. In short, before you can do any data science work, you must discover how to access the data in all its myriad forms. Real data requires a lot of work to use and fortunately, Python is up to the task of manipulating it as needed.

This chapter helps you understand the techniques required to access data in a number of forms and locations. For example, memory streams represent a form of data storage that your computer supports natively; flat files exist on your hard drive; relational databases commonly appear on networks (although smaller relational databases, such as those found in Access, could appear on your hard drive as well); and web-based data usually appears on the Internet. You won't visit every form of data storage available (such as that stored on a point-of-sale, or POS, system). Quite possibly, an entire book on the topic wouldn't suffice to cover the topic of data formats in any detail. However, the techniques in this chapter do demonstrate how to access data in the formats you most commonly encounter when working with real-world data.

TIP

The scikit-learn library includes a number of *toy* data sets (small data sets meant for you to play with). These data sets are complex enough to perform a number of tasks, such as experimenting with Python to perform data science tasks. Because this data is readily available, and making the examples too complicated to understand is a bad idea, this book relies on these toy data sets as input for many of the examples. Even though the book does use these toy data sets for the sake of reducing complexity and making the examples clearer, the techniques that the book demonstrates work equally well on real-world data that you access using the techniques shown in this chapter.

You don't have to type the source code for this chapter in by hand. In fact, it's a lot easier if you use the downloadable source (see Book 5, Chapter 2 for download instructions).

WARNING

It's essential that the `Colors.txt`, `Titanic.csv`, `Values.xls`, `Colorblk.jpg`, and `XMLData.xml` files that come with the downloadable source code appear in the same folder (directory) as your Notebook files. Otherwise, the examples in the following sections fail with an input/output (IO) error. The file location varies according to the platform you're using. For example, on a Windows system, you find the notebooks stored in the `C:\Users\`*Username*`\CAIO4D2E` folder, where *Username* is your login name. (The book assumes that you've used the prescribed folder location of `CAIO4D2E`, as described in the "Defining the code repository" section of Book 5, Chapter 2.) To make the examples work, simply upload the five files from the downloadable source folder into your Notebook folder.

Uploading, Streaming, and Sampling Data

Storing data in local computer memory represents the fastest and most reliable means to access it. The data could reside anywhere. However, you don't actually interact with the data in its storage location. You load the data into memory from the storage location and then interact with it in memory. This is the technique the book uses to access all the toy data sets found in the scikit-learn library.

REMEMBER

Data scientists call the columns in a database *features* or *variables*. The rows are *cases*. Each row represents a collection of variables that you can analyze.

Uploading small amounts of data into memory

The most convenient method that you can use to work with data is to load it directly into memory. This section uses the `Colors.txt` file, shown in Figure 3-1, for input.

FIGURE 3-1:
Format of the
`Colors.txt` file.

The example also relies on native Python functionality to get the task done. When you load a file (of any type), the entire data set is available at all times and the loading process is quite short. Listing 3-1 shows an example of how this technique works.

LISTING 3-1: **Loading the Colors Data Set**

```python
with open("Colors.txt", 'r') as open_file:
    print('Colors.txt content:\n' + open_file.read())
```

The example begins by using the `open()` method to obtain a `file` object. The `open()` function accepts the filename and an access mode. In this case, the access mode is read (`r`). It then uses the `read()` method of the file object to read all the data in the file. If you were to specify a size argument as part of `read()`, such as `read(15)`, Python would read only the number of characters that you specify or stop when it reaches the End Of File (`EOF`). When you run this example, you see the following output:

```
Colors.txt content:
Color Value
Red 1
Orange 2
```

```
Yellow 3
Green 4
Blue 5
Purple 6
Black 7
White 8
```

WARNING

The entire data set is loaded from the library into free memory. Of course, the loading process will fail if your system lacks sufficient memory to hold the data set. When this problem occurs, you need to consider other techniques for working with the data set, such as streaming it or sampling it. In short, before you use this technique, you must ensure that the data set will actually fit in memory. You won't normally experience any problems when working with the toy data sets in the scikit-learn library.

Streaming large amounts of data into memory

Some data sets will be so large that you won't be able to fit them entirely in memory at one time. In addition, you may find that some data sets load slowly because they reside on a remote site. Streaming answers both needs by making it possible to work with the data a little at a time. You download individual pieces, making it possible to work with just part of the data and to work with it as you receive it, rather than waiting for the entire data set to download. Listing 3-2 shows an example of how you can stream data using Python.

LISTING 3-2: **Streaming the Colors Data Set**

```python
with open("Colors.txt", 'r') as open_file:
    for observation in open_file:
        print('Reading Data: ' + observation)
```

This example relies on the Colors.txt file, which contains a header, and then a number of records that associate a color name with a value. The open_file file object contains a pointer to the open file.

As the code performs data reads in the for loop, the file pointer moves to the next record. Each record appears one at a time in observation. The code outputs the value in observation using a print statement. You should receive this output:

```
Reading Data: Color Value
Reading Data: Red 1
```

```
Reading Data: Orange 2
Reading Data: Yellow 3
Reading Data: Green 4
Reading Data: Blue 5
Reading Data: Purple 6
Reading Data: Black 7
Reading Data: White 8
```

Python streams each record from the source. This means that you must perform a read for each record you want.

Generating variations on image data

At times, you need to import and analyze image data. The source and type of the image does make a difference. A good starting point is to simply read a local image in, obtain statistics about that image, and display the image on-screen, as shown in Listing 3-3.

LISTING 3-3: **Importing and Analyzing an Image**

```
import matplotlib.image as img
import matplotlib.pyplot as plt
%matplotlib inline
image = img.imread("Colorblk.jpg")
print(image.shape)
print(image.size)
plt.imshow(image)
plt.show()
```

The example begins by importing two matplotlib libraries, image and pyplot. The image library reads the image into memory, while the pyplot library displays it on-screen.

After the code reads the file, it begins by displaying the image shape property — the number of horizontal pixels, vertical pixels, and pixel depth. Figure 3-2 shows that the image is 100 x 100 x 3 pixels. The image size property is the combination of these three elements, or 30,000 bytes.

The next step is to load the image for plotting using imshow(). The final call, plt. show(), displays the image on-screen, as shown in Figure 3-2. This technique represents just one of a number of methods for interacting with images using Python so that you can analyze them in some manner.

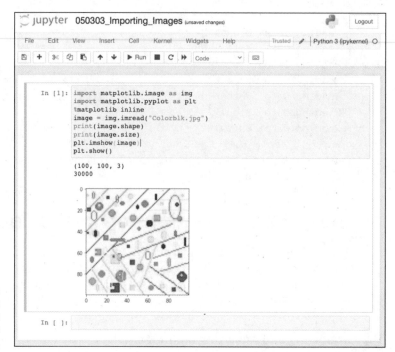

FIGURE 3-2:
The test image is
100 pixels high
and 100 pixels
long.

Sampling data in different ways

Data streaming obtains all the records from a data source. You may find that you
don't need all the records. You can save time and resources by simply sampling the
data. This means retrieving records a set number of records apart, such as every
fifth record, or by making random samples. Listing 3-4 shows how to retrieve
every other record in the Colors.txt file.

LISTING 3-4: **Retrieving Every Other Record**

```
n = 2
with open("Colors.txt", 'r') as open_file:
    for j, observation in enumerate(open_file):
        if j % n==0:
            print('Reading Line: ' + str(j) + ' Content: ' + observation)
```

The basic idea of sampling is the same as streaming. However, in this case, the
application uses enumerate() to retrieve a row number. When j % n == 0, the
row is one that you want to keep and the application outputs the information. In
this case, you see the following output:

```
Reading Line: 0 Content: Color Value
Reading Line: 2 Content: Orange 2
Reading Line: 4 Content: Green 4
Reading Line: 6 Content: Purple 6
Reading Line: 8 Content: White 8
```

The value of n is important in determining which records appear as part of the data set. Try changing n to 3. The output will change to sample just the header and rows 3 and 6.

You can perform random sampling as well. All you need to do is randomize the selector, as shown in Listing 3-5.

LISTING 3-5: **Random Sampling**

```python
from random import random
sample_size = 0.25
with open("Colors.txt", 'r') as open_file:
    for j, observation in enumerate(open_file):
        if random()<=sample_size:
            print('Reading Line: ' + str(j) + ' Content: ' + observation)
```

To make this form of selection work, you must import the random class. The random method outputs a value between 0 and 1. However, Python randomizes the output so that you don't know what value you receive. The sample_size variable contains a number between 0 and 1 to determine the sample size. For example, 0.25 selects 25 percent of the items in the file.

The output will still appear in numeric order. For example, you won't see Green come before Orange. However, the items selected are random, and you won't always get precisely the same number of return values. The spaces between return values will differ as well. Here is an example of what you might see as output (although your output will likely vary):

```
Reading Line: 1 Content: Red 1
Reading Line: 4 Content: Green 4
Reading Line: 8 Content: White 8
```

Working with Real Data

Accessing Data in Structured Flat-File Form

In many cases, the data you need to work with won't appear within a library, such as the toy data sets in the scikit-learn library. Real-world data usually appears in a file of some type. A flat file presents the easiest kind of file to work with. The data appears as a simple list of entries that you can read one at a time into memory. Depending on the requirements for your project, you can read all or part of the file.

A problem with using native Python techniques is that the input isn't intelligent. For example, when a file contains a header, Python simply reads it as yet more data to process, rather than as a header. You can't easily select a particular column of data. The pandas library used in the sections that follow makes it much easier to read and understand flat-file data. Classes and methods in the pandas library interpret (parse) the flat-file data to make it easier to manipulate.

REMEMBER

The least formatted and therefore easiest-to-read flat-file format is the text file. However, a text file also treats all data as strings, so you often have to convert numeric data into other forms. A comma-separated value (CSV) file provides more formatting and more information, but it requires a little more effort to read. At the high end of flat-file formatting are custom data formats, such as an Excel file, which contains extensive formatting and could include multiple data sets in a single file.

The following sections describe these three levels of flat-file data set and show how to use them. These sections assume that the file structures the data in some way. For example, the CSV file uses commas to separate data fields. A text file might rely on tabs to separate data fields. An Excel file uses a complex method to separate data fields and to provide a wealth of information about each field. You can work with unstructured data as well, but working with structured data is much easier because you know where each field begins and ends.

Reading from a text file

Text files can use a variety of storage formats. However, a common format is to have a header line that documents the purpose of each field, followed by another line for each record in the file. The file separates the fields using tabs. Refer to Figure 3-1 for an example of the `Colors.txt` file used for the example in this section.

Native Python provides a wide variety of methods you can use to read such a file. However, it's far easier to let someone else do the work. In this case, you can use the pandas library to perform the task. Within the pandas library, you find a set of *parsers*, code used to read individual bits of data and determine the purpose of each bit according to the format of the entire file. Using the correct parser is essential if you want to make sense of file content. In this case, you use the `read_table` method to accomplish the task, as shown in Listing 3-6.

LISTING 3-6: **Using read_table**

```
import pandas as pd
color_table = pd.io.parsers.read_table("Colors.txt")
print(color_table)
```

The code imports the pandas library, uses the `read_table` method to read `Colors.txt` into a variable named `color_table`, and then displays the resulting memory data on-screen using the `print` function. Figure 3-3 shows the output from Listing 3-6.

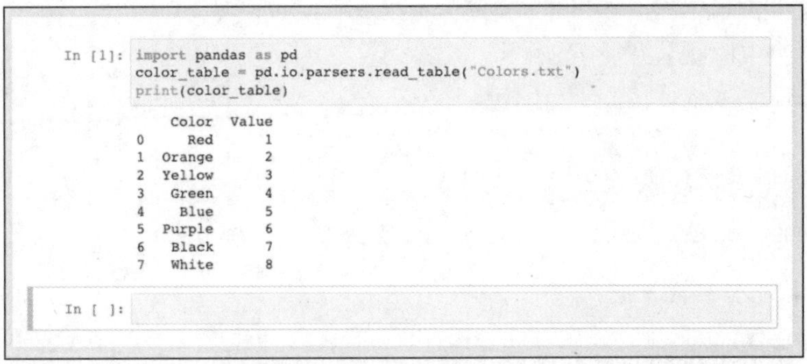

FIGURE 3-3:
Reading a table
with pandas.

© John Wiley & Sons

Notice that the parser correctly interprets the first row as consisting of field names. It numbers the records from 0 through 7. Using `read_table()` method arguments, you can adjust how the parser interprets the input file, but the default settings usually work best. You can read more about the `read_table()` arguments at `http://pandas.pydata.org/pandas-docs/version/0.23.0/generated/pandas.read_table.html`.

Reading CSV-delimited format

A CSV file provides more formatting than a simple text file. In fact, CSV files can become quite complicated. There is a standard that defines the format of CSV files, and you can see it at `https://tools.ietf.org/html/rfc4180`. The CSV file used for this example is quite simple:

>> A header defines each of the fields

>> Fields are separated by commas

>> Records are separated by linefeeds

>> Strings are enclosed in double quotes

>> Integers and real numbers appear without double quotes

Figure 3-4 shows the raw format for the `Titanic.csv` file used for this example. You can see the raw format using any text editor.

FIGURE 3-4:
The raw format of a CSV file is still text and quite readable.

© John Wiley & Sons

Applications such as Excel can import and format CSV files so that they become easier to read. Figure 3-5 shows the same file in Excel.

FIGURE 3-5:
Use an application such as Excel to create a formatted CSV presentation.

© John Wiley & Sons

Excel actually recognizes the header as a header. If you were to use features such as data sorting, you could select header columns to obtain the desired result. Fortunately, pandas also makes it possible to work with the CSV file as formatted data, as shown in Listing 3-7.

LISTING 3-7: **Using pandas with a CSV File**

```
import pandas as pd
titanic = pd.io.parsers.read_csv("Titanic.csv")
X = titanic[['age']]
print(X)
```

Notice that the parser of choice this time is read_csv(), which understands CSV files and provides you with new options for working with it. (You can read more about this parser at http://pandas.pydata.org/pandas-docs/version/0.23.0/generated/pandas.read_csv.html.) Selecting a specific field is quite easy — you just supply the field name as shown. The output from Listing 3-7 is shown in Figure 3-6.

```
In [1]: import pandas as pd
        titanic = pd.io.parsers.read_csv("Titanic.csv")
        X = titanic[['age']]
        print(X)

              age
        0     29.0000
        1      0.9167
        2      2.0000
        3     30.0000
        4     25.0000
        ...      ...
        1304  14.5000
        1305  9999.0000
        1306  26.5000
        1307  27.0000
        1308  29.0000

        [1309 rows x 1 columns]

In [ ]:
```

FIGURE 3-6:
The result of loading a CSV with pandas.

© John Wiley & Sons

TIP

Of course, a human-readable output like this one is nice when working through an example, but you might also need the output as a list. To create the output as a list, you simply change the third line of code to read X = titanic[['age']].values. Notice the addition of the values property. The resulting output is shown in Figure 3-7.

```
In [1]: import pandas as pd
        titanic = pd.io.parsers.read_csv("Titanic.csv")
        X = titanic[['age']].values
        print(X)

        [[29.        ]
         [ 0.91670001]
         [ 2.        ]
         ...
         [26.5       ]
         [27.        ]
         [29.        ]]

In [ ]:
```

FIGURE 3-7:
Displaying results
as a list.

© John Wiley & Sons

Reading Excel and other Microsoft Office files

Excel and other Microsoft Office applications provide highly formatted content. You can specify every aspect of the information these files contain. The Values.xls file used for this example provides a listing of sine, cosine, and tangent values for a random list of angles. You can see this file in Figure 3-8.

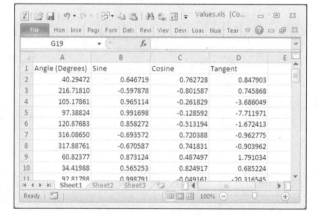

FIGURE 3-8:
An Excel file is
highly formatted
and might
contain
information of
various types.

© John Wiley & Sons

When you work with Excel or other Microsoft Office products, you begin to experience some complexity. For example, an Excel file can contain more than one worksheet, so you need to tell pandas which worksheet to process. In fact, you can choose to process multiple worksheets, if desired. When working with other Office products, you have to be specific about what to process. Just telling pandas to process something isn't good enough. Listing 3-8 shows an example of working with the Values.xls file.

LISTING 3-8: **Working with an Excel File**

```
import pandas as pd
xls = pd.ExcelFile("Values.xls")
trig_values = xls.parse('Sheet1', index_col=None, na_values=['NA'])
print(trig_values)
```

The code begins by importing the pandas library as normal. It then creates a pointer to the Excel file using the `ExcelFile` constructor. This pointer, `xls`, lets you access a worksheet, define an index column, and specify how to present empty values. The index column is the one that the worksheet uses to index the records. Using a value of `None` means that pandas should generate an index for you. The `parse` method obtains the values you request. You can read more about the Excel parser options at `https://pandas.pydata.org/pandas-docs/stable/reference/api/pandas.ExcelFile.parse.html`.

TIP

You don't absolutely have to use the two-step process of obtaining a file pointer and then parsing the content. You can also perform the task using a single step like this:

```
trig_values = pd.read_excel("Values.xls", 'Sheet1', index_col=None,
    na_values=['NA'])
```

Because Excel files are more complex, using the two-step process is often more convenient and efficient because you don't have to reopen the file for each read of the data.

Sending Data in Unstructured File Form

Unstructured data files consist of a series of bits. The file doesn't separate the bits from each other in any way. You can't simply look into the file and see any structure because there isn't any to see. Unstructured file formats rely on the file user to know how to interpret the data. For example, each pixel of a picture file could consist of three 32-bit fields. Knowing that each field is 32-bits is up to you. A header at the beginning of the file may provide clues about interpreting the file, but even so, it's up to you to know how to interact with the file.

The example in this section shows how to work with a picture as an unstructured file. The example image is a public domain offering from `http://commons.wikimedia.org/wiki/Main_Page`. To work with images, you need to access the scikit-image library (`http://scikit-image.org/`), which is a free-of-charge collection of algorithms used for image processing. You can find a tutorial for this library at http://scipy-lectures.github.io/packages/scikit-image/. The first task is to be able to display the image on-screen using the code in Listing 3-9. (This code can require a little time to run. The image is ready when the busy indicator disappears from the Notebook tab.)

LISTING 3-9: **Image Processing with the scikit-image Library**

```
from skimage.io import imread
from skimage.transform import resize
from matplotlib import pyplot as plt
import matplotlib.cm as cm
example_file = ("http://upload.wikimedia.org/wikipedia/commons/7/7d/Dog_face.
    png")
image = imread(example_file, as_gray=True)
plt.imshow(image, cmap=cm.gray)
plt.show()
```

The code begins by importing a number of libraries. It then creates a string that points to the example file online and places it in example_file. This string is part of the imread() method call, along with as_gray, which is set to True. The as_gray argument tells Python to turn any color images into grayscale. Any images that are already in grayscale remain that way.

Now that you have an image loaded, it's time to render it (make it ready to display on-screen). The imshow() function performs the rendering and uses a grayscale color map. The show() function actually displays image for you, as shown in Figure 3-9.

You now have an image in memory and you may want to find out more about it. When you run the following code, you discover the image type and size:

```
print("data type: %s, shape: %s" %
(type(image), image.shape))
```

The output from this call tells you that the image type is a numpy.ndarray and that the image size is 90 pixels by 90 pixels. The image is actually an array of pixels that you can manipulate in various ways. For example, if you want to crop the image, you can use the following code to manipulate the image array:

```
image2 = image[5:70,0:70]
plt.imshow(image2, cmap=cm.gray)
plt.show()
```

FIGURE 3-9:
The image appears on-screen after you render and show it.

© John Wiley & Sons

The `numpy.ndarray` in `image2` is smaller than the one in `image`, so the output is smaller as well. Figure 3-10 shows typical results. The purpose of cropping the image is to make it a specific size. Both images must be the same size for you to analyze them. Cropping is one way to ensure that the images are the correct size for analysis.

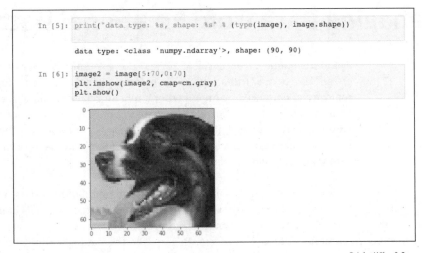

FIGURE 3-10:
Cropping the image makes it smaller.

© John Wiley & Sons

Another method that you can use to change the image size is to resize it. The following code resizes the image to a specific size for analysis:

```
image3 = resize(image2, (30, 30), mode='symmetric')
plt.imshow(image3, cmap=cm.gray)
print("data type: %s, shape: %s" %
(type(image3), image3.shape))
```

The output from the `print()` function tells you that the image is now 30 pixels by 30 pixels in size. You can compare it to any image with the same dimensions.

After you have all the images the right size, you need to flatten them. A data set row is always a single dimension, not two dimensions. The image is currently an array of 30 pixels by 30 pixels, so you can't make it part of a data set. The following code flattens `image3` so that it becomes an array of 900 elements that is stored in `image_row`.

```
image_row = image3.flatten()
print("data type: %s, shape: %s" %
(type(image_row), image_row.shape))
```

Notice that the type is still a `numpy.ndarray`. You can add this array to a data set and then use the data set for analysis purposes. The size is 900 elements, as anticipated.

Managing Data from Relational Databases

Databases come in all sorts of forms. For example, AskSam (http://asksam. en.softonic.com/) is a kind of free-form textual database. However, the vast majority of data used by organizations rely on relational databases because these databases provide the means for organizing massive amounts of complex data in an organized manner that makes the data easy to manipulate. The goal of a database manager is to make data easy to manipulate. The focus of most data storage is to make data easy to retrieve.

REMEMBER

Relational databases accomplish both the manipulation and data retrieval objectives with relative ease. However, because data storage needs come in all shapes and sizes for a wide range of computing platforms, there are many different relational database products. In fact, for the data scientist, the proliferation of different Database Management Systems (DBMSs) using various data layouts is one of the main problems you encounter with creating a comprehensive data set for analysis.

The one common denominator between many relational databases is that they all rely on a form of the same language to perform data manipulation, which does make the data scientist's job easier. The Structured Query Language (SQL) lets you perform all sorts of management tasks in a relational database, retrieve data as needed, and even shape it in a particular way so that the need to perform additional shaping is unnecessary.

Creating a connection to a database can be a complex undertaking. For one thing, you need to know how to connect to that particular database. However, you can divide the process into smaller pieces. The first step is to gain access to the database engine. You use two lines of code similar to the following code (but the code presented here is not meant to execute and perform a task):

```
from sqlalchemy import create_engine
engine = create_engine('sqlite:///:memory:')
```

After you have access to an engine, you can use the engine to perform tasks specific to that DBMS. The output of a read method is always a DataFrame object that contains the requested data. To write data, you must create a DataFrame object or use an existing one. You normally use these methods to perform most tasks:

>> read_sql_table(): Reads data from a SQL table to a DataFrame object

>> read_sql_query(): Reads data from a database using a SQL query to a DataFrame object

>> read_sql(): Reads data from either a SQL table or query to a DataFrame object

>> DataFrame.to_sql(): Writes the content of a DataFrame object to the specified tables in the database

The sqlalchemy library provides support for a broad range of SQL databases. The following list contains just a few of them:

>> SQLite

>> MySQL

>> PostgreSQL

>> SQL Server

>> Other relational databases, such as those you can connect to using Open Database Connectivity (ODBC)

You can discover more about working with databases at `https://docs.sqlalchemy.org/en/latest/core/engines.html`. The techniques that you discover in this book using the toy databases also work with relational databases.

Interacting with Data from NoSQL Databases

In addition to standard relational databases that rely on SQL, you find a wealth of databases of all sorts that don't have to rely on SQL. These Not only SQL (NoSQL) databases are used in large data storage scenarios in which the relational model can become overly complex or can break down in other ways. The databases generally don't use the relational model. Of course, you find fewer of these DBMSes used in the corporate environment because they require special handling and training. Still, some common DBMSes are used because they provide special functionality or meet unique requirements. The process is essentially the same for using NoSQL databases as it is for relational databases:

1. Import required database engine functionality.

2. Create a database engine.

3. Make any required queries using the database engine and the functionality supported by the DBMS.

The details vary quite a bit, and you need to know which library to use with your particular database product. For example, when working with MongoDB (`www.mongodb.org`), you must obtain a copy of the PyMongo library (`https://pymongo.readthedocs.io/en/stable/`) and use the `MongoClient` class to create the required engine.

The MongoDB engine relies heavily on the `find()` function to locate data. Following is a pseudocode example of a MongoDB session. (You won't be able to execute this code in Notebook; it's shown only as an example.)

```
import pymongo
import pandas as pd
from pymongo import Connection
connection = Connection()
db = connection.database_name
input_data = db.collection_name
data = pd.DataFrame(list(input_data.find()))
```

Accessing Data from the Web

It would be incredibly difficult (perhaps impossible) to find an organization today that doesn't rely on some sort of web-based data. Most organizations use web services of some type. A *web service* is a kind of web application that provides a means to ask questions and receive answers. Web services usually host a number of input types. In fact, a particular web service may host entire groups of query inputs.

Another type of query system is the microservice. Unlike the web service, *microservices* have a specific focus and provide only one specific query input and output. Using microservices has specific benefits that are outside the scope of this book to address, but essentially they work like tiny web services, so that's how this book addresses them.

Accessing XML data

One of the most beneficial data access techniques to know when working with web data is accessing XML. All sorts of content types rely on XML, even some web pages. Working with web services and microservices often means working with XML. With this in mind, the example in this section works with XML data found in the XMLData.xml file, shown in Figure 3-11. In this case, the file is simple and uses only a couple of levels. XML is hierarchical and can become quite a few levels deep.

APIs AND OTHER WEB ENTITIES

A data scientist may have a reason to rely on various web Application Programming Interfaces (APIs) to access and manipulate data. In fact, the focus of an analysis might be the API itself. This book doesn't discuss APIs in any detail because each API is unique, and APIs operate outside the normal scope of what a data scientist might do. For example, you might use a the JavaScript Fetch API or Axios (www.axios.com) to access data; then you can manipulate it in various ways using JavaScript when working with a web application. However, the techniques for doing so are more along the lines of writing an application than employing a data science technique.

It's important to realize that APIs can be data sources and that you might need to use one to achieve some data input or data-shaping goals. In fact, you find many data entities that resemble APIs but don't appear in this book. Windows developers can create Component Object Model (COM) applications that output data onto the web that you could possibly use for analysis purposes. In fact, the number of potential sources is nearly endless. This book focuses on the sources that you use most often and in the most conventional manner. Keeping your eyes open for other possibilities, though, is always a good idea.

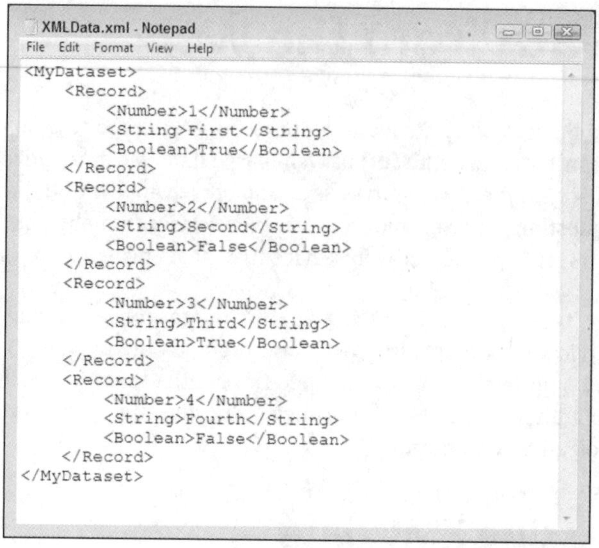

FIGURE 3-11:
XML is a hierarchical format that can become quite complex.

© John Wiley & Sons

The technique for working with XML, even simple XML, can be a bit harder than anything else you've worked with so far. Listing 3-10 shows the code for this example.

LISTING 3-10: **Working with XML Data**

```python
from lxml import objectify
import pandas as pd
xml = objectify.parse(open('XMLData.xml'))
root = xml.getroot()
df = pd.DataFrame(columns=('Number', 'String', 'Boolean'))

for i in range(0,4):
    obj = root.getchildren()[i].getchildren()
    row = dict(zip(['Number', 'String', 'Boolean'],[obj[0].text, obj[1].text,
obj[2].text]))
    row_s = pd.Series(row)
    row_s.name = i
    df = df.append(row_s)

print(df)
```

The example begins by importing libraries and parsing the data file using the objectify.parse() method. Every XML document must contain a root node, which is <MyDataset> in this case. The root node encapsulates the rest of the content, and every node under it is a child. To do anything practical with the document, you must obtain access to the root node using the getroot() method.

The next step is to create an empty DataFrame object that contains the correct column names for each record entry: Number, String, and Boolean. As with all other pandas data handling, XML data handling relies on a DataFrame. The for loop fills the DataFrame with the four records from the XML file (each in a <Record> node).

The process looks complex but follows a logical order. The obj variable contains all the children for one <Record> node. These children are loaded into a dictionary object in which the keys are Number, String, and Boolean to match the DataFrame columns.

There is now a dictionary object that contains the row data. The code creates an actual row for the DataFrame next. It gives the row the value of the current for loop iteration. It then appends the row to the DataFrame. To see that everything worked as expected, the code prints the result, which looks like this:

```
   Number  String  Boolean
0       1   First     True
1       2  Second    False
2       3   Third     True
3       4  Fourth    False
```

Using read_xml

If you're using a pandas version 1.4 or newer, you'll get a warning message when you run the previous code. The message says that the append method is deprecated and will be removed in a future version. If your code runs and produces the correct output, the warning message is nothing to worry about.

If you do see this warning message, or if you're reading this book in a far future time when the append method actually is removed from pandas, you can use a much easier method of working with XML data: the pandas.read_xml method. Listing 3-11 shows how to do the same thing as Listing 3-10, but using read_xml instead.

LISTING 3-11: **Using pandas.read_xml**

```
import pandas as pd
df = pd.read_xml('XMLData.xml')

print(df)
```

USING THE JSON ALTERNATIVE

You shouldn't get the idea that all data you work with on the web is in XML format. You may need to consider other popular alternatives as part of your development plans. One of the most popular today is JavaScript Object Notation (JSON) (www.json.org), which you learned about in Book 4, Chapter 8. JSON usually takes less space, is faster to use, and is easier to work with than XML (see www.w3schools.com/js/js_json_xml.asp for details). Consequently, you may find that your next project relies on JSON output, rather than XML, when dealing with certain web services and microservices.

If your data formatting choices consisted of just XML and JSON, you might feel that interacting with data is quite manageable. However, a lot of other people have ideas of how to format data so that you can parse it quickly and easily. In addition, developers now have a stronger emphasis on understanding the data stream, so some formatting techniques emphasize human readability. You can read about some of these other alternatives at https://insights.dice.com/2018/01/05/5-xml-alternatives-to-consider/. One of the more important of these alternatives is YAML — Yet Another Markup Language or YAML Ain't Markup Language, depending on whom you talk to and which resources you use (https://yaml.org/spec/1.2.2/). Be prepared to do your homework when working through the particulars of any new projects.

Yes, that's really all there is to it! If you get an error when you try to run Listing 3-11, you can upgrade to the latest version of pandas by entering the following command into the Terminal (on macOS or Linux) or the Anaconda Prompt (on Windows):

```
pip install pandas --upgrade
```

6
Data Analysis with Python

Contents at a Glance

Chapter **1**

Conditioning Your Data

"In God we trust. All others must bring data."

— W. EDWARDS DEMING

The characteristics, content, type, and other elements that define your data in its entirety make up the data's *shape*. The shape of your data determines the kinds of tasks you can perform with it. In order to make your data amenable to certain types of analysis, you must shape it into a different form. Think of the data as clay and you as the potter, because that's the sort of relationship that exists. However, instead of using your hands to shape the data, you rely on functions and algorithms to perform the task. This chapter helps you understand the tools you have available to shape data and the ramifications of shaping it.

Also in this chapter, you consider the problems associated with shaping. For example, you need to know what to do when data is missing from a data set. It's important to shape the data correctly or you end up with an analysis that simply doesn't make sense. Likewise, some data types, such as dates, can present problems. Again, you need to tread carefully to ensure that you get the desired result so that the data set becomes more useful and amenable to analysis of various sorts.

The goal of some types of data shaping is to create a larger data set. In many cases, the data you need to perform an analysis on doesn't appear in a single database or in a particular form. You need to shape the data and then combine it so that you have a single data set in a known format before you can begin the analysis. Combining data successfully can be an art form because data often defies simple analysis or quick fixes.

You don't have to type the source code for this chapter by hand. In fact, it's a lot easier if you use the downloadable source. The source code for this chapter appears in the CAIO4DE2_0601_Getting Your Data in Shape.ipynb source code file available at www.dummies.com/go/codingallinonefd2e.

Juggling between NumPy and pandas

One of the most essential tools for working with data in Python is NumPy. NumPy is a library for working with arrays of data. There is no question that you need NumPy at all times. In fact, the pandas library, which you learned about in Book 5, Chapter 3, is built on top of NumPy. However, you do need to choose between NumPy and pandas when performing tasks. You need the low-level functionality of NumPy to perform some tasks, but pandas makes things so much easier that you'll want to use it as often as possible. The following sections describe when to use each library in more detail.

Knowing when to use NumPy

It's essential to realize that developers built pandas on top of NumPy. As a result, every task you perform using pandas also goes through NumPy. To obtain the benefits of pandas, you may pay a performance penalty that some testers say is 100 times slower than NumPy for a similar task (see https://penandpants.com/2014/09/05/performance-of-pandas-series-vs-numpy-arrays). Given that computer hardware can make up for a lot of performance differences today, the speed issue may not be a concern at times, but when speed is essential, NumPy is always the better choice.

Knowing when to use pandas

You use pandas to make writing code easier and faster. Because pandas does a lot of the work for you, you could make a case for saying that using pandas also reduces the potential for coding errors. The essential consideration, though, is that the pandas library provides rich time-series functionality, data alignment, NA-friendly statistics, groupby, merge, and join methods. Normally, you need to code these features when using NumPy, which means you keep reinventing the wheel.

IT'S ALL IN THE PREPARATION

This book may seem to spend a lot of time massaging data and little time on actually analyzing it. However, the majority of a data scientist's time is spent preparing data because the data is seldom in any order to perform analysis. To prepare data for use, a data scientist must

- Get the data.

- Aggregate the data.

- Create data subsets.

- Clean the data.

- Develop a single data set by merging various data sets together.

Fortunately, you don't need to die of boredom while wading your way through these various tasks. Using Python and the various libraries it provides makes the task a lot simpler, faster, and more efficient. The better you know how to use Python to speed your way through these repetitive tasks, the sooner you begin having fun performing various sorts of analysis on the data.

As this book progresses, you'll discover just how useful pandas can be for performing such tasks as *binning* (a data preprocessing technique designed to reduce the effect of observational errors) and working with a *data frame* (a two-dimensional labeled data structure with columns that can potentially contain different data types) so that you can calculate statistics on it. All you need to know at this point is that pandas makes your work considerably easier.

Validating Your Data

When it comes to data, no one really knows what a large database contains. Yes, everyone has seen bits and pieces of it, but when you consider the size of some databases, viewing it all would be physically impossible. Because you don't know what's in there, you can't be sure that your analysis will actually work as desired and provide valid results. In short, you must validate your data before you use it to ensure that the data is at least close to what you expect it to be. This means performing tasks such as removing duplicate records before you use the data for any sort of analysis (duplicates would unfairly weight the results).

CHECKING YOUR VERSION OF PANDAS

The examples in this section depend on your having a minimum version of pandas 0.23.0 installed on your system. However, your version of Anaconda may have a previous pandas version installed instead. Use the following code to check your version of pandas:

```
import pandas as pd
print(pd.__version__)
```

You see the version number of pandas you have installed. Another way to check the version is to open the Anaconda Prompt, type `pip show pandas`, and press Enter. If you have an older version, open the Anaconda Prompt, type `pip install pandas --upgrade`, and press Enter. The update process will occur automatically, along with a check of associated packages. When working with Windows, you may need to open the Anaconda prompt using the Administrator option (right-click the Anaconda Prompt entry in the Start menu and choose Run as Administrator from the context menu).

The latest version of pandas that the code in this book has been tested on is version 1.3.5. If you have a newer version, you may see errors or warnings when you run the code. To downgrade your version of pandas, open the Anaconda Prompt and type `conda install -c conda-forge pandas=1.3.5`. Whether you upgrade or downgrade, you'll need to restart Jupyter Notebook for the change to take effect.

REMEMBER

However, you do need to consider what validation actually does for you. It doesn't tell you that the data is correct or that there won't be values outside the expected range. Validation ensures that you can perform an analysis of the data and reasonably expect that analysis to succeed. Later, you need to perform additional data massaging to obtain the sort of results that you need.

Figuring out what's in your data

Figuring out what your data contains is important because checking data by hand is sometimes simply impossible due to the number of observations and variables. In addition, hand verifying the content is time consuming, error prone, and, most important, really boring. Finding duplicates is important because you end up

>> Spending more computational time to process duplicates, which slows your algorithms down.

>> Obtaining false results because duplicates implicitly overweigh the results. Because some entries appear more than once, the algorithm considers these entries more important.

As a data scientist, you want your data to enthrall you, so it's time to get it to talk to you — not figuratively, of course, but through the wonders of pandas, as shown in Listing 1-1.

LISTING 1-1: **Figuring Out What's In Your Data**

```
from lxml import objectify
import pandas as pd
xml = objectify.parse(open('XMLData2.xml'))
root = xml.getroot()
df = pd.DataFrame(columns=('Number', 'String', 'Boolean'))
for i in range(0,4):
    obj = root.getchildren()[i].getchildren()
    row = dict(zip(['Number', 'String', 'Boolean'],
                    [obj[0].text, obj[1].text,
                     obj[2].text]))
    row_s = pd.Series(row)
    row_s.name = i
    df = df.append(row_s)

search = pd.DataFrame.duplicated(df)
print(df)
print()
print(search[search == True])
```

This example shows how to find duplicate rows. It relies on a modified version of the XMLData.xml file, XMLData2.xml, which contains a simple repeated row in it. A real data file contains thousands (or more) of records and possibly hundreds of repeats, but this simple example does the job. The example begins by reading the data file into memory using the same technique you explore in Book 6, Chapter 2. It then places the data into a DataFrame.

TIP

Place the XMLData2.xml data file in the same directory as your Python program.

At this point, your data is corrupted because it contains a duplicate row. However, you can get rid of the duplicated row by searching for it. The first task is to create a search object containing a list of duplicated rows by calling pd.DataFrame.duplicated(). The duplicated rows contain a True next to their row number.

Of course, now you have an unordered list of rows that are and aren't duplicated. The easiest way to determine which rows are duplicated is to create an index in which you use search == True as the expression. Following is the output you see

Conditioning Your Data

from this example. Notice that row 1 is duplicated in the `DataFrame` output and that row 1 is also called out in the `search` results:

```
   Number String Boolean
0       1  First    True
1       1  First    True
2       2 Second   False
3       3  Third    True
1    True
dtype: bool
```

DEALING WITH DEPRECATED LIBRARY ISSUES

One of the major advantages of working with Python is the huge number of packages that it supports. Unfortunately, not every package receives updates quickly enough to avoid using deprecated features in other packages. A *deprecated feature* is one that still exists in the target package, but the developers of that package plan to remove it in an upcoming update. Consequently, you receive a deprecated package warning when you run your code. Even though the deprecation warning doesn't keep your code from running, it does tend to make people leery of your application. After all, no one wants to see what appears to be an error message as part of the output. The fact that Notebook displays these messages in light red by default doesn't help matters.

These messages look something like this:

```
/var/folders/cf/tfv1tkwj5mq_nvkcxn0fdjzr0000gn/T/
    ipykernel_3375/957726744.py:13: FutureWarning: The frame.
    append method is deprecated and will be removed from pandas
    in a future version. Use pandas.concat instead.
```

One way to deal with this problem is to downgrade your version of pandas, as mentioned in the Checking Your Version of Pandas sidebar, by using the following command at the Anaconda prompt:

```
conda install -c conda-forge pandas=1.3.5
```

The problem with this approach is that it can also cause problems for any code that uses the newer features found in the latest versions of pandas.

Another solution is to simply admit that the problem exists by documenting it as part of your code. Documenting the problem and its specific cause makes it easier to check for the problem later after a package update. To do this, you add the two lines of code shown here:

```
import warnings
warnings.filterwarnings("ignore")
```

The call to `filterwarnings()` performs the specified action, which is `"ignore"` in this case. To cancel the effects of filtering the warnings, you call `resetwarnings()`. Notice that the `module` attribute is the same as the source of the problems in the warning messages. You can also define a broader filter by using the `category` attribute. This particular call is narrow, affecting only one module.

Removing duplicates

To get a clean data set, you want to remove the duplicates. Fortunately, you don't have to write any weird code to get the job done — pandas does it for you, as shown in Listing 1-2.

LISTING 1-2: **Removing Duplicates**

```
from lxml import objectify
import pandas as pd

xml = objectify.parse(open('XMLData2.xml'))
root = xml.getroot()
df = pd.DataFrame(columns=('Number', 'String', 'Boolean'))
for i in range(0,4):
    obj = root.getchildren()[i].getchildren()
    row = dict(zip(['Number', 'String', 'Boolean'],
                   [obj[0].text, obj[1].text,
                    obj[2].text]))
    row_s = pd.Series(row)
    row_s.name = i
    df = df.append(row_s)

print(df.drop_duplicates())
```

As with the previous example, you begin by creating a DataFrame that contains the duplicate record. To remove the errant record, all you need to do is call drop_duplicates(). Here's the result you get:

```
   Number String Boolean
0       1  First    True
2       2 Second   False
3       3  Third    True
```

Creating a data map and data plan

You need to know about your data set — that is, how it looks statically. A *data map* is an overview of the data set. You use it to spot potential problems in your data, such as

>> Redundant variables

>> Possible errors

>> Missing values

>> Variable transformations

Checking for these problems goes into a *data plan*, which is a list of tasks you have to perform to ensure the integrity of your data. Listing 1-3 shows a data map, A, with two data sets, B and C.

LISTING 1-3: **Creating a Data Map and Data Plan**

```
import pandas as pd
pd.set_option('display.width', 55)
df = pd.DataFrame({'A': [0,0,0,0,0,1,1],
'B': [1,2,3,5,4,2,5],
'C': [5,3,4,1,1,2,3]})
a_group_desc = df.groupby('A').describe()
print(a_group_desc)
```

In this case, the data map uses 0s for the first series and 1s for the second series. The groupby() function places the data sets, B and C, into groups. To determine whether the data map is viable, you obtain statistics using describe(). What you end up with is a data set B, series 0 and 1, and data set C, series 0 and 1, as shown in the following output:

```
        B                                                      \
   count mean           std  min   25%  50%   75%  max
A
0    5.0  3.0  1.581139  1.0  2.00  3.0  4.00  5.0
1    2.0  3.5  2.121320  2.0  2.75  3.5  4.25  5.0


        C
   count mean           std  min   25%  50%   75%  max
A
0    5.0  2.8  1.788854  1.0  1.00  3.0  4.00  5.0
1    2.0  2.5  0.707107  2.0  2.25  2.5  2.75  3.0
```

These statistics tell you about the two data set series. The breakup of the two data sets using specific cases is the *data plan*. As you can see, the statistics tell you that this data plan may not be viable because some statistics are relatively far apart.

The default output from `describe()` shows the data unstacked. Unfortunately, the unstacked data can print out with an unfortunate break, making it very hard to read. To keep this from happening, you can set the width you want to use for the data by calling `pd.set_option('display.width', 55)`. You can set a number of pandas options this way, by using the information found at `https://pandas.pydata.org/pandas-docs/stable/generated/pandas.set_option.html`.

Although the unstacked data is relatively easy to read and compare, you may prefer a more compact presentation. In this case, you can stack the data using the following code:

```
stacked = a_group_desc.stack()
print(stacked)
```

Using `unstack()` creates a new presentation. Here's the output shown in a compact form:

```
              B         C
A
0 count  5.000000  5.000000
  mean   3.000000  2.800000
  std    1.581139  1.788854
  min    1.000000  1.000000
  25%    2.000000  1.000000
  50%    3.000000  3.000000
  75%    4.000000  4.000000
  max    5.000000  5.000000
1 count  2.000000  2.000000
  mean   3.500000  2.500000
  std    2.121320  0.707107
```

```
     min    2.000000  2.000000
     25%    2.750000  2.250000
     50%    3.500000  2.500000
     75%    4.250000  2.750000
     max    5.000000  3.000000
```

Of course, you may not want all the data that describe() provides. Perhaps you really just want to see the number of items in each series and their mean. Here's how you reduce the size of the information output:

```
print(a_group_desc.loc[:,(slice(None),['count','mean']),])
```

Using loc lets you obtain specific columns. Here's the final output from the example showing just the information you absolutely need to make a decision:

```
         B           C
    count mean count mean
A
0    5.0  3.0   5.0  2.8
1    2.0  3.5   2.0  2.5
```

Manipulating Categorical Variables

In data science, a *categorical variable* is one that has a specific value from a limited selection of values. The number of values is usually fixed. Many developers will know categorical variables by the moniker *enumerations*. Each of the potential values that a categorical variable can assume is a *level*.

To understand how categorical variables work, say that you have a variable expressing the color of an object, such as a car, and that the user can select blue, red, or green. To express the car's color in a way that computers can represent and effectively compute, an application assigns each color a numeric value, so blue is 1, red is 2, and green is 3. Normally when you print each color, you see the value rather than the color.

If you use pandas.DataFrame (http://pandas.pydata.org/pandas-docs/dev/generated/pandas.DataFrame.html), you can still see the symbolic value (blue, red, and green), even though the computer stores it as a numeric value. Sometimes you need to rename and combine these named values to create new symbols. Symbolic variables are just a convenient way of representing and storing qualitative data.

When using categorical variables for machine learning, it's important to consider the algorithm used to manipulate the variables. Some algorithms can work directly with the numeric variables behind the symbols, while other algorithms require that you encode the categorical values into binary variables. For example, if you have three levels for a color variable (blue, red, and green), you have to create three binary variables:

- » One for blue (1 when the value is blue, 0 when it is not)
- » One for red (1 when the value is red, 0 when it is not)
- » One for green (1 when the value is green, 0 when it is not)

Creating categorical variables

Categorical variables have a specific number of values, which makes them incredibly valuable in performing a number of data science tasks. For example, imagine trying to find values that are out of range in a huge data set. In Listing 1-4, you see one method for creating a categorical variable and then using it to check whether some data falls within the specified limits.

LISTING 1-4: **Creating Categorical Variables**

```
import pandas as pd

car_colors = pd.Series(['Blue', 'Red', 'Green'],dtype='category')

car_data = pd.Series(
    pd.Categorical(['Yellow', 'Green', 'Red', 'Blue', 'Purple'],
                   categories=car_colors, ordered=False))
find_entries = pd.isnull(car_data)
print(car_colors)
print()
print(car_data)
print()
print(find_entries[find_entries == True])
```

The example begins by creating a categorical variable, car_colors. The variable contains the values Blue, Red, and Green as colors that are acceptable for a car. Notice that you must specify a dtype property value of category.

The next step is to create another series. This one uses a list of actual car colors, named car_data, as input. Not all the car colors match the predefined acceptable values. When this problem occurs, pandas outputs Not a Number (NaN) instead of the car color.

Of course, you could search the list manually for the nonconforming cars, but the easiest method is to have pandas do the work for you. In this case, you ask pandas which entries are null using `isnull()` and place them in `find_entries`. You can then output just those entries that are actually null. Here's the output you see from the example:

```
0 Blue
1 Red
2 Green
dtype: category
Categories (3, object): [Blue, Green, Red]
0 NaN
1 Green
2 Red
3 Blue
4 NaN
dtype: category
Categories (3, object): [Blue, Green, Red]
0 True
4 True
dtype: bool
```

Looking at the list of `car_data` outputs, you can see that entries 0 and 4 equal NaN. The output from `find_entries` verifies this fact for you. If this were a large data set, you could quickly locate and correct errant entries in the data set before performing an analysis on it.

Renaming levels

There are times when the category names you use are inconvenient or otherwise wrong for a particular need. Fortunately, you can rename the categories as needed using the technique shown in Listing 1-5.

LISTING 1-5: **Renaming Levels**

```
import pandas as pd

car_colors = pd.Series(['Blue', 'Red', 'Green'],
                       dtype='category')
car_data = pd.Series(
    pd.Categorical(
        ['Blue', 'Green', 'Red', 'Blue', 'Red'],
        categories=car_colors, ordered=False))
```

```
car_colors.cat.categories = ["Purple", "Yellow", "Mauve"]
car_data.cat.categories = car_colors

print(car_data)
```

All you need to do is set the `cat.categories` property to a new value, as shown. Here is the output from this example:

```
0 Purple
1 Yellow
2 Mauve
3 Purple
4 Mauve
dtype: category
Categories (3, object): [Purple, Yellow, Mauve]
```

Combining levels

A particular categorical level might be too small to offer significant data for analysis. Perhaps there are only a few of the values, which may not be enough to create a statistical difference. In this case, combining several small categories might offer better analysis results. Listing 1-6 shows how to combine categories.

LISTING 1-6: **Combining Levels**

```
import pandas as pd

car_colors = pd.Series(['Blue', 'Red', 'Green'],
                       dtype='category')
car_data = pd.Series(
    pd.Categorical(
        ['Blue', 'Green', 'Red', 'Green', 'Red', 'Green'],
        categories=car_colors, ordered=False))

car_data = car_data.cat.set_categories(["Blue", "Red", "Green", "Blue_Red"])
print(car_data.loc[car_data.isin(['Red'])])

car_data.loc[car_data.isin(['Red'])] = 'Blue_Red'
car_data.loc[car_data.isin(['Blue'])] = 'Blue_Red'
car_data = car_data.cat.set_categories(["Green", "Blue_Red"])

print()
print(car_data)
```

What this example shows you is that there is only one `Blue` item and only two `Red` items, but there are three `Green` items, which places `Green` in the majority. Combining `Blue` and `Red` first, you add the `Blue_Red` category to `car_data`. Then you change the `Red` and `Blue` entries to `Blue_Red`, which creates the combined category. As a final step, you can remove the unneeded categories.

However, before you can change the `Red` entries to `Blue_Red` entries, you must find them. This is where a combination of calls to `isin()`, which locates the `Red` entries, and `loc[]`, which obtains their index, provides precisely what you need. The first `print` statement shows the result of using this combination. Here's the output from this example:

```
2      Red
4      Red
dtype: category
Categories (4, object): ['Blue', 'Red', 'Green', 'Blue_Red']

0      Blue_Red
1         Green
2      Blue_Red
3         Green
4      Blue_Red
5         Green
dtype: category
Categories (2, object): ['Green', 'Blue_Red']
```

Notice that there are now three `Blue_Red` entries and three `Green` entries. The `Blue` and `Red` categories are no longer in use. The result is that the levels are now combined as expected.

Dealing with Dates in Your Data

Dates can present problems in data. For one thing, dates are stored as numeric values. However, the precise value of the number depends on the representation for the particular platform and could even depend on the users' preferences. For example, Excel users can choose to start dates in 1900 or 1904 (https://support. microsoft.com/en-us/kb/180162). The numeric encoding for each is different, so the same date can have two numeric values depending on the starting date.

In addition to problems of representation, you also need to consider how to work with time values. Creating a time value format that represents a value the user can understand is hard. For example, you might need to use Greenwich Mean Time (GMT) in some situations but a local time zone in others. Transforming between various times is also problematic. With this in mind, the following sections provide you with details on dealing with time issues.

Formatting date and time values

Obtaining the correct date and time representation can make performing analysis a lot easier. For example, you often have to change the representation to obtain a correct sorting of values. Python provides two common methods of formatting date and time. The first technique is to call str(), which simply turns a datetime value into a string without any formatting. The strftime() function requires more work because you must define how you want the datetime value to appear after conversion. When using strftime(), you must provide a string containing special directives that define the formatting. You can find a listing of these directives at strftime.org.

Now that you have some idea of how time and date conversions work, it's time to see an example. Listing 1-7 creates a datetime object and then converts it into a string using two different approaches.

LISTING 1-7: **Formatting Date and Time Values**

```
import datetime as dt

now = dt.datetime.now()

print(str(now))
print(now.strftime('%a, %d %B %Y'))
```

In this case, you can see that using str() is the easiest approach. However, as shown by the following output, it may not provide the output you need. Using strftime() is infinitely more flexible.

```
2022-02-27 05:50:39.309668
Sun, 27 February 2022
```

Using the right time transformation

Time zones and differences in local time can cause all sorts of problems when performing analysis. For that matter, some types of calculations simply require a time shift in order to get the right results. No matter what the reason, you may need to transform one time into another time at some point. Listing 1-8 shows some techniques you can employ to perform the task.

LISTING 1-8: **Using the Right Time Transformation**

```
import datetime as dt

now = dt.datetime.now()
timevalue = now + dt.timedelta(hours=2)

print(now.strftime('%H:%M:%S'))
print(timevalue.strftime('%H:%M:%S'))
print(timevalue - now)
```

The `timedelta()` function makes the time transformation straightforward. You can use any of these parameter names with `timedelta()` to change a time and date value:

>> days

>> seconds

>> microseconds

>> milliseconds

>> minutes

>> hours

>> weeks

You can also manipulate time by performing addition or subtraction on time values. You can even subtract two time values to determine the difference between them. Here's the output from this example:

```
05:51:52
07:51:52
2:00:00
```

Notice that now is the local time, timevalue is two time zones different from this one, and there is a two-hour difference between the two times. You can perform all sorts of transformations using these techniques to ensure that your analysis always precisely shows the time-oriented values you need.

Dealing with Missing Data

Sometimes the data you receive is missing information in specific fields. For example, a customer record might be missing an age. If enough records are missing entries, any analysis you perform will be skewed and the results of the analysis weighted in an unpredictable manner. Having a strategy for dealing with missing data is important. The following sections give you some ideas on how to work through these issues and produce better results.

Finding the missing data

It's essential to find missing data in your data set to avoid getting incorrect results from your analysis. Listing 1-9 shows how you could obtain a listing of missing values without too much effort.

LISTING 1-9: **Finding the Missing Data**

```
import pandas as pd
import numpy as np

s = pd.Series([1, 2, 3, np.NaN, 5, 6, None])

print(s.isnull())

print()
print(s[s.isnull()])
```

A data set could represent missing data in several ways. In this example, you see missing data represented as np.NaN (NumPy Not a Number) and the Python None value.

Use the isnull() method to detect the missing values. The output shows True when the value is missing. By adding an index into the data set, you obtain just the entries that are missing. The example shows the following output:

```
0      False
1      False
2      False
3       True
4      False
5      False
6       True
dtype: bool
```

```
3    NaN
6    NaN
dtype: float64
```

Encoding missingness

After you figure out that your data set is missing information, you need to consider what to do about it. The three possibilities are to ignore the issue, fill in the missing items, or remove (drop) the missing entries from the data set. Ignoring the problem could lead to all sorts of problems for your analysis, so it's the option you use least often. Listing 1-10 shows one technique for filling in missing data or dropping the errant entries from the data set.

LISTING 1-10: **Encoding Missingness**

```
import pandas as pd
import numpy as np

s = pd.Series([1, 2, 3, np.NaN, 5, 6, None])

print(s.fillna(int(s.mean())))
print()
print(s.dropna())
```

The two methods of interest are `fillna()`, which fills in the missing entries, and `dropna()`, which drops the missing entries. When using `fillna()`, you must provide a value to use for the missing data. This example uses the mean of all the values, but you could choose a number of other approaches. Here's the output from this example:

```
0    1
1    2
2    3
3    3
4    5
5    6
6    3
dtype: float64

0    1
1    2
2    3
4    5
5    6
dtype: float64
```

**TECHNICAL
STUFF**

Working with a series is straightforward because the data set is so simple. When working with a `DataFrame`, however, the problem becomes significantly more complicated. You still have the option of dropping the entire row. When a column is sparsely populated, you might drop the column instead. Filling in the data also becomes more complex because you must consider the data set as a whole, in addition to the needs of the individual feature.

Imputing missing data

The previous section hints at the process of *imputing* missing data (ascribing characteristics based on how the data is used). The technique you use depends on the sort of data you're working with. Listing 1-11 shows a technique you can use to impute missing data values.

LISTING 1-11: **Imputing Missing Data**

```
import pandas as pd
import numpy as np
from sklearn.impute import SimpleImputer

s = [[1, 2, 3, np.NaN, 5, 6, None]]

imp = SimpleImputer(strategy='mean')
imp.fit([[1, 2, 3, 4, 5, 6, 7]])

x = pd.Series(imp.transform(s).tolist()[0])

print(x)
```

In this example, s is missing some values. The code creates a `SimpleImputer` to replace these missing values. The `strategy` parameter defines how to replace the missing values.

Before you can impute anything, you must provide statistics for the `Simple Imputer` to use by calling `fit()`. The code then calls `transform()` on s to fill in the missing values. However, the output is no longer a series. To create a series, you must convert the `SimpleImputer` output to a list and use the resulting list as input to `Series()`. Here's the result of the process with the missing values filled in:

```
0    1.0
1    2.0
2    3.0
3    4.0
4    5.0
```

Conditioning Your Data

```
5    6.0
6    7.0
dtype: float64
```

Slicing and Dicing: Filtering and Selecting Data

You may not need to work with all the data in a data set. In fact, looking at just one particular column might be beneficial, such as age, or a set of rows with a significant amount of information. You perform two steps to obtain just the data you need to perform a particular task:

1. **Filter rows to create a subject of the data that meets the criterion you select (such as all the people between the ages of 5 and 10).**

2. **Select data columns that contain the data you need to analyze.**

   For example, you probably don't need the individuals' names unless you want to perform some analysis based on name.

The act of slicing and dicing data gives you a subset of the data suitable for analysis. The following sections describe various ways to obtain specific pieces of data to meet particular needs.

Slicing rows

Slicing can occur in multiple ways when working with data, but the technique of interest in this section is to slice data from a row of 2D or 3D data. A 2D array may contain temperatures (x axis) over a specific timeframe (y axis). Slicing a row would mean seeing the temperatures at a specific time. In some cases, you might associate rows with cases in a data set.

A 3D array might include an axis for place (x axis), product (y axis), and time (z axis) so that you can see sales for items over time. Perhaps you want to track whether sales of an item are increasing, and specifically where they are increasing. Slicing a row would mean seeing all the sales for one specific product for all locations at any time. Listing 1-12 demonstrates how to perform this task.

LISTING 1-12:
Slicing Rows

```
x = np.array([[[1, 2, 3], [4, 5, 6], [7, 8, 9],],
              [[11,12,13], [14,15,16], [17,18,19],],
              [[21,22,23], [24,25,26], [27,28,29]]])
x[1]
```

In this case, the example builds a 3D array. It then slices row 1 of that array to produce the following output:

```
array([[11, 12, 13],
       [14, 15, 16],
       [17, 18, 19]])
```

Slicing columns

Using the examples from the previous section, slicing columns would obtain data at a 90-degree angle from rows. In other words, when working with the 2D array, you would want to see the times at which specific temperatures occurred. Likewise, you might want to see the sales of all products for a specific location at any time when working with the 3D array. In some cases, you might associate columns with features in a data set. Listing 1-13 demonstrates how to perform this task using the same array as in the previous section.

LISTING 1-13:
Slicing Columns

```
x = np.array([[[1, 2, 3], [4, 5, 6], [7, 8, 9],],
              [[11,12,13], [14,15,16], [17,18,19],],
              [[21,22,23], [24,25,26], [27,28,29]]])
x[:,1]
```

Notice that the indexing now occurs at two levels. The first index refers to the row. Using the colon (:) for the row means to use all the rows. The second index refers to a column. In this case, the output will contain column 1. Here's the output you see:

```
array([[ 4,  5,  6],
       [14, 15, 16],
       [24, 25, 26]])
```

REMEMBER

This is a 3D array. Therefore each of the columns contains all the z axis elements. What you see is every row — 0 through 2 for column 1 with every z axis element 0 through 2 for that column.

Dicing

The act of dicing a data set means to perform both row and column slicing such that you end up with a data wedge. For example, when working with the 3D array, you might want to see the sales of a specific product in a specific location at any time. Listing 1-14 demonstrates how to perform this task using the same array as in the previous two sections.

Dicing

```
x = np.array([[[1, 2, 3], [4, 5, 6], [7, 8, 9],],
              [[11,12,13], [14,15,16], [17,18,19],],
              [[21,22,23], [24,25,26], [27,28,29]]]])

print(x[1,1])
print(x[:,1,1])
print(x[1,:,1])
print()
print(x[1:2, 1:2])
```

This example dices the array in four different ways. First, you get row 1, column 1. Of course, what you may actually want is column 1, z axis 1. If that's not quite right, you could always request row 1, z axis 1 instead. Then again, you may want rows 1 and 2 of columns 1 and 2. Here's the output of all four requests:

```
[14 15 16]
[ 5 15 25]
[12 15 18]

[[[14 15 16]]]
```

Concatenating and Transforming

Data used for data science purposes seldom comes in a neat package. You may need to work with multiple databases in various locations — each of which has its own data format. It's impossible to perform analysis on such disparate sources of information with any accuracy. To make the data useful, you must create a single data set (by *concatenating*, or combining, the data from various sources).

Part of the process is to ensure that each field you create for the combined data set has the same characteristics. For example, an age field in one database might appear as a string, but another database could use an integer for the same field. For the fields to work together, they must appear as the same type of information.

The following sections help you understand the process involved in concatenating and transforming data from various sources to create a single data set. After you have a single data set from these sources, you can begin to perform tasks such as analysis on the data. Of course, the trick is to create a single data set that truly represents the data in all those disparate data sets — modifying the data would result in skewed results.

Adding new cases and variables

You often find a need to combine data sets in various ways or even to add new information for the sake of analysis. The result is a combined data set that includes either new cases or variables. Listing 1-15 shows techniques for performing both tasks.

LISTING 1-15: **Adding New Cases and Variables**

```
import pandas as pd
df = pd.DataFrame({'A': [2,3,1],
                   'B': [1,2,3],
                   'C': [5,3,4]})

df1 = pd.DataFrame({'A': [4],
                    'B': [4],
                    'C': [4]})
df = df.append(df1)
df = df.reset_index(drop=True)
print(df)

df.loc[df.last_valid_index() + 1] = [5, 5, 5]
print()
print(df)

df2 = pd.DataFrame({'D': [1, 2, 3, 4, 5]})

df = pd.DataFrame.join(df, df2)
print()
print(df)
```

The easiest way to add more data to an existing `DataFrame` is to rely on the `append()` method. You can also use the `concat()` method (a technique shown in Book 6, Chapter 1). In this case, the three cases found in `df` are added to the single case found in `df1`. To ensure that the data is appended as anticipated, the columns in `df` and `df1` must match. When you append two `DataFrame` objects in this manner, the new `DataFrame` contains the old index values. Use the `reset_index()` method to create a new index to make accessing cases easier.

You can also add another case to an existing `DataFrame` by creating the new case directly. Any time you add a new entry at a position that is one greater than the `last_valid_index()`, you get a new case as a result.

Sometimes you need to add a new variable (column) to the `DataFrame`. In this case, you rely on `join()` to perform the task. The resulting `DataFrame` will match cases with the same index value, so indexing is important. In addition, unless you want blank values, the number of cases in both `DataFrame` objects must match. Here's the output from this example:

```
A B C
0 2 1 5
1 3 2 3
2 1 3 4
3 4 4 4
A B C
0 2 1 5
1 3 2 3
2 1 3 4
3 4 4 4
4 5 5 5
A B C D
0 2 1 5 1
1 3 2 3 2
2 1 3 4 3
3 4 4 4 4
4 5 5 5 5
```

Removing data

At some point, you may need to remove cases or variables from a data set because they aren't required for your analysis. In both cases, you rely on the `drop()` method to perform the task. The difference in removing cases or variables is in how you describe what to remove, as shown in Listing 1-16.

LISTING 1-16: **Removing Data**

```
import pandas as pd

df = pd.DataFrame({'A': [2,3,1],
                   'B': [1,2,3],
                   'C': [5,3,4]})
df = df.drop(df.index[[1]])
print(df)

df = df.drop(columns='B')
print()
print(df)
```

The example begins by removing a case from `df`. Notice how the code relies on an index to describe what to remove. You can remove just one case (as shown), ranges of cases, or individual cases separated by commas. The main concern is to ensure that you have the correct index numbers for the cases you want to remove.

Removing a column is different. This example shows how to remove a column using a column name. You can also remove a column by using an index. Here's the output from this example:

```
  A B C
0 2 1 5
2 1 3 4

  A C
0 2 5
2 1 4
```

Sorting and shuffling

Sorting and shuffling are two ends of the same goal — to manage data order. In the first case, you put the data into order, while in the second, you remove any systematic patterning from the order. In general, you don't sort data sets for the purpose of analysis because doing so can cause you to get incorrect results. However, you might want to sort data for presentation purposes. Listing 1-17 shows sorting and shuffling.

LISTING 1-17: **Sorting and Shuffling**

```
import pandas as pd
import numpy as np
df = pd.DataFrame({'A': [2,1,2,3,3,5,4],
                   'B': [1,2,3,5,4,2,5],
                   'C': [5,3,4,1,1,2,3]})
df = df.sort_values(by=['A', 'B'], ascending=[True, True])
df = df.reset_index(drop=True)
print(df)
index = df.index.tolist()
np.random.shuffle(index)
df = df.loc[df.index[index]]
df = df.reset_index(drop=True)

print()
print(df)
```

It turns out that sorting the data is a bit easier than shuffling it. To sort the data, you use the sort_values() method and define which columns to use for indexing purposes. You can also determine whether the index is in ascending or descending order. Make sure to always call reset_index() when you're done so that the index appears in order for analysis or other purposes.

To shuffle the data, you first acquire the current index using df.index.tolist() and place it in index. A call to random.shuffle() creates a new order for the index. You then apply the new order to df using loc[]. As always, you call reset_index() to finalize the new order. Here's the output from this example (but note that the second output may not match your output because it has been shuffled):

```
   A  B  C
0  1  2  3
1  2  1  5
2  2  3  4
3  3  4  1
4  3  5  1
5  4  5  3
6  5  2  2

   A  B  C
0  2  1  5
1  4  5  3
2  5  2  2
3  3  5  1
4  2  3  4
5  1  2  3
6  3  4  1
```

Aggregating Data at Any Level

Aggregation is the process of combining or grouping data together into a set or list. The data may or may not be alike. However, in most cases, an aggregation function combines several rows together statistically using algorithms such as average, count, maximum, median, minimum, mode, or sum. There are several reasons to aggregate data:

>> Make it easier to analyze.

>> Obfuscate personal data for privacy or other reasons.

>> Create a combined data element from one data source that matches a combined data element in another source.

The most important use of data aggregation is to promote anonymity in order to meet legal or other concerns. Sometimes even data that should be anonymous turns out to provide identification of an individual using the proper analysis techniques. For example, researchers have found that it's possible to identify individuals based on just three credit card purchases (see www.computerworld. com/article/2877935/how-three-small-credit-card-transactions-could-reveal-your-identity.html). Listing 1-18 shows how to perform aggregation tasks.

LISTING 1-18: **Aggregating Data at Any Level**

```python
import pandas as pd
df = pd.DataFrame({'Map': [0,0,0,1,1,2,2],
'Values': [1,2,3,5,4,2,5]})
df['S'] = df.groupby('Map')['Values'].transform(np.sum)
df['M'] = df.groupby('Map')['Values'].transform(np.mean)
df['V'] = df.groupby('Map')['Values'].transform(np.var)
print(df)
```

In this case, you have two initial features for this DataFrame. The values in Map define which elements in Values belong together. For example, when calculating a sum for Map index 0, you use the Values 1, 2, and 3.

To perform the aggregation, you must first call groupby() to group the Map values. You then index into Values and rely on transform() to create the aggregated data using one of several algorithms found in NumPy, such as np.sum. Here are the results of this calculation:

```
Map Values S   M   V
0 0      1 6 2.0 1.0
1 0      2 6 2.0 1.0
2 0      3 6 2.0 1.0
3 1      5 9 4.5 0.5
4 1      4 9 4.5 0.5
5 2      2 7 3.5 4.5
6 2      5 7 3.5 4.5
```

Chapter **2**

Shaping Data

"It is a capital mistake to theorize before one has data."

— SHERLOCK HOLMES

Book 6, Chapter 1 demonstrates techniques for working with data as an entity — as something you work with in Python. However, data doesn't exist in a vacuum. It doesn't just suddenly appear in Python for absolutely no reason at all. As demonstrated in Book 5, Chapter 3, you load the data. However, loading may not be enough — you may have to shape the data as part of loading it. That's the purpose of this chapter. You discover how to work with a variety of container types in a way that makes it possible to load data from a number of complex container types, such as HTML pages. In fact, you even work with graphics, images, and sounds.

REMEMBER

As you progress through the book, you discover that data takes all kinds of forms and shapes. As far as the computer is concerned, data consists of 0s and 1s. Humans give the data meaning by formatting, storing, and interpreting it in a certain way. The same group of 0s and 1s could be a number, date, or text, depending on the interpretation. The data container provides clues as to how to interpret the data, so that's why this chapter is so important as you use Python to discover data patterns. You will find that you can discover patterns in places where you might have thought patterns couldn't exist.

You don't have to type the source code for this chapter manually. In fact, it's a lot easier if you use the downloadable source available at www.dummies. com/go/codingallinonefd2e. The source code for this chapter appears in the CAIO4D2E_0602_Shaping_Data.ipynb source code file.

Working with HTML Pages

HTML pages contain data in a hierarchical format. You often find HTML content in a strict HTML form or as XML. The HTML form can present problems because it doesn't always necessarily follow strict formatting rules. XML does follow strict formatting rules because of the standards used to define it, which makes it easier to parse. However, in both cases, you use similar techniques to parse a page. The first section that follows describes how to parse HTML pages in general.

Sometimes you don't need all the data on a page. Instead you need specific data, which is where XPath comes into play. You can use XPath to locate specific data on the HTML page and extract it for your particular needs.

Parsing XML and HTML

Simply extracting data from an XML file as you do in Book 5, Chapter 3 may not be enough. The data may not be in the correct format. Using the approach in Book 5, Chapter 3, you end up with a DataFrame containing three columns of type str. Obviously, you can't perform much data manipulation with strings. Listing 2-1 shapes the XML data from Book 5, Chapter 3 to create a new DataFrame containing just the <Number> and <Boolean> elements in the correct format.

LISTING 2-1: **Parsing XML and HTML**

```
from lxml import objectify
import pandas as pd
from distutils import util
xml = objectify.parse(open('XMLData.xml'))
root = xml.getroot()
df = pd.DataFrame(columns=('Number', 'Boolean'))
for i in range(0, 4):
    obj = root.getchildren()[i].getchildren()
    row = dict(zip(['Number', 'Boolean'],
                   [obj[0].pyval,
                    bool(util.strtobool(obj[2].text))]))
```

```
        row_s = pd.Series(row)
        row_s.name = obj[1].text
        df = df.append(row_s)

print(type(df.loc['First']['Number']))
print(type(df.loc['First']['Boolean']))
```

The DataFrame df is initially instantiated as empty, but as the code loops through the root node's children, it extracts a list containing the following

>> A <Number> element (expressed as an int)

>> An ordinal element (a string)

>> A <Boolean> element (expressed as a string)

The code uses this list to increment df. In fact, the code relies on the ordinal number element as the index label and constructs a new individual row to append to the existing DataFrame. This operation programmatically converts the information contained in the XML tree into the right data type to place into the existing variables in df. The number elements are already available as int type; the conversion of the <Boolean> element is a little harder. You must convert the string to a numeric value using the strtobool() function in distutils.util. The output is a 0 for False values and a 1 for True values. However, that's still not a Boolean value. To create a Boolean value, you must convert the 0 or 1 using bool().

TIP

This example also shows how to access individual values in the DataFrame. Notice that the name property now uses the <String> element value for easy access. You provide an index value using loc and then access the individual feature using a second index. The output from this example is

```
<class 'int'>
<class 'bool'>
```

Using XPath for data extraction

Using XPath to extract data from your data set can greatly reduce the complexity of your code and potentially make it faster as well. Listing 2-2 shows an XPath version of the example in the previous section. Notice that this version is shorter and doesn't require the use of a for loop.

LISTING 2-2: **Using XPath for Data Extraction**

```
from lxml import objectify
import pandas as pd
from distutils import util

xml = objectify.parse(open('XMLData.xml'))
root = xml.getroot()
map_number = map(int, root.xpath('Record/Number'))
map_bool = map(str, root.xpath('Record/Boolean'))
map_bool = map(util.strtobool, map_bool)
map_bool = map(bool, map_bool)
map_string = map(str, root.xpath('Record/String'))

data = list(zip(map_number, map_bool))
df = pd.DataFrame(data,
                  columns=('Number', 'Boolean'),
                  index = list(map_string))

print(df)
print(type(df.loc['First']['Number']))
print(type(df.loc['First']['Boolean']))
```

The example begins just like the previous example, by importing data and obtaining the root node. At this point, the example creates a data object that contains record number and Boolean value pairs. Because the XML file entries are all strings, you must use the map() function to convert the strings to the appropriate values. Working with the record number is straightforward — all you do is map it to an int. The xpath() function accepts a path from the root node to the data you need, which is 'Record/Number' in this case.

Mapping the Boolean value is a little more difficult. As in the previous section, you must use the util.strtobool() function to convert the string Boolean values to a number that bool() can convert to a Boolean equivalent. However, if you try to perform just a double mapping, you'll encounter an error message saying that lists don't include a required function, tolower().To overcome this obstacle, you perform a triple mapping and convert the data to a string using the str() function first.

Creating the DataFrame is different, too. Instead of adding individual rows, you add all the rows at one time by using data. Setting up the column names is the same as before. However, now you need some way of adding the row names, as in the previous example. This task is accomplished by setting the index parameter to a mapped version of the xpath() output for the 'Record/String' path. Here's the output you can expect:

```
      Number Boolean
First   1    True
Second  2    False
Third   3    True
Fourth  4    False
<type 'numpy.int64'>
<type 'numpy.bool_'>
```

Working with Raw Text

Even though it might seem as if raw text wouldn't present a problem in parsing because it doesn't contain any special formatting, you do have to consider how the text is stored and whether it contains special words. The multiple forms of Unicode can present interpretation problems that you need to consider as you work through the text. Using regular expressions can help you locate specific information within a raw text file. You can use regular expressions for both data cleaning and pattern matching. The following sections help you understand the techniques used to shape raw text files.

Dealing with Unicode

Text files are pure text — this much is certain. The way the text is encoded can differ. For example, a character can use seven, eight, or more bits for encoding purposes. The use of special characters can differ as well. In short, the interpretation of bits used to create characters differs from encoding to encoding. You can see a host of encodings at `www.i18nguy.com/unicode/codepages.html`.

REMEMBER

Sometimes you need to work with encodings other than the default encoding set within the Python environment. When working with Python 3.*x*, you must rely on Universal Transformation Format 8-bit (UTF-8) as the encoding used to read and write files. This environment is always set for UTF-8, and trying to change it causes an error message. The article at `https://docs.python.org/3/howto/unicode.html` provides insights on how to get around the Unicode problems in Python.

WARNING

Dealing with encoding incorrectly can prevent you from performing tasks such as importing modules or processing text. Make sure to test your code carefully and completely to ensure that any problem with encoding won't affect your ability to run the application. Good additional articles to read on this topic appear at `http://blog.notdot.net/2010/07/Getting-unicode-right-in-Python` and `http://web.archive.org/web/20120722170929/http://boodebr.org/main/python/all-about-python-and-unicode`.

Stemming and removing stop words

Stemming is the process of reducing words to their stem (or root) word. This task isn't the same as understanding that some words come from Latin or other roots, but instead makes like words equal to each other for the purpose of comparison or sharing. For example, the words *cats, catty,* and *catlike* all have the stem *cat.* The act of stemming helps you analyze sentences by tokenizing them in a more efficient way because the machine learning algorithm has to learn about the stem *cat* and not about all its variants.

Removing suffixes to create stem words and generally tokenizing sentences are only two parts of the process, however, of creating something like a natural language interface. Languages include a great number of glue words that don't mean much to a computer but have significant meaning to humans, such as *a, as, the, that,* and so on in English. These short, less useful words are *stop* words. Sentences don't make sense without them to humans, but for your computer, they can act as a means of stopping sentence analysis.

The act of stemming and removing stop words simplifies the text and reduces the number of textual elements so that just the essential elements remain. In addition, you keep just the terms that are nearest to the true sense of the phrase. By reducing phrases in such a fashion, a computational algorithm can work faster and process the text more effectively.

WARNING

This example requires the use of the Natural Language Toolkit (NLTK), which Anaconda doesn't install by default. To use this example, you must download and install NLTK using the instructions found at `www.nltk.org/install.html` for your platform. Make certain that you install the NLTK for whatever version of Python you're using for this book when you have multiple versions of Python installed on your system. After you install NLTK, you must also install the packages associated with it. The instructions at `www.nltk.org/data.html` tell you how to perform this task (install all the packages to ensure you have everything).

The example in Listing 2-3 demonstrates how to perform stemming and remove stop words from a sentence. It begins by training an algorithm to perform the required analysis using a test sentence. Afterward, the example checks a second sentence for words that appear in the first.

LISTING 2-3: **Stemming and Removing Stop Words**

```
from sklearn.feature_extraction.text import *
from nltk import word_tokenize
from nltk.stem.porter import PorterStemmer
stemmer = PorterStemmer()
```

```
def stem_tokens(tokens, stemmer):
    stemmed = []
    for item in tokens:
        stemmed.append(stemmer.stem(item))
    return stemmed

def tokenize(text):
    tokens = word_tokenize(text)
    stems = stem_tokens(tokens, stemmer)
    return stems

vocab = ['Sam loves swimming so he swims all the time']
vect = CountVectorizer(tokenizer=tokenize,
                       stop_words='english')
vec = vect.fit(vocab)

sentence1 = vec.transform(['George loves swimming too!'])

print(vec.get_feature_names_out())
print(sentence1.toarray())
```

At the outset, the example creates a vocabulary using a test sentence and places it in vocab. It then creates a CountVectorizer, vect, to hold a list of stemmed words, but excludes the stop words. The tokenizer parameter defines the function used to stem the words. The stop_words parameter refers to a pickle file that contains stop words for a specific language, which is English in this case. There are also files for other languages, such as French and German. (You can see other parameters for the CountVectorizer() at https://scikit-learn.org/stable/modules/generated/sklearn.feature_extraction.text.CountVectorizer.html.) The vocabulary is fitted into another CountVectorizer, vec, which is used to perform the actual transformation on a test sentence using the transform() function. Here's the output from this example.

```
['love', 'sam', 'swim', 'time']
[[1 0 1 0]]
```

The first output shows the stemmed words. Notice that the list contains only *swim*, not *swimming* and *swims*. All the stop words are missing as well. For example, you don't see the words *so, he, all,* or *the*.

The second output shows how many times each stemmed word appears in the test sentence. In this case, a *love* variant appears once and a *swim* variant appears once as well. The words *sam* and *time* don't appear in the second sentence, so those values are set to 0.

Introducing regular expressions

Regular expressions present the data scientist with an interesting array of tools for parsing raw text. At first, it may seem daunting to figure out precisely how regular expressions work. However, sites such as `https://regexr.com/` let you play with regular expressions so that you can see how the use of various expressions performs specific types of pattern matching. Of course, the first requirement is to discover *pattern matching*, which is the use of special characters to tell a parsing engine what to find in the raw text file. Table 2-1 provides a list of pattern-matching characters and tells you how to use them.

TABLE 2-1   Pattern-Matching Characters Used in Python

Character	Interpretation
`(re)`	Groups regular expressions and remembers the matched text.
`(?: re)`	Groups regular expressions without remembering matched text.
`(?#...)`	Indicates a comment, which isn't processed.
`re?`	Matches 0 or 1 occurrence of preceding expression (but no more than 0 or 1 occurrence).
`re*`	Matches 0 or more occurrences of the preceding expression.
`re+`	Matches 1 or more occurrences of the preceding expression.
`(?> re)`	Matches an independent pattern without backtracking.
`.`	Matches any single character except the new line (\n) character (adding the m option allows it to match the new line character as well).
`[^...]`	Matches any single character or range of characters not found within the brackets.
`[...]`	Matches any single character or range of characters that appears within the brackets.
`re{ n, m}`	Matches at least n and at most m occurrences of the preceding expression.
`\n, \t, etc.`	Matches control characters such as new lines (\n), carriage returns (\r), and tabs (\t).
`\d`	Matches digits (which is equivalent to using [0–9]).
`a|b`	Matches either a or b.
`re{ n}`	Matches exactly the number of occurrences of preceding expression specified by n.
`re{ n,}`	Matches n or more occurrences of the preceding expression.
`\D`	Matches nondigits.
`\S`	Matches nonwhitespace.

Character	Interpretation
\B	Matches nonword boundaries.
\W	Matches nonword characters.
\1...\9	Matches nth grouped subexpression.
\10	Matches nth grouped subexpression if it matched already (otherwise the pattern refers to the octal representation of a character code).
\A	Matches the beginning of a string.
^	Matches the beginning of the line.
\z	Matches the end of a string.
\Z	Matches the end of string (when a new line exists, it matches just before new line).
$	Matches the end of the line.
\G	Matches the point where the last match finished.
\s	Matches whitespace (which is equivalent to using [\t\n\r\f]).
\b	Matches word boundaries when outside the brackets; matches the backspace (0x08) when inside the brackets.
\w	Matches word characters.
(?= re)	Specifies a position using a pattern (this pattern doesn't have a range).
(?! re)	Specifies a position using pattern negation (this pattern doesn't have a range).
(?-imx)	Toggles the i, m, or x options temporarily off within a regular expression (when this pattern appears in parentheses, only the area within the parentheses is affected).
(?imx)	Toggles the i, m, or x options temporarily on within a regular expression (when this pattern appears in parentheses, only the area within the parentheses is affected).
(?-imx: re)	Toggles the i, m, or x options within parentheses temporarily off.
(?imx: re)	Toggles the i, m, or x options within parentheses temporarily on.

Using regular expressions helps you manipulate complex text before using other techniques described in this chapter. In Listing 2-4, you see how to extract a telephone number from a sentence no matter where the telephone number appears. This sort of manipulation is helpful when you have to work with text of various origins and in irregular format. You can see some additional telephone number manipulation routines at www.diveintopython.net/regular_expressions/phone_numbers.html. The big thing is that this example helps you understand how to extract any text you need from text you don't.

LISTING 2-4: **Introducing Regular Expressions**

```
import re

data1 = 'My phone number is: 800-555-1212.'
data2 = '800-555-1234 is my phone number.'

pattern = re.compile(r'(\d{3})-(\d{3})-(\d{4})')

dmatch1 = pattern.search(data1).groups()
dmatch2 = pattern.search(data2).groups()

print(dmatch1)
print(dmatch2)
```

The example begins with two telephone numbers placed in sentences in various locations. Before you can do much, you need to create a pattern. Always read a pattern from left to right. In this case, the pattern is looking for three digits, followed by a dash, three more digits, followed by another dash, and finally four digits.

To make the process faster and easier, the code calls the `compile()` function to create a compiled version of the pattern so that Python doesn't have to re-create the pattern every time you need it. The compiled pattern appears in `pattern`.

The `search()` function looks for the pattern in each of the test sentences. It then places any matched text that it finds into groups and outputs a tuple into one of two variables. Here's the output from this example.

```
('800', '555', '1212')
('800', '555', '1234')
```

Using the Bag of Words Model and Beyond

The goal of most data imports is to perform some type of analysis. Before you can perform analysis on textual data, you must tokenize every word within the data set. The act of tokenizing the words creates a *bag of words*. You can then use the bag of words to train *classifiers*, a special kind of algorithm used to break words down into categories. The following section provides additional insights into the bag of words model and shows how to work with it.

GETTING THE 20 NEWSGROUPS DATA SET

The examples in the sections that follow rely on the 20 Newsgroups data set (qwone. com/~jason/20Newsgroups) that's part of the scikit-learn installation. The host site provides some additional information about the data set, but essentially it's a good data set to use to demonstrate various kinds of text analysis.

You don't have to do anything special to work with the data set because scikit-learn already knows about it. However, when you run the first example, you see the message `"WARNING:sklearn.datasets.twenty_newsgroups:Downloading dataset from http://people.csail.mit.edu/jrennie/20Newsgroups/20news-bydate.tar. gz (14 MB)."` All this message tells you is that you need to wait for the data download to complete. There is nothing wrong with your system. Look at the left side of the code cell in IPython Notebook and you see the familiar `In [*]:` entry. When this entry changes to show a number, the download is complete. The message doesn't go away until the next time you run the cell.

Understanding the bag of words model

In order to perform textual analysis of various sorts, you need to first tokenize the words and create a bag of words from them. The bag of words uses numbers to represent words, word frequencies, and word locations that you can manipulate mathematically to see patterns in the way that the words are structured and used. The bag of words model ignores grammar and even word order — the focus is on simplifying the text so that you can easily analyze it.

The creation of a bag of words revolves around Natural Language Processing (NLP) and Information Retrieval (IR). Before you perform this sort of processing, you normally remove any special characters (such as HTML formatting from a web source), remove the stop words, and possibly perform stemming as well (as described in the "Stemming and removing stop words" section, earlier this chapter). For the purpose of this example, you use the 20 Newsgroups data set directly. Listing 2-5 shows an example of how you can obtain textual input and create a bag of words from it.

LISTING 2-5:   **Understanding the Bag of Words Model**

```
from sklearn.datasets import fetch_20newsgroups
from sklearn.feature_extraction.text import *

categories = ['comp.graphics', 'misc.forsale',
              'rec.autos', 'sci.space']
```

(continued)

LISTING 2-5: **_(continued)_**

```
twenty_train = fetch_20newsgroups(subset='train',
    categories=categories,
    shuffle=True,
    random_state=42)
count_vect = CountVectorizer()
X_train_counts = count_vect.fit_transform(
    twenty_train.data)

print("BOW shape:", X_train_counts.shape)
caltech_idx = count_vect.vocabulary_['caltech']
print('"Caltech": %i' % X_train_counts[0, caltech_idx])
```

REMEMBER

A number of the examples you see online are unclear as to where the list of categories they use come from. The host site at http://qwone.com/~jason/20Newsgroups/ provides you with a listing of the categories you can use. The category list doesn't come from a magic hat somewhere, but many examples online simply don't bother to document some information sources. Always refer to the host site when you have questions about issues such as data set categories.

The call to fetch_20newsgroups() loads the data set into memory. You see the resulting training object, twenty_train, described as a _bunch._ At this point, you have an object that contains a listing of categories and associated data, but the application hasn't tokenized the data, and the algorithm used to work with the data isn't trained.

Now that you have a bunch of data to use, you can begin creating a bag of words with it. The bag of words process begins by assigning an integer value (an index of a sort) to each unique word in the training set. In addition, each document receives an integer value. The next step is to count every occurrence of these words in each document and create a list of document and count pairs so that you know which words appear and how often in each document.

Naturally, some words from the master list aren't used in some documents, thereby creating a _high-dimensional sparse data set._ The scipy.sparse matrix is a data structure that lets you store only the nonzero elements of the list in order to save memory. When the code makes the call to count_vect.fit_transform(), it places the resulting bag of words into X_train_counts. You can see the resulting number of entries by accessing the shape property and the counts for the word "Caltech" in the first document:

```
BOW shape: (2356, 34750)
"Caltech": 3
```

Working with n-grams

An *n-gram* is a continuous sequence of items in the text you want to analyze. The items are phonemes, syllables, letters, words, or base pairs. The *n* in n-gram refers to a size. An n-gram that has a size of one, for example, is a unigram. The example in this section uses a size of three, making a trigram. You use n-grams in a probabilistic manner to perform tasks such as predicting the next sequence in a series, which wouldn't seem very useful until you start thinking about applications such as search engines that try to predict the word you want to type based on the previous letters you've supplied. However, the technique has all sorts of applications, such as in DNA sequencing and data compression. Listing 2-6 shows how to create n-grams from the 20 Newsgroups data set.

LISTING 2-6: **Working with n-Grams**

```
from sklearn.datasets import fetch_20newsgroups
from sklearn.feature_extraction.text import *

categories = ['sci.space']

twenty_train = fetch_20newsgroups(subset='train',
    categories=categories,
    remove=('headers','footers','quotes'),
    shuffle=True,
    random_state=42)

count_chars = CountVectorizer(analyzer='char_wb',
    ngram_range=(3,3),
    max_features=10)
count_chars.fit(twenty_train['data'])

count_words = CountVectorizer(analyzer='word',
    ngram_range=(2,2),
    max_features=10,
    stop_words='english')
count_words.fit(twenty_train['data'])

X = count_chars.transform(twenty_train.data)

print(count_chars.get_feature_names_out())
print(X[1].todense())
print(count_words.get_feature_names_out())
```

The beginning code is the same as in the previous section. You still begin by fetching the data set and placing it into a bunch. However, in this case, the vectorization process takes on new meaning. The arguments process the data in a special way.

In this case, the `analyzer` parameter determines how the application creates the n-grams. You can choose words (`word`), characters (`char`), or characters within word boundaries (`char_wb`). The `ngram_range` parameter requires two inputs in the form of a tuple: The first determines the minimum n-gram size and the second determines the maximum n-gram size. The third argument, `max_features`, determines how many features the vectorizer returns. In the second vectorizer call, the `stop_words` argument removes the terms contained in the English pickle file (see the "Stemming and removing stop words" section, earlier in the chapter, for details). At this point, the application fits the data to the transformation algorithm.

The example provides three outputs. The first shows the top ten trigrams for characters from the document. The second is the n-gram for the first document. It shows the frequency of the top ten trigrams. The third is the top ten trigrams for words. Here's the output from this example:

```
[' an', ' in', ' of', ' th', ' to', 'he ', 'ing', 'ion',
'nd ', 'the']
[[0 0 2 5 1 4 2 2 0 5]]
['anonymous ftp', 'commercial space', 'gamma ray',
'nasa gov', 'national space', 'remote sensing',
'sci space', 'space shuttle', 'space station',
'washington dc']
```

Implementing TF-IDF transformations

The *Term Frequency times Inverse Document Frequency (TF-IDF)* transformation is a technique used to help compensate for words found relatively often in different documents, which makes it hard to distinguish between the documents because they are too common (stop words are a good example). What this transformation is really telling you is the importance of a particular word to the uniqueness of a document. The greater the frequency of a word in a document, the more important it is to that document. However, the measurement is offset by the document size — the total number of words the document contains — and by how often the word appears in other documents.

Even if a word appears many times inside a document, that doesn't imply that the word is important for understanding the document itself; in many documents, you find stop words with the same frequency as the words that relate to the document's general topics. For example, if you analyze documents with scifi-related discussions (such as in the 20 Newsgroups data set), you may find that many of them deal with UFOs; therefore, the acronym *UFO* can't represent a distinction between different documents. Moreover, longer documents contain more words than shorter ones, and repeated words are easily found when the text is abundant.

REMEMBER

In fact, a word found a few times in a single document (or possibly a few others) could prove quite distinctive and helpful in determining the document type. If you are working with documents discussing scifi and automobile sales, the acronym *UFO* can be distinctive because it easily separates the two topic types in your documents.

Search engines often need to weight words in a document in a way that helps determine when the word is important in the text. You use words with a higher weight to index the document so that when you search for those words, the search engine will retrieve that document. This is the reason that the TD–IDF transformation is used quite often in search engine applications.

Getting into more details, the TF–IDF part of the TF–IDF equation determines how frequently the term appears in the document, while the IDF part of the equation determines the term's importance because it represents the inverse of the frequency of that word among all the documents. A large IDF implies a seldom-found word and that the TF–IDF weight will also be larger. A small IDF means that the word is common, and that will result in a small TF–IDF weight. You can see some actual calculations of this particular measure at www.tfidf.com. Listing 2-7 shows an example of how to calculate TF–IDF using Python.

LISTING 2-7: **Implementing TF-IDF Transformations**

```
from sklearn.datasets import fetch_20newsgroups
from sklearn.feature_extraction.text import *
categories = ['comp.graphics', 'misc.forsale',
              'rec.autos', 'sci.space']
twenty_train = fetch_20newsgroups(subset='train',
                                  categories=categories,
                                  shuffle=True,
                                  random_state=42)
count_vect = CountVectorizer()
X_train_counts = count_vect.fit_transform(twenty_train.data)
tfidf = TfidfTransformer().fit(X_train_counts)
X_train_tfidf = tfidf.transform(X_train_counts)
caltech_idx = count_vect.vocabulary_['caltech']

print('"Caltech" scored in a BOW:')
print('count: %0.3f' % X_train_counts[0, caltech_idx])
print('TF-IDF: %0.3f' % X_train_tfidf[0, caltech_idx])
```

This example begins much like the other examples in this section have, by fetching the 20 Newsgroups data set. It then creates a word bag, much like the example in the "Understanding the bag of words model" section, earlier in this chapter. However, now you see something you can do with the word bag.

In this case, the code calls upon `TfidfTransformer()` to convert the raw newsgroup documents into a matrix of TF-IDF features. The `use_idf` controls the use of inverse-document-frequency reweighting, which it turned on in this case. The vectorized data is fitted to the transformation algorithm. The next step, calling `tfidf.transform()`, performs the actual transformation process. Here's the result you get from this example:

```
"Caltech" scored in a BOW:
count: 3.000
TF-IDF: 0.123
```

Notice how the word *Caltech* now has a lower value in the first document compared to the example in the previous paragraph, where the counting of occurrences for the same word in the same document scored a value of 3. To understand how counting occurrences relates to TF-IDF, compute the average word count and average TF-IDF:

```
import numpy as np
count = np.mean(X_train_counts[X_train_counts>0])
tfif = np.mean(X_train_tfidf[X_train_tfidf>0])
print('mean count: %0.3f' % np.mean(count))
print('mean TF-IDF: %0.3f' % np.mean(tfif))
```

The results demonstrate that no matter how you count occurrences of *Caltech* in the first document or use its TF-IDF, the value is always double the average word, revealing that it is a keyword for modeling the text:

```
mean count: 1.698
mean TF-IDF: 0.064
```

REMEMBER

TF-IDF helps you to locate the most important word or n-grams and exclude the least important ones. It is also very helpful as an input for linear models, because they work better with TF-IDF scores than word counts.

Working with Graph Data

Imagine data points that are connected to other data points, such as how one web page is connected to another web page through hyperlinks. Each of these data points is a *node.* The nodes connect to each other using *links.* Not every node links to every other node, so the node connections become important. By analyzing the nodes and their links, you can perform all sorts of interesting tasks in data science, such as defining the best way to get from work to your home using streets and highways. The following sections describe how graphs work and how to perform basic tasks with them.

Understanding the adjacency matrix

An *adjacency matrix* represents the connections between nodes of a graph. When there is a connection between one node and another, the matrix indicates it as a value greater than 0. The precise representation of connections in the matrix depends on whether the graph is directed (where the direction of the connection matters) or undirected.

A problem with many online examples is that the authors keep them simple for explanation purposes. However, real-world graphs are often immense and defy easy analysis simply through visualization. Just think about the number of nodes that even a small city would have when considering street intersections (with the links being the streets themselves). Many other graphs are far larger, and simply looking at them will never reveal any interesting patterns. Data scientists call the problem in presenting any complex graph using an adjacency matrix a *hairball*.

One key to analyzing adjacency matrices is to sort them in specific ways. For example, you might choose to sort the data according to properties other than the actual connections. A graph of street connections might include the date the street was last paved, making it possible for you to look for patterns that direct someone based on the streets that are in the best repair. In short, making the graph data useful becomes a matter of manipulating the organization of that data in specific ways.

Using NetworkX basics

Working with graphs could become difficult if you had to write all the code from scratch. Fortunately, the NetworkX package for Python makes it easy to create, manipulate, and study the structure, dynamics, and functions of complex networks (or graphs). Even though this book covers only graphs, you can use the package to work with digraphs and multigraphs as well.

The main emphasis of NetworkX is to avoid the whole issue of hairballs. The use of simple calls hides much of the complexity of working with graphs and adjacency matrices from view. Listing 2-8 shows how to create a basic adjacency matrix from one of the NetworkX-supplied graphs.

LISTING 2-8:
Creating the Initial Graph

```
import networkx as nx
G = nx.cycle_graph(10)
A = nx.adjacency_matrix(G)
print(A.todense())
```

TECHNICAL STUFF

This book uses version 2.6 of NetworkX. If you get errors or warnings when you run the above code, install NetworkX version 2.6 by opening a Terminal window (on macOS) or the Anaconda Prompt (on Windows) and entering `pip install networkx==2.6`.

The example begins by importing the required package. It then creates a graph using the `cycle_graph()` template. The graph contains ten nodes. Calling `adjacency_matrix()` creates the adjacency matrix from the graph. The final step is to print the output as a matrix, as shown here:

```
[[0 1 0 0 0 0 0 0 0 1]
 [1 0 1 0 0 0 0 0 0 0]
 [0 1 0 1 0 0 0 0 0 0]
 [0 0 1 0 1 0 0 0 0 0]
 [0 0 0 1 0 1 0 0 0 0]
 [0 0 0 0 1 0 1 0 0 0]
 [0 0 0 0 0 1 0 1 0 0]
 [0 0 0 0 0 0 1 0 1 0]
 [0 0 0 0 0 0 0 1 0 1]
 [1 0 0 0 0 0 0 0 1 0]]
```

TIP

You don't have to build your own graph from scratch for testing purposes. The NetworkX site documents a number of standard graph types that you can use, all of which are available in IPython. The list appears at https://networkx.org/documentation/stable/reference/classes/index.html.

It's interesting to see how the graph looks after you generate it. Listing 2-9 displays the graph for you. Figure 2-1 shows the result of the plot.

LISTING 2-9:
Visualizing the Graph

```
import matplotlib.pyplot as plt
%matplotlib inline
nx.draw_networkx(G)
plt.show()
```

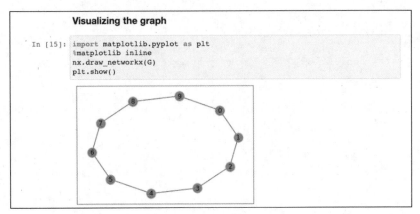

FIGURE 2-1:
Plotting the
original graph.

© John Wiley & Sons

The plot shows that you can add an edge between nodes 1 and 5. Listing 2-10 shows the code needed to perform this task using the add_edge() function. Figure 2-2 shows the result.

LISTING 2-10: **Adding to the Graph**

```
G.add_edge(1,5)
nx.draw_networkx(G)
plt.show()
```

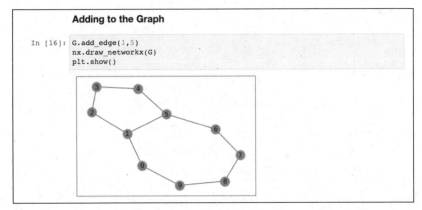

FIGURE 2-2:
Plotting the graph
addition.

© John Wiley & Sons

Chapter **3**

Getting a Crash Course in MatPlotLib

"If we have data, let's look at data. If all we have are opinions, let's go with mine."

— JIM BARKSDALE

ost people visualize information better when they see it in graphic, versus textual, format. Graphics help people see relationships and make comparisons with greater ease. Even if you can deal with the abstraction of textual data with ease, performing data analysis is all about communication. Unless you can communicate your ideas to other people, the act of obtaining, shaping, and analyzing the data has little value beyond your own personal needs. Fortunately, Python makes the task of converting your textual data into graphics relatively easy using MatPlotLib, which is actually a simulation of the MATLAB application. You can see a comparison of the two at `https://pyzo.org/python_vs_matlab.html`.

TIP

If you already know how to use MATLAB, moving over to MatPlotLib is relatively easy because they both use the same sort of state machine to perform tasks and have a similar method of defining graphic elements. A number of people feel that MatPlotLib is superior to MATLAB because you can do things like perform tasks using less code when working with MatPlotLib than when using MATLAB (see http://phillipmfeldman.org/Python/Advantages_of_Python_Over_Matlab. html). Others have noted that the transition from MATLAB to MatPlotLib is relatively straightforward (see https://vnoel.wordpress.com/2008/05/03/bye-matlab-hello-python-thanks-sage). However, what matters most is what you think. You may find that you like to experiment with data using MATLAB and then create applications based on your findings using Python with MatPlotLib. It's a matter of personal taste rather than one of a strictly correct answer.

REMEMBER

You don't have to type the source code for this chapter manually. In fact, it's a lot easier if you use the downloadable source code available at www.dummies. com/go/codingallinonefd2e. The source code for this chapter appears in the CAIO4D2E_0603_Getting_a_Crash_Course_in_MathPlotLib.ipynb source code.

Starting with a Graph

A graph or chart is simply a visual representation of numeric data. MatPlotLib makes a large number of graph and chart types available to you. Of course, you can choose any of the common graph and graph types such as bar charts, line graphs, or pie charts. As with MATLAB, you also have access to a huge number of statistical plot types, such as box plots, error bar charts, and histograms. You can see a gallery of the various graph types that MatPlotLib supports at https://matplotlib.org/stable/gallery/index.html. However, it's important to remember that you can combine graphic elements in an almost infinite number of ways to create your own presentation of data no matter how complex that data might be. The following sections describe how to create a basic graph, but remember that you have access to a lot more functionality than these sections tell you about.

Defining the plot

Plots show graphically what you've defined numerically. To define a plot, you need some values, the matplotlib.pyplot module, and an idea of what you want to display, as shown in Listing 3-1.

LISTING 3-1: **Defining the Plot**

```
import matplotlib.pyplot as plt
%matplotlib inline
values = [1, 5, 8, 9, 2, 0, 3, 10, 4, 7]
plt.plot(range(1,11), values)
plt.show()
```

In this case, the code tells the `plt.plot()` function to create a plot using x axis values between 1 and 11 and y axis values as they appear in values. Calling `plot.show()` displays the plot in a separate dialog box, as shown in Figure 3-1. Notice that the output is a line graph. Book 6, Chapter 4 shows you how to create other chart and graph types.

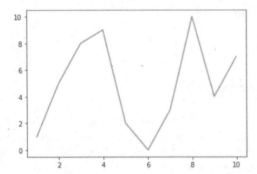

FIGURE 3-1:
Creating a basic
plot that shows
just one line.

Drawing multiple lines and plots

You encounter many situations in which you must use multiple plot lines, such as when comparing two sets of values. To create such plots using MatPlotLib, you simply call `plt.plot()` multiple times — once for each plot line — as shown in Listing 3-2.

LISTING 3-2: **Drawing Multiple Lines and Plots**

```
values = [1, 5, 8, 9, 2, 0, 3, 10, 4, 7]
values2 = [3, 8, 9, 2, 1, 2, 4, 7, 6, 6]
import matplotlib.pyplot as plt
plt.plot(range(1,11), values)
plt.plot(range(1,11), values2)
plt.show()
```

When you run this example, you see two plot lines, as shown in Figure 3-2. Even though you can't see it in the printed book, the line graphs are different colors so that you can tell them apart.

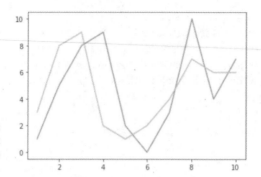

FIGURE 3-2:
Defining a plot
that contains
multiple lines.

Saving your work

Jupyter Notebook makes it easy to include your graphs within the notebooks you create, so that you can define reports that everyone can easily understand. When you do need to save a copy of your work to disk for later reference or to use it as part of a larger report, you save the graphic programmatically using the `plt.savefig()` function, as shown in Listing 3-3.

LISTING 3-3: Saving Your Work

```
import matplotlib.pyplot as plt
%matplotlib auto
values = [1, 5, 8, 9, 2, 0, 3, 10, 4, 7]
plt.plot(range(1,11), values)
plt.ioff()
plt.savefig('MySamplePlot.png', format='png')
```

In this case, you must provide a minimum of two inputs. The first input is the filename. You may optionally include a path for saving the file. The second input is the file format. In this case, the example saves the file in Portable Network Graphic (PNG) format, but you have other options: Portable Document Format (PDF), Postscript (PS), Encapsulated Postscript (EPS), and Scalable Vector Graphics (SVG).

REMEMBER

Note the presence of `%matplotlib auto`. Using this call removes the inline display of the graph. You do have options for other MatPlotLib backends, depending on which version of Python and MatPlotLib you use. For example, some developers prefer the `notebook` backend to the `inline` backend because it provides additional functionality. However, to use the `notebook` backend, you must also restart the kernel, and you may not always see what you expect. To see the backend list, use `%matplotlib -l`. In addition, calling `plt.ioff()` turns plot interaction off.

Setting the Axis, Ticks, Grids

It's hard to know what the data actually means unless you provide a unit of measure or at least some means of performing comparisons. The use of axes, ticks, and grids make it possible to illustrate graphically the relative size of data elements so that the viewer gains an appreciation of comparative measure. You won't use these features with every graphic, and you may employ the features differently based on viewer needs, but it's important to know that these features exist and how you can use them to help document your data within the graphic environment.

TECHNICAL STUFF

The following examples use %matplotlib notebook so that you can see the difference between it and %matplotlib inline. The two inline displays rely on a different graphic engine. Consequently, you must choose Kernel ➪ Restart to restart the kernel before you run any of the examples in the sections that follow.

Getting the axes

The axes define the x and y plane of the graphic. The x axis runs horizontally, and the y axis runs vertically. In many cases, you can allow MatPlotLib to perform any required formatting for you. However, sometimes you need to obtain access to the axes and format them manually. Listing 3-4 shows how to obtain access to the axes for a plot.

LISTING 3-4: **Setting the Axes**

```
import matplotlib.pyplot as plt
%matplotlib notebook
values = [0, 5, 8, 9, 2, 0, 3, 10, 4, 7]
ax = plt.axes()
plt.plot(range(1,11), values)
plt.show()
```

The reason you place the axes in a variable, ax, instead of manipulating them directly is to make writing the code simpler and more efficient. In this case, you simply turn on the default axes by calling plt.axes(); then you place a handle to the axes in ax. A *handle* is a sort of pointer to the axes. Think of it as you would a frying pan. You wouldn't lift the frying pan directly but would instead use its handle when picking it up.

Formatting the axes

Simply displaying the axes won't be enough in many cases. You want to change the way MatPlotLib displays them. For example, you may not want the highest value t to reach to the top of the graph. Listing 3-5 shows just a small number of tasks you can perform after you have access to the axes.

LISTING 3-5: **Formatting the Axes**

```
import matplotlib.pyplot as plt
%matplotlib notebook
values = [0, 5, 8, 9, 2, 0, 3, 10, 4, 7]
ax = plt.axes()
ax.set_xlim([0, 11])
ax.set_ylim([-1, 11])
ax.set_xticks([1, 2, 3, 4, 5, 6, 7, 8, 9, 10])
ax.set_yticks([0, 1, 2, 3, 4, 5, 6, 7, 8, 9, 10])
plt.plot(range(1,11), values)
plt.show()
```

In this case, the set_xlim() and set_ylim() calls change the axes limits — the length of each axis. The set_xticks() and set_yticks() calls change the ticks used to display data. The ways in which you can change a graph using these calls can become quite detailed. For example, you can choose to change individual tick labels if you want. Figure 3-3 shows the output from this example. Notice how the changes affect how the line graph displays.

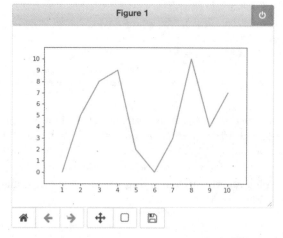

FIGURE 3-3:
Specifying how the axes should appear to the viewer.

© John Wiley & Sons

TECHNICAL STUFF

As you can see by viewing the differences between Figures 3-1, 3-2, and 3-3, %matlplotlib notebook produces a significantly different display. The controls at the bottom of the display let you pan and zoom the display, move between views you've created, and download the figure to disk. The button to the right of the Figure 1 heading in Figure 3-3 lets you stop interacting with the graph after you've finished working with it. Any changes you've made to the presentation of the graph remain afterward so that anyone looking at your notebook will see the graph in the manner you intended for them to see it. The ability to interact with the graph ends when you display another graph.

Adding grids

Grid lines make it possible to see the precise value of each element of a graph. You can more quickly determine both the x and y coordinate, which allow you to perform comparisons of individual points with greater ease. Of course, grids also add noise and make seeing the actual flow of data harder. The point is that you can use grids to good effect to create particular effects. Listing 3-6 shows how to add a grid to the graph in the previous section.

LISTING 3-6: **Adding Grids**

```
import matplotlib.pyplot as plt
%matplotlib notebook
values = [0, 5, 8, 9, 2, 0, 3, 10, 4, 7]
ax = plt.axes()
ax.set_xlim([0, 11])
ax.set_ylim([-1, 11])
ax.set_xticks([1, 2, 3, 4, 5, 6, 7, 8, 9, 10])
ax.set_yticks([0, 1, 2, 3, 4, 5, 6, 7, 8, 9, 10])
ax.grid()
plt.plot(range(1,11), values)
plt.show()
```

All you really need to do is call the grid() function. As with many other MatPlot-Lib functions, you can add parameters to create the grid precisely as you want to see it. For example, you can choose whether to add the x grid lines, y grid lines, or both. The output from this example appears in Figure 3-4.

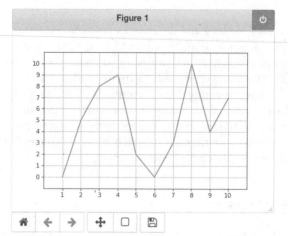

FIGURE 3-4:
Adding grids
makes the values
easier to read.

Defining the Line Appearance

Just drawing lines on a page won't do much for you if you need to help the viewer understand the importance of your data. In most cases, you need to use differ- ent line styles to ensure that the viewer can tell one data grouping from another. However, to emphasize the importance or value of a particular data grouping, you need to employ color. The use of color communicates all sorts of ideas to the viewer. For example, green often denotes that something is safe, while red com- municates danger. The following sections help you understand how to work with line style and color to communicate ideas and concepts to the viewer without using any text.

Working with line styles

Line styles help differentiate graphs by drawing the lines in various ways. Using a unique presentation for each line helps you distinguish each line so that you can call it out (even when the printout is in shades of gray). You could also call out a particular line graph by using a different line style for it (and using the same style for the other lines). Table 3-1 shows the various MatPlotLib line styles.

The line style appears as a third argument to the `plot()` function call. You simply provide the desired string for the line type, as shown in Listing 3-7.

MAKING GRAPHICS ACCESSIBLE

Avoiding assumptions about someone's ability to see your graphic presentation is essential. For example, someone who is color blind may not be able to tell that one line is green and the other red. Likewise, someone with low-vision problems may not be able to distinguish between a line that is dashed and one that has a combination of dashes and dots. Using multiple methods to distinguish each line helps ensure that everyone can see your data in a manner that is comfortable to each person.

TABLE 3-1 ## MatPlotLib Line Styles

Character	Line Style
'_'	Solid line
'__'	Dashed line
'_.'	Dash-dot line
':'	Dotted line

LISTING 3-7: **Working with Line Styles**

```
import matplotlib.pyplot as plt
%matplotlib inline
values = [1, 5, 8, 9, 2, 0, 3, 10, 4, 7]
values2 = [3, 8, 9, 2, 1, 2, 4, 7, 6, 6]
plt.plot(range(1,11), values, '--')
plt.plot(range(1,11), values2, ':')
plt.show()
```

In this case, the first line graph uses a dashed line style, while the second line graph uses a dotted line style. You can see the results of the changes in Figure 3-5.

Using colors

Color is another way in which to differentiate line graphs. Of course, this method has certain problems. The most significant problem occurs when someone makes a black-and-white copy of your colored graph — hiding the color differences as shades of gray. Another problem is that someone with color blindness may not be able to tell one line from the other. All this said, color does make for a brighter, eye-grabbing presentation. Table 3-2 shows the colors that MatPlotLib supports.

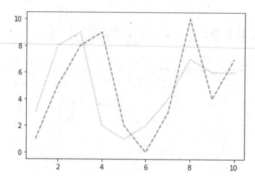

FIGURE 3-5:
Line styles help
differentiate
between plots.

TABLE 3-2

MatPlotLib Colors

Character	Color
'b'	Blue
'g'	Green
'r'	Red
'c'	Cyan
'm'	Magenta
'y'	Yellow
'k'	Black
'w'	White

As with line styles, the color appears in a string as the third argument to the `plot()` function call. In this case, the viewer sees two lines — one in red and the other in magenta. The actual presentation looks like Figure 3-2, but with specific colors, rather than the default colors used in that screenshot. Listing 3-8 shows how to style two lines in different colors.

LISTING 3-8: **Using Colors**

```
values = [1, 5, 8, 9, 2, 0, 3, 10, 4, 7]
values2 = [3, 8, 9, 2, 1, 2, 4, 7, 6, 6]
import matplotlib.pyplot as plt
plt.plot(range(1,11), values, 'r')
plt.plot(range(1,11), values2, 'm')
plt.show()
```

Adding markers

Markers add a special symbol to each data point in a line graph. Unlike line style and color, markers tend to be a little less susceptible to accessibility and printing issues. Even when the specific marker isn't clear, people can usually differentiate one marker from the other. Table 3-3 shows the list of markers that MatPlotLib provides.

TABLE 3-3

MatPlotLib Markers

Character	Marker Type
'.'	Point
','	Pixel
'o'	Circle
'v'	Triangle 1 down
'^'	Triangle 1 up
'<'	Triangle 1 left
'>'	Triangle 1 right
'1'	Triangle 2 down
'2'	Triangle 2 up
'3'	Triangle 2 left
'4'	Triangle 2 right
's'	Square
'p'	Pentagon
'*'	Star
'h'	Hexagon style 1
'H'	Hexagon style 2
'+'	Plus
'x'	X
'D'	Diamond
'd'	Thin diamond
'|'	Vertical line
'_'	Horizontal line

As with line style and color, you add markers as the third argument to a `plot()` call. In Listing 3-9, you see the effects of combining line style with a marker to provide a unique line graph presentation.

<table>
<tr><td>LISTING 3-9:</td><td>Adding Markers</td></tr>
</table>

```
import matplotlib.pyplot as plt
%matplotlib inline
values = [1, 5, 8, 9, 2, 0, 3, 10, 4, 7]
values2 = [3, 8, 9, 2, 1, 2, 4, 7, 6, 6]
plt.plot(range(1,11), values, 'o--')
plt.plot(range(1,11), values2, 'v:')
plt.show()
```

Notice how the combination of line style and marker makes each line stand out in Figure 3-6. Even when printed in black and white, you can easily differentiate one line from the other, which is why you may want to combine presentation techniques.

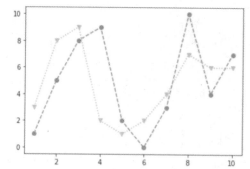

FIGURE 3-6: Markers help to emphasize individual values.

Using Labels, Annotations, and Legends

To fully document your graph, you usually have to resort to labels, annotations, and legends. Each of these elements has a different purpose, as follows:

>> **Label:** Provides positive identification of a particular data element or grouping. The purpose is to make it easy for the viewer to know the name or kind of data illustrated.

» **Annotation:** Augments the information the viewer can immediately see about the data with notes, sources, or other useful information. In contrast to a label, the purpose of annotation is to help extend the viewer's knowledge of the data rather than simply identify it.

» **Legend:** Presents a listing of the data groups within the graph and often provides cues (such as line type or color) to make identification of the data group easier. For example, all the red points may belong to group A, while all the blue points may belong to group B.

The following sections help you understand the purpose and usage of various documentation aids provided with MatPlotLib. These documentation aids help you create an environment in which the viewer is certain as to the source, purpose, and usage of data elements. Some graphs work just fine without any documentation aids, but in other cases, you might find that you need to use all three in order to communicate with your viewer fully.

Adding labels

Labels help people understand the significance of each axis of any graph you create. Without labels, the values portrayed don't have any significance. In addition to a moniker, such as rainfall, you can also add units of measure, such as inches or centimeters, so that your audience knows how to interpret the data shown. Listing 3-10 shows how to add labels to your graph.

LISTING 3-10: **Adding Labels**

```
import matplotlib.pyplot as plt
%matplotlib inline
values = [1, 5, 8, 9, 2, 0, 3, 10, 4, 7]
plt.xlabel('Entries')
plt.ylabel('Values')
plt.plot(range(1,11), values)
plt.show()
```

The call to `xlabel()` documents the x axis of your graph, while the call to `ylabel()` documents the y axis of your graph. Figure 3-7 shows the output of this example.

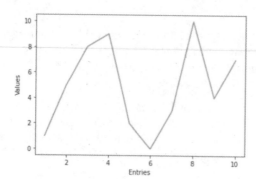

FIGURE 3-7:
Using labels to
identify the axes.

Annotating the chart

You use annotation to draw special attention to points of interest on a graph. For example, you may want to point out that a specific data point is outside the usual range expected for a particular data set. Listing 3-11 shows how to add annotation to a graph.

LISTING 3-11: **Annotating the Chart**

```
import matplotlib.pyplot as plt
%matplotlib inline
values = [1, 5, 8, 9, 2, 0, 3, 10, 4, 7]
plt.annotate(xy=[1,1], s='First Entry')
plt.plot(range(1,11), values)
plt.show()
```

**TECHNICAL
STUFF**

If you're using a newer version of MatPlotLib, you may get an error when you run Listing 3-11, saying that annotate() is missing a required attribute. If this happens, change s='First Entry' to text='First Entry'.

The call to annotate() provides the labeling you need. You must provide a location for the annotation by using the xy parameter, as well as provide text to place at the location by using the s parameter. The annotate() function also provides other parameters that you can use to create special formatting or placement on-screen. Figure 3-8 shows the output from this example.

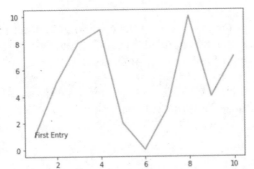

FIGURE 3-8:
Annotation can identify points of interest.

Creating a legend

A legend documents the individual elements of a plot. Each line is presented in a table that contains a label for it so that people can differentiate the lines. For example, one line may represent sales from the first store location and another line may represent sales from a second store location, so you include an entry in the legend for each line that is labeled first and second. Listing 3-12 shows how to add a legend to your plot.

LISTING 3-12: **Creating a Legend**

```
import matplotlib.pyplot as plt
%matplotlib inline
values = [1, 5, 8, 9, 2, 0, 3, 10, 4, 7]
values2 = [3, 8, 9, 2, 1, 2, 4, 7, 6, 6]
line1 = plt.plot(range(1,11), values)
line2 = plt.plot(range(1,11), values2)
plt.legend(['First', 'Second'], loc=4)
plt.show()
```

The call to legend() occurs after you create the plots, not before, as with some of the other functions described in this chapter. You must provide a handle to each of the plots. Notice how line1 is set equal to the first plot() call and line2 is set equal to the second plot() call.

The default location for the legend is the upper-right corner of the plot, which proved inconvenient for this particular example. Adding the `loc` parameter lets you place the legend in a different location. See the `legend()` function documentation at `https://matplotlib.org/stable/api/_as_gen/matplotlib.pyplot.legend.html#matplotlib.pyplot.legend` for additional legend locations. Figure 3-9 shows the output from this example.

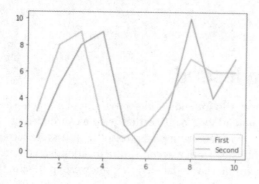

FIGURE 3-9:
Using legends
to identify
individual lines.

Chapter **4**

Visualizing the Data

"Those who rule data will rule the entire world."

— MASAYOSHI SON

Book 6, Chapter 3 helped you understand the mechanics of working with MatPlotLib, which is an important first step toward using it. This chapter takes the next step in helping you use MatPlotLib to perform useful work. The main goal of this chapter is to help you visualize your data in various ways. Creating a graphic presentation of your data is essential if you want to help other people understand what you're trying to say. Even though you can see what the numbers mean in your mind, other people will likely need graphics to see what point you're trying to make by manipulating data in various ways.

The chapter starts by looking at some basic graph types that MatPlotLib supports. You don't find the full list of graphs and plots listed in this chapter — it would take an entire book to explore them all in detail. However, you do find the most common types.

In this chapter, you begin exploring specific sorts of plotting as it relates to data science. Of course, no book on data science would be complete without exploring scatterplots, which are used to help people see patterns in seemingly unrelated data points. Because much of the data that you work with today is time-related or geographic in nature, the chapter devotes two special sections to these topics. You also get to work with both directed and undirected graphs, which is fine for social media analysis.

You don't have to type the source code for this chapter manually. In fact, it's a lot easier if you use the downloadable source available at www.dummies.com/go/ codingallinonefd2e. The source code for this chapter appears in the CAIO4D2E_ Visualizing_the_Data.ipynb source code.

REMEMBER

Choosing the Right Graph

The kind of graph you choose determines how people view the associated data, so choosing the right graph from the outset is important. For example, if you want to show how various data elements contribute toward a whole, you really need to use a pie chart. On the other hand, when you want people to form opinions on how data elements compare, you use a bar chart. The idea is to choose a graph that naturally leads people to draw the conclusion that you need them to draw about the data that you've carefully massaged from various data sources. (You also have the option of using line graphs — a technique demonstrated in Book 6, Chapter 3.) The following sections describe the various graph types and provide you with basic examples of how to use them.

Showing parts of a whole with pie charts

Pie charts focus on showing parts of a whole. The entire pie would be 100 percent. The question is how much of that percentage each value occupies. Listing 4-1 shows how to create a pie chart with many of the special features in place.

LISTING 4-1: **Showing Parts of a Whole with Pie Charts**

```
import matplotlib.pyplot as plt
%matplotlib inline

values = [5, 8, 9, 10, 4, 7]
colors = ['b', 'g', 'r', 'c', 'm', 'y']
labels = ['A', 'B', 'C', 'D', 'E', 'F']
explode = (0, 0.2, 0, 0, 0, 0)

plt.pie(values, colors=colors, labels=labels,
        explode=explode, autopct='%1.1f%%',
        counterclock=False, shadow=True)
plt.title('Values')

plt.show()
```

The essential part of a pie chart is the values. You could create a basic pie chart using just the values as input.

The `colors` parameter lets you choose custom colors for each pie wedge. You use the `labels` parameter to identify each wedge. In many cases, you need to make one wedge stand out from the others, so you add the `explode` parameter with a list of explode values. A value of 0 keeps the wedge in place — any other value moves the wedge out from the center of the pie.

Each pie wedge can show various kinds of information. This example shows the percentage occupied by each wedge with the `autopct` parameter. You must provide a format string to format the percentages.

TIP

Some parameters affect how the pie chart is drawn. Use the `counterclock` parameter to determine the direction of the wedges. The `shadow` parameter determines whether the pie appears with a shadow beneath it (for a 3D effect). You can find other parameters at `https://matplotlib.org/stable/api/pyplot_summary.html`.

In most cases, you also want to give your pie chart a title so that others know what it represents. You do this using the `title()` function. Figure 4-1 shows the output from this example.

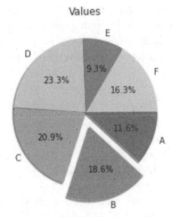

FIGURE 4-1:
Pie charts show
a percentage
of the whole.

Creating comparisons with bar charts

Bar charts make comparing values easy. The wide bars and segregated measurements emphasize the differences between values, rather than the flow of one value to another as a line graph would do. Fortunately, you have all sorts of methods at your disposal for emphasizing specific values and performing other tricks. Listing 4-2 shows just some of the things you can do with a vertical bar chart.

LISTING 4-2: **Creating Comparisons with Bar Charts**

```
import matplotlib.pyplot as plt
%matplotlib inline

values = [5, 8, 9, 10, 4, 7]
widths = [0.7, 0.8, 0.7, 0.7, 0.7, 0.7]
colors = ['b', 'r', 'b', 'b', 'b', 'b']

plt.bar(range(0, 6), values, width=widths,
color=colors, align='center')

plt.show()
```

To create even a basic bar chart, you must provide a series of x coordinates and the heights of the bars. The example uses the range() function to create the x coordinates, and the values variable contains the heights.

Of course, you may want more than a basic bar chart, and MatPlotLib provides a number of ways to get the job done. In this case, the example uses the width parameter to control the width of each bar, emphasizing the second bar by making it slightly larger. The larger width would show up even in a black-and-white printout. It also uses the color parameter to change the color of the target bar to red (the rest are blue).

As with other chart types, the bar chart provides some special features that you can use to make your presentation stand out. The example uses the align parameter to center the data on the x coordinate (the standard position is to the left). You can also use other parameters, such as hatch, to enhance the visual appearance of your bar chart. Figure 4-2 shows the output of this example.

TIP

This chapter helps you get started using MatPlotLib to create a variety of chart and graph types. Of course, more examples are better, so you can also find some more advanced examples on the MatPlotLib site at https://matplotlib.org/stable/gallery/index.html. Some of the examples, such as those that demonstrate animation techniques, become quite advanced, but with practice you can use any of them to improve your own charts and graphs.

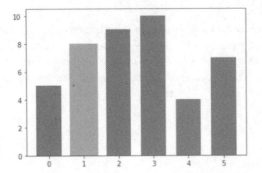

FIGURE 4-2:
Bar charts make it
easier to perform
comparisons.

Showing distributions using histograms

Histograms categorize data by breaking it into *bins*, where each bin contains a subset of the data range. A histogram then displays the number of items in each bin so that you can see the distribution of data and the progression of data from bin to bin. In most cases, you see a curve of some type, such as a bell curve. Listing 4-3 shows how to create a histogram with randomized data.

LISTING 4-3: **Showing Data Progressions Using Histograms**

```
import numpy as np
import matplotlib.pyplot as plt
%matplotlib inline


x = 20 * np.random.randn(10000)
plt.hist(x, 25, range=(-50, 50), histtype='stepfilled',
        align='mid', color='g', label='Test Data')
plt.legend()
plt.title('Step Filled Histogram')

plt.show()
```

In this case, the input values are a series of random numbers. The distribution of these numbers should show a type of bell curve. As a minimum, you must provide a series of values, x in this case, to plot. The second argument contains the number of bins to use when creating the data intervals. The default value is 10. Using the range parameter helps you focus the histogram on the relevant data and exclude any outliers.

You can create multiple histogram types. The default setting creates a bar chart. You can also create a stacked bar chart, stepped graph, or filled stepped graph (the type shown in the example). In addition, it's possible to control the orientation of the output, with vertical as the default.

As with most other charts and graphs in this chapter, you can add special features to the output. For example, the `align` parameter determines the alignment of each bar along the baseline. Use the `color` parameter to control the colors of the bars. The `label` parameter doesn't actually appear unless you also create a legend (as shown in this example). Figure 4-3 shows typical output from this example.

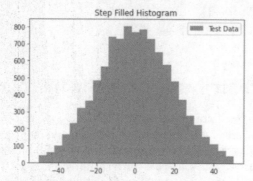

FIGURE 4-3: Histograms let you see distributions of numbers.

REMEMBER

Data generated using the random function changes with every call. Every time you run the example, you see slightly different results because the random-generation process differs.

Depicting groups using box plots

Box plots provide a means of depicting groups of numbers through their *quartiles* (three points dividing a group into four equal parts). A box plot may also have lines, called *whiskers,* indicating data outside the upper and lower quartiles. The spacing shown within a box plot helps indicate the skew and dispersion of the data. Listing 4-4 shows how to create a box plot with randomized data.

LISTING 4-4: **Depicting Groups of Numbers Using Box Plots**

```
import numpy as np
import matplotlib.pyplot as plt
%matplotlib inline

spread = 100 * np.random.rand(100)
center = np.ones(50) * 50
flier_high = 100 * np.random.rand(10) + 100
```

```
flier_low = -100 * np.random.rand(10)
data = np.concatenate((spread, center,
                        flier_high, flier_low))
plt.boxplot(data, sym='gx', widths=.75, notch=True)

plt.show()
```

To create a usable data set, you need to combine several different number-generation techniques, as shown at the beginning of the example. Here are how these techniques work:

>> spread: Contains a set of random numbers between 0 and 100.

>> center: Provides 50 values directly in the center of the range of 50.

>> flier_high: Simulates outliers between 100 and 200.

>> flier_low: Simulates outliers between 0 and -100.

The code combines all these values into a single data set using concatenate(). Being randomly generated with specific characteristics (such as a large number of points in the middle), the output will show specific characteristics but will work fine for the example.

The call to boxplot() requires only data as input. All other parameters have default settings. In this case, the code sets the presentation of outliers to green Xs by setting the sym parameter. You use widths to modify the size of the box (made extra-large in this case to make the box easier to see). Finally, you can create a square box or a box with a notch using the notch parameter (which normally defaults to False). Figure 4-4 shows typical output from this example.

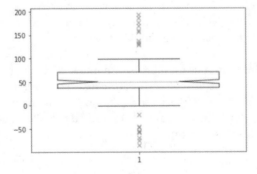

FIGURE 4-4: Use box plots to present groups of numbers.

The box shows the three data points as the box, with the line in the middle being the median. The two black horizontal lines connected to the box by whiskers show the upper and lower limits (for four quartiles). The outliers appear above and below the upper and lower limit lines as Xs.

Seeing data patterns using scatterplots

Scatterplots show clusters of data rather than trends (as with line graphs) or discrete values (as with bar charts). The purpose of a scatterplot is to help you see data patterns. Listing 4-5 shows how to create a scatterplot using randomized data.

LISTING 4-5: **Seeing Data Patterns Using Scatterplots**

```
import numpy as np
import matplotlib.pyplot as plt

x1 = 5 * np.random.rand(40)
x2 = 5 * np.random.rand(40) + 25
x3 = 25 * np.random.rand(20)
x = np.concatenate((x1, x2, x3))

y1 = 5 * np.random.rand(40)
y2 = 5 * np.random.rand(40) + 25
y3 = 25 * np.random.rand(20)
y = np.concatenate((y1, y2, y3))

plt.scatter(x, y, s=[100], marker='^', c='m')
plt.show()
```

The example begins by generating random x and y coordinates. For each x coordinate, you must have a corresponding y coordinate. It's possible to create a scatterplot using just the x and y coordinates.

It's possible to dress up a scatterplot in a number of ways. In this case, the s parameter determines the size of each data point. The marker parameter determines the data point shape. You use the c parameter to define the colors for all the data points, or you can define a separate color for individual data points. Figure 4-5 shows the output from this example.

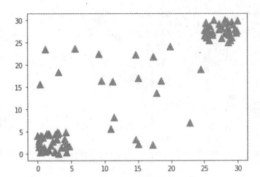

FIGURE 4-5:
Use scatterplots
to show groups of
data points and
their associated
patterns.

Creating Advanced Scatterplots

Scatterplots are especially important for data science because they can show data patterns that aren't obvious when viewed in other ways. You can see data groupings with relative ease and help the viewer understand when data belongs to a particular group. You can also show overlaps between groups and even demonstrate when certain data is outside the expected range. Showing relationships in the data is an advanced technique that you need to know in order to best use MatPlotLib. The following sections demonstrate how to perform these advanced techniques on the scatterplot you created earlier in the chapter.

Depicting groups

Color is the third axis when working with a scatterplot. Using color lets you highlight groups so that others can see them with greater ease. Listing 4-6 shows how you can use color to show groups within a scatterplot.

LISTING 4-6: **Depicting Groups**

```
import numpy as np
import matplotlib.pyplot as plt

x1 = 5 * np.random.rand(50)
x2 = 5 * np.random.rand(50) + 25
x3 = 30 * np.random.rand(25)
x = np.concatenate((x1, x2, x3))

y1 = 5 * np.random.rand(50)
y2 = 5 * np.random.rand(50) + 25
```

(continued)

LISTING 4-6: *(continued)*

```
y3 = 30 * np.random.rand(25)
y = np.concatenate((y1, y2, y3))

color_array = ['b'] * 50 + ['g'] * 50 + ['r'] * 25

plt.scatter(x, y, s=[50], marker='D', c=color_array)
plt.show()
```

The example works essentially the same as the scatterplot example in the previous section, except that this example uses an array for the colors. Unfortunately, if you're seeing this in the printed book, the differences between the shades of gray in Figure 4-6 will be hard to see. However, the first group is blue, followed by green for the second group. Any outliers appear in red.

FIGURE 4-6:
Color arrays can make the scatterplot groups stand out better.

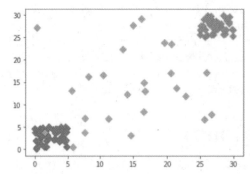

Showing correlations

In some cases, you need to know the general direction that your data is taking when looking at a scatterplot. Even if you create a clear depiction of the groups, the actual direction that the data is taking as a whole may not be clear. In this case, you add a trendline to the output. Listing 4-7 is an example of adding a trendline to a scatterplot that includes groups but isn't quite as clear as the scatterplot shown in Figure 4-6.

LISTING 4-7: **Showing Correlations**

```
import numpy as np
import matplotlib.pyplot as plt
import matplotlib.pylab as plb
%matplotlib inline
```

```
x1 = 15 * np.random.rand(50)
x2 = 15 * np.random.rand(50) + 15
x3 = 30 * np.random.rand(25)
x = np.concatenate((x1, x2, x3))

y1 = 15 * np.random.rand(50)
y2 = 15 * np.random.rand(50) + 15
y3 = 30 * np.random.rand(25)
y = np.concatenate((y1, y2, y3))

color_array = ['b'] * 50 + ['g'] * 50 + ['r'] * 25
plt.scatter(x, y, s=[90], marker='*', c=color_array)
z = np.polyfit(x, y, 1)
p = np.poly1d(z)
plb.plot(x, p(x), 'm-')

plt.show()
```

The code for creating the scatterplot is essentially the same as in the example in the "Depicting groups" section, earlier in the chapter, but the plot doesn't define the groups as clearly. Adding a trendline means calling the NumPy `polyfit()` function with the data, which returns a vector of coefficients, p, that minimizes the least-squares error. Least-square regression is a method for finding a line that summarizes the relationship between two variables, x and y in this case, at least within the domain of the explanatory variable x. The third `polyfit()` parameter expresses the degree of the polynomial fit.

The vector output of `polyfit()` is used as input to `poly1d()`, which calculates the actual data points on the y axis. The call to `plot()` creates the trendline on the scatterplot. You can see a typical result of this example in Figure 4-7.

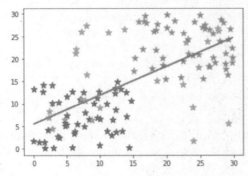

FIGURE 4-7:
Scatterplot
trendlines can
show you the
general data
direction.

Plotting Time Series

Nothing is truly static. When you view most data, you see an instant of time — a snapshot of how the data appeared at one particular moment. Of course, such views are both common and useful. However, sometimes you need to view data as it moves through time — to see it as it changes. Only by viewing the data as it changes can you expect to understand the underlying forces that shape it. The following sections describe how to work with data on a time-related basis.

Representing time on axes

Many times, you need to present data over time. The data could come in many forms, but generally you have some type of time tick (one unit of time), followed by one or more features that describe what happens during that particular tick. Listing 4-8 shows a simple set of days and sales on those days for a particular item in whole (integer) amounts.

LISTING 4-8: **Representing Time on Axes**

```
import pandas as pd
import matplotlib.pyplot as plt
import datetime as dt
%matplotlib inline

start_date = dt.datetime(2022, 7, 30)
end_date = dt.datetime(2022, 8, 5)
daterange = pd.date_range(start_date, end_date)
sales = (np.random.rand(len(daterange)) * 50).astype(int)
df = pd.DataFrame(sales, index=daterange,
                  columns=['Sales'])
df.loc['Jul 30 2022':'Aug 05 2022'].plot()
plt.ylim(0, 50)
plt.xlabel('Sales Date')
plt.ylabel('Sale Value')
plt.title('Plotting Time')

plt.show()
```

The example begins by creating a DataFrame to hold the information. The source of the information could be anything, but in this example, the data is generated randomly.

Using `loc[]` lets you select a range of dates from the total number of entries available. Notice that this example uses only some of the generated data for output. It then adds some amplifying information about the plot and displays it on-screen. The call to `plot()` must specify the x and y values in this case or you get an error. Figure 4-8 shows typical output from the randomly generated data.

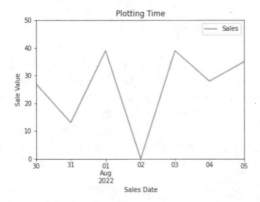

FIGURE 4-8:
Use line graphs to show the flow of data over time.

Plotting trends over time

As with any other data presentation, sometimes you really can't see what direction the data is headed in without help. Listing 4-9 starts with the plot from the previous section and adds a trendline to it.

LISTING 4-9: **Plotting Trends Over Time**

```
import numpy as np
import pandas as pd
import matplotlib.pyplot as plt
import datetime as dt
%matplotlib inline

start_date = dt.datetime(2022, 7, 29)
end_date = dt.datetime(2022, 8, 7)
daterange = pd.date_range(start_date, end_date)
sales = (np.random.rand(len(daterange)) * 50).astype(int)
df = pd.DataFrame(sales, index=daterange,
                  columns=['Sales'])
lr_coef = np.polyfit(range(0, len(df)), df['Sales'], 1)
lr_func = np.poly1d(lr_coef)
trend = lr_func(range(0, len(df)))
df['trend'] = trend
```

(continued)

LISTING 4-9: *(continued)*

```
df.loc['Jul 30 2022':'Aug 05 2022'].plot()
plt.xlabel('Sales Date')
plt.ylabel('Sale Value')
plt.title('Plotting Time')
plt.legend(['Sales', 'Trend'])

plt.show()
```

REMEMBER

The "Showing correlations" section, earlier in this chapter, shows how most people add a trendline to their graph. In fact, this is the approach that you often see used online. You'll also notice that a lot of people have trouble using this approach in some situations. This example takes a slightly different approach by adding the trendline directly to the DataFrame. If you print df after the call to df['trend'] = trend, you see trendline data similar to the values shown here:

```
Sales trend
2022-07-29 6 18.890909
2022-07-30 13 20.715152
2022-07-31 38 22.539394
2022-08-01 22 24.363636
2022-08-02 40 26.187879
2022-08-03 39 28.012121
2022-08-04 36 29.836364
2022-08-05 21 31.660606
2022-08-06 7 33.484848
2022-08-07 49 35.309091
```

Using this approach makes it ultimately easier to plot the data. You call plot() only once and avoid relying on the MatPlotLib, pylab, as shown in the example in the "Showing correlations" section. The resulting code is simpler and less likely to cause the issues you see online.

When you plot the initial data, the call to plot() automatically generates a legend for you. MatPlotLib doesn't automatically add the trendline, so you must also create a new legend for the plot. Figure 4-9 shows typical output from this example using randomly generated data.

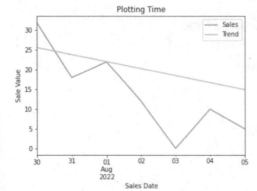

FIGURE 4-9:
Add a trendline
to show the
average direction
of change in a
chart or graph.

Visualizing Graphs

A *graph* is a depiction of data showing the connections between data points using lines. The purpose is to show that some data points relate to other data points, but not all the data points that appear on the graph. Think about a map of a subway system. Each of the stations connects to other stations, but no single station connects to all the stations in the subway system. Graphs are a popular data science topic because of their use in social media analysis. When performing social media analysis, you depict and analyze networks of relationships, such as friends or business connections, from social hubs such as Facebook, Twitter, or LinkedIn.

REMEMBER

The two common depictions of graphs are *undirected*, where the graph simply shows lines between data elements, and *directed*, where arrows added to the line show that data flows in a particular direction. For example, consider a depiction of a water system. The water would flow in just one direction in most cases, so you could use a directed graph to depict not only the connections between sources and targets for the water but also to show water direction by using arrows. The following sections help you understand the two types of graphs better and show you how to create them.

Developing undirected graphs

As previously stated, an undirected graph simply shows connections between nodes. The output doesn't provide a direction from one node to the next. For example, when establishing connectivity between web pages, no direction is implied. Listing 4-10 shows how to create an undirected graph.

LISTING 4-10: **Developing Undirected Graphs**

```
import networkx as nx
import matplotlib.pyplot as plt
%matplotlib inline

G = nx.Graph()
H = nx.Graph()
G.add_node(1)
G.add_nodes_from([2, 3])
G.add_nodes_from(range(4, 7))
H.add_node(7)
G.add_nodes_from(H)
G.add_edge(1, 2)
G.add_edge(1, 1)
G.add_edges_from([(2,3), (3,6), (4,6), (5,6)])
H.add_edges_from([(4,7), (5,7), (6,7)])
G.add_edges_from(H.edges())
nx.draw_networkx(G)

plt.show()
```

In contrast to the canned example found in Book 6, Chapter 2, this example builds the graph using a number of different techniques. It begins by importing the NetworkX package you use in Book 6, Chapter 2. To create a new undirected graph, the code calls the Graph() constructor, which can take a number of input arguments to use as attributes. However, you can build a perfectly usable graph without using attributes, which is what this example does.

The easiest way to add a node is to call add_node() with a node number. You can also add a list, dictionary, or range() of nodes using add_nodes_from(). In fact, you can import nodes from other graphs if you want.

REMEMBER

Even though the nodes used in the example rely on numbers, you don't have to use numbers for your nodes. A node can use a single letter, a string, or even a date. Nodes do have some restrictions. For example, you can't create a node using a Boolean value.

Nodes don't have any connectivity at the outset. You must define connections (edges) between them. To add a single edge, you call add_edge() with the numbers of the nodes that you want to add. As with nodes, you can use add_edges_from() to create more than one edge using a list, dictionary, or another graph as input. Figure 4-10 shows the output from this example (your output may differ slightly but should have the same connections).

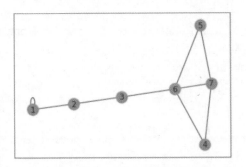

Developing directed graphs

You use directed graphs when you need to show a direction, say from a start point to an end point. When you get a map that shows you how to get from one specific point to another, the starting node and ending node are marked as such, and the lines between these nodes (and all the intermediate nodes) show direction.

TIP

Your graphs need not be boring. You can dress them up in all sorts of ways so that the viewer gains additional information. For example, you can create custom labels, use specific colors for certain nodes, or rely on color to help people see the meaning behind your graphs. You can also change edge line weight and use other techniques to mark a specific path between nodes as the better one to choose. Listing 4-11 shows many (but not nearly all) the ways in which you can dress up a directed graph and make it more interesting.

LISTING 4-11: **Developing Direct Graphs**

```
import networkx as nx
import matplotlib.pyplot as plt
%matplotlib inline


G = nx.DiGraph()
G.add_node(1)
G.add_by nodes_from([2, 3])
G.add_nodes_from(range(4, 6))
nx.add_path(G,[6, 7, 8])
G.add_edge(1, 2)
G.add_edges_from([(1,4), (4,5), (2,3), (3,6), (5,6)])
colors = ['r', 'g', 'g', 'g', 'g', 'm', 'm', 'r']
labels = {1:'Start', 2:'2', 3:'3', 4:'4',
          5:'5', 6:'6', 7:'7', 8:'End'}
```

(continued)

LISTING 4-11:   **(continued)**

```
sizes = [800, 300, 300, 300, 300, 600, 300, 800]
nx.draw_networkx(G, node_color=colors, node_shape='D',
                 with_labels=True, labels=labels,
node_size=sizes)

plt.show()
```

The example begins by creating a directional graph using the DiGraph() constructor. You should note that the NetworkX package also supports MultiGraph() and MultiDiGraph() graph types. You can see a listing of all the graph types at https://networkx.org/documentation/stable/reference/classes/index.html.

Listing 4-11 requires version 2+ of NetworkX. If you get an error when you run it, you can upgrade NetworkX using the following command:

```
pip install networkx==2.6
```

Adding nodes is much like working with an undirected graph. You can add single nodes using add_node() and multiple nodes using add_nodes_from(). The add_path() call lets you create nodes and edges at the same time. The order of nodes in the call is important. The flow from one node to another is from left to right in the list supplied to the call.

REMEMBER

Adding edges is much the same as working with an undirected graph, too. You can use add_edge() to add a single edge or add_edges_from() to add multiple edges at one time. However, the order of the node numbers is important. The flow goes from the left node to the right node in each pair.

This example adds special node colors, labels, sizes, and a shape (only one shape is used) to the output. You still call on draw_networkx() to perform the task. However, adding the parameters shown changes the appearance of the graph. Note that you must set with_labels to True in order to see the labels provided by the labels parameter. Figure 4-11 shows the output from this example.

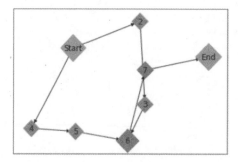

FIGURE 4-11:
Use directed graphs to show direction between nodes.

7
Career Building with Coding

Contents at a Glance

Chapter **1**

Exploring Coding Career Paths

We shall not cease from exploration, and the end of all our exploring will be to arrive where we started and know the place for the first time.

— T.S. ELIOT

For many people, the words "coding career" evoke an image of a person sitting in a dimly lit room typing incomprehensible commands into a computer. The stereotype has persisted for decades — just watch actors such as Matthew Broderick in *War Games* (1983), Keanu Reeves in *The Matrix* (1999), or Jesse Eisenberg in *The Social Network* (2010). Fortunately, these movies are not accurate representations of reality. Just like a career in medicine can lead to psychiatry, gynecology, or surgery, a career in coding can lead to an equally broad range of options.

In this chapter, you see how coding can augment your existing job across a mix of functions, and you explore increasingly popular careers based primarily on coding.

Augmenting Your Existing Job

Many people find coding opportunities in their existing job. It usually starts innocently enough, and with something small. For example, you may need a change made to the text on the company's website, but the person who would normally do that is unavailable before your deadline. If you knew how to alter the website's code, you could perform your job faster or more easily. This section explores how coding might augment your existing job.

Creative design

Professionals in creative design include those who

>> Shape how messages are delivered to clients.

>> Create print media such as brochures and catalogs.

>> Design for digital media such as websites and mobile applications.

CHOOSING A CAREER PATH

Coding career paths are extremely varied. For some people, the path starts with using code to more efficiently perform an existing job. For others, coding is a way to transition to a new career. As varied as the career path is, so too are the types of companies that need coders.

As more people carry Internet-capable mobile phones, businesses of every type are turning to coders to reach customers and to optimize existing operations. No business is immune. For example, FarmLogs is a company that collects data from farm equipment to help farmers increase crop yields and forecast profits. FarmLogs needs coders to build the software that collects and analyzes data, and farmers with large operations may need coders to customize the software.

To build or customize software, you'll need to learn new skills. Surprisingly, the time required to learn and start coding can range from an afternoon of lessons to a ten-week crash course to more time-intensive options, such as a four-year undergraduate degree in computer science.

Traditionally, digital designers, also known as visual designers, created *mockups*, static illustrations detailing layout, images, and interactions, and then sent these mockups to developers who would create the web or mobile product. This process worked reasonably well for everyday projects, but feedback loops started becoming longer as mockups became more complex. For example, a designer would create multiple mockups of a website, and then the developer would implement them to create working prototypes, after which the winning mockup would be selected. As another example, the rise of mobile devices has led to literally thousands of screen variations between mobile phones and tablets created by Apple, Samsung, and others. Project timelines increased because designers had to create five or more mockups to cover the most popular devices and screen sizes.

As a designer, one way to speed up this process is to know just enough code to create working prototypes of the initial mockups that are responsive, which means one prototype renders on both desktop and mobile devices. Then project managers, developers, and clients can use these early prototypes to decide which versions to further develop and which to discard. Additionally, because responsive prototypes follow a predictable set of rules across all devices, creating additional mockups for each device is unnecessary, which further decreases design time. As mobile devices have become more popular, the demand for designers who understand how to create good user interactions (UI) and user experiences (UX) has greatly increased.

TIP

Prototyping tools such as InVision and Axure provide a middle option between creating static illustrations and coding clickable prototypes by allowing designers to create working prototypes without much coding. Still, a person with basic coding skills can improve a prototype generated with these tools by making it more interactive and realistic. Designers who can design and code proficiently are referred to as "unicorns" because they are rare and in high demand.

Content and editorial

Professionals in content and editorial perform tasks such as the following:

» Maintain the company's presence on social networks such as Twitter and Facebook.

» Create short posts for the company blog and for email campaigns.

» Write longer pieces for articles or presentations.

At smaller companies, content creation is usually mixed with other responsibilities. At larger companies, creating content is a full-time job. Whether you're blogging for a startup or reporting for *The Wall Street Journal*, writers of all types face the same challenges of identifying relevant topics and backing it up with data.

Traditionally, content was written based on a writer's investigation and leads from a small group of people. For example, you might write a blog post about a specific product's feature because a major customer asked about it during a sales call. But what if most of your smaller customers, whom you don't speak with regularly, would benefit from a blog post about some other product feature?

As a writer, you can produce more relevant content by writing code to analyze measurable data and use the conclusions to author content. I Quant NY (http://iquantny.tumblr.com), an online blog, is one shining example of data driving content creation. In 2014, the site's author, Ben Wellington, analyzed public data on New York City parking tickets, bike usage, and traffic crashes, and wrote about his conclusions. His analysis led to original stories and headlines in major newspapers such as *The New York Times* and *New York Post* (see Figure 1-1).

FIGURE 1-1:
Article about a ticket-generating fire hydrant.

Human resources

Those who work in human resources might be expected to do the following:

>> Source and screen candidates for open company jobs.

>> Manage payroll, benefits, performance, and training for employees.

>> Ensure company compliance with relevant laws and resolve disputes.

Traditionally, HR professionals have not performed much coding in the workplace. The human- and process-driven components of the job generally outweighed the need for automation that coding typically provides. For example, a dispute between co-workers is usually resolved with an in-person meeting organized by HR, not by a computer program. However, the recruiting function in HR may benefit from coding. Hiring employees has always been challenging, especially for technical positions where the demand for employees far exceeds the supply of available and qualified candidates.

If you're responsible for technical recruiting and want to increase the number of candidates you reach out to and source, one solution is to develop some coding experience that enables you to discover people who may not meet the traditional hiring criteria. For example, a company might ordinarily look for developers from a specific university with at least a 3.0 grade point average.

However, increasingly developers are self-taught and may have dropped out or not attended university at all. A technical recruiter who can evaluate code that self-taught developers have written and made publicly available on sites such as GitHub or Bitbucket can qualify candidates who previously would have been rejected. Additionally, recruiters working with technical candidates improve outcomes by being able to speak their language.

Companies such as Google and Facebook have taken a technical approach to managing the expensive and difficult problem of finding and retaining employees. These companies perform people analytics on their employees by looking at everyone who applies and analyzing factors that contribute to hiring, promotion, and departure, such as undergraduate GPA, previous employer, interview performance, and on-the-job reviews. At Google, this analysis requires some serious coding because more than two million people apply each year.

Product management

Product managers, especially those working on software and hardware products, perform tasks like the following:

>> Manage processes and people to launch products on time and on budget, maintain existing products, and retire old products.

>> Connect all departments that create a product, including sales, engineering, marketing, design, operations, and quality control.

>> Guide the product definition, roadmap, and business model based on understanding the target market and customers.

The product manager's role can vary greatly because it is a function of the company culture and the product being built. This is especially true for technical products; in some companies, product managers define the problem and engineers design hardware and software to solve those problems. In other companies, product managers not only define the problem but also help design the technical solution.

One of the hardest challenges and main responsibilities of a product manager is to deliver a product on time and within budget. Timelines can be difficult to estimate, especially when new technology is used or existing technology is used in a new way. When you manufacture, say, a chair, it has a set product definition. For a product with a technical component, additional features can creep into the project late in development, or a single feature might be responsible for the majority of time or cost overruns. The product manager helps to keep these variables in check.

The product manager working on a technical product who has some coding skill will be able to better estimate development cycles and anticipate the moving pieces that must come together. In addition, solving technical challenges that arise and understanding the tradeoffs of one solution versus another are easier with some coding background.

TIP

Business analysts or integration specialists translate business requirements from customers into technical requirements that are delivered to project managers and that are eventually implemented by backend engineers.

Sales and marketing

Sales and marketing professionals perform tasks such as

>> Segment existing customers and identify new potential customers.

>> Generate and convert prospective leads into sold customers.

>> Craft product and brand images to reflect company and customer values.

Salespeople and marketers expend a great deal of effort placing the right message at the right time before the right customer. For decades, these messages were delivered in newspapers, in magazines, and on television and radio. Measuring their effect in these channels was difficult, part art and part science. With the movement of messages to the Internet, we can now measure and analyze every customer view and click. Online marketing has created another problem: Online customers generate so much data that much of it goes unanalyzed.

The salesperson or marketer who can code is able to better target customers online. If you're a salesperson, generating leads is the start of the sales funnel, and coding enables you to find and prioritize online website visitors as potential customers. For example, when Uber launched their mobile application, it was available only in San Francisco. The company tracked and analyzed the location of users who opened the app to decide which city to launch in next.

If you're in marketing, identifying *whom* to market to is as important as identifying *what* message to market. Website visitors reveal behavioral and demographic data about themselves, including location, web pages visited, visit duration, and often gender, age, employer, and past online purchases. Even moderately successful websites generate tens of millions of records a month, and coding can help spot trends such as the 25-to-29-year-old females in Nebraska who are suddenly interested in but aren't purchasing your product. Marketing messages become more efficient when you know the segments you're targeting and how they are responding.

Legal

Professionals providing legal services might perform the following tasks:

>> Identify and manage legal risks in agreements and transactions.

>> Ensure ongoing compliance with relevant laws and regulations.

>> Review documents such as prior cases, business records, and legal filings.

>> Resolve disputes through litigation, mediation, and arbitration.

Historically, the legal profession has been resilient to advances in technology. I include it here because if lawyers who code are able to more efficiently perform their jobs, professionals in any other industry should be able to benefit from coding as well.

Coding knowledge may not assist a lawyer with delivering a passionate argument in court or finalizing a transaction between two Fortune 500 companies, but the bulk of a lawyer's time is spent on document review, a task that could benefit from coding knowledge.

When reviewing legal documents, a lawyer might read previous cases in a litigation, check existing patent filings before filing a new patent, or examine a company's contracts in preparation for a merger. All these tasks involve processing large amounts of text, and current legal tools enable, for example, wildcard searching (such as using *new** to find New York, New Jersey, and New Hampshire).

However, the use of *regular expressions* — code that searches for patterns in text — could help lawyers review documents faster and more efficiently. See Figure 1-2.

For example, suppose you are a government lawyer investigating an investment bank for fraudulently selling low-quality mortgages. The investment bank has produced two million documents, and you want to find every email address mentioned in these documents. You could spend months reviewing every page and noting the email addresses, or you could spend a few minutes writing a regular expression that returns every email address automatically.

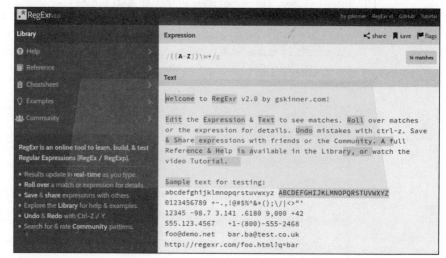

© John Wiley & Sons

TECHNICAL
STUFF

As the government lawyer reviewing those documents, one of many regular expressions you could use to find email addresses is .+@.+\..+. Much like the * wildcard character, each symbol represents a pattern to match. This regular expression first looks for a least one character before and after the @ symbol, and at least one character before and after a period that appears following the @ symbol. This pattern matches the username@domain.com email address format.

Finding a New Coding Job

The career changer looking to transition to a coding job can choose from a variety of roles. This section describes the most popular coding jobs today. In these roles at the entry level, your coding knowledge will be used daily. As you become more skilled and senior, however, your people-management responsibilities will increase while the number of lines of code you write will decrease. For example, Mark Zuckerberg wrote the code for the initial version of Facebook and continued to write code for two years after the website launched, after which he stopped coding for almost six years to focus on managing the team's growth.

Some coding roles may appeal to you to more than others. In addition to understanding jobs available in the market, some self-reflection can help you make the best choice possible. As you review the role descriptions in this section, take a personal inventory of

>> Tasks you enjoy and dislike in your current role

>> Skills you already possess, and the skills you will need to learn

>> Interests you want to pursue that will make you excited about working every day

Although no job is completely secure, the demand for technical roles is high and continues to grow. The U.S. government estimates that employment in computer science and information technology occupations will grow by 13 percent from 2020 to 2030, adding around 667,600 jobs. The median income for computer and information technology jobs in 2020 was more than double the median annual wage for all occupations.

Frontend web development

Web developers create websites. There are two types of web developers: frontend developers and backend developers. Each requires different skills and tasks, which are discussed in this section.

Frontend web developers code everything visible on the web page, such as the layout, image placement and sizing, input features including buttons and text boxes, and the site's general look and feel. These effects are created with three major programming languages: HTML (Hypertext Markup Language), which is used to place content on the page, CSS (Cascading Style Sheets), which styles the text and further contributes to its appearance, and JavaScript, which adds interactivity.

In addition to these three languages, frontend developer job postings reveal a common set of skills that employers are looking for:

>> **SEO (search engine optimization):** Creating web pages for humans might seem like the only goal, but machines, specifically search engines, are the primary way most users find websites. Search engines "view" web pages differently than humans, and certain coding techniques can make it easier for search engines to index an individual web page or an entire website.

>> **Cross-browser testing:** Users navigate web pages by using four major browsers (Chrome, Firefox, Edge, and Safari), each with two or three active versions in addition to mobile versions of each browser. As a result, a web developer must be skilled in testing websites across eight or more browser versions. Developing for older browsers is typically more difficult because

they support fewer features and require more code to achieve the same effect as modern browsers.

» **CSS tools:** Developers use precompilers and CSS frameworks to make coding in CSS easier:

- *Precompilers* extend CSS functionality with features such as variables and functions, which make it easier to read and maintain CSS code.

  CSS frameworks, such as Bootstrap and Foundation, provide prewritten HTML and CSS code that makes it easier to develop a website with a consistent look across desktop and mobile devices.

TIP

Proficiency in all precompilers and frameworks is unnecessary, but knowledge of one precompiler and framework can be helpful.

» **JavaScript frameworks:** Developers use prewritten JavaScript code called a *JavaScript framework* to add features to web pages. Some popular JavaScript frameworks are ReactJS, Vue.js, and Svelte. Proficiency in the over 30 JavaScript frameworks is unnecessary, but knowing one or two can be helpful.

None of the work a web developer does would be possible without product managers and designers. Developers work with product managers to ensure that the product scope and timelines are reasonable. Additionally, product managers make sure that the technical and nontechnical teams are communicating and aligned. Developers also work with designers who create *mockups*, or illustrations of the website, images, and the flow users take to move between web pages. After the mockups are created, frontend developers code the website to match the mockups as closely as possible.

Backend web development

Backend web developers code everything that is not visible on the web page but is necessary to support the frontend developer's work. Backend development happens in the following three places:

» **Server:** The *server* is the computer hosting the coding files that include the website application and the database. When you visit www.google.com, for example, your web browser requests the web page from Google servers, which respond with a copy of the web page you see in your browser.

» **Application:** The *application* handles the content in web pages sent to users and the changes made to the database. Applications are written using programming languages like Ruby, Python, and PHP, and run only on the server. Proficiency in one language is usually sufficient.

>> **Database:** The *database* stores website and user data so it is available for future browsing sessions. The simplest database is an Excel spreadsheet, which is ill suited for web development. Databases such as PostgreSQL and MongoDB are optimized for website use; usually only one of these databases is used per website.

As an example of backend web development, suppose that you visit www. amazon.com using your web browser. Your computer makes a request to the Amazon server, which runs an application to determine what web content to serve you. The application queries a database, and past purchases and browsing show that you have an interest in technology, legal, and travel books. The application creates a web page that displays books matching your interests and sends it to your computer. You see a book on bike trails in New York and click to purchase it. After you enter your credit card and shipping details, the application stores the information in a database on the server for easy checkout in the future.

For backend developers, one major part of the job is writing code for the application and database to render web pages in the browser. Employers are interested in additional skills such as these:

>> **Scaling:** Backend developers must change and optimize application code, servers, and databases to respond to increases in website traffic. Without the right planning, a mention of your website on a morning talk show or in the newspaper could result in a "website not available" error message instead of thousands of new customers. *Scaling* involves balancing the cost of optimizing the website with leaving the configuration as-is.

>> **Analytics:** Every online business, whether large or small, has key website performance indicators, such as new user signups and retention of existing users. Backend developers can implement and track these metrics by querying information from the website database.

>> **Security:** Websites with a substantial number of users become a target for all types of security risks. Attackers may automate signups, in which fake profiles post spam that promotes unrelated products. Additionally, you may receive a massive amount of traffic in a short period of time, called a *denial of service attack,* which prevents legitimate customers from accessing your website. Or attackers might try to detect weaknesses in your servers to gain unauthorized access to sensitive information such as email addresses, passwords, and credit card numbers. In 2021, major data breaches were uncovered at large corporations including Facebook, T-Mobile, Neiman Marcus, and Kaseya. Prevention of these attacks rests, in part, with backend developers.

The backend developer is a part of the product team and works closely with frontend developers and product managers. Unlike frontend developers, backend developers do not interact frequently with designers because the job is not as visual or based on website appearance.

Mobile application development

Mobile application developers create applications that run on cell phones, tablets, and other mobile devices. Mobile applications can be more challenging to create than browser-based websites because users expect the same functionality on a device without a dedicated keyboard and with a smaller screen.

REMEMBER

In 2014, users purchased and spent more time on mobile devices than traditional PC desktops, marking a major milestone. Today, it's estimated that 55 percent of global Internet traffic comes from mobile devices.

Up to 90 percent of time users spend on mobile devices is spent using native apps that are downloaded from an app store. The two most popular app stores are

» The Apple App Store, which hosts apps for iOS devices such as iPhones and iPads

» The Google Play Store, which hosts apps for phones and tablets running the Android operating system

Developers code apps for iOS devices by using the Objective-C and Swift programming languages, and they code apps for Android devices by using Java or Kotlin. Cross-platform mobile app development frameworks, such as Flutter and React Native, make it possible for programmers to write their apps once (using the JavaScript or Dart programming languages) and compile them for both Android and iOS.

Mobile developers are in high demand as mobile usage overtakes browsing on traditional PCs. In addition to creating apps, employers also value these skills:

» **Location services:** The service most frequently integrated into and used in mobile applications is location. Maps, reservation, and transportation applications all become more useful when they take into account your current location.

» **Application testing:** The number of devices that a mobile developer has to consider is staggering. In addition, an errant line of code can cause a mobile application to install incorrectly or to leak memory until the application crashes. Mobile application-testing software automates the process of testing your application across a variety of device types, saving a huge amount of time and a drawer full of phones. Mobile developers who can integrate testing software such as Crashlytics into their applications will get the data needed to continuously improve their application code.

Mobile application developers work with designers to create easy and intuitive mobile experiences, with backend developers to ensure that data submitted by or received from the phone is in sync with data on the website, and with product managers so that the application launches smoothly.

Data analysis

Data analysts sift through large volumes of data, looking for insights that help drive the product or business forward. This role marries programming and statistics in the search for patterns in the data. Popular examples of data analysis in action include the recommendation engines used by Amazon to make product suggestions to users based on previous purchases and by Netflix to make movie suggestions based on movies watched.

The data analyst's first challenge is simply importing, cleaning, and processing the data. A website can generate daily millions of database entries of users' data, requiring the use of complicated techniques, referred to as *machine learning*, to create classifications and predictions from the data. For example, half a billion messages are sent per day using Twitter; some hedge funds analyze this data and classify whether a person talking about a stock is expressing a positive or negative sentiment. These sentiments are then aggregated to see whether a company has a positive or negative public opinion before the hedge fund purchases or sells any stock.

Any programming language can be used to analyze data, but the most popular programming languages used for the task are R, Python, and SQL. Publicly shared code in these three languages makes it easier for individuals entering the field to build on another person's work. While crunching the data is important, employers also look for data analysts with skills in the following:

>> **Visualization:** Just as important as finding insight in the data is communicating that insight. Data visualization uses charts, graphs, dashboards, infographics, and maps, which can be interactive, to display data and reduce the complexity such that one or two conclusions appear obvious, as shown in Figure 1-3 (courtesy of I Quant NY). Common data visualization tools include D3.js, a JavaScript graphing library, and ArcGIS for geographic data.

>> **Distributed storage and processing:** Processing large amounts of data on one computer can be time-intensive. One option is to purchase a single faster computer. Another option, called *distributed storage and processing*, is to purchase multiple machines and divide the work. For example, imagine that

we want to count the number of people living in Manhattan. In the distributed storage and processing approach, you might ring odd-numbered homes, I would ring even-numbered homes, and when we finished, we would total our counts.

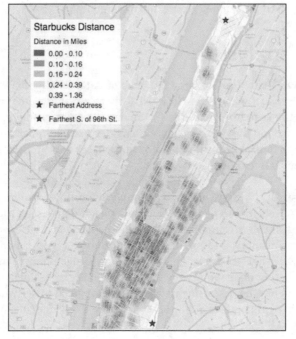

FIGURE 1-3:
The two Manhattan addresses farthest away from Starbucks.

Data analysts work with backend developers to gather data needed for their work. After the data analysts have drawn conclusions from the data and come up with ideas on improving the existing product, they meet with the entire team to help design prototypes to test the ideas on existing customers.

» Coding outside class in clubs and
hackathons

» Securing an internship to learn on
the job

Chapter **2**

Exploring Undergraduate and Graduate Degrees

"When I was in college, I wanted to be involved in things that would change the world."

— ELON MUSK

Going to college to learn how to code is probably the most traditional and expensive path you can take. A bachelor's degree, designed to take four years, is rooted in the tradition of the English university system and was made popular by the GI Bill after World War II. More recently, the two-year associate degree has become more popular. It costs less than a bachelor's degree, but many are designed as a way to eventually transfer to a four-year bachelor degree program.

But when it comes to computer programmers, you likely know more people who didn't graduate from college than did. Entrepreneurs such as Bill Gates, Steve Jobs, Mark Zuckerberg, and Larry Ellison dropped out of college to create technology companies worth billions of dollars. Still, the world's biggest technology companies continue to hire mainly college graduates.

Whether you're thinking about going to college, are already in college, or attended college and want another degree, this chapter is for you. This chapter explores learning to code in college or graduate school, and then building your credibility with an internship.

Getting a College Degree

The recent media attention on coding, with movies such as *The Social Network* and TV shows such as *Silicon Valley*, might make it seem like everyone in college is learning how to program. Although computer science (CS) graduates earn some of the highest salaries in the United States (see Figure 2-1), less than 3 percent of students major in computer science, and less than 1 percent of AP exams taken in high school are in computer science.

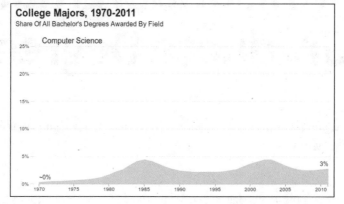

FIGURE 2-1: Bachelor's degrees awarded in CS over 40 years, courtesy of NPR.

Source: Digest of Educational Statistics; credit: Quoctrung Bui/NPR

The supply of students is low but is improving relative to the jobs that are available. Companies such as Apple, Microsoft, Yahoo!, Facebook, and Twitter recruit computer science engineers from schools such as Carnegie Mellon, MIT, and Stanford. It's not just the companies you read about in the news that are hiring either. CS graduates are in high demand — in 2020, there were an estimated 1.4 million computing jobs but only 400,000 trained computer science students to fill those jobs.

Yet far more important to employers than the name of the school you went to is what you did while you were in school. Employers will ask how you challenged yourself with your course load, and the applications you built and why.

College computer science curriculum

College CS courses offer a sweeping survey of entire computer systems from the hardware used to allocate memory to the high-level software that runs programs and the theories used to write that software. As a result, you gain a great sense of why computer systems behave as they do, which gives you the foundation to advance a technology or a programming language when the need arises.

This approach differs dramatically from the learning you'd typically do by yourself or in a boot camp, where the focus is only on software development in a specific language such as Python or Ruby. Given the typical 12-week duration of a boot camp, there isn't much time for anything else.

The core CS curriculum across universities is similar. Table 2-1 compares select core curriculum classes required as part of the Computer Science degree at Stanford and Penn State — a private university on the West Coast and a public university on the East Coast, respectively. Both have introductory classes to acquaint you with programming topics, math classes that cover probability, hardware classes for low-level programming and memory storage, software classes for designing algorithms, and higher level classes that cover advanced topics such as artificial intelligence and networking.

TABLE 2-1

CS Select Core Curriculum at Stanford and Penn State

Course Name	Course Description	Stanford	Penn State
Programming Abstractions	Intro to programming using C++ with sorting and searching	CS 106B	CMPSC 121
Programming with Web Applications	Intro to graphics, virtual machines, and programming concepts using Java	N/A	CMPSC 221
Math Foundations of Computing	Topics include proofs, logic, induction, sets, and functions	CS 103	CMPSC 360
Probability	Probability and statistics relevant to computer science	CS 109	STAT 318
Algorithms	Algorithm types (e.g., random) and complexity	CS 161	CMPSC 465
Hardware Systems	Machine registers, assembly language, and compilation	CS 107	CMPSC 311
Computer Systems	Storage and file management, networking, and distributed systems	CS 110	N/A

(continued)

TABLE 2-1 *(continued)*

Course Name	Course Description	Stanford	Penn State
Operating Systems	Designing and managing operating and system tasks	CS 140	CMPSC 473
Computer and Network Security	Principles of building and breaking secure systems	CS 155	CMPSC 443
Intro to Artificial Intelligence	AI concepts such as searching, planning, and learning	CS 121	CMPSC 448
Intro to Databases	Database design and using SQL and NoSQL systems	CS 145	CMPSC 431W

Until recently, universities generally did not teach web programming courses. As web programming has increased in popularity, this has begun to change — for example, Stanford offers a web programming class (CS 142) that teaches HTML, CSS, and Ruby on Rails, and Penn State has a similar class that teaches web programming with Java.

TECHNICAL VERSUS PRACTICAL EDUCATION

As you look at the courses offered in the Stanford and Penn State CS programs, you'll notice that the overwhelming majority speak to the theory of computer science and aren't always used every day. For example, as a person interested in software development, you likely aren't going to use much if any of your hardware systems courses. Note that some classes will be very relevant — algorithms and databases are two topics frequently used in web programming.

However, understanding the theory is useful. For example, database systems were initially created assuming that storage was expensive and the amount of data that needed to be stored would grow linearly. The reality turned out to be different — the cost of hardware plummeted and hard drives became bigger and cheaper, while people generated more data at a faster pace than ever before. Computer scientists, with a solid understanding of databases, took advantage of cheap hardware and created distributed databases, which store data across multiple computers instead of a single one.

Whether or not you should learn programming in college comes down to your goal. If you want to one day be in a position to change the industry or work on cutting-edge technology, the theory you learn studying computer science is without substitute or comparison. There are few other places where you can engage with a professional, in this case a professor, of a high caliber to push the limits of fundamental understanding. Also, specific programming languages and technologies are constantly changing, while the underlying concepts and theories stay the same. Some of the most popular programming languages in use today, including Python, Java, Ruby, and JavaScript, are 30 years old, while Go, R, Swift, and Dart are less than ten years old.

On the other hand, if your goal is to use these concepts to make a living in the industry instead of trying to change the industry, you could learn to code in a less expensive and less time-intensive way than obtaining a computer science degree.

Doing extracurricular activities

Many students complement their coursework by applying what they've learned in a tangible way. Your coursework will include project work, but projects assigned in class may not have changed in a few years to make it easier for the instructor to provide support and grade your work. Also, with so many technologies constantly popping up, using your coding skills outside the classroom will help build confidence and skill.

One option is to code side projects, which are personal coding projects that perform some small basic utility and can be built in a short amount of time, over a weekend to a few months at most. For example, not many people know that before Mark Zuckerberg built Facebook, he had coded many side projects, including an instant messaging client for his dad's dental practice, an MP3 player that suggested the next song to listen to, and a tool that helped students choose their semester schedule based on which classes their friends were enrolling in. In another example, three students at Tufts University wanted an easy way to find the cheapest place to buy all their textbooks. They created a site called GetchaBooks, which lets students select the classes they would be taking in a semester and then retrieved the full list of books needed and the total prices across many stores to find the cheapest price. Although the site is no longer actively developed, all the code is open sourced and can be viewed at `github.com/getchabooks/getchabooks`.

In addition to coding on your own, coding and discussing technology topics with others can be more engaging. On-campus clubs are usually formed by students and cater to almost every interest. You can find clubs on robotics, financial technologies such as Bitcoin, technology investing from the venture capital stage to the public equities stage, and more.

The Dorm Room Fund is a student-run venture capital firm with locations in San Francisco, Boston, New York, and Philadelphia that invests in student-run companies. Backed by First Round Capital, the goal is to nurture and support young technology companies, teach students how to evaluate and invest in technology companies, and find the next billion-dollar company on a college campus.

The most intense extracurricular pursuit for a student is participating in hackathons. A *hackathon* is a one-day to weekend-long event with the goal of brainstorming, designing, and building a small useful app. Hackathons are most popular among students, who often stay up all night coding their apps, while the hosts are often technology companies. However, some of the largest hackathons, such as Cal Hacks, which is hosted by UC Berkeley, and PennApps, which is hosted by the University of Pennsylvania (see Figure 2-2), are organized by students and attended by thousands of students from schools around the country.

FIGURE 2-2:
Students show a mentor their mobile application at PennApps.

Daniel Ge / Flickr / CC BY-SA 2.0

Two-year versus four-year school

You may not be able to afford the time, expense, or commitment demanded by a four-year degree. Even though some colleges offer financial aid, not earning money for four years or earning a far-reduced wage may not be feasible, especially if you have to support yourself or family members.

One alternative to the Bachelor of Arts (BA) degree is the Associate of Arts (AA) degree, which is typically granted by community colleges or technical schools. You can complete an AA degree in two years. In addition to taking less time, according to the College Board, tuition and fees are on average $4,000 per year, compared to $10,560 per year at public four-year institutions. Courses are also offered during evenings and on weekends, so students can work while attending school. When evaluating an institution that grants the AA degree, review the instructors teaching the courses and make sure they are experienced practitioners in the field. Additionally, see the types of jobs recent graduates went on to do and the employers they worked for to make sure that both match with your goals.

A close relative of the AA degree is a certificate granted by a school of continuing education. Certificates are noncredit offerings completed within a year. They usually cost less than $10,000 but don't result in a degree. To get the most bang for your buck, get your certificate from a school with a good regional or even national reputation. For example, NYU has a Certificate in Web Development that teaches web development basics with HTML, CSS, and JavaScript along with more advanced topics such as PHP, a popular programming language for the web, and SQL, a language used to query databases. (See Figure 2-3.) Learning these topics in a structured way from an instructor can help jumpstart your learning so you can teach yourself additional topics on your own.

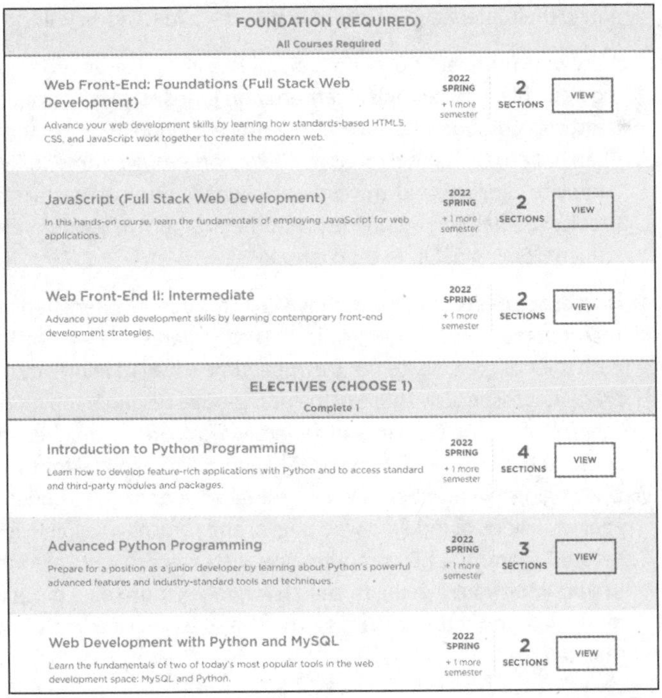

FIGURE 2-3:
NYU's Certificate in Web Development offers classes in JavaScript and Python.

Credit: Courtesy of NYU

When enrolling in a certificate program, keep in mind that instructor quality can be highly variable. Make sure you talk to current students or find some student reviews before signing up for either the certificate program or courses that the certificate requires.

Enrolling in an Advanced Degree Program

The options for learning how to code never seem to end, and advanced degrees typically appeal to a particular group of people. While not necessary for either learning to code or obtaining a coding job, an advanced degree can help accelerate your learning and differentiate you from other job candidates. Here are the two types of advanced degree programs:

>> **Master's degree:** A technical degree that allows you to explore and specialize in a particular area of computer science such as artificial intelligence, security, database systems, or machine learning. Based on the course load, the degree typically takes one or two years of full-time, in-person instruction to complete. Upon completion, the degree can be a way for a student who pursued a nontechnical major to transition into the field and pursue a coding job. Alternatively, some students use the master's degree experience as a way to gauge their interest in or improve their candidacy for a PhD program.

TIP

A growing number of part-time online master's degree programs are becoming available. For example, Stanford and Johns Hopkins both offer a master's degree in Computer Science with a concentration in one of ten topics as part of an online part-time degree that takes on average three to five years to complete. Similarly, Northwestern University offers a master's degree in Predictive Analytics, an online part-time program in big data that teaches students SQL, NoSQL, Python, and R.

>> **Doctorate degree:** A program typically for people interested in conducting research into a specialized topic. PhD candidates can take six to eight years to earn their degree, so it's not the most timely way to learn how to code. PhD graduates, especially those with cutting-edge research topics, differentiate themselves in the market and generally work on the toughest problems in computer science. For example, Google's core search algorithm is technically challenging in a number of ways — it takes your search request, compares it against billions of indexed web pages, and returns a result in less than a second. Teams of PhD computer scientists work to write algorithms that predict what you're going to search for, index more data (such as from social networks), and return results to you five to ten milliseconds faster than before.

TIP

Students who enroll and drop out of PhD programs early have often done enough coursework to earn a master's degree, usually at no cost to the student because PhD programs are typically funded by the school.

Graduate school computer science curriculum

The master's degree school curriculum for computer science usually consists of 10 to 12 computer science and math classes. You start with a few foundational classes, and then specialize by focusing on a specific computer science topic. The PhD curriculum follows the same path, except after completing the coursework, you propose a previously unexplored topic to further research, spend three to five years conducting original research, and then present and defend your results before other professors appointed to evaluate your work.

Table 2-2 is a sample curriculum to earn a master's degree in CS with a concentration in Machine Learning from Columbia University. Multiple courses can be used to meet the degree requirements, and the courses offered vary by semester.

The curriculum, which in this case consists of ten classes, begins with three foundational classes, and then quickly focuses on an area of concentration. Concentrations vary across programs, but generally include the following:

>> **Security:** Assigning user permissions and preventing unauthorized access, such as preventing users from accessing your credit card details on an e-commerce site

>> **Machine learning:** Finding patterns in data, and making future predictions, such as predicting what movie you should watch next based on the movies you've already seen and liked

>> **Network systems:** Protocols, principles, and algorithms for how computers communicate with each other, such as setting up wireless networks that work well for hundreds of thousands of users

>> **Computer vision:** Duplicating the ability of the human eye to process and analyze images, such as counting the number of people who enter or exit a store based on a program analyzing a live video feed

>> **Natural language processing:** Automating the analysis of text and speech, such as using voice commands to convert speech to text

TABLE 2-2

Columbia University MS in Computer Science

Course Number	Course Name	Course Description
W4118	Operating Systems I	Design and implementation of operating systems including topics such as process management and synchronization
W4231	Analysis of Algorithms I	Design and analysis of efficient algorithms including sorting and searching
W4705	Natural Language Processing	Natural language extraction, summarization, and analysis of emotional speech
W4252	Computational Learning Theory	Computational and statistical possibilities and limitations of learning
W4771	Machine Learning	Machine learning with classification, regression, and inference models
W4111	Intro to Databases	Understanding of how to design and build relational databases
W4246	Algorithms for Data Science	Methods for organizing, sorting, and searching data
W4772	Advanced Machine Learning	Advanced machine learning tools with applications in perception and behavior modeling
E6232	Analysis of Algorithms II	Graduate course on design and analysis of efficient approximation algorithms for optimization problems
E6998	Advanced Topic in Machine Learning	Graduate course covers current research on Bayesian networks, inference, Markov models, and regression

Performing research

Students are encouraged in master's degree programs and required in PhD programs to conduct original research. Research topics vary from the theoretical, such as estimating how long an algorithm will take to find a solution, to the practical, such as optimizing a delivery route given a set of points.

Sometimes this academic research is commercialized to create products and companies worth hundreds of millions to billions of dollars. For example, in 2003 university researchers created an algorithm called Farecast that analyzed 12,000 airline ticket prices. Later, it could analyze billions of ticket prices in real time and predict whether the price of your airline ticket would increase, decrease, or stay the same. Microsoft purchased the technology for $100 million and incorporated it into its Bing search engine.

In another example, Shazam was based on an academic paper that analyzed how to identify an audio recording based on a short, low-quality sample, usually an audio recording from a mobile phone. Today, Shazam lets a user record a short snippet of a song, identifies the song title, and offers the song for purchase. The company has raised over $100 million in funding for operations and is privately valued at over $1 billion. Both products were based on published research papers that identified a problem that could be addressed with technology and presented a technology solution that solved existing constraints with high accuracy.

Your own research may not lead to the creation of a billion-dollar company, but it should advance, even incrementally, a solution for a computer science problem or help eliminate an existing constraint.

Interning to Build Credibility

Your classroom work helps create a theoretical foundation but can be divorced from the real world. Actual real-world problems often have inaccurate or incomplete data and a lack of obvious solutions. One way to bridge the gap from the classroom to the real world is to take on an internship.

Internships are 10- to 12-week engagements, usually over the summer, with an employer on a discrete project. The experience is meant to help an intern assess whether the company and the role are a good fit for permanent employment and for the company to assess the intern's abilities.

The competition for interns is just as strong as it is for full-time employees, so interns can expect to be paid. Top tech companies pay interns between $6,000 and $8,000 per month, with Palantir, LinkedIn, and Twitter topping the list. After the internship is finished, companies offer successful interns anywhere from $5,000 to $100,000 signing bonuses to return to the firm to work full time.

Types of internship programs

Companies structure their internship program differently, but the following configurations are more common than others:

>> **Summer internship:** The majority of internships happen during the summer. Because of the work involved in organizing an intern class, larger companies usually have a formal process with application deadlines and fixed dates when interviews for the internship are conducted. After offers are extended, companies ideally screen projects given to interns to make sure the work is

interesting and substantive. There are also a significant number of social events so that full-time employees and interns can meet in an environment outside work.

>> **School-year internship:** Some internships take place during the school year, from September to May. These programs are usually smaller, hiring is on an as-needed basis, and the entire process is less formalized. Usually, the intern does more work to find divisions who need extra help, networks with managers of those divisions, and then finally interviews for and accepts an internship position. You can get a more realistic view of what working at the company is like because there likely aren't many other interns working with you, and you might be able to integrate more closely with the team.

>> **Fellowship:** Many students get the itch to try a longer professional experience before graduation. These experiences, called fellowship programs, last six to twelve months and give a person enough time to work on a project to make a substantive contribution. For undergraduates, the work confirms an existing interest or creates an interest in a new area of technology. For graduate students, the work can highlight the difference between theory and practice, inform an area of research, or help them break into a new industry.

TIP

Positions for internships are often more selective than positions for full-time jobs, so apply early and for more than one internship position. If you don't receive an internship, try again for a full-time position. Companies have large hiring needs, and one purpose for hiring summer interns is to ensure that the interns have a great time at the company so when they return to campus they tell other students, who then feel more comfortable applying.

Securing an internship

Much of the advice for obtaining a full-time job applies to securing an internship offer as well. There are a few strategies to keep in mind when pursuing an internship.

Choose products and companies you're passionate about. As an intern, you join a company for three months at most, and much of that time is spent meeting new people, understanding the company, and fitting into existing processes. As a passionate power user of the product, your excitement will naturally show, and your ideas will give the company a sense for what you want to work on and provide a fresh and valuable perspective to the team, which likely feels that they have already explored every possible idea. Be able to describe how you use the product and what additional features would help increase your engagement or retention.

For any product that has a public profile, link to your profile so team members can easily see how frequently you use the product.

After you've chosen a few companies, start looking for current students who have worked at the company as well as school alumni who currently work at the company. Reach out by email and schedule short phone calls or a coffee chat no longer than 30 minutes to try and build a connection. Current students can share information about their experience, tell you which groups have the greatest need, and share some of the company culture, such as what the company values. Alumni will be able to share much of the same information, but they can also send a recommendation to HR on your behalf or may be able to hire you.

There is a balance between the response rate, ability to help, and seniority of a person you reach out to. Try to reach for the most senior alumni you can find at a company, because a quick email from them to HR will guarantee an interview, but recognize that they may not always have the time to respond. Alternatively, more junior employees will likely have more time to chat with you but likely do not have as much influence over interview or hiring decisions.

Finally, include a mix of startups and more established companies in your search process. Given the number of interviews they do, established companies can be formulaic in their interview and hiring decisions, often looking for candidates from specific schools with a minimum GPA. If you aren't attending a top school or have below a 3.0 (out of 4.0) GPA, you should still apply to the larger companies and include an explanation for your lower GPA if one applies. Another option is to apply to startups, which will likely care more about the products you've built than your grade in chemistry. The trade-off is that startups likely have less time and people to help train you and a smaller selection of projects for you to choose from. After you join a company and finish a brief orientation period, you'll often need to start coding right away and contributing to the product.

Chapter **3**

Training on the Job

*I hated every minute of training, but I said, 'Don't quit. Suffer now and live
the rest of your life as a champion.'*

— MUHAMMAD ALI

As an employee, whether you're a marketer, a sales person, or a designer, you likely find that technology dominates more and more of your conversations with your boss, co-workers, and clients. Perhaps your boss wants to know which customer segments the company should target with online advertising, and you need to analyze millions of customer records to provide an answer. Or maybe a client wants to add or change a feature and will double the contract if the process can be done in six weeks, and you need to know whether it's possible. More tangibly, you might find yourself performing mundane and repetitive tasks that you know a computer could do.

You have probably found that an ability to code could help you perform your current job more efficiently. Companies are also noticing the value of having non-technical employees learn to code, and offering various on-site training options and support. This chapter shows you how to learn to code on the job and ways to incorporate what you've learned into your job.

Taking a Work Project to the Next Level

As a busy professional with a full work schedule, you need a tangible project to work toward and keep you motivated while you learn how to code. Think of all the tasks you perform during the week — how many could be automated if you had the right tools and skills?

The following sample tasks can be done more efficiently with some coding and could help you think of a goal of your own:

>> **Spreadsheet consolidation:** You have fifteen team members who submit timesheets to you using spreadsheets, and you create a consolidated weekly report by manually cutting and pasting entries from each spreadsheet.

>> **Content updates:** You cut and paste the latest press stories every week into a content management system to update the company's website.

>> **Data retrieval:** You work for a financial services company, and monitor acquisitions and sales made by ten private equity firms. Every day you visit each firm's website to look for updates.

>> **Quality assurance:** You test updates made to the company's website by clicking the same set of links to make sure they work as expected.

>> **Prototyping designs:** You create website designs, but it's difficult to explain to clients the user experience and interactions through static illustrations.

Whatever task you choose, make sure that you can describe how to complete it from start to finish. For example, the steps to complete the data retrieval task might be listed as follows:

1. Visit the first firm's website and download the list of companies on the acquisitions page.

2. Permanently store the list. If the acquisition list has previously been retrieved, compare the list downloaded today with yesterday's version and note any additions or deletions.

3. Display the additions or deletions.

4. Repeat Steps 1–3 for the next firm, until all the firm websites have been visited.

5. Repeat Steps 1–4 daily.

You may be part of a technical process, such as a designer who hands off mockups to a developer to create. Instead of automating your existing work, you could try to complete work the technical team normally does after you. For example, if you do customer or sales support, you regularly receive customer and client feedback and file support tickets for issues that require an engineer. The number of support tickets always exceeds the number of engineers, so choose a low-priority non-mission-critical issue to fix.

TIP

Don't worry about choosing a task that seems too simple. Fixing an issue on a live site currently in use is always more complex than it initially appears. However, try to choose a work-related task so you can ask for help from co-workers.

Learning on the Job and After Work

After you've selected a task, you need to learn some coding to be able to fix the issue. Given that you're already working, going back to school or taking a hiatus from work to learn full-time is likely not feasible. Your next best option is to learn coding on the job, ideally with your company's support. Companies are increasingly supporting employees who want to expand their technical skill set by providing resources to help them learn and by incentivizing those who learn tangible skills.

WISTIA CODE SCHOOL

Companies are starting to recognize the demand for coding education and the benefits of having more employees who can code. Wistia, a video-hosting and analytics company, hosts a code school so that nontechnical employees can learn how to code. Employees work as customer champions, or customer support agents, and are paired with a developer who conducts an hourly mentoring session every week for five to six months.

Normally, people learning to code usually practice their skills on personal projects. One advantage Wistia employees have is that the programming skills they learn are used to solve real problems that customers are experiencing. Solving coding issues, no matter how small, for a live website is difficult because the fix will immediately affect customers using the website.

As employees learn more, they still refer complex issues to the technical staff but are able to handle the easier technical problems themselves, resulting in quicker resolution times.

Training on the job

You are likely familiar with the compliance and leadership training available at your company, especially in medium- to large-sized firms. However, you may have never looked for the technical training options available to you. Here are some tips to get started learning on the job:

>> **Virtual training resources:** Corporate training libraries such as Safari, Skillsoft, Lynda, and Pluralsight are popular among companies, and are a good place to start learning programming fundamentals. Each provider has a mix of text and video content, which you can read and view on-demand. Additionally, look for company generated wikis and other training resources that describe internal programming tools and procedures.

>> **In-person training programs:** Company employees often teach orientation training courses to introduce new engineers to basic concepts and the way to code in the company. Additionally, outside vendors may occasionally conduct specific training courses on more advanced programming topics and languages. Ask whether you can view the list of training topics typically made available to engineers, and then attend introductory training sessions.

TIP

>> **Let your supervisor know that learning to code is a development goal, and include it in any reviews:** Your supervisor can help you access training programs not traditionally offered to nontechnical employees. Additionally, letting as many co-workers as possible know about your goals will increase your accountability and motivation.

>> **Support from company developers:** Your company likely has developers who already assist you with the technical side of your projects. Whether you've chosen a project to improve the efficiency of your own workflow or are trying to complete work a developer would typically do, make sure to recruit a developer, usually one you already have a relationship with, so you have a resource to help you answer questions when you get stuck.

TIP

Your co-workers, especially on technical teams, are just as busy as you are. Before asking for help, try finding the answer by reviewing internal materials, using a search engine, or posting a question on a question-and-answer site such as Stack Overflow. Include where you looked because developers might use the same resources to answer questions.

Learning after work

Your company may be too small to have on-site technical training, or your office may not have any developers. Don't fret! You can take classes after work to learn how to code. Look for classes that meet twice a week in the evenings, and set aside time to do coursework during the weekend.

Companies often partially or fully reimburse the cost for employees who successfully complete a job-related course. Think of a few tangible ways that learning to code would help you do your job better or take on a new project and then make the pitch to your manager. If you receive approval, make sure to keep up with the coursework so you're ready to contribute at work after the class is over.

A few places teach in-person coding classes designed for working professionals. Because a live instructor is teaching and assisting you, many charge a fee.

TIP

Lower cost and free options are usually taught exclusively online, though completion rates for in-person classes are usually higher than online classes.

Here are some places where you can learn to code from a live instructor:

>> **General Assembly:** Teaches part-time classes across a range of subjects, and has a presence in major cities in the United States and internationally. Topics include frontend, backend, data science, and mobile development. Classes typically meet twice a week for three hours over 12 weeks. General Assembly is one of the largest companies teaching coding classes. You can view their classes at www.generalassemb.ly.

>> **Nucamp:** A low-cost online bootcamp that offers classes in full stack web and mobile development. Classes include online text and video content, with a four-hour live online session each Saturday, led by a live instructor.

>> **Local boot camps:** As coding has become more popular, coding boot camps have sprung up in many cities around the world. Many of these boot camps offer part-time programs that don't require you to quit your job. You can search boot camps by subject, location, and cost by using Course Report, available at www.coursereport.com, and CourseHorse, available at www.coursehorse.com.

TIP

Before signing up, make sure you review the instructor, the physical location, and the cost, which should be no more than $4,000 for a part-time program with 70 hours of instruction. Course Report profiles ten part-time boot camps at www.coursereport.com/blog/learn-web-development-at-these-10-part-time-bootcamps.

>> **College courses:** Traditionally, college computer science courses were theoretical, but colleges have recently started offering more applied web development and data science courses. Check your local university or community college's continuing education departments to see what's offered. For example, the City College of New York offers an Intro to Web Development class with 16 hours of instruction for $280.

>> **Library classes:** Public libraries offer desktop productivity and other computer classes and have recently started offering web development

classes as well. For example, the New York Public Library has a free, ten-week program called Project_<code>, in which you build a website for a small business.

Freelancing to Build Confidence and Skills

You've taken training classes at work, found a coding mentor, and solved your first problem by using code. Congratulations! So where do you go from here? Like a foreign language, if you stop coding you'll forget what you've learned. The most important thing is to keep coding and building your confidence and skills.

Here are a few ideas for you to practice coding in the workplace:

» **Clone a website:** Unlike programs that may have code you can't access, company websites allow you to see and save text and images. You may not be able to re-create all the functionality, but choose a specific company's web page and try creating a copy of the layout, images, and text. This process will help you practice your HTML, CSS, and JavaScript skills.

» **Build a mobile app:** People purchase more mobile devices and spend more time on them than desktops and laptops. Still, some companies have been slow to adapt and don't have a mobile presence. Create a mobile website using HTML and CSS, or a native application using Swift for the iPhone, Java for Android devices, or Flutter for both!

» **Code a small workplace utility app:** There are many tasks that everyone at your company and in your office performs. Your co-workers come to the office around the same time, eat lunch at the same places, and leave work using the same modes of transportation. They also share the same frustrations, some of which might be solved with a simple program. Try building an app that solves a small workplace annoyance — no one knows what would appeal to your co-workers better than you. For example, build a website that sends an email to those who opt-in whenever there is a traffic jam on the highway that everyone uses to leave work. Similarly, you could build an app that sends an alert if any of the restaurants close to work fails a health inspection. The goal here is to learn a new technology to solve a problem and get real feedback from other users.

After you've practiced and built a few things, publish your code on a hosting service such as GitHub and create a portfolio website pulling everything you've built into one place. You'll be able to share and others will be able to find your work, and the progression in your coding skills will be visible for anyone to see.

TIP

If you are stuck and can't think of anything to build, try freeCodeCamp, available at www.freecodecamp.com. The website, shown in Figure 3-1, connects working professionals with nonprofits who need a website or app built. After you complete the challenges, you'll start working on a vetted nonprofit project. Current projects include an animal adoption database for Latin America through the nonprofit People Saving Animals, and a charity fundraiser website for the Save a Child's Heart Foundation.

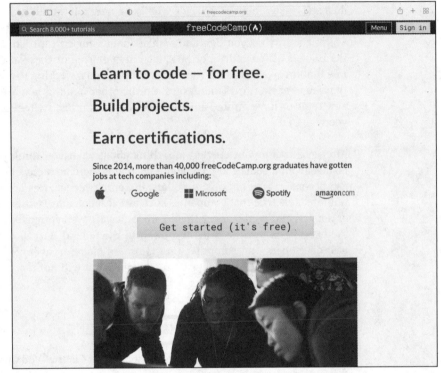

FIGURE 3-1:
freeCodeCamp
connects
professionals
who code
together for
nonprofits.

© *John Wiley & Sons*

Transitioning to a New Role

Like any skill, coding can take a lifetime to master, but after you learn a little you may find that you want to move into a technology-based role. The first step is to do a self-assessment and evaluate what you like and dislike about your current role, and how that matches with the technology role you want. You'll likely also need input from others; networking and chatting with developers you trust will help give you a balanced view of the job. If you decide to take the leap, you have the big advantage of being inside a company, so you'll know what they need before a job posting is ever written.

Assessing your current role

You've worked hard to get to where you are — perhaps you just landed a job in a competitive industry or have been working and advancing in your role for a few years. In either case, if you're thinking about switching to a coding job, you should do a self-assessment and decide whether a new role would be a better fit for you.

Think about what you like and dislike about your current job. For some people, the issue is office politics or poor team dynamics, but these are present in every role that involves working with other people, and switching to a coding job carries the risk of seeing the same issues. On the other hand, if you are ready to learn a new topic or have limited advancement opportunities, switching roles could be a good idea.

After evaluating your current job, think about what you think you would like or dislike about a coding job. For some, tech jobs seem attractive because companies can become worth billions of dollars and employee salaries are reportedly in the millions. It is true that companies such as Facebook and Twitter are worth billions of dollars, and engineers at these companies are well compensated, but these are the exceptions not the rule. According to the federal Bureau of Labor Statistics, web developers and computer programmers make on average between $77,000 and $89,000, which is higher than many jobs but will not make you a millionaire overnight.

Networking with developers

One major benefit you have over other job seekers is that you probably work with developers who hold the position you're trying to obtain. Seek out some of these developers, either from people you already work with or in a department that you think is interesting.

After you connect with a few people, ask them how they spend their days, what they enjoy and what they would change about their job, and for any advice they have for you on how to make the transition. These types of conversations happen less frequently than you might think, so don't be shy about reaching out — you might be surprised to find that some developers are happy to chat with you because they are wondering how to transition into a nontechnical or business role.

The biggest constraint any company faces when hiring externally is not finding people who are technically capable of doing the job but finding people who will fit in with the company and the team culturally. As a current employee, you've already passed one culture screen, and you're in a good position to learn about how you might fit in with the existing developer culture at the company. After you build relationships with developers, maintain them and keep them updated on your goals. At some point, they'll likely be asked how serious you are and whether you'd be a good fit.

Identifying roles that match your interest and skills

Technical roles are just as numerous and varied as nontechnical roles. The positions include data analysts who analyze big data, traffic analysts who monitor website traffic and patterns, web developers who create website frontends and backends, app developers who create mobile web apps and native apps for mobile devices, and quality assurance testers who test for and help solve bugs in new releases.

Apply for roles in which you have a strong interest. If you like working with statistics and math, a data analyst or traffic analytics role might suit you best. Or if you're a visual person and like creating experiences others can see, consider a frontend developer role.

No matter the role, you should aim for a junior title and be committed to learning a lot on the job. Don't be afraid of starting over. For example, if you've been in marketing for four years and are interested in being a web developer, you will likely start as a junior developer. Your previous job experience will help you be a better team member and manager, which could help you advance more quickly, but you'll need to show that you're able to complete basic technical tasks first. Also, no matter the role, you'll be spending a lot of time learning on the job, and will be relying on your co-workers to teach you, so choose your role and team carefully.

Chapter **4**

Coding Career Myths

The tech profession is filled with myths and rumors. It can be hard to separate fact from fiction, especially given the reports of eye-popping salaries and prices for company acquisitions in the news. After you cut through the hype, the tech industry is like any other, with demand for talent far exceeding supply.

The following are ten myths about coding that just aren't true. These myths mainly apply to people learning to code for the first time. Read on to separate myth from reality.

You Must Be Good at Math

Developers who are building cutting-edge games, data scientists trying to create the next big machine-learning algorithm, or engineers working in the financial services industry likely need some proficiency in physics, statistics, or financial math. However, many developers, such as those building e-commerce applications or typical web pages, do not need much more math than basic addition and subtraction, and high school algebra.

A good deal of math operates and powers applications, but there often isn't a need to understand everything that is happening. Computer languages and programs are designed to manage complexity by requiring that you understand the inputs and outputs — but not what happens in between, a concept called *abstraction.* For example, when driving a car, you don't need to understand how the internal combustion engine works or the physics behind converting the energy from the piston to the wheels. To drive a car you need to understand how to operate the accelerator, the brake, and the clutch for stick-shift cars. Similarly, programs have functions that perform operations, but you need to understand only the inputs you send a function and the output it returns.

In other words, you need to be able to understand math and have some basic math skills, but you do not need to be the next Einstein to be able to program.

You Must Have Studied Engineering

Many people who study engineering learn how to program, but you do not need to be an engineer to learn how to code. Engineering teaches skills that are useful to programmers, such as how to solve a problem step-by-step as well as working within and then designing around real-world constraints. These are useful skills, but you can learn them outside the engineering curriculum.

Many topics that are part of an engineering curriculum vary in usefulness for learning how to code. Topics such as algorithms can be directly applicable, especially if you're working on cutting-edge problems. Other topics, such as assembly language and computational theory, provide a good background but are rarely used by most coders.

If your goal is to push the cutting edge of computer programs, a degree in computer engineering might be useful. However, if you want to create a website to solve a problem, learning to code in three to six months is probably sufficient to start.

You Can Learn Coding in a Few Weeks

Like any passion or profession, coding is an art and coders hone their skills over decades. Although you don't need decades of study to start coding, the amount of time needed to learn depends on your goals. For example:

» **One week:** Learn enough HTML to put text, images, and other basic content on the page. You'll be able to operate site builders to create and customize informational websites.

» **One month:** Develop your frontend CSS skills so you can position and style elements on the page. You'll also be able to edit sites built with website builders such as Wix, Weebly, or SquareSpace. For data science, you can learn to import and handle large data sets and use Python or R to find insights about the data.

» **Three to six months:** Learn frontend and backend development skills to take a concept, build a working prototype that can store data in a database, and then code a version that can handle hundreds of thousands of users. In addition, learn how to use a programming language's external libraries to add additional functionality, user management, and version control systems such as Git so multiple people can work on a project at the same time. For data science, you'll be able to build an interactive visualization using a JavaScript library such as d3.js. Whether learning web development or data science, it will take approximately 800 hours of effort to be proficient enough to be hired for a job.

You Need a Great Idea to Start Coding

Learning to code is a lengthy process, filled with ups and downs. You might get stuck for days or see much progress. During periods of inevitable frustration, having a bigger idea or a concrete reason to motivate you to keep learning can be helpful. Instead of trying to build the next Facebook, YouTube, or Google, try to build something that solves a problem you've personally faced. Or, focus on building a clone of something that already exists or that exists in a different form. There's no need for anyone to build a replica of Twitter, for example, but could you do it? It doesn't seem that complex, after all. You might be surprised by the challenges you face and how much you learn while working on such a project.

Ruby Is Better than Python

You might wonder what language to learn first, especially given all the choices out there. You could start with Ruby, Python, JavaScript, PHP, Swift, Dart, Objective-C — the list goes on. To resolve this debate, you might search for which language is the best, or which language to learn first. You'll find articles and posts advocating one language or another. Unlike comparing TVs or toasters, a clear winner is unlikely to emerge. Sometimes you can spend more time deciding which language to learn first than getting down to learning the language.

The most important thing is to learn a few easy scripting languages first and then choose one all-purpose beginner programming language to learn thoroughly.

Usually, beginners start with HTML, CSS, and JavaScript. These languages are the most forgiving of syntax mistakes and the easiest to learn. Then, after you learn these basics, choose Python or Ruby if you are interested in web development. You'll find many online tutorials and help for both.

If you plan on doing work with a content management system such as WordPress or Drupal, consider learning PHP.

Don't spend too much time deciding which language to learn first, and don't try to learn all of them at the same time. Sometimes people hit a roadblock with one language, give up, and start learning another language. However, the end result is learning a little bit about many languages, instead of mastering a single language and being able to build a complete and functioning application.

Only College Graduates Receive Coding Offers

Both Bill Gates and Mark Zuckerberg left college before graduating to start their own technology companies. To encourage more college dropouts, Peter Thiel, the billionaire founder of PayPal and investor in Facebook, created a fellowship to pay students $100,000 to start businesses and forgo school. Still, whether you can get a coding offer without a degree varies by company type:

>> **Elite technology companies:** Google, Apple, Facebook, Microsoft, Twitter, and Yahoo! are some of the world's most elite technology companies. Because of their sheer size and name recognition, they employ recruiters who screen for certain attributes, such as college affiliation. College graduates from top

schools apply to these companies in overwhelming numbers. Although it is not impossible to be hired at one of these companies without a college degree, it is very difficult.

>> **Fortune 1000 companies:** Large companies such as Verizon and AT&T hire thousands of engineers a year, making their initial requirements for hiring slightly more flexible. These companies typically look for a college degree or two to three years of relevant experience with a specific programming language.

>> **Startups and small companies:** Startups are sympathetic to non-degree holders, and many startup employees are currently in college or are college dropouts. Although startups don't require a college degree, a great deal of emphasis is given on what you've built previously and your ability to code under tight deadlines. Well-funded startups are often a good place to gain experience because they need talent to keep growing and often compensate employees as well as the more mature companies do.

>> **Freelancing and contracting:** When working for contracting websites such as Upwork or for yourself, the main consideration is whether you can complete the job. Few employers check whether you have a college degree; a portfolio of past work, even if it was unpaid, is much more important to securing the job and conveying the confidence that you'll be able to deliver the project on time and within budget.

You Must Have Experience

Studies have shown that there is no correlation between experience and performance in software development. For the new programmer, after you master some basic skills, your performance is affected by much more than the amount of time you've spent on a job. Despite the research, however, some companies still screen for years of experience when filling open positions.

Much of the same logic that applies to getting a coding job without a college degree applies here as well. Elite technology companies receive so many resumes and are in such high demand that they can be more selective and look first at experienced candidates. Fortune 1000 companies usually take one of two approaches: They look for a minimum one to two years of experience, or they understand that as a new hire you'll need training and use existing staff to help support you.

Startups and small companies typically pay the least attention to the number of years of experience and more attention to your previous projects. Your contributions to an open-source project or a weekend project that attracted real users will generate plenty of interest and enthusiasm for you as a candidate. Although it can be easier to get your foot in the door at a startup, remember that the company's small size likely means there are fewer people and less money to devote to your training and support, so much of your learning will be self-supported.

TIP

Companies of any size willing to invest in developing your programming abilities will typically look for a positive attitude, a willingness to learn, and the persistence to keep trying to solve problems and overcome obstacles.

Tech Companies Don't Hire Women or Minorities

Whether in the *Law and Order: SVU* portrayal of women in technology or the national media reports of the high-powered lawsuit filed by Ellen Pao around her treatment in the technology industry, the tech industry has not had the best track record for being welcoming of women and minorities.

Admittedly, the numbers show a story that has improved but still has plenty of room to grow, with the tech industry workforce made up of 29 percent women and 22 percent minority workers, which is below the national averages for both groups. A recent Deloitte Global report predicts that large global technology firms, on average, will reach nearly 33 percent overall female representation in their workforces in 2022, up slightly more than 2 percentage points from 2019.

Although many contributing causes have been identified, including the lack of a pipeline of candidates studying computer science or applying to tech firms, many leading companies and nonprofits are actively trying to increase the recruitment and support of women and minorities in the workplace.

On the corporate side, larger companies are creating programs that train and increase the number of pathways to join the workforce. For example, Google launched a $50 million campaign called Made with Code to highlight women in tech and provide opportunities for girls to learn to code.

Similarly, nonprofit organizations such as Code 2040 connect Black and Latino talent to companies. On the training side, nonprofits such as Yes We Code, Girls Who Code, Black Girls Code, and Women Who Code teach technical skills to increase the number of women and minorities entering the jobs pipeline.

TIP

Many colleges offer scholarships that can subsidize or completely cover the cost of attendance for women and minorities pursuing science and engineering degrees.

The Highest Paying Coding Jobs
Are in San Francisco

Many of the most famous tech companies, including Apple, Facebook, Google, Twitter, and Yahoo!, are located in Silicon Valley. While these and other companies in the San Francisco and Silicon Valley area hire a large number of tech workers each year, that paints only part of the picture.

Cities across the United States pay tech salaries comparable to San Francisco but have a much lower cost of living, as shown in Table 4-1. Two numbers to keep in mind when evaluating a city are the average salaries paid to tech workers and the average cost of living. Salary minus rent provides a simple and rough estimate of take-home pay, though it doesn't take into account taxes, transportation, and cost of goods and services.

TABLE 4-1

Salary and Median Rent by City

City	Annual Salary	Annual Rent	Salary Less Rent
San Francisco, CA	$96,500	$35,160	$61,340
Seattle, WA	$84,500	$20,760	$63,740
Boston, MA	$91,000	$32,400	$58,600
Austin, TX	$81,500	$18,600	$62,900
Chicago, IL	$76,000	$19,320	$56,680
New York, NY	$84,000	$37,200	$46,800
Detroit, MI	$73,000	$13,080	$59,920

Sources: CareerBuilder.com, Zumper.com median rent prices

Although San Francisco does pay the most of any city in the country, it looks less attractive after subtracting the cost of rent from annual pay. By contrast, cities such as Austin and Seattle offer strong salaries with a much lower cost of living.

TIP

A cost of living calculator will help you compare salaries in different cities. See, for example, the NerdWallet cost of living calculator by visiting www.nerdwallet. com/cost-of-living-calculator.

CHAPTER 4 **Coding Career Myths** 859

Your Previous Experience Isn't Relevant

Coding skill is one important factor that tech companies evaluate when hiring coders. But just as important is your domain knowledge and ability to work and lead a team. For example, perhaps you're a lawyer looking to switch careers and become a coder. Your legal knowledge will far exceed that of the average programmer, and if you target companies making software for lawyers, your perspective will be valuable.

Similarly, whether you previously were in finance or marketing, the issues around managing and leading teams are similar. It is natural for a team of people to disagree, have trouble communicating, and end up short of the intended goal. Your previous experiences handling this type of situation and turning it into a positive outcome will be valued in a tech company, where much of the coding is performed in teams.

Finally, your current or previous job might not seem technical, but others like you have made the transition into a coding job. People from a variety of professions — such as lawyers, teachers, and financial analysts — have learned how to code and found ways to incorporate their past work experiences into their current coding careers.

Index

Special Characters

A

education *(continued)*

extracurricular activities, 833–834

getting college degree, 830

graduate degrees, 836–839

master's degree, 836

overview, 829–830

research, 838–839

technical versus practical, 832–834

two-year versus four-year school, 834–836

undergraduate degrees, 829–836

element nodes, 308

Element object

methods, 318–319

properties, 316–317

elements, HTML

appending, 325

attaching events to, 331

choosing, 81–83

creating, 325

defined, 170

getting and setting values, 349–351

laying out, 113–122

naming, 112–113

overview, 47–49

removing, 325–326

styling, 107–111

using, 52–57

ElevatedButton widget., 574

elevation parameter, 453–454

elite technology companies, 856–857

Ellison, Larry, 829

else statement, 242–243

Emacs (code editor), 176

email value, 343

embeds property, 314

emulator, 402, 416

encapsulation, 519–523

encoding property, 346

enctype attribute, 341

enctype property, 346

ending tags, 170

end-of-line comments, 483–484

end-of-line doc comments, 484

enum, creating, 593

enum feature, 454

enumeration, 454, 740

equality (==) operator, 231, 686

error event, 329

errors, 38

escaping quotes, 207

event, 504

event handler, 504

events

bubbling up, 335–336

capturing, 335–336

handling

inline, 330

overview, 329–330

using addEventListener method, 331–337

using element properties, 331–332

overview, 327–329

turning off propagation, 336–337

every method, 221

Excel files, 718–719

@exception tag, 261

exclamation point (!), 628

Expanded widget, 549–560

experience, 857–858, 860

explode parameter, 797

@exports tag, 261

expressions, 226, 477–480, 645

eXtensible Markup Language. *See* XML

extension keyword, 603–608

extracurricular activities, 833–834

F

Facebook, 29, 30

fat arrow (=>), 489

features, deprecated, 736–737

fellowships, 840

field, 518

file value, 343

filename extensions, 405

fillna( ) method, 748

filter method, 221

finite machine diagram, 628

First Round Capital, 834

firstChild property, 311–313, 316

firstElementChild property, 316

FlatButton dialog box, 624

Flex class, 562

flex property, 138–139

flex value, 560–562

flex-basis property, 137, 139

Flexbox

aligning on cross-axis, 134–135

aligning on main axis, 136

changing order of, 139–140

creating boxes, 129–130

dimension, 130–132

items, 129

modifying flexible boxes, 137–139

multi-line containers, 133–134

overview, 123, 128–129

practicing with CodeSandbox. io, 140–141

wrapping items in container, 133–134

flex-direction property, 130–132, 135

flex-grow property, 137–139

Flexible class, 562

flex-shrink property, 138

flex-wrap property, 133–134

Flickr, 57

float property, 120

R

radio buttons
  building radio group, 593
  creating, 590–592
  creating enum, 593
  displaying user's choice, 595–596
radio value, 343
ramdom sampling, 712
random.shuffle( ), 756
range( ) function, 797–799
range value, 343
raw text files, shaping data in
  introducing regular expressions, 765–768
  removing stop words, 764–765
  stemming stop words, 764–765
  Unicode, 763
React Native, 30, 393
ReactJS, 824
read_sql( ) method, 723
read_sql_query( ) method, 723
read_sql_table( ) method, 723
read_xml, 727–728
readability, 679
readyState property, 314
real devices, 402
recommendation engines, 827
recursion, 271–272
recursive functions, 271–273
Reddfit.com, 679
reduce method, 221
reduceRight method, 221
references, passing arguments by, 267
referrer property, 314
regular expressions, 765–768, 821
relational databases, 722–724
removeAttribute( ) method, 319

removeAttributeNode( ) method, 319
removeChild( ) method, 319
removeEventListener( ) method, 315, 319
removeFirstParagraph( ) function., 326
renameNode( ) method, 315
replaceChild( ) method, 319
repository
  creating folders, 699–700
  creating notebooks, 700–702
  exporting notebooks, 702
  importing notebooks, 703–704
  overview, 699
  removing notebooks, 703
Representational State Transfer (REST), 650
research, performing, 838–839
Reset button, 601
reset event, 328
reset method, 347
reset value, 343
reset_index( ) method, 755–756
resize event, 329
resizeBy( ) method, 304
resizeTo( ) method, 305
resources, 293
responsive design, 124–128
REST (Representational State Transfer), 650
return statement, 474
@return tag, 261
return value, 472–475
@returns tag, 261
reverse method, 220
root element node, 308
round (n, d) function, 683
routes
  defined, 613
  named, creating, 629–632

RouteSettings constructor call, 618
rows
  nesting, 545–546
  slicing, 750–751
  stretching, 70–72
Ruby
  creator of, 14
  as one of first languages to learn, 856
  overview, 27
Runes type, 485
runtime, 387, 388

S

Safari, 845
salaries, 859
sales
  careers in, 820–821
  coding in, 12
same-origin policy, 375–377
scaffold, 451
Scaffold constructor, 451–453
scaling, 825
scatterplots
  creating, 803–805
  depicting groups, 803–804
  overview, 802–803
  showing correlations, 804–805
school-year internships, 840
scikit-image library, 719–722
scraping, 12
screen property, 299
screenLeft property, 299
screenTop property, 299
screenX property, 299
screenY property, 299
script element, 183–185
scroll event, 329
scrollBy( ) method, 305
scrollHeight property, 317

About the Authors

Nikhil Abraham is currently the CFO of Udacity, a venture-backed education technology startup that teaches its students how to code and that bridges the gap between real-world skills, relevant education, and employment. Prior to joining Udacity, he worked at Codecademy. At Codecademy, he helped technology, finance, media, and advertising companies teach their employees how to code. With his help, thousands of marketing, sales, and recruiting professionals have written their first lines of code and built functional applications. In addition to his day job, he has lectured at the University of Chicago Law School and created a course that teaches students how to solve legal problems using open data and software.

Prior to joining startups, Nikhil worked in a variety of fields, including management consulting, investment banking, and law; he also founded a Y Combinator-backed technology education startup. He received a JD and MBA from the University of Chicago and a BA in quantitative economics from Tufts University.

Nikhil is a recent transplant from Manhattan, New York, and now lives in Mountain View, California. Content from Nikhil's books *Coding For Dummies* and *Getting a Coding Job For Dummies* appears in this book.

Barry Burd received an MS degree in computer science at Rutgers University and a PhD in mathematics at the University of Illinois. As a teaching assistant in Champaign-Urbana, Illinois, he was elected five times to the university-wide List of Teachers Ranked as Excellent by Their Students.

Since 1980, Barry has been a professor in the department of mathematics and computer science at Drew University in Madison, New Jersey. He has spoken at conferences in the United States, Europe, Australia, and Asia. He is the author of several articles and books, including *Java For Dummies*, *Beginning Programming with Java For Dummies*, and *Java Programming for Android Developers For Dummies*, all from Wiley.

Barry lives in Madison, New Jersey, with his wife of 40 years. In his spare time, he enjoys eating chocolate and avoiding exercise. Content from Barry's book *Flutter For Dummies* appears in this book.

Eva Holland is an experienced writer, trainer, and cofounder of WatzThis?. Eva has written, designed, and taught online, in-person, and video courses. She has created curriculum for web development, mobile web development, and search engine optimization (SEO). Prior to founding WatzThis?, Eva served as COO of MWS, where she provided astute leadership, management, and vision that guided the company to its goals. Content from Eva's book *Coding with JavaScript For Dummies* appears in this book.

Luca **Massaron** is a data scientist and marketing research director who specializes in multivariate statistical analysis, machine learning, and customer insight, with more than a decade of experience in solving real-world problems and generating value for stakeholders by applying reasoning, statistics, data mining, and algorithms. From being a pioneer of web audience analysis in Italy to achieving the rank of top ten Kaggler on kaggle.com, he has always been passionate about everything regarding data and analysis and about demonstrating the potentiality of data-driven knowledge discovery to both experts and nonexperts. Content from Luca's books *Machine Learning For Dummies* and *Python for Data Science For Dummies* appears in this book.

Chris Minnick has been a full-stack developer for over 25 years, a trainer for over 10 years, and a writer for much longer than he can remember. He has taught web and mobile development, ReactJS, and advanced JavaScript at many of the world's largest companies as well as at colleges, public libraries, co-working spaces, and meetups.

Minnick has written over a dozen books about coding and two novels about clowns. He is also a painter, musician, swimmer, and avid indoorsman. Visit his website at `https://www.chrisminnick.com`.

Original content and content from Chris's book *Coding with JavaScript For Dummies* appears in this book.

John Mueller is a freelance author and technical editor. He has writing in his blood, having produced 100 books and more than 600 articles to date. His technical editing skills have helped more than 63 authors refine the content of their manuscripts. John has provided technical editing services to both *Data Based Advisor* and *Coast Compute* magazines. It was during his time with *Data Based Advisor* that John was first exposed to MATLAB, and he has continued to follow the progress in MATLAB development ever since. During his time at Cubic Corporation, John was exposed to reliability engineering and has continued his interest in probability. Be sure to read John's blog at `http://blog.johnmuellerbooks.com`. Content from John's book *Machine Learning For Dummies* and *Python for Data Science For Dummies* appears in this book.

Dedication

For my dad, who told me I'd never amount to anything, but who also bought me my first three computers.

— Chris Minnick

Author's Acknowledgments

This book would not have been possible without the help, support, experience, and wisdom provided by my friends, family, colleagues, and the team at Wiley. Thanks to everyone whose writing appears in this book. It was a pleasure and a privilege to work on a book with so many amazing minds. I would love to thank you all by name, but they tell me the book is already way too long. Thanks to you, the reader, for beginning or continuing your coding journey with me.

—Chris Minnick

Publisher's Acknowledgments

Executive Editor: Steve Hayes

Project Editor: Kezia Endsley

Copy Editor: Kezia Endsley

Proofreader: Penny Stuart

Production Editor: Tamilmani Varadharaj

Cover Image: © shutterstock/antoniodiaz

Dummies is the global leader in the reference category and one of the most trusted and highly regarded brands in the world. No longer just focused on books, customers now have access to the dummies content they need in the format they want. Together we'll craft a solution that engages your customers, stands out from the competition, and helps you meet your goals.

Advertising & Sponsorships

Connect with an engaged audience on a powerful multimedia site, and position your message alongside expert how-to content. Dummies.com is a one-stop shop for free, online information and know-how curated by a team of experts.

- Targeted ads
- Video
- Email Marketing
- Microsites
- Sweepstakes sponsorship

20 MILLION PAGE VIEWS EVERY SINGLE MONTH

15 MILLION UNIQUE VISITORS PER MONTH

43% OF ALL VISITORS ACCESS THE SITE VIA THEIR MOBILE DEVICES

700,000 NEWSLETTE SUBSCRIPTION TO THE INBOXES OF

300,000 UNIQUE INDIVIDUALS EVERY WEEK

# of dummies

Custom Publishing

Reach a global audience in any language by creating a solution that will differentiate you from competitors, amplify your message, and encourage customers to make a buying decision.

- Apps
- Books
- eBooks
- Video
- Audio
- Webinars

Brand Licensing & Content

Leverage the strength of the world's most popular reference brand to reach new audiences and channels of distribution.

For more information, visit **dummies.com/biz**

PERSONAL ENRICHMENT

Staying Sharp
9781119187790
USA $26.00
CAN $31.99
UK £19.99

Facebook
Carolyn Abram
9781119179030
USA $21.99
CAN $25.99
UK £16.99

Guitar
Mark Phillips
Jon Chappell
9781119293354
USA $24.99
CAN $29.99
UK £17.99

Investing
Eric Tyson, MBA
9781119293347
USA $22.99
CAN $27.99
UK £16.99

Beekeeping
Howland Blackiston
9781119310068
USA $22.99
CAN $27.99
UK £16.99

Digital Photography
Julie Adair King
9781119235606
USA $24.99
CAN $29.99
UK £17.99

Meditation
Stephan Bodian
9781119251163
USA $24.99
CAN $29.99
UK £17.99

Pregnancy
ALL-IN-ONE
9781119235491
USA $26.99
CAN $31.99
UK £19.99

Samsung Galaxy S7
Bill Hughes
9781119279952
USA $24.99
CAN $29.99
UK £17.99

iPhone
Edward C. Baig
Bob "Dr. Mac" LeVitus
9781119283133
USA $24.99
CAN $29.99
UK £17.99

Crocheting
Karen Manthey
Susan Brittain
9781119287117
USA $24.99
CAN $29.99
UK £16.99

Nutrition
Carol Ann Rinzler
9781119130246
USA $22.99
CAN $27.99
UK £16.99

PROFESSIONAL DEVELOPMENT

Windows 10
Andy Rathbone
9781119311041
USA $24.99
CAN $29.99
UK £17.99

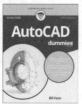

AutoCAD
Bill Fane
9781119255796
USA $39.99
CAN $47.99
UK £27.99

Excel 2016
Greg Harvey, PhD
9781119293439
USA $26.99
CAN $31.99
UK £19.99

QuickBooks 2017
Stephen L. Nelson, MBA, CPA, MS in Taxation
9781119281467
USA $26.99
CAN $31.99
UK £19.99

macOS Sierra
Bob "Dr. Mac" LeVitus
9781119280651
USA $29.99
CAN $35.99
UK £21.99

LinkedIn
Joel Elad, MBAs
9781119251132
USA $24.99
CAN $29.99
UK £17.99

Windows 10
ALL-IN-ONE
Woody Leonhard
9781119310563
USA $34.00
CAN $41.99
UK £24.99

SharePoint 2016
Rosemarie Withee
Ken Withee
9781119181705
USA $29.99
CAN $35.99
UK £21.99

Fundamental Analysis
Matt Krantz
9781119263593
USA $26.99
CAN $31.99
UK £19.99

Networking
Doug Lowe
9781119257769
USA $29.99
CAN $35.99
UK £21.99

Office 2016
Wallace Wang
9781119293477
USA $26.99
CAN $31.99
UK £19.99

Office 365
Rosemarie Withee
Ken Withee
Jennifer Reed
9781119265313
USA $24.99
CAN $29.99
UK £17.99

Salesforce.com
Liz Kao
Jon Paz
9781119239314
USA $29.99
CAN $35.99
UK £21.99

Coding
Nikhil Abraham
9781119293323
USA $29.99
CAN $35.99
UK £21.99

dummies.com

dummies®
A Wiley Brand